THE CASSELL ATLAS OF WORLD HISTORY

The
ANCIENT & CLASSICAL WORLDS

VOLUME ONE

John Haywood

with

**Freeman • Paul Garwood
Judith Toms**

CASSELL

Project director	Peter Furtado
Cartographic manager	Richard Watts
Advisory editors	Jeremy Black Professor of History, University of Exeter, UK
	K.M. Chaudhuri Vasco da Gama Professor of European Exploration, European University Institute, Florence, Italy
	Barry Cunliffe Professor of European Archaeology, University of Oxford, UK
	Brian M. Fagan Professor of Anthropology, University of California, Santa Barbara, USA
	J.E. Spence Associate Fellow, Royal Institute of International Affairs, UK
Academic advisors	J.I. Catto Oriel College, University of Oxford, UK
	Professor Robin Cohen University of Warwick, UK
	Professor J.H. Elliott Regius Professor of Modern History, University of Oxford, UK
	Professor Harold James Princeton University, New Jersey, USA
	Professor Maldwyn A. Jones University of London, UK
	Dr Stuart Kewley University of Cambridge, UK
	Dr Stewart Lone Australian Defence Force Academy
	Dr Oswyn Murray Balliol College, University of Oxford, UK
	Professor A.J.S. Reid The Australian National University
	Professor Francis Robinson Royal Holloway, University of London, UK
	Professor John K. Thornton Millersville University, Pennsylvania, USA

This page:
Saharan rock paintings, c.3500 BC

Opposite above:
Chinese bronze horse, c.AD 200

Opposite below:
Gold mask from Mycenae, c.1500 BC

Art director	Ayala Kingsley
Art editor	Martin Anderson
Cartographic editor	Tim Williams
Editors	Susan Kennedy
	Peter Lewis
(Encyclopedic dictionary)	BCS Publishing
Cartographer	Nathalie Johns
Picture research	Claire Turner
Production	Clive Sparling
Editorial assistance	Marian Dreier
Typesetter	Brian Blackmore
Illustrations	Charles Raymond
Proof reader	Lynne Elson
Index	Ann Barrett

AN ANDROMEDA BOOK

Produced and prepared by
Andromeda Oxford Ltd
11–13 The Vineyard
Abingdon
Oxfordshire OX14 3PX

© Andromeda Oxford Ltd 2000

First published in the UK
by Cassell plc
Wellington House
125 Strand
London WC2R 0BB

ISBN 0–304–35515–1

10 9 8 7 6 5 4 3 2 1

Printed and bound in Singapore

Contents

Part 1
The Ancient World
(4,000,000 – 500 BC)

INTRODUCTION

OUTLINE OF WORLD HISTORY

1.01 Human origins • 4,000,000–100,000 years ago
1.02 Peopling the Earth • 100,000–10,000 years ago
1.03 The rise of agriculture • 10,000–500 BC
1.04 The world • 2000 BC
1.05 The world • 1000 BC
1.06 The world • 500 BC
1.07 The spread of writing • 3000 BC–AD 1500

THE MIDDLE EAST

1.08 The first farmers of the Middle East • 10,000–6000 BC
1.09 Advanced farmers of the Middle East • 6500–4300 BC
1.10 The first cities of Mesopotamia • 4300–2334 BC
1.11 The first empires • 2334–1595 BC
1.12 The Hittite and Assyrian empires • 1595–1000 BC
1.13 The Assyrian and Babylonian empires • 1000–539 BC
1.14 The Bible lands • 1000–587 BC
1.15 The Achemenid empire of Persia • 559–480 BC

AFRICA

1.16 Early farming in Africa • 7000–500 BC
1.17 The foundation of ancient Egypt • 6000–2040 BC
1.18 Middle and New Kingdom Egypt • 2040–332 BC

EUROPE AND THE MEDITERRANEAN

1.19 Upper Paleolithic Europe • 35,000 years ago–5000 BC
1.20 Neolithic Europe • 5000–2000 BC
1.21 Bronze Age Europe • 2000–500 BC
1.22 The first civilizations of the Mediterranean • 2000–1100 BC
1.23 Phoenician and Greek expansion in the Mediterranean • 900–500 BC
1.24 The emergence of the Greek city-states • 1100–500 BC
1.25 Etruscans, Greeks and Carthaginians • 800–480 BC

ASIA AND THE AMERICAS

1.26 The first civilizations of south Asia • 6000–500 BC
1.27 The first civilizations of east Asia • 6000–500 BC
1.28 The first civilizations of the Americas • 4000–500 BC

1.29 ENCYCLOPEDIC DICTIONARY

Part 2
The Classical World
(500 BC – AD 600)

INTRODUCTION

OUTLINE OF WORLD HISTORY

2.01 The world • 323 BC
2.02 The world • 200 BC
2.03 The world • 1 BC
2.04 The world • AD 400
2.05 The world • AD 600
2.06 The growth of the world religions • 600 BC–AD 600

GREECE AND THE MIDDLE EAST

2.07 The Persian wars and 5th-century Greece • 499–435 BC
2.08 The Peloponnesian war and the rise of Macedon • 435–336 BC
2.09 The conquests of Alexander the Great • 336–300 BC
2.10 The Hellenistic world • 301–30 BC
2.11 Parthian and Sasanian Persia • 238 BC–AD 636

ROME AND THE MEDITERRANEAN

2.12 Early Rome and the Punic wars • 509–201 BC
2.13 The growth of the Roman empire • 201 BC–AD 117
2.14 Economy and society of the Roman empire • 27 BC–AD 305
2.15 Crisis and recovery of the Roman empire • AD 117–376
2.16 The fall of the western Roman empire • AD 376–480
2.17 Justinian and the origins of the Byzantine empire • AD 480–629

EUROPE

2.18 The Celts • 500 BC–AD 600
2.19 The Germans and the Slavs • 750 BC–AD 600
2.20 The steppe nomads • 900 BC–AD 600

AFRICA

2.21 Early states of Africa • 500 BC–AD 600

SOUTH AND EAST ASIA

2.22 Mauryan India • 550 BC–AD 100
2.23 Kushan and Gupta India • AD 50–570
2.24 China from warring states to first empires • 480 BC–AD 220
2.25 China disunited and the rise of Japan • AD 220–600
2.26 The Pacific and southeast Asia • 2000 BC–AD 600

THE AMERICAS

2.27 South America and Mexico • 500 BC–AD 700
2.28 The ancient Maya • 300 BC–AD 800

2.29 ENCYCLOPEDIC DICTIONARY

ACKNOWLEDGMENTS

INDEX

Part 1

The Ancient

Four million years of biological and cultural evolution are covered in this story of the development of humankind from its origins on the African savanna to the appearance of literate civilizations and classical empires. The story is the product of research in many disciplines, but the central thread comes from thousands of archeological excavations, from inconspicuous scatters of stone tools and animal bones to hunting camps, farm villages and spectacular cities.

Archeologists study and explain changes in societies, indeed in humanity itself, over immensely long periods of time. Why, for example, did some societies begin farming? How and why did humans cross from Siberia into Alaska and colonize the Americas? The archeologist tries to account for such developments in terms of social organization as well as technology and environmental change.

The key intellectual framework for our most distant past derives from the evolutionary theories of Charles Darwin, formulated in 1859. The theory of evolution by natural selection made it possible to imagine a vast antiquity in which human evolution unfolded over hundreds of thousands, if not millions, of years. Darwin and his contemporaries could only guess at the timescales involved. Today, study of the DNA in our body cells tells us that the hominid line – culminating in Homo sapiens sapiens – separated from the other apes between four and five million years ago. Today, archeology tells us that human ancestors appeared in Africa and moved out to populate the rest of the world almost two million years ago, and that modern humanity may also have originated there. With its help, we can not only wonder at the art of 30,000 years ago, but also build up chronologies based on scientific analysis as well as on techniques of stylistic comparison. Archeology reveals that literate civilizations developed independently in many places around the world. Historians using written sources, and archeologists using material remains, can then collaborate in piecing together a narrative of these civilizations.

Modern scholars think of evolution like the branches of a tree, with new species emerging as endlessly proliferating limbs and twigs derived from a trunk of remote common ancestors. Human societies have evolved in many ways; but there are similarities, especially in social and political organization and in the ways in which people make their livings. A flexible

classification of human societies into "prestate societies" and "state-organized societies" was made by the American anthropologist Elman Service. The simplest prestate societies were small family bands, egalitarian groups with communal leadership based on experience. Usually hunters and gatherers of plant foods, bands prevailed for an immensely long time, until farming began. Some bands survived to modern times.

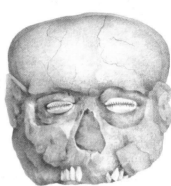

Decorated skull from Jericho, c.8000 BC

Early farmers lived in permanent villages and needed new institutions to settle quarrels and establish land ownership. Many village societies were "tribes", egalitarian groups with kin-based organization to regulate ownership and undertake communal tasks. "Chiefdoms" were a development of tribes; power was held by a few people who controlled trade and

Using this Atlas

This atlas is part of a three-volume chronological set covering the Ancient and Classical (1), Medieval and Early Modern (2), 19th Century and Modern (3) worlds. To help the user pinpoint straight away which era any particular map relates to, pages are numbered first by the part, and then by 2-page spread within that part for each volume. Thus, map spread 14 in part 1 is identified by the page number 1.14.

World map spreads outline global history on the date shown. Different typographical categories (see table opposite) denote different kinds of political or social entity. The text on these spreads includes many cross-references to other relevant spreads. The timelines here are organized by region.

Regional map spreads cover a part of the world over a specific period. Maps for a continent or major region are grouped in a section, named in the heading on the right-hand side of the spread. These sections also appear in the Contents page.

Maps are shown in true cartographic projections. North is

WORLD

accumulated wealth. "State-organized societies" or civilizations operated on a larger scale; they involved cities and saw the development of a writing system. Early civilizations were centralized, with a supreme ruler at the head of a stratified society.

Four major themes dominate the early chapter of our history: the origins of humanity, the evolution and spread of humans, the beginnings of agriculture, and the emergence of civilizations. All are bound up with the ways in which food has been secured. For 99 percent of all human history, people lived by hunting and gathering. Our earliest ancestors probably used speed and opportunism to scavenge their meat from lion and leopard kills. Hunting may have begun with modern humans. Stone-tipped spears, barbed antler projectiles and spear-throwers allowed hunters to shoot from a safe distance. When the bow-and-arrow came into use some 10,000 years ago, humans could hunt animals of every size and birds on the wing. As the ice sheets retreated, the quest for food intensified and permanent settlements began to emerge at favored sites.

Edible plants formed the essential diet of humans for four million years. Our ancestors knew which plants to eat as staples, and which to fall back on in lean times. It was only when populations rose at the end of the Ice Age that people began to plant wild grasses and tubers to extend the range. And, in a remarkably short time – perhaps three thousand years – farming and the domestication of animals spread.

Farming accelerated the pace of change. At first, civilizations like those of the Egyptians, the Shang and the Sumerians were self-sufficient, but states grew increasingly reliant on each other. By 500 BC, empires played a leading role. But the first four million years had created human cultural diversity and laid the foundations of our own world ■

Chavín textile of fanged god, c.400 BC

generally at the top of the page. Some distortion is evident in those maps that cover huge areas of the world (e.g. Asia). Where necessary, location maps have been included.

Each regional map has certain standard features: thick grey lines denote major borders, thin grey lines internal borders. Campaigns or journeys are shown by lines with arrowheads; thicker grey arrows are used for mass movements of people. Trade routes are thinner lines, with arrowheads when the trade is one-way. All map-key items are referred to in text. The main text explains and amplifies the information on the map.

The timelines on regional maps are arranged in geographical or thematic sections. Civilizations, cultures, and dynasties are shown with colored bands; broad historical phases (such as "Bronze Age") are indicated with grey bands. Every regional map also has several numbered "pointers", whose captions offer further historical detail on the places marked. Finally, the panel bottom right cross-refers to other spreads with related information, listing their numbers and themes.

TYPOGRAPHICAL CONVENTIONS

World maps

FRANCE	state or empire
Belgian Congo	dependency or territory
Mongols	tribe, chiefdom or people
Anasazi culture	cultural group

Regional maps

HUNGARY	state or empire
Bohemia	dependency or territory
Slavs	tribe, chiefdom or people
ANATOLIA	geographical region
⚔	battle
•	site or town

An encyclopedic section contains an A–Z guide to the people, places, and events of each period. It is cross-referenced within the section and to the information on the maps. The index provides detailed references to the text, timelines, pointer captions and map keys. Map locations are not indexed due to limited space.

Human evolution began as the Earth's climate started to cool during the Miocene epoch (25–5 million years ago), and culminated about one million years ago in the Pleistocene Ice Age. During the early Miocene the global climate was warmer than today. Widespread tropical forests in Africa and Eurasia supported diverse populations of early hominoid apes, including a common ancestor of gorillas, chimpanzees and humans.

By the end of the Miocene ice caps had formed at the Poles, and drier conditions in Africa caused tropical forests to shrink. In east Africa, probably the birthplace of the hominids, this was exacerbated by geological movements that led to the uplift of the East African plateau and the formation of the Rift Valley. The ancestral hominids were confined to shrinking "islands" of forest surrounded by open woodland and savanna. As a result they learned to walk on two legs, allowing them to cover long distances on the ground.

The oldest known hominid, 4.4-million-year-old *Ardipithecus ramidus*, was probably bipedal, and the slightly later species *Australopithecus afarensis* certainly was, although (like later australopithecines) it retained a good tree-climbing ability. By 3 million years ago the australopithecines had evolved into two types, known as robusts and graciles. The robusts (named for their massive jaws and teeth) were not human ancestors. The gracile *Australopithecus africanus* had smaller teeth and jaws, and lived on plant foods and meat scavenged from the carcasses of the savanna's herd animals. The first hominid to be considered human, *Homo habilis*, appeared about 2.4 million years ago. This lived in a similar way to the gracile australopithecines, but had a larger brain – almost half the size of a modern human's, compared with a third, for australopithecines and chimpanzees. Whereas the australopithecines used simple tools such as stones and sticks, *Homo habilis* made sharp flakes and chipped pebble tools for butchering large animals. This simple toolmaking culture is known as the Oldowan, for the early hominid fossil site of Olduvai Gorge in the Rift Valley.

About 1.9 million years ago *Homo habilis* was replaced by *Homo erectus*, with a brain size about two-thirds that of modern humans. Over the next million years this proportion grew to three-quarters, the brain evolving rapidly as the climate fluctuated from dry glacial periods to moister, warmer inter-glacial periods. There was little time to adapt physically to new conditions, and intelligent animals that could cope by modifying their

| 0 | 600 km |
| 0 | 400 mi |

Hadar
Aa
Bodo
He
Middle
Awash
Ar
Melka
Kunture
Gadeb
Omo
Ra, other
Ra
Ileret
Ra, Hh, He
West Turkana
He
Koobi Fora
Ra, Hh, He
Chesowanja
Ra
Olorgasailie
Peninj
Ra
Olduvai Gorge
Ndutu
Ra, Hh, He.
other
Laetoli
Aa, other

Kalambo Falls

Kabwe
other

1,600,000 Earliest evidence of the use of fire, at Chesowanja, Kenya and Swartkrans (South Africa)

1,800,000 Populations of *Homo erectus* reach south and southeast Asia

c.2,000,000 Stone choppers, from Olduvai Gorge, Tanzania, initiate the Oldowan culture

c.3,500,000 "Lucy", the most complete *Australopithecus afarensis* found, lives at Hadar, Ethiopia

c.3,600,000 Hominid bipedal footsteps from this date have been found at Laetoli, Tanzania

c.2,400,000 Date of the oldest known stone tools, from Hadar, Ethiopia and the start of the African Lower Paleolithic

1,000,000 Beginning of the modern (Pleistocene) Ice Age

1,000,000 *Homo erectus* reaches Europe and Asia

TIMELINE						
	4,000,000 years ago (ya)	3,000,000 ya	2,000,000 ya	1,500,000 ya	1,000,000

Homo habilis

Homo erectus

Ardipithecus ramidus

Australopithecus afarensis

Australopithecus africanus

Robust Australopithecines

Oldowan culture

LOWER PALEOLITHIC

PLIOCENE EPOCH

TERTIARY PERIOD

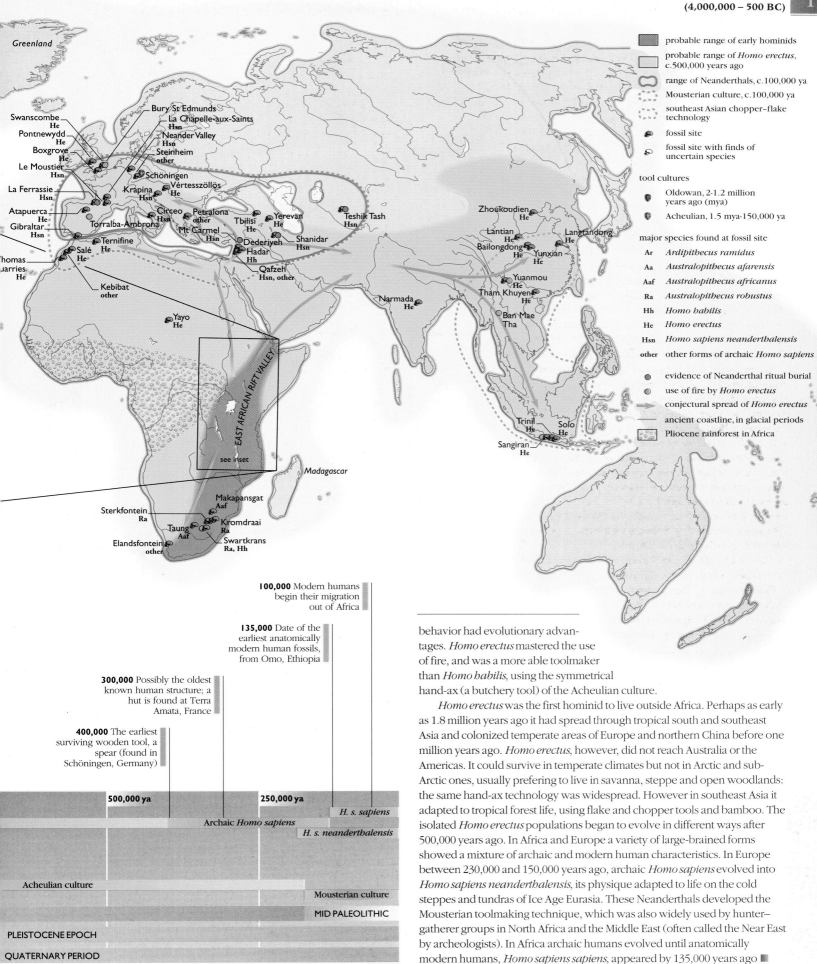

Greenland

Swanscombe
He
Pontnewydd
He
Boxgrove
He
Le Moustier
Hsn
La Ferrassie
Hsn
Atapuerca
He
Gibraltar
Hsn
Thomas
Quarries
He
Salé
He

Bury St Edmunds
La Chapelle-aux-Saints
Hsn
Neander Valley
Hsn
Steinheim
other
Schöningen
Krapina
Hsn
Circeo
Hsn
Torralba-Ambrona
Ternifine
He
Kebibat
other

Vértesszöllös
He
Petralona
other
Mt Carmel
Hsn
Tbilisi
He
Yerevan
He
Dederiyeh
He
Shanidar
Hsn
Hadar
Hh
Qafzeh
Hsn, other

Teshik Tash
Hsn

Yayo
He

EAST AFRICAN RIFT VALLEY

see inset

Madagascar

Makapansgat
Aaf
Sterkfontein
Ra
Taung
Aaf
Kromdraai
Ra
Swartkrans
Ra, Hh
Elandsfontein
other

Zhoukoudien
He
Lantian
He
Bailongdong
He
Langtandong
He
Yunxian
He
Yuanmou
He
Tham Khuyen
He
Ban Mae
Tha
Narmada
He

Trinil
He
Solo
He
Sangiran
He

	probable range of early hominids
	probable range of *Homo erectus*, c.500,000 years ago
	range of Neanderthals, c.100,000 ya
	Mousterian culture, c.100,000 ya
	southeast Asian chopper–flake technology
	fossil site
	fossil site with finds of uncertain species

tool cultures

| | Oldowan, 2-1.2 million years ago (mya) |
| | Acheulian, 1.5 mya-150,000 ya |

major species found at fossil site

Ar	*Ardipithecus ramidus*
Aa	*Australopithecus afarensis*
Aaf	*Australopithecus africanus*
Ra	*Australopithecus robustus*
Hh	*Homo habilis*
He	*Homo erectus*
Hsn	*Homo sapiens neanderthalensis*
other	other forms of archaic *Homo sapiens*

	evidence of Neanderthal ritual burial
	use of fire by *Homo erectus*
	conjectural spread of *Homo erectus*
	ancient coastline, in glacial periods
	Pliocene rainforest in Africa

100,000 Modern humans begin their migration out of Africa

135,000 Date of the earliest anatomically modern human fossils, from Omo, Ethiopia

300,000 Possibly the oldest known human structure; a hut is found at Terra Amata, France

400,000 The earliest surviving wooden tool, a spear (found in Schöningen, Germany)

500,000 ya   **250,000 ya**

H. s. sapiens

Archaic *Homo sapiens*

H. s. neanderthalensis

Acheulian culture

Mousterian culture

MID PALEOLITHIC

PLEISTOCENE EPOCH

QUATERNARY PERIOD

behavior had evolutionary advantages. *Homo erectus* mastered the use of fire, and was a more able toolmaker than *Homo habilis*, using the symmetrical hand-ax (a butchery tool) of the Acheulian culture.

    Homo erectus was the first hominid to live outside Africa. Perhaps as early as 1.8 million years ago it had spread through tropical south and southeast Asia and colonized temperate areas of Europe and northern China before one million years ago. *Homo erectus*, however, did not reach Australia or the Americas. It could survive in temperate climates but not in Arctic and sub-Arctic ones, usually prefering to live in savanna, steppe and open woodlands: the same hand-ax technology was widespread. However in southeast Asia it adapted to tropical forest life, using flake and chopper tools and bamboo. The isolated *Homo erectus* populations began to evolve in different ways after 500,000 years ago. In Africa and Europe a variety of large-brained forms showed a mixture of archaic and modern human characteristics. In Europe between 230,000 and 150,000 years ago, archaic *Homo sapiens* evolved into *Homo sapiens neanderthalensis*, its physique adapted to life on the cold steppes and tundras of Ice Age Eurasia. These Neanderthals developed the Mousterian toolmaking technique, which was also widely used by hunter–gatherer groups in North Africa and the Middle East (often called the Near East by archeologists). In Africa archaic humans evolved until anatomically modern humans, *Homo sapiens sapiens*, appeared by 135,000 years ago ∎

The earliest known anatomically modern *Homo sapiens sapiens* had appeared in Africa by 135,000 years ago (ya). By 90,000 years ago anatomically modern humans existed in the Middle East; by 75,000 years ago they were in east Asia and by 40,000 in Europe and Australia. By the end of the Ice Age 10,000 years ago, only some oceanic islands, Antarctica and some parts of the high Arctic remained completely uninhabited.

Two rival explanations have been offered for these facts. One argues that the modern human races developed directly from the regional *Homo erectus* populations: modern Africans evolved from *Homo erectus* via African archaic *Homo sapiens*; modern Europeans from *Homo erectus* via European archaic *Homo sapiens* and Neanderthals and so on. Critics point out that parallel evolution of this sort over such a wide area is implausible and that there is no supporting fossil evidence. The second explanation, known as the single-origins or "out of Africa" model, is supported by genetic evidence suggesting that all modern humans derive from African ancestors who lived between about 285,000 and 150,000 years ago, and that all modern non-African humans are descendants of a single group of this ancestral population that migrated out of Africa around 100,000 years ago. According to this model, the descendants of this group spread across Eurasia. The anatomically modern humans had better developed speech abilities than the archaic natives, who could not compete with the newcomers and gradually became extinct.

This model is more compatible with the fossil and archeological evidence than the first. Between 120,000 and 90,000 years ago the African climate was more moist than it is today and bands of hunters and gatherers could have crossed the Sahara. The earliest known fossils of modern humans outside Africa date to about 90,000 years ago and were found in Israel – just the place and date predicted by the single-origins theory. Only in Africa have forms intermediate between archaic and modern humans been found. In Europe, the Neanderthals and early modern humans formed distinct populations that coexisted for over 10,000 years: the Neanderthals did not evolve into modern humans. In east and southeast Asia, the *Homo erectus* populations were replaced by modern humans with no trace of intermediate forms.

When the first modern humans reached the Middle East, the global climate was beginning to enter one of the most severe glacial periods of the Ice Age. Human technology was probably inadequate for survival in the arctic climates of Europe and central Asia, and these areas were left to the hardier Neanderthals. Instead the moderns moved east, reaching China and southeast Asia around 75,000 years ago. Here they developed boat- or raft-building skills and

Map labels

BERINGIA

modern humans reach Alaska around 15,000

Bluefish Cave 15–12,000

Cordilleran Ice Sheet

Laurentide Ice Sheet

ice free corridor opens c.12–14,000

Marmes 10,500

Folsom

Clovis

Clovis sites occupied around 11,500–11,000

Little Salt Spring

Tepexpan 11–10,000

Pedra Pintada 11,200–10,500

Guitarrero Cave c.10,000

Monte Verde 12,500

modern humans reach Patagonia 11,000

Fell's Cave 11,000

Timeline

115,000 Onset of the last glaciation of the (Pleistocene) Ice Age

90,000 Anatomically modern humans living at Qafzeh, Israel

40,000 Anatomically modern humans begin to colonize Europe: they live alongside the indigenous Neanderthals

32,000–14,000 Period of cave art traditions in Europe

TIMELINE		
The Americas		
Europe		
Middle East		
Africa		
East and South Asia		

100,000 years ago   80,000 ya   60,000 ya   40,000 ya   30,000 ya

c.120,000 Middle Stone Age flake-tool technology is well established in tropical Africa

c.75,000 Glaciation causes Africa to become arid: the Sahara becomes impassable by humans

45,000 Date of the oldest known musical instrument, a flute, found in north Africa

35,000 Anatomically modern humans hunt large game in Eurasia

120,000–90,000 Periods of higher rainfall make the Sahara habitable by humans

75,000 Anatomically modern humans inhabit China and southeast Asia

35,000 Australian aboriginal hunter–gatherer traditions emerge

28,000 The Solomon Islands are settled

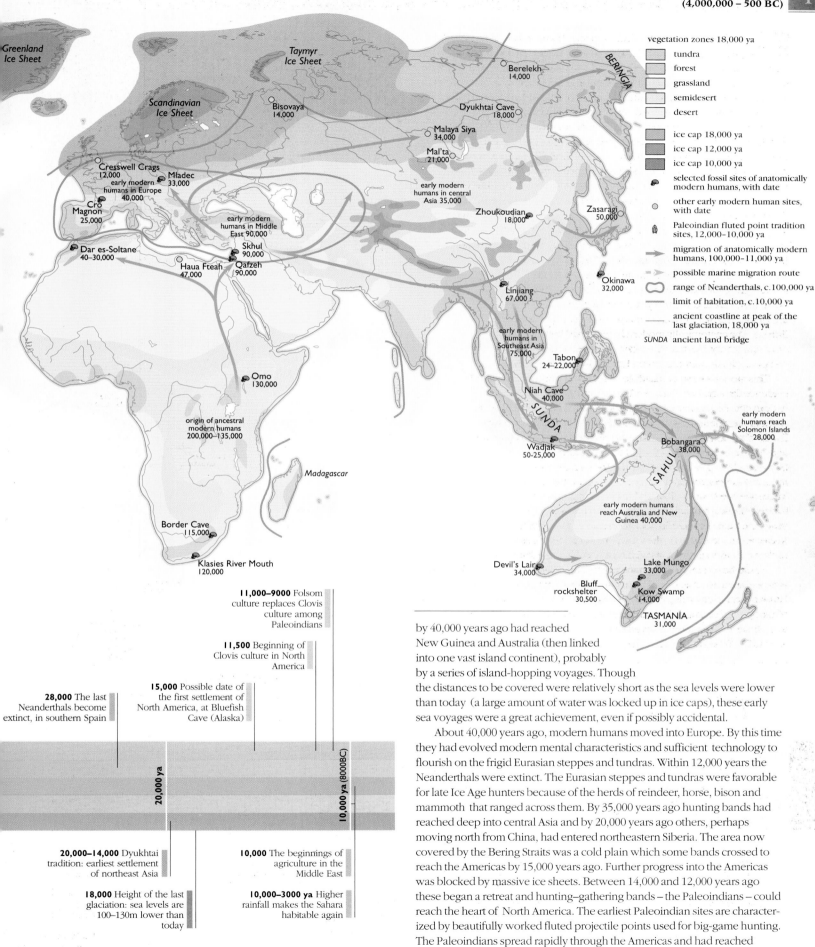

vegetation zones 18,000 ya

- tundra
- forest
- grassland
- semidesert
- desert

- ice cap 18,000 ya
- ice cap 12,000 ya
- ice cap 10,000 ya

selected fossil sites of anatomically modern humans, with date

other early modern human sites, with date

Paleoindian fluted point tradition sites, 12,000–10,000 ya

migration of anatomically modern humans, 100,000–11,000 ya

possible marine migration route

range of Neanderthals, c.100,000 ya

limit of habitation, c.10,000 ya

ancient coastline at peak of the last glaciation, 18,000 ya

SUNDA ancient land bridge

Greenland Ice Sheet

Taymyr Ice Sheet

Scandinavian Ice Sheet

Berelekh 14,000

Dyukhtai Cave 18,000

BERINGIA

Bisovaya 14,000

Malaya Siya 34,000

Mal'ta 21,000

early modern humans in central Asia 35,000

Zasaragi 50,000

Cresswell Crags 12,000

Mladec 33,000

early modern humans in Europe 40,000

Zhoukoudian 18,000

Cro Magnon 25,000

early modern humans in Middle East 90,000

Dar es-Soltane 40–30,000

Skhul 90,000

Haua Fteah 47,000

Qafzeh 90,000

Okinawa 32,000

Linjiang 67,000

early modern humans in Southeast Asia 75,000

Tabon 24–22,000

Omo 130,000

Niah Cave 40,000

SUNDA

origin of ancestral modern humans 200,000–135,000

Madagascar

early modern humans reach Solomon Islands 28,000

Bobangara 38,000

Wadjak 50–25,000

SAHUL

early modern humans reach Australia and New Guinea 40,000

Border Cave 115,000

Klasies River Mouth 120,000

Devil's Lair 34,000

Lake Mungo 33,000

Bluff rockshelter 30,500

Kow Swamp 14,000

TASMANIA 31,000

11,000–9000 Folsom culture replaces Clovis culture among Paleoindians

11,500 Beginning of Clovis culture in North America

15,000 Possible date of the first settlement of North America, at Bluefish Cave (Alaska)

28,000 The last Neanderthals become extinct, in southern Spain

20,000 ya

10,000 ya (8000BC)

20,000–14,000 Dyukhtai tradition: earliest settlement of northeast Asia

18,000 Height of the last glaciation: sea levels are 100–130m lower than today

10,000 The beginnings of agriculture in the Middle East

10,000–3000 ya Higher rainfall makes the Sahara habitable again

by 40,000 years ago had reached New Guinea and Australia (then linked into one vast island continent), probably by a series of island-hopping voyages. Though the distances to be covered were relatively short as the sea levels were lower than today (a large amount of water was locked up in ice caps), these early sea voyages were a great achievement, even if possibly accidental.

About 40,000 years ago, modern humans moved into Europe. By this time they had evolved modern mental characteristics and sufficient technology to flourish on the frigid Eurasian steppes and tundras. Within 12,000 years the Neanderthals were extinct. The Eurasian steppes and tundras were favorable for late Ice Age hunters because of the herds of reindeer, horse, bison and mammoth that ranged across them. By 35,000 years ago hunting bands had reached deep into central Asia and by 20,000 years ago others, perhaps moving north from China, had entered northeastern Siberia. The area now covered by the Bering Straits was a cold plain which some bands crossed to reach the Americas by 15,000 years ago. Further progress into the Americas was blocked by massive ice sheets. Between 14,000 and 12,000 years ago these began a retreat and hunting–gathering bands – the Paleoindians – could reach the heart of North America. The earliest Paleoindian sites are characterized by beautifully worked fluted projectile points used for big-game hunting. The Paleoindians spread rapidly through the Americas and had reached Patagonia in South America by 11,000 years ago ∎

Farming communities arose independently in many parts of the world between 10,000 and 5000 BC as a response to the environmental changes that followed the end of the Ice Age. The warmer climate was a mixed blessing: sea levels rose as the ice sheets melted, flooding huge areas of lowland hunting grounds. The savannas, steppes and tundras, all abundant in big game, shrank as the forests advanced.

In many areas, hunter–gatherers began to exploit small game birds, fish and plants to a greater extent than before. It was among these communities that agriculture first arose. Probably the first stage was planting the seeds of favored wild plant foods to guarantee their continuing availability. Next was the domestication of food plants by breeding strains with desirable characteristics. Because their seeds had a high carbohydrate content and were easy to store, the most important domesticated plant foods were strains of the cereals – wheat, barley, oats, rice, millet and maize – that still form the staple food crops today. Relatively few animal species have been domesticated; most of those have been herd animals, whose tendency to "follow the leader" makes them easier to manage. Animal domestication began with the management and selective culling of wild herds. Penning the animals followed, then selective breeding for desirable qualities. Most early centers of agriculture were rich in wild plants and animals suitable for domestication. Elsewhere agriculture relied on the introduction of crops and livestock from established farming areas.

Some communities of hunter–gatherers moved from casual cultivation of wild plants (incipient agriculture) to a full farming economy far more quickly than others. Farmers have to work harder than hunter–gatherers, and few made the transition willingly. Rising populations probably forced many to adopt cultivation to supplement wild food supplies. In the Fertile Crescent of the Middle East, where farming first developed, (▷ 1.08) the transition from incipient agriculture to dependence on domesticated cereals took only three centuries, 8000–7700 BC, and domesticated animals replaced hunted wild animals a millennium later. In Mesoamerica a full farming way of life developed within a few centuries of the domestication of maize (▷ 1.28). In eastern North America hunting and gathering remained the main source of food for some three millennia after the first cultivation of domesticated food around 2500 BC. Even farmers who grew most of their food still exploited wild food sources.

Agriculture led to far-reaching technological developments. Most hunter–gatherers had to carry everything from camp to camp: farmers were sedentary, so weight became less critical. New tools, such as polished stone

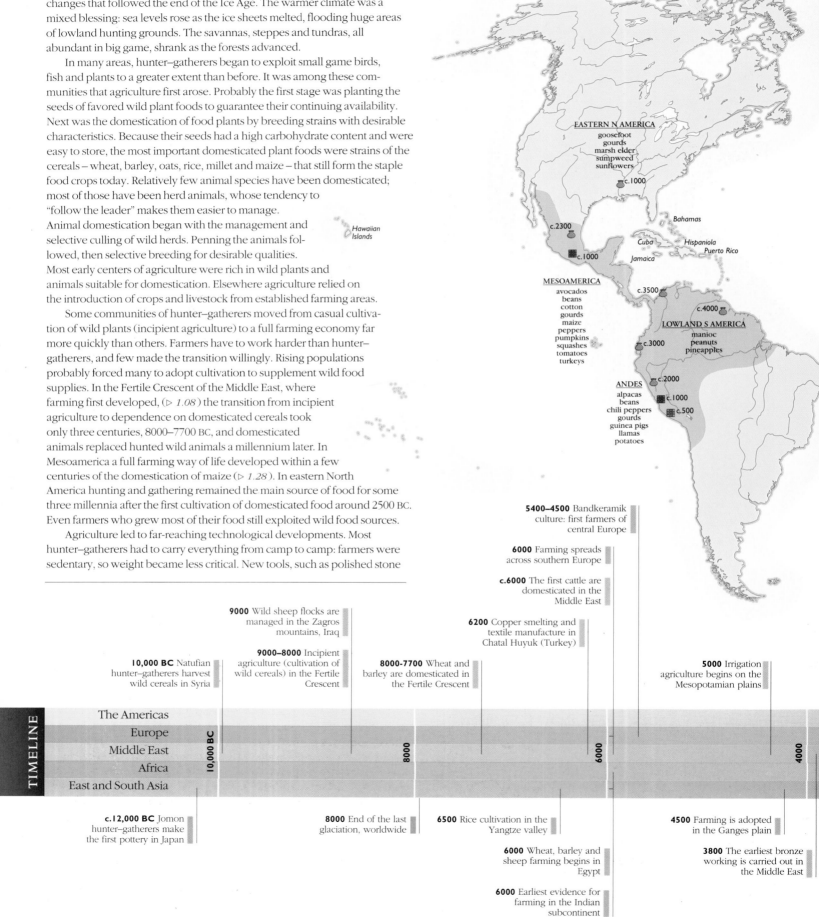

EASTERN N AMERICA
goosefoot
gourds
marsh elder
sumpweed
sunflowers
c.1000

Hawaiian Islands

Bahamas

Cuba *Hispaniola* *Puerto Rico*
Jamaica

c.2300
c.1000

MESOAMERICA
avocados
beans
cotton
gourds
maize
peppers
pumpkins
squashes
tomatoes
turkeys

c.3500
c.4000

LOWLAND S AMERICA
manioc
peanuts
pineapples

c.3000

ANDES
alpacas
beans
chili peppers
gourds
guinea pigs
llamas
potatoes

c.2000
c.1000
c.500

5400–4500 Bandkeramik culture: first farmers of central Europe

6000 Farming spreads across southern Europe

c.6000 The first cattle are domesticated in the Middle East

6200 Copper smelting and textile manufacture in Chatal Huyuk (Turkey)

9000 Wild sheep flocks are managed in the Zagros mountains, Iraq

9000–8000 Incipient agriculture (cultivation of wild cereals) in the Fertile Crescent

10,000 BC Natufian hunter–gatherers harvest wild cereals in Syria

8000-7700 Wheat and barley are domesticated in the Fertile Crescent

5000 Irrigation agriculture begins on the Mesopotamian plains

TIMELINE		10,000 BC		8000		6000		4000
The Americas								
Europe								
Middle East								
Africa								
East and South Asia								

c.12,000 BC Jomon hunter–gatherers make the first pottery in Japan

8000 End of the last glaciation, worldwide

6500 Rice cultivation in the Yangtze valley

4500 Farming is adopted in the Ganges plain

6000 Wheat, barley and sheep farming begins in Egypt

3800 The earliest bronze working is carried out in the Middle East

6000 Earliest evidence for farming in the Indian subcontinent

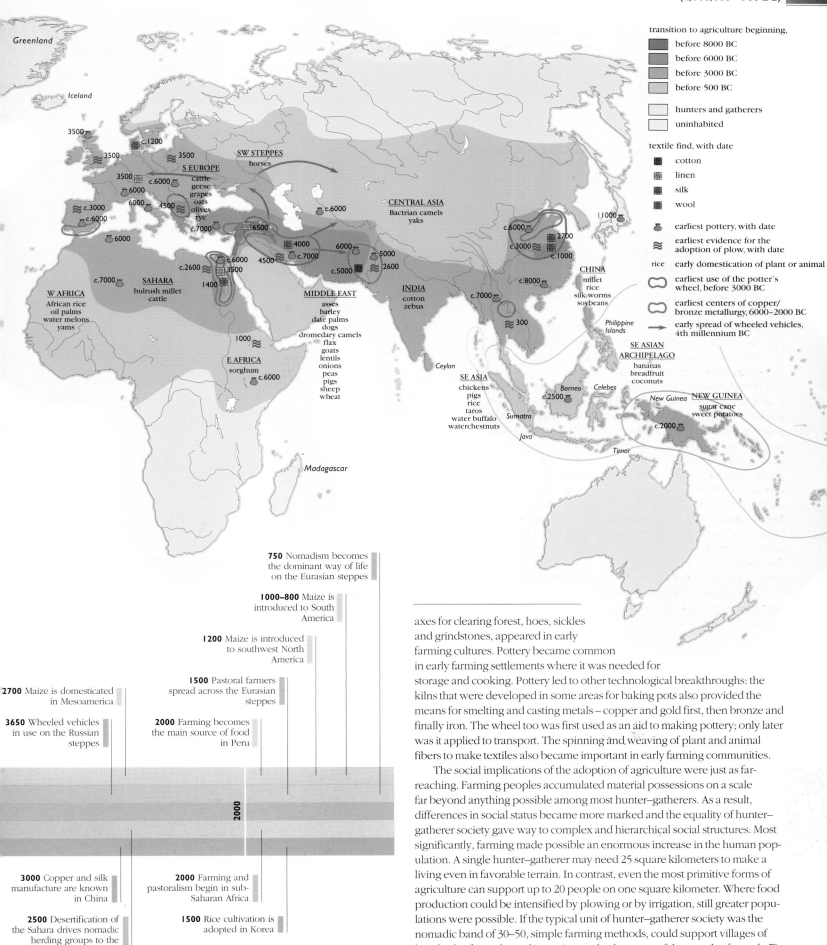

Greenland

Iceland

3500

3500

c.1200

3500

SW STEPPES
horses

S EUROPE
cattle
geese
grapes
oats
olives
rye

3500

c.6000

6000

c.3000

4500

c.6000

6000

6000

6500

c.6000

CENTRAL ASIA
Bactrian camels
yaks

c.6000

11000

c.6000

2700

c.3000

c.1000

4000

c.7000

6000

5000

c.5000

4500

2600

CHINA
millet
rice
silk worms
soybeans

c.8000

c.2600

3500

1400

W AFRICA
African rice
oil palms
water melons
yams

c.7000

SAHARA
bulrush millet
cattle

MIDDLE EAST
asses
barley
date palms
dogs
dromedary camels
flax
goats
lentils
onions
peas
pigs
sheep
wheat

INDIA
cotton
zebus

c.7000

300

Philippine
Islands

SE ASIAN
ARCHIPELAGO
bananas
breadfruit
coconuts

1000

E AFRICA
sorghum

c.6000

Ceylon

SE ASIA
chickens
pigs
rice
taros
water buffalo
waterchestnuts

Borneo

Celebes

c.2500

New Guinea

NEW GUINEA
sugar cane
sweet potatoes

c.2000

Sumatra

Java

Timor

Madagascar

Legend:

transition to agriculture beginning,

before 8000 BC

before 6000 BC

before 3000 BC

before 500 BC

hunters and gatherers

uninhabited

textile find, with date

cotton

linen

silk

wool

earliest pottery, with date

earliest evidence for the
adoption of plow, with date

rice   early domestication of plant or animal

earliest use of the potter's
wheel, before 3000 BC

earliest centers of copper/
bronze metallurgy, 6000–2000 BC

early spread of wheeled vehicles,
4th millennium BC

Timeline:

750 Nomadism becomes
the dominant way of life
on the Eurasian steppes

1000–800 Maize is
introduced to South
America

1200 Maize is introduced
to southwest North
America

1500 Pastoral farmers
spread across the Eurasian
steppes

2700 Maize is domesticated
in Mesoamerica

2000 Farming becomes
the main source of food
in Peru

3650 Wheeled vehicles
in use on the Russian
steppes

2000

3000 Copper and silk
manufacture are known
in China

2000 Farming and
pastoralism begin in sub-
Saharan Africa

2500 Desertification of
the Sahara drives nomadic
herding groups to the
edges of the desert

1500 Rice cultivation is
adopted in Korea

axes for clearing forest, hoes, sickles
and grindstones, appeared in early
farming cultures. Pottery became common
in early farming settlements where it was needed for
storage and cooking. Pottery led to other technological breakthroughs: the
kilns that were developed in some areas for baking pots also provided the
means for smelting and casting metals – copper and gold first, then bronze and
finally iron. The wheel too was first used as an aid to making pottery; only later
was it applied to transport. The spinning and weaving of plant and animal
fibers to make textiles also became important in early farming communities.

The social implications of the adoption of agriculture were just as far-
reaching. Farming peoples accumulated material possessions on a scale
far beyond anything possible among most hunter–gatherers. As a result,
differences in social status became more marked and the equality of hunter–
gatherer society gave way to complex and hierarchical social structures. Most
significantly, farming made possible an enormous increase in the human population. A single hunter–gatherer may need 25 square kilometers to make a
living even in favorable terrain. In contrast, even the most primitive forms of
agriculture can support up to 20 people on one square kilometer. Where food
production could be intensified by plowing or by irrigation, still greater populations were possible. If the typical unit of hunter–gatherer society was the
nomadic band of 30–50, simple farming methods, could support villages of
hundreds of people, and intensive methods, towns of thousands of people ∎

By 2000 BC the revolutionary impact of agriculture had become clear. Farming was practiced on every continent and would overtake hunting and gathering as the way of life of most people well before the Christian era.

Not all early farming societies developed the same level of complexity. Poor soil, climate, endemic diseases of humans or livestock or a lack of suitable crops limited development in many areas. The greater the resources possessed by a society, the more complex it could become; in a few favorable environments (such as the northwest of North America), hunter-gatherer societies too achieved greater levels of social complexity.

Most early farming societies were kinship-based tribes of hundreds or a few thousand people living in villages or dispersed homesteads. Although they recognized ties of kinship, religion or language with others, each tribe was essentially independent. Differences of rank and status existed but leaders could rarely exercise coercive power over other tribes' people. Archeologically, such societies (known to anthropologists as "segmentary societies") can be recognized by communal burial practices, the remains of permanent homesteads and villages and communal works such as the megalithic tombs of prehistoric western Europe. In 2000 BC segmentary farming societies were dominant in south and southeast Asia, New Guinea, north Africa, northern Europe and parts of Mesoamerica and South America.

Where intensive agricultural techniques could be used, largescale hierarchical communities of up to 20,000 people, known as "chiefdoms", could develop. Rank and status were linked to lineage: the senior person of the senior lineage was the chief, who was thereby the ruler of the whole community. Chieftains could exercise coercive power, often through a warrior class, and support specialist craftsmen. Archeologically, chiefdoms show major construction projects requiring large resources of labor and wealth, such as Stonehenge in southern Britain (▷ *1.20*). In chiefdoms the quantity and quality of grave goods placed with burials indicate the rank and status of the individual and a few burials are lavishly furnished. Chiefdoms commonly had a dominant central site such as a stronghold or ceremonial center, and smaller satellite settlements. In 2000 BC chiefdoms were established in the Middle East and southwest central Europe, in China and the Andes. In western Europe segmentary farming societies were giving way to chiefdoms at this time.

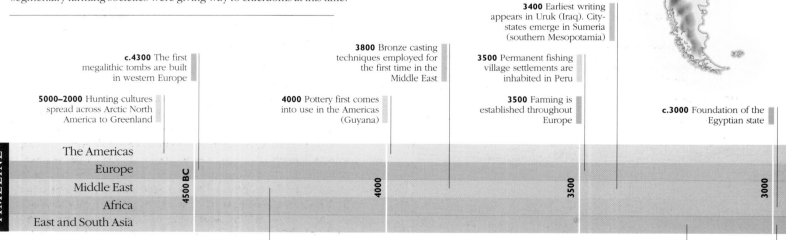

3400 Earliest writing appears in Uruk (Iraq). City-states emerge in Sumeria (southern Mesopotamia)

c.4300 The first megalithic tombs are built in western Europe

3800 Bronze casting techniques employed for the first time in the Middle East

3500 Permanent fishing village settlements are inhabited in Peru

5000–2000 Hunting cultures spread across Arctic North America to Greenland

4000 Pottery first comes into use in the Americas (Guyana)

3500 Farming is established throughout Europe

c.3000 Foundation of the Egyptian state

TIMELINE				
The Americas				
Europe	4500 BC	4000	3500	3000
Middle East				
Africa				
East and South Asia				

4300–3100 Uruk period in Mesopotamia. The first cities are built.

3200–1800 Chinese Longshan advanced farming cultures; first towns are built in China

3000 Ancestral Austronesians migrate from Taiwan to the Philippines

3000–1700 Pastoral farming is established on the central Asian steppes (Afanasevo culture)

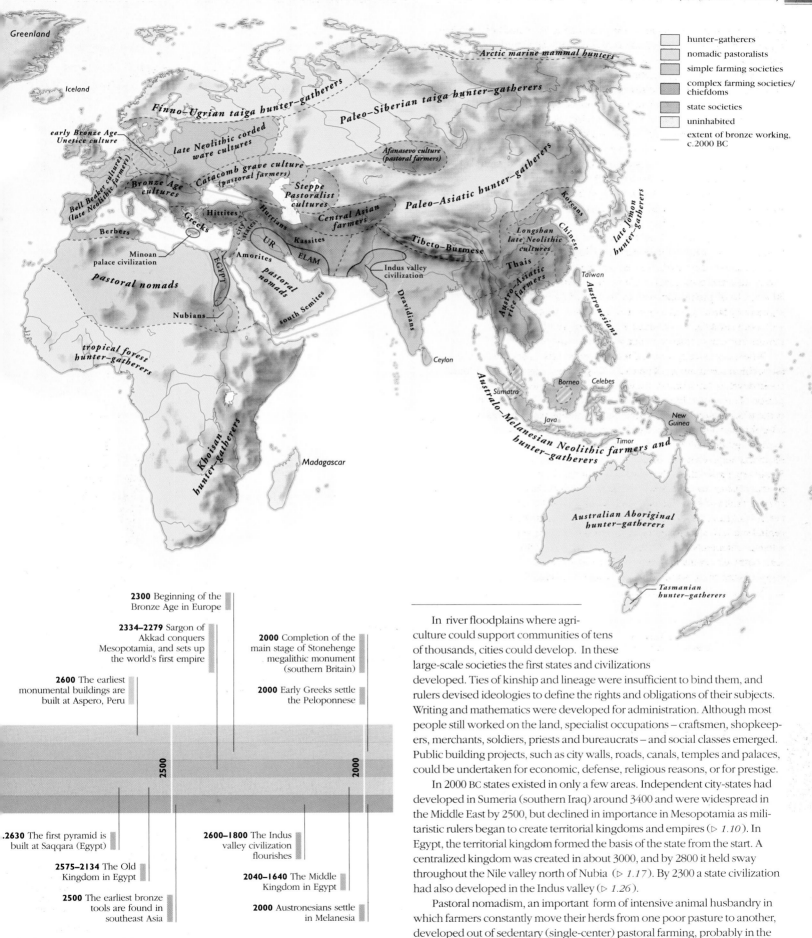

hunter–gatherers
nomadic pastoralists
simple farming societies
complex farming societies/
chiefdoms
state societies
uninhabited
extent of bronze working,
c.2000 BC

Greenland

Iceland

Arctic marine mammal hunters

Finno–Ugrian taiga hunter–gatherers

Paleo–Siberian taiga hunter–gatherers

*early Bronze Age
Unetice culture*

*late Neolithic corded
ware cultures*

*Afanasevo culture
(pastoral farmers)*

*Bell Beaker cultures
(late Neolithic farmers)*

*Catacomb grave culture
(pastoral farmers)*

*Steppe
Pastoralist
cultures*

Paleo–Asiatic hunter–gatherers

Koreans

*Bronze Age
cultures*

*Central Asian
farmers*

*late Jomon
hunter–gatherers*

Greeks

Hittites

Hurrians

Berbers

*CITY
STATES*

UR

Kassites

Chinese

*Longshan
late Neolithic
cultures*

*Minoan
palace civilization*

ELAM

Amorites

EGYPT

Tibeto–Burmese

Taiwan

Pastoral nomads

*Pastoral
nomads*

*Indus valley
civilization*

Thais

Austronesians

Nubians

south Semites

Dravidians

*Austro-Asiatic
rice farmers*

*tropical forest
hunter–gatherers*

Ceylon

Borneo

Celebes

Sumatra

*Khoisan
hunter–gatherers*

Java

Madagascar

*New
Guinea*

Timor

*Australo–Melanesian Neolithic farmers and
hunter–gatherers*

*Australian Aboriginal
hunter–gatherers*

*Tasmanian
hunter–gatherers*

2300 Beginning of the
Bronze Age in Europe

2334–2279 Sargon of
Akkad conquers
Mesopotamia, and sets up
the world's first empire

2000 Completion of the
main stage of Stonehenge
megalithic monument
(southern Britain)

2600 The earliest
monumental buildings are
built at Aspero, Peru

2000 Early Greeks settle
the Peloponnese

2500

2000

.2630 The first pyramid is
built at Saqqara (Egypt)

2600–1800 The Indus
valley civilization
flourishes

2575–2134 The Old
Kingdom in Egypt

2040–1640 The Middle
Kingdom in Egypt

2500 The earliest bronze
tools are found in
southeast Asia

2000 Austronesians settle
in Melanesia

In river floodplains where agriculture could support communities of tens
of thousands, cities could develop. In these
large-scale societies the first states and civilizations
developed. Ties of kinship and lineage were insufficient to bind them, and
rulers devised ideologies to define the rights and obligations of their subjects.
Writing and mathematics were developed for administration. Although most
people still worked on the land, specialist occupations – craftsmen, shopkeep-
ers, merchants, soldiers, priests and bureaucrats – and social classes emerged.
Public building projects, such as city walls, roads, canals, temples and palaces,
could be undertaken for economic, defense, religious reasons, or for prestige.

In 2000 BC states existed in only a few areas. Independent city-states had
developed in Sumeria (southern Iraq) around 3400 and were widespread in
the Middle East by 2500, but declined in importance in Mesopotamia as militaristic rulers began to create territorial kingdoms and empires (▷ 1.10). In
Egypt, the territorial kingdom formed the basis of the state from the start. A
centralized kingdom was created in about 3000, and by 2800 it held sway
throughout the Nile valley north of Nubia (▷ 1.17). By 2300 a state civilization
had also developed in the Indus valley (▷ 1.26).

Pastoral nomadism, an important form of intensive animal husbandry in
which farmers constantly move their herds from one poor pasture to another,
developed out of sedentary (single-center) pastoral farming, probably in the
Sahara where desertification spread after 3000 BC ▪

T he fragility of the first civilizations was evident during the second millennium BC. Sumeria had vanished as a political entity shortly before 2000 BC, though its achievements were built upon by the Babylonian and Assyrian states which arose in the early second millennium (▷ 1.11). The rivalry between these two states was to endure until the middle of the first millennium. The other major power of the Middle East was the Hittite kingdom of Anatolia. One of the secrets of Hittite success is thought to have been their early mastery of iron working, in about 1500 BC. Meanwhile, Egypt expanded far south into Nubia and north into the Levant (▷ 1.18). In the eastern Mediterranean, the Minoans of Crete were replaced by the Mycenaean civilization that emerged on the Greek mainland around 1600. Around 1400 the Mycenaeans conquered Crete and introduced the Greek language; they also settled on Cyprus and in Anatolia (▷ 1.22).

This civilized world was thrown into chaos about 1200 by a wave of invasions. Mycenae was destroyed by invaders from the north, plunging Greece into a 400-year-long "dark age". Thracians, Phrygians and Anatolian Luvians overthrew the Hittite empire and nomadic Aramaeans occupied much of Mesopotamia. Egypt was invaded by mysterious Sea Peoples. Their fleets were driven from the Nile, but they settled in the Levant where they were known as the Philistines.

By 1000 stability was returning. The Hittites survived though as a shadow of their former selves. The Aramaeans had settled and were assimilating with the urbanized peoples of the conquered territories: their language became the common tongue of the Middle East for the next millennium. Assyria and Babylon were beginning to recover (▷ 1.12). The Levant was a mosaic of tiny states: of these, the Phoenician city-states and Israel acquired a historical importance out of all proportion to their size (▷ 1.14). Egyptian power was in decline and the Nubians, after a millennium of Egyptian domination, set up the kingdom of Kush. In sub-Saharan Africa, the transition to a farming way of life was beginning.

In Asia, the Indus valley civilization had collapsed around 1700; about 200 years later the Aryans, an Indo-European pastoralist people, migrated into India. In northern China the Neolithic Longshan cultures developed into the urbanized Shang state around 1766, marking the start of Chinese civilization. Around 1122 the Shang dynasty was ousted by the ruler of the Zhou sub-kingdom (▷ 1.27).

The Austronesian farming peoples continued to colonize the southeast Asian archipelagoes; by 2000 they had bypassed New Guinea and settled the western Pacific Bismarck archipelago around 1500 BC. The Lapita culture,

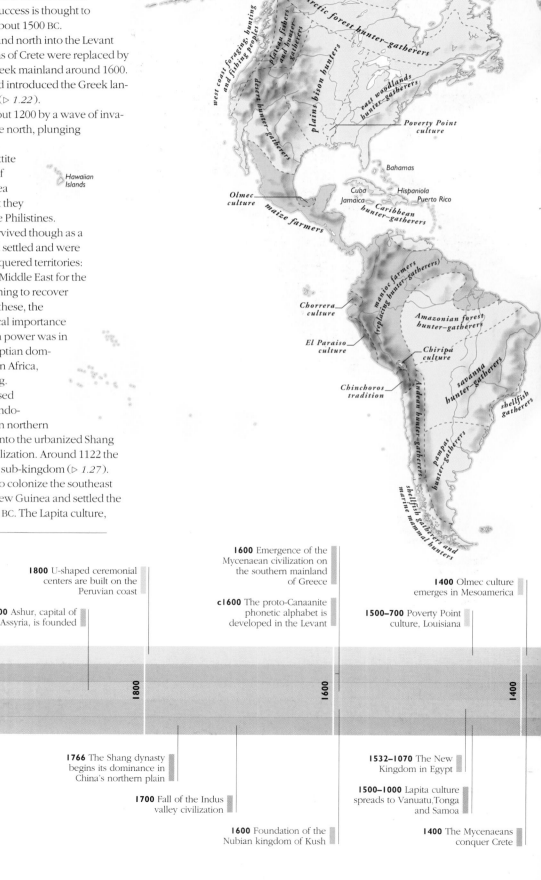

| | 2000–1500 Wessex culture introduces bronze working to the British Isles | 1800 U-shaped ceremonial centers are built on the Peruvian coast | 1600 Emergence of the Mycenaean civilization on the southern mainland of Greece | 1400 Olmec culture emerges in Mesoamerica |
| | 2300–1500 Emergence of the first permanent farming villages in Mesoamerica | c.1900 Ashur, capital of Assyria, is founded | c1600 The proto-Canaanite phonetic alphabet is developed in the Levant | 1500–700 Poverty Point culture, Louisiana |

TIMELINE		2000	1800	1600	1400
The Americas					
Europe					
Middle East					
Africa					
East and South Asia					

	2040–1640 The Middle Kingdom in Egypt	1766 The Shang dynasty begins its dominance in China's northern plain		1532–1070 The New Kingdom in Egypt
	2000–1600 The Minoan palace civilization flourishes on Crete	1700 Fall of the Indus valley civilization		1500–1000 Lapita culture spreads to Vanuatu, Tonga and Samoa
	2000 Cattle raising begins in highland east Africa		1600 Foundation of the Nubian kingdom of Kush	1400 The Mycenaeans conquer Crete

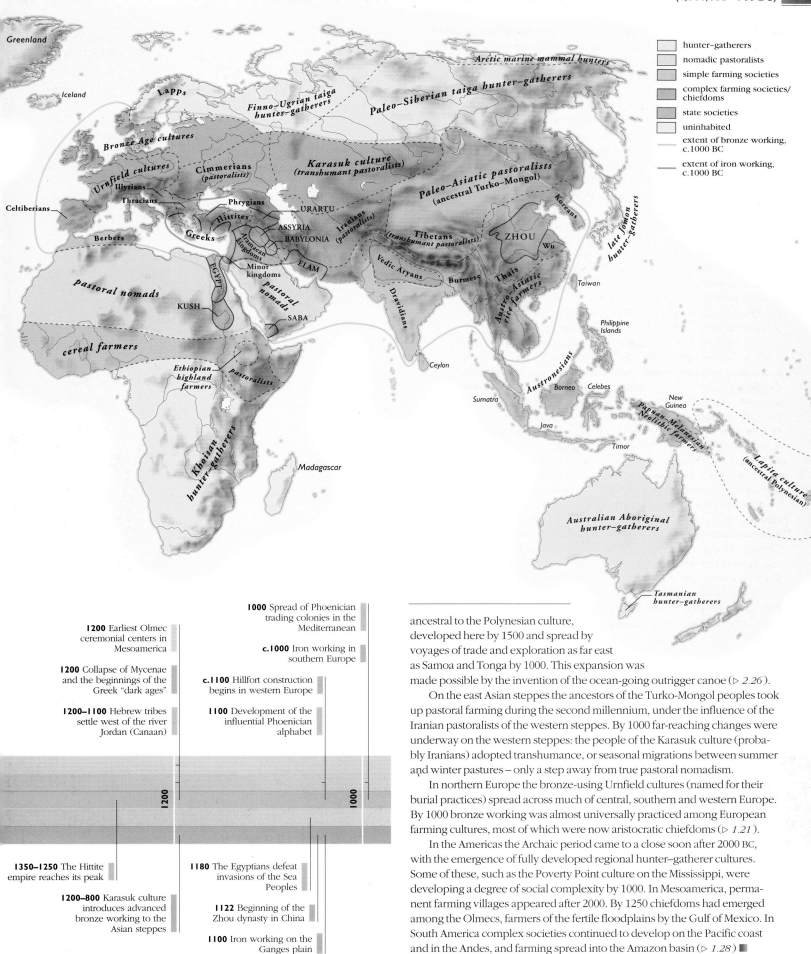

Greenland

Iceland

Arctic marine mammal hunters

Lapps

Finno-Ugrian taiga hunter-gatherers

Paleo-Siberian taiga hunter-gatherers

Bronze Age cultures

Urnfield cultures

Cimmerians
(pastoralists)

*Karasuk culture
(transhumant pastoralists)*

*Paleo-Asiatic pastoralists
(ancestral Turko-Mongol)*

Illyrians

Thracians

Celtiberians

Phrygians

URARTU

Hittites

Greeks

Berbers

Iranians
(pastoralists)

Koreans

ZHOU

ASSYRIA

Aramaean
kingdoms

BABYLONIA

Tibetans
(transhumant pastoralists)

Wu

Minor
kingdoms

ELAM

EGYPT

Vedic Aryans

Burmese

Thais

*late Jomon
hunter-gatherers*

KUSH

*Pastoral
nomads*

Dravidians

*Austro-Asiatic
rice farmers*

Taiwan

SABA

Pastoral nomads

cereal farmers

*Ethiopian
highland
farmers*

pastoralists

*Philippine
Islands*

Ceylon

Austronesians

Borneo

Celebes

New
Guinea

Sumatra

*Papuan-Melanesian
Neolithic farmers*

*Lapita culture
(ancestral Polynesian)*

Java

Timor

*Khoisan
hunter-gatherers*

Madagascar

*Australian Aboriginal
hunter-gatherers*

*Tasmanian
hunter-gatherers*

	hunter-gatherers
	nomadic pastoralists
	simple farming societies
	complex farming societies/ chiefdoms
	state societies
	uninhabited
	extent of bronze working, c.1000 BC
	extent of iron working, c.1000 BC

1200 Earliest Olmec
ceremonial centers in
Mesoamerica

1200 Collapse of Mycenae
and the beginnings of the
Greek "dark ages"

1200–1100 Hebrew tribes
settle west of the river
Jordan (Canaan)

1000 Spread of Phoenician
trading colonies in the
Mediterranean

c.1000 Iron working in
southern Europe

c.1100 Hillfort construction
begins in western Europe

1100 Development of the
influential Phoenician
alphabet

1200

1000

1350–1250 The Hittite
empire reaches its peak

1200–800 Karasuk culture
introduces advanced
bronze working to the
Asian steppes

1180 The Egyptians defeat
invasions of the Sea
Peoples

1122 Beginning of the
Zhou dynasty in China

1100 Iron working on the
Ganges plain

ancestral to the Polynesian culture,
developed here by 1500 and spread by
voyages of trade and exploration as far east
as Samoa and Tonga by 1000. This expansion was
made possible by the invention of the ocean-going outrigger canoe (▷ 2.26).

On the east Asian steppes the ancestors of the Turko-Mongol peoples took
up pastoral farming during the second millennium, under the influence of the
Iranian pastoralists of the western steppes. By 1000 far-reaching changes were
underway on the western steppes: the people of the Karasuk culture (probably Iranians) adopted transhumance, or seasonal migrations between summer
and winter pastures – only a step away from true pastoral nomadism.

In northern Europe the bronze-using Urnfield cultures (named for their
burial practices) spread across much of central, southern and western Europe.
By 1000 bronze working was almost universally practiced among European
farming cultures, most of which were now aristocratic chiefdoms (▷ 1.21).

In the Americas the Archaic period came to a close soon after 2000 BC,
with the emergence of fully developed regional hunter–gatherer cultures.
Some of these, such as the Poverty Point culture on the Mississippi, were
developing a degree of social complexity by 1000. In Mesoamerica, permanent farming villages appeared after 2000. By 1250 chiefdoms had emerged
among the Olmecs, farmers of the fertile floodplains by the Gulf of Mexico. In
South America complex societies continued to develop on the Pacific coast
and in the Andes, and farming spread into the Amazon basin (▷ 1.28) ■

The number and size of organized states in the Middle East, India and the Mediterranean rose sharply between 1000 and 500 BC. A succession of empires dominated the Middle East. The first was the Assyrian empire which stretched from the Zagros mountains to Egypt by the 7th century. Assyrian rule was harsh and in 625 the Babylonians rebelled and seized most of the empire for themselves (▷ 1.13). Then the Iranian Medes pushed west, conquering the Caucasus and eastern Anatolia. In 550 Cyrus II "the Great", an Iranian king, seized the Median kingdom and founded the Persian empire. He then took western Anatolia and the Babylonian empire. By 500 the Persian empire extended from Egypt to the Indus (▷ 1.15).

State-organized societies had also spread throughout the Mediterranean world. By 700 Greece was a patchwork of independent city-states: by 500 these cities, and Athens in particular, entered a period of intellectual creativity unparalleled in world history (▷ 1.24). The Greeks and Phoenicians also founded trading colonies throughout the Mediterranean. Although the Phoenicians lost their independence by 500, Carthage, their colony in north Africa, was the leading power of the western Mediterranean. The Greek cities of Sicily and southern Italy had a powerful influence, notably on the Etruscans who dominated northern Italy by 500. North of the Alps the Urnfield cultures of central Europe were replaced by the aristocratic iron-using Celtic Hallstatt culture c.600 (▷ 1.25).

States reappeared in the Indian subcontinent in the 9th century. The focus this time was the Ganges plain where Vedic Aryan chiefdoms began to coalesce into kingdoms and republics. By 500 the largest was the kingdom of Magadha. At the same time the Aryans extended southward, conquering the Dravidians and imposing Hindu religion on them (▷ 1.26). The Chinese Zhou kingdom expanded to the southeast after 1000, but what it gained in area it lost in internal cohesion. The Zhou kingdom was a decentralized feudal state and by the 8th century the powerful warlords had so undermined the power of the monarchy that it was power-less to prevent the kingdom from breaking up (▷ 1.27). Meanwhile the first chiefdoms emerged around 500 in Korea and in Van Lang in southeast Asia.

One far-reaching development of the early first millennium was the change in lifestyle of the Iranian peoples (Scythians, Sarmatians, Sakas and Yue Qi) of the Eurasian steppes from transhumant (seasonal) pastoralism to nomadic pastoralism. The steppe peoples had been pioneers in the use of horses: they had domesticated them for their meat around 4000 BC, they had harnessed them to wagons (4th millennium) and war chariots (2nd millennium) and by 1000 BC they had mastered

800 Zapotecs develop hieroglyphic script in Mesoamerica

800–500 Greek coloniza-tion of the Mediterranean and Black Sea

800 Emergence of the Etruscan civilization in Italy

900–700 Nomadism becomes the dominant way of life on the Eurasian steppes

1000 Emergence of the kingdom of Israel

700–100 Adena culture burial mound builders in the eastern woodlands of North America

700 City-states flourish in Greece and the Aegean

c.750 Emergence of the Celtic Hallstatt Iron Age culture north of the Alps

750–705 Assyrian power reaches its peak

612 The collapse of the Assyrian empire

TIMELINE	1000	900	800	700	600
The Americas					
Europe					
Middle East					
Africa					
East and South Asia					

1000–500 Formative period of Hinduism

900 The first states emerge on the Ganges plain

814 Foundation of the Phoenician colony of Carthage

712–671 Egypt is ruled by a Kushite dynasty from Nubia

600 Iron and bronze working develop in west Africa

800 The Aryans expand into southern India

600 Introduction of iron working into China

770–481 The "Springs and Autumns" period in China: the Zhou kingdom breaks up into minor states

c.590 The Nubian capital established at Meroë

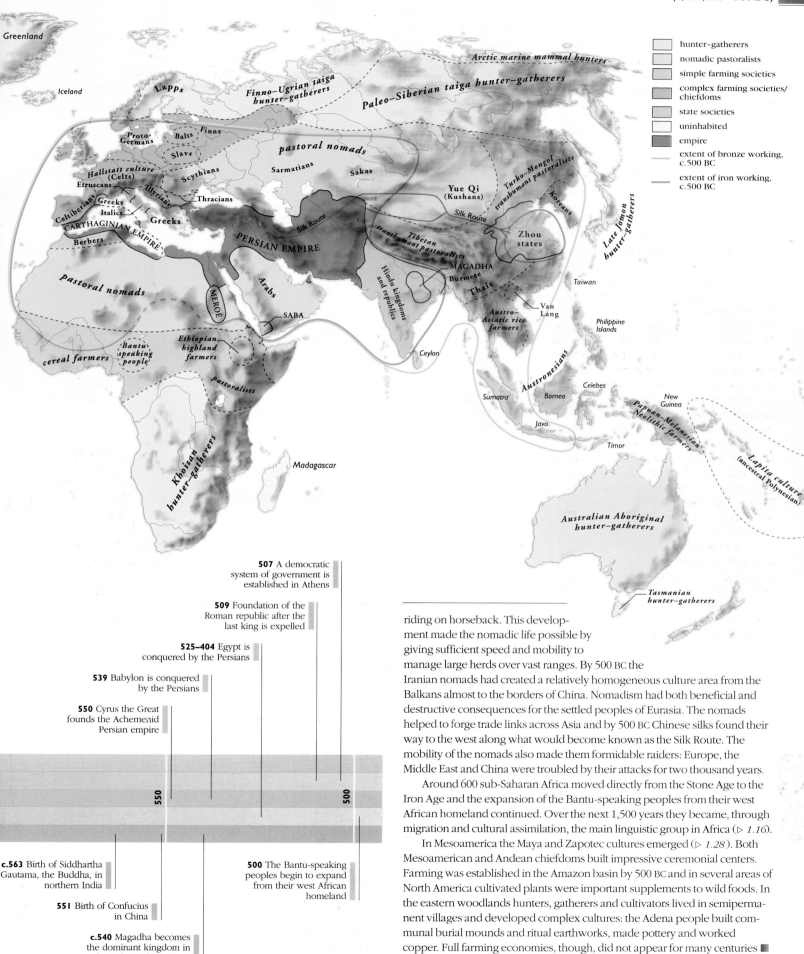

Greenland

Iceland

Lapps

Finno–Ugrian taiga
hunter–gatherers

Paleo–Siberian taiga hunter–gatherers

Arctic marine mammal hunters

Proto-
Germans

Balts   Finns

Slavs

Hallstatt culture
(Celts)

Etruscans

Greeks

Italics

Celtiberians

CARTHAGINIAN EMPIRE

Berbers

pastoral nomads

Scythians

Sarmatians

Sakas

Illyrians

Thracians

Greeks

PERSIAN EMPIRE

Silk Route

Yue Qi
(Kushans)

Turko–Mongol
transhumant pastoralists

Korenas

Zhou
states

Silk Route

Tibetan
transhumant pastoralists

Late Jomon
hunter–gatherers

Taiwan

Pastoral nomads

Arabs

MEROË

SABA

Hindu kingdoms
and republics

MAGADHA

Burmese

Thais

Van
Lang

Philippine
Islands

cereal farmers

Bantu
speaking
people

Ethiopian
highland
farmers

Austro-
Asiatic rice
farmers

Ceylon

Austronesians

Celebes

Sumatra

Borneo

New
Guinea

Madagascar

Java

Timor

Papuan–Melanesian
Neolithic farmers

Lapita culture
(ancestral Polynesian)

*Khoisan
hunter–gatherers*

*Australian Aboriginal
hunter–gatherers*

*Tasmanian
hunter–gatherers*

hunter-gatherers	
nomadic pastoralists	
simple farming societies	
complex farming societies/
chiefdoms	
state societies	
uninhabited	
empire	

— extent of bronze working,
c.500 BC

— extent of iron working,
c.500 BC

507 A democratic
system of government is
established in Athens

509 Foundation of the
Roman republic after the
last king is expelled

525–404 Egypt is
conquered by the Persians

539 Babylon is conquered
by the Persians

550 Cyrus the Great
founds the Achemenid
Persian empire

550   500

c.563 Birth of Siddhartha
Gautama, the Buddha, in
northern India

551 Birth of Confucius
in China

c.540 Magadha becomes
the dominant kingdom in
the Indian subcontinent

500 The Bantu-speaking
peoples begin to expand
from their west African
homeland

riding on horseback. This development made the nomadic life possible by
giving sufficient speed and mobility to
manage large herds over vast ranges. By 500 BC the
Iranian nomads had created a relatively homogeneous culture area from the
Balkans almost to the borders of China. Nomadism had both beneficial and
destructive consequences for the settled peoples of Eurasia. The nomads
helped to forge trade links across Asia and by 500 BC Chinese silks found their
way to the west along what would become known as the Silk Route. The
mobility of the nomads also made them formidable raiders: Europe, the
Middle East and China were troubled by their attacks for two thousand years.

Around 600 sub-Saharan Africa moved directly from the Stone Age to the
Iron Age and the expansion of the Bantu-speaking peoples from their west
African homeland continued. Over the next 1,500 years they became, through
migration and cultural assimilation, the main linguistic group in Africa (▷ 1.16).

In Mesoamerica the Maya and Zapotec cultures emerged (▷ 1.28). Both
Mesoamerican and Andean chiefdoms built impressive ceremonial centers.
Farming was established in the Amazon basin by 500 BC and in several areas of
North America cultivated plants were important supplements to wild foods. In
the eastern woodlands hunters, gatherers and cultivators lived in semiperma-
nent villages and developed complex cultures: the Adena people built communal burial mounds and ritual earthworks, made pottery and worked
copper. Full farming economies, though, did not appear for many centuries ■

Writing was invented as an aid to administration in communities that had grown so complex that human memory could no longer store all the information needed for efficient government. The earliest known writing has been found on clay tablets from the Sumerian city of Uruk (in modern Iraq), from about 3400 BC but, as this was already a complete system with over seven hundred signs, development must have begun much earlier.

The earliest Sumerian signs are pictographs – for example the sign for barley is a simplified picture of an ear of barley. More complex ideas were expressed by combining signs: thus a head and a bowl together meant "to eat". The signs were inscribed on wet clay tablets which were then dried. This proved to be a very durable medium and many thousands of clay tablets have survived (▷ 1.10). After about 2900 BC the signs were gradually simplified and inscribed with a rectangular-ended reed stylus. This left wedge-shaped strokes from which this script derives its name (cuneiform, from the Latin *cuneus*, "wedge").

Cuneiform was gradually refined so that a sign could also stand for the phonetic value of the word: if this system were used for modern English, the sign for "man" could also be used in combination with another sign, such as that for "age", to make another word, "manage". Syllable signs were also introduced, enabling cuneiform to record accurately all elements of human speech. Most early Sumerian documents were accounts and records of transactions. It was not until about 2400 that writing was used to record law codes, letters, chronicles, religious beliefs or for literature.

The Sumerian writing systems were widely adapted to other languages. Elamite and Indus valley pictographic derive from Sumerian pictographic (▷ 1.26) and although Egyptian hieroglyphic writing (a system that is almost as old as the Sumerian) was unique, the idea was probably based on Sumerian pictographs (▷ 1.17). Cuneiform was adapted successfully to the Akkadian, Assyrian, Babylonian, Elamite, Hittite, Hurrian and Urartian languages among others. Nevertheless, hundreds of different signs had to be learned, and scribes needed several years to master cuneiform and hieroglyphic scripts; as a result literacy remained the preserve of a tiny minority of specialists, and the cultural impact of its introduction was limited.

In the early 16th century BC the much simpler proto-Canaanite phonetic alphabet, with only 28 letters that stood for syllables which could be combined to spell out the sound of a word, was developed in the Levant or eastern Mediterranean coastal region (▷ 1.12). The letters were based on Egyptian hieroglyphs. By 1000 BC many variants of the proto-Canaanite script had developed, most important among them the Phoenician, Aramaic and the Arabian Sabean and Nabatean alphabets. The Aramaic alphabet was adopted by the Assyrians by the 8th century and replaced cuneiform as the main script of the Middle East. Adaptations of Aramaic were introduced into India in the 7th century and became the basis of modern Indian scripts and, ultimately, of the Indian-derived scripts of southeast and central Asia. Nabatean developed into the Arabic script in the 7th century AD while Sabean crossed the Red Sea to form the basis of Ethiopic, which was the only independent script to emerge in sub-Saharan Africa.

The Phoenician alphabet was the basis of the Old Hebrew and Greek alphabets. The Greeks adapted the Phoenician alphabet in the 8th century by introducing separate letters for consonant and vowel sounds (▷ 1.23). This was more precise than any syllabic alphabet. The Greek alphabet was in turn adapted to form new scripts by the peoples of Anatolia, the Balkans and Italy, including the Etruscans whose script was developed by the Romans into the Latin alphabet. Alphabetic scripts were easier to learn and use and they permitted literacy to become a widespread accomplishment, rather than just the preserve of professional scribes and administrators.

China, Mesoamerica and Polynesia each saw the independent development of writing. In Shang Dynasty China, a script with both pictographic and phonetic elements appeared around 1600 BC. Most early examples record the

results of divinations on animal bones, but the script was also used for record-keeping (▷ 1.27). This script was constantly refined and standardized over the centuries, and the modern Chinese writing system is still based on its principles. The Chinese script became the basis of Japanese and Korean scripts (though the Koreans later adopted an alphabetic script).

In Mesoamerica the Zapotecs began to develop a hieroglyphic script about 800 BC, from which the later Mesoamerican scripts derive (▷ 1.28). Of these, only the Mayan was a fully developed literary language capable of expressing all aspects of spoken language. Writing did not develop in the Andean civilizations although the Inca *quipu,* a mnemonic device made of knotted strings, fulfilled some of the functions of a simple script. Colored strings symbolized different commodities or services while the number of knots represented quantities held or required.

Another script to arise independently of any other was the hieroglyphic script developed in the Polynesian chiefdoms of Easter Island about AD 1500. Known as Rongorongo, it fell out of use before Europeans reached Easter Island and has not been deciphered ■

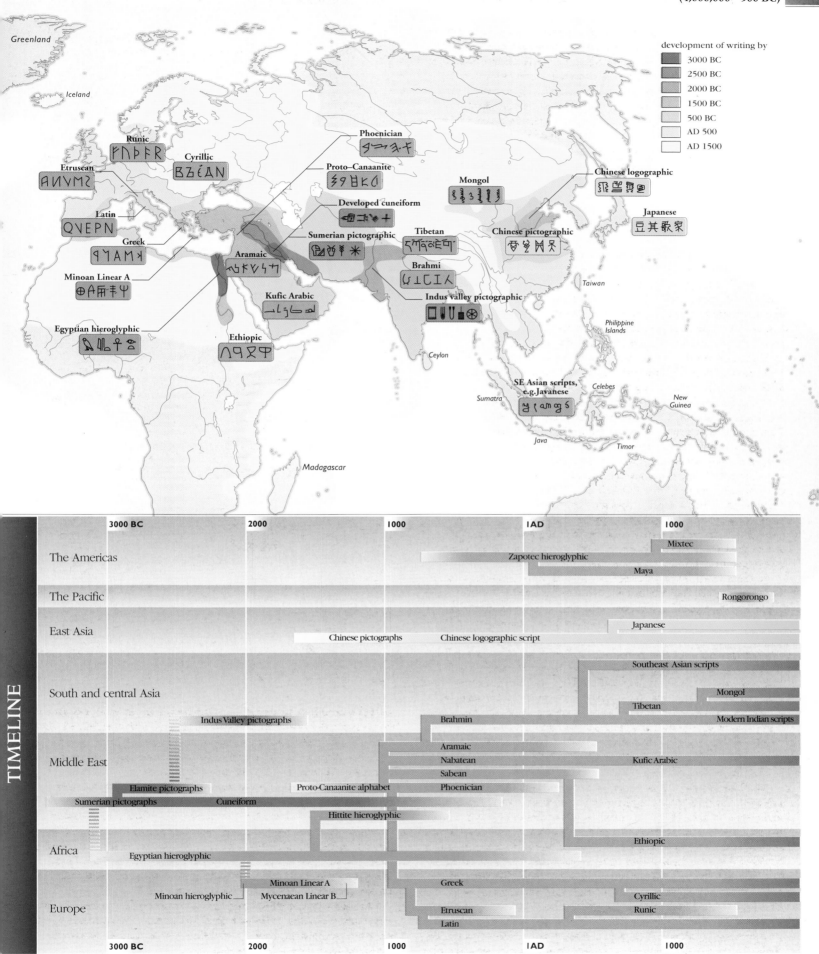

Greenland

Iceland

Runic

Cyrillic

Etruscan

Phoenician

Proto–Canaanite

Chinese logographic

Mongol

Latin

Developed cuneiform

Greek

Sumerian pictographic

Chinese pictographic

Japanese

Aramaic

Tibetan

Minoan Linear A

Brahmi

Kufic Arabic

Indus valley pictographic

Taiwan

Egyptian hieroglyphic

Ethiopic

Philippine Islands

Ceylon

SE Asian scripts, e.g.Javanese

Celebes

Sumatra

New Guinea

Java

Timor

Madagascar

development of writing by

- 3000 BC
- 2500 BC
- 2000 BC
- 1500 BC
- 500 BC
- AD 500
- AD 1500

TIMELINE

	3000 BC	2000	1000	IAD	1000
The Americas				Zapotec hieroglyphic	Mixtec / Maya
The Pacific					Rongorongo
East Asia		Chinese pictographs	Chinese logographic script	Japanese	
South and central Asia		Indus Valley pictographs	Brahmin	Southeast Asian scripts / Tibetan	Mongol / Modern Indian scripts
Middle East	Sumerian pictographs	Elamite pictographs / Cuneiform	Proto-Canaanite alphabet	Aramaic / Nabatean / Sabean / Phoenician	Kufic Arabic
			Hittite hieroglyphic		
Africa	Egyptian hieroglyphic				Ethiopic
Europe		Minoan hieroglyphic / Minoan Linear A / Mycenaean Linear B	Greek / Etruscan / Latin		Cyrillic / Runic

| | 3000 BC | 2000 | 1000 | IAD | 1000 |

The earliest communities to rely on farming for most of their food grew up in the area known as the Fertile Crescent. This region of good soils and light but reliable rainfall extends in an arc from the foothills of Iraq's Zagros mountains, through south Turkey to western Syria, the Lebanon and Israel. Toward the end of the Ice Age it was colonized by plants such as wild emmer and einkorn wheat, wild barley, wild pulses, and almond, oak and pistachio trees. The supply of cereals and nuts was so rich that in some areas the hunter–gatherer population could settle in semi-permanent villages.

Among these sedentary hunter–gatherers were the Natufians of the Levant, whose way of life developed about 10,500 BC. Except for short stays at seasonal camps, the Natufians lived in villages of substantial wooden huts with stone foundations. They hunted gazelle intensively but their staple food was wild cereals, which they harvested with bone-handled reaping knives, stored in stone jars and processed with querns, grindstones, and mortars and pestles. Settled living and abundant food led them to abandon the egalitarianism of the nomadic hunter–gatherer band. A wide variation in the range and quality of goods found in individual burials points to the existence of social ranking.

During the 9th millennium they began to cultivate wild cereals close to their settlements. In some places, such as at Tell Mureybet in Syria, wild cereals may even have been introduced to areas where they did not naturally occur. The climate was changing and the natural range of wild cereals was shrinking, so these developments were probably an attempt to secure the food supply. Around 8000 BC these early farmers learned to breed wild cereals selectively for characteristics that increased the yield and made them easier to harvest. Within a few centuries domesticated strains of barley, emmer and einkorn wheat had appeared. Although cultivated plants were important to the economies of these transitional, or "proto-Neolithic", farmers, hunting and gathering continued to be crucial sources of food. As the population began to outstrip the environment's

capacity to support the old lifestyle, the dependence on farming increased. By about 7500 BC communities with a full farming economy had developed, marking the proper beginning of the Neolithic or "New Stone Age" (the period between the adoption of agriculture and that of metal working).

One of the most impressive proto-Neolithic sites is at Jericho, where a walled settlement of 1,500 people had grown up near a permanent spring by about 8000 BC. Domesticated barley and emmer wheat, pulses and figs were cultivated, but wild animals – gazelle and wild sheep and goats – were also important food sources. The people lived in huts built of sun-dried mud bricks, the earliest known use of what became the most important building material of the Middle East. Mud brick was easy to produce; when a house fell into disrepair it was simply knocked down and replaced by a new one. Over the centuries, successive rebuildings on the same site produced a high mound of debris,

Map labels:
spread of domesticated emmer wheat and barley to southeast Europe, 7th millennium
Aegean Sea
Lake Tuz
Ashikli Huyuk
Hacilar
Suberde
Can Has
TAURUS
Cyprus
Khirokitia
Mediterranean Sea

Legend:
- wild strains of einkorn wheat only
- wild strains of emmer and einkorn wheat, and barley
- distribution of wild sheep and goats
- southeastern limit of range of aurochs
- southern limit of dry farming
- area of Epipaleolithic Natufian sites, 10,500–8500
- proto–Neolithic settlement, 8500–7500
- aceramic Neolithic farming village, 7500–6500
- aceramic site with population of over 1000
- obsidian source
- distribution of Armenian obsidian
- distribution of Anatolian obsidian
- modern coastline and drainage where altered

0   300 km
0   200 mi

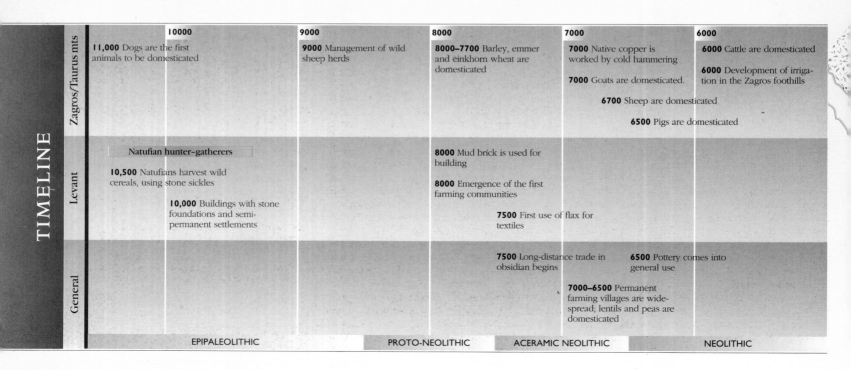

TIMELINE		10000	9000	8000	7000	6000
	Zagros/Taurus mts	**11,000** Dogs are the first animals to be domesticated	**9000** Management of wild sheep herds	**8000–7700** Barley, emmer and einkorn wheat are domesticated	**7000** Native copper is worked by cold hammering **7000** Goats are domesticated. **6700** Sheep are domesticated **6500** Pigs are domesticated	**6000** Cattle are domesticated **6000** Development of irrigation in the Zagros foothills
	Levant	Natufian hunter–gatherers **10,500** Natufians harvest wild cereals, using stone sickles **10,000** Buildings with stone foundations and semi-permanent settlements		**8000** Mud brick is used for building **8000** Emergence of the first farming communities **7500** First use of flax for textiles		
	General			**7500** Long-distance trade in obsidian begins **7000–6500** Permanent farming villages are wide-spread; lentils and peas are domesticated	**6500** Pottery comes into general use	

EPIPALEOLITHIC   PROTO-NEOLITHIC   ACERAMIC NEOLITHIC   NEOLITHIC

Black Sea

CAUCASUS MOUNTAINS

Kura

Ardks

Caspian Sea

hunter–gatherers

ANATOLIA

Kizil Irmak

Murat

Lake Van

Lake Urmia

◆ Acigol

◆ Chiftlik

5

Bingol ◆

Nemrut Dag

Cafer Huyuk ⬠ Chayonu

Gritille

Ceyhan

Orontes

MESOPOTAMIA

Tigris

2

Zawi Chemi Shanidar

Qermez Dere

Tell Aswad

6

Karim Shahir

Jarmo

Great Zab

ZAGROS MOUNTAINS

Tell Mureybet

Abu Hureyra

1

Euphrates

Bouqras

Ganj Dareh

Diyala

Tepe Guran

Tepe Abdul Hosein

Ugarit

Syrian Desert

Tamarkhan

Karkheh

LEVANT

Labwe

Ali Kosh

8

Choga Bonut

Tell Ramad

Beisamoun

Nahal Oren

Munhatta

Hatula

Ain Ghazal

Bou Gosh

Jericho

El Khiam

3

Nahal Hemar

4

Beidha

Basta

Persian Gulf

HUMAN skulls, like this one found at Jericho, were often buried separately. Sometimes they were decorated with paint, shells and modeled clay features.

---

called a *tell* in Arabic, *huyuk* in Turkish and *tepe* in Persian. These settlement mounds are the most characteristic archeological sites of the region.

Farming also began to develop in southern Anatolia and the Zagros mountains. In the mountains hunter–gatherers intensified their management of flocks of wild sheep and goats. Animal bones from a settlement at Zawi Chemi Shanidar (9000 BC) show that the inhabitants killed mainly immature sheep. Since hunting would have resulted in a more random distribution of ages, the sheep had probably been penned and selectively culled. Pollen samples also suggest that wild cereals were cultivated at Zawi Chemi Shanidar. By the 7th millennium, domesticated sheep and goats were an important part of the economy of villages such as Chayonu (now in eastern Turkey).

Farming had not yet begun on the greater part of the fertile but almost rainless Mesopotamian plain. Only along the eastern edges, which caught some of the rainfall of the Zagros mountains, was farming possible before the development of irrigation and heat-resistant cereal strains in the 6th millennium.

The early farming communities had no pottery; this period of the Neolithic is known as the aceramic or prepottery Neolithic. The first pottery appeared by 7000 BC, but such was its usefulness for cooking and storage that its use had become widespread within five centuries. By this time bread wheat had also been developed, flax – the raw material of linen cloth – had been domesticated, as had the pig, and cattle were introduced from southeastern Europe where farming was just beginning.

The sedentary way of life meant that communities became less self-sufficient and long-distance trade, particularly in salt and toolmaking stone, became more important. The finest toolmaking stone, obsidian (volcanic glass), was traded over long distances. Obsidian from Anatolia has been found in early Neolithic sites almost as far south as the Red Sea, while obsidian from the region by Lake Van reached the Mediterranean and the Persian Gulf.

---

1 Abu Hureyra was a village of 300-400 people, living by hunting gazelles and harvesting wild cereals, c.9500.

2 Zawi Chemi Shanidar, a summer settlement c.9000, shows evidence for intensive management of wild sheep herds.

3 Jericho was a permanent settlement by 8500 BC, and was walled by 8000.

4 Nahal Hemar, an aceramic Neolithic site, has the earliest evidence for textile manufacture (flax).

5 At Chayonu, native copper was used 7300-6500 to make tools and ornaments.

6 Before 6000 BC Mesopotamia was only sparsely populated with hunter–gatherers.

7 Cultivation of emmer wheat and barley began in southeast Europe c.6000 BC, probably as a result of trade contacts with the Middle East.

8 Ali Kosh was one of the earliest farming communities on the Mesopotamian plain, founded 8000 BC.

See also 1.03 (rise of agriculture),
1.09 (MiddleEast), 1.16 (Africa)

By the time that pottery came into widespread use in the Fertile Crescent, around 6500 BC, the densest concentration of farming settlements was still to be found in the uplands of the Levant, southern Anatolia and the Zagros mountains, where there was reliable rainfall. Most villages had no more than a few hundred inhabitants and had social structures with relatively little distinction between rich and poor; the simple subsistence economies were based on cereals and herds of sheep, goats or cattle.

An important exception was the town-sized settlement which grew up around 6700 BC at Chatal Huyuk in Turkey. This settlement of densely packed mud-brick houses is the largest Neolithic settlement yet found. Long-distance trade in obsidian from nearby volcanoes, and improved agricultural yields resulting from the adoption of simple irrigation techniques, may have played a role in the town's growth. Chatal Huyuk had rich artistic traditions of wall-painting and sculpture, and a great many elaborately decorated shrines have been found. Many other crafts were practiced, including weaving, basketry, copper working (the earliest known evidence of copper smelting has been found here), fine stone toolmaking and pottery. Chatal Huyuk, however, was a precocious development. The local environment could not sustain longterm urban growth: the site was abandoned after about a thousand years and the pattern of dispersed settlements, typical of the rest of Neolithic Anatolia, was resumed.

The conditions for sustainable urban growth were first achieved in Mesopotamia. Farming was still confined to the fringes of the Mesopotamian plain in 6500 BC but it had spread throughout the region by 5500. The expansion of farming settlement across the plain is reflected by a series of cultures, each of which can be identified by a distinctive pottery style. The first of these was the Hassuna culture (6500–6000), centered on northern Mesopotamia and mostly within the dry farming zone. The Hassuna people grew emmer, einkorn and barley, bred sheep, goats, pigs and cattle and hunted a little. There is evidence for copper and lead

smelting and the Hassuna culture was the earliest to produce painted pottery and fire it in purpose-built kilns. Stamp seals, later used widely in Mesopotamia to indicate ownership, were also first used in the Hassuna culture.

The Hassuna culture was replaced around 6000 by the Halafian culture. A storehouse excavated at Arpachiyeh, containing a concentration of fine pottery, jewelry, sculpture and flint and obsidian tools, suggests that the Halafians were ruled by chiefs who amassed considerable personal wealth and controlled the community's trade contacts. The influence of the Halafian culture was confined almost entirely to the dry farming zone but the same was not true of the contemporary, and overlapping,

Legend:

- earliest centers of copper working, 6000
- spread of copper working by 4500
- Hassuna culture, 6500–6000
- Samarran culture, 6000–5500
- Halafian culture, 6000–5400
- Ubaid culture, 5900–4300

settlement, though not necessarily occupied continuously throughout the period
- established before 6000
- established 6000–5400
- established 5400–4300
≈ evidence of irrigation, c.6000
Uruk Ubaid period temple
- early pottery kilns
- find of Ubaid pottery outside main cultural area
- obsidian source
- copper source
...... southern limit of dry farming
—— modern coastline and drainage where altered

0 _____ 300 km
0 _____ 200 mi

Mediterranean Sea

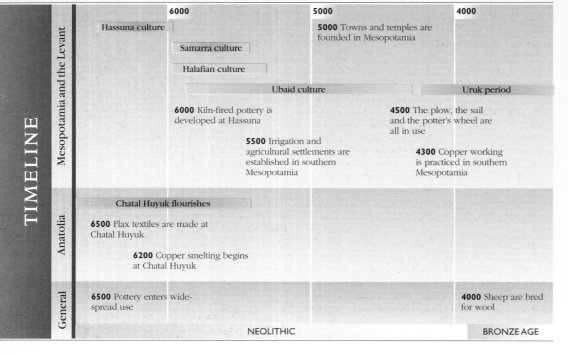

		6000	5000	4000
Mesopotamia and the Levant		Hassuna culture	**5000** Towns and temples are founded in Mesopotamia	
		Samarra culture		
		Halafian culture		
		Ubaid culture		Uruk period
		6000 Kiln-fired pottery is developed at Hassuna	**4500** The plow, the sail and the potter's wheel are all in use	
		5500 Irrigation and agricultural settlements are established in southern Mesopotamia	**4300** Copper working is practiced in southern Mesopotamia	
Anatolia		Chatal Huyuk flourishes		
		6500 Flax textiles are made at Chatal Huyuk.		
		6200 Copper smelting begins at Chatal Huyuk		
General		**6500** Pottery enters widespread use	**4000** Sheep are bred for wool	
		NEOLITHIC		BRONZE AGE

1 Chatal Huyuk had a population of about 6000 people, mainly farmers, between 6700–5700 BC.

2 Tell Umm Dabaghiyeh was a permanent hunter settlement c.6000, trading hides for grain with the northern farmers.

3 Choga Mami is the site of the earliest known irrigation canals; 5500 BC.

4 The fertile but rainless south Mesopotamia plain was colonized by farmers after the development of irrigation c.5500 BC.

5 Kilns were first used for firing pottery in Hassuna c.6000 BC.

6 The Ubaid settlement of Tell Awayli had a grain storehouse with a total area of 200 square meters.

7 Eridu was the oldest town in southern Mesopotamia. It had a large temple and a population of five thousand by the end of the Ubaid period.

8 Ubaid pottery from Ur found here indicates trade links between Mesopotamia and Arabia.

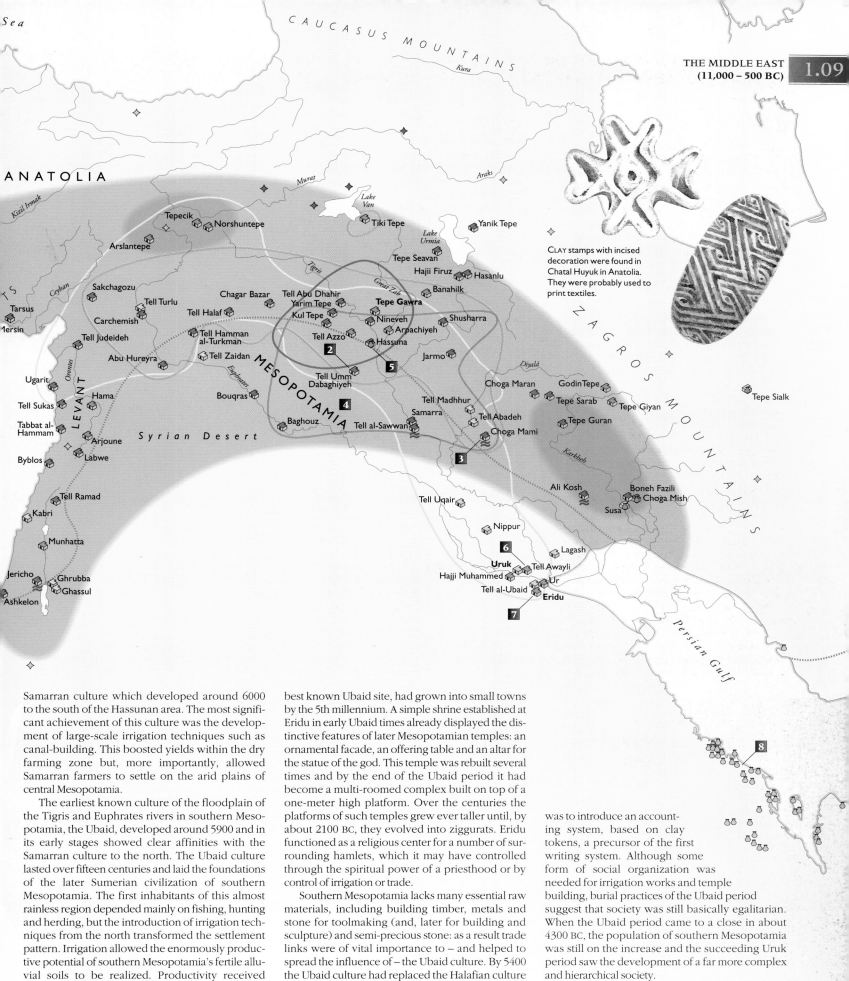

Sea

CAUCASUS MOUNTAINS

Kura

ANATOLIA

Kizil Irmak

Murat

Araks

Lake Van

Tigris

Lake Urmia

Tepecik
Norshuntepe
Arslantepe

Tiki Tepe

Yanik Tepe

Tepe Seavan

Hajii Firuz
Hasanlu

TS

Ceyhan

Sakchagozu

Tell Turlu

Carchemish

Chagar Bazar
Tell Halaf

Tell Abu Dhahir
Yarim Tepe
Kul Tepe

Banahilk

Tepe Gawra

Shusharra

CLAY stamps with incised
decoration were found in
Chatal Huyuk in Anatolia.
They were probably used to
print textiles.

Tarsus

Mersin

Tell Judeideh

Tell Hamman
al-Turkman

Tell Azzo

Nineveh
Arpachiyeh
Hassuna

Great Zab

ZAGROS MOUNTAINS

Abu Hureyra

Tell Zaidan

2

Jarmo

Diyala

Ugarit

Orontes

Hama

MESOPOTAMIA

5

Tell Umm
Dabaghiyeh

Choga Maran

GodinTepe
Tepe Sarab
Tepe Giyan

Tepe Sialk

LEVANT

Tell Sukas
Tabbat al-
Hammam

Bouqras

4

Tell Madhhur
Samarra
Tell Abadeh

Tepe Guran

Baghouz

Tell al-Sawwan

Choga Mami

Karkheh

Arjoune
Labwe

Syrian Desert

Byblos

3

Ali Kosh

Boneh Fazili
Choga Mish

Tell Ramad

Tell Uqair

Susa

Kabri

Nippur

Munhatta

6

Lagash

Jericho

Ghrubba
Ghassul

Uruk
Hajji Muhammed

Tell Awayli
Ur

Persian Gulf

Ashkelon

Tell al-Ubaid
Eridu

7

8

Samarran culture which developed around 6000 to the south of the Hassunan area. The most significant achievement of this culture was the development of large-scale irrigation techniques such as canal-building. This boosted yields within the dry farming zone but, more importantly, allowed Samarran farmers to settle on the arid plains of central Mesopotamia.

The earliest known culture of the floodplain of the Tigris and Euphrates rivers in southern Mesopotamia, the Ubaid, developed around 5900 and in its early stages showed clear affinities with the Samarran culture to the north. The Ubaid culture lasted over fifteen centuries and laid the foundations of the later Sumerian civilization of southern Mesopotamia. The first inhabitants of this almost rainless region depended mainly on fishing, hunting and herding, but the introduction of irrigation techniques from the north transformed the settlement pattern. Irrigation allowed the enormously productive potential of southern Mesopotamia's fertile alluvial soils to be realized. Productivity received another boost in the 5th millennium with the invention of the plow. Intensive agriculture meant that the population rose rapidly and many new farming villages were founded. Some of these, like Eridu, the

best known Ubaid site, had grown into small towns by the 5th millennium. A simple shrine established at Eridu in early Ubaid times already displayed the distinctive features of later Mesopotamian temples: an ornamental facade, an offering table and an altar for the statue of the god. This temple was rebuilt several times and by the end of the Ubaid period it had become a multi-roomed complex built on top of a one-meter high platform. Over the centuries the platforms of such temples grew ever taller until, by about 2100 BC, they evolved into ziggurats. Eridu functioned as a religious center for a number of surrounding hamlets, which it may have controlled through the spiritual power of a priesthood or by control of irrigation or trade.

Southern Mesopotamia lacks many essential raw materials, including building timber, metals and stone for toolmaking (and, later for building and sculpture) and semi-precious stone: as a result trade links were of vital importance to – and helped to spread the influence of – the Ubaid culture. By 5400 the Ubaid culture had replaced the Halafian culture in northern Mesopotamia while Ubaid pottery manufactured around Ur has been found throughout the Persian Gulf region.

An important innovation of the Ubaid culture

was to introduce an accounting system, based on clay tokens, a precursor of the first writing system. Although some form of social organization was needed for irrigation works and temple building, burial practices of the Ubaid period suggest that society was still basically egalitarian. When the Ubaid period came to a close in about 4300 BC, the population of southern Mesopotamia was still on the increase and the succeeding Uruk period saw the development of a far more complex and hierarchical society.

See also 1.03 (the rise of agriculture),
1.10 (earliest cities), 1.20 (southeast Europe)

The world's first cities and states emerged in the region of Sumeria in southern Mesopotamia in the Uruk period (4300–3100), named for the oldest and largest Sumerian city. States, with their social classes, centralized government and well-organized trade, became important mechanisms for coordinating flood control (important in this region) and other public works. Early Sumerian cities were dominated by temple complexes, and the priesthood probably took the lead in this organization. The Tigris and Euphrates rivers are subject to violent floods and unpredictable changes of course, events which must have seemed like the acts of capricious gods (the biblical story of the flood is of Sumerian origin). The priests claimed to be able to propitiate the gods, and this may have given them the authority to be accepted as rulers of their cities.

Most Sumerian cities of the Uruk period had a population between two and eight thousand people, although Uruk itself, the largest, had over 10,000; by 2700 BC this had risen to about 50,000. Most of these were farmers who traveled out each day to the surrounding fields. However, the food surpluses they produced were great and Sumerian society became the first to have the resources to support large numbers of people in specialist occupations: sculptors, potters, bronze-casters, stonemasons, bakers, brewers and weavers.

The temples became centers of redistribution where the surplus food of the countryside and craft products were gathered to be given out as rations, or traded abroad for raw materials that could not be found locally. These trade links ranged from India and Afghanistan to Egypt, and played an important part in spreading the influence of Sumerian civilization throughout the Middle East. It was a complex task to manage the redistribution of produce. Keeping track of all the transactions was beyond the ability of unaided memory and by around 3400 a system of pictographic writing, probably derived

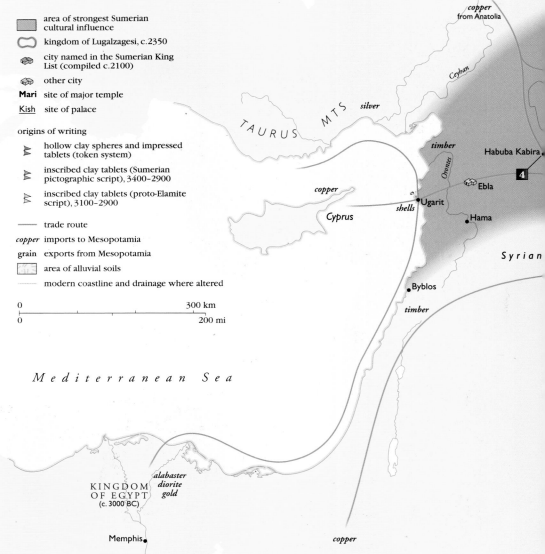

area of strongest Sumerian cultural influence

kingdom of Lugalzagesi, c.2350

city named in the Sumerian King List (compiled c.2100)

other city

Mari site of major temple

<u>Kish</u> site of palace

origins of writing

hollow clay spheres and impressed tablets (token system)

inscribed clay tablets (Sumerian pictographic script), 3400–2900

inscribed clay tablets (proto-Elamite script), 3100–2900

trade route

copper imports to Mesopotamia

grain exports from Mesopotamia

area of alluvial soils

modern coastline and drainage where altered

0   300 km

0   200 mi

from an earlier token system, had been developed.

Sumerian civilization entered a new and troubled phase in the Early Dynastic period (2900–2334 BC). Massive defensive walls were built around the cities, bronze weapons were produced in increasing quantities and war begins to feature prominently as a subject of official art with rulers often being shown trampling on their enemies. This period also saw writing applied to purposes other than administration, as rulers began to record their glorious deeds to ensure their posthumous reputations. The gap between rich and poor widened and slavery appears in the records for the first time. Secular leaders now appear alongside the priest-kings. Some had the title *sangu* (accountant), suggesting that bureaucrats had achieved equal status with the priests. Others were called *lugal* (literally "big man"): these may have been war leaders, elected in times of emergency in the past, who had succeeded in making their power permanent. To show that their rule had divine approval these secular rulers built palaces next to the temple precincts, where they lived in opulence. In death they were given rich burials, such as those excavated at the Royal Cemetery at Ur, accompanied by the luxuries of their everyday lives and even their sacrificed retainers. Lacking the spiritual authority of the priesthood, the new secular rulers established their authority through law codes,

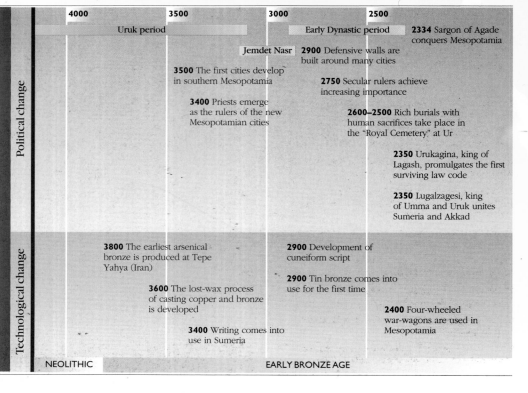

TIMELINE

	4000	3500	3000	2500
		Uruk period	Early Dynastic period	**2334** Sargon of Agade conquers Mesopotamia
			Jemdet Nasr	**2900** Defensive walls are built around many cities
Political change		**3500** The first cities develop in southern Mesopotamia		**2750** Secular rulers achieve increasing importance
		3400 Priests emerge as the rulers of the new Mesopotamian cities		**2600–2500** Rich burials with human sacrifices take place in the "Royal Cemetery" at Ur
				2350 Urukagina, king of Lagash, promulgates the first surviving law code
				2350 Lugalzagesi, king of Umma and Uruk unites Sumeria and Akkad
Technological change		**3800** The earliest arsenical bronze is produced at Tepe Yahya (Iran)	**2900** Development of cuneiform script	
		3600 The lost-wax process of casting copper and bronze is developed	**2900** Tin bronze comes into use for the first time	
		3400 Writing comes into use in Sumeria		**2400** Four-wheeled war-wagons are used in Mesopotamia
	NEOLITHIC		EARLY BRONZE AGE	

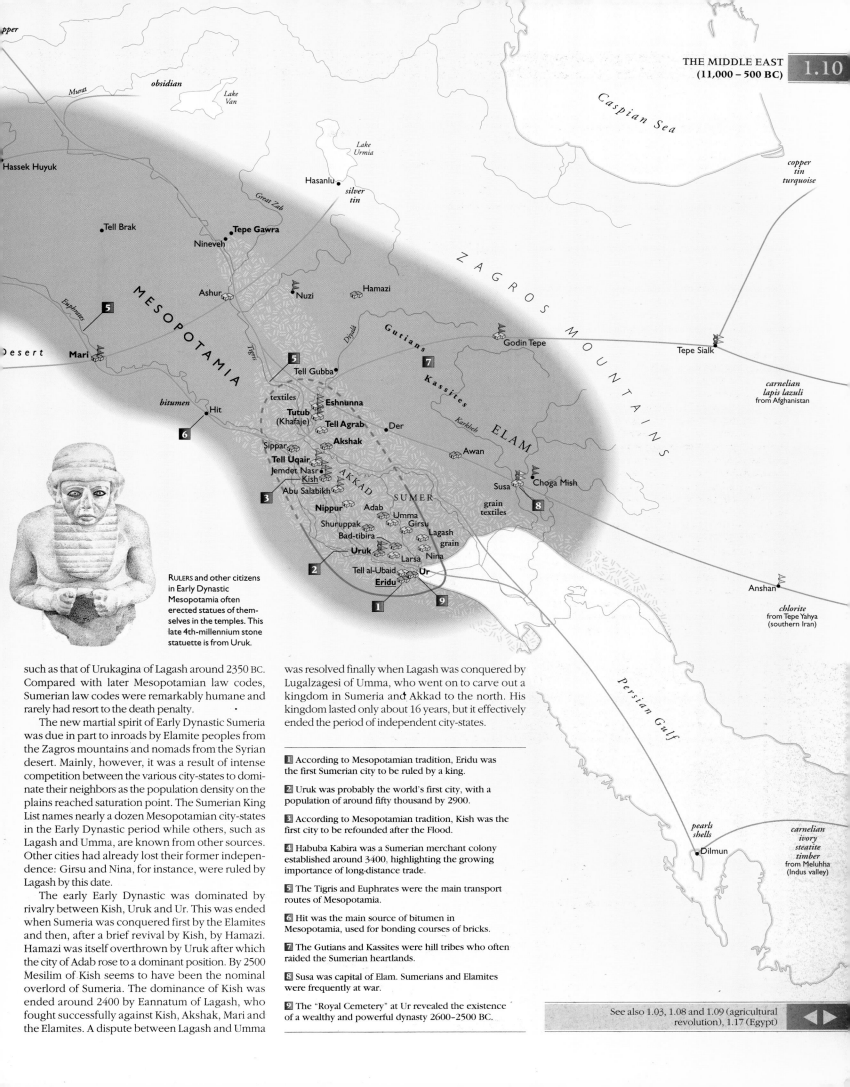

Caspian Sea

pper

Murat

obsidian

*Lake
Van*

Hassek Huyuk

copper
tin
turquoise

Hasanlu

*silver
tin*

Great Zab

Tell Brak

Tepe Gawra

Nineveh

M E S O P O T A M I A

Ashur

Nuzi

Hamazi

Z A G R O S

Euphrates

5

Tigris

Diyala

Gutians

Godin Tepe

Tepe Sialk

Mari

Desert

bitumen

Hit

6

textiles

Eshnunna

Tutub
(Khafaje)

Tell Agrab

Sippar

Akshak

Tell Uqair

Jemdet Nasr

Kish

Abu Salabikh

3

Tell Gubba

5

Kassites

E L A M

Karkheh

Der

M O U N T A I N S

*carnelian
lapis lazuli
from Afghanistan*

A K K A D

Nippur

Adab

Shuruppak

Bad-tibira

Uruk

Larsa

2

Tell al-Ubaid

Eridu

1

S U M E R

Umma

Girsu

Lagash
grain

Nina

Ur

9

Awan

Susa

Choga Mish

*grain
textiles*

8

7

Anshan

*chlorite
from Tepe Yahya
(southern Iran)*

RULERS and other citizens
in Early Dynastic
Mesopotamia often
erected statues of them-
selves in the temples. This
late 4th-millennium stone
statuette is from Uruk.

Persian Gulf

*pearls
shells*

Dilmun

*carnelian
ivory
steatite
timber
from Meluhha
(Indus valley)*

such as that of Urukagina of Lagash around 2350 BC.
Compared with later Mesopotamian law codes,
Sumerian law codes were remarkably humane and
rarely had resort to the death penalty.

The new martial spirit of Early Dynastic Sumeria
was due in part to inroads by Elamite peoples from
the Zagros mountains and nomads from the Syrian
desert. Mainly, however, it was a result of intense
competition between the various city-states to dominate their neighbors as the population density on the
plains reached saturation point. The Sumerian King
List names nearly a dozen Mesopotamian city-states
in the Early Dynastic period while others, such as
Lagash and Umma, are known from other sources.
Other cities had already lost their former independence: Girsu and Nina, for instance, were ruled by
Lagash by this date.

The early Early Dynastic was dominated by
rivalry between Kish, Uruk and Ur. This was ended
when Sumeria was conquered first by the Elamites
and then, after a brief revival by Kish, by Hamazi.
Hamazi was itself overthrown by Uruk after which
the city of Adab rose to a dominant position. By 2500
Mesilim of Kish seems to have been the nominal
overlord of Sumeria. The dominance of Kish was
ended around 2400 by Eannatum of Lagash, who
fought successfully against Kish, Akshak, Mari and
the Elamites. A dispute between Lagash and Umma

was resolved finally when Lagash was conquered by
Lugalzagesi of Umma, who went on to carve out a
kingdom in Sumeria and Akkad to the north. His
kingdom lasted only about 16 years, but it effectively
ended the period of independent city-states.

1 According to Mesopotamian tradition, Eridu was
the first Sumerian city to be ruled by a king.

2 Uruk was probably the world's first city, with a
population of around fifty thousand by 2900.

3 According to Mesopotamian tradition, Kish was the
first city to be refounded after the Flood.

4 Habuba Kabira was a Sumerian merchant colony
established around 3400, highlighting the growing
importance of long-distance trade.

5 The Tigris and Euphrates were the main transport
routes of Mesopotamia.

6 Hit was the main source of bitumen in
Mesopotamia, used for bonding courses of bricks.

7 The Gutians and Kassites were hill tribes who often
raided the Sumerian heartlands.

8 Susa was capital of Elam. Sumerians and Elamites
were frequently at war.

9 The "Royal Cemetery" at Ur revealed the existence
of a wealthy and powerful dynasty 2600-2500 BC.

See also 1.03, 1.08 and 1.09 (agricultural
revolution), 1.17 (Egypt)

By the end of the Early Dynastic period Sumeria, though still wealthy and populous, was being overtaken by Akkad as the leading center of Mesopotamian civilization. The rise of Akkad is reflected in the career of the first great conqueror known to history, Sargon "the Great" of Agade (r.2334–2279). Sargon's origins are obscure. He claimed that his father had been a date-grower and that he himself had been an official to the king of the Akkadian city of Kish. How he came to power is unknown but he may have staged a coup against his employer to become king of Kish. Sargon's first task was to eliminate the most powerful ruler in Mesopotamia, Lugalzagesi of Umma and Uruk, which he did in three hard-fought battles. He went on to conquer the rest of Sumeria, Akkad and Elam before pushing west to the Mediterranean and Anatolia. The island of Dilmun (Bahrain) and parts of Iran may also have been conquered. Sargon united peoples of many different ethnic and cultural identities to create an entirely new kind of state, an empire. To celebrate his conquests he founded the city of Agade, which has yet to be located. His empire reached its peak of power under his grandson Naram-Sin (r.2254–2218) but thereafter declined and collapsed about 2193, probably as a result of invasions by the Gutians and Amorites. For eighty years the old pattern of competing city-states returned until a Sumerian revival occurred.

Using diplomacy as much as force, Ur-Nammu (r.2112–2095), the first king of the Third Dynasty of Ur, built a new empire stretching as far north as Assyria. Ur-Nammu's reign saw the construction of the first ziggurats, the high temple platforms that are Mesopotamia's most distinctive monuments. About 2034 the empire of the Third Dynasty came under pressure from the nomadic Amorites of the Syrian desert but it was a knockout blow from the Elamites, who sacked Ur in 2004, that led to the fall of the empire. Sumeria never regained its preeminence.

The two centuries following the fall of the Third Dynasty are a confusion of minor states and of inroads by the Amorites. The Amorites were a strong influence in the rise of the two states that were to dominate the next one and a half millennia of Mesopotamian history: Assyria and Babylon. Assyria emerged as an important trading power in the 19th century BC but it was only after the Amorite Shamshi-Adad took the capital Ashur, along with most of northern Mesopotamia, in about 1813 that it became a major territorial power. An Amorite dynasty had also set up at Babylon around 1894 and when Hammurabi came to the throne in 1792 Babylon controlled most of Akkad (subsequently known as Babylonia). Five years later Hammurabi marched south and conquered Sumeria. In 1781 Shamshi-Adad died and, weakened by attacks from Eshnunna and the Elamites, most of his kingdom was under Hammurabi's control by 1757. Two years later Hammurabi conquered the last Mesopotamian power, Eshnunna. Babylon now became the religious and cultural center of Mesopotamia.

In the 17th century BC new and threatening powers began to gather on the borders of Mesopotamia. The most important of these were the Hurrians and the Hittites. The Hurrians were a tribal people from Armenia who overran Assyria around 1680. The Hittites were an Indo-European people who had invaded Anatolia from Thrace about 1800 and had emerged as a powerful kingdom by 1650.

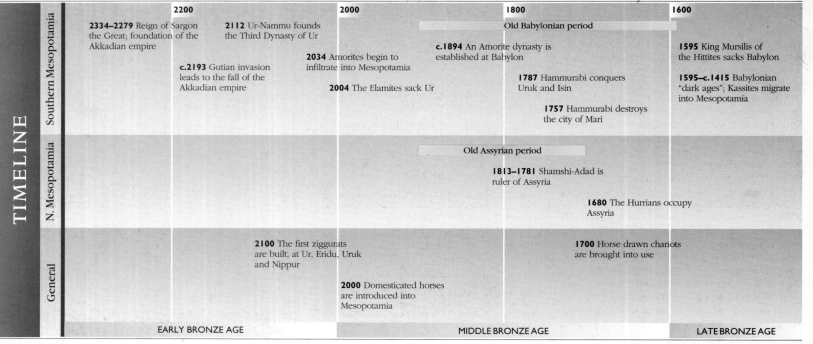

TIMELINE

Southern Mesopotamia

	2200		2000		1800		1600

2334–2279 Reign of Sargon the Great; foundation of the Akkadian empire

2112 Ur-Nammu founds the Third Dynasty of Ur

Old Babylonian period

c.1894 An Amorite dynasty is established at Babylon

1595 King Mursilis of the Hittites sacks Babylon

c.2193 Gutian invasion leads to the fall of the Akkadian empire

2034 Amorites begin to infiltrate into Mesopotamia

1787 Hammurabi conquers Uruk and Isin

1595–c.1415 Babylonian "dark ages"; Kassites migrate into Mesopotamia

2004 The Elamites sack Ur

1757 Hammurabi destroys the city of Mari

N. Mesopotamia

Old Assyrian period

1813–1781 Shamshi-Adad is ruler of Assyria

1680 The Hurrians occupy Assyria

General

2100 The first ziggurats are built; at Ur, Eridu, Uruk and Nippur

1700 Horse drawn chariots are brought into use

2000 Domesticated horses are introduced into Mesopotamia

EARLY BRONZE AGE | MIDDLE BRONZE AGE | LATE BRONZE AGE

Hurrians

Lake Van

Murat

Lake Urmia

SUBARTU [5]

Chagar Bazar (Ashnakkum)

Shubat-Enlil

Harran

Tell Brak

Nineveh

Qatara (Tell al-Rimah)

Shusharra

Tuttul

Ekallatum

Ashur [2]

Nuzi

MESOPOTAMIA

ASSYRIA

Great Zab

Tigris

Euphrate

1757

Desert

Terqa

Mari [8]

1757

Hit

1760

Z A G R O S

Diyala

Gutians

Kassites

1784

Mu-ti [4]

Eshnunna

Dur-Apilsin (Dur-Kurigalzu)

Der

Sippar [1]

1755

Agade?

Babylon

Kish

Abu Salabikh

Nippur

Borsippa

Isin

Adab

Shuruppak

AKKAD

EMUTBAL

Tell Wilaya

Susa

ELAM

Karkheh

1762

1787

1787

1763

Uruk

SUMER

Larsa

Eridu

Ur [7]

Lagash

[9]

Amorites

Lullubians

M O U N T A I N S

MARHASHI

HEAD of an Akkadian king, cast in copper. It probably portrays Naram-Sin (the grandson of Sargon) who called himself "god of Agade".

Persian Gulf

DILMUN [6]

empire of Sargon "the Great" of Agade, c.2279

territories possibly part of Sargon's empire

empire of the Third Dynasty of Ur, 2112–2004

Babylonian empire under Hammurabi, c.1750

kingdom of Shamshi–Adad, c.1813–1781

limit of Egyptian influence, c.1850

city

Kish royal palace

preserved palace archive of clay tablets

Ur capital of empire

ziggurat

Ur III, 2112–2004

old Babylonian, 1900–1700

campaign of Hammurabi, with date

Hittite campaign against Babylon, c.1595

defensive barrier

modern coastline and drainage where altered

0   300 km
0   200 mi

When the Hittite king Mursilis invaded and sacked Babylon in 1595, Mesopotamia entered a dark age that lasted almost two centuries. The Kassites migrated into the region from the east and by 1415 Babylonia had reemerged as a Kassite kingdom.

The most notable characteristic of the early Mesopotamian empires was instability. The success of a state was very dependent on the abilities of its ruler. Government was an expression of the king's will: a strong ruler could carve out an empire for himself but if his successor were indolent or weak the empire would decline. Part of the reason for this was the mechanism of government of the empires themselves. Conquered states were not occupied, garrisoned or subjected to a centrally controlled provincial government; instead, tribute was imposed and native rulers were given the duty of collecting and delivering it to the imperial power. This system worked well under strong emperors, but if imperial power was weakened, a vassal state could assert its independence simply by stopping payment of the tribute. Also, Mesopotamia lacked defensible frontiers and was vulnerable to invasions and infiltration from the Syrian desert or the Zagros mountains. The inhabitants of these regions were eager to share in the wealth and fertility of the plains. They might overthrow states, but were not seeking to destroy Mesopotamian civilization itself; indeed, those – like the Kassites and Amorites – who did succeed in settling on the plains quickly adopted Mesopotamian customs and became assimilated with the native population.

[1] Sargon's capital Agade has not been located but is believed to have been near Babylon.

[2] Ashur developed as a major trading power in the 19th century BC with links with Iran, Anatolia and the Persian Gulf.

[3] An Assyrian merchant colony was founded at Kultepe in the 19th century BC, part of a network that extended as far as the Black Sea.

[4] The Mu-ti defensive wall was built between the Tigris and Euphrates by King Shu-Sin of Ur (r.2037–2029) to protect Akkad and Sumer from invasion.

[5] Shubat-Enlil was the capital of Shamshi-Adad, the Amorite king of Assyria c.1813–1781.

[6] Later traditions held that Sargon the Great led a fleet against Dilmun; if true, this was the first recorded naval campaign in history.

[7] After the sack of Ur by the Elamites in 2004, Sumeria never regained its former influence.

[8] More than 20,000 inscribed clay tablets have been recovered from the royal archives at Mari.

[9] The temple of the god Enlil at Nippur was the most important Sumerian religious center; control of Nippur conferred the right to rule all Sumer and Akkad.

See also 1.03 (rise of agriculture); 1.09 (Mesopotamia); 1.16 (early Africa)

In the two centuries following the Hittite sack of Babylon in 1595, the kingdom of Mittani controlled most of northern Mesopotamia and, at its peak, southern Anatolia. Mittani was founded about 1550 by the Hurrians, who had begun to encroach on northern Mesopotamia early in the previous century. As its power spread west into the Levant (the part of the Fertile Crescent bordering the Mediterranean), Mittani came into conflict with the Egyptians. Under Tuthmosis I (r.1504–1492), Egypt controlled all of the Levant and established a frontier on the Euphrates.

The Egyptians were unable to maintain this frontier and over the next century Mittani regained control over the northern Levant and pushed the Egyptians south of the Orontes river. Then, during the reign of Tuthmosis IV (r.1401–1391) Egypt and Mittani formed an alliance. The peace initiative probably came from Mittani which was faced with a revival of Hittite power in the north, while in the east the Assyrians had won back their independence. When Egypt became preoccupied with internal affairs during the reign of Akhenaten (r.1353–1335), Mittani was left exposed.

The Hittite king Suppiluliumas (r.1344–1322) spent the early part of his reign establishing Hittite dominance in Anatolia, and then in about 1340 sacked Washukanni, Mittani's capital, before sweeping on into the Levant. Mittani began to crumble and when he launched a second campaign around 1328 (or 1323) the western half of the kingdom fell. Suppiluliumas established a puppet ruler at Washukanni, intending western Mittani to become a buffer state against Assyria. As such it was a failure, and fell to the Assyrians by 1300.

The Hittites, who now held the same commanding position in the Levant that Mittani had held in the 15th century, incurred the enmity of Egypt, where a new dynasty had come to power in 1307, eager to reestablish Egypt's position in the Levant. By 1290 the Egyptians had recovered Canaan, which had become independent under Akhenaten, and in 1285 pharaoh Ramesses II (r.1290–1224) launched a major invasion of Hittite territory. The Hittite king

Muwatallis II (r.1295–1271) was prepared and, in a battle between two fleets of chariots at Qadesh, Ramesses was defeated (though he claimed a great victory). The Egyptians withdrew and Hittite control was extended as far south as Damascus. Relations between the two empires remained difficult until 1258 when they agreed an alliance, as the Hittites were alarmed at the growth of Assyrian power.

Assyrian expansion had begun under Ashur-uballit I (r.1363–1328), who seized Nineveh from the crumbling Mittanian kingdom in about 1330, and was continued in the 13th century. Tukulti-Ninurta I (r.1243–1207) waged campaigns against the Hittites and the Kassite kingdom of Babylonia and built an empire that stretched from the upper Euphrates to the Persian Gulf. However, the empire fell apart after he was murdered by discontented nobles.

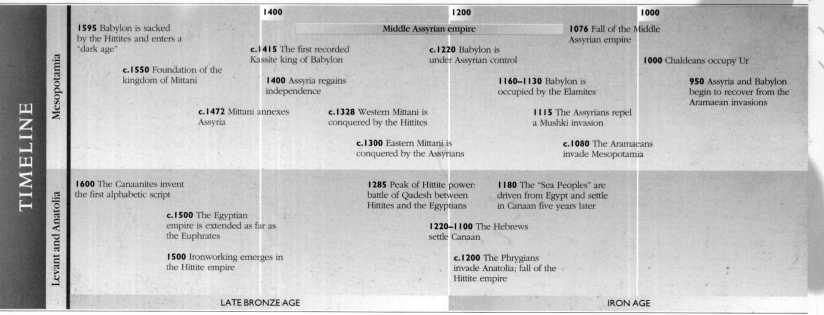

TIMELINE

Mesopotamia

1595 Babylon is sacked by the Hittites and enters a "dark age"

c.1550 Foundation of the kingdom of Mittani

c.1472 Mittani annexes Assyria

c.1415 The first recorded Kassite king of Babylon

1400 Assyria regains independence

Middle Assyrian empire

c.1328 Western Mittani is conquered by the Hittites

c.1300 Eastern Mittani is conquered by the Assyrians

c.1220 Babylon is under Assyrian control

1160–1130 Babylon is occupied by the Elamites

1115 The Assyrians repel a Mushki invasion

1076 Fall of the Middle Assyrian empire

c.1080 The Aramaeans invade Mesopotamia

1000 Chaldeans occupy Ur

950 Assyria and Babylon begin to recover from the Aramaean invasions

Levant and Anatolia

1600 The Canaanites invent the first alphabetic script

c.1500 The Egyptian empire is extended as far as the Euphrates

1500 Ironworking emerges in the Hittite empire

1285 Peak of Hittite power: battle of Qadesh between Hittites and the Egyptians

1220–1100 The Hebrews settle Canaan

c.1200 The Phrygians invade Anatolia; fall of the Hittite empire

1180 The "Sea Peoples" are driven from Egypt and settle in Canaan five years later

LATE BRONZE AGE

IRON AGE

Black Sea

CAUCASUS MOUNTAINS

Caspian Sea

Kaskas

1

Hattusas
(Boghazkoy)

HATTI

Mushki
(Mysians)

Kizil Irmak

Kanesh

c.1340

Malatya

Hurrians

c.1328

Murat

Urartians

Lake
Van

Lake
Urmia

Ceyhan

KIZZUWATNA

Tarsus

Carchemish

2

Washukanni
(Tell al-Fakhariyeh)

MITTANI

Aleppo

5

1115

Tigris

Great Zab

Nineveh

Arbil

Kalhu

ASSYRIA

Kar-Tukulti-Ninurta

Nuzi

Ashur

Ugarit

LEVANT

Orontes

Arvad

6

Qadesh
1285

4

Byblos

Damascus

Tyre

Syrian Desert

Euphrates

Tadmor
(Palmyra)

Aramaeans

MESOPOTAMIA

Djala

Gutians

Hit

Dur-Kurigalzu

Der

Sippar

Babylon

BABYLONIA

3

Nippur

Isin

Susa

ELAM

Al-Untash-Napirisha

ZAGROS MTS

Uruk

Ur

CANAAN

Jerusalem

Chaldeans

Persian Gulf

HITTITE metalworkers of
around 1200 BC
demonstrate their skill with
this silver ceremonial
drinking cup in the shape
of a stag.

Hebrews

Legend

major kingdom, c.1400

- Hittite
- Hurrian kingdom of Mittani
- Assyria
- Kassite kingdom of Babylon
- New Kingdom of Egypt

- maximum extent of Hittite empire, c.1322
- Mycenaean civilization, c.1300
- maximum extent of the Middle Assyrian empire, 1243-1207
- maximum northern expansion of Egyptian kingdom of Tuthmosis I, 1504-1492
- ■ capital city
- → campaign of Suppiluliumas, 1344-1323

campaign of Assyrian king

- → Adad-nirari, 1305-1274
- → Shalmaneser I, 1273-1244
- → Tukulti-Ninurta I, 1243-1207
- → Tiglath-pileser I, 1115-1076

- → migration, 12th and 11th centuries
- modern coastline and drainage where altered

0   300 km
0   200 mi

Around 1200 new waves of migrations brought chaos to the region. Shortly after 1205 the Hittite kingdom collapsed, destroyed by the Phrygians, who had entered Anatolia from Thrace. At the same time Egypt came under attack from a group known to the Egyptians as the Sea Peoples. Their origin is uncertain. Some may have come from the Aegean islands and Anatolian coast but they were joined by others already settled in the Levant and Libya. The Sea Peoples were driven from Egypt in 1180 but settled in Canaan where they became known as the Philistines. Nomadic Hebrew tribes, related to the Aramaeans, were also moving into Canaan.

At the end of the 12th century Assyria was attacked by a confederation of Mushki (probably Mysians – relatives of the Phrygians) and native Anatolian peoples including the Kaskas and Hurrians. The new Assyrian king Tiglath-pileser I (r.1115–1076), forced the invaders to retreat into Anatolia, but he had less success against the nomadic Aramaeans who, despite 28 campaigns against them, had made considerable settlements in Assyria before his death. Tiglath-pileser's successors failed

to contain the Aramaeans and by 1000 Assyria was reduced to its heartland around Ashur and Nineveh.

Babylonia's main problem from the 14th to 12th centuries was the kingdom of Elam. Devastating Elamite invasions of Babylon in the mid 12th century led to the fall of the Kassite dynasty. Babylon recovered under a native dynasty around 1130 and defeated the Elamites so thoroughly that they disappeared from history for 300 years. Then, in the 11th century Babylonia, like Assyria, had problems with migrating nomads – Aramaeans in the north, Chaldeans in the south – and, also like Assyria, was unable to do much about them. The nomads' tribal structures provided no central authority to destroy or negotiate with, and they had no cities that could be taken nor crops to be burned. The powerful Assyrian and Babylonian armies had no target to attack.

The period saw key technological advances, glass, glazed pottery and bricks and iron-smelting all appearing for the first time. Iron did not supplant bronze as the main metal for tools and weapons until around 900, but its use was widespread by 1200, the date accepted as the start of the Iron Age.

1 Hattusas became the Hittite capital in about 1650, and was destroyed about 1200, probably by Phrygian invaders.

2 Tell al-Fakhariyeh is the likely site of Washukanni, capital of Mittani, sacked by the Hittites in 1340 and the Assyrians c.1304-1274.

3 Babylon was sacked by the Hittites in 1595, and was under Kassite rule by 1415, held by the Assyrians 1220-1213 and the Elamites 1160-1130.

4 The Egyptians and Hittites clashed at Qadesh over control of Syria; this is the first battle in history well enough recorded for historians to reconstruct its course.

5 Tiglath-pileser I defeated an invading army of 20,000 Mushki in the upper Tigris valley.

6 On reaching the Mediterranean, Tiglath-pileser I went sailing and claimed to have harpooned a whale.

See also 1.13 (later Assyria); 1.14 (Bible lands);
1.18 (Egypt)

By the 10th century the Aramaeans had begun to abandon their nomadic lifestyle and to settle in city-states across a wide area of the Levant and northern Mesopotamia. Simultaneously the Chaldeans were undergoing the same process in southern Mesopotamia. By settling down, the Aramaeans and Chaldeans lost most of the advantages that their loose nomadic organization had given them over the old military powers, and these now began to revive.

Like the Amorites a millennium earlier, the Aramaeans and Chaldeans adopted Mesopotamian culture but the Aramaeans, at least, kept their identity; their language and alphabet was the common tongue of the region by 500 BC. Mesopotamia experienced no further immigrations in this period but Anatolia and Iran saw the arrival of several waves of Iranian peoples, including the Medes and the Persians, who had both formed powerful kingdoms by the 6th century.

Of the Hittites, Assyria and Babylon, the three powers who had dominated the region before 1200, the Hittites made the least impressive recovery. With their heartland lost to the Phrygians, the Neo-Hittites (as they are now called) formed a number of small states in southern Anatolia, of which the most successful were Carchemish, Kummukhu (Commagene) and Khilakku (Cilicia). The Neo-Hittites were conquered by Assyria in the 8th century after which their identity became lost.

The Assyrian heartland around Ashur and Nineveh had survived the Aramaean invasions relatively unscathed and formed a strong base for recovery. The old pattern, established during the Middle Assyrian period, of expansion under able warrior kings followed by contraction under weak kings was continued in the new Assyrian empire.

Expansion began again in the reign of Adad-nirari II (r.911–891) and by the reign of Ashurnasirpal II (r.883–859) the empire dominated northern Mesopotamia and received tribute from the Levant as far south as Tyre. During Ashurnasirpal's reign Ashur, Assyria's ancient capital, declined in importance and was superseded by a new purpose-built capital at Kalhu.

In 854 a coalition of Levantine states tried to halt the expansion of Assyrian power in the region. The coalition met Shalmaneser III (r.858–824) in battle at Qarqar on the Orontes and, though Shalmaneser claimed complete victory, Assyrian power in the Levant did suffer a setback. Relations between Assyria and Babylon had been good since about 911 when the two states became allies. Shalmaneser gave military support to the Babylonians against the Chaldeans and also gave them assistance against internal enemies.

After Shalmaneser's reign Assyria was crippled by internal problems and went into decline for sixty years. Recovery and expansion began again in the reign of Tiglath-pileser III (r.744–727), who assumed overlordship over Babylon, reconquered the Levant and exacted tribute from Israel and Judah. Tiglath-pileser was responsible for a complete overhaul of the administration of the empire to assert central power. Hereditary provincial governors in the Assyrian heartlands were replaced by a hierarchy of officials under direct royal control. Traveling inspectors were sent out to examine the performance of local officials. A post system was introduced and officials were required to send regular reports to the capital. Representatives were appointed to the courts of vassal states to safeguard the interests of Assyria. Large numbers of subject peoples were resettled to prevent local opposition. Finally, in

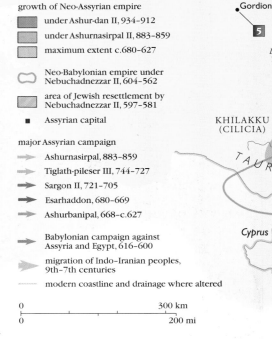

growth of Neo-Assyrian empire			
	under Ashur-dan II, 934–912		
	under Ashurnasirpal II, 883–859		
	maximum extent c.680–627		
	Neo-Babylonian empire under Nebuchadnezzar II, 604–562		
	area of Jewish resettlement by Nebuchadnezzar II, 597–581		
■	Assyrian capital		

major Assyrian campaign

Ashurnasirpal, 883–859

Tiglath-pileser III, 744–727

Sargon II, 721–705

Esarhaddon, 680–669

Ashurbanipal, 668–c.627

Babylonian campaign against Assyria and Egypt, 616–600

migration of Indo-Iranian peoples, 9th–7th centuries

- - - - modern coastline and drainage where altered

| 0 | | 300 km |
| 0 | | 200 mi |

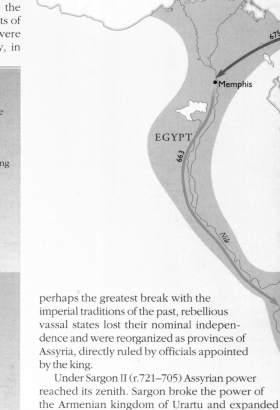

perhaps the greatest break with the imperial traditions of the past, rebellious vassal states lost their nominal independence and were reorganized as provinces of Assyria, directly ruled by officials appointed by the king.

Under Sargon II (r.721–705) Assyrian power reached its zenith. Sargon broke the power of the Armenian kingdom of Urartu and expanded Assyrian dominions with campaigns against the Chaldeans (who had seized Babylon), Elamites and Hebrews. Sargon's last campaign ended in defeat, however, and he was killed in battle in Anatolia in 705. Sargon's successor Sennacherib (r.704–681) was preoccupied with rebellions in Judah, with Babylon

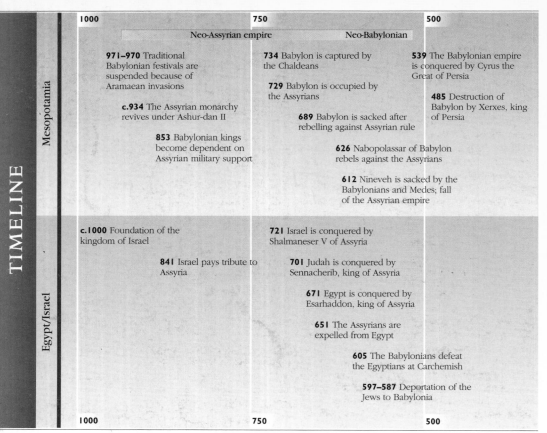

TIMELINE

	1000	750	500
		Neo-Assyrian empire	Neo-Babylonian

Mesopotamia

971–970 Traditional Babylonian festivals are suspended because of Aramaean invasions

c.934 The Assyrian monarchy revives under Ashur-dan II

853 Babylonian kings become dependent on Assyrian military support

734 Babylon is captured by the Chaldeans

729 Babylon is occupied by the Assyrians

689 Babylon is sacked after rebelling against Assyrian rule

626 Nabopolassar of Babylon rebels against the Assyrians

612 Nineveh is sacked by the Babylonians and Medes; fall of the Assyrian empire

539 The Babylonian empire is conquered by Cyrus the Great of Persia

485 Destruction of Babylon by Xerxes, king of Persia

Egypt/Israel

c.1000 Foundation of the kingdom of Israel

841 Israel pays tribute to Assyria

721 Israel is conquered by Shalmaneser V of Assyria

701 Judah is conquered by Sennacherib, king of Assyria

671 Egypt is conquered by Esarhaddon, king of Assyria

651 The Assyrians are expelled from Egypt

605 The Babylonians defeat the Egyptians at Carchemish

597–587 Deportation of the Jews to Babylonia

| 1000 | 750 | 500 |

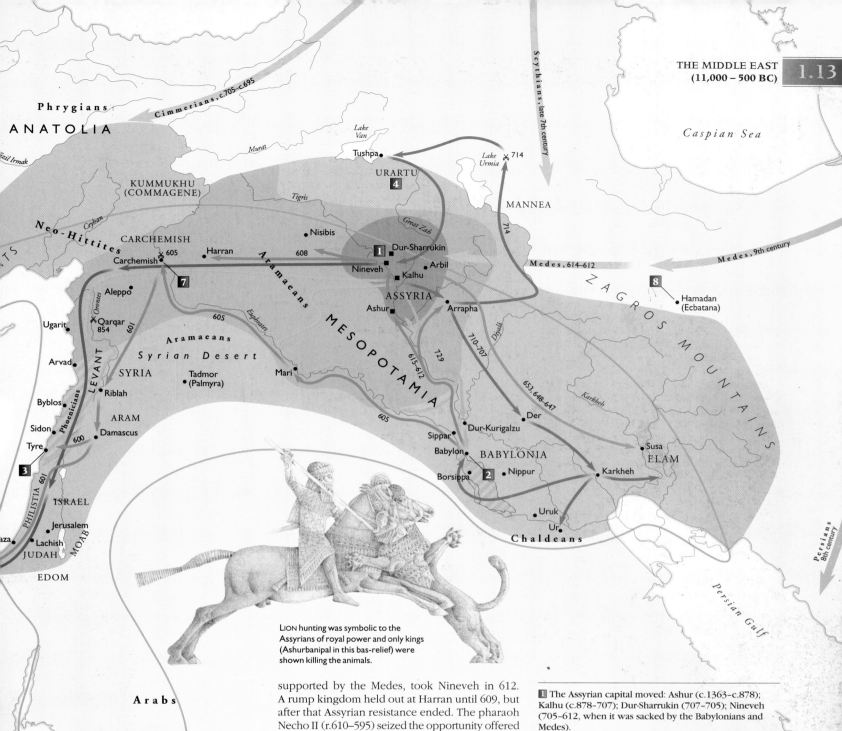

LION hunting was symbolic to the Assyrians of royal power and only kings (Ashurbanipal in this bas-relief) were shown killing the animals.

and with Chaldean and Elamite attacks in the south. Assyrian expansion was renewed under Esarhaddon (r.680–669), who began the conquest of Egypt, and Ashurbanipal (r.668–c.627), who completed it and took great stores of booty back to Nineveh. This last conquest, however, succeeded only in over-extending the empire while Ashurbanipal's increasingly tyrannical rule spread discontent everywhere. Egypt regained its independence by 651 and, despite his subsequent conquest of Elam in 648, Ashurbanipal's reign ended in chaos. The Babylonian king Nabopolassar (626–605) rebelled against Assyrian rule and after ten years of fighting drove the Assyrians from Babylon.

In 615 Nabopolassar took the offensive and, supported by the Medes, took Nineveh in 612. A rump kingdom held out at Harran until 609, but after that Assyrian resistance ended. The pharaoh Necho II (r.610–595) seized the opportunity offered by the collapse of Assyrian power to reoccupy the Levant but was defeated by the Babylonian crown prince Nebuchadnezzar at Carchemish in 605. The Babylonians followed up their victory by occupying virtually all of the territory previously held by Assyria. Nebuchadnezzar came to the throne in the following year and spent his reign (r.604–562) consolidating his empire, rebuilding the city of Babylon in imperial splendor and ruling very much within the Assyrian tradition.

Nebuchadnezzar's dynasty lasted only until 556 when it was overthrown in a palace coup. An official, Nabonidus (r.555–539), was chosen as king but his religious unorthodoxy soon made him unpopular in the Babylonian heartland. When the Persian king Cyrus the Great invaded in 539, Babylon surrendered without a fight, bringing to a quiet end an imperial tradition that was almost two thousand years old. Mesopotamian civilization survived for some centuries but gradually declined under the influence of Persian, and subsequently Hellenistic, culture, and had died out by the beginning of the Christian era.

1 The Assyrian capital moved: Ashur (c.1363–c.878); Kalhu (c.878–707); Dur-Sharrukin (707–705); Nineveh (705–612, when it was sacked by the Babylonians and Medes).

2 Though overshadowed militarily by Assyria before 626, Babylon was the dominant religious and cultural center of Mesopotamia.

3 Tyre was the leading Phoenician city; in the 9th century the Phoenicians established trade routes to the western Mediterranean.

4 Urartu developed as a rival to Assyria in the 8th century; its power was broken by Sargon II in 714.

5 Gordion was the capital of the Phrygians; its last king Mitas (Midas) killed himself after being conquered by the Cimmerians around 695.

6 Thebes, the most southerly point reached by the Assyrians, was sacked by Ashurbanipal in 663.

7 Pharaoh Necho II's attempt to seize the Levant was ended by the Babylonians at Carchemish.

8 Hamadan became the capital of a powerful Median empire after the fall of Assyria.

See also 1.12 (Early Assyria and Babylon); 1.14 (Bible lands); 1.15 (Persians); 1.18 (Egypt)

The Hebrew kingdoms of the Bible lands were dwarfed in scale and longevity by the great empires of the Middle East, yet their significance in world history is at least as great. The period of the independent monarchy, from the time of David to the Babylonian conquest in 587, was a formative time for Judaism and gave Jews a sense of historical destiny, driving them to preserve their religion and identity through centuries of foreign rule, exile and worldwide dispersal. Christianity and Islam both owe so much to Judaism that neither religion would have its present form had Judaism not survived.

The Hebrews migrated into Canaan in the early 12th century BC, a time when the great powers of the region were neutralized by troubles of various kinds. In their initial attacks under Joshua, the Hebrews occupied most of Canaan, which they settled in tribal units under chieftains (the "judges" of the biblical Book of Judges). However, many Canaanite enclaves remained and Hebrew expansion to the southwest was blocked by the Philistines who had settled in the area after being repulsed from Egypt in 1180. Most of the Canaanite enclaves were mopped up in the 11th century, but the Hebrews began to lose ground in the southwest to the Philistines.

The need for effective defense against the Philistines led the Hebrew tribes to unite under a monarchy. According to the Bible, the first king of the Hebrews was Saul (r.c.1020–c.1006), but it was his successor David who was responsible for consolidating the monarchy and creating the first Hebrew state. David conquered the Philistines, Ammonites, Moabites and Edomites and forced several of the Aramaean tribes of the Levant to accept his overlordship. These were great achievements, but he was aided by the temporary impotence of the powers who might otherwise have intervened. It was also to his advantage that the Aramaeans of the Levant (who had moved into the area after the fall of the Hittite empire) had settled in urban communities by 1000, and so were more vulnerable to attack than the still-nomadic Mesopotamian Aramaeans. Perhaps the most important event of David's reign was his capture of Jerusalem from the Canaanite Jebusites. By making Jerusalem his capital David ensured its lasting importance as a religious center.

David was succeeded by his son Solomon. Solomon's reign was largely peaceful, but maintaining his splendid court life and ambitious building projects, including the temple at Jerusalem, proved burdensome to his people. Some Hebrews were used as forced labor and territory was ceded to Tyre in return for supplying craftsmen and materials. He was criticized for tolerating the pagan religious practices of the many non-Hebrew wives he had acquired from diplomatic marriages. When his successor Rehoboam (r.928–911) dealt tactlessly with the economic complaints of the northern tribes, the kingdom split in two halves, Israel and Judah, and most of the non-Hebrew provinces fell away.

probable border of the kingdom of Saul, c.1006

kingdom of David and Solomon
border, 1006–928
under direct rule
vassal states and tributaries
campaigns of David, c.1006–965
Canaanite enclaves conquered by David
area ceded to Tyre by Solomon
fortress built by Solomon
other major building project by Solomon

0   200 km
0   150mi

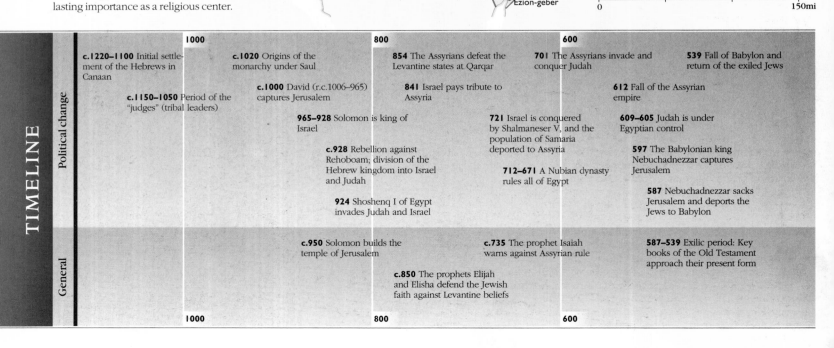

Political change

c.1220–1100 Initial settlement of the Hebrews in Canaan

c.1150–1050 Period of the "judges" (tribal leaders)

c.1020 Origins of the monarchy under Saul

c.1000 David (r.c.1006–965) captures Jerusalem

965–928 Solomon is king of Israel

c.928 Rebellion against Rehoboam; division of the Hebrew kingdom into Israel and Judah

924 Shoshenq I of Egypt invades Judah and Israel

854 The Assyrians defeat the Levantine states at Qarqar

841 Israel pays tribute to Assyria

721 Israel is conquered by Shalmaneser V, and the population of Samaria deported to Assyria

712–671 A Nubian dynasty rules all of Egypt

701 The Assyrians invade and conquer Judah

612 Fall of the Assyrian empire

609–605 Judah is under Egyptian control

597 The Babylonian king Nebuchadnezzar captures Jerusalem

587 Nebuchadnezzar sacks Jerusalem and deports the Jews to Babylon

539 Fall of Babylon and return of the exiled Jews

General

c.950 Solomon builds the temple of Jerusalem

c.850 The prophets Elijah and Elisha defend the Jewish faith against Levantine beliefs

c.735 The prophet Isaiah warns against Assyrian rule

587–539 Exilic period: Key books of the Old Testament approach their present form

Map labels

Legend:
- border of former kingdom of Solomon
- greatest extent of kingdom of Israel
- greatest extent of kingdom of Judah
- border of state gaining independence from kingdoms of Israel or Judah
- kingdom of Egypt, 924
- Assyrian empire, 722
- Babylonian empire, 597

campaigns in Israel and Judah
- pharaoh Shoshenq I, 924
- Sennacherib, 701

0 ____ 150 km
0 ____ 100 mi

Cyprus

Aleppo

Euphrates

Orontes

6

×Qarqar
854

Ugarit

Hamath

Syrian Desert

ARAM

Arvad

LEVANT

Riblah

Tadmor

Byblos

ARAM-ZOBAH

Mediterranean Sea

Sidon

Damascus

Tyre

Dan

ARAM-DAMASCUS

Acco

Hazor

7

Sea of Chinnereth
(Sea of Galilee)

Megiddo

Beth-shean

8

Jordan

Samaria   Shechem

Joppa

5

KINGDOM OF ISRAEL

AMMON
Rabbah

Eltekeh
701

9

Gezer

×

Jerusalem

Ashkelon

Bethlehem

Gaza   Lachish

MOAB
independent of
Israel, 843 BC

Arad

Salt Sea
(Dead Sea)

PHILISTIA

KINGDOM
OF JUDAH

EGYPT

EDOM
independent of
Judah, 843 BC

Ezion-geber

HEBREW captives march into
exile after the fall of
Lachish in 701.
Sennacherib commis-
sioned this relief to
record his
triumph.

Main text

Disunity was a luxury the Hebrews could ill afford, as the power of both Egypt and Assyria was reviving. In 924 the pharaoh Shoshenq I (r.945–924) led a campaign through Philistia, Judah and Israel, sacking many cities and imposing tribute, although both kingdoms survived. In the 9th century relations between Israel and Judah was usually hostile and Israel often suffered attacks from Aram–Damascus, which was frequently allied to Judah. Under Omri and Ahab Israel became the most powerful kingdom in the region and played a leading role in attempts by the Levantine states to check the growing power of Assyria under Shalmaneser III. However, under Ahab's successor Jehu, Israel was forced to pay tribute to Assyria. In the early 8th century the king-doms enjoyed relative peace and prosperity with Assyria in a period of decline, until Tiglath-pileser III (r.744–727) overran the Levant and forced vassal status on Israel and Judah. When Hoshea, king of Israel, rebelled against Assyria in 724 his capital Samaria was taken after a three-year siege and its population deported to Assyria. Despite receiving Egyptian support, a rebellion by Hezekiah, the king of Judah, was also put down by the Assyrians. As Assyrian power entered terminal decline in the 630s, Judah briefly regained independence under Josiah (r.640–609) who extended his authority over the old kingdom of Israel until he was killed in battle with the Egyptians at Megiddo. The Egyptians occupied the Levant but were defeated by the Babylonians at Carchemish in 605, after which Judah became a vassal state of Babylon.

In 597 Judah rebelled against Babylonian rule and was crushed by Nebuchadnezzar. Jerusalem was captured, the temple plundered and many of its citizens were deported to Babylonia. Ten years later Judah rebelled again but Jerusalem was taken after an eighteen-month siege. This was the end for inde-pendent Judah. Its last king Zedekiah was blinded and imprisoned with most of his nobles and more Hebrews were deported. Many others fled into exile in Egypt. Though a disaster in political terms, the Babylonian captivity was a creative period in Jewish history. Exile caused a great deal of religious reflec-tion and it was the period when much of the Old Testament was written up in something close to its present form. Nor perhaps were the conditions of the exile extremely harsh. When Cyrus of Persia destroyed the Babylonian empire in 539 and gave the Jews leave to return home, thousands chose to remain where they were. Many others remained in Egypt. It was the beginning of the Diaspora.

1 Saul was killed in battle against the Philistines at Gilboa c.1006.

2 Hebron was David's capital before his capture of Jerusalem from the Jebusite Canaanites c.1000.

3 The Aramaeans of Hamath submitted after David defeated the Aramaeans of Zobah and Damascus.

4 Solomon built a fleet at Ezion-geber to trade on the Red Sea with east Africa and Arabia.

5 Northern tribes rebelled against Rehoboam and formed the breakaway kingdom of Israel.

6 A coalition of Levantine states including Israel briefly checked Assyrian expansion at Qarqar, 854 BC.

7 Aram–Damascus emerged as a major rival to Israel in the 850s, but was conquered by Assyria in 732.

8 Samaria, the capital of Israel, was taken by the Assyrians in 721 after a three-year siege.

9 Jerusalem, capital of Judah, was sacked after the rebellion of 587, and its population deported to Babylon; they stayed until 539 when the victorious Achemenid Persians allowed them to return.

See also 1.07 (writing), 1.13 (Assyrians and Babylonians), 1.23 (eastern Mediterranean)

The Persians who took Babylon in 539 were comparative newcomers to the region. An Indo-Iranian people, the Persians had followed their close relations the Medes from central Asia to Iran in the 8th century. The founder of the Persian monarchy was Achemenes, who gave his name to the dynasty, but it is uncertain when he ruled. In 648, when Ashurbanipal destroyed the Elamite kingdom and occupied western Elam, the Persians seized the opportunity to take its eastern territories. Despite this Persia was overshadowed by, and often subject to, the powerful Median kingdom. It was in the reign of Cyrus the Great that Persia rose to empire.

Cyrus' career as a great conqueror started when his nominal overlord, the Median king Astyages, invaded Persia around 550 following a rebellion. Astyages was deserted by his army and captured when he met Cyrus in battle at Pasargadae. Cyrus followed up this easy victory by taking the Median capital at Hamadan (Ecbatana). Cyrus was now the most powerful ruler in the region. In 547 he repulsed an invasion of Media by King Croesus of Lydia, who withdrew to his capital Sardis and disbanded his army for the winter. Cyrus, however, had nothing against winter campaigns and, when he arrived unexpectedly, Sardis fell after a siege of only fourteen days. Leaving his generals to complete the conquest of Lydia and the Ionian Greeks, Cyrus marched east to push deep into central Asia. In 539 he crowned his career by conquering Babylonia. Discontent over the religious unorthodoxy of its king Nabonidus was rife and, by posing as a servant of the god Marduk and restorer of orthodoxy, he was even welcomed in Babylon.

In little more than a decade Cyrus had built the largest empire the world had yet seen, with remarkably little hard campaigning. Clearly the close relationship between the Medes and Persians aided in what was more of a dynastic takeover than a conquest, and in Mesopotamia the experience of incorporation in the Assyrian and Babylonian empires had long-since mixed cultures, weakened local identities and accustomed people to imperial rule. As a result there was little spirit of resistance to what amounted, in practice, to no more than the advent of a new imperial dynasty. Cyrus was diplomat as well as soldier and the consolidation of his empire owed much to his moderation. Demands for tribute were modest, he did not interfere with local customs, upheld the rights of the local priesthood and left local institutions of government intact.

Cyrus was killed in 530 on campaign against the Sakas in central Asia and was succeeded by his son Cambyses. Cambyses added Egypt and Libya to the empire before dying in mysterious circumstances,

Legend

	Persia at the accession of Cyrus, 559
	conquered by Cyrus, 559–550
	conquered by Cyrus, 550–530
	conquered by Cambyses, 530–522
	conquered by Darius, 521–486
	tributary region or vassal state
	border of pre-Achemenid state
	uncertain border of pre-Achemenid state
	border of Persian empire, 496
	royal road
■	capital of Persian empire
Susa	major royal palace
LYDIA	conquered state
Caria	region paying tribute to Persia in 500
	modern coastline and drainage where altered

major Persian campaign
- Cyrus
- Cyrus, conjectural
- Cambyses
- Darius
- Darius, conjectural
- Xerxes

Map labels

Scythians
Scythians
513
513
THRACE
Black Sea
Skudra — horses, weapons
Bosporus
Sinope
MACEDON
480
Cappadocia — 300 talents of silver, clothing, horses
480
Hellespont
547–546
LYDIA
GREEK CITY STATES
Pteria
547
Kizil Irmak
2
Plataea 479
Marathon 490
Salamis 480
Athens
Sardis 547–546
Lydia — 500 talents of silver, vessels
Lake Tuz
Cilician Gates
Sparta
7
MTS
Ionia — clothing, vessels
TAURUS
Crete
Xanthus
Rhodes
Cilicia — 360 white horses
Aleppo
Caria — 400 talents of silver with Ionia, chariots, weapons
Cyprus — 350 talents of silver with Palestine and Phoenicia
Sy... char... jewe... vess...
Mediterranean Sea
Sidon
Tyre
Phoenicia
Syr...
Barca
Cyrene
Libya — chariots, goats
Jerusalem
525
Pelusium
525
Palestine
4
525
5
Siwa Oasis
Memphis
526
KINGDOM OF EGYPT
Arabia — camels, cloth, frankincense
Ta...
Egypt — 700 talents of silver, bulls, cloth
El Kharga Oasis
Thebes
526
Nile
523
Red Sea
Kingdom of Meroë (Nubia) — elephant tusks, giraffe, vessels
6

Timeline

TIMELINE

Persian empire

- **c.850** The Medes migrate into Iran from central Asia.
- **c.750** The Persians migrate into southern Iran from central Asia
- **c.640** Persia becomes a vassal state of Media
- **c.630–553** Life of Zoroaster, the prophet of Iran and founder of the Parsee religion
- **559** Accession of Cyrus, who seizes the Median throne in 550
- **547–546** Cyrus captures Lydia
- **539** Cyrus takes Babylon
- **525–523** Cambyses (r.530–522) conquers Egypt
- **520** Darius (r.521–486) campaigns against the pointed-hat Scythians
- **518** Conquest of the Indus valley by the Persians
- **513** Darius invades southeast Europe
- **499** The Ionian Greeks rebel against Persian rule
- **490** The Greeks defeat the Persians at Marathon
- **480** The Greeks halt Xerxes (r.486–465) at Salamis

General

- **612** Fall of Nineveh and collapse of Assyria's empire
- **562** Decline of Babylon after the death of Nebuchadnezzar
- **520** Darius links the Nile and Red Sea by a canal
- **507** Kleisthenes lays the basis for democracy in Athens

| | 0 | | 600 km |
| | 0 | | 400 mi |

GOLD bracelets like this were shown as part of the Lydians' tribute, depicted on reliefs at Persepolis

Aral Sea

Sakas

Syr Dar'ya

Sogdiana
horses, jewelry, weapons

[3]
Kyreskhata

Marakanda (Samarkand)

Amu Dar'ya

Bactria
360 talents of silver, camels, vessels

Pointed-hat Scythians
250 talents of silver, clothing, jewelry, horses

Pointed-hat Scythians

Caspian Sea

Indus

HINDU KUSH

Bactra

Capisa

Peshawar (Caspatyrus?)

Kabul

Taxila

CAUCASUS MTS

Colchis
25 boys, 25 girls

Turan Lowland

Chorasmia
300 talents of silver with Parthia and Aria, horses, jewelry, weapons

546–539

Aria
camels, lionskin cloaks, vessels

Gandhara
170 talents of silver, bulls, weapons

Chenab

Araks

Armenia
400 talents of silver, clothing, horses, vessels

Lake Van

Van

Lake Urmia

Media
450 talents of silver, animal hides, clothing, jewelry, vessels, weapons

EMPIRE

Parthia
camels, vessels

520

Herat

Helmand

Ihelum

Murat

547

Tigris

MEDIAN

ZAGROS

Nineveh

Arbil

Assyria
animal hides, cloth, eunuchs, metals, rams, vessels

Diyala

Hamadan

Dasht-e Lut

Kandahar

c.518

Sutlej

BABYLONIAN EMPIRE

539

Elam
300 talents of silver, lioness & cubs, weapons

550

Drangiana
camels, lionskin cloaks, vessels

Sind
360 talents of gold dust, axes, weapons

HINDU KINGDOMS

Desert

Euphrates

539

Opis

Sippar

Babylon

Nippur

Susa

MOUNTAINS

[1]

550

Pasargadae

Persepolis

Sagartia
600 talents of silver, cloth, horses

Arachosia
animal hides, camels, vessels

Babylonia
1000 talents of silver with Assyria, bulls, cloth, eunuchs, vessels

PERSIA

Indus

Persian Gulf

Maka

Gulf of Oman

Arabian Sea

---

possibly murdered by his brother Smerdis. Smerdis was quickly overthrown and killed by Darius (r.521–486), a member of a junior Achemenid house. Darius faced rebellions from one end of the empire to the other but suppressed them all within a year. By 520 he was secure enough to campaign against the Caspian Scythians. In 518 he extended Persian control as far as, and possibly a little beyond, the Indus and in 513 he crossed into Europe; though he conquered Thrace, the expedition failed in its main objective of subduing the Black Sea Scythians. This failure encouraged a rebellion by the Ionian Greeks in 499. This was put down in 494 and Darius dispatched an expedition to punish the mainland Greeks for supporting the rebels. When this force was defeated by the Athenians at Marathon in 490, Darius began to plan for the conquest of Greece. The expedition was finally launched by his son Xerxes, but the decisive defeat of his fleet at Salamis in 480 and of his army at Plataea the following year brought the expansion of the empire to a halt.

Darius reorganized the empire into about twenty provinces under governors, or satraps, often relatives or close friends of the king. The system of taxation was regularized and fixed tributes, based on the wealth of each province, were introduced. Only Persia, which was not a conquered province, was exempt. The Assyrian imperial post system was expanded and the roads improved. Local garrison commanders remained directly responsible to the king. The official capital of the empire under Cyrus had been Pasargadae, but Hamadan was effectively the administrative capital. Darius moved the administrative capital to Susa and founded a new official capital at Persepolis. Under Darius the imperial administration used various local languages transcribed into cuneiform and written on clay tablets for documents, but his successors abandoned this system in favor of writing on parchment using the widespread Aramaic language and alphabet.

The Persian empire was a thoroughly cosmopolitan state which united elements of all the major civilizations of its time except the Chinese. By throwing together peoples from so many backgrounds, the empire promoted the diffusion and mixing of cultures and ended the isolation of the old civilizations.

[1] Astyages, king of Media, was defeated by Cyrus at Pasargadae; Cyrus then took Hamadan and seized the Median throne.

[2] Cyrus repulsed a Lydian invasion at Pteria, then captured the Lydian capital Sardis and King Croesus.

[3] Kyreskhata was the strongest of a chain of forts built by Cyrus to protect the northern frontier.

[4] After a hard-fought battle at Pelusium Cambyses captured Memphis (525) and took pharaoh Psammeticus III to Susa in chains.

[5] A Persian force sent by Cambyses to capture Siwa vanished in the desert.

[6] Darius built a bridge of boats over the Bosporus (513) to invade Europe; Xerxes did the same over the Hellespont in 480.

[7] Persian expansion to the west was decisively halted by the Greeks at the naval battle of Salamis.

See also 1.14 (Babylon); 1.24 (Greece)

The end of the Ice Age, about 10,000 years ago, brought major climatic changes. Africa had been an arid continent during the last glaciation: rainforests were small and the Sahara desert formed a virtually impenetrable barrier between central and northern Africa. When the last glaciation ended rainfall increased over the whole continent, with most of the Sahara now able to support semi-arid grassland, diverse wildlife and large permanent lakes. Some 9,000 years ago hunter–gatherer bands lived in most of the area, exploiting game, lake-fish and wild plants of all kinds. Most groups became sedentary around favored watercourses or lakes and produced pottery decorated with a wavy-line motif while they exploited wild plants and hunted over the semi-arid neighborhood. They have yielded bone fishing harpoons, small stone tools and a pottery style decorated with wavy line patterns.

Some of Africa's earliest farming communities developed among these Saharan groups, perhaps as early as 6000 BC. Even though wetter than today, the Sahara suffered long drought cycles that affected the availability of both game and wild plant foods. One survival strategy was to supplement cereal grass yields by planting small gardens in areas where these wild grasses flourished. Over many centuries this resulted in a permanent dependence on crops such as bulrush millet, sorghum and African rice.

In the eastern Sahara, farming based on barley and wheat and domesticated indigenous wild cattle was established by 6500 BC. Farming probably began in the Nile valley soon after. A period of low Nile floods around this time probably reduced supplies of fish and other aquatic animals on which the local hunter–gatherers depended, and forced them to adopt farming. The fertile soils and reliable water supply of the Nile valley made it the richest and most densely populated farming area in Africa by the 4th millennium BC. Wheat and barley spread from Egypt throughout north Africa and to the Ethiopian highlands by about 500 BC, but they were unsuited to the climate of tropical Africa.

Another early center of agriculture in Africa was the Ethiopian highlands, where farming may have begun by 5000 BC based on teff, an indigenous Ethiopian cereal, and finger millet, a cereal of unknown origin. Other Ethiopian domesticates included noog, an oil plant, and ensete, a relative of the banana grown for its starchy root. Of these, only finger millet became important outside Ethiopia. Ethiopia's relative isolation meant that many food plants, including barley, flax, emmer wheat, peas and lentils, developed strains unique to the area.

Farming along the margins of the west African forest zone had begun by the 2nd millennium with indigenous plants such as yams, cowpeas and the oil palm. African rice, adapted to grow in flooded savanna waterholes, became a staple west of the Bandama river. Farmers spread using a technique of shifting agriculture in clearings cut or burned out of the forest.

The introduction of cattle, sheep and goats about 5000 BC revolutionized farming in the central Sahara. By the 4th millennium cattle- and sheep-herding and limited cultivation of cereals were widespread. The herders were seminomadic, and drove their animals between seasonal pastures. The Saharan herders left a vivid record of their way of life in thousands of naturalistic rock paintings found widely across the central Sahara. By about 3000 BC desertification intensified, perhaps in part because of overgrazing. The herders' response was to move out to the Sahel region of semi-arid savanna at its southern margins. South of the Sahara, cattle-herding was restricted by areas of dense rainforest and by the widespread tsetse fly. However, herder groups spread onto the east African highlands by 2000 BC and moved south.

Copper was worked in the southern Sahara in the 2nd millennium, but sub-Saharan Africa moved straight from the Stone Age to the Iron Age. Knowledge of iron working may have developed indigenously in the southern Sahara; alternatively it may have been introduced either down the Nile valley or from the Phoenician colonies in north Africa. Iron was being worked in the Nubian kingdom of Kush by about 600 BC, while it is attested in northern Nigeria at about the same time, where the Nok culture developed by the late 6th century.

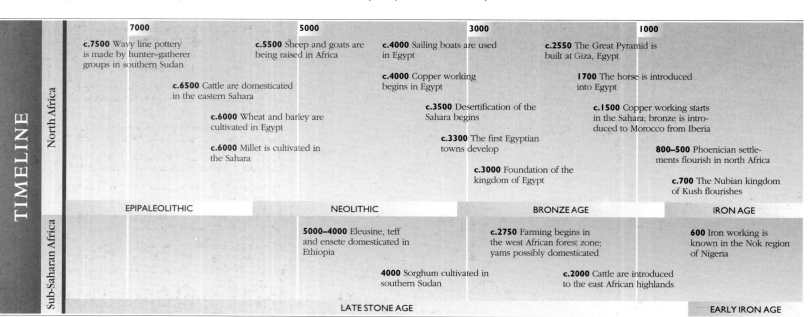

TIMELINE

North Africa

c.7500 Wavy line pottery is made by hunter–gatherer groups in southern Sudan

c.6500 Cattle are domesticated in the eastern Sahara

c.6000 Wheat and barley are cultivated in Egypt

c.6000 Millet is cultivated in the Sahara

c.5500 Sheep and goats are being raised in Africa

c.4000 Sailing boats are used in Egypt

c.4000 Copper working begins in Egypt

c.3500 Desertification of the Sahara begins

c.3300 The first Egyptian towns develop

c.3000 Foundation of the kingdom of Egypt

c.2550 The Great Pyramid is built at Giza, Egypt

1700 The horse is introduced into Egypt

c.1500 Copper working starts in the Sahara; bronze is introduced to Morocco from Iberia

800–500 Phoenician settlements flourish in north Africa

c.700 The Nubian kingdom of Kush flourishes

EPIPALEOLITHIC — NEOLITHIC — BRONZE AGE — IRON AGE

Sub-Saharan Africa

5000–4000 Eleusine, teff and ensete domesticated in Ethiopia

4000 Sorghum cultivated in southern Sudan

c.2750 Farming begins in the west African forest zone; yams possibly domesticated

c.2000 Cattle are introduced to the east African highlands

600 Iron working is known in the Nok region of Nigeria

LATE STONE AGE — EARLY IRON AGE

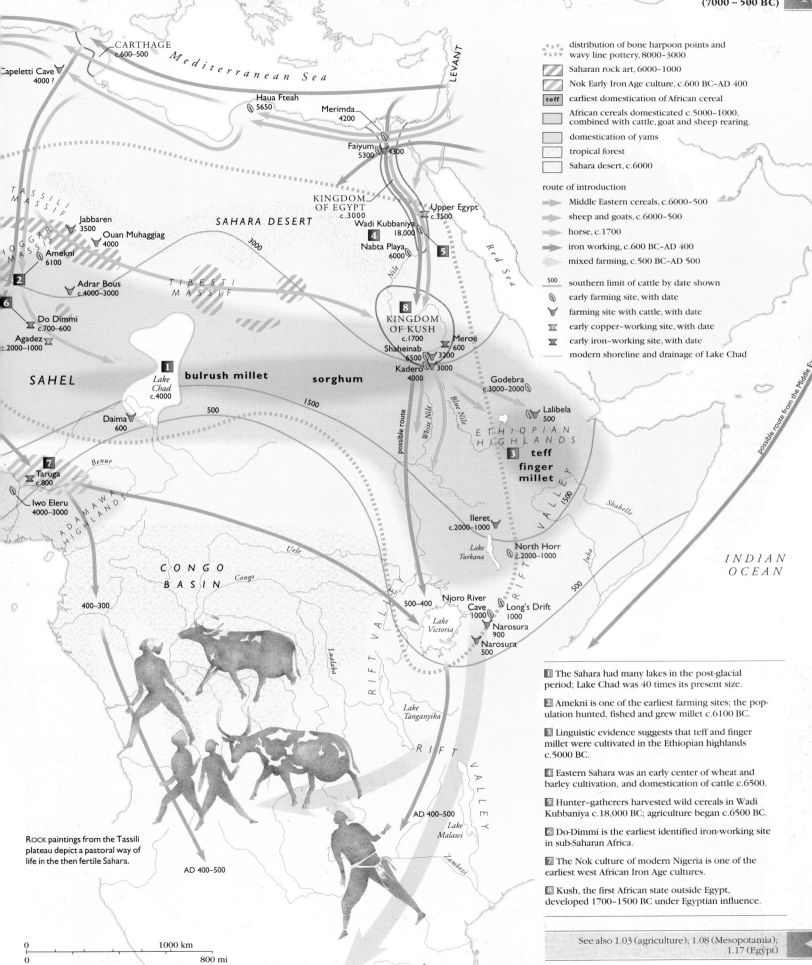

CARTHAGE
c.600–500

Mediterranean Sea

LEVANT

Capeletti Cave
4000 ?

Haua Fteah
5650

Merimda
4200

Faiyum
5300   4300

KINGDOM
OF EGYPT
c.3000

Upper Egypt
c.3500

Wadi Kubbaniya
18,000

Nabta Playa
6000

SAHARA DESERT

TASSILI
MASSIF

HOGGAR MASSIF

Jabbaren
3500

Ouan Muhaggiag
4000

Amekni
6100

Adrar Bous
c.4000–3000

TIBESTI
MASSIF

3000

2

6

Do Dimmi
c.700–600

Agadez
c.2000–1000

SAHEL

1

bulrush millet

Lake Chad
c.4000

sorghum

Daima
600

500

1500

8

KINGDOM
OF KUSH
c.1700

Shaheinab
6500

Meroë
600

Kadero   3200
4000   3000

Godebra
c.3000–2000

Red Sea

Nile

Lalibela
500

ETHIOPIAN
HIGHLANDS

3

teff
finger
millet

1500

White Nile

Blue Nile

possible route

7

Taruga
c.800

Iwo Eleru
4000–3000

Benue

ADAMAWA HIGHLANDS

Ileret
c.2000–1000

Lake Turkana

North Horr
c.2000–1000

Shabelle

RIFT VALLEY

1500

possible route from the Middle East or India

*INDIAN
OCEAN*

CONGO
BASIN

Uele

Congo

400–300

Lualaba

500–400

Njoro River
Cave
1000

Long's Drift
1000

Narosura
900

Narosura
500

Lake
Victoria

Juba

500

RIFT VALLEY

Lake
Tanganyika

RIFT VALLEY

AD 400–500

Lake
Malawi

ROCK paintings from the Tassili
plateau depict a pastoral way of
life in the then fertile Sahara.

AD 400–500

Zambezi

Limpopo

herding reaches
southern Africa
around AD 1

0   1000 km
0   800 mi

Legend

- distribution of bone harpoon points and wavy line pottery, 8000–3000
- Saharan rock art, 6000–1000
- Nok Early Iron Age culture, c.600 BC–AD 400
- **teff** earliest domestication of African cereal
- African cereals domesticated c.5000–1000, combined with cattle, goat and sheep rearing.
- domestication of yams
- tropical forest
- Sahara desert, c.6000

route of introduction
- Middle Eastern cereals, c.6000–500
- sheep and goats, c.6000–500
- horse, c.1700
- iron working, c.600 BC–AD 400
- mixed farming, c.500 BC–AD 500

- 500 southern limit of cattle by date shown
- early farming site, with date
- farming site with cattle, with date
- early copper-working site, with date
- early iron-working site, with date
- modern shoreline and drainage of Lake Chad

1 The Sahara had many lakes in the post-glacial period; Lake Chad was 40 times its present size.

2 Amekni is one of the earliest farming sites; the population hunted, fished and grew millet c.6100 BC.

3 Linguistic evidence suggests that teff and finger millet were cultivated in the Ethiopian highlands c.5000 BC.

4 Eastern Sahara was an early center of wheat and barley cultivation, and domestication of cattle c.6500.

5 Hunter-gatherers harvested wild cereals in Wadi Kubbaniya c.18,000 BC; agriculture began c.6500 BC.

6 Do-Dimmi is the earliest identified iron-working site in sub-Saharan Africa.

7 The Nok culture of modern Nigeria is one of the earliest west African Iron Age cultures.

8 Kush, the first African state outside Egypt, developed 1700–1500 BC under Egyptian influence.

See also 1.03 (agriculture); 1.08 (Mesopotamia);
1.17 (Egypt)

Ancient Egypt was totally dependent on the Nile. Below the First Cataract, the Nile flows through a narrow valley and, except where it broadens out into the Delta, its flood plain is nowhere more than a few kilometers wide, often less. The flood plain was probably the most favorable area for agriculture anywhere in the ancient world. The Nile flooded annually in the late summer, falling in the autumn and leaving the fields moist and fertilized with fresh silt ready for sowing. The crops grew through the warm Egyptian winter and were harvested in the spring before the next cycle of flooding. Egypt had little need of the complex irrigation systems and flood defenses of Mesopotamia, where the rivers flooded in spring, after the start of the growing season. Canals, however, were used to spread the floodwaters and increase the cultivable area. High yields were possible year after year: the farmers' surpluses were taken to state storehouses for distribution to administrators, craftsmen and priests, for trade or to build up reserves against the famine that would follow if the Nile flood failed. The Nile was also Egypt's main highway. The prevailing winds in Egypt blow north to south, enabling boats to travel upstream under sail and return downstream with the flow. Few settlements were far from the river, making it relatively easy to transport heavy loads of grain or stone over long distances. On either side of the narrow 800-kilometer (500-mile) fertile strip was the desert which isolated Egypt from the influence of other civilizations and protected it from invaders: Egyptian civilization was over 1,300 years old before it suffered its first major invasion.

Farming began in the Nile valley before 6000 BC and by 4000 BC it was populated by subsistence farmers. Chiefdoms and towns appeared by 3300. In the narrow confines of the valley competition was probably intense. Eventually, the southern chiefdoms amalgamated into an Upper Egyptian kingdom, which gained control over Lower Egypt. The first king known to have ruled all Egypt was Narmer, king of Upper Egypt who may have conquered Lower Egypt about 3000. This unification was consolidated by the foundation of Memphis as a new capital.

By the same date the hieroglyphic system of writing had appeared. The system worked on similar principles to the Sumerian pictographic script; hieroglyphs were developed for use in record keeping and as labels in the late Predynastic period. Early hieroglyphs appear on a slate palette which Narmer had carved to commemorate his victories. This palette shows that the principle of theocratic kingship that would be the basis of the ancient Egyptian state was already well established. During the ensuing Early Dynastic period (2920– 2575) the kings developed an efficient administration which made possible a dramatic increase in royal power at the beginning of the Old Kingdom (2575–2134), named for the kingdom ruled from Memphis by a succession of four dynasties.

The annual Nile flood was seen as a gift from the gods. The king claimed to be able to control the flood, but if the flood failed, his authority could be called into question. He was believed to be of divine descent and was held to be immortal. At his death immense effort was put into preserving his body and to providing it with a suitably regal tomb furnished with the luxuries of everyday life. Early royal tombs were built on platforms known as *mastabas*, but these were superseded by pyramids in the reign of King Djoser (r.2630–2611). Pyramid building climaxed in about 2550 with the 146-meter-high Great Pyramid, built for Khufu, and the slightly smaller pyramid of his son Khephren. These enormous buildings are impressive evidence of the power the kings exercised over their subjects. However the large pyramids strained the resources of the kingdom: later ones were more modest and no more royal pyramids were built after the 17th century BC, by which time ideas of the afterlife had changed.

Egypt was governed by an efficient central and local bureaucracy. The kingdom was treated as the personal property of the king and the central bureaucracy was an extension of the royal household. The highest official was the vizier, who supervised the administration of justice and taxation. Below the vizier were chancellors, controllers of stores and other officials, supported by a staff of scribes trained in mathematics and writing. For the purposes of local government, Egypt was divided into provinces, or *nomes*, under governors selected from the royal or noble families.

During the 5th Dynasty (2465–2323) the monarchy was weakened by granting out lands as rewards and favors to the nobility. The provincial governorships became hereditary and drifted out of the control of the king. A period of low Nile floods then began around 2150, bringing famine and starvation, and the remaining royal authority crumbled. The Old Kingdom state collapsed and Egypt was divided between rival dynasties in Upper and Lower Egypt in what is known as the First Intermediate period.

THIS pottery lion, with a stylized mane resembling a headcloth, was found in the temple at Hierakonpolis. It dates from about the 3rd Dynasty.

Mediterranean Sea

to Libya

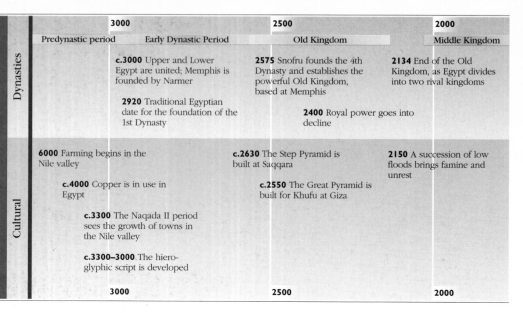

TIMELINE

		3000		2500		2000	
		Predynastic period	Early Dynastic Period		Old Kingdom	Middle Kingdom	
Dynasties		**c.3000** Upper and Lower Egypt are united; Memphis is founded by Narmer		**2575** Snofru founds the 4th Dynasty and establishes the powerful Old Kingdom, based at Memphis		**2134** End of the Old Kingdom, as Egypt divides into two rival kingdoms	
		2920 Traditional Egyptian date for the foundation of the 1st Dynasty		**2400** Royal power goes into decline			
Cultural		**6000** Farming begins in the Nile valley		**c.2630** The Step Pyramid is built at Saqqara		**2150** A succession of low floods brings famine and unrest	
		c.4000 Copper is in use in Egypt		**c.2550** The Great Pyramid is built for Khufu at Giza			
		c.3300 The Naqada II period sees the growth of towns in the Nile valley					
		c.3300–3000 The hieroglyphic script is developed					
		3000		2500		2000	

1 The First Cataract was the traditional southern frontier of Egypt through most of its history.

2 Hierakonpolis and Naqada were the first towns to develop in Egypt, c.3300.

3 Saqqara is the site of the oldest pyramid, the Step Pyramid, c.2630.

4 Giza is the site of the largest pyramids, including the Great Pyramid of Khufu.

5 The mountains of the Eastern Desert were the chief source of minerals.

6 Graffiti show that the Egyptians were exploiting Sinai's mineral wealth as early as the 3rd Dynasty (2649–2575).

7 The Egyptians maintained a trading post at Buhen in Nubia during the Old Kingdom.

8 Memphis was capital of Egypt for most of the Early Dynastic period and Old Kingdom.

to the Levant

timber
from Lebanon

SINAI

**LOWER
EGYPT**

Nile River Delta

Buto

Tell el-Rub'a

natron

Great Bitter
Lake

natron

Wadi
Natrun

Heliopolis

4

*quartzite
limestone*

6

*copper
turquoise*

Abu Rawash

Giza

Zawyet el-Aryan

Abusir

Memphis

Saqqara

8

3

Dahshur

Gulf of Suez

copper

Legend

- ☐ fertile area
- conjectural borders of Kingdom of Upper Egypt, c.3000
- southern border of Old Kingdom
- border of Kingdoms of Upper and Lower Egypt, 2134–2040

Old Kingdom pyramids, 2650–2040
- single
- multiple
- non-royal

- capital of Old Kingdom
- Predynastic and Early Dynastic royal tomb, c.3250–2650
- later Old Kingdom tomb, c.2500-2100
- → military expansion of Upper Egypt, c.3000
- ➤ campaign in the Early Dynastic and Old Kingdom
- *lead* source of commodity
- desert route
- modern coastline and drainage where altered

0   300 km
0   200 mi

Maidum

Seila

*basalt
dolerite
gypsum*

Faiyum

Nile

Birket Qarun
(ancient shoreline)

Abu Rawash

Herakleopolis

Dishasha

flint

MIDDLE EGYPT

Bahariya
Oasis

Sawaris

Gebel el-Teir

Tihna

Zawyet el-Amwat

Bahr Yusuf

Beni Hasan
limestone

Deir el-Malik

Sheik Sa'id

alabaster

Quseir el-Amarna

Deir el-Gabrawi

Sheik Atiya

Meir

Dara

Asyut

Hammamiya

Qaw el-Kebir

**Eastern
Desert**

copper

Red Sea

*porphyry
granite
jasper*

copper

lead

5

copper

Farafra
Oasis

**Western
Desert**

TERRACOTTA figure of a
dancing woman from the
Predynastic Naqada I
culture.

Akhmim

Nag el-Deir

Hagarsa

limestone

UPPER

Abydos

Nile

Dendara

Nag el-Gaziriyah

Koptos

Naqada

Tukh

2

Thebes

Gebelan

El-Mo'alla

EGYPT

granite

limestone

El-Kab

El-Kula

Hierakonpolis

Edfu

2

*gold
feldspar
emeralds*

to the Red Sea

alum

El-Kharga
Oasis

El-Dakhla
Oasis

Balat

Kurkur
Oasis

lead

Qubbet el-
Hawa

amethyst

Elephantine

1st Cataract

*lead
granite
diorite
steatite
quartzite*

1

7

to Buhen

*ebony
gold
ivory
from Nubia*

See also 1.07 (writing); 1.10 (Mesopotamia);
1.18 (Middle and New Kingdoms)

The reunification of Egypt in 2040 BC by Men-tuhotpe II (r.2061–2010), of the Theban dynasty of Upper Egypt, marks the start of the Middle Kingdom. A few decades later royal authority and political stability had been restored and the power of the provincial governors reduced. To rebuild a loyal administration, the Middle Kingdom rulers promoted propagandist literature, while statuary presented the king as the care-worn "good shepherd" of his people. Pyramid building was revived, though more modestly than in the Old Kingdom.

Egypt's neighbors were now becoming organized into chiefdoms and petty kingdoms, and the Middle Kingdom rulers had to pursue a more aggressive foreign policy than their predecessors. Under Amenemhet I (r.1991–1962), Lower Nubia was conquered; the frontier at the Second Cataract was garrisoned and heavily fortified by his successors. Egyptian influence was extended over the Levant during the reign of Senwosret III (r.1878–1841) and local rulers were forced to become vassals of Egypt. During the 18th century the bureaucracy began to grow out of control and for much of the time the effective rulers of Egypt were the viziers. In the 17th century there was considerable immigration from the Levant into the Delta. Most immigrants were absorbed into the lower classes of Egyptian society but one, Khendjer, became king around 1745 BC.

From around 1640 much of Egypt was ruled by the Hyksos, a Semitic people from the Levant, who gradually took over Lower Egypt, which they ruled from their capital at Avaris. Upper Egypt remained independent under a Theban dynasty but control over Lower Nubia was lost to the nascent kingdom of Kush. Hyksos rule, in what is known as the Second Intermediate period, made Egypt more open to foreign influences. Bronze came into widespread use, war chariots were introduced, as were weapons such as the composite bow and scale armor. New fashions in dress, musical instruments, domestic animals and crops were adopted through Hyksos influence. Otherwise, the Hyksos accepted Egyptian traditions and historical continuity was unbroken.

Under the Theban king Seqenenre II (died c.1555) the Egyptians began a long struggle to expel the Hyksos which was finally completed by Ahmose in 1532. This victory marks the beginning of the New Kingdom, under which the power and influence of ancient Egypt reached its peak. The Hyksos invasion had shown the Egyptians that their borders were no longer secure, and the New Kingdom was overtly militaristic and expansionist, reaching its greatest extent around 1500 under the warrior king Tuthmosis I. Tuthmosis conquered the entire Levant and established a frontier on the Euphrates. Lower Nubia was reconquered and Kush was overrun to beyond the Fourth Cataract. The primary motive of expansion into the Levant was to establish a buffer zone between Egypt and the aggressive powers of the Middle East; in Nubia, which had rich gold deposits, the motive was economic. In the Levant, local rulers were kept under the supervision of Egyptian officials and key cities were garrisoned. Nubia was subjected to full colonial government under a viceroy directly responsible to the king. Nubia was a great source of wealth to the New Kingdom, but the Egyptians faced a constant struggle to control the Levant, against local rebellions and expansionist powers such as the Hittite empire.

The power of Egypt declined after the reign of Amenophis IV (r.1353–1335). Amenophis, who changed his name to Akhenaten, was a radical religious reformer who attempted to replace Egypt's traditional polytheism with the monotheistic cult of the Aten, or sun disk. Akhenaten founded a new capital and promoted radically new art styles to symbolize the break with the past, but there was little popular enthusiasm for the new religion, which was abandoned after his death. In the ensuing period of political instability, Egypt lost control of the Levant to the Hittites. Campaigns by the kings (or pharaohs as they were now known) Sethos I (r.1306–1290) and Ramesses II "the Great" (r.1290–1224) to restore the Egyptian position were only partially successful and Ramesses eventually made peace with the Hittites.

Around 1200 the entire region was disrupted by

Legend

Middle Kingdom (12th Dynasty, 1991-1783)
- zone of direct control
- zone of dominance

Second Intermediate period
- Hyksos Kingdom (15th Dynasty, 1640-1532)
- Theban (17th Dynasty, 1646-1550)
- Kingdom of Kush
- maximum extent of New Kingdom under Tuthmosis I, 1504-1492

- royal capital, with dynasty
- city

royal tomb
- Middle Kingdom
- New Kingdom

fort or garrison
- Middle Kingdom
- New Kingdom

- sacked c.1200, probably by Sea Peoples
- Giza temple
- desert route used for communication between the Hyksos and Kushite allies
- gold deposit
- major migration
- modern coastline and drainage where altered

Libyans

0   300 km
0   200 mi

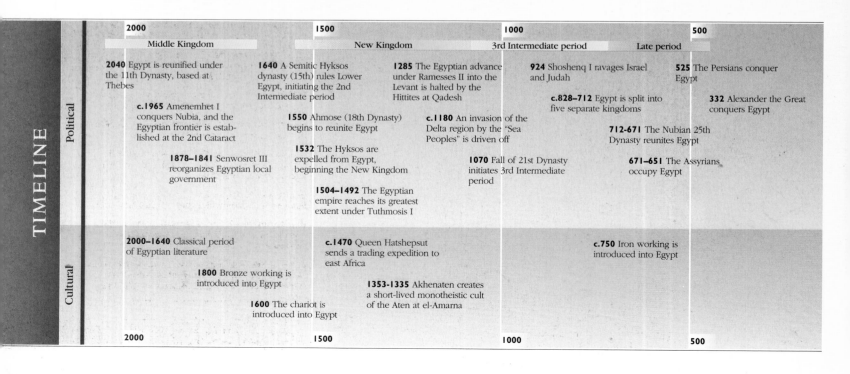

TIMELINE

		2000	1500	1000	500
		Middle Kingdom	New Kingdom	3rd Intermediate period Late period	

Political

2040 Egypt is reunified under the 11th Dynasty, based at Thebes

c.1965 Amenemhet I conquers Nubia, and the Egyptian frontier is established at the 2nd Cataract

1878–1841 Senwosret III reorganizes Egyptian local government

1640 A Semitic Hyksos dynasty (15th) rules Lower Egypt, initiating the 2nd Intermediate period

1550 Ahmose (18th Dynasty) begins to reunite Egypt

1532 The Hyksos are expelled from Egypt, beginning the New Kingdom

1504–1492 The Egyptian empire reaches its greatest extent under Tuthmosis I

1285 The Egyptian advance under Ramesses II into the Levant is halted by the Hittites at Qadesh

1180 An invasion of the Delta region by the "Sea Peoples" is driven off

1070 Fall of 21st Dynasty initiates 3rd Intermediate period

924 Shoshenq I ravages Israel and Judah

c.828–712 Egypt is split into five separate kingdoms

712-671 The Nubian 25th Dynasty reunites Egypt

671–651 The Assyrians occupy Egypt

525 The Persians conquer Egypt

332 Alexander the Great conquers Egypt

Cultural

2000–1640 Classical period of Egyptian literature

1800 Bronze working is introduced into Egypt

1600 The chariot is introduced into Egypt

c.1470 Queen Hatshepsut sends a trading expedition to east Africa

1353-1335 Akhenaten creates a short-lived monotheistic cult of the Aten at el-Amarna

c.750 Iron working is introduced into Egypt

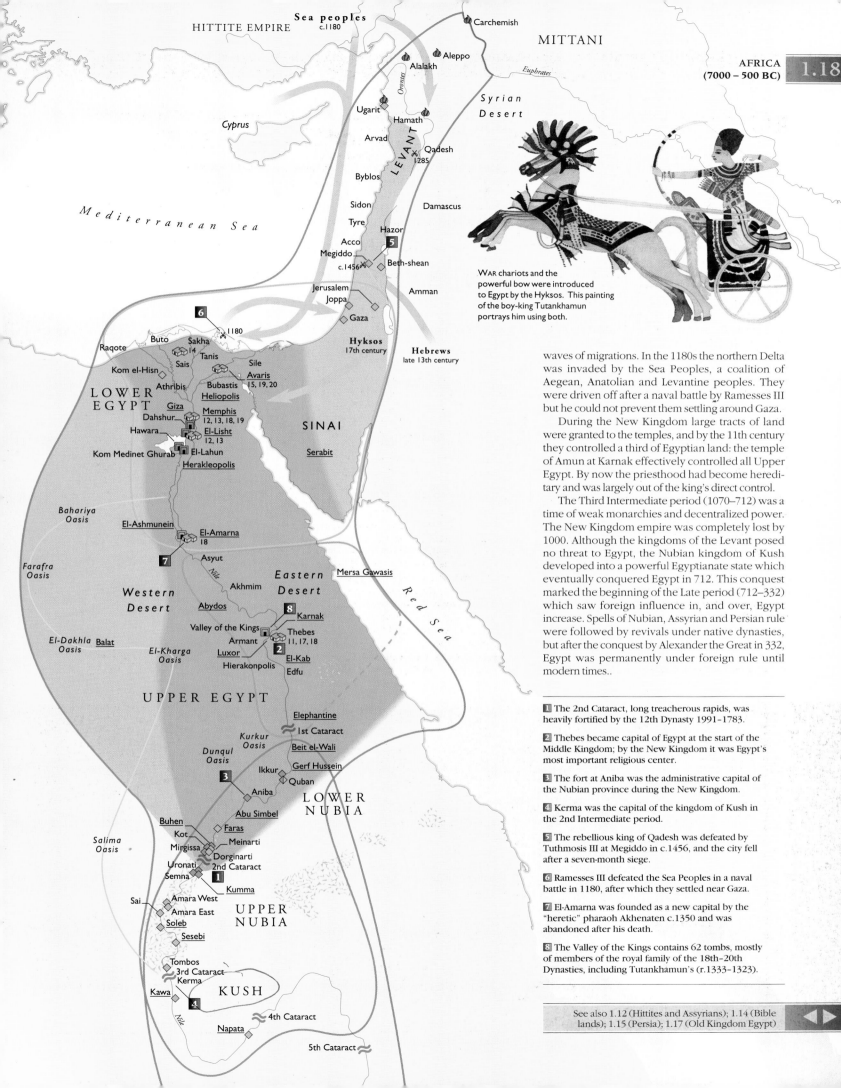

Map labels:

Sea peoples c.1180
HITTITE EMPIRE
MITTANI
Carchemish
Aleppo
Alalakh
Euphrates
Cyprus
Ugarit
Hamath
Orontes
Arvad
Qadesh ×1285
Syrian Desert
Byblos
LEVANT
Sidon
Damascus
Tyre
Acco
Hazor
Megiddo c.1456
Beth-shean
Amman
Jerusalem
Joppa
Gaza
Hyksos 17th century
Hebrews late 13th century

Mediterranean Sea

Raqote
Buto
Sakha 14
Tanis
1180
Sile
Avaris 15, 19, 20
Sais
Kom el-Hisn
Athribis
Bubastis
LOWER EGYPT
Giza
Heliopolis
Memphis 12, 13, 18, 19
Dahshur
El-Lisht 12, 13
Hawara
Kom Medinet Ghurab
El-Lahun
Herakleopolis
SINAI
Serabit

BaharIya Oasis
El-Ashmunein
El-Amarna 18
Farafra Oasis
Asyut
Western Desert
Akhmim
Eastern Desert
Mersa Gawasis
Abydos
Karnak
Valley of the Kings
Thebes 11, 17, 18
Armant
Luxor
El-Kab
Hierakonpolis
Edfu
El-Dakhla Oasis
Balat
El-Kharga Oasis

UPPER EGYPT

Red Sea

Elephantine
1st Cataract
Kurkur Oasis
Beit el-Wali
Gerf Hussein
Dunqul Oasis
Ikkur
Quban
Aniba
LOWER NUBIA
Buhen
Faras
Kot
Meinarti
Mirgissa
Dorginarti
Salima Oasis
Uronati
Semna
2nd Cataract
Kumma
Sai
Amara West
Amara East
UPPER NUBIA
Soleb
Sesebi
Tombos
3rd Cataract
Kerma
Kawa
KUSH
4th Cataract
Napata
5th Cataract
Nile

WAR chariots and the powerful bow were introduced to Egypt by the Hyksos. This painting of the boy-king Tutankhamun portrays him using both.

waves of migrations. In the 1180s the northern Delta was invaded by the Sea Peoples, a coalition of Aegean, Anatolian and Levantine peoples. They were driven off after a naval battle by Ramesses III but he could not prevent them settling around Gaza.

During the New Kingdom large tracts of land were granted to the temples, and by the 11th century they controlled a third of Egyptian land: the temple of Amun at Karnak effectively controlled all Upper Egypt. By now the priesthood had become hereditary and was largely out of the king's direct control.

The Third Intermediate period (1070–712) was a time of weak monarchies and decentralized power. The New Kingdom empire was completely lost by 1000. Although the kingdoms of the Levant posed no threat to Egypt, the Nubian kingdom of Kush developed into a powerful Egyptianate state which eventually conquered Egypt in 712. This conquest marked the beginning of the Late period (712–332) which saw foreign influence in, and over, Egypt increase. Spells of Nubian, Assyrian and Persian rule were followed by revivals under native dynasties, but after the conquest by Alexander the Great in 332, Egypt was permanently under foreign rule until modern times..

1 The 2nd Cataract, long treacherous rapids, was heavily fortified by the 12th Dynasty 1991–1783.

2 Thebes became capital of Egypt at the start of the Middle Kingdom; by the New Kingdom it was Egypt's most important religious center.

3 The fort at Aniba was the administrative capital of the Nubian province during the New Kingdom.

4 Kerma was the capital of the kingdom of Kush in the 2nd Intermediate period.

5 The rebellious king of Qadesh was defeated by Tuthmosis III at Megiddo in c.1456, and the city fell after a seven-month siege.

6 Ramesses III defeated the Sea Peoples in a naval battle in 1180, after which they settled near Gaza.

7 El-Amarna was founded as a new capital by the "heretic" pharaoh Akhenaten c.1350 and was abandoned after his death.

8 The Valley of the Kings contains 62 tombs, mostly of members of the royal family of the 18th–20th Dynasties, including Tutankhamun's (r.1333–1323).

See also 1.12 (Hittites and Assyrians); 1.14 (Bible lands); 1.15 (Persia); 1.17 (Old Kingdom Egypt)

Anatomically modern humans from Africa reached what is now the Middle East some 90,000 years ago, but it was not until the beginning of the Upper Paleolithic period, about 40,000 years ago, that they were able to move into Europe. Unlike the indigenous Neanderthals, who were physically adapted to the harsh Ice Age climate, the early anatomically modern humans were poorly equipped to survive in Europe until, some 50,000–40,000 years ago, they also acquired a fully modern human mental capacity. This enabled them to adapt to the cold climate through technological and social innovation, and compete on more than equal terms with the Neanderthals. The Neanderthals became extinct about 28,000 years ago. Whether it was as a result of a war of extermination or because superior modern human hunting techniques drove them into marginal environments is a subject of debate: current archeological opinion favors the latter.

Two parallel toolmaking traditions, the Châtelperronian and the Aurignacian, are found in Europe during the 10–12,000 years that modern humans and Neanderthals shared the continent. The Châtelperronian is apparently a development of the Mousterian tool culture and is thought to have been used by the Neanderthals. The Aurignacian has similarities with contemporary tool cultures in the Middle East and is therefore thought to have been introduced to Europe by anatomically modern humans. The Aurignacian and the succeeding Gravettian tool cultures both are fairly uniform over wide areas but later Upper Paleolithic tool cultures show greater variety between different regions. These variations are often in style rather than function and probably served as a way of expressing emerging ethnic identities. Typical Upper Paleolithic stone tools include scrapers, sharpened blades, burins – engraving tools used for antler harpoons – and bone points and needles were also used. The Solutrean culture introduced a sophisticated technique of pressure flaking which produced beautiful leaf shaped spear heads.

The most impressive characteristics of the Upper Paleolithic cultures are their art traditions, both decorated artifacts and cave-wall painting. The earliest Upper Paleolithic art dates from around 31,000 years ago but the traditions reached their peak in the Magdalenian (17,000–11,000 years ago), in the cave paintings of sites such as Lascaux and Altamira. The greatest concentration of Upper Paleolithic cave art is to be found in southwest France and northern Spain, an area with a particularly dense population at the time. The function of cave art is unknown but it is thought to have played a religious role. The most distinctive decorated artifacts are female "Venus" figurines made around 25,000 years ago. These have been found across Europe – evidence, perhaps, of a widespread religious cult.

Despite the cold, the tundras and steppes of Ice Age Europe were a very favorable environment for hunters, being filled with easily tracked herds of large grazing mammals. Upper Paleolithic hunters used a combination of semi-permanent base-camps – often sited at bottlenecks on animal migration routes, such as river crossings – and seasonal camps where particular game species were intensively exploited. Caves and south-facing rock shelters were favored camp sites, but in more exposed areas tents and huts were built.

The end of the last glaciation, around 10,000 years ago (8000 BC) marks the end of the Upper Paleolithic and the beginning of the Mesolithic

Upper Paleolithic, 40,000–10,000 years ago

- ▨ Levantine Aurignacian culture
- ▨ Aurignacian culture
- ◆ cave site
- ✋ cave site with painting
- ● open site
- ▲ open site with structure
- ⚱ "Venus" figurine find

Mesolithic, 10,000–6000 ya (8000–4000 BC)

- ⚱ major site
- 🐚 site with shell midden
- ▨ maximum extent of ice sheet during last glaciation, c.18,000 ya
- ▨ extent of ice sheet, 7000 BC
- ⋯ northern limit of deciduous woodland, c.18,000 ya
- ⋯ northern limit of deciduous woodland, 7000 BC
- ⇨ migration of anatomically modern humans from Middle East, c.40,000 ya
- - - ancient course of Thames/Rhine, 7000 BC
- — modern coastline and drainage where altered

```
0                    800 km
0                    600 mi
```

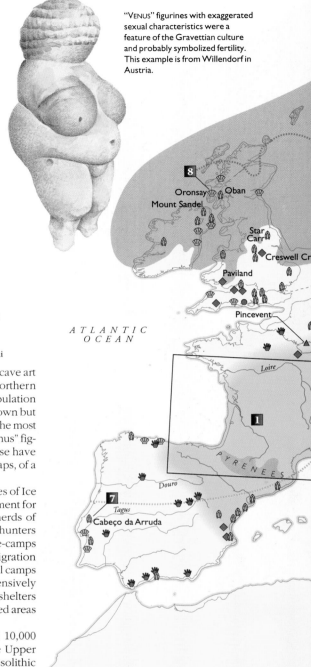

"VENUS" figurines with exaggerated sexual characteristics were a feature of the Gravettian culture and probably symbolized fertility. This example is from Willendorf in Austria.

Oronsay · Oban
Mount Sandel
Star Carr
Creswell Cra[g]
Paviland
Pincevent
ATLANTIC OCEAN
Loire
PYRENEES
Douro
Tagus
Cabeço da Arruda

TIMELINE

	40,000 years ago (ya)	30,000	20,000	10,000 ya (8000 BC)
	Mousterian / Châtelperronian / Aurignacian	Gravettian	Solutrean / Magdalenian	
Cultural	c.41,000 Blade tool technology introduced to Europe	c.30,000 The earliest cave paintings in southwest France and northern Spain	c.20,000 The pressure-flaking technique of tool manufacture is adopted	14,000 Production of cave paintings at Altamira, Spain
		25,000–22,000 "Venus" figurines are found widely from Spain to Russia	17,000 The cave paintings at Lascaux, France, are made	8000 (6000 BC) Beginning of the transition to a farming way of life in southeast Europe
			16,000 Microlithic tools are developed	
Physical	c.40,000 The first anatomically modern humans enter Europe	c.28,000 The last remaining Neanderthals become extinct in Spain	18,000–15,000 The Ice Age is in its coldest phase	10,000 End of the last glaciation
	MID PALEOLITHIC	UPPER PALEOLITHIC		MESOLITHIC

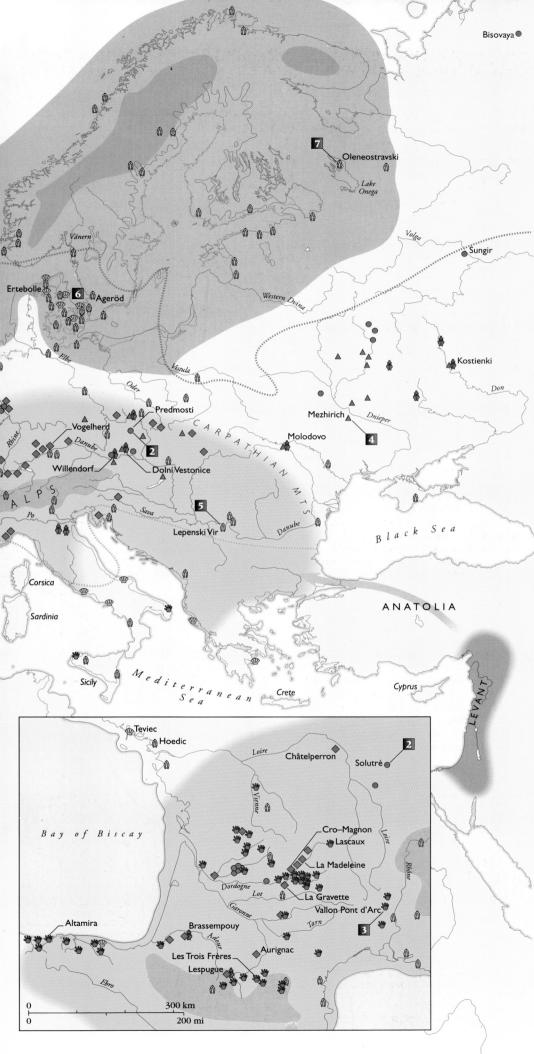

period. As the climate became warmer, sea levels rose and dense forests advanced over most of Europe, bringing the big-game hunting way of life to an end. Large mammals were now fewer and more elusive, but a far greater diversity of plant foods, shellfish, fish, birds and small mammals was available. Mesolithic hunter–gatherers introduced many new devices to exploit these new food sources. The most important technological change was a reliance on microliths – small stone blades or flakes – used in combination to make composite tools such as knives, harpoons, fish spears and lightweight arrow heads. Nets, fish traps, shellfish scoops and dug-out canoes also came into widespread use for the first time in the Mesolithic.

Many areas of northern Europe which had previously been uninhabitable because of extreme cold or ice sheets received their first modern human inhabitants during the Mesolithic, while some which had been relatively densely populated, such as southwest France and the southwest steppes, became comparatively depopulated. The densest population moved to areas such as the Atlantic coast and southern Scandinavia. Hunter–gatherers here were able to adopt an increasingly sedentary way of life, making fewer and shorter migrations between camps. In southern Scandinavia and eastern Europe there were even permanent settlements occupied all year round. Task groups set out from these settlements to spend short periods at temporary seasonal camps to exploit locally abundant food resources.

The Mesolithic period came to an end with the adoption of the Neolithic farming way of life, a process which began about 6000 BC in southeast Europe and about two thousand years later in the British Isles and Scandinavia. In extreme northerly areas, an essentially Mesolithic way of life continued until the domestication of the reindeer early in the Christian era.

---

1 In the Upper Paleolithic, southwest France had light woodland for fuel, sheltered valleys with many caves, and lay across major animal migration routes; it was therefore Europe's most densely populated area.

2 Upper Paleolithic hunters used temporary camps to exploit particular game species. Solutré was a base for horse hunters, Predmosti for mammoth.

3 Cave paintings of woolly rhinoceros, horses and buffalo found at Vallon Pont d'Arc in 1994 are, at 30,000 years old, the oldest yet found.

4 On the treeless steppes, mammoth bones were used to build huts; a well-known example, c.18,000 years old, was found at Mezhirich.

5 The well-preserved Mesolithic settlement of Lepenski Vir includes many fish-head sculptures, perhaps indicating worship of a fish-deity.

6 Denmark, with marine, freshwater and terrestrial food sources in close proximity, was densely populated in the Mesolithic.

7 The first cemeteries, such as those at Cabeço da Arruda and Oleneostravski (about 170 burials each) date from the late Mesolithic (c.4250 BC).

8 Late Mesolithic hunter–gatherers (c.4000–3400 BC) visited Oronsay island several times a year for fish and shellfish.

See also 1.02 (peopling the earth);
1.08 (Middle East); 1.20 (Neolithic Europe)

The spread of agriculture through Europe was a complex process of small-scale migrations by farming peoples and the adoption of farming techniques by Mesolithic hunter–gatherers. It took time to develop crop strains suited to the colder and wetter climates of central, western and northern Europe. Hunter–gatherers readily adopted some aspects of the material culture of neighboring farmers, such as pottery and polished stone axes, but only adopted food production when natural food sources were in short supply. In many areas, Mesolithic hunter–gatherers were already semi-sedentary, so the transition to a settled farming way of life was probably easily made when it became necessary.

Farming, based on cereals, legumes, sheep, goats and cattle, first began in Europe in Greece and the Balkans around 6500 BC. This pattern of farming spread from the Balkans around the Mediterranean coasts to southern France and Spain by 5000. Whether the adoption of farming in Europe was an indigenous development or was influenced by the farming societies of the Middle East is doubtful. Southeastern Europe was within the range of wild einkorn wheat, cattle, pigs and sheep and farming may have developed as a result of experimentation with cultivation and animal husbandry by indigenous hunter–gatherers. Cattle may have been domesticated independently in southeast Europe but some crops, such as emmer wheat and barley, were certainly introduced from the Middle East.

The earliest farming culture of central Europe is the Bandkeramik or Linear Pottery culture. This originated in the northern Balkans around 5400 BC and over a few centuries spread north and west across the band of fertile and easily worked loess soils that extends across Europe from Romania to the Rhineland. When the population of a village became too large, a daughter settlement was simply founded a few kilometers away. The indigenous Mesolithic hunter–gatherer bands were not displaced by the Bandkeramik people, who settled on vacant lands between them, usually along rivers. However, the steady encroachment by the farmers placed pressure on the hunter–gatherers' resources and they were gradually forced to adopt farming too: gradually the two populations became assimilated. After a delay of several centuries, the farming way of life spread

from central Europe into western Europe, then Britain and Scandinavia and the southwest steppes.

Farming in central and northern Europe was very different from that in the south. The cold winters led to spring sowing of crops (autumn sowing prevailed in southern Europe, the Middle East and north Africa) and there was greater emphasis on cattle and pigs, which were better suited to grazing in woodland than sheep and goats.

Neolithic settlements were generally small, with populations of only forty to sixty. The most common type of building was the wooden longhouse that accommodated both people and livestock. Except in treeless areas such as the Orkney Islands, where stone houses were built, settlements have left few traces; burials and ritual structures provide most evidence of the nature of Neolithic societies. In most of Europe the dead were buried in individual graves in cemeteries with offerings of stone tools, pottery and ornaments. There is little variation in the quantity and quality of grave goods, indicating that these communities were not divded between rich and poor. In many areas the dead were buried communally in megalithic tombs which remained in use for many generations. The tombs were usually covered with mounds of earth, and may have served as territorial markers as well as burial places, the presence of the community's ancestors legitimizing the ownership of the present generation. The Atlantic coast of western Europe, where the earliest megalithic tombs were built, was already relatively densely populated in Mesolithic times. Population pressure may have been felt after the introduction of agriculture, leading to a new concern with territoriality.

In the later Neolithic and the early Bronze Age, northwest Europe saw the construction of megalithic stone circles and circular earth structures known as henges. Some circles have astronomical alignments or form part of a complex ritual landscape but their exact functions are unknown. Some monuments are so large that they must have been built by chiefdoms able to command the resources

TIMELINE		6000	5000	4000	3000	2000
	South, east & central Europe	c.6500 Farming starts to appear in the Balkans c.6500 Cattle are domesticated in the Balkans c.6000 Farming spreads to Italy	c.5400 The Bandkeramik farming culture of central Europe begins c.5000 Hierarchical societies emerge in southeast Europe	c.4000 The horse is domesticated on the southwestern steppes c.4500 Copper smelting begins in the Balkans c.4500 The plow is in use in southeast Europe	c.3300 Copper smelting begins in central Europe c.3200 Wheeled vehicles are in use in the Balkans and the southwestern steppes	c.2500 Bronze is made in central Europe c.2300 Bronze is in use in southeast Europe c.2000 The Minoan palace civilization emerges in Crete
	West and north Europe			c.4500 Farming begins in western Europe c.4300 The first megalithic tombs are built, in Brittany c.4000 Farming is introduced into Britain and Scandinavia	c.2900 Cord Impressed Pottery cultures appear in northern Europe c.2500 Bell Beaker cultures appear in western Europe c.2400 Copper is first in use in western Europe	c.2000 The main stage of Stonehenge is completed in southern Britain

NEOLITHIC   BRONZE AGE

earliest farming cultures

- early Aegean and Anatolian Painted Ware cultures, 7000–6000
- Balkan Painted and Impressed Pottery cultures, 6500–4000
- Impressed Pottery cultures, 6000–4000
- Bandkeramik or Linear Pottery culture, 5400–4500
- Bowl cultures, 4500–3300
- Tripolye–Cucuteni cultures, 4200–3800
- Funnel-necked Beaker cultures, 4200–2800

- megalithic monument building, 4300–2000
- stone circle or alignment
- megalithic tomb
- excavation of early farming village
- other site
- spread of copper working by 4500
- spread of copper working by 3000
- general direction of the spread of farming, 6000–3000

0   600 km
0   400 mi

BELL-BEAKER drinking cups with incised decoration have been found in graves all over western Europe. Pollen grains found in the bottom of some indicate that they had contained a mead-like drink.

and populations of wide areas. The emergence of more hierarchical societies in the later Neolithic is also reflected in burial practices. In cultures such as the Cord Impressed Ware culture of eastern Europe and the Bell Beaker cultures in western Europe, variations in the quality and quantity of grave goods in burials indicate differences of wealth and status in farming societies. In many areas these changes are associated with the introduction of copper and gold metallurgy.

Metallurgy developed separately in the northern Balkans around 4800 BC and in southern Spain about fifteen centuries later. Both copper and gold were used to make small tools and ornaments. At first only native metals were used, cold-hammered into shape, but by 4500 copper ores were being mined in the Balkans for smelting. Copper was smelted in Spain, Italy and probably Britain by 2400. Copper tools had few advantages over stone ones, but the elites valued metal for display objects. Only in the Bronze Age did metal tools begin to replace stone tools in everyday use.

1 Starcevo was one of the earliest farming settlements in the Balkans, 6000–4000 BC. Hunting and gathering, cereals and cattle were all important.

2 Horses were domesticated in the Tripolye–Cucuteni cultures in the 4th millennium BC.

3 Incised clay tablets from Tartaria show that a simple system of notation had developed in the Balkans by 5000.

4 Copper ores were being mined at Rudna Glava in 4500 BC, the earliest known in the world.

5 A major stone temple complex was built at Tarxien c.3500–2400 BC.

6 Some three thousand standing stones aligned in multiple rows make Carnac one of the largest megalithic sites. Its purpose is unknown.

7 The stone circle at Stonehenge was built in several phases spanning the Neolithic and Bronze Age (c.3000–1500 BC).

8 An "ice man", whose body was found in 1991, froze to death in the Otztaler Alps c.3350–3120 BC.

See also 1.03 (spread of agriculture); 1.08 (Middle East); 1.19 (Mesolithic Europe)

The Bronze Age saw chiefdoms and warrior elites established across most of Europe. Beyond the Aegean, states were not formed until the Iron Age was well advanced and in northern and eastern Europe not until the early Middle Ages. The chiefdoms were competitive communities: fortifications were built in great numbers and new weapons such as swords and halberds were invented. Superb crafted display objects – ornaments, weapons, "parade-ground" armor, tableware, cult objects – made of bronze and precious metals, express the competitiveness of the period. Long-distance trade, particularly in tin and amber, arose to satisfy the demand for metals and other precious objects in areas where such resources were lacking. The increase in trade aided the spread of ideas and fashions and led to a high degree of cultural uniformity.

The earliest known use of bronze in Europe, in the Unetice culture in central Europe about 2500 BC, was probably an independent development and not the result of influence from the Middle East. Bronze came into use in southeast Europe, the Aegean and Italy two hundred years later, followed by Spain and, finally, the British Isles in about 1800. Scandinavia, with no workable deposits of copper or tin, continued in the Stone Age until the middle of the 2nd millennium BC. By this time bronze had entered Scandinavia, brought by traders in exchange for amber and, probably, furs.

Bronze technology led to a rapid increase in the use of metals. Bronze weapons and tools kept an edge better than stone or copper, could easily be resharpened and when broken could be melted down and recast. It was expensive, however, and its use was largely confined to the social elites in the early Bronze Age. Stone tools, sometimes copying the style of prestigious bronze tools, continued in everyday use. Large quantities of bronze artifacts, often of the highest quality, were buried or sunk in bogs as offerings to the gods.

The social distinctions of Bronze Age society are apparent in burial practices: a minority of burials being richly furnished with grave goods and the majority with few offerings. In the earlier Bronze

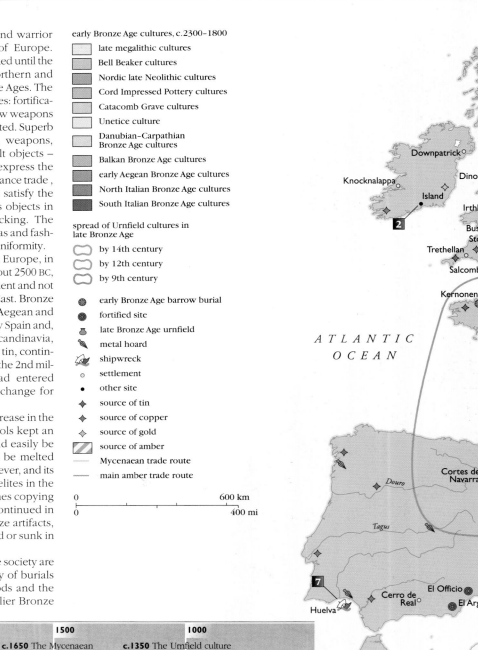

early Bronze Age cultures, c.2300–1800
- late megalithic cultures
- Bell Beaker cultures
- Nordic late Neolithic cultures
- Cord Impressed Pottery cultures
- Catacomb Grave cultures
- Unetice culture
- Danubian–Carpathian Bronze Age cultures
- Balkan Bronze Age cultures
- early Aegean Bronze Age cultures
- North Italian Bronze Age cultures
- South Italian Bronze Age cultures

spread of Urnfield cultures in late Bronze Age
- by 14th century
- by 12th century
- by 9th century

- early Bronze Age barrow burial
- fortified site
- late Bronze Age urnfield
- metal hoard
- shipwreck
- settlement
- other site
- source of tin
- source of copper
- source of gold
- source of amber
- Mycenaean trade route
- main amber trade route

| 0 | | 600 km |
| 0 | | 400 mi |

Age three distinct burial practices are found. In southeast Europe the normal practice was burial of rich and poor alike in flat grave cemeteries. In most of eastern, northern and western Europe, the poor were buried in flat graves but the rich were buried under earth mounds known as barrows. Barrows required a communal effort to build and are evidence of the power of the elites. In some parts of western Europe Neolithic-style communal burials in megalithic tombs continued until about 1200 BC.

In southern and central Europe, large villages, often fortified, developed but in northern and western Europe the settlement pattern was one of dispersed homesteads. Population rose across Europe and agricultural settlers moved into many marginal upland areas. These were abandoned late in the Bronze Age, perhaps because of climatic deterioration or because the poor soils had been exhausted. As agricultural land rose in value, clear boundaries were laid out between communities in

TIMELINE

	2000	1500	1000
South and east Europe	**c.2500–1800** The Unetice culture appears in central Europe **c.2300** Bronze working begins in southeast Europe **c.2000** Hillforts are built in central Europe **c.2000** The first European state emerges, in Crete **c.2000** Trade routes across Europe appear for amber and metals	**c.1650** The Mycenaean civilization develops and traders are active in south Italy	**c.1350** The Urnfield culture appears in central Europe **c.1200** Fall of the Mycenaean civilization **c.1000** Iron comes into widespread use in Greece **c.750** Beginning of the Hallstatt ("Celtic") Iron Age
West and north Europe	**c.2000** The Wessex culture flourishes in Britain, with rich barrow burials **c.2000** The main stage of Stonehenge, in southern Britain, is completed		**1100** Hillforts are built in western Europe **1000** Urnfield cultures spread to western Europe **c.700** Iron in widespread use throughout Europe
	NEOLITHIC	BRONZE AGE	IRON AGE

sub-Neolithic forest hunters and gatherers

Tromøy
Rickeby
Hallunda
Vänern
Vättern
Kvarnby
Bulbjerg
Trundholm
Brudevaelte
Egtved
Kivik
Voldtofte
Lake Peipus
Rezne
Western Dvina
Drenthe
Barger-Oosterveld
Perleberg
Pustinka
Biskupin
Jankowo
Kamieniec
Toterfout
Court St Etienne
Nieder-Neundorf
Schweinert
Miejsce
Leubingen
Grossenheim
Bad Nauheim
Helmsdorf
Iwanowice
Ivanja
Moska
Donec group
Flörsheim
Postoloprty
Elbe
Oder
Vistula
Spissky Stvrtok
Gedinne
Heidesheim
Unetice
Veterov
Barca
Rostov
Havré
Mannheim
Blucina
Vélatice
Hagenam
Kelheim
Danube
Unter-Radl
Malé Kosihy
Usatove
Wasserburg
Ettins
Mohi
Füzesabony
Suciu du Sus
Tudoromo
Rixheim
Baldegg
Volders
Nitriansky Hrádok
Caka
Vál
Monteoru
Kamenka
Cortaillod
Wittnauer Horn
Hölting
Ptuj
Kisapostag
Tószeg
Periam
Crestaulta
Ledro
Bled
Angarano
Dobova
Sava
Czorvas
CARPATHIAN MTS
Polada
Canegrate
Po
Gomalova
Vattina
ALPS
Fontanella
Gîrla Mare
Danube
Ezerovo
Bismantora
Cirna
Tarnava
Ezerovo
Luni
Ezero
Corsica
Filitosa
Allumiere
Narce
Danja Slatina
Nuraghe Albucci
Phlegraean Fields
Scoglio del Tonno
Barumini
Sardinia
Black Sea
ANATOLIA
Hittites
Lipara
Millazzo
Troy
Sicily
Mycenae
Borg in-Nadur
Malta
Cyprus
Crete
Knossos
Minoan civilization
Mediterranean Sea

VOTIVE offerings, thrown into the bogs, include this bronze and gold "chariot of the sun" from Trundholm (Denmark).

many areas, especially northwest Europe, and farmland was enclosed into small fields that could be managed more intensively. Farmers benefited from the introduction of heavier plows, wheeled vehicles and horses. European wild oats were domesticated at this time, probably as horse fodder.

Around 1350 the Urnfield culture, named for its distinctive burial practices, appeared in Hungary. Bodies were cremated and the ashes buried in funerary urns in flat grave cemeteries of hundreds, even thousands, of graves. As with earlier Bronze Age burial customs, a minority of graves included rich offerings, weapons and armor. Some of these graves were covered with barrows, demonstrating a degree of continuity with the past, but this was by no means universal: the powers enjoyed by chieftains in the early Bronze Age may have been undermined to an extent by the emergence of a warrior class. By the 9th century Urnfield customs had spread over most of continental Europe. Except in the west where it

was probably taken by migrating Celtic peoples, the Urnfield culture spread mainly as a result of the wide-ranging contacts on trade links. The later Bronze Age saw increased militarization, with extensive fortress building in western Europe and the introduction of the bronze slashing sword. Bronze armor was introduced, but probably for display only: it offers less protection than leather.

Small numbers of iron artifacts appeared in many areas about 1200. However, iron tools first became common only around 1000 in Greece and two hundred and fifty years later in northern Europe.

1 Bronze Age settlements along the northern fringes of the Alps were often built on islands in lakes for defense.

2 One of the last megalithic tombs to be used was at Island, in Ireland; it was still in use about 1200 BC about a millennium later than most megalithic tombs.

3 At Leubingen, an early Bronze Age barrow contains the remains of an elderly man accompanied by a girl, pottery, stone and bronze tools and weapons, and gold jewelry.

4 A late Bronze Age dismantled wooden "temple" was deliberately sunk into a peat bog at Barger-Oosterveld.

5 The Urnfield cemetery at Kelheim of 900–800 BC had more than 10,000 burials.

6 Defensive towers called *nuraghe* were built about 1800 BC in Sardinia; similar structures are found in Corsica and the Balearic islands.

7 A shipwreck from 800 BC off the southwest coast of Spain included more than 200 bronze weapons made in the Loire region.

See also 1.20 (Neolithic Europe);
1.22 (Minoans and Mycenaeans)

Europe's first cities and states developed on the Aegean island of Crete around 2000 BC, where the Minoans developed a system of intensive agriculture based on wheat, olives and vines. Olives and vines grew well on rough hillsides and produced valuable commodities for long-distance trade, allowing good plowland to be kept for wheat production. Sheep were kept on Crete's mountain pastures and their wool supplied a textile industry that exported cloth to Egypt. Minoan pottery and metalwork was in demand throughout the eastern Mediterranean.

By 2000 BC Minoan society was controlled from palaces at Knossos, Phaistos, Mallia and Khania, probably the capitals of small kingdoms. A number of smaller palaces were probably subordinate centers. The palaces, which incorporated vast storehouses for grain, oil and other products, were centers for redistributing produce collected as taxes or tribute for rations to support administrators, craftsmen or traders. The Minoans had a hieroglyphic script by 2000, but this was superseded by a syllabic script three centuries later. Neither script has been deciphered so the ethnic identity of the Minoans is unknown, but they did not speak an Indo-European language and were therefore not Greeks.

Around 1700 most of the Minoan palaces were destroyed by fire, probably as a result of warfare between the palace states; they were subsequently rebuilt, but only Knossos regained its former splendor, taking control of the whole island and reducing the other palaces to tributary status. In 1626 the palaces were damaged by ash falls and earthquakes resulting from a volcanic eruption on the nearby island of Thera. The palaces were rebuilt and the Minoan civilization endured until it collapsed in about 1450 after conquest by the Mycenaeans.

The Mycenaeans, or Achaeans as they probably called themselves, were a Greek-speaking people who had moved to the Greek peninsula from the Balkans around 2000 BC. By around 1600 small kingdoms based on fortified towns were beginning to develop and a system of writing, based on the Cretan syllabic script, had been adopted. The earliest

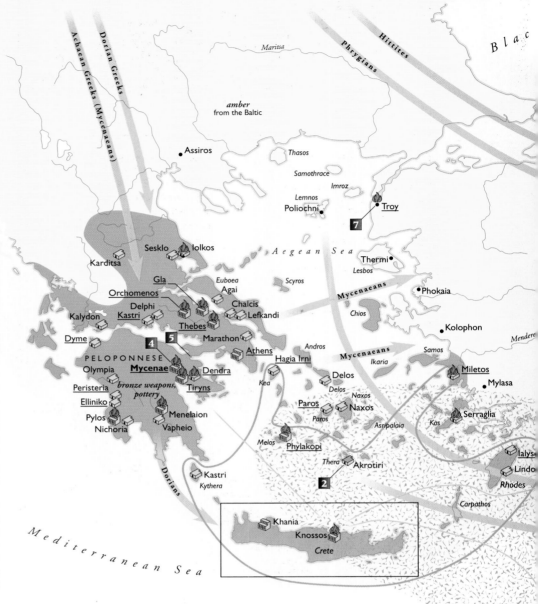

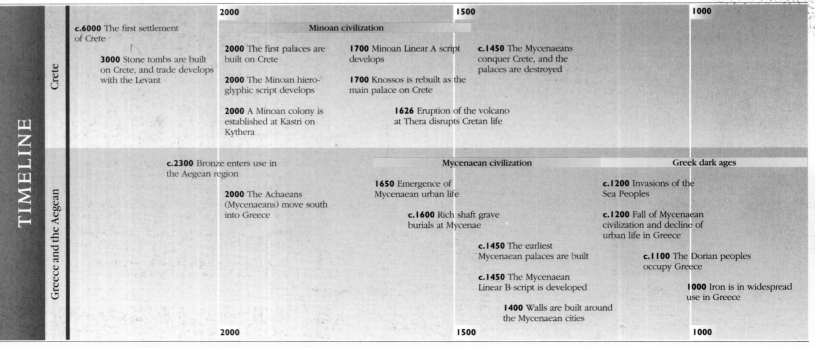

TIMELINE

	2000	1500	1000
Crete	**c.6000** The first settlement of Crete	**Minoan civilization**	
	3000 Stone tombs are built on Crete, and trade develops with the Levant	**2000** The first palaces are built on Crete	**1700** Minoan Linear A script develops	**c.1450** The Mycenaeans conquer Crete, and the palaces are destroyed
		2000 The Minoan hieroglyphic script develops	**1700** Knossos is rebuilt as the main palace on Crete	
		2000 A Minoan colony is established at Kastri on Kythera	**1626** Eruption of the volcano at Thera disrupts Cretan life	
Greece and the Aegean	**c.2300** Bronze enters use in the Aegean region	**Mycenaean civilization**	**Greek dark ages**
		1650 Emergence of Mycenaean urban life	**c.1200** Invasions of the Sea Peoples
	2000 The Achaeans (Mycenaeans) move south into Greece	**c.1600** Rich shaft grave burials at Mycenae	**c.1200** Fall of Mycenaean civilization and decline of urban life in Greece
		c.1450 The earliest Mycenaean palaces are built	**c.1100** The Dorian peoples occupy Greece
		c.1450 The Mycenaean Linear B script is developed	**1000** Iron is in widespread use in Greece
		1400 Walls are built around the Mycenaean cities	
	2000	1500	1000

MINOAN CRETE

S e a

Crete

Khania
Monastiraki
Arkhanes
Knossos
Mallia
Palaikastro
Hagia Triadha
Phaistos
Gournia
Kato Zakro
Myrtos

| 0 | 60 km |
| 0 | 40 mi |

Legend

- Minoan civilization, c.1600
- Minoan influence, c.1600
- Mycenaean civilization, c.1300
- Mycenaean colonization, late 13th century BC
- Minoan city, with palace
- other Minoan settlement
- Mycenaean city, with palace
- other Mycenaean settlement
- **Knossos** capital city
- **Troy** fortified settlement
- site damaged or destroyed by Mycenaeans, c.1450
- site damaged or destroyed by invaders from the north, or "Sea Peoples", c.1200
- mountain-top shrine on Crete
- sacred cave on Crete
- shipwreck
- probable trading route of the Ulu Burun ship
- *ivory* source of objects in the cargo of the Ulu Burun wreck, 14th century BC
- major migration, c.2000
- major migration, c.1200
- area affected by ash falls from the eruption of Thera, 1626

HITTITE EMPIRE

Carchemish

Sea Peoples
Mersin
Tarsus
Alalakh
Aleppo

tin ingots

Orontes

Ugarit

6
Cape Gelidonya

Sea Peoples

Hamath

Mycenaeans

Lapethos
Chytroi
Soloi
Enkomi
8
Idalion
Tamassos
Kition
Paphos
Amathous
Kourion
Cyprus copper ingots, pottery

amphoras, bronze, dye, glass, ivory, olives, resin, weapons

Sea Peoples

PALESTINE

cylinder seals from Mesopotamia

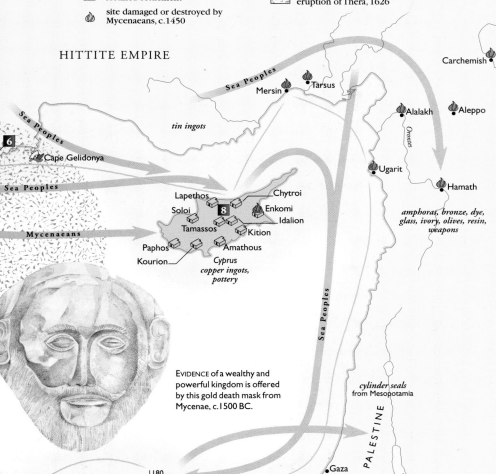

EVIDENCE of a wealthy and powerful kingdom is offered by this gold death mask from Mycenae, c.1500 BC.

1180

bronze weapons, ebony, scarab brooches

Avaris
3

EGYPT

Gaza

Memphis

Nile

| 0 | 300 km |
| 0 | 200 mi |

evidence of Mycenaean civilization is a series of richly furnished shaft graves at Mycenae, dating to between 1650 and 1550. The grave goods reveal a wealthy warrior society and include hoards of bronze weapons, gold, silver and electrum table-ware, jewelry and gold deathmasks. Mycenaean warriors rode to battle in horse-drawn chariots, but fought on foot with spear, sword and dagger. The towns were well defended, especially after the 14th century, by strong walls, built with massive blocks of stone and bastioned gateways. From the 15th century, Mycenaean rulers were buried in vaulted *tholos* (beehive shaped) tombs in which rituals related to a cult of kingship could be performed.

Each Mycenaean stronghold was ruled over by a king with a warrior aristocracy. The kings con-trolled many craftsmen – the king of Pylos employed about four hundred bronzesmiths – and hundreds of mainly female slaves. The royal palaces were smaller than those on Crete. According to a survey pre-served in Homer's *Iliad*, known as the Catalog of Ships, there were some twenty kingdoms theoreti-cally acknowledging the leadership of Mycenae.

Around 1450 the Mycenaeans expanded in the Aegean, conquering Crete and founding Miletos on the Anatolian coast: they may also have raided Egypt and the Hittite empire and, perhaps, they sacked Troy. They traded throughout the eastern Mediter-ranean and as far west as Malta, Sicily and Italy.

The Mycenaean civilization came to a violent end around 1200. Most of the major centers were sacked, town life came to an end and writing fell out of use. The whole Aegean entered a dark age which lasted about four centuries. The attackers were probably the Sea Peoples who also brought chaos to Egypt and the Levant. Some Mycenaeans sought refuge on Cyprus and on the coast of Anatolia; others may have joined with the Sea Peoples – Mycenaean influ-ence is evident in Palestine where some of them settled. A power vacuum developed in Greece into which another Greek-speaking people, the Dorians, migrated around 1100, overrunning the Pelo-ponnese, Crete and Rhodes: of the old Mycenaean centers only Athens retained its independence.

1 Knossos, the greatest of the Cretan palaces, was first built around 2000 and was rebuilt several times after earthquake damage or war.

2 The Minoan city of Akrotiri was preserved by ashfalls after the volcanic eruption on Thera in 1626.

3 Avaris was an Egyptian city which contained a Minoan colony founded in about 1550.

4 Mycenae had rich tombs and massive defenses built between 1600 and 1200. According to Homer, its king Agamemnon led the Greeks in the Trojan War.

5 A defensive wall was built across the Isthmus of Corinth in the late 13th century to protect the Peloponnese from invasion from the north.

6 A 14th-century shipwreck found at Ulu Burun near Kas had a cargo from around the east Mediterranean.

7 Troy was sacked twice in the 13th century, and again in 1100.

8 Mycenaeans reached Cyprus in the 15th century but the main settlement was 300 years later.

See also 1.12 (Sea Peoples); 1.18 (Egypt); 1.24 (Greek city-states)

As the eastern Mediterranean recovered from the disruptions of the late second millennium, the Phoenicians and Greeks began to establish trade routes and colonies throughout the western Mediterranean and, in the case of the Greeks, the Black Sea.

The first to extend their trade routes into the western Mediterranean were the Phoenicians, a Levantine people culturally and linguistically closely related to the Canaanites. The Phoenician homeland had the best natural harbors on the coastline of the Levant, where small ports had grown up as early as the third millennium BC, trading cedar wood, purple dye and other commodities with Egypt. The leading Phoenician ports had developed into independent city-states by 1500 BC. In the earliest records the Phoenician cities were ruled by hereditary kings, but by the 6th century monarchy had been replaced by elected officials. The Phoenician cities never exercised control far inland and for the greater part of their history they were dominated by one or other of the region's great powers.

The earliest evidence of Phoenician expansion overseas is at Kition, originally a Mycenaean colony, on Cyprus about 1000 BC. Cyprus was an important source of copper and had had close trade links with Phoenicia for centuries before this. The main period of Phoenician expansion, however, extended from the late 9th century to the mid 7th century. The main concentration of Phoenician colonies were in Tunisia, Sicily and Sardinia, which gave them control over the main approaches to the western Mediterranean. By the 7th century Carthage, a Tyrian colony, had become the leading Phoenician city in the west. By the 8th century Phoenician trade routes extended through the Straits of Gibraltar and some way along the Atlantic coasts of Spain and Morocco. At first the Phoenicians maintained only seasonal trading posts in this area, but permanent colonies, such as Tingis and Gades, were established in the 7th century. Phoenician colonies technically remained subject to their parent cities, but they were forced to become independent when Phoenicia was conquered by the Babylonians in the 6th century.

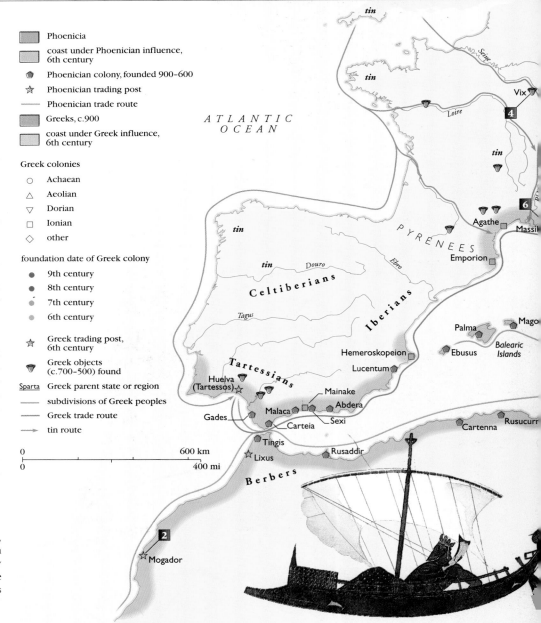

Legend:

- Phoenicia
- coast under Phoenician influence, 6th century
- Phoenician colony, founded 900–600
- ☆ Phoenician trading post
- —— Phoenician trade route
- Greeks, c.900
- coast under Greek influence, 6th century

Greek colonies
- ○ Achaean
- △ Aeolian
- ▽ Dorian
- □ Ionian
- ◇ other

foundation date of Greek colony
- ● 9th century
- ● 8th century
- ◔ 7th century
- ● 6th century

- ☆ Greek trading post, 6th century
- ▽ Greek objects (c.700–500) found
- Sparta Greek parent state or region
- —— subdivisions of Greek peoples
- —— Greek trade route
- → tin route

0 — 600 km
0 — 400 mi

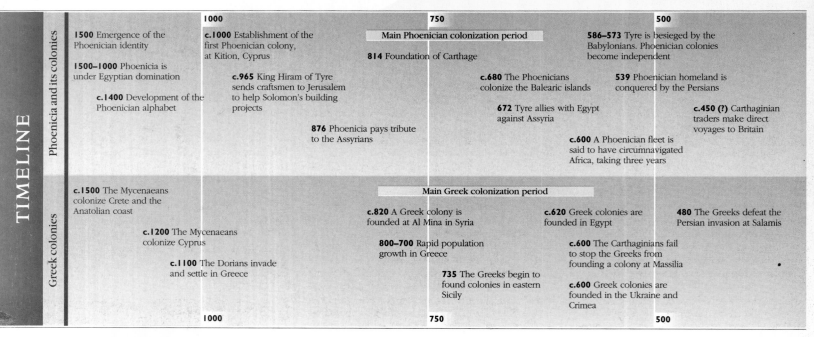

TIMELINE

	1000	**750**	**500**
Phoenicia and its colonies	**1500** Emergence of the Phoenician identity **1500–1000** Phoenicia is under Egyptian domination **c.1400** Development of the Phoenician alphabet	**c.1000** Establishment of the first Phoenician colony, at Kition, Cyprus **c.965** King Hiram of Tyre sends craftsmen to Jerusalem to help Solomon's building projects **876** Phoenicia pays tribute to the Assyrians	*Main Phoenician colonization period* **814** Foundation of Carthage **c.680** The Phoenicians colonize the Balearic islands **672** Tyre allies with Egypt against Assyria **c.600** A Phoenician fleet is said to have circumnavigated Africa, taking three years	**586–573** Tyre is besieged by the Babylonians. Phoenician colonies become independent **539** Phoenician homeland is conquered by the Persians **c.450 (?)** Carthaginian traders make direct voyages to Britain
Greek colonies	**c.1500** The Mycenaeans colonize Crete and the Anatolian coast **c.1200** The Mycenaeans colonize Cyprus **c.1100** The Dorians invade and settle in Greece	**c.820** A Greek colony is founded at Al Mina in Syria **800–700** Rapid population growth in Greece **735** The Greeks begin to found colonies in eastern Sicily	*Main Greek colonization period* **c.620** Greek colonies are founded in Egypt **c.600** The Carthaginians fail to stop the Greeks from founding a colony at Massilia **c.600** Greek colonies are founded in the Ukraine and Crimea	**480** The Greeks defeat the Persian invasion at Salamis

GORGON's head handles and a frieze of soldiers and chariots embellish this head-height bronze *krater* (a vessel for mixing wine and water). Of 6th-century Greek manufacture, it was found at Vix, France

SHIPBUILDING and navigation were essential skills. This detail of a vase painting c.540 shows the god Dionysus at sea (having escaped capture by pirates).

Map labels

Rhine · Elbe · Danube · Sava · Po · ALPS

Celts

Spina · Etruscan city states · Volaterrae · Volci · Graivisca · Alalia · *Corsica* · *Sardinia* · Tharros · Caralis · Icis · Nora

Illyrians · **Italics** · **Epirotes**

Kymai · Neapolis · Pithekoussai · Poseidonia · Elea · Skidros · Terina · Taras · Satyrion · Metapontum · Sybaris · Kroton · Hipponion · Himera · Soleis · Metauros · Panormus · Mylai · Motya · Katana · Naxos · Minoa · Akragas · Gela · Leontinoi · Kamarina · Syracuse · Rhegion · Lokroi · Melite · *Malta*

Utica · Hippo Regius · Carthage · Hadrumetum · Girba · Sabrata · Oea · Leptis Magna · Kinyps

Achaeans · *ACHAEA* · Chalcis · Locris · Megara · Corinth · Athens · Sparta · *Dorians*

Epidamnos · Apollonia · Methone · Stageiros · Mende · Poteidaia · Torone · Thasos · Ainos · Sestos · Ilium · Abydos · Lesbos · Phokaia · Smyrna · Samos · Miletos

Macedonians · **Thracians** · Kallatis · Odessos · Mesembria · Apollonia · Byzantium · Chalcedon · Kardia · Cyzicus

Aeolians · **Ionians** · **Lydians** · **Phrygians** · **Lycians**

Phaselis · Nagidos · Side · Kelenderis · Soloi · Al Mina · Ugarit · *Cyprus* · Kition · Arvad · Berytus · Byblos · Tyre · Sidon · Jerusalem · Hebrew kingdoms · *LEVANT* · **ASSYRIA** · *Euphrates* · *Tigris* · COLCHIS

Thera · *Crete* · *Rhodes*

Mediterranean Sea

Black Sea · Tanais · Dioskurias · Phasis · Trapezus · Kerasous · Sinope · Sesamos · Kytoros · Herakleia · Phanagoria · Kimmerikon · Pantikapaion · Theodosia · Berezean Island · Olbia · Tyras · Istros

Scythians [3]

Naukratis · Memphis · Daphnai · *Nile* · **EGYPT** [7]

Cyrene · Apollonia · Ptolemais · Taucheira · Barca · Aziris · Platea Island · Euesperides · *CYRENAICA*

For almost three centuries after the collapse of the Mycenaean civilization, Greece remained impoverished and isolated. Recovery began around 900 as the Greeks reestablished trade links with the Levant and Italy. By the 8th century prosperity had returned, urban life was restored and the Greek population was rising rapidly. The earliest Greek overseas colonies, such as Al Mina in Syria and Pithekoussai and Kymai in Italy, were motivated by trade. The earliest long-distance trade was in iron ore, slaves and luxury goods; in return the Greeks offered wine and acted as middlemen. Even before the end of the 8th century, colonies had also become a way for the Greek cities to resettle surplus population. Often colonists were chosen by lot. Most active as colonizers were the Ionian Greeks, descendants of the Mycenaeans, and the Dorians. The Greek colonies, unlike Phoenician colonies, were founded from the outset to be independent states in their own right, although relations with the parent states often remained close.

The Greeks initially looked west. The first major colonizing efforts in the 8th century were in southern Italy and Sicily, where there were many good harbors and fertile agricultural land to support the colonists. Relations with the native peoples were poor, but that did not prevent Greek culture from having a great impact in Italy, especially on the Etruscans in the north. The Italian colonies were initially highly successful – Syracuse, for example, was the most populous Greek city in the 5th century – but the constant hostility of the natives sapped their strength and by the 3rd century they were in decline. Further west in the Mediterranean, the Greeks faced the opposition of the Phoenicians but Massilia was founded around 600. The Celtic chiefs of Gaul prospered greatly from trade with the Greeks, as the superb quality of Greek artifacts found in burials, such as that at Vix, shows.

In the 7th and 6th centuries the effort of colonization shifted to the coasts of Thrace and the Black Sea. The Greek colonies here traded luxury goods with the steppe peoples for wheat to feed the cities of the Greek homeland. The same period also saw colonies founded in Cyrenaica and Egypt. The Greek colonies in Egypt became politically influential and through them the Greeks gained a deep knowledge of Egyptian art and architecture.

[1] Carthage was the most important Phoenician colony, founded in 814. It became a powerful independent state in the 6th century.

[2] Phoenician trading posts on the African coast, such as Mogador, were occupied for only part of the year.

[3] The Scythians traded grain with the Greek Black Sea colonies in return for luxury goods

[4] The burial mound at Vix of a 6th-century Celtic princess has yielded some of the finest Greek bronze-work yet found.

[5] Syracuse, founded by Corinth around 733, became the wealthiest and most powerful of the western Greek colonies.

[6] Massilia, founded around 600 to exploit the tin trade, declined after 500 when the trade routes shifted to the Atlantic and the Alpine passes.

[7] Greek mercenaries played a key role in Egyptian armies around 600.

See also 1.14 (Bible lands), 1.22 (Mycenaeans), 1.24 (Mainland Greece), 1.25 (Carthage)

During the dark ages (1200–800 BC), the Greeks lived in tribal communities under chiefs or kings who combined the roles of warleader and chief priest but who had to consult a council of elders and the warrior aristocracy. Their subjects sometimes paid tribute to the kings, but there was no regular system of taxation. There were no palaces, and kings lived in houses distinguished from those of their subjects only by their greater size. Town life almost ceased and such long-distance trade as survived was controlled by the Phoenicians. War, hunting and lavish displays of hospitality were the hallmarks of dark-age Greek culture. One of the most important developments of the period was that iron replaced bronze.

By the 9th century power began to pass to the hereditary aristocracy, and by the end of the 7th century only Sparta, Argos and Thera still had monarchies. Little is known about the institutions of aristocratic government but it was under their rule that trade and city life revived in Greece and that Greek colonization overseas began. The *polis* (city-state) became the dominant form of political organization. The cities dominated the countryside and became the main centers of political power, commerce and cultural life. The revival of trade made it necessary to re-invent writing in the 8th century, as the Mycenaean script had been entirely forgotten. The Greeks adopted the Phoenician consonantal alphabet and by adding separate signs for vowels turned it into a far more flexible and simple writing system. As a result writing became a common accomplishment in Greece. This was to be a major factor in the brilliant flowering of Greek civilization in the 6th and 5th century.

In the 7th century aristocratic government became unpopular. New military tactics, involving large numbers of heavily armed infantry, deprived them of their status as a warrior elite. There was discontent also among the newly rich who, not having aristocratic birth, were excluded from political power. In many Greek city-states these discontents led, between 660 and 485, to revolutions under popular leaders known as "tyrants" (a term describing rulers who had gained power through their own efforts, rather than by virtue of birth). Most tyrannies endured only a few decades before they were overthrown and replaced with "oligarchies", in which the aristocracy was influential but had no monopoly on power. Other Greek city-states reformed their constitutions without revolutions and by the 6th century most were ruled by oligarchies: the remaining strongholds of aristocratic power were in the north of Greece, where there were few cities, and in Sicily.

The most far-reaching political upheavals took place in Athens. Faced with mounting internal problems, the Athenians sought to avoid revolution by

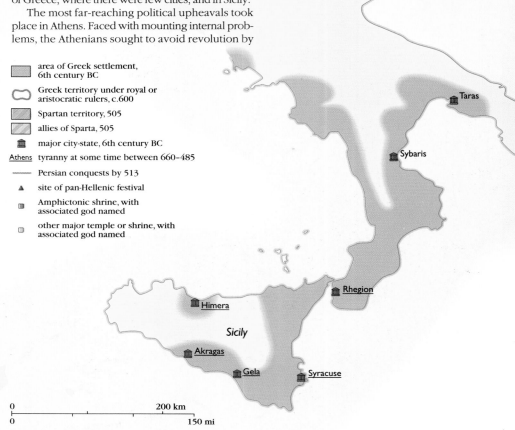

	area of Greek settlement, 6th century BC
	Greek territory under royal or aristocratic rulers, c.600
	Spartan territory, 505
	allies of Sparta, 505
🏛	major city-state, 6th century BC
Athens	tyranny at some time between 660–485
—	Persian conquests by 513
▲	site of pan-Hellenic festival
▪	Amphictonic shrine, with associated god named
▫	other major temple or shrine, with associated god named

Illyria

Taras

Sybaris

Rhegion

Himera

Sicily

Akragas

Gela

Syracuse

0   200 km
0   150 mi

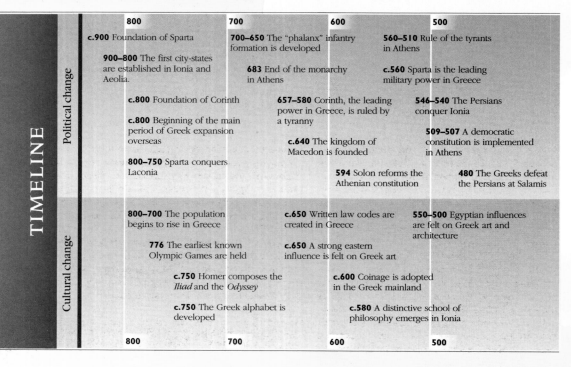

TIMELINE

Political change

800	700	600	500
c.900 Foundation of Sparta	**700–650** The "phalanx" infantry formation is developed	**560–510** Rule of the tyrants in Athens	
900–800 The first city-states are established in Ionia and Aeolia.	**683** End of the monarchy in Athens	**c.560** Sparta is the leading military power in Greece	
c.800 Foundation of Corinth	**657–580** Corinth, the leading power in Greece, is ruled by a tyranny	**546–540** The Persians conquer Ionia	
c.800 Beginning of the main period of Greek expansion overseas	**c.640** The kingdom of Macedon is founded	**509–507** A democratic constitution is implemented in Athens	
800–750 Sparta conquers Laconia	**594** Solon reforms the Athenian constitution	**480** The Greeks defeat the Persians at Salamis	

Cultural change

800	700	600	500
800–700 The population begins to rise in Greece	**c.650** Written law codes are created in Greece	**550–500** Egyptian influences are felt on Greek art and architecture	
776 The earliest known Olympic Games are held	**c.650** A strong eastern influence is felt on Greek art		
c.750 Homer composes the *Iliad* and the *Odyssey*	**c.600** Coinage is adopted in the Greek mainland		
c.750 The Greek alphabet is developed	**c.580** A distinctive school of philosophy emerges in Ionia		

| 800 | 700 | 600 | 500 |

1 A century of far-reaching political reforms transformed Athens from a backwater in 600 into a leading state in 500.

2 Regarded by the Greeks as a barbarian kingdom, Macedon had a mixed population of Illyrians, Thracians and Dorian Greeks.

3 Olympia was the wealthiest religious center in Greece; pan-Hellenic games were held in honor of Zeus every four years from 776 BC to AD 393.

4 The oracle of Apollo at Delphi was widely consulted by the Greek states on important political matters; it was famous for its ambiguous answers.

5 Corinth benefited from its strategic position on the isthmus between the Gulf of Corinth and the Aegean Sea to become a major trading power.

6 The Ionians were the most culturally sophisticated Greeks in the 7th and 6th centuries, taking advantage of close links with the Middle Eastern civilizations.

7 Argos was a bitter rival of Sparta for control of the Peloponnese from the 7th to the 5th century.

8 Coinage was introduced by Lydian kings in about 700; its use had spread to Greece by about 600.

BURIED under the ruins of the Acropolis when the Persians attacked Athens in 480, this marble *kore* (maiden) would once have been brightly painted.

Black Sea

Danube

Olt

Thracians

Marisa

Herakleia

Byzantium

Chalcedon

Strymon

Abdera

Thasos

Thasos

Lampsakos

Cyzicus

Sestos

Abydos

Samothrace

Imroz

Lemnos

Poteidaia

Axios

MACEDON

2

Lake Prespa

Aliakmon

Mt Olympos
(Zeus)

EPIRUS

Corcyra

Corfu

Dodona
(Zeus)

Pinios

THESSALY

PINDOS MOUNTAINS

Vjose

Ambracia

Acheloos

ACARNANIA

AETOLIA

PHOCIS

Delphi
(Apollo)

Anthela
(Apollo)

Kephisos

Kephallenia

Alacomenae
(Apollo)

Chalcis

Eretria

Euboea

Northern Sporades

BOEOTIA

Thebes

ACHAEA

Sikyon

5

Megara

ATTICA

Eleusis (Demeter)

Athens

Nemea
(Zeus)

Corinth
(Poseidon)

Zakynthos

ELIS

Olympia
(Zeus)

ARCADIA

Mantineia

Tegea

Argos
(Hera)

Aegina

1

Epidauros (Asclepios)

Calauria
(Poseidon)

7

3

MESSENIA

KYNOURIA

Sparta

LACONIA

KYTHERA
(Aphrodite)

Melos

Delos
(Apollo)

Naxos

Paros

Naxos

Thera

Andros

Ikaria

Aegean Sea

Lesbos

Mytilene

AEOLIA

Phokaia

Chios

Chios

Klasomenai

Kolophon

Ephesos
(Artemis)

LYDIA
conquered by Persians
547–546

8

Gediz

Menderes

Samos

IONIA

6

Miletos

Didyma
(Apollo)

Halikarnassos

Kos

Kos

Knidos
(Aphrodite)

Ialysos

Kameiros

Rhodes

Lindos

LYCIA

Carpathos

Mediterranean Sea

Kydonia

Crete

Knossos

Itanos

Gortyn

4

appointing Solon to reform the constitution in 594. The result was a compromise that satisfied nobody and in 546 the tyrant Peisistratus seized power. Peisistratus was an effective and popular ruler who broke the aristocratic hold on power and did much to address the problems of the peasantry. Peisistratos was succeeded by his less able son Hippias who was overthrown by an aristocratic faction in 510. After three years of internal strife the aristocratic party was defeated. The reformer Kleisthenes "took the people into partnership" and introduced a democratic constitution which gave all 45,000 male citizens the right to attend the assembly and vote on all major decisions and appointments.

By actively involving its citizens in government, Athens had become a self-confident and assertive

state by 500, but for most of the 6th century the most powerful state was Sparta, which had taken the lead in developing new infantry tactics in which armored spearmen fought in a close-packed phalanx, presenting an impenetrable hedge of spears to the enemy. Sparta formed a league of similar cities based on a hoplite franchise, through which it dominated the Peloponnese.

The first Greeks to fall under Persian power were the Ionians on the Anatolian coast. Since about 600 the Ionians had paid tribute to the kings of Lydia but relations were good: the Greeks adopted coinage as a result of Lydian influences and the Lydians themselves became increasingly Hellenized. Persian rule was not particularly oppressive but it was more unpopular than the loose control of the Lydians.

Despite their rivalries, Greeks had a strong sense of common identity by the 8th century, expressed through the name they gave themselves – Hellenes – and by religion. All Greeks worshiped the same gods and celebrated pan-Hellenic festivals, such as the Olympic Games, during which hostilities had to cease. The neutrality of shrines of pan-Hellenic importance was protected and supported by leagues (*amphictonies*) of neighboring states, such as the Amphictony of Delphi. A cultural heritage had also emerged, epitomized by the epic poems of Homer, which were composed in the 8th century.

See also 1.15 (Persia), 1.22 (Minoans and Mycenaeans), 1.25 (western Mediterranean)

The first cities and states in the western Mediterranean developed in the early Iron Age. The first were the Etruscan city-states of northern Italy, which had emerged by 800 BC. Then in the 8th century many cities were founded on the coasts of southern Italy, France, Spain and north Africa by Phoenician and Greek colonists. The Greeks had a strong impact on the Etruscan civilization while the Phoenician colonies in Spain influenced the growth of cities and states among the native Tartessian, Turdetanian and Iberian peoples by 500 BC.

The origin of the Etruscans is uncertain. Their language was unrelated to any other European language, suggesting that the Etruscans may have migrated into Italy from the Middle East. There is no convincing evidence of this, however, and it is more likely that the Etruscans were an indigenous people. The forerunner of the Etruscan civilization was the Villanova culture – the first iron-using culture in Italy – which developed in Tuscany around 900 and later spread north into the Po valley. This culture itself seems to have developed out of local Urnfield cultures. In Tuscany the Villanova culture was replaced by the Etruscan civilization in the 8th century BC but it survived in the Po valley until the 6th century, when the area was overrun by the Etruscans.

Etruria was rich in iron and copper ores, had good agricultural land and a coastline with many natural harbors, which encouraged the Etruscans to become active seafarers and traders. Most early Etruscan cities were sited a few kilometers from the coast, close enough for convenience but not vulnerable to pirate raids. Each city was an independent state ruled by a king but the twelve most important cities were loosely united in the Etruscan league. From the 8th century the Etruscans faced competition from Greek and Phoenician colonies in the western Mediterranean. The foundation of the Greek colony at Massilia around 600 was a particularly serious development as it shut the Etruscans out of the important trans-Gallic tin routes. To some extent this was offset by Etruscan expansion into the Po valley in the 6th century, which brought them control of the transalpine and Adriatic trade routes

and diverted some trade away from the Greek colonies. With Carthaginian help, the Etruscans succeeded in driving the Greeks out of Corsica in 535 but attacks on the Greeks at Kymai (Cumae) in southern Italy were repulsed in 524, 505 and 474. Despite these hostilities, Etruscan culture had become very Hellenized by the 6th century.

The other major group of peoples in Italy were the Italic speakers who had probably migrated into Italy from central Europe during Urnfield times. Though most of the Italic peoples were still organized into tribes in 500 BC, city-states had developed among the Latins as a result of Etruscan influence. The leading Latin city was Rome. The Romans expelled their Etruscan king in 509 and founded a republic but Rome was still little more than a market town.

Carthage was not the earliest Phoenician colony in north Africa but its fine harbor and strategic position had made it into the most important by the mid 7th century.

Legend:
- Villanova early Iron Age culture, c.900
- Etruria, c.600
- area under Etruscan domination, c.500
- Carthaginian empire, c.500
- area settled and controlled by Greeks, c.500
- Iberian peoples
- Tartessian–Turdetanian peoples
- Italic peoples
- Illyrian peoples
- Celtic and related peoples, c.500
- Hallstatt heartland, c.700
- ■ Etruscan city
- ■ Greek city
- • other city
- trans-Gallic tin route
- transalpine trade route
- → major migration

```
0                      400 km
0               300 mi
```

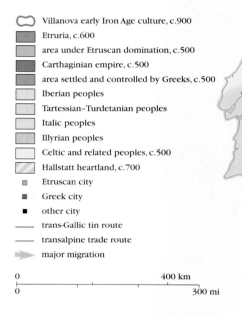

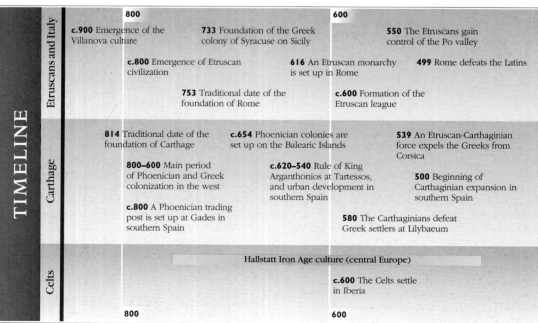

TIMELINE

Etruscans and Italy

800		600
c.900 Emergence of the Villanova culture	**733** Foundation of the Greek colony of Syracuse on Sicily	**550** The Etruscans gain control of the Po valley
c.800 Emergence of Etruscan civilization	**616** An Etruscan monarchy is set up in Rome	**499** Rome defeats the Latins
753 Traditional date of the foundation of Rome		**c.600** Formation of the Etruscan league

Carthage

814 Traditional date of the foundation of Carthage	**c.654** Phoenician colonies are set up on the Balearic Islands	**539** An Etruscan-Carthaginian force expels the Greeks from Corsica
800–600 Main period of Phoenician and Greek colonization in the west	**c.620–540** Rule of King Arganthonios at Tartessos, and urban development in southern Spain	**500** Beginning of Carthaginian expansion in southern Spain
c.800 A Phoenician trading post is set up at Gades in southern Spain	**580** The Carthaginians defeat Greek settlers at Lilybaeum	

Celts

Hallstatt Iron Age culture (central Europe)

c.600 The Celts settle in Iberia

| 800 | 600 |

1 By 600 BC, Tartessos was the capital of a wealthy kingdom, and the region saw rapid urban growth under Phoenician and Carthaginian influence in the 6th century.

2 The Hallstatt Iron Age culture (c.750–450) is named for a rich cemetery at an ancient salt-mining center in the Austrian Alps.

3 The stone defenses of the 6th-century Celtic fort at Heuneburg show the influence of Greek architecture.

4 Until the end of the 6th century, the main importance of the small market town of Rome was its control of the main crossing point of the river Tiber.

5 The Lipari Islands were the base for Greek pirates in the 6th and 5th centuries.

6 A joint Carthaginian-Etruscan force defeated the Greeks off Corsica in 539, halting Greek colonization in the western Mediterranean.

7 Populonia was the main iron-working center of Italy from the 6th century; around 10,000 tonnes of iron ore were imported from Elba and smelted there annually.

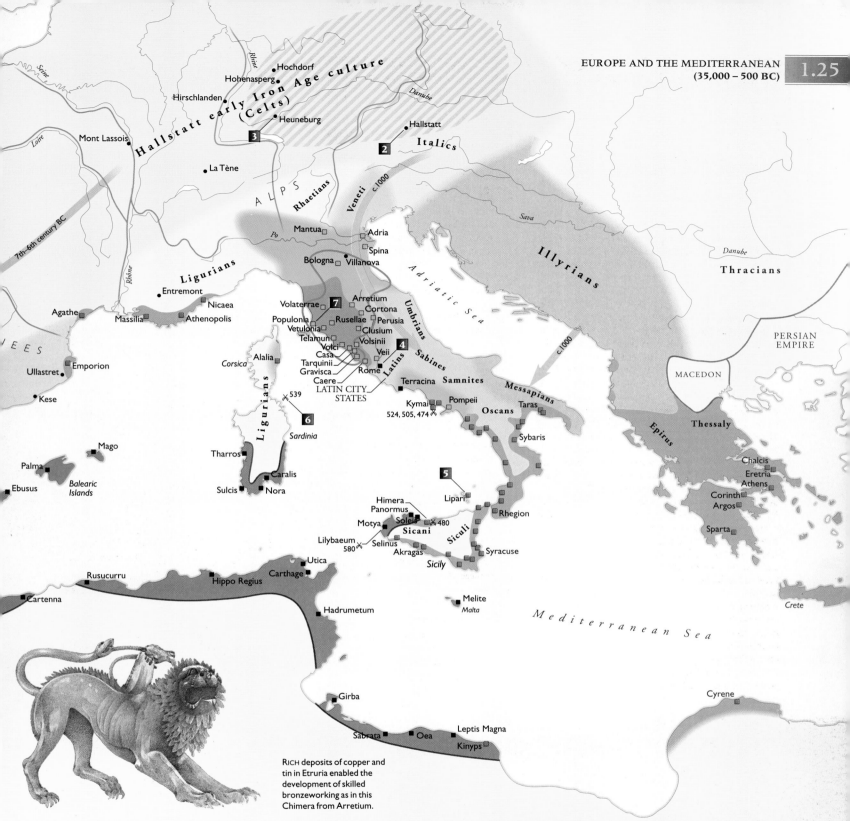

Rhine

Seine

Loire

Hochdorf

Hohenasperg

Hirschlanden

Mont Lassois

Hallstatt early Iron Age culture (Celts)

Heuneburg

3

La Tène

ALPS

Danube

Hallstatt

2

Italics

7th–6th century BC

Rhaetians

Veneti c.1000

Po

Mantua

Adria

Spina

Sava

Danube

Bologna

Villanova

Illyrians

Thracians

Ligurians

Rhône

Entremont

Nicaea

Agathe

Massilia

Athenopolis

Volaterrae

7

Arretium

Cortona

Perusia

Adriatic Sea

Populonia

Rusellae

Vetulonia

Clusium

Telamun

Volsinii

Umbrians

c.1000

PERSIAN
EMPIRE

Volci

Casa

Veii

4

Sabines

MACEDON

EES

Ullastret

Emporion

Corsica

Alalia

Tarquinii

Grafrom

Caere

Rome

Latins

Terracina

Samnites

Messapians

Epirus

Thessaly

Kese

Sardinia

539

6

LATIN CITY
STATES

Kymai

524, 505, 474

Pompeii

Oscans

Taras

Chalcis

Mago

Tharros

Sybaris

Eretria

Athens

Palma

Balearic
Islands

Caralis

5

Lipari

Rhegion

Corinth

Argos

Ebusus

Sulcis

Nora

Himera

Panormus

Soleis

480

Sparta

Motya

Sicani

Siculi

Lilybaeum

580

Selinus

Akragas

Syracuse

Sicily

Rusucurru

Utica

Cartenna

Hippo Regius

Carthage

Melite

Malta

Crete

Hadrumetum

Mediterranean Sea

Girba

Cyrene

Sabrata

Oea

Leptis Magna

Kinyps

RICH deposits of copper and tin in Etruria enabled the development of skilled bronzeworking as in this Chimera from Arretium.

Although technically still subject to its parent city Tyre, Carthage had by this time begun its own independent colonization of the Balearic Islands. In 580 Carthage intervened in Sicily to protect Motya against the Greek city of Selinus and shortly after to support the Phoenician colonies in Sardinia against the natives. These actions established Carthage as the protector of the Phoenician colonies in the west, and by 500 it had become the capital of a loose-knit maritime empire which dominated the western Mediterranean trade routes. The Greeks, however, succeeded in gaining control of most of Sicily in 480.

The area most influenced by the Phoenicians and Carthaginians was southern Spain. Gades (Cadiz) was an important Phoenician trading post from at least the 8th century, if not earlier, and Huelva –

almost certainly the ancient city of Tartessos – was a port with trading links with the Greeks, Phoenicians and Atlantic Europe by around 800. Excavations at Huelva have yielded huge quantities of imported pottery. Huelva's prosperity was based on exports of silver and other metals from southern Spain and of tin from Galicia, Brittany and Cornwall. By the 6th century a Tartessian kingdom had developed and fortified towns were being founded in the Guadalquivir valley. Phoenician techniques were incorporated into local metalworking and sculpture and a script based on the Phoenician alphabet was adopted. Urban development was also beginning in the Iberian area on the east coast of Spain by 500. Here too a Phoenician-based script was adopted.

The dominant influence in west and central

Europe in the 7th and 6th centuries was the Hallstatt culture, which is generally identified with the Celts. The Hallstatt culture began to develop in the 12th century BC from the Urnfield cultures of the upper Danube region. Bronze-using in its earlier stages, the Hallstatt culture adopted iron working in about 750. In the early 7th century the Celts spread west across Germany and France and by the early 6th century they had crossed the Pyrenees and occupied over half of the Iberian peninsula. The Celts there were quickly assimilated with the native peoples to produce a distinctive Celtiberian culture.

See also 1.21 (Bronze Age Europe), 1.23 (Greek and Phoenician colonization)

The first civilization of south Asia emerged in the Indus river valley around 2600 BC. The Indus civilization covered the greatest geographical extent of the Bronze Age civilizations. In its origins it resembled the Mesopotamian civilization, arising on the arid flood plain of a great and unpredictable river where the need for large-scale irrigation and flood defense schemes led to the development of a well-organized hierarchical society.

The first farming communities in south Asia developed at sites such as Mehrgarh in the mountains of Baluchistan as early as 6000 BC and spread from there into the Indus valley in the 4th millennium. There was considerable interaction between the valley settlements and those in the highlands. Highland peoples took their flocks to winter in the valley and traded metals, semiprecious stones and timber for grain and other foodstuffs. The early farming communities of the Indus valley showed no signs of social ranking, but the transition to a hierarchical society occurred very rapidly in about 2600 BC. This may have been a result of the establishment of trading contacts with Mesopotamia. Towns grew up in the Indus valley as a result of this trade. The metals and other products of the highlands were gathered in the towns and sent on to Mesopotamia: a shipment of 5,900 kilograms of copper was recorded on one occasion. The growth of trade also led to the development of small towns, such as Nindowari, in the highlands.

Most of the cities and towns in the Indus valley were small but two, Mohenjo-Daro and Harappa (from which the Indus civilization gets its alternative name, "Harappan"), had populations of around 30,000–40,000, placing them among the largest Bronze Age cities anywhere. Both Mohenjo-Daro and Harappa, as well as several of the smaller cities such as Kalibangan, had impressive mud-brick city walls, a citadel with public buildings and granaries and streets laid out on a grid pattern. The civilization was literate but its pictographic script has not been deciphered. As a result, the identity of the Indus people is unknown: they may have been related to the modern Dravidian peoples of southern India.

By 1800 BC the Indus cities were in decline and a century later they had been abandoned. Writing fell

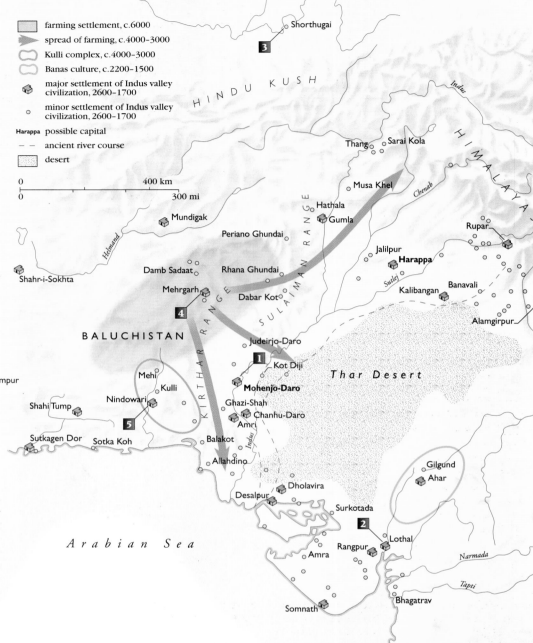

farming settlement, c.6000
spread of farming, c.4000–3000
Kulli complex, c.4000–3000
Banas culture, c.2200–1500
major settlement of Indus valley civilization, 2600–1700
minor settlement of Indus valley civilization, 2600–1700
Harappa possible capital
– – ancient river course
desert

0   400 km
0   300 mi

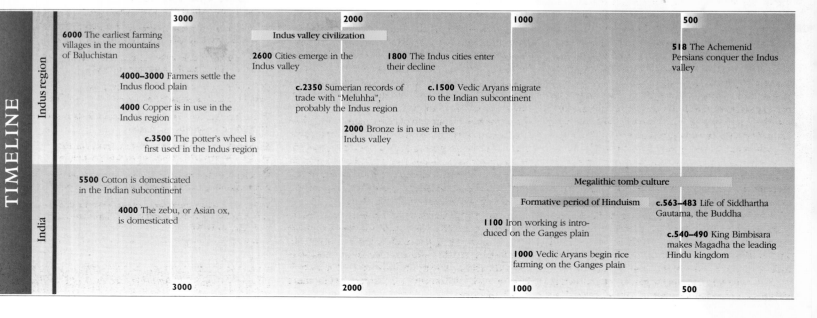

		3000	2000	1000	500
Indus region			Indus valley civilization		
		6000 The earliest farming villages in the mountains of Baluchistan			**518** The Achemenid Persians conquer the Indus valley
			2600 Cities emerge in the Indus valley	**1800** The Indus cities enter their decline	
		4000–3000 Farmers settle the Indus flood plain	**c.2350** Sumerian records of trade with "Meluhha", probably the Indus region	**c.1500** Vedic Aryans migrate to the Indian subcontinent	
		4000 Copper is in use in the Indus region			
		c.3500 The potter's wheel is first used in the Indus region	**2000** Bronze is in use in the Indus valley		
India		**5500** Cotton is domesticated in the Indian subcontinent		Megalithic tomb culture	
				Formative period of Hinduism	**c.563–483** Life of Siddhartha Gautama, the Buddha
		4000 The zebu, or Asian ox, is domesticated		**1100** Iron working is introduced on the Ganges plain	**c.540–490** King Bimbisara makes Magadha the leading Hindu kingdom
				1000 Vedic Aryans begin rice farming on the Ganges plain	
		3000	2000	1000	500

Map Labels

Taxila
GANDARA
Aryans from central Asia, mid 2nd millennium
KURU
HIMALAYAS
Indus
Sutlej
Hastinapura
PANCHALA
Ahichhattra
KOSALA
6
SURASENA
Atranjikhera
Sravasti
Lumbini
Thar Desert
Bairat
Ganges
MALLA
VRIJJI
Mathura
Tilaura-kot
Kusinagara
Vaisali
Yamuna
VATSA
Campa
MATSYA
CHEDI
KASI
Rajgir
ANGA
Ahar
9
AVANTI
Kausambi
MAGADHA
7
Arabian Sea
Ujjain
Vidisha
Māhismati
Narmada
Tamluk
Tapti
Mahanadi
ASSAKA
Bay of Bengal
Deccan
Godavari
Krishna
EASTERN GHATS
WESTERN GHATS
8
Brahmagiri
Kaveri
Sinhalese settlement of Ceylon, c.500 BC
Ceylon
Veddas

Legend

- Indus valley civilization
- Banas culture
- distribution of Painted Grey ware pottery, 1000–500
- distribution of Black-and-Red ware pottery, 2nd and 1st millennium BC
- area of early Iron Age megalithic tombs
- Persian empire, 518
- city, c.500
- other important site
- KASI *mahajanapada* ("great realm"), c.550
- major migration
- Persian conquest of Indus valley, c.518
- ancient river course
- desert

0 — 600 km
0 — 400 mi

ALOOF and solemn, the "priest-king" statuette from Mohenjo-Daro wears a decorated robe with one shoulder bare, a way of showing reverence.

Main Text

out of use. To date, no entirely convincing explanation has been found for the abandonment of these cities. Life in the countryside continued unchanged for several centuries, suggesting at least that the civilization did not fall as a result of outside invasion. Sometime around 1500 BC the Aryans, a semi-nomadic Indo-European pastoralist people, migrated into the Indian subcontinent from central Asia and occupied the northern half of the territory once covered by the Indus civilization. Some aspects of Indus culture were absorbed by the Aryans and the pottery styles of the late Indus Banas culture survived, then slowly spread across most of southern India, but all memory of the civilization itself was lost; it was rediscovered only in the 1920s.

For five centuries, the semi-nomadic Aryans left little physical trace of their presence, but a mythic record of their migrations and wars with the indigenous peoples has been preserved in the *Vedic Hymns*. These, the holiest books of the Hindu religion, were transmitted orally for centuries until they were written down in the 6th century BC. Around 1100 BC the Aryans adopted iron working, possibly independently of outside influence, and soon afterward they moved east and began to settle down in villages on the Ganges plain as rice farmers. The

appearance, round 1000–800 BC, across the Ganges plain, of the Painted Grey ware pottery style has been linked to the Aryan settlement of the area. By 900 small tribal kingdoms and aristocratic tribal republics, known collectively as *janapadas*, were developing across the Ganges plain. By 700 they had coalesced to form 16 *mahajanapadas* ("great realms"). By 500 BC Magadha, under its energetic king Bimbisara, had emerged as the most powerful. Hand in hand with the process of state formation was the growth of cities, many which, like Ujjain and Kausambi, had mud-brick defensive walls. This was a period of great developments in religion: it was the formative period of the Hindu religion and the late 6th century witnessed the lives and teachings of Mahavira, the founder of Jainism, and of Siddhartha Gautama, the Buddha.

By 500 BC the Gangetic civilization extended as far south as the River Godavari. South of this were iron-using, tribally organized farming peoples, many of whom buried their dead in megalithic cists (box-shaped tombs). Only towards the end of the 1st millennium did state formation and urban development start in this area.

1 Mohenjo-Daro is the first known planned city, built on a massive brick platform to protect it from floods.

2 Lothal was a port with a brick-lined artificial harbor; it had trading links with Mesopotamia.

3 Shorthugai was a colony possibly founded to exploit the trade in lapis lazuli from the Hindu Kush.

4 Mehrgarh was one of the earliest farming settlements in south Asia, flourishing about 6000.

5 The Kulli complex of towns centered on Nindowari had close trade links with the Indus valley.

6 Lumbini was the birthplace of Siddhartha Gautama, the Buddha; he died at Kusinagara.

7 Magadha was the leading Hindu kingdom in 500 BC, later forming the center of the Mauryan empire.

8 Brahmagiri is a major site of the south Indian Iron Age megalithic, with 300 tombs and stone circles.

9 Black-and-Red ware pottery appeared in the Banas region in late Indus times and spread across southern India after 1800 BC.

See also 1.10 (Mesopotamia); 1.15 (Persia)

The first civilization of east Asia developed in the Yellow river valley in the 18th century BC from indigenous Neolithic cultures. Farming began as early as 5800 BC on the broad band of loess soils that stretches across the Yellow river basin. By 5000 millet farming villages of the Yangshao culture were spread across much of the region. At the same time rice farming communities were spreading among the wetlands of the Yangtze valley. Rice farming spread to the Yellow river valley in the late 4th millennium and the Longshan cultures emerged. In favorable areas, the Longshan cultures practiced intensive rice cultivation using irrigation. The population rose, copper came into use, regional trading networks developed and a warrior class emerged. There is evidence of warfare, such as rammed earth fortifications and massacres of prisoners. A system of divination based on the use of "oracle bones" was developed.

According to Chinese traditions, civilization was founded by the emperor Huang Di around 2698 BC while the first dynasty, the Xia, was founded by Yu the Great in about 2205. However, there is no evidence for states in China in the 3rd millennium BC.

The first historically and archeologically attested Chinese dynasty is the Shang. This was founded about 1766 BC by King Tang, around the time of the appearance of the Erlitou culture. Cities with monumental buildings began to develop craft specialization and advanced bronze-casting techniques were adopted. The appearance of rich burials points to the emergence of a powerful ruling elite. A pictographic script came into use: the modern Chinese script is its direct descendant. Shang cultural influence extended across most of northern China and as far south as the Yangtze river. Like many early states, the Shang kingdom combined directly run provinces and vassal states.

Around 1122 the Shang king Di-xin was defeated and overthrown by his vassal king Wu of Zhou. The dynasty established by Wu became the longest lived of Chinese history and the early centuries of its rule were looked back on as a golden age. To legitimize their rule after their usurpation of the Shang, the Zhou rulers introduced the theory of the "Mandate

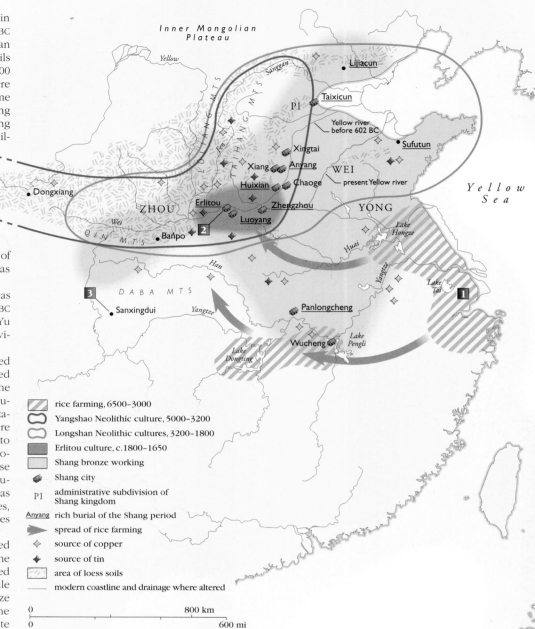

rice farming, 6500–3000
Yangshao Neolithic culture, 5000–3200
Longshan Neolithic cultures, 3200–1800
Erlitou culture, c.1800–1650
Shang bronze working
Shang city
PI   administrative subdivision of Shang kingdom
Anyang   rich burial of the Shang period
spread of rice farming
source of copper
source of tin
area of loess soils
modern coastline and drainage where altered

0 _____ 800 km
0 _____ 600 mi

TIMELINE		3000	2000	1000	500
		Longshan cultures	Shang dynasty	Western Zhou	Eastern Zhou (to 256 BC)
Political change					Springs and Autumns	Warring states (to 221 BC)
		c.3200 The first ranked societies in China are found in the Longshan culture	c.2205–1766 Traditional dates of the probably legendary Xia dynasty	c.1400–1122 The Shang capital is at Anyang	
					481–480 End of the Springs and Autumns period, and start of the Warring States period
		c.3000 Towns and complex fortifications are built	c.1766 Foundation of the Shang dynasty by king Tang	c.1122 King Wu of Zhou overthrows the Shang	
				770 The Zhou capital is moved from Hao to Luoyang; royal authority declines	
			c.1557 The Shang capital is moved to Zhengzhou		
Cultural change		6500 Rice farming begins in the Yangtze valley	c.1900 The earliest Chinese bronzes are made, at Erlitou	c.1350 The war chariot is introduced into China	551–479 Life of Confucius, philosopher and sage
		c.5800 Beginning of millet farming in northern China	c.1600 Origins of pictographic writing in China	c.800 Rapid increase in the number of towns in China	
		c.3000 Introduction of the potter's wheel in China	c.1400–1122 Royal burials at Anyang include human sacrifices	c.600 Earliest use of iron in China	
		3000	2000	1000	500

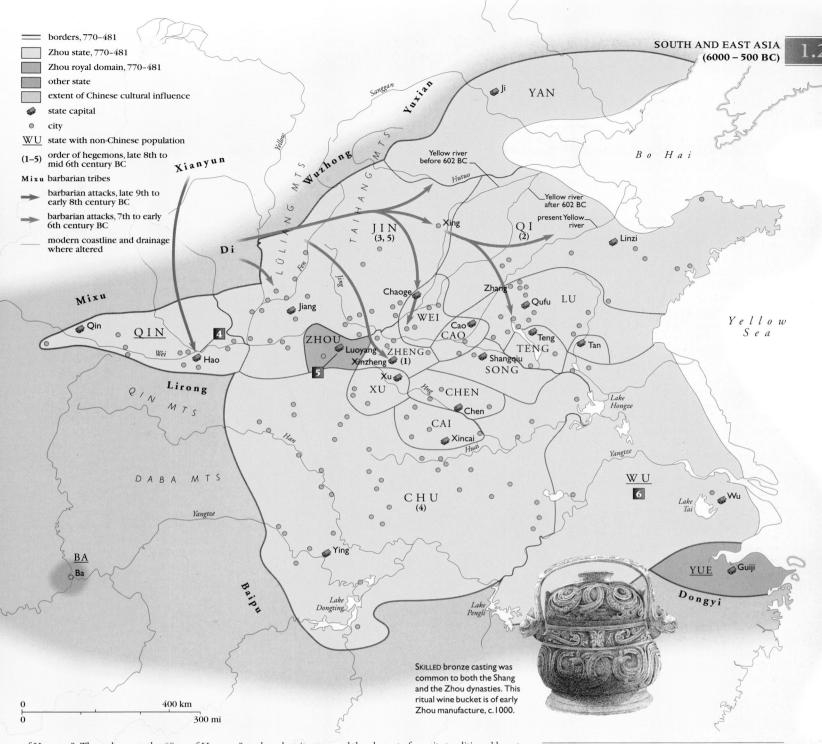

borders, 770–481
Zhou state, 770–481
Zhou royal domain, 770–481
other state
extent of Chinese cultural influence
state capital
city
WU state with non-Chinese population
(1–5) order of hegemons, late 8th to mid 6th century BC
Mixu barbarian tribes
barbarian attacks, late 9th to early 8th century BC
barbarian attacks, 7th to early 6th century BC
modern coastline and drainage where altered

SKILLED bronze casting was common to both the Shang and the Zhou dynasties. This ritual wine bucket is of early Zhou manufacture, c.1000.

of Heaven". The ruler was the "Son of Heaven" and "All under Heaven" was his lawful domain so long as he was just and moral. Should a ruler become unjust, Heaven would send him a warning and if he failed to reform, the Mandate would be given to another. Di-xin had been a sadist so Heaven had transferred the right to rule to the Zhou. This theory, which could be used both to condemn disobedience to the ruler and to justify successful usurpation, remained central to Chinese imperial ideology.

The Zhou kingdom was a decentralized feudal state, divided into fiefs governed by dukes chosen from among the king's relatives and trusted supporters. Only the royal domain was directly ruled by the king. In 770 barbarian attacks on Hao forced the Zhou to move their capital to Luoyang. This event was a turning-point in the history of the dynasty and marks the beginning of the period of disorder and fragmentation known as the Springs and Autumns period (after the title of the annals of the state of Lu).

Luoyang was more centrally situated than Hao

but it removed the dynasty from its traditional heartland in the west; its authority began to decline. By this time the king controlled less land than most of his dukes who now became, in effect, the rulers of independent states, making almost constant war on one another. However, the dukes continued to recognize the sovereignty of the king and also recognized the duke of the leading state of the time as hegemon (with general primacy over all other states). The Springs and Autumns period turned into the Warring States period (480–221), which saw the decline of feudal relationships and the rise of a professional bureaucracy.

The Springs and Autumns period was a brutal age but it saw great creativity in literature and religious and philosophical thought. The end of the period saw Confucius found the ethical system, which remains fundamental to Chinese thought. Iron working was adopted around 600, probably in Wu, though iron tools and weapons did not replace bronze in everyday use until the 2nd century BC.

1 More than a hundred wet-rice farming villages (using flooded fields) were established in this region 6500–4000 BC.

2 Erlitou was the site of the first Chinese bronzes c.1900 BC; it was probably also the first Shang capital.

3 The city and ritual offering pits at Sanxingdui, discovered in the 1990s, are evidence of a bronze-using civilization contemporary with the Shang.

4 Hao, in the original Zhou heartland, was abandoned as the capital in 770 after barbarian attacks. The move initiated a decline in Zhou authority.

5 The Zhou royal domain was limited to a small area around Luoyang by the 7th century.

6 Wu, the dominant state in southern China in the late 6th century, was destroyed by Yue in 473 BC.

See also 1.03 (agriculture)

The domestication of maize around 2700 made possible the development of permanent farming villages in Mesoamerica by 2300. Most early farmers practiced slash-and-burn agriculture, which cannot support dense populations. However, on fertile river flood-plains in the tropical forests of southeastern Mexico, reliable rainfall and year-round warmth made it possible to raise four crops of maize a year, which provided the economic base for the Olmec civilization.

By 1250 BC the Olmec lived in chiefdoms or small states ruled by a powerful hereditary elite. The most important sites were ceremonial centers with earth pyramid mounds and monumental stone sculptures of gods and chiefs. Associated with the ceremonial centers were settlements of two to three thousand people. The ritual centers were periodically destroyed and sculptures defaced or buried. Though possibly due to warfare between chiefdoms or states, it is more likely that this served a ritual purpose, marking the end of calendrical cycles, the death of a ruler or the accession of a new dynasty. Trade and gift exchange played an important part in the Olmec way of life. The Olmec lands have few natural resources and the raw materials for everyday tools, stone sculpture and status enhancing display objects had to be imported over long distances. Gift exchange played an important part in the diffusion of Olmec culture as the emerging elites of neighboring communities took up Olmec beliefs and artifacts to enhance their prestige. Late in their history, the Olmec developed a rudimentary hieroglyphic script which was used mainly for astronomical inscriptions. They used – and may have originated – both the Mesoamerican 260-day sacred year and the 52-year "long-count" calendar.

The Maya originated about 1200 BC in the Guatemalan highlands, developing from earlier Archaic cultures, and began to spread out into the lowlands of the Yucatán peninsula around 1000. By draining and canalizing swamps the Maya were able to

CARVED in rare blue jade, this tiny bust of a woman has the distinctive monumental quality which characterizes all Olmec sculpture.

Payón
Capacha
El Opeño
Tlatilco • Valley of Mexico
Cuicuilco • El Trapiche
Gualupita • Tlapacoya • El Viejón
Chalcatzinco • Los Bocas
Oxtotitlan • Tehuacán Valley
Juxtiahuaca • Tres Zapotes
Monte Negro • Laguna de los Cerros
San José Mogote
Las Limas • La Venta
Dainzú • San Lorenzo
Oaxaca Valley • Balancán
Monte Albán
Padre Piedra • Nakbe • Cuello
Pijijiapan • Lamanai
Xoc • Uaxactún
Altar de • Tikal
Sacrificios
Salinas la Blanca • Izapa
Abaj Takalik • Copán
Kaminaljuyú
Chalchuapa
Komchen
Dzibilchaltun
Yucatán Peninsula

Gulf of Mexico

PACIFIC OCEAN

Olmec, c.1250–400
Maya, c.1000
Maya, c.800
Zapotec, c.1400–400
◈ Olmec ceremonial center
• site with Olmec or Olmec influenced art
— Olmec trade route
◆ source of basalt
◆ source of hematite
◆ source of jade
◆ source of obsidian
◇ source of serpentine
— northern limit of farming cultures, c.500 BC

0 ————— 600 km
0 ————— 400 mi

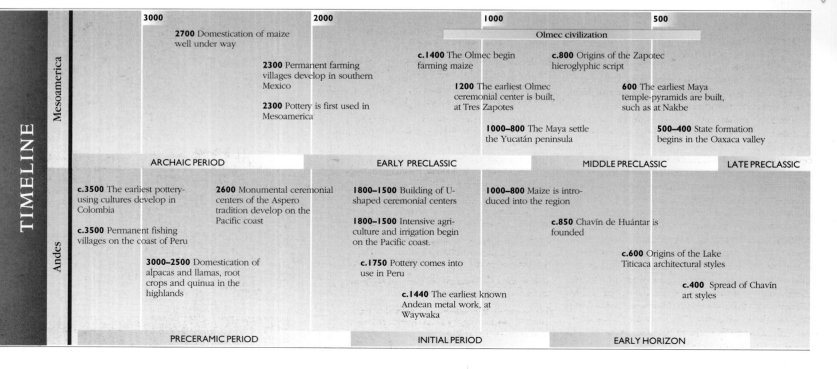

Mesoamerica

3000	2000	1000	500
		Olmec civilization	
2700 Domestication of maize well under way		**c.1400** The Olmec begin farming maize	**c.800** Origins of the Zapotec hieroglyphic script
	2300 Permanent farming villages develop in southern Mexico	**1200** The earliest Olmec ceremonial center is built, at Tres Zapotes	**600** The earliest Maya temple-pyramids are built, such as at Nakbe
	2300 Pottery is first used in Mesoamerica	**1000–800** The Maya settle the Yucatán peninsula	**500–400** State formation begins in the Oaxaca valley
ARCHAIC PERIOD	EARLY PRECLASSIC	MIDDLE PRECLASSIC	LATE PRECLASSIC

Andes

c.3500 The earliest pottery-using cultures develop in Colombia	**2600** Monumental ceremonial centers of the Aspero tradition develop on the Pacific coast	**1800–1500** Building of U-shaped ceremonial centers	**1000–800** Maize is introduced into the region
c.3500 Permanent fishing villages on the coast of Peru		**1800–1500** Intensive agriculture and irrigation begin on the Pacific coast	**c.850** Chavín de Huántar is founded
	3000–2500 Domestication of alpacas and llamas, root crops and quinua in the highlands	**c.1750** Pottery comes into use in Peru	**c.600** Origins of the Lake Titicaca architectural styles
		c.1440 The earliest known Andean metal work, at Waywaka	**c.400** Spread of Chavín art styles
PRECERAMIC PERIOD	INITIAL PERIOD	EARLY HORIZON	

produce sufficient food to support a complex society and by 600 towns, such as Nakbe and Komchen, with monumental temple pyramids, were developing. Complex societies also developed among the Zapotec people of the Oaxaca valley by the 1st millennium BC. Here food production was increased by simple irrigation techniques and terracing. By 400 BC there were at least seven small states in the valley, the most important of which was centered on Monte Albán, and a system of hieroglyphic writing had been developed. In the Valley of Mexico highly productive agriculture using *chinampas* – raised fields built on reclaimed swamps – led to the development of trading networks, a market economy, craft specialization and large villages by around 200 BC.

The earliest complex societies in South America developed on the desert coast of Peru in settled fishing communities during the Preceramic period (3750–1800 BC). The marine resources of this area are unusually rich and these communities were able to free labor for the construction of temples and ceremonial centers under the direction of village leaders. One of the earliest such centers was built at Aspero around 2600: it consisted of six mounds nine meters high, topped with masonry ceremonial structures. Cotton, squash and gourds (used as floats for fishing nets) were cultivated but farming did not make a significant contribution to the diet. In the highlands, herding alpacas or llamas and cultivation of root crops such as potatoes, ullucu and oca or quinua, a cereal, gradually replaced hunting and gathering during the Preceramic; permanent villages with small ceremonial buildings also developed.

During the Initial Period (1800–800 BC) the area of cultivable land in the coastal lowlands was greatly extended through irrigation works, diverting water from the rivers which flowed from the Andes through the desert to the coast. Pottery was adopted. Huge U-shaped ceremonial centers, requiring the control of considerable resources of labor, food supplies and raw materials, were constructed: one at Garagay is estimated to have required 3.2 million work-days to complete. These sites were probably focal points for local chiefdoms but burial practices show few distinctions of wealth or rank. Interaction between the fishing communities on the coast and the farming communities in the desert river valleys and the mountains was considerable, with salt, seaweed and dried fish from the coast being exchanged for carbohydrate foods such as root crops and grain from the highlands and river valleys.

The Early Horizon (about 800–200 BC) saw the development of sophisticated architecture and complex sculptural styles at the highland ceremonial center of Chavín de Huántar. The Chavín style was the culmination of styles which had originated as early as 1200 in other Andean and coastal sites and by 400 its influence had spread over a wide area of coastal and highland Peru. Chavín had a population of two to three thousand at its peak in the 4th century but thereafter it declined, without developing into a full urban civilization. Complex societies, united by common beliefs, also developed in the Lake Titicaca basin during the Early Horizon. Particularly important is the ceremonial center at Chiripa, built 600–400 BC, in which can be seen the origins of the architectural styles of the 5th-century AD Tiahuanaco state. Maize became an important crop in the Andes during this period.

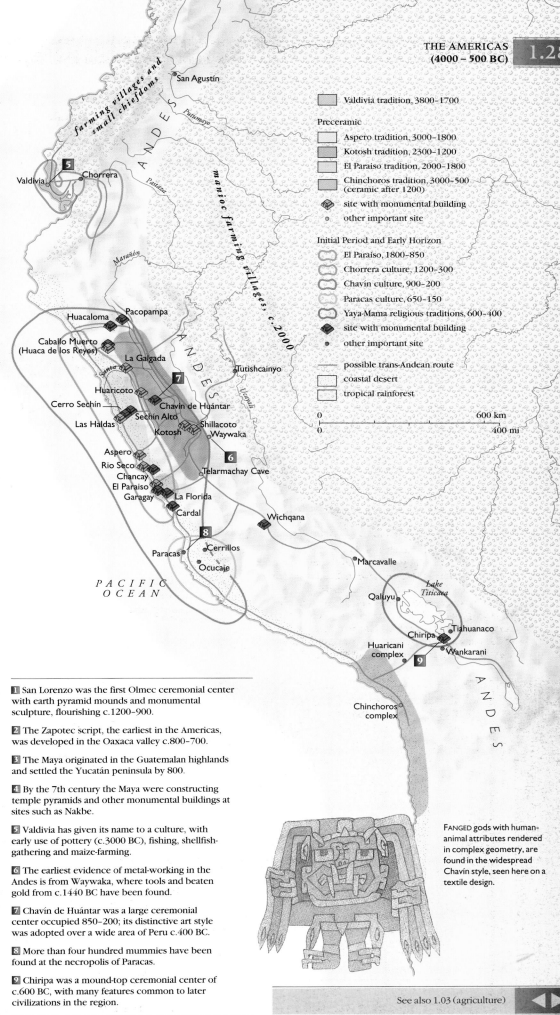

Valdivia tradition, 3800–1700

Preceramic

Aspero tradition, 3000–1800

Kotosh tradition, 2300–1200

El Paraiso tradition, 2000–1800

Chinchoros tradition, 3000–500 (ceramic after 1200)

site with monumental building

other important site

Initial Period and Early Horizon

El Paraiso, 1800–850

Chorrera culture, 1200–300

Chavin culture, 900–200

Paracas culture, 650–150

Yaya-Mama religious traditions, 600–400

site with monumental building

other important site

possible trans-Andean route

coastal desert

tropical rainforest

0 ———— 600 km

0 ———— 400 mi

1 San Lorenzo was the first Olmec ceremonial center with earth pyramid mounds and monumental sculpture, flourishing c.1200–900.

2 The Zapotec script, the earliest in the Americas, was developed in the Oaxaca valley c.800–700.

3 The Maya originated in the Guatemalan highlands and settled the Yucatán peninsula by 800.

4 By the 7th century the Maya were constructing temple pyramids and other monumental buildings at sites such as Nakbe.

5 Valdivia has given its name to a culture, with early use of pottery (c.3000 BC), fishing, shellfish-gathering and maize-farming.

6 The earliest evidence of metal-working in the Andes is from Waywaka, where tools and beaten gold from c.1440 BC have been found.

7 Chavín de Huántar was a large ceremonial center occupied 850–200; its distinctive art style was adopted over a wide area of Peru c.400 BC.

8 More than four hundred mummies have been found at the necropolis of Paracas.

9 Chiripa was a mound-top ceremonial center of c.600 BC, with many features common to later civilizations in the region.

FANGED gods with human-animal attributes rendered in complex geometry, are found in the widespread Chavín style, seen here on a textile design.

See also 1.03 (agriculture)

Cross-referencing
References to other dictionary entries are identified in small capitals (e.g. ACROPOLIS*); references to map spreads are denoted by the use of an arrow (e.g.* ▷ 1.21*).*

Dating
For the purposes of this dictionary, the end of the Paleolithic period of early human prehistory, about 10,000 BC/12,000 years ago (i.e. the end of the Pleistocene Ice Age), is taken as the boundary between geological and historical time. Earlier dates are therefore given in years ago (ya), while dates after the end of the Paleolithic are given using the conventional BC/AD system.

Chinese spellings
Since 1979 the standard international system for the transliteration of Chinese names into Roman characters has been Pinyin, and this is the system used throughout this dictionary.

ABU SIMBEL
The site of two massive rock temples built by the Egyptian PHARAOH RAMESSES II (r.c.1290–1224 BC) on the Nile, 250 kilometers (155 miles) south of Aswan. The largest temple is fronted by four colossal statues of Ramesses. The smaller temple is dedicated to Ramesses' queen, Nefertari. In the 1960s, the temples were lifted and reconstructed above the waters of Lake Nasser. ▷ 1.18

ACHAEA, ACHAEANS
A region in the northwestern Peloponnese. The Achaeans were one of the peoples of Greece mentioned by HOMER as fighting at TROY. They were divided among a number of settlements, which shared common citizenship and COINAGE. Achaea formed a confederacy with other Peloponnesian cities in the Hellenistic period, but was overwhelmed by ROME in 146 BC. ▷ 1.23, 1.24

ACHEMENES
Founding ancestor of the ACHEMENID royal dynasty of Persia. He probably ruled the kingdom of Parsumash in western Iran in the early 7th century BC as a vassal of the MEDIAN EMPIRE. Achemenes may have led an army against King SENNACHERIB of ASSYRIA in 681 BC. ▷ 1.15

ACHEMENID EMPIRE
Persian empire ruled by the Achemenid dynasty (550–331 BC), named after its founding ancestor, ACHEMENES. The empire was established by CYRUS II (559–530 BC), who took over the MEDIAN throne (550 BC) and conquered LYDIA, BABYLONIA, Bactria and GANDHARA. By the reign of DARIUS I (522–530 BC), the empire extended from Greece to the Indus, and from the Persian Gulf to the Aral Sea, with an administrative capital at SUSA and royal center at PERSEPOLIS. This period is often regarded as a golden age of Persian artistic and architectural achievement, and was important for the cultural contacts made possible between the Mediterranean civilizations and those of the Middle East and south Asia.

The empire was administered by 20 provincial governors (satraps), with a regular system of tribute and a large army of regular soldiers and levies controlled by the king. Imperial expansion came to an end after defeats by the Greeks in 490 and 480 BC. The empire gradually declined until it was conquered by Alexander the Great, who deposed the last of the Achemenids, Darius III, in 330 BC. ▷ 1.15, 1.26

ACHEULIAN
Cultural tradition of the LOWER PALEOLITHIC period that originated in Africa and spread to Europe with HOMO ERECTUS populations, about 1.5–0.2 million ya. The Acheulian is distinguished by the use of hand-axes, multi-purpose animal butchery and processing tools with a continuous, sharp working edge and a tapered or pointed end, that were designed for piercing, chopping, cutting and scraping. ▷ 1.01

ACROPOLIS
Literally the "high part" of any Greek city, often used as a center for defense. The most famous acropolis is in Athens; it became the ceremonial and religious center of the city and home of the Parthenon.

ADAD-NIRARI II
King of ASSYRIA (r.911–891 BC), who initiated renewed Assyrian expansion and the establishment of the Neo-Assyrian empire. He undertook campaigns against ARAMAEANS and Babylonians, securing Assyrian dominance in central MESOPOTAMIA. ▷ 1.13

ADENA
Complex HUNTER-GATHERER and farming culture of the middle Ohio river valley, in the eastern woodlands of North America (c.1000 BC–AD 100). Adena communities lived in permanent villages and had a rich material culture including pottery, smoking pipes, and COPPER, mica and seashell ornaments. Their mixed hunting, fishing, food-gathering and farming economy supported a large population, and their impressive burial and ceremonial monuments (such as Great Serpent Mound) suggest the development of social ranking and chiefly authority. This cultural tradition was elaborated by the succeeding Hopewell culture. ▷ 1.06

AEOLIA, AEOLIAN GREEKS
According to legend, the Aeolian Greeks fled from the Greek mainland after the collapse of the MYCENAEAN world in the 11th century BC. They came to settle on the west coast of Asia Minor, including the island of Lesbos, where they retained a distinctive dialect and developed their own style of architecture. Like other Greeks, they developed city-states (POLIS) from the 8th century BC. ▷ 1.23, 1.24

AFANASEVO CULTURE
NEOLITHIC culture of southern Siberia from about 2300 to 1500 BC, in the steppe/taiga region to the north of the Altai mountains, along the upper reaches of the Yenisey and Ob rivers. It had a mixed hunting, farming and herding economy (domestic SHEEP, CATTLE and HORSES), a ROUND BARROW funerary tradition, and decorated pottery and COPPER metallurgy. Similar cultures occupied the steppes further to the west, from the Altai to southern Russia. ▷ 1.04

AGADE
See AKKAD

AGAMEMNON
Legendary king of MYCENAE and leader of the Greek forces to TROY. His quarrel with the hero Achilles is the main theme of HOMER's epic, the ILIAD. On his return to Mycenae he was murdered by his wife, Clytemnestra, and her lover, Aegisthus. ▷ 1.22

AHAB
King of ISRAEL (r.c.874–853 BC) and son of Omri. Often at war with JUDAH and ARAM-DAMASCUS, in 854 BC he led the alliance of Levantine states that were opposed to Assyrian expansion. ▷ 1.14

AHMOSE
Egyptian PHARAOH (r.1550–1525 BC) who successfully drove the HYKSOS from Egypt and led campaigns into Syria and southwards into NUBIA. Ahmose firmly established the foundations of the NEW KINGDOM (1532–1070 BC). ▷ 1.18

AKHENATEN
Egyptian PHARAOH (r.1353–1335 BC), also known as Amenophis IV, who reacted against the power of the priests at the sacred city of THEBES by establishing a monotheistic religion based on Aten, the sun disk, whose rays were shown in paintings as shining on Akhenaten ("glory of the sun disk") and his family. He set up his own capital at Akhetaten (now known as EL-AMARNA) in Middle Egypt. After his death Akhenaten was treated as a heretic, and the old gods were restored. ▷ 1.18

AKKAD
A region of south MESOPOTAMIA lying between the Euphrates and Tigris rivers to the northwest of SUMERIA. It was named after the unlocated city of Agade and was founded by SARGON OF AGADE in about 2300 BC, probably near BABYLON on the Euphrates. Akkad was the power base of Sargon's short-lived Akkadian dynasty, which established the first imperial STATE in world history (c.2330–2193 BC). At the height of its power, under Sargon's grandson, NARAM-SIN

(c.2254–2218 BC), the Akkadian empire dominated all of Mesopotamia, the northern LEVANT and possibly southeast Anatolia and western Iran, before collapsing as a result of internal weakness and AMORITE and GUTIAN invasions. The Akkadians established their Semitic dialect as the official language and adopted Sumerian CUNEIFORM as a writing system. Akkadian formed the basis for later Babylonian and Assyrian writing. ▷ 1.04, 1.07, 1.10, 1.11

ALEUTS
Culture inhabiting the Aleutian Islands in the north Pacific, which extend from southwest Alaska towards the east coast of Siberia. The Aleuts had colonized the islands from the Alaskan mainland by about 2000 BC, living primarily by hunting marine and land mammals, and fishing. They had complex fishing technologies, sea-going boats and notable art traditions, particularly ceremonial masks, and bone and ivory carvings. ▷ 1.04, 1.05, 1.06

ALIGNMENT (MEGALITHIC)
Ceremonial monuments of the European NEOLITHIC that were probably used for processions and consist of large stones erected in lines. They are found mainly in Brittany (notably at CARNAC) and in western Britain (c.4000–2000 BC). Timber versions may also have existed. ▷ 1.20

ALTAMIRA
Cave site in northern Spain famous for its UPPER PALEOLITHIC paintings of bison and other animal and anthropomorphic figures. The cave was used by hunting communities over a long period, though the paintings are probably associated with SOLUTREAN and MAGDALENIAN occupation levels, (c.22,000–17,000 ya). ▷ 1.19

AMALEKITES
A group of nomadic tribes in southern JUDAH and Sinai in the early 1st millennium BC. The Amalekites were enemies of the HEBREWS, often raiding ISRAEL, but by the 8th century BC they were no longer a major threat. ▷ 1.14

AMENEMHET I
Egyptian PHARAOH of the MIDDLE KINGDOM (r.1991–1962 BC), who founded the 12th Dynasty and enforced strong Egyptian control over NUBIA. He initiated the practice of installing his son as co-ruler, so as to ensure a smoother succession from one pharaoh to the next. ▷ 1.18

AMENOPHIS IV
See AKHENATEN

AMORITES
Semitic people of Arabia, originally nomadic, who are mentioned in Mesopotamian records from about 2400 to 2000 BC, when their invasions contributed to the collapse of the

Akkadian empire (c.2193 BC) and later the Third Dynasty of UR (c.2000 BC). In the early 2nd millennium BC, Amorite kings established ruling dynasties in many Babylonian and Assyrian cities, assimilating Sumero-Akkadian culture. Amorites also settled in parts of Palestine in this period, and were sometimes associated with the CANAANITES. ▷ 1.11, 1.13

AMPHICTONIES
Leagues of cities associated with a particular Greek shrine (e.g. DELPHI). *Amphictonies* would oversee the arrangements for visitors and punish those who offended the dignity of the shrine. ▷ 1.24

ANDEAN CIVILIZATIONS
The cultures of the Andean region and adjacent coastal areas of western South America that developed CHIEFDOMS and later STATE systems, ceremonial centers, cities, and complex iconography and material culture. The history of Andean civilizations is divided into the following periods: PRECERAMIC (c.3750–2000 BC), INITIAL (2000–900 BC), EARLY HORIZON (900–200 BC), Early Intermediate (200 BC–AD 500), Middle Horizon (AD 500–1000), Late Intermediate (AD 1000–1475) and Late Horizon (AD 1475–1530). ▷ 1.04, 1.05, 1.06, 1.28

ANYANG
The last and most enduring of the SHANG capital cities ("Yin", c.1400–1100 BC), situated on a tributary of the Yellow river in Honan province, China. The urban settlement surrounded a palace and temple complex built on a massive, rammed earth platform. All the buildings were constructed of timber and clay, with thatch roofs, some elaborately painted. Stone and jade carvings, ORACLE BONES and evidence of bronze working and pottery manufacture have been found at the site. The royal cemetery nearby had at least 14 richly furnished tombs with grave goods that included magnificently decorated bronze vessels and other objects, and human and animal sacrifices. ▷ 1.27

ARAM, ARAMAEANS
Nomadic people who originally lived in Aram, a desert region in modern Syria, Jordan and western Iraq. The Aramaeans are first mentioned in Assyrian inscriptions in about 1100 BC, when they raided and settled in MESOPOTAMIA and the LEVANT. By 1000 BC Aramaean kingdoms were established from the Levant to BABYLONIA (where they were known as CHALDEANS). Western Aramaean kingdoms were eventually destroyed by the Assyrian king TIGLATH-PILESER III in 740–720 BC, while Aramaean dynasties in the east merged with the Babylonians. ▷ 1.12, 1.13, 1.14

ARAM-DAMASCUS
ARAMAEAN kingdom founded in about 1100 BC, with a capital at Damascus. It was a

major enemy of ISRAEL from the 10th to 8th centuries BC, until it was annexed by the Assyrians in 732 BC. ▷ 1.14

ARAMAIC LANGUAGE
Semitic language widely adopted in the Middle East following the ARAMAEAN migrations and the development of written Aramaic, using a phonetic script derived from the CANAANITE alphabet (by c.1100 BC). This became the main script used in the Middle East when it was adopted by the Assyrians from about 800 BC, replacing CUNEIFORM. ▷ 1.07, 1.12, 1.13, 1.15

ARCADIA
The central region of the Peloponnese. Although it is relatively unfertile, the Roman poet Virgil portrayed it as a haven of rural bliss, an image that has remained in the European imagination. ▷ 1.24

ARCHAIC PERIOD
A period of MESOAMERICAN CIVILIZATION from about 7000 to 2000 BC, in which HUNTER-GATHERER societies intensified food collection practices and modified plant habitats, domesticating several plant species, notably MAIZE (by c.2700 BC). Population growth, the development of permanent village settlements, intensive farming systems, the use of CERAMICS and long-distance OBSIDIAN exchange are all evident in Mexico by the late 3rd millennium BC.

ARCHAIC PERIOD (GREECE)
The period in Greek history before the Classical period, usually dated from about 750 to 480 BC. It saw the major expansion of the Greeks throughout the Mediterranean, the consolidation of the city-state (POLIS) and the appearance of important PAN-HELLENIC sites, such as OLYMPIA (the four-yearly OLYMPIC GAMES) and DELPHI (the ORACLE). The period also witnessed the birth of the Greek orders of architecture, the first marble sculptures and early lyric poetry. ▷ 1.24

ARDIPITHECUS RAMIDUS
The divergence of the evolutionary lineages of hominids and apes occurred about 6 million ya. Fossil remains of the earliest known hominid, *Ardipithecus ramidus* (found in Ethiopia), dating from about 4.4 million ya, show that it was a small animal about the size of a chimpanzee. It is not yet known whether it had developed the upright, bipedal gait characteristic of modern humans. This species probably evolved into the early australopithecines. ▷ 1.01

ARGOS
Greek city-state in the eastern Peloponnese and according to legend, the first to develop the HOPLITE phalanx as a means of defense. Argos was also a long-term rival of SPARTA, with whom it fought many wars between the 7th and 5th centuries BC. ▷ 1.24

ARVAD
City on the Levantine coast (modern Tripoli in Lebanon), probably founded by about 1000 BC. It was later the capital of a PHOENICIAN city-state, at times owing allegiance to a succession of Assyrian, BABYLONIAN and ACHEMENID kings. ▷ 1.12, 1.13, 1.14

ARYANS
Pastoralist people from central Asia with an INDO-EUROPEAN LANGUAGE, who invaded Iran and India in about 1500 BC. They may have been related to the KASSITES, who invaded the Middle East in about 1600 BC. The Aryans are described in Indian epic poems, the Rigvedas, which were first composed orally in archaic Sanskrit (c.1500–800 BC) and only later recorded in writing. They absorbed aspects of local culture and, by 900 BC, ruled most of northern India, establishing small kingdoms, which coalesced into larger states in the following centuries. The relevance of the Aryans to the question of Indo-European language origins is much disputed, and the identification of an Aryan "race" has no foundation in biological anthropology. ▷ 1.05, 1.06, 1.26

ARZAWA
Kingdom in western Anatolia that was conquered on several occasions by the HITTITES, and a vassal of the Hittite empire for a period in the 17th century BC. Arzawa was at its most powerful from the 15th to 14th centuries BC, but was reconquered by the Hittites in about 1300 BC and later became embroiled in power struggles within the Hittite empire. The collapse of the Hittites in about 1200 BC left Arzawa fragmented and it lost its separate political identity. ▷ 1.12

ASHUR
City in north MESOPOTAMIA situated on the river Tigris, at a strategic point on trade routes from SUMERIA to Anatolia and the LEVANT. It was founded in the 3rd millennium BC and had become a major trade center by about 1800 BC, when it was siezed by the Amorite king, SHAMSHI-ADAD. An Akkadian dynasty ruled Ashur from about 1600 BC, overthrowing Mittanian domination in about 1330 BC, and renaming their kingdom ASSYRIA (after Ashur). It remained the Assyrian capital until about 878 BC, and continued to be the religious capital when the political center moved elsewhere. The city was destroyed by the BABYLONIANS in 614 BC. ▷ 1.11, 1.12, 1.13

ASHURBANIPAL
The last great king of ASSYRIA (r.668–627 BC). He completed the conquest of Egypt, installing Necho I as vassal ruler. Assyrian garrisons were later expelled, but Egypt was no longer a threat to Assyrian dominance. He suppressed rebellions in the LEVANT, expelled the CIMMERIANS, reconquered BABYLONIA and conquered ELAM by 639 BC. Ashurbanipal greatly overstretched the resources of the empire, while his tyrannical rule created wide discontent. After his death the empire rapidly declined, due to MEDIAN invasions and the resurgence of BABYLON. ▷ 1.13, 1.15

ASHURNASIRPAL II
King of ASSYRIA (r.883–859 BC). Ashurnasirpal III conquered north MESOPOTAMIA and the Levantine coast, using cavalry on a large scale, and enforced Assyrian dominance by means of terror tactics and the resettlement of conquered populations. He moved the royal capital to KALHU. ▷ 1.13

ASPERO TRADITION
Cultural tradition of the Andean PRECERAMIC PERIOD that produced the first ceremonial monument complexes in South America (c.3000–1800 BC), with sedentary settlement and an increasing reliance on agriculture. It is named after the site of Aspero, one of the earliest ceremonial sites in lowland Peru, consisting of six large earthen mounds with masonry temples (c.2600 BC). ▷ 1.04, 1.28

ASSYRIA
Region of north MESOPOTAMIA centered on the Upper Tigris in modern Iraq. The name derives from ASHUR, an early city-state that was siezed by SHAMSHI-ADAD (c.1800 BC), who established a short-lived empire (the Old Assyrian period). The Akkadian dynasty, which ruled Assyria from about 1600 BC, were vassals of MITTANI or BABYLON until Ashuruballit I overthrew Mittanian domination in about 1330 BC. This initiated the Middle Assyrian empire (c.1330–1076 BC), which at its greatest extent under Tukulti-Ninurta I (r.1243–1207 BC) controlled Mesopotamia and dominated most of the LEVANT, Anatolia and ELAM. The empire collapsed in the face of ARAMAEAN invasions.

The Neo-Assyrian empire (c.911–612 BC), the period of Assyria's greatest expansion and cultural achievement, was initiated by ADAD-NIRARI II (r.911–891 BC) and maintained by a series of powerful and warlike kings. The empire reached its greatest extent under ASHURBANIPAL (668–627 BC), but disintegrated after his death and was destroyed by the MEDES and Babylonians in 612 BC. Assyrian imperialism is notable for its military innovations (the mass production of iron weaponry, huge professional armies and mass cavalry tactics), and its extreme ruthlessness (the use of terror and resettlement of conquered populations). The Assyrians are also noted for their architectural and sculptural achievements, especially monumental temples, fortifications, narrative friezes depicting campaigns and hunts, and huge gateway statues of winged bulls. ▷ 1.11, 1,12, 1.13

ATTICA
The territory of Athens, extending for 2,500 square kilometers (965 square miles) around the city. Originally controlled by aristocratic clans, by the 5th century BC its inhabitants were well integrated into the city's democratic system through their membership of demes, local "village" communities. ▷ 1.24

AURIGNACIAN CULTURE
The earliest UPPER PALEOLITHIC stone tool industry in Europe (c.40,000–29,000 ya), associated with the colonization of the region by anatomically modern humans. It was characterized by a diverse new range of specialized stone and bone tools, such as burins, scrapers and projectile points, and by the appearance of complex works of art, including engraved pebbles, bone and ivory carvings, clay figurines and cave paintings (by 30,000 ya). ▷ 1.19

AUSTRALOPITHECUS AFARENSIS
The earliest australopithecine hominid, living about 4 million to 3 million ya. Fossil remains have been found at HADAR in Ethiopia and at LAETOLI in Tanzania. Lightly built and fully bipedal (though not a tool user), this species evolved into two later types of hominid – gracile AUSTRALOPITHECUS AFRICANUS and the larger AUSTRALOPITHECUS ROBUSTUS – and was possibly ancestral to the genus Homo. ▷ 1.01

AUSTRALOPITHECUS AFRICANUS
Hominid that lived in Africa about 3 million to 2 million ya and was contemporary with the related, but more heavily built, AUSTALOPITHECUS ROBUSTUS. Fossils from Taung and Makapansgat in South Africa and KOOBI FORA in Tanzania suggest that this was a small, gracile hominid with teeth similar to those of humans. It is possibly the ancestor of HOMO HABILIS, though the human genus may have evolved from AUSTRALOPITHECUS AFARENSIS at an earlier date. ▷ 1.01

AUSTRALOPITHECUS ROBUSTUS
A heavily-built hominid that lived in Africa about 3 to 1 million ya, alongside the gracile AUSTRALOPITHECUS AFRICANUS and the earliest humans. It was characterized by massive jaws and teeth that were adapted to the consumption of tough vegetable foods rather than meat. Fossil remains have been found in eastern and southern Africa (notably at KOOBI FORA, OMO, OLDUVAI, SWARTKRANS and Sterkfontein). This species probably became extinct when HOMO ERECTUS, a sophisticated tool user, began to colonize new habitats, becoming more numerous and marginalizing australopithecine populations. ▷ 1.01

AVEBURY HENGE
Late NEOLITHIC enclosure in southern Britain, built in about 2800–2500 BC. It consists of a massive circular embankment, about 425 meters (1,394 feet) in diameter with an interior quarry ditch, enclosing the three largest STONE CIRCLES in Europe. The site was approached by an avenue of standing stones,

1.6 kilometers (1 mile) long, which lead from another stone circle (the Sanctuary). SILBURY HILL is located to the south. ▷ 1.20

BA
Early state with a non-Chinese population near the confluence of the Yangtze and Jialing rivers in Sichuan province, China. Ba became a feudal state, with Chinese overlords, that owed allegiance to the Western ZHOU in the 11th century BC. It was incorporated into the QIN empire from the late 4th century BC. ▷ 1.27

BABYLON
City on the Euphrates and the most important religious and cultural center of ancient MESOPOTAMIA. Probably founded in the mid-3rd millennium BC, it was the capital of an AMORITE dynasty from about 1895 BC, the best-known ruler being HAMMURABI, until it was destroyed by the HITTITES in 1595 BC. It was the capital of a KASSITE dynasty from 1570 until 1158 BC, when it was sacked by the Elamites.

Babylon was subsequently ruled by a series of short-lived ARAMAEAN and CHALDEAN dynasties under Assyrian dominance, until the restoration of Babylonian independence in 626 BC. It was reconstructed by NEBUCHADNEZZAR (c.600 BC) to become the largest city in the world, covering 1,000 hectares (2,500 acres) with a population of over 100,000, and was defended by a massive double wall on both sides of the Euphrates. The most famous buildings in Babylon date from this period, including the ZIGGURAT of Marduk (the Tower of Babel) and the Ishtar Gate. The Greek historian Herodotus also mentions the Hanging Gardens, possibly part of one of the two palace complexes. Babylon was captured by the Persians in 539 BC and a revolt in 482 BC led to the widespread destruction of its ancient temples and fortifications. ▷ 1.11, 1.12, 1.13, 1.14, 1.15, 1.23

BABYLONIA
A region of south MESOPOTAMIA named after the city of BABYLON. It became a province of the Third Dynasty of UR in the late 3rd millennium BC and was established as an independent kingdom during the Old Babylonian period (c.1895–1595 BC), under the AMORITE dynasty founded by king Sumuabum (c.1895). Expansion into northern Mesopotamia by King HAMMURABI in about 1790–1755 BC briefly established Babylonia as the leading imperial power in the Middle East. After Hammurabi's death, Babylonia declined and after Babylon was sacked by the HITTITES in 1595 BC, it was so weakened that it was unable to resist a KASSITE invasion (c.1570 BC). Under the Kassites, Babylonia became a powerful state once again, and was frequently at war with its ASSYRIAN, Elamite and ARAMAEAN neighbors. This dynasty was swept away when the Elamites sacked Babylon in 1157 BC, opening the way to a

series of Aramaean and CHALDEAN dynasties. Babylonia became a mere vassal of the Assyrian empire from the mid-9th century BC, until its revival in the 7th century BC.

During the Neo-Babylonian empire (c.626–539 BC), Babylonian independence was reasserted by King NABOPOLASSAR, who attacked Assyria and destroyed NINEVEH in 612 BC, ending Assyrian power and taking over their domains. His son, NEBUCHADNEZZAR, defeated the Egyptians in 605 BC, ensuring supremacy in the Middle East. The empire lasted until 539 BC, when Babylonia was taken over by CYRUS the Great, becoming the wealthiest satrapy of the ACHEMENID EMPIRE. The rich cultural heritage of SUMER and AKKAD was adopted by later Babylonian rulers, who maintained their religious, artistic, architectural and literary traditions until conquest by the Persians in the 6th century BC. ▷ 1.12, 1.13, 1.15

BANAS CULTURE
Culture of the Banas valley, Rajasthan, influenced by the late INDUS CIVILIZATION, with stone and clay houses, Black-and-Red ware pottery and bronze tools. The principal settlement at Ahar is dated from about 2200 to 1500 BC. The Banas culture survived the collapse of the Indus civilization and Black-and-Red ware pottery became widespread across southern India after 1800 BC. ▷ 1.26

BANDKERAMIK CULTURE
The earliest farming culture of the central European NEOLITHIC, from 5400 to 4500 BC, characterized by distinctive round-based decorated pottery, large timber LONGHOUSES, and slash-and-burn horticulture. It spread through a gradual colonization process from the Balkans across the loess lands of central Europe, as far as Poland, the Netherlands and France, exploiting domestic plant and animal species that were derived from the Near East. ▷ 1.20

BANTU
An African language group that originated in the equatorial region of Cameroon. Bantu-speaking herders and farmers, with their iron-working technology, spread eastwards and southwards from about 500 BC, replacing or influencing indigenous populations. Bantu speakers were dominant throughout central and southern Africa by AD 400. ▷ 1.06

BARLEY
Cereal plant native to the temperate regions of the Old World, from China to southern Europe and Egypt. Two varieties of barley were domesticated in the Middle East by 8000 BC. It was one of the staple crops of NEOLITHIC farming communities. ▷ 1.03, 1.08, 1.09, 1.16

BARROW, LONG
A type of early NEOLITHIC burial monument found in Europe in about 5000–2500 BC,

consisting of an elongated rectangular, trapezoidal or oval mound built of earth or rock. The mounds cover one or more burials, often collective deposits of disarticulated skeletons, sometimes housed in timber or MEGALITHIC mortuary houses. ▷ 1.20

BARROW, ROUND
Multi-period burial monument found in many parts of the Old World, especially associated with NEOLITHIC and BRONZE AGE cultures of temperate Europe from about 3000 to 1000 BC, and steppe cultures (such as the SCYTHIANS) from about 3000 to 200 BC. Built of turf, earth and/or rock, sometimes with timber structures and mortuary houses, they usually cover single articulated burials, some with lavish grave goods. ▷ 1.21

BASILEUS
Literally Greek for "king", the word is normally used to describe Greek nobles of the 10th to 8th centuries BC, a class portrayed by HOMER. A CATTLE-owning aristocracy, they idealized feasting and the heroism of war. In the medieval Byzantine empire the word was used to describe the emperor.

BELL BEAKER CULTURES
Late NEOLITHIC and early BRONZE AGE cultures of Europe associated with distinctive decorated drinking vessels (beakers) and other objects, including COPPER and bronze items, often found as grave goods with single burials under ROUND BARROWS in about 2800–1800 BC. This tradition emerged in the Rhineland and the Netherlands and spread to Britain, central Europe, Atlantic France and Spain, probably adopted by local populations as a cult package. ▷ 1.04, 1.20, 1.21

BERINGIA
Continental shelf between Siberia and Alaska that was exposed as dry land several times during the last glaciation (c.45,000–40,000 ya; 33,000–28,000 ya; 22,000–12,000 ya), forming the Bering land-bridge across which humans migrated from Asia to America. The date of this is disputed, but PALEOINDIAN populations were present in North America by about 15,000–12,000 ya. ▷ 1.02

BIBLE LANDS
A region of the Middle East comprising most of modern Israel, Jordan, Lebanon and Syria. It is referred to in detail in the Old Testament, during the period of HEBREW colonization from the 12th century BC until the destruction of the last of the Hebrew kingdoms in about 587 BC. ▷ 1.14

BIMBISARA
King of Magadha (c.520–491 BC), one of the major Indian states of the Gangetic civilization. He expanded his territory by annexing neighboring kingdoms, forming the core area of the later Mauryan Empire. He was a friend and patron of the BUDDHA. ▷ 1.26

BOEOTIA
Region of central Greece, neighboring ATTICA, that was a fertile area of many settlements, the most prominent of which was Thebes. Its central position made it the focus of many wars between surrounding city-states. ▷ 1.24

BOOK OF THE DEAD
A book of spells that was designed to help Egyptians make the transition into the next world safely. Usually written on papyrus, it was placed beside the mummified body of the deceased.

BOW AND ARROW
A hunting and fighting weapon used for precision killing at a distance from the target. The earliest preserved examples are MESOLITHIC in date, but stone and bone arrow points found in Europe and Africa suggest that they were first used by modern humans about 20,000 ya. The bow was introduced into the Americas from Asia in about 2000 BC. ▷ 1.18

BOWL CULTURES
First farming cultures of northwest Europe (c.4500–3300 BC), with regional traditions of round-based CERAMICS, tomb building (PASSAGE GRAVES and LONG BARROWS), and ceremonial enclosures. These cultures developed from MESOLITHIC communities who adopted ceramics and agriculture, at first perhaps more for ritual than subsistence purposes. ▷ 1.20

BOXGROVE
LOWER PALEOLITHIC fossil beach in southern Britain with the earliest human remains yet found in Europe (HOMO ERECTUS), about 500,000 years old. ACHEULIAN hand-axes and animal remains found *in situ* on the ancient beach surface provide important information about tool manufacture and butchery practices, with implications for early human cognition. ▷ 1.01

BRONZE AGE
A subdivision of the THREE AGE SYSTEM. It is now recognized that the idea of a Bronze Age is of limited value, being applicable only to Eurasia and north Africa, beginning at different times in different regions (e.g. c.4000 BC in MESOPOTAMIA and c.2000 BC in China), and being too general to describe the great variety of bronze-using cultures. ▷ 1.04, 1.05, 1.06, 1.09, 1.10, 1.11, 1.12, 1.16, 1.20, 1.21, 1.26, 1.27

BUDDHA (SIDDHARTHA GAUTAMA)
Founder of the Buddhist religion who was born at LUMBINI in north India in about 563 BC, son of the king of the Sakyas. He renounced his royal status and embarked on a period of learning, formulating a doctrine of personal spiritual enlightenment that attracted a growing number of disciples. He

was highly regarded by King BIMBISARA of Magadha. His teachings inspired a religious movement that spread rapidly, though it did not become a major organized religion until the 3rd century BC. The Buddha died at Kusinagara in about 483 BC. ▷ 1.06, 1.26

BYBLOS
NEOLITHIC settlement on the Levantine coast that became a major trading center, especially for the export of cedar wood to Egypt, by 2500 BC. It was the main city of PHOENICIA in the 11th century BC, but later declined as its rivals SIDON and TYRE grew more powerful. ▷ 1.09, 1.10, 1.11, 1.12, 1.13, 1.14

CALENDAR
Once it was realized that there was a regular year of 365 days, calendars came into operation to mark the passing of the year. They could be based on the cycles of the moon (hence the 12 months of the Egyptian, Greek and Roman calendars), or the sun. Any calendar based on full (e.g. 365) days is bound to become inaccurate with time (the true length of a year is approximately 365 ¼ days), so additional days or even months have to be entered to maintain accuracy. The Roman emperor Julius Caesar adapted an Egyptian solar calendar to solve inaccuracies in the Roman calendar, and it is this Julian calender, with some modifications (Pope Gregory, 1582), that is used today. The practice of dividing a day or night into 12 hours is Egyptian, and that of dividing hours into 60 minutes, Babylonian.

CAMBYSES II
ACHEMENID king of Persia (r.529–522 BC) and the son of CYRUS II. He annexed Egypt after the Battle of Pelusium and the capture of MEMPHIS in 525 BC, but failed to conquer the Nubian state of MEROË. He was possibly murdered in Syria in 522 BC by his brother, SMERDIS, who was deposed by DARIUS. ▷ 1.15

CANAANITES
Semitic people who had settled in the LEVANT, from Sinai to the Orontes river, by about 2000 BC, and established small city-states with a shared religion and alphabet. The Canaanites were culturally heterogenous with elements of pre-Semitic, Semitic and Mesopotamian culture, and Egyptian, Anatolian and Aegean influences. In southern Palestine they were conquered by the Israelites and PHILISTINES (c.1200 BC), the last enclaves being annexed by king DAVID in the early 10th century BC. Further north, the PHOENICIANS were partly descended from the Canaanites and maintained some Canaanite cultural traditions. ▷ 1.05, 1.07, 1.11, 1.12, 1.14, 1.23

CANAANITE ALPHABET
The Canaanite language appears to have been an early form of HEBREW. The CANAANITES developed the first known

phonetic alphabet, which was widely adapted in the LEVANT and Middle East from the late 2nd millennium BC. The PHOENICIAN version of this alphabet was the basis for the Old HEBREW, GREEK and LATIN (via Etruscan) alphabets. ▷ 1.07, 1.12, 1.14, 1.23

CARCHEMISH
City situated on the upper Euphrates, that was strategically placed to command the main trade routes from MESOPOTAMIA to the LEVANT and Anatolia. It was important in the 2nd millennium BC as a trading city and the administrative center of MITTANI (c.1500–1350 BC), a vassal state dominated by the HITTITES (c.1350–1200 BC), and the most powerful of the Neo-Hittite city-states (c.1200–880 BC). Carchemish later became a vassal of the Neo-Asyrian empire and was annexed by SARGON II in 716 BC. In 605 BC it was the site of a battle between the Egyptians and Babylonians, which ended Egyptian attempts to regain their power in the Near East. ▷ 1.12, 1.13, 1.14

CARNAC
NEOLITHIC ceremonial center to the north of the Gulf of Morbihan in Brittany, with a dense concentration of MEGALITHIC tombs and alignments (c.4500–2000 BC). The alignments consist of parallel lines of menhirs (standing stones) in several segments on a line about 4 kilometers (2.5 miles) in length, some with enclosures at the ends, that were probably used for processions and other rituals. ▷ 1.20

CATACOMB GRAVE CULTURES
Early BRONZE AGE pastoral nomad cultures of the south Russian steppes (c.2300–1800 BC), characterized by ROUND BARROWS covering burial chambers, some of which contain wheeled vehicles. This was one phase of the longer Kurgan tradition (*kurgan* means "mound"), preceded by the Pit Grave culture, (c.3500–2300 BC) and followed by the Timber Grave phase. SCYTHIAN round-barrow burials are a later version of this tradition. ▷ 1.21

CATTLE
Animals derived from the wild aurochs (*Bos primigenius*), that were domesticated in Anatolia and the Balkans by about 6500 BC, giving rise to *Bos taurus* breeds in Europe and the Middle East, and *Bos indicus* (or humped zebu) breeds in India and east Asia. Central to early farming economies for meat and leather, cattle were increasingly exploited for dairy products and traction from about 4500 BC. The water buffalo (*Bubalus bubalis*) is derived from a different ruminant species domesticated in Asia by about 5000 BC. ▷ 1.03, 1.05, 1.08, 1.16, 1.20

CAUSEWAYED CAMP
A type of NEOLITHIC enclosure found in Britain (e.g. WINDMILL HILL) and Denmark, built in about 3800–3000 BC, that consists of one or more ditch and bank circuits

interrupted by causeways. Most had settlement or ceremonial functions (including possible exposure of the dead). ▷ 1.20

CAVE AND ROCK ART

The earliest examples of art, consisting of paintings and engravings on the walls of caves and rock shelters, produced by the UPPER PALEOLITHIC hunters of Europe, Africa and Australia. In Africa and Australia these traditions continued into modern times. In the case of Upper Paleolithic Europe, the cave art is associated with modern humans, dating mostly from about 25,000 to 10,000 ya, and is dominated by representations of animals, some of them extraordinarily naturalistic, human figures, hand prints and abstract symbols. Especially impressive friezes survive at LASCAUX (France) and ALTAMIRA (Spain). These paintings are believed to have had considerable religious and social significance. ▷ 1.02, 1.16, 1.19

CERAMICS

Materials and objects made of fired clay, including pottery (containers and other vessels) and terracotta (fine building materials, clay tablets and statuary). The earliest known fired-clay objects are the "Venus" figurines and animal models of the UPPER PALEOLITHIC GRAVETTIAN CULTURE of Europe. The use of pottery is sometimes equated with early farming cultures, though the first NEOLITHIC societies of the LEVANT (9th millennium BC) were aceramic, while the HUNTER-GATHERER JOMON CULTURE of Japan made pottery from about 12,500 ya. ▷ 1.04, 1.06, 1.08, 1.10, 1.12, 1.17, 1.27

CHALDEANS

ARAMAEAN people of northern Arabia who settled in MESOPOTAMIA in the early 1st millennium BC, establishing ruling dynasties in several cities. The famous Chaldean 11th dynasty of BABYLON destroyed the Assyrians and re-established the Babylonian empire. ▷ 1.12, 1.13

CHAMBERED TOMB

A type of collective burial monument found in many parts of the world, that consists of a stone mortuary chamber covered by an earth or stone mound. The earliest examples are the early NEOLITHIC MEGALITHIC tombs of Europe, such as PASSAGE GRAVES and chambered LONG BARROWS, built by the earliest farming societies in France and Britain in about 4500–3400 BC, with later types found throughout western Europe. ▷ 1.20

CHATAL HUYUK

An exceptionally large early agricultural settlement, sometimes described as a town, that is situated on the edge of the Konya plateau in southern Anatolia and dates from about 6500 BC. The densely-clustered clay-built houses were entered through rooftop openings, some with shrine rooms which

contained clay-modeled bull's heads and frescoes. The settlement had a mixed farming economy that supported a population of about 6,000 people, importing materials such as OBSIDIAN for tools. There is evidence in late occupation levels of early COPPER WORKING. ▷ 1.03, 1.09

CHÂTELPERRONIAN CULTURE

Initial stage of the European UPPER PALEOLITHIC, defined by a distinctive set of stone tools, including backed knives. Dating from about 40,000 to 30,000 ya, it was once thought to be the earliest cultural evidence of modern humans in Europe, though it is now believed to be a product of late Neanderthal populations, copying the AURIGNACIAN blade-tool technologies of the modern human communities. ▷ 1.19

CHAVÍN DE HUÁNTAR

Ceremonial center in the Andes, occupied from about 850 to 200 BC, with several large temple platforms and sunken courts linked by pavements and stairs. The stone buildings, especially gates, are decorated with relief carvings of humans and animals. The site gives its name to the Chavín style of art and architecture (c.900–200 BC), and is probably related to a religious cult that had spread throughout the Andes and coastal Peru by 400 BC. ▷ 1.06, 1.28

CHAYONU

A rare transitional HUNTER-GATHERER and early agricultural settlement in north MESOPOTAMIA, occupied from about 8500 to 6500 BC. It is also notable for the very early evidence (c.7300 BC) of COPPER metallurgy (cold hammering of "native" copper in its free metallic state) to make tools and ornaments. ▷ 1.08

CHESOWANJA

LOWER PALEOLITHIC site in ancient lake sediments and tuffs at Lake Baringo, Kenya, dating from about 2.4 to 1.3 million ya, with remains of AUSTRALOPITHECUS ROBUSTUS, layers containing OLDOWAN chopper tools, and a later ACHEULIAN hand-ax industry. There is also possible evidence of the earliest controlled use of FIRE (c.1.6 million ya). ▷ 1.01

CHIEFDOM

A type of social system characterized by centralized chiefly and religious authority, tribute-giving, the exhange and redistribution of prestige goods, the building of ceremonial centers, alliance networks, and competition between polities. Chiefdoms are usually regarded as an evolutionary stage following tribal or simple ranked societies, and preceding the development of STATES and urbanism, and are recognized in many parts of the world at different times. ▷ 1.04, 1.05, 1.06

CHINCHOROS TRADITION

Long-lived HUNTER-GATHERER culture of the coastal region of South America, in modern

north Chile, spanning both the PRECERAMIC and INITIAL periods (3000–500 BC). As well as fishing and hunting equipment, the Chinchorros had knowledge of basketry and textiles, and made pottery from about 1200 BC. ▷ 1.04, 1.06, 1.15

CHINESE LANGUAGE AND SCRIPT

Chinese is a language group of the Sino-Tibetan language family and consists of a number of separate languages, though all use a common writing system. The earliest Chinese scripts were pictographic, of the SHANG period (from c.1600 BC), when they were used for recording divinations. Refinements to this writing system gave rise to a LOGOGRAPHIC SCRIPT from about 900 BC (standardized in the 3rd century BC), in which each sign represented a unit of meaning rather than sound. This script is the world's oldest continually used writing system. ▷ 1.07, 1.27

CHIRIPA CULTURE

Culture of the Andean EARLY HORIZON PERIOD named after the ceremonial center at Chiripa (600–400 BC), at the south end of Lake Titicaca, Bolivia. Little is known about its origins or development, but the communities of the Titicaca Basin probably shared a religious tradition (YAYA-MAMA), and the architectural styles seen at Chiripa are similar to those of the later Tiahuanaco state in the same area in about AD 500. ▷ 1.05, 1.28

CHOGA MAMI

Early agricultural settlement of the 7th to 6th millennia BC, to the east of the Tigris river on the edge of the Mesopotamian plains. It is the site of the earliest recorded canal IRRIGATION system, built by about 5500 BC. ▷ 1.09

CHORRERA CULTURE

Early farming culture in southern Ecuador with a sophisticated CERAMIC tradition spanning the INITIAL and EARLY HORIZON periods (1200–300 BC), which expanded from the long-settled VALDIVIA coastal region into the Andean highlands to grow MAIZE and manioc. ▷ 1.05, 1.06, 1.28

CHU

Major feudal state of the ZHOU kingdom in southern China in about 1100–250 BC, with a capital at Ying. It was constantly at war with its powerful northern enemy, JIN, during the later SPRINGS AND AUTUMNS PERIOD and briefly became the leading state (hegemon) in about 710–690 BC, under King Zhuang. It lost its position as the pre-eminent southern Zhou state as its rivals, WU and YUE, grew more powerful in the late 6th century BC. ▷ 1.27

CIMMERIANS

Nomadic people of the steppes to the north of the Caucasus who migrated southwards in the 8th century BC. They were repulsed by the Assyrians and driven into Anatolia, where they conquered PHRYGIA (705–696 BC) and LYDIA (652 BC). Their power was broken by the Lydians and Babylonians in the late 7th century BC. ▷ 1.13

CLOVIS CULTURE
Earliest distinct PALEOINDIAN culture of North America (c.9500–9000 BC), characterized by stone tools, including projectile points with concave bases (Clovis points) used for big-game hunting of mammoths and bison. The origins of the Clovis culture are unclear but must lie in the preceding little-known Lower Lithic Paleoindian traditions. ▷ 1.02

COINAGE
Stamped pieces of metal were first given to the Greek mercenaries of the king of LYDIA in about 600 BC and spread quickly into the Greek world. (Coinage was invented independently in China at about the same time.) At first they were used for state transactions and for the receipt of taxes. By the end of the 6th century BC, many Greek cities were minting their own smaller coins in silver, and these were used for everyday transactions. The use of coin faces for propaganda and for the glorification of a city, ruler or successful victory was soon widespread. Coinage quickly spread from Greece to Italy, and then the rest of Europe. ▷ 1.24

COLCHIS
An area enclosed by the Caucasus mountains, stretching from the east coast of the Black Sea. The coastline was colonized by the Greek city of MILETOS in the 6th century BC, and the area was later absorbed into the Roman province of Cappadocia. ▷ 1.15, 1.23

CONFUCIUS
Chinese philosopher and teacher born in 551 BC in the state of LU, who was a member of the minor aristocracy, or bureaucratic class. Confucius advocated moral rectitude, education for all, service to the state and responsible government. His writings established an influential ethical code for the exercise of power and citizenship. He died in 479 BC. ▷ 1.06, 1.27

COPPER WORKING
Copper was one of the first metals used for making tools and ornaments. It is easily worked and may exist in a pure form, though it usually requires extraction from ores by smelting. Copper working began independently in different parts of the world: in MESOPOTAMIA by about 7000 BC, China by about 3000 BC and the Americas by about 1000 BC. In the western Old World, a Copper Age is sometimes identified as a separate period. ▷ 1.08, 1.27, 1.28

CORD IMPRESSED WARE CULTURE
Late NEOLITHIC culture of central Europe that influenced the farming societies of northern

Europe from the Meuse to the Volga in 3000–2400 BC. It is distinguished by its pottery beakers with cord-impressed decoration, stone battle-axes, and burials under ROUND BARROWS. The Cord Impressed Ware culture marked a new emphasis on PASTORALISM and social hierarchy, and was a precursor of the BELL BEAKER cultures of western Europe. ▷ 1.04, 1.20

CORINTH
The leading Greek city-state of the 7th century BC, heavily involved in Mediterranean trading and shipbuilding, and the pioneer of Doric architecture. Corinth's central position meant that it was drawn into the wars of the 5th and 4th centuries BC, at first in support of SPARTA (Peloponnesian War) and then against it. The Romans sacked Corinth in 146 BC, but later founded a new colony there, which regained the original city's prosperity. It was the home of an early Christian community made famous by the letters it received from St Paul. ▷ 1.22, 1.23, 1.24

CORTAILLOD
Early farming and fishing village beside Lake Neuchâtel in Switzerland, that gave its name to the early NEOLITHIC of the north Alpine region in about 3800–3000 BC. Cortaillod settlements are famous for the preservation of wooden houses and artifacts in the lake sediments. ▷ 1.20

COTTON
Seed-hair fiber from plants of the genus *Gossypium*, found in sub-tropical regions and cultivated for making textiles and thread. The earliest use of cotton was in the Indian sub-continent, where it was domesticated by 5000 BC, and in South America, where cotton textiles of the 3rd millennium BC have been recorded (ASPERO culture). ▷ 1.03, 1.26, 1.28

CROESUS
King of LYDIA (r.c.560–546 BC) who lives on in legend for his immense wealth. Croesus had many links with the Greek world, but found himself isolated when he attacked CYRUS of Persia, who defeated him and annexed his kingdom to the ACHEMENID EMPIRE (546–545 BC). ▷ 1.15

CUMAE
See KYMAI

CUNEIFORM
Writing system invented in MESOPOTAMIA in the 3rd millennium BC, derived from Sumerian pictographs that were refined to include phonetic and syllabic values. Early inscriptions were written in Sumerian, but cuneiform was widely adopted in the Middle East for writing other languages, notably AKKADIAN. It fell out of use as ARAMAIC LANGUAGES and versions of CANAANITE phonetic alphabets became widespread in the 1st millennium BC. ▷ 1.07, 1.10, 1.15

CYRUS II (THE GREAT)
King of Persia (r.559–30 BC) who founded the ACHEMENID EMPIRE by overthrowing his MEDIAN overlord, King Astyages, and appropriating his extensive empire. He confirmed his position by destroying his main rival to the west, CROESUS of LYDIA, in Asia Minor (547–546 BC) and annexing BABYLONIA (539 BC). Cyrus was known for his diplomacy as well as his use of force. His eastern campaigns and fortress-building (546–530 BC) consolidated the empire, but Cyrus was killed in battle on the frontier in 530 BC. ▷ 1.13, 1.14, 1.15

DARIUS I (THE GREAT)
Achemenid king of Persia (r.521–486 BC) who ruled the ACHEMENID EMPIRE when it was at the height of its power. He seized the throne after the death of CAMBYSES and secured the northern frontiers by defeating the SCYTHIANS. He conquered the Indus valley by 518 BC and Thrace by 513 BC, but failed to conquer Greece (490 BC). He reorganized the empire by establishing a federal system of satrapies, efficient taxation and postal systems, and a new military organization. He marked his reign by building a new royal capital at PERSEPOLIS. ▷ 1.15

DAVID
King of ISRAEL (r.c.1006–965 BC), proclaimed ruler of JUDAH and later of Israel after the death of King SAUL. David conquered JERUSALEM and made it the capital of a united kingdom in about 1000 BC. He defeated the PHILISTINES and consolidated the kingdom of Israel by dominating vassal states such as EDOM, MOAB and ARAM-DAMASCUS. ▷ 1.14

DELPHI
Important shrine of Apollo, situated on the slopes of Mount Parnassus, central Greece. Its famous ORACLE attracted visitors from all parts of the Greek world, and the Pythian Games held at the shrine were second only to those held at OLYMPIA. The site was crowded with treasuries, temples and statues donated by cities and supplicants. Delphi played an important role during the period of Greek colonization, advising migrants where they should settle. ▷ 1.24

DI-XIN
Last king of the SHANG dynasty of China, who was overthrown by his vassal, King WU of the ZHOU family, at the Battle of Chaoge in 1122 BC. He was later seen as a sadistic despot who was morally unfit to rule, and was therefore justly removed according to the doctrine known as the "Mandate of Heaven", under which political power was subject to divine judgement. ▷ 1.27

DIASPORA
Greek word meaning "dispersion" that is used to describe the scattering of Jewish populations and their exile from Palestine.

The first Diaspora took place in 587 BC, when NEBUCHADNEZZAR, king of BABYLON, suppressed a revolt in JUDAH and forcibly resettled HEBREW communities in BABYLONIA. When CYRUS the Great of Persia permitted a return to their homeland in 539 BC, many Jews stayed behind. Later Diaspora scattered the Jews still further. ▷ 1.14

DILMUN

Early state and trading center in the Persian Gulf that is mentioned in Sumerian records and was probably on the island of Bahrain, where a large fortified city existed in about 2800–1800 BC. Dilmun was at the center of a thriving trade system, largely based on commerce between MESOPOTAMIA and the Indus valley in the 3rd millennium BC. It may have been conquered by SARGON OF AGADE, becoming part of the Akkadian empire in the 23rd century BC. ▷ 1.11

DJOSER

Founder of the 3rd Dynasty of Egyptian PHARAOHS, Djoser ruled from 2677 until 2648 BC. He is chiefly remembered for his burial place, the STEP PYRAMID at SAQQARA, designed by the architect Imhotep. ▷ 1.17

DOG

The first animal to be tamed by humans, the wolf probably being its main ancestral species. There is evidence of early domestic dogs in several parts of the world, with the earliest in the Middle East (c.3000 ya), though earlier hunters may have initiated the domestication process. Dogs were used for protection, herding and food (in the Americas), and as pets. ▷ 1.08

DOLMEN

Term used by early European archeologists to describe MEGALITHIC tomb chambers of the NEOLITHIC period, especially those consisting of upright orthostats with a large capstone on top. The term is now rarely used, except to describe the "portal-dolmen", a specific type of tomb. ▷ 1.20

DORIANS

One of the tribes of Greeks whose foundation myths told of their arrival in the Peloponnese after the fall of TROY. Some archeologists and historians have dated this to about 1100 BC, but others point to a later foundation (c.900 BC) of the main Dorian city, SPARTA. By the 5th century BC the Dorians were deadly rivals of the IONIANS, whose mother city was Athens. ▷ 1.12, 1.22, 1.23, 1.24

DRAVIDIANS

People of southern India, sometimes regarded as the original pre-ARYAN HUNTER-GATHERER population, which adopted farming from the 4th millennium BC. The ethnic and racial distinctiveness of the Dravidians is open to question, and the term is now used mainly to describe speakers of the Dravidian languages, widely spoken in southern India. ▷ 1.04, 1.05, 1.06, 1.26

DUR-KURIGALZU

City in south MESOPOTAMIA near to the confluence of the Tigris and Diyala rivers, founded in the 14th century BC by a KASSITE king of BABYLON, Kurigalzu I or Kurigalzu II. The city contained a ZIGGURAT and temples dedicated to Sumerian gods, as well as a royal palace. ▷ 1.12, 1.13

DYUKHTAI TRADITION

UPPER PALEOLITHIC stone-tool industry (c.20,000–12,000 ya) that represents the first human colonization of far northeast Asia (eastern Siberia). It is characterized by bifacial spear points for big-game hunting. Communities from this region migrated east-wards in this period and eventually crossed BERINGIA to colonize the Americas. ▷ 1.02

EARLY HORIZON period

Period of ANDEAN CIVILIZATION from about 900 to 200 BC. It is marked by the spread of the Chavín artistic and temple-building tradition across the formerly diverse regional cultures of the central Andes, after which coastal areas adopted highland architectural styles. This process of cultural integration may have been due to the adoption of a single religious cult. The decline of Chavín influence after 200 BC resulted in the renewed regionalization of cultures such as the Mochica, Nazca and Lima. ▷ 1.28

EARLY DYNASTIC period

Period of MESOPOTAMIAN CIVILIZATION (c.2900–2334 BC) that saw the emergence of the first documented royal dynasties in the region. A definitive chronology for the period has not been established, due to the fragmentary nature of the sources. The end of the period is marked by the accession of SARGON OF AGADE in 2334 BC, which is the first reliable established date in the history of the Middle East. ▷ 1.10

EARLY PRECLASSIC period

Period of MESOAMERICAN CIVILIZATION from about 2000 to 800 BC, marked by the adoption of farming, the growth of village settlements and the use of pottery throughout Mesoamerica. Most significant was the development of complex hierarchical societies with large settlements and ceremonial centers, such as the Maya, OLMECS and ZAPOTECS, and the emergence of the Olmec civilization in the lowland region to the south of the Gulf of Mexico from about 1200 BC. Extensive trade networks, religious architecture and monumental stone sculpture all appeared in this period. ▷ 1.05, 1.28

EDOM

Region of Palestine between the Dead Sea and the Gulf of Aqaba, occupied by the Edomites from the 14th to the 6th centuries BC. Although well-placed to exploit the Red Sea trade route, Edom was often dominated by ISRAEL or JUDAH (c.1000–843 BC). The region lost its political and cultural identity following its conquest by the Babylonians in about 600 BC. ▷ 1.13, 1.14

EGYPTIAN CIVILIZATION

Ancient Egypt was blessed with annual floods of the Nile, which brought fertile silt and water, making the lower Nile valley the most favorable agricultural area in the ancient world. After 2,500 years of settled cultivation, a unified Egyptian kingdom was created by NARMER (r.c.3000 BC). The Egyptian hiero-glyphic writing system and styles of art and architecture emerged with unification. Ancient Egypt was a highly centralized state focused on the semi-divine king (or PHARAOH, as he was later called). The kings showed their authority through grand building projects, such as PYRAMID complexes and temples. Egypt enjoyed long periods of stability (under the OLD KINGDOM, MIDDLE KINGDOM and NEW KINGDOM), broken by periods of fragmentation (Intermediate periods).

Egyptian society was highly ritualized; every activity was related to the gods, who were appeased through elaborate rituals in temples or by means of magic and spells in the home. Those who behaved correctly were promised an afterlife, though this depended on their body being preserved through MUMMIFICATION after death. The Egyptians were expert craftsmen in fields such as sculpture, architecture, painting and jewelry-making. They also had a reputation for wisdom in science, astronomy, mathematics and medicine, though there is little evidence of creative thinking in these areas.

By 1070 BC Egypt was in decline and after the 8th century BC it was usually under foreign rule, but its civilization survived until it was undermined by Christianity in the fourth century AD. ▷ 1.05, 1.07, 1.10, 1.13, 1.14, 1.15, 1.16, 1.17, 1.18, 1.23

EL PARAISO TRADITION

Cultural tradition of coastal Peru in about 1800–850 BC, that was contemporary with the Andean KOTOSH TRADITION. The largest PRECERAMIC monument complex in South America is named after El Paraiso; it consists of massive mounds forming U-shaped plat-forms, with a temple at the end and central sunken courts. This style of architecture was widely adopted along the coast, together with IRRIGATION farming and pottery, from about 1800 BC. ▷ 1.28

ELAM

Plains region to the east of MESOPOTAMIA, between the Zagros mountains and the Persian Gulf. Cultural developments in Mesopotamia were closely paralleled in Elam, where cities, states and writing (proto-Elamite pictographs) existed by about 3500 BC. The

KINGS OF EGYPT

LATE PREDYNASTIC PERIOD
c.3000 BC

Zekhen
Narmer

EARLY DYNASTIC PERIOD
2920–2575

1st Dynasty	2920–2770
Menes	
Djer	
Djet	
Wadj	
Den	
Adjib	
Semerkhet	
Qa'a	

2nd Dynasty	2770–2649
Hotepsekhemwy	
Reneb	
Ninetjer	
Peribsen	
Khasekhemwy	

3rd Dynasty	2649–2575
Zanakht	2649–2630
Djoser	2630–2611
Sekhemkhet	2611–2603
Khaba	2603–2599
Huni	2599–2575

OLD KINGDOM
2575–2134

4th Dynasty	2575–2465
Snefru	2575–2551
Khufu (Cheops)	2551–2528
Radjedef	2528–2520
Khephren	2520–2494
Menkaure (Mycerinus)	2490–2472
Shepseskaf	2472–2467

5th Dynasty	2465–2323
Userkaf	2465–2458
Sahure	2458–2446
Kakai	2446–2426
Ini	2426–2419
Raneferef	2419–2416
Izi	2416–2392
Menkauhor	2396–2388
Izezi	2388–2356
Unas	2356–2323

6th Dynasty	2323–2150
Teti	2323–2291
Pepi I	2289–2255
Nemtyemzaf	2255–2246
Pepi II	2246–2152

7th/8th Dynasty	2150–2134
Numerous kings, including Neferkare	

1st INTERMEDIATE PERIOD
2134–2040

9th/10th Dynasty	2134–2040
Several kings called	
Khety	
Merykare	
Ity	

11th Dynasty	2134–2040
Inyotef I (Sehertawy)	2134–2118
Inyotef II (Wahankh)	2118–2069
Inyotef III	2069–2061
(Nakhtnebtepnufer)	
Mentuhotpe II	2061–2010

MIDDLE KINGDOM
2040–1640

11th Dynasty	2040–1991
Mentuhotpe II	2061–2010
(ruler of all Egypt from 2040)	
Mentuhotpe III	2010–1998
Mentuhotpe IV	1998–1991

12th Dynasty	1991–1783
Amenemhet I	1991–1962
Senwosret I	1971–1926
Amenemhet II	1929–1982
Senwosret II	1987–1878
Senwosret III	1878–1841?
Amenemhet III	1844–1797
Amenemhet IV	1799–1787
Nefrusobk	1787–1783

13th Dynasty	1783–after 1640
About 70 kings, including	
Wegaf 1	1783–1779
Amenemhet V	
Harnedjheriotef	
Amenyqemau	
Sebekhotpe 1	c.1750
Hor	
Amenemhet VII	
Sebekhotpe II	
Khendjer	
Sebekhotpe III	c.1745
Neferhotep I	c.1741–1730
Sebekhotpe IV	c.1730–1720
Sebekhotpe V	c.1720–1715
Aya	c.1704–1690
Mentuemzaf	
Dedumose II	
Neferhotep III	

14th Dynasty	
A group of kings probably contemporary with the 13th or 15th Dynasty	

2nd INTERMEDIATE PERIOD
1640–1532

15th Dynasty (Hyksos)	
Salitis	
Sheshi	
Khian	
Apophis	c.1585–1542
Khamudi	c.1542–1532

16th Dynasty	
Minor Hyksos rulers, contemporary with the 15th Dynasty	

17th Dynasty	1640–1550
Numerous kings, including	
Inyotef V	c.1640–1635
Sebekemzaf I	
Nebireyeraw	
Sebekemzaf II	
Ta'o (or Djehuti'o) I	
Ta'o (or Djehuti'o) II	
Kamose	c.1555–1550

NEW KINGDOM
1532–1070

18th Dynasty	1550–1307
Ahmose	1550–1525
(ruler of all Egypt from 1532)	
Amenophis I	1525–1504
Tuthmosis I	1504–1492
Tuthmosis II	1492–1479
Tuthmosis III	1479–1425
Hatshepsut	1473–1458
Amenophis II	1427–1401
Tuthmosis IV	1401–1391
Amenophis III	1391–1353
Amenophis IV (Akhenaten)	1353–1335
Smenkhkare	1335–1333
Tutankhamun	1333–1323
Aya	1323–1319
Haremhab	1319–1307

19th Dynasty	1307–1196
Ramesses I	1307–1306
Sethos I	1306–1290
Ramesses II	1290–1224
Merneptah	1224–1214
Sethos II	1214–1204
Siptah	1204–1198
Twosre	1198–1196

20th Dynasty	1196–1070
Sethnakhte	1196–1194
Ramesses III	1194–1163
Ramesses IV	1163–1156
Ramesses V	1156–1151
Ramesses VI	1151–1143
Ramesses VII	1143–1136
Ramesses VIII	1136–1131
Ramesses IX	1131–1112
Ramesses X	1112–1100
Ramesses XI	1100–1070

Elamites briefly conquered SUMERIA and sacked UR in 2004 BC, and were a major threat to Mesopotamian states in the 2nd millennium BC. In the 13th century BC Elam emerged as a powerful unified kingdom, under a series of warrior kings who conquered much of south Mesopotamia, but it declined rapidly from about 1110 BC, when the capital at SUSA was captured by the Babylonians, later becoming a vassal of Assyrian and Babylonian empires, and one of the richest satrapies of the ACHEMENID EMPIRE. Little is known about Elamite society or religion; its artistic and architectural achievements were predominantly BABYLONIAN in style. ▷ 1.10, 1.11, 1.12, 1.13, 1.15

EL-AMARNA

Modern name for the site of Akhetaten, the capital of the "heretic" PHARAOH AKHENATEN, in Middle Egypt from 1350 to 1325 BC. The city was abandoned at Akhenaten's death and the site remained well-preserved. The ceremonial procession way and great royal hall for public audiences have been recognized as well as residential suburbs. The site also contained the famous El-Amarna letters, detailing the relationship between Egypt and the cities and states of the Near East. ▷ 1.18

ELEUSIS

Important sanctuary west of Athens, known throughout the Greek world for its Mysteries into which suppliants could be initiated. The presiding goddesses were Demeter and her daughter Persephone, themselves at the center of complex cults of fertility and rebirth. ▷ 1.24

ELIJAH

Biblical prophet of the 9th century BC who, with the prophet ELISHA, asserted a monotheistic religious doctrine and successfully encouraged the Israelites to reject CANAANITE beliefs and the worship of Baal (c.860–853 BC). ▷ 1.14

ELISHA

Biblical prophet who, with his mentor ELIJAH, persuaded the Israelites to reject the god Baal. He directed the civil war that led to the death of King AHAB (853 BC) and Jehu's seizure of the throne. Elisha succeeded Elijah as the most influential religious figure in ISRAEL. ▷ 1.14

ENLIL

Sumerian deity (Bel in Akkadian) of the air, winds and farming. One of a triad of gods (with An and Enki), Enlil was especially important because of his role in ensuring fertility and agricultural productivity. Control of the cult center at NIPPUR was essential for Sumerian and Akkadian kings. ▷ 1.11

ENSETE

Plant of the banana family that produces an edible root, domesticated in Ethiopia at a very early date (by c.4000 BC). It is one of several indigenous farming innovations based on local plants (including teff and finger MILLET) that were independent of Middle Eastern agriculture. ▷ 1.16

EPIPALEOLITHIC

Period in the post-glacial period prior to the adoption of agriculture, in which HUNTER-GATHERER societies – including cultures in the LEVANT (such as the NATUFIANS) and north Africa – continued to use UPPER PALEOLITHIC stone-tool and hunting technologies. ▷ 1.08, 1.16

EPIRUS

An area of northwestern Greece known from early times for its ORACLE to Apollo at Dodona. Gradually Hellenized by Greek colonies on the coast, the area was united into a single kingdom under a chieftain from the central Molossian tribe in the 4th century BC. Epirus' greatest period of prosperity then followed. Its most famous king was Pyrrhus. The kingdom collapsed in the 3rd century BC and, in 167 BC, Epirus was conquered by the Romans, who reputedly enslaved 150,000 of its inhabitants. ▷ 1.24, 1.25

ERIDU

Sumerian city to the south of UR, referred to in ancient king lists as the first city of SUMER. Founded in the mid-6th millennium BC, Eridu was one of the leading cities of MESOPOTAMIA by the EARLY DYNASTIC period (c.2500 BC), and was continuously occupied until about 600 BC. Its political importance declined after the rise of the Third Dynasty of Ur. ▷ 1.09, 1.10, 1.11

ERLITOU CULTURE

The first bronze-using culture of China (c.1900–1650 BC), named after the city of Erlitou situated on the Yellow river in the heartland of the later Shang state. The Erlitou culture is probably equivalent to the first phase of the SHANG civilization and is notable for its sophisticated cast-bronze work. ▷ 1.27

ERTEBOLLE CULTURE

Late MESOLITHIC HUNTER-GATHERER-fisher culture of Denmark (c.6000–3500 BC). It is characterized by its distinctive stone tools, massive shell middens at coastal sites, cemeteries with grave goods, and the adoption of pottery, polished stone axes and agricultural methods from neighboring farmers. Several canoes and examples of wood-carved art have been found in water-logged sediments. ▷ 1.19

ESARHADDON

King of ASSYRIA (r.680–669 BC), who re-established peaceful dominion over BABYLONIA but lost contol of the northern provinces due to SCYTHIAN and CIMMERIAN invasions. Esarhaddon suppressed revolts in the LEVANT and conquered Egypt, but failed to consolidate Assyrian rule. Esarhaddon's successor, ASHURBANIPAL, was forced to reconquer the country. ▷ 1.13

ESHNUNNA

City on the Diyali river in central MESOPOTAMIA and an important city-state of the EARLY DYNASTIC period. It was conquered by the Akkadians (c.2250 BC) and later ruled by the Third Dynasty of UR, before regaining its independence in about 2000 BC. It was the last major Mesopotamian state to be conquered by HAMMURABI of BABYLON (1755 BC). ▷ 1.10, 1.11

ETRUSCANS

The leading pre-Roman people of Italy, located between the Tiber and Arno rivers, with offshoots in the Po valley and Campania. Recognizable in the early IRON AGE Villanovan cultural group of the 9th and 8th centuries BC, the Etruscans soon developed prosperous city-states supported by agriculture, COPPER and iron deposits, and extensive trading contacts throughout the Mediterranean. The leading cities were loosely organized in the league of Twelve Cities (the Etruscan league), which met periodically at the sanctuary of Voltumna in central Etruria. From 396 BC, with the fall of Veii, the Etruscans gradually came under Roman control and their assimilation was complete by the end of the republic. They were famed for their artistic skills, and many Etruscan wall-paintings, terracottas and bronzes have been discovered in tombs and sanctuaries dating from the 7th to the 1st centuries BC. ▷ 1.06, 1.07, 1.23, 1.25

FERTILE CRESCENT

Region of the ancient Middle East in which the earliest agricultural economies and sedentary village societies developed (c.9000–7000 BC), with domesticated cereals (einkorn and emmer WHEAT, and BARLEY) and animal species (SHEEP and GOAT). These species co-existed in the wild in the crescent-shaped region extending from the southern LEVANT, through northwest Syria to the Zagros mountains in Iran. ▷ 1.08, 1.09

FIRE, EARLIEST USE

The earliest evidence of the controlled use of fire by hominids (probably HOMO ERECTUS) is dated to about 1.6 million ya, at CHESOWANJA, Kenya and at SWARTKRANS, South Africa. Consistent fire making, however, was probably a later development associated with the human colonization of temperate regions after about 600,000 ya. The earliest evidence of the use of fire in Europe comes from near Bury St Edmunds in eastern England and dates from about 400,000 ya. ▷ 1.01

FLOOD, THE

Biblical story with earlier origins in Middle Eastern culture. CUNEIFORM tablets dating from about 2000 BC, found at NINEVEH and other sites in MESOPOTAMIA, record parts of the "Epic of Gilgamesh" (the earliest surviving literary tale). It includes an account of a great flood that left only one family alive. ▷ 1.10

FOLSOM CULTURE

Early PALEOINDIAN culture (c.9000–8000 BC) of the North American plains and adjacent regions, characterized by stone projectile points with concave bases (Folsom points) used in big-game hunting, especially of bison (mammoths were extinct by this period). The Folsom culture developed as a regional specialization of the preceding CLOVIS tradition. ▷ 1.02

FUNNEL-NECKED BEAKER CULTURE

The earliest NEOLITHIC culture of northern Europe (c.4200–2800 BC), with distinctive necked pottery styles, MEGALITHIC CHAMBERED TOMBS and long mounds, settlements of small timber buildings or LONGHOUSES, and enclosures. It is associated with the first use of PLOWS, animal traction and wheeled transport in north-central Europe. ▷ 1.20

GADES

City on the Atlantic coast of Spain (modern Cadiz), founded as a seasonal trading post (possibly before 1000 BC) by PHOENICIANS from the LEVANT. It had become a major trading center by the 8th century BC and probably part of the powerful native kingdom of TARTESSOS by about 600 BC. It was controlled by the Carthaginians from about 500 BC. ▷ 1.23, 1.25

GANDHARA

Satrapy of the ACHEMENID EMPIRE in the mountainous region of east Afghanistan and northwest Pakistan. Gandhara was strategically important as a focus for trade routes from Iran and central Asia to India through the Khyber Pass, and sent silver, bulls and weapons as tribute to the Persian king. After the conquest of the Achemenid empire by Alexander the Great, Gandhara came under Greek rule (the last Greek principalities in the area were extinguished at about the time of Jesus Christ). The Gandhara style of art, a fusion of Greek and Indian influences that developed in the last centuries BC, became the most important style of Buddhist art in southeast Asia. ▷ 1.15

GAVRINIS

Island in the Gulf of Morbihan in Brittany, France, on which a large, early NEOLITHIC PASSAGE GRAVE was built in the 4th millennium BC. It is notable for its elaborate carved stone decoration, bearing abstract curvilinear designs and depictions of stone axes. ▷ 1.20

GERMANS, PROTO-

Peoples of north and north-central Europe who spoke proto-Germanic languages and shared cultural features during the IRON AGE.

Their origins are uncertain but proto-Germanic languages probably developed in the late BRONZE AGE (by c.800 BC). ▷ 1.06

GEZER

A major CANAANITE city of the 2nd millennium BC, sometimes held by the Egyptians. It was refortified by King SOLOMON of ISRAEL in about 950 BC, before abandonment in about 900 BC. Early examples of the Canaanite alphabet (c.1800 BC) and of HEBREW writing (the GEZER calendar, c.1000 BC) have been discovered at the site. ▷ 1.14

GIRSU

See LAGASH

GOAT

Animal first domesticated in the highland regions of the Middle East, with early evidence (c.7500 BC) from sites such as Jarmo in the foothills of the Zagros mountains. Goats were used as a source of milk and cheese, WOOL, meat and leather. ▷ 1.03, 1.08, 1.16, 1.20

GORDION

City in Anatolia, the capital of the Phrygian kingdom from about 800 BC. It was destroyed by the CIMMERIANS in 695 BC, when the last king of the PHRYGIANS, MITAS, was killed. The city was re-established as a provincial center by the ACHEMENID empire in the 6th century BC. ▷ 1.13

GRAVETTIAN CULTURE

A phase (c.28,000–23,000 ya) of the European UPPER PALEOLITHIC that is characterized by a stone-tool industry with small pointed blades used for big-game hunting (bison, horse, reindeer and mammoth). It is divided into two regional groups: the western Gravettian, mostly known from cave sites in France, and the eastern Gravettian, with open sites of specialized mammoth hunters on the plains of central Europe and Russia. Some early examples of CAVE ART, and the famous "Venus" figurines were made by Gravettian artists. ▷ 1.19

GREEK ALPHABET

The Greeks adopted an alphabet from the PHOENICIANS in about 750 BC, but adapted it for their own use by adding vowels. There were 23 standard letters, but some city-states used variations. The alphabet was passed on to Italy in the 8th century BC and, as adapted by the Romans, forms the basis of the Western alphabet. ▷ 1.07

GUTIANS

Tribal people of the hill region between the Mesopotamian plains and the Zagros mountains. The Gutians raided SUMERIA and AKKAD, and briefly dominated the lowlands in the 22nd century BC. Mesopotamian kings often attempted to conquer them and they finally lost their cultural identity when

the Assyrian empire expanded during the 9th century BC. ▷ 1.10, 1.11, 1.12

HADAR

Site of hominid fossil finds in Ethiopia, where the remains, dating about 3 million ya, of 30 individuals of the species AUSTRALOPITHECUS AFARENSIS – including the most complete skeleton of an early hominid (LUCY) – have been discovered in ancient lake silts. ▷ 1.01

HALAFIAN CULTURE

Late NEOLITHIC culture (c.6000–5400 BC) of central and north MESOPOTAMIA, named after the site of Tell Halaf. It is characterized by burnished and painted pottery, small villages of clay-built houses, a mixed dry-farming economy and evidence of weaving. The Halafians used stone tools, imported OBSIDIAN, and made increasing use of COPPER and bronze. Storehouses and prestige goods suggest the development of chiefly authority and social ranking. ▷ 1.09

HALLSTATT CULTURE

The general term for the late BRONZE AGE URNFIELD CULTURES (Hallstatt phases A and B, c.1150–750 BC) and the early IRON AGE cultures (Hallstatt C and D, c.750–450 BC) of central and western Europe, named after the cemetery and salt-mining center at Hallstatt in Austria. Each phase of the culture is characterized by distinctive metalwork and burial practices, with the appearance of iron and large HILLFORTS at the beginning of Hallstatt C. From about 600 BC, there is evidence of increasing trade in luxury goods, and of other contacts with Greek and Etruscan cities in the Mediterranean. ▷ 1.06, 1.25

HAMMURABI

AMORITE king of BABYLON (r.1792–1750 BC). Hammurabi inherited a strong state from his father, SIN-MUBALLIT, and later conquered most of MESOPOTAMIA (c.1764–1750 BC), capturing the Assyrian capital at SHUBAT-ENLIL, and defeating his last major rival, ESHNUNNA, in 1755 BC. His empire stretched from SUMERIA to north Syria, but he failed to establish an effective bureaucracy and the empire declined after his death. Hammurabi is most famous for his law code, one of the earliest to have survived. Though not a complete legal system, it provides a valuable source for the structure of early Babylonian society. The code is heavily reliant on retaliatory punishments involving the death or mutilation of offenders, or members of their family. ▷ 1.11

HAO

The first capital city of the ZHOU DYNASTY from about 1122 to 770 BC, situated on the WEI river in the Zhou heartland (the state of QIN) in northwest China. It was attacked by an alliance of barbarian tribes and rebellious noblemen in 771 BC, prompting the Zhou to move their capital to LUOYANG. ▷ 1.27

HARAPPA

Second largest city of the INDUS CIVILIZATION, with an estimated population of 30,000, situated beside the river Ravi in modern northeast Pakistan. Founded in the mid-3rd millennium BC on the site of a pre-Indus settlement, the city consisted of a heavily fortified citadel, a cereal-processing and storage complex and a planned workers' quarter, with uniform housing units on a grid layout. It was probably abandoned after 1800 BC. ▷ 1.26

HASSUNA CULTURE

NEOLITHIC cultural phase (c.6500–6000 BC) marking the first agricultural settlement of the central Mesopotamian plains, with small villages of clay-built houses, a mixed dry-farming economy, the first permanent kilns for pottery manufacture, distinctive painted CERAMICS, the use of COPPER, and stamp seals to denote ownership. It developed directly into the succeeding SAMARRAN and HALAFIAN cultural traditions. ▷ 1.09

HATSHEPSUT

Appointed regent to her stepson, TUTHMOSIS III, on her husband's death, Hatshepsut seized power in Egypt in 1473 BC to become the only female PHARAOH. She shrewdly used "male" images of herself when appropriate to maintain loyalties. The reliefs on her impressive burial complex at Deir el-Bahri detail a famous voyage to the exotic kingdom of Punt. After her death in 1458 BC her memory was erased by later pharaohs. ▷ 1.18

HATTI

Assyrian name for the people of central Anatolia who spoke a non-INDO-EUROPEAN LANGUAGE (Hattian) in the late 3rd millennium BC. This region was occupied from about 2000 BC by the Indo-European HITTITES, who are sometimes confusingly identified with the Hatti, though the latter were one of several distinct populations ruled by Hittite kings. ▷ 1.12

HATTUSAS

(Modern Boghazkoy) Settlement in central Anatolia first occupied in the 3rd millennium BC. It was a major HITTITE city by 1800 BC and the capital from about 1650 until its destruction by the PHRYGIANS (c.1200 BC). By the New Kingdom period (c.1450–1190 BC) the city extended across several hills and deep valleys, with a fortified royal residence, an upper town with temples and official buildings, and a lower town with a Great Temple and merchants' houses. ▷ 1.12

HEBREW LANGUAGE AND ALPHABET

Semitic language closely related to CANAANITE. "Old Hebrew" was spoken in Palestine until the 3rd century BC. The earliest examples of written Hebrew date to the 10th century BC, using a version of the phonetic PHOENICIAN alphabet (notably the GEZER calendar), which was later supplanted by an ARAMAIC script. ▷ 1.07

HEBREWS

People with a shared language and religious identity whose ancestors may once have lived in northwest MESOPOTAMIA before settling in Palestine (Canaan) in the mid-2nd millennium BC. Some Hebrews probably migrated to Egypt, where they lived as serfs before returning to the LEVANT in the late 13th century BC (the biblical stories of Moses and JOSHUA), colonizing areas previously dominated by CANAANITE and PHILISTINE cities. The monotheistic religious doctrine of Judaism was firmly established in the 9th century BC. ▷ 1.12, 1.14, 1.18, 1.23

HELLENES

The name the Greeks called themselves. It originally referred only to the inhabitants of a small area of central Greece, but gradually came to refer to all Greeks. ▷ 1.24

HELOT

The helots were the enslaved population of MESSENIA (southwest Peloponnese), brought into subjection when SPARTA conquered the area in the 8th century BC. They were tied to the land and forced to produce food for their Spartan overlords, who could then train full-time to maintain their supremacy.

HENGE

Circular ceremonial enclosure of the late NEOLITHIC period in Britain (c.3000–2000 BC). Henges are usually symmetrical in plan and typically have a ditch on the inside of the bank, varying from about 50 to 450 meters (165 to 150 feet) in diameter. Some enclose either STONE CIRCLES (e.g. AVEBURY) or timber circles (e.g. DURRINGTON WALLS). The larger sites suggest a complex social organization, perhaps indicative of CHIEFDOMS. The STONEHENGE enclosure, from which they take their name, is not a classic henge. ▷ 1.20

HEUNEBURG

HILLFORT of the HALLSTATT period situated on the Upper Danube in south Germany that was refortified in the 6th century BC using Greek-style building methods, with mud-brick walls on stone foundations with projecting bastions. Imports of Greek wine amphorae and tableware indicate Mediterranean trade contacts. A royal burial mound, with grave goods that may have included silk fabrics, is located nearby. ▷ 1.25

HIEROGLYPHS

A distinctive script that emerged in Egypt in about 3200 BC. It consisted of more than 1,000 signs and took many years for scribes to master. Traditionally used for carved inscriptions on religious or royal monuments, it fell into disuse in early Christian times and remained undeciphered until the early 19th century.

HILLFORTS

Fortified hilltop enclosures of the European late BRONZE AGE and IRON AGE (c.1100–50 BC), with stone, earth, and/or timber ramparts. Hillforts had diverse functions: as settlement centers and refuges, royal residences and defended storage complexes. The largest and most elaborately fortified sites date mainly from the middle Iron Age (c.600–200 BC). ▷ 1.05

HINDUISM

Religion of the Indian subcontinent with a complex set of beliefs and practices, which refer to a pantheon of deities, numerous sacred texts and a sacred geography of temples and shrines. Hinduism is difficult to characterize, however, as it has no single founder, doctrine, or authoritative scripture, and no ecclesiastical organization. Some features may be traced back to the INDUS CIVILIZATION and DRAVIDIAN traditions of the late 3rd millennium BC, but the earliest Hindu scriptures are the Vedas, hymns composed from about 1500 BC by ARYAN settlers in India. By 500 BC the principal features of historical Hinduism were codified in the Vedic texts, the caste system, and religious law books that defined moral lifestyles. ▷ 1.26

HIPPIAS

TYRANT of Athens (r.527–510 BC) who succeeded his father, PEISISTRATUS. He was responsible for extensive building programs in Athens. Increasingly tyrannical, he was overthrown by the Athenians, who were helped by the Spartans, in 510 BC. The Persians attempted to restore him as a manageable ruler of Athens in 490 BC. ▷ 1.24

HIRAM

PHOENICIAN king of TYRE (r.c.969–936 BC) and an ally of ISRAEL. He contributed craftsmen and materials for the building of SOLOMON's Temple at JERUSALEM, and received tribute and territory on the Levantine coast in return. ▷ 1.23

HIT

Settlement on the middle Euphrates where the river runs into the lowland floodplains of southern MESOPOTAMIA. Important nearby sources of bitumen were intensively exploited by the Mesopotamians for bonding courses of mud brick in building work. ▷ 1.10

HITTITES

People with an INDO-EUROPEAN LANGUAGE who settled in Anatolia (c.2000 BC), possibly from the Ukraine or Caucasus. They founded several kingdoms that dominated native populations, including the non-Indo-European HATTI; by about 1750 BC a unified Hittite state had emerged. The Hittite state was organized on a devolved feudal basis, which could be unstable when succession to the throne was disputed. The high king had supreme power, partly theocratic in nature (after death he gained the status of a god). Little is known about Hittite religion or art.

The later history of the Hittites can be divided into three main periods: the Old Kingdom period, New Kingdom (Empire) period and Neo-Hittite period. During the Old Kingdom period (1750–1450 BC), the Hittites established a capital at Kussara, and then at Hattusas (c.1650 BC), extending their rule into north MESOPOTAMIA. Under King MURSILIS they briefly annexed ASSYRIA and sacked BABYLON (1595 BC), but could not sustain their conquests. Hittite power declined in the 16th century BC in the face of Egyptian and Mittanian expansion and internal instability, and reached a low point in the 15th century BC, when little is known about Hittite affairs.

Under the New Kingdom (Empire) period (c.1450–1190 BC) the revival of the Hittite empire took place, as MITTANI power waned and the Egyptians were distracted by internal affairs. The empire reached its greatest extent in about 1325 BC under King SUPPILULIUMAS, who consolidated Hittite rule in Anatolia and conquered the northern parts of Syria and the LEVANT. Confrontations with the Egyptians in the early 13th century BC over control of the Levant ended in stalemate. The collapse of the empire (c.1205–1190 BC) is attributed to PHRYGIAN invasions (which destroyed the capital at Hattusas), attacks by the SEA PEOPLES and political fragmentation.

After the Phrygian conquests, during the Neo-Hittite period (1190–700 BC), Hittite cultural identity was maintained only in small city-states and kingdoms in south Anatolia and north Syria, the most powerful being CARCHEMISH. Their independence, and the last remnants of Hittite culture, were finally destroyed by the Assyrians in the 8th century BC. ▷ 1.11, 1.12, 1.13, 1.14, 1.18, 1.21, 1.22

HOMER

Greek poet who is associated with the final composition of the two great Greek epics, the ILIAD and the ODYSSEY, in the late 8th century BC. The Ionic dialect of the poems suggests that he may have come from Asia Minor, the eastern Aegean or Euboea. Homer probably brought together earlier oral poems and consolidated them into coherent stories. ▷ 1.22, 1.24

HOMINOID APES

Large primates belonging to three main groups (*Sivapithecus*, *Dryopithecus* and *Proconsul*) that evolved in the MIOCENE EPOCH and spread throughout the Old World. The evolutionary lineage of hominids, including humans, probably diverged from other apes only 6 million ya. ▷ 1.01

HOMO ERECTUS

Human species that had evolved in Africa from HOMO HABILIS by about 1.5 million ya. Though probably slightly taller, *Homo erectus* was physically similar to modern humans. Its

brain size ranged from two-thirds that of a modern human in early examples of the species, to three-quarters in later examples. *Homo erectus* developed more effective technology than *Homo habilis*, notably the use of hand axes, wooden spears and FIRE. *Homo erectus* was so successful adaptively that populations grew to colonize a wide range of new habitats, spreading from Africa to Eurasia, reaching Britain (BOXGROVE), China (ZHOUKOUDIEN) and Indonesia (Sangiran). Between 500,000 and 100,000 ya *Homo erectus* evolved into anatomically modern HOMO SAPIENS SAPIENS in Africa. In Europe it evolved into HOMO SAPIENS NEANDERTHALENSIS, while in southeast Asia it may have survived until about 60,000 ya, becoming extinct only with the arrival of anatomically modern humans in the region. ▷ 1.01, 1.02

HOMO HABILIS

The earliest human species, probably evolved from AUSTRALOPITHECUS AFARENSIS or AUSTRALOPITHECUS AFRICANUS, that lived in eastern and southern Africa, about 2.5–1.5 million ya. Fossils from OLDUVAI GORGE, KOOBI FORA and SWARTKRANS show that this gracile hominid had hands that were capable of the precise manipulation of objects, and discoveries of contemporary stone tools suggest that *Homo habilis* was the first tool-using hominid. Its brain size was about half that of a modern human. ▷ 1.01

HOMO SAPIENS

Although the origins of *Homo sapiens* ("Wise Man") are debated, this species probably evolved from HOMO ERECTUS populations in Africa and Eurasia, with some distinct regional traits, such as the cold-adapted groups in Europe (which later developed into the NEANDERTHALS). As a sophisticated tool user, *Homo sapiens* developed effective hunting equipment for the first time (projectiles for close-impact spearing of animals), had a wider range of specialized tool industries, may have built shelters, and were adept at using FIRE. ▷ 1.01, 1.02

HOMO SAPIENS NEANDERTHALENSIS

(NEANDERTHAL man) Specialized cold-adapted human species that evolved in west Eurasia and the Middle East from late HOMO ERECTUS, about 230,000–150,000 ya. The recent recovery of Neanderthal DNA has shown that they were not ancestral to modern humans. The Neanderthals had short, thick skeletal frames to reduce surface body area exposed to the cold, and heavy facial structures to protect the sinuses and lungs from cold air. They used MIDDLE PALEOLITHIC tools, hunted a range of animals, lived in open settlements and cave sites, and were the first humans to express aesthetic qualities and religious beliefs (formal burials). They became extinct about 28,000 ya, as more numerous and versatile HOMO SAPIENS SAPIENS populations colonized their territories. ▷ 1.01, 1.02, 1.19

HOMO SAPIENS SAPIENS

Anatomically modern man, a regional human adaptation that evolved in Africa about 150,000–100,000 ya, with enhanced cognitive and linguistic capabilities, increasingly complex technologies and social institutions, and new forms of cultural expression in art and ritual. The adaptational success of modern humans, with developed UPPER PALEOLITHIC tool-kits, led to population growth and rapid global colonization, spreading from Africa to east Asia by about 75,000 ya, to Europe by about 40,000 ya, and to the Americas by about 15,000 ya, replacing existing human groups (HOMO SAPIENS variants). All humans today are descendents of the *Homo sapiens sapiens* population that evolved in Africa. ▷ 1.01, 1.02

HOPLITE

Greek infantry soldier of the 7th to 4th centuries BC, notable for his large shield (hoplon), which – joined alongside those of others – enabled him to fight in a heavily protected line. Hoplite battles consisted of tightly packed bodies of troops (phalanxes), about 12 ranks deep, pushing and jabbing their opponents until one side gave way.

HORSE, DOMESTICATION

Probably first domesticated as a food source in the steppe region of southeast Europe and central Asia in the 4th millennium BC, the use of horses as draft animals for pulling wagons and chariots developed in this region from about 2500 BC and spread to the Middle East by about 1700 BC. Horse-riding equipment was invented by the pastoralist cultures of the Eurasian steppes (c.1500–1000 BC), enabling them to adopt a fully nomadic way of life. ▷ 1.03, 1.06, 1.11, 1.19, 1.20, 1.21, 1.22, 1.23

HUANG DI

Mythical third emperor of China and founder of Chinese civilization, traditionally dated to 2698 BC, who "invented" wooden houses, wheeled transport, the bow, writing and moral government. His reign was regarded as a golden age of order and prosperity. ▷ 1.27

HUELVA

See TARTESSOS

HUNTER-GATHERERS

People that depend on wild resources for their subsistence by hunting wild animals, fishing, and gathering plant foods and other materials. All humans were hunter-gatherers until the development of farming about 10,000 ya, each group adapting to local ecological conditions, with highly specialized social and economic systems. By 500 BC agriculture was the dominant mode of livelihood in most parts of the world, and hunter-gatherers were restricted to Arctic regions, North America, parts of South America, southern Africa and Australia. ▷ 1.01, 1.02, 1.03, 1.04, 1.05, 1.06, 1.08, 1.16, 1.19, 1.20

HURRIANS

People closely related to the Urartians, from the area to the southwest of the Caspian Sea, who moved into MESOPOTAMIA and Anatolia in the late 3rd millennium BC. They settled in northern Mesopotamia and Syria, overran ASSYRIA in about 1680 BC, and had established the powerful kingdom of MITTANI by about 500 BC. ▷ 1.11, 1.12

HYKSOS

Literally "chiefs of foreign lands", Semitic peoples who migrated from Asia to the Nile Delta in the 17th century BC, and whose influence spread throughout Lower Egypt at a time when central Egyptian government was weak (the 2nd Intermediate period). They were expelled from Egypt by AHMOSE I in about 1550 BC. ▷ 1.18

ICE AGES

The cold phases of the PLEISTOCENE EPOCH, a period of extreme oscillation in global temperatures with extensions and contractions of the polar ice sheets. The long-accepted sequence of four glacial/inter-glacial phases from 750,000 ya, recognized in the northern hemisphere, is now known to be too simplistic. Recent studies of polar ice cores and ocean sediments have identified at least 22 major warm and cold phases in the same period. ▷ 1.01, 1.02, 1.08, 1.16, 1.18, 1.19

ICE MAN

The frozen body of a man, dating from about 3350–3120 BC, discovered in an Alpine glacier on the Italian–Austrian border. Preserved equipment lying nearby included leather clothing, a fur hat, BOWS AND ARROWS, COPPER and stone tools, and a backpack made of wood and animal skins. The man had several small linear tatoos on his arms, legs and back. The discovery revealed that metal tools had come into use in west-central Europe far earlier than previously supposed. ▷ 1.20

ILIAD

One of Europe's great epics, traditionally ascribed to HOMER, which tells the story of the hero Achilles during the Greek siege of TROY. A poem about war and the pity of war, it explores the nature of heroism and leadership. It was probably brought to its final form in about 750 BC, but contains material that may be dated to MYCENAEAN times. ▷ 1.24

IMPRESSED POTTERY CULTURES

The earliest farming societies (c.6000–4000 BC) of the west Mediterranean region, characterized by pottery with impressed decoration, such as the Cardial Wares of southern France, and village settlements. Their farming economy, based on cereals, legumes and domestic animals, probably spread along the coast from the Balkans. ▷ 1.20, 1.21

INDO-EUROPEAN LANGUAGES

Group of related languages spoken in Europe, the Middle East and India, the origins of which are disputed. The prevailing view is that they derive from dialects spoken in the west Eurasian steppe region in the 4th to 3rd millennia BC, which spread as a result of population migrations. An alternative argument sees Indo-European origins in the adoption of Middle Eastern farming and associated economic and social practices, which spread throughout the Indo-European area in the NEOLITHIC period, from about 7000 to 5000 BC. ▷ 1.11, 1.12, 1.26

INDO-IRANIAN PEOPLES

Peoples who spoke Indo-Iranian languages, the easternmost branch of the INDO-EUROPEAN LANGUAGE group, who were probably originally pastoral nomads of the central Eurasian steppes. These included the ARYANS, who migrated into northern India in the mid-2nd millennium BC, and the CIMMERIANS, SCYTHIANS, MEDES and Persians who migrated into different parts of the Middle East, Anatolia and Ukraine in the 9th–7th centuries BC. ▷ 1.13, 1.26

INDUS CIVILIZATION

A civilization that had emerged in the Indus valley by 2500 BC, with consistent features across a vast area from the Hindu Kush to the Arabian Sea, and from Baluchistan to Gujarat. STATE formation and URBANIZATION in the early 3rd millennium BC may have been partly stimulated by trade with MESOPOTAMIA. Planned towns, built of mud brick, included walled citadels with monumental buildings, civic granaries and housing areas. The two largest centers, at HARAPPA and MOHENJO-DARO, were probably capital cities, though their relative status is unknown.

The Indus economy was based on IRRIGATION farming of cereals, RICE, legumes and COTTON, with CATTLE for dairy products and traction. Domesticated elephants and camels were also exploited. Evidence exists of long-distance trade in silver, COPPER and lapis lazuli, with distant trading colonies such as SHORTHUGAI in the Hindu Kush, and maritime trade with SUMERIA. Little is known about Indus political organization or religion, but features such as the ritual bath at Mohenjo-Daro are found in later Hindu contexts. Monumental art works are rare, but terracotta figurines, painted pottery, stone seals and an undeciphered pictographic script give the impression of a complex cultural life.

The decline and collapse of the Indus civilization in about 2000–1700 BC has not been fully explained, though flooding, soil degradation, over-population and political fragmentation have been suggested, with the final collapse of an already impoverished society at the time of the ARYAN invasions. Urban state cultures did not develop again in the Indian subcontinent for several centuries. ▷ 1.07, 1.26

INITIAL PERIOD

Period of ANDEAN CIVILIZATION from about 2000 to 900 BC, marked by full dependence on agriculture, farming villages, impressive ceremonial and temple complexes, IRRIGATION systems in the coastal lowlands, and the widespread introduction of pottery and COTTON-weaving. Marked regional cultures in this period gave way after 900 BC to the spread of the Chavín tradition. ▷ 1.28

IONIA, IONIAN GREEKS

A division of the Greek peoples, traditionally descendants of settlers from the Ionian "mother city" of Athens, found in communities on the central-western coast and islands of Asia Minor. Ionians pioneered the Ionic style of architecture and fostered early Greek philosophy. ▷ 1.23

IRON AGE

A subdivision of the THREE AGE SYSTEM that commences and ends at different times in different regions (it could be argued that it continued until the modern industrial era, c.AD 1750). It is misleading as a means of characterizing very complex and varied iron-using cultures. Iron metallurgy was practiced in Anatolia by about 1500 BC and spread rapidly throughout the Old World, except southern Africa, from 1100 to 500 BC. ▷ 1.05, 1.06, 1.12, 1.16, 1.21, 1.24, 1.26, 1.27

IRRIGATION

A means of controlling plant growth by ensuring and regulating water supply to produce consistent harvests and intensify production. Irrigation agriculture was a key factor in the development of complex civilizations in many parts of the world, particularly in MESOPOTAMIA and the Indus valley from the 6th to 3rd millennia BC, north China by 4000 BC, and in Mesoamerica and South America from the 2nd to 1st millennia BC. ▷ 1.03, 1.09, 1.17, 1.26, 1.27, 1.28

ISAIAH

HEBREW prophet of the mid-8th century BC who warned the Israelites about the impending threat of Assyrian conquest (c.735 BC), which he saw in a vision and interpreted as a sign of divine condemnation of Israelite godlessness. ▷ 1.14

ISIN

City in south MESOPOTAMIA, ruled by an AMORITE dynasty by about 2000 BC. It briefly dominated SUMERIA in the 20th century BC, but lost its political independence to Larsa and then BABYLON from about 1800 BC. It reasserted its independence in the 12th and 11th centuries BC, when several kings of Isin dominated BABYLONIA. ▷ 1.11, 1.12

ISRAEL, ANCIENT

HEBREW kingdom founded in the late 11th century BC by King SAUL and consolidated by DAVID (c.1006–965 BC). It reached its greatest extent under SOLOMON (c.965–928 BC), who dominated the region from Sinai to the Euphrates, but split into the two separate kingdoms of JUDAH and Israel in about 920 BC. Thereafter, as Egyptian and Assyrian power revived and internal disunity and hostilities with Judah continued, Israel declined and by the mid-8th century BC it had become a vassal of the Assyrian empire. A rebellion by Hoshea in 727–724 BC was crushed, resulting in the annexation of Israel and the deportation of much of the population. ▷ 1.13, 1.14

ITALICS

Indigenous peoples of Italy from the early IRON AGE, excluding the ETRUSCANS, Greeks and PHOENICIANS. The main groups are the Veneti, UMBRIANS, SABINES, LATINS, SAMNITES, LIGURIANS and OSCANS. They were generally organized into tribes in the earlier 1st millennium BC, and spoke INDO-EUROPEAN Italic languages. ▷ 1.23, 1.25

JANAPADAS

Collective name for the small Hindu kingdoms that developed on the Gangetic plains from about 1000 BC, based on intensive WHEAT and RICE cultivation. These coalesced into 16 larger states (*mahajanapadas*) by about 700 BC. ▷ 1.26

JEBUSITES

People of mixed cultural origins, predominantly CANAANITE, whose city-state, centered on JERUSALEM, was conquered by King DAVID of ISRAEL in about 1000 BC. ▷ 1.14

JEMDET NASR

Transitional phase of Sumerian history, from about 3200 to 2900 BC, at the end of the URUK PERIOD. It was marked by distinctive painted pottery, rich metalwork, the wider use of writing, urban growth and the appearance of monumental sculpture. It precedes the EARLY DYNASTIC period. ▷ 1.10

JERICHO

Important early farming settlement situated in the Jordan valley at the north end of the Dead Sea. The first settlement dates to the late 9th millennium BC, when a NATUFIAN HUNTER-GATHERER village was replaced by the earliest-known town, with a stone defensive wall and mud-brick houses, inhabited by an aceramic farming community. Occupation of the site saw several phases of abandonment and renewal, with a major urban settlement in the 3rd millennium BC, and an urban revival by the CANAANITES in the early 2nd millennium BC. Jericho was occupied by the Israelites in the 12th century BC. ▷ 1.08, 1.09

JERUSALEM

City in Palestine that was founded in the 3rd millennium BC and was a major CANAANITE center by about 2000 BC. Occupied by the JEBUSITES in the late 2nd millennium BC, the

city was captured by King DAVID in about 1000 BC and made the capital of ISRAEL. Jerusalem was massively rebuilt by SOLOMON (c.965–928 BC), with elaborate fortifications and the Great Temple. It was the capital of JUDAH from 922 BC to 586 BC, when the city was destroyed and the population deported by King NEBUCHADNEZZAR of BABYLON. The city was rebuilt when the HEBREWS were allowed to return to Palestine by CYRUS the Great in 538 BC. There was a further major phase of building during the reign of Herod the Great (37–4 BC), but the city suffered serious destruction during the Jewish revolts against Roman rule in the 1st and 2nd centuries AD. ▷ 1.12, 1.13, 1.14, 1.15, 1.23

JIN

Major feudal state of the ZHOU kingdom in northern China in about 1100–250 BC, with a capital at Jiang. It twice became the leading state (hegemon) during the SPRINGS AND AUTUMNS PERIOD: in the late 7th century BC under Duke Wen, and in the early 6th century under Duke Diao. It was constantly at war with its powerful southern neighbor, CHU. Both states declined in the late 6th century as other southern states, WU and Yue, grew more powerful. ▷ 1.27

JOMON CULTURE

Complex HUNTER-GATHERER and early farming culture of Japan, dating from 14,000–2300 ya (300 BC). It is notable for making the earliest pottery in the world (c.13,000 ya). Early Jomon communities were already semi-sedentary, with a rich fishing, food-collecting and hunting economy, living much of the year in permanent settlements of round houses. This tradition continued in the Middle and Late Jomon periods, with a gradual transition to agriculture from about 4000 BC (MILLET, buckwheat and CATTLE), and RICE farming from about 300 BC. ▷ 1.03, 1.04, 1.05, 1.06

JOSHUA

HEBREW warrior who succeeded Moses as leader of the Israelites. According to the Bible he led the invasion of Canaan, though other evidence indicates a more episodic process of conquest and peaceful colonization during the 12th–11th centuries BC. ▷ 1.14

JOSIAH

King of JUDAH (r.c.640–609 BC) who restored its independence and undertook religious reforms, destroying idols and establishing the Great Temple at JERUSALEM as the only official place of worship. His territorial ambitions ended in defeat by the Egyptians at MEGIDDO. ▷ 1.14

JUDAH

Region of Palestine named after one of the tribes of ISRAEL. It became an independent HEBREW kingdom in 922 BC, when civil war led to the division of Israel, and remained

loyal to King REHOBOAM and the Davidic dynasty. Judah remained a separate state, often at war with Israel and other neighbors, until it was conquered by the Assyrians in about 730 BC. King JOSIAH briefly restored independence in about 630 BC, but died fighting the Egyptians. Judah became a vassal state of the neo-Babylonian empire in 605 BC, but rebellions in 597 and 587 BC led to the annexation of the kingdom and the deportion of its population to BABYLONIA. ▷ 1.13, 1.14, 1.18

KALHU

City in ASSYRIA situated on the upper Euphrates, also known as Nimrud, founded by King Shalmaneser I in about 1260 BC. The city was refounded on a larger scale by ASHURNASIRPAL II (c.878 BC) to replace ASHUR as the Assyrian capital (until 707 BC), with massive defences 8 kilometers (5 miles) in circumference, a citadel, a huge ZIGGURAT and palaces richly adorned with sculpted friezes. The city was destroyed by the Babylonians and MEDES in 612 BC. ▷ 1.13

KANESH

City in Anatolia founded in the 3rd millennium BC (the Kultepe TELL site), outside which an Assyrian merchant colony was established in the 19th century BC. Important clay tablets from the Assyrian quarter have revealed details of the Mesopotamian–Anatolian trade in textiles and metals, and of political relations before the rise of the HITTITES. ▷ 1.11, 1.12

KARASUK CULTURE

BRONZE AGE pastoral nomad culture of the Siberian steppes (c.1200–700 BC) that succeeded the AFANASEVO-Andronovo tradition. They were skilled bronze workers, with distant cultural contacts, particularly with late-SHANG China to the east. ▷ 1.05

KARNAK

A vast complex of Egyptian temples on the outskirts of THEBES in Upper Egypt. The most vigorous period of building was the NEW KINGDOM, and the greatest temple that of the god Amun. ▷ 1.18

KASKAS

Tribal people of the mountain areas of northern Anatolia in about 1600–1200 BC. They are mentioned by the HITTITES, who saw them as a major threat because of raiding. Campaigns to control the Kaskas were largely unsuccessful, and in the 14th century BC the Hittites had to build forts to protect their northern frontier. ▷ 1.12

KASSITES

People from the Zagros mountains (Iran–Iraq border) who spoke an INDO-EUROPEAN LANGUAGE and settled in MESOPOTAMIA in the 16th century BC. They established royal dynasties in several cities, notably BABYLON, imposing a system of feudal rule. They were rapidly assimilated by Babylonian aristocracies and native populations. The dynasty that ruled Babylon was destroyed by the Elamites in the mid-12th century BC. ▷ 1.11, 1.12, 1.13

KAUSAMBI

Pre-Mauryan city in the Ganges valley, India, founded by about 800 BC, when it was probably the capital of Kuru (one of the 16 Gangetic *mahajanapadas* or "great realms"). In the 6th century BC the city was enclosed by brick ramparts more than 5 kilometers (3 miles) in circumference. ▷ 1.26

KERMA

Town on the Nile in Upper NUBIA, the capital of the KUSH peoples during the 2nd Intermediate period (during which Egypt was unable to exercise control over Nubia). It gives its name to the Kerma culture (c.2500–1500 BC). ▷ 1.18

KHEPHREN

Fourth PHARAOH (r.2558–2532 BC) of the 4th Dynasty of Egypt, whose monument is the second of the three great PYRAMIDS at Giza. The GREAT SPHINX is part of his burial complex. ▷ 1.17

KHILAKKU

Neo-Hittite kingdom of Cilicia, south Anatolia (c.1200–750 BC), formerly a province of the HITTITE empire. Although elements of Hittite culture survived, from about 900 BC the region was increasingly influenced by Greek colonies on the coast. Khilakku was conquered by the Assyrians in the mid-8th century BC. ▷ 1.13

KHOISAN

Holocene HUNTER-GATHERERS of southern Africa, with related languages (the Khoisan language group) and similar stone-tool technologies and economies evident in the archeological record from about 8000 BC. Although some Khoisan peoples adopted animal-herding from 500 BC, they were increasingly marginalized by BANTU colonists in the 1st millennium AD; a few groups survived into the modern era (e.g. San Bushmen and Hottentots). ▷ 1.04, 1.05, 1.06

KHUFU

Second PHARAOH (r.2589–2566 BC) of the 4th Dynasty of Egypt, responsible for the Great PYRAMID at Giza, the construction of which earned him a reputation for tyranny. Virtually nothing else is known about him. ▷ 1.17

KISH

City in south MESOPOTAMIA that, according to Sumerian tradition, was the first to be founded after the FLOOD. Established by about 3000 BC, the city was a major rival of URUK and UR in the EARLY DYNASTIC PERIOD and King Mesilim of Kish appears to have been pre-eminent in SUMERIA in the early 25th

century BC. The city lost its independence after 2400 BC but remained a prestigious religious center. ▷ 1.10, 1.11

KIZZUWATNA

Kingdom in Cilicia, south Anatolia, mentioned in HITTITE texts in the 2nd millennium BC. Although powerful in the 15th century BC, its status depended on Hittite imperial fortunes, as Kizzuwatna was usually a vassal state. After the collapse of the Hittites in about 1200 BC, the region fragmented into several Neo-Hittite kingdoms. ▷ 1.12

KLEISTHENES

Athenian statesman who was responsible for an important program of constitutional reform in 508–507 BC. It saw the encouragement of local democracy throughout ATTICA and the reorganization of citizens into new tribes, breaking down traditional regional alliances and allowing all to focus their political energies on the city-state (POLIS) itself. The reforms paved the way for full democracy in 461 BC. ▷ 1.15, 1.24

KLEOMENES

King of SPARTA (r.520–490 BC), remembered for his aggressive foreign policy. He crushed Sparta's old enemy, ARGOS, organized the remaining Peloponnesian cities into the so-called Spartan (Peloponnesian) league (an alliance of states under the leadership of Sparta), and ousted the TYRANT HIPPIAS from Athens (510 BC). ▷ 1.24

KNOSSOS

One of the oldest inhabited sites in CRETE and, from 2000 BC, the site of the most impressive and sophisticated palace complex of the MINOAN CIVILIZATION. It was even designed to withstand earthquakes. At its height in about 1600 BC, the palace and its rulers probably controlled most of the island. It was also a center for sophisticated religious rituals, including bull-leaping. The palace appears to have been taken over by the MYCENAEANS (c.1450 BC) and probably collapsed with their civilization in about 1200 BC. ▷ 1.22

KOOBI FORA

Site of early hominid fossil finds on the east side of Lake Turkana in Kenya, east Africa. The deep deposits of ancient lake sediments contain remains of AUSTRALOPITHECUS ROBUSTUS, HOMO HABILIS and HOMO ERECTUS, as well as evidence of stone-tool working (chopper and flake tools) and animal butchery sites dating from about 2.5 to 1.3 million ya. ▷ 1.01

KOSALA

One of the *mahajanapadas* ("great realms"), an ancient kingdom of northern India, which rose to prominence in the 6th century BC. It was the setting for several stories in Sanskrit literature, including the *Ramayana*. Its capital

was Ayodhya (later moved to Sravasti). In about 500 BC it controlled most of the trade routes in the Ganges basin, but in the following decades it was conquered by Magadha.

KOTOSH TRADITION

Cultural tradition of the PRECERAMIC and INITIAL periods in the Andean highlands of South America from about 2300 to 1200 BC. It is characterized by the development of permanent villages, root crops and cereal farming, camelid herding, monumental architecture, and the earliest pottery in the Andes region (from c.1750 BC). It is named after the site of a temple complex. ▷ 1.28

KOW SWAMP

Early cemetery in south Australia, with formal burials of about 50 individuals dating from about 14,000 to 8000 ya (6000 BC). It is the largest burial population of the late PLEISTOCENE period. Although all anatomically modern humans (HOMO SAPIENS SAPIENS), the skulls have robust archaic features. Grave goods found in some of the burials included shells and stone tools. ▷ 1.02

KULLI

Early BRONZE AGE urban culture of the highland area to the west of the Indus in Baluchistan, with distinctive painted pottery and carved stone vessels. Towns such as Nindowari and Kulli, founded in the early 4th millennium BC, traded in metals with the Indus valley and were possibly influenced by Mesopotamian trade contacts along the coast. The Kulli region fell within the territory of the INDUS CIVILIZATION in the mid-3rd millennium BC. ▷ 1.26

KULTEPE

See KANESH

KUSH

The land of Kush lay to the south of Egypt in NUBIA and was controlled by the strong Egyptian dynasties. In the so-called Kushite period (747–656 BC), kings from Kush controlled Egypt in their turn. They later moved their capital further up the Nile to MEROË (fl.c.300 BC–AD 350). ▷ 1.16, 1.18

KYMAI (CUMAE)

Located at modern Cuma in Campania, this was a Euboean colony founded in about 740 BC. It dominated coastal Campania from 700 to 474 BC, but fell to the OSCANS in 421 BC. Kymai was an ally of ROME in the Punic wars and flourished under the empire. The Cumaean sibyl and the cult of Apollo was important in Augustan ideology, and the area was a popular location for elite Roman villas. The site declined in the 3rd and 4th centuries AD. ▷ 1.23, 1.25

LA VENTA

Largest OLMEC ceremonial center, situated on an island surrounded by swamps, near the

Gulf of Mexico. The main monument complex had a linear arrangement of platforms, pavements, shrines and enclosures oriented on the Great Pyramid, a 30-meter (100-foot) high clay mound. These were adorned with fine stone sculptures and offerings of jade figurines. The principal monuments were built from about 1000 BC, and the site was violently destroyed in about 400 BC.

LACHISH

City in Palestine founded in the mid-3rd millennium BC and a CANAANITE town and religious center from about 1500 BC. It was occupied by the Israelites in the 10th century BC and fortified by REHOBOAM. Lachish was sacked in 701 BC by the Assyrian king SENNACHERIB, who had the event recorded in reliefs at his palace at NINEVEH. The city was again sacked, by the Babylonians, in 588–587 BC and was finally abandoned in the 2nd century BC. ▷ 1.14

LACONIA

Mountainous region in the central-southern Peloponnese and the home territory of SPARTA, which drew on the fertility of the Eurotas valley between the main mountain ranges. The word "laconic" reflects the tradition that the Spartans – unlike most Greeks – were uncommunicative by nature. ▷ 1.24

LAETOLI

Site of hominid fossil finds close to OLDUVAI GORGE in Tanzania, east Africa. Remains of AUSTRALOPITHECUS AFARAENSIS were found in wind-blown sediments, together with remarkable footprints, about 3.6 million years old, of fully bipedal hominids preserved in ancient muds. Later discoveries included the early remains of HOMO SAPIENS dating from about 120,000 ya. ▷ 1.01

LAGASH

Sumerian city that became a major city-state in the EARLY DYNASTIC PERIOD and briefly dominated south MESOPOTAMIA after King Eannatum conquered the city of KISH (c.2400 BC). Control of Lagash later fell to UMMA and to SARGON of AGADE, but its power revived in the 22nd century BC when it was rebuilt by Gudea, a vassal king of GUTIAN overlords. The city declined after its capture by Larsa in about 2100 BC. ▷ 1.09, 1.10, 1.11

LASCAUX

Cave site in southwest France, famous for its magnificent UPPER PALEOLITHIC paintings and engravings of animals, especially aurochs, red deer and horses. The cave was probably used for ritual purposes in the MAGDALENIAN period (c.17,000–14,000 ya). ▷ 1.19

LATINS, LATIUM

The Latins were an ITALIC group occupying the area between the Tiber and Campania, known in antiquity as Latium Vetus. By the 6th century BC the main settlements had become city-states. ROME, also a Latin city, had conquered the whole area by 300 BC, and the Latial cities declined as Rome developed and as the area was disturbed by warfare during the late republic. ▷ 1.25

LEPENSKI VIR

Late MESOLITHIC settlement of the 7th millennium BC, beside the river Danube in Serbia. The community was semi-sedentary, living in permanent trapezoidal houses, with a complex fishing and hunting economy. Several houses had human burials in the floors, and notable carved stone statuettes of human heads, some with fish-like features. ▷ 1.19

LEVANT

East Mediterrannean region between Anatolia and Sinai, extending inland to the Arabian desert. Sometimes described as the "Near East", it comprises the modern countries of Israel, Palestine, Lebanon, west Jordan and west Syria. The earliest farming societies developed in this region in the 9th millennium BC. It was a key area of URBANIZATION and STATE formation from the 4th millennium BC, and the main stage for imperial struggles between Egypt, ASSYRIA, MITTANI, the HITTITES and the Israelites in the 2nd–1st millennia BC. ▷ 1.07, 1.08, 1.09, 1.10, 1.11, 1.12, 1.13, 1.14, 1.18, 1.23

LIGURIANS

Indigenous group of southern France and northeast Italy that became Celticized from the 3rd century BC, through amicable relations with neighboring Gauls. Greek settlements developed on the Mediterranean coast from about 600 BC, and the area was conquered by the Romans between 238 and 117 BC. No archeological culture can be equated with the Ligurians. ▷ 1.23, 1.25

LINEAR A SCRIPT

Script that evolved in CRETE in about 1800 BC and was used by the Minoans to record quantities of goods, the ownership of produce and – in some cases – religious texts. Linear A signs stand for syllables. The script has not been deciphered, and disappeared in about 1450 BC. ▷ 1.22

LINEAR B SCRIPT

Script similar to LINEAR A but in a different language, that first appeared on CRETE in about 1450 BC and spread to the Greek mainland. Linear B script was used to record quantities of goods and administrative matters. Decipherment by Michael Ventris in 1952 revealed the language to be an early form of GREEK and showed that the Mycenaeans had adopted the script from Linear A. ▷ 1.22

LINEAR POTTERY culture

See BANDKERAMIK CULTURE

LINEN (FLAX)

Woven fabric made from cultivated plant fiber (flax), first produced in the Middle East in the 7th millennium BC. This plant and associated weaving technologies spread across the Middle East to Anatolia and Europe: there is evidence of linen clothing in Egypt and at NEOLITHIC lake villages in Switzerland by the 4th millennium BC. ▷ 1.03, 1.08, 1.09, 1.16

LLAMA

Camelid domesticated in the Andes of South America, possibly as early as the 5th millennium BC, closely related to the alpaca, wild guanaco and vicuna. Llamas were mainly used as pack animals and as sources of WOOL, food and leather. ▷ 1.03, 1.28

LOGOGRAPHIC SCRIPTS

Writing systems in which signs represent units of meaning (morphemes) rather than units of sound, as in phonographic scripts. The most widely used logographic script is CHINESE, which developed in the 1st millennium BC and has thousands of signs, each with a different meaning or set of meanings depending on the context of use. ▷ 1.07

LONGHOUSES, NEOLITHIC

Elongated rectangular or trapezoidal buildings of the early Neolithic BANDKERAMIK CULTURE of central Europe (c.5500–4500 BC). Longhouses were massive constructions, up to 50 meters (160 feet) in length, some with rows of entire tree trunks set in pits to support the superstructure. They probably housed extended families of between 20 and 40 people, similar to more recent examples in southeast Asia and North America. ▷ 1.20

LONGSHAN CULTURE

Late NEOLITHIC culture (c.3200–1800 BC) of the Yellow river region in northern China, with distinctive wheel-thrown pottery, polished stone tools, ORACLE BONES for divination, and intensive RICE cultivation. Their large settlements, rammed earth fortifications and evidence of warfare and prestige goods indicate a CHIEFDOM society that was more complex and hierarchical than the preceding YANGSHAO farming culture. ▷ 1.04, 1.05, 1.27

LOS MILLARES

Important Copper Age settlement in southern Spain, consisting of a heavily fortified village protected by several outlying citadels, with a large cemetery of collective tombs nearby. The scale and prosperity of the site in the 3rd millennium BC was based on a rich agricultural economy, control of local COPPER sources and trade in prestige goods. ▷ 1.20, 1.21

LOTHAL

Southern port of the INDUS CIVILIZATION, situated at the head of the Gulf of Khambat, Gujarat. The rectangular town was enclosed by a brick wall, with a citadel, granaries, and a housing and craft-working quarter. Outside the town was a large brick-built basin, possibly a dock or reservoir. Artifacts from the site indicate trade contacts with the Persian Gulf. ▷ 1.26

LU
Large feudal state of the ZHOU kingdom, with a capital city at Qufu, in about 1100–250 BC. It was the home of the philosopher CONFUCIUS (c.551–479 BC), who served as a bureaucrat. Lu played only a minor role in the power struggles of the SPRINGS AND AUTUMNS PERIOD as the authority of the Zhou dynasty declined (from c.770 BC). ▷ 1.27

LUCY (AUSTRALOPITHECUS AFARENSIS)
The most complete fossil remains (about 40 percent) of an individual AUSTRALOPITHECUS AFARENSIS hominid, about 3.5 million years old, found at HADAR in Ethiopia. Nicknamed "Lucy" by the excavators, the female australopithecine was bipedal and stood only about 1.2 meters (4 feet) tall. ▷ 1.01

LUGALZAGESI
King of the city of UMMA (c.2375–2350 BC) in south MESOPOTAMIA. He established a short-lived empire by conquering the pre-eminent city of LAGASH, along with KISH, UR and URUK, but was in turn conquered by SARGON of AGADE, who took over his dominions. ▷ 1.10, 1.11

LULLUBIANS
Tribal people of the Zagros mountains who are mentioned in Akkadian inscriptions of the late 3rd millennium BC, when they raided or traded with lowland communites. The Lullubians were later absorbed by the Elamite kingdom. ▷ 1.11

LUMBINI
Mythical grove in the foothills of the Himalayas where Queen Maha Maya gave birth to Siddhartha Gautama, the future BUDDHA, in about 563 BC. ▷ 1.26

LUOYANG
City to the south of the Yellow river in Honan province, northern China, founded in the 12th century BC. It became the capital of the ZHOU state in about 770 BC, after their ancient capital at HAO was exposed to barbarian attacks. The city was captured by QIN in about 256 BC. ▷ 1.27

LUVIANS
People of southwest Anatolia in the 2nd millennium BC, who spoke an INDO-EUROPEAN LANGUAGE that was related to HITTITE and Lydian. The Luvians may have contributed to the collapse of the Hittite empire. The latest hieroglyphic Luvian inscriptions date from the 7th century BC, and Lycian (written from about 600 to 200 BC) is believed to derive from a Luvian dialect. ▷ 1.05, 1.12

LUXOR
The site of an important NEW KINGDOM temple to the Egyptian god Amun. Each year, at the Festival of Opet, when the Nile began reflooding, a cult statue of the god was carried from his temple at KARNAK to a ceremony at Luxor symbolizing the sexual relationship between the god and the mother of the reigning PHARAOH. ▷ 1.18

LYDIA, LYDIANS
An area of central Asia Minor consolidated as a kingdom under the Mermnad dynasty (c.700–545 BC). Lydia exploited its central position on trade routes to become conspicuously wealthy, and is credited with the invention of COINAGE in about 600 BC. It was absorbed into the ACHEMENID EMPIRE in 545 BC, after the defeat of its last king, CROESUS. ▷ 1.15, 1.23, 1.24

MAES HOWE
Famous early NEOLITHIC PASSAGE GRAVE in ORKNEY, dating from the early 3rd millennium BC, with a finely built MEGALITHIC tomb structure covered by an enormous mound and surrounded by a rock-cut ditch. The passage is oriented towards sunset at the midwinter solstice. ▷ 1.20

MAGDALENIAN
The last cultural phase (c.17,000–11,000 ya) of the UPPER PALEOLITHIC period in western and central Europe. The Magdalenian communities were specialized reindeer hunters, and later turned to sea-mammal hunting using distinctive bone harpoons. They are also renowned for their works of art and the most accomplished and impressive cave paintings are Magdalenian in date, including those at LASCAUX and ALTAMIRA. ▷ 1.19

MAGNA GRAECIA
"Greater Greece", the name given to southern Italy (sometimes including Sicily) after its extensive colonization by the Greeks from the 8th century BC. ▷ 1.25

MAHAJANAPADAS
See JANAPADAS

MAIZE
Cereal plant that was domesticated in Mesoamerica in the early 3rd millennium BC. By about 2300 BC, maize formed the staple crop of farming communities in Mesoamerica, spreading to South America in about 1000–800 BC and to the southwestern deserts of North America by about AD 300. With the development of cold-resistant strains, maize also became a staple food crop in the eastern woodlands of North America by about AD 800. Maize cultivation facilitated surplus production and reliable food storage, which led to the development of permanent villages and population growth. ▷ 1.03, 1.28

MANNEANS
People to the east of Lake Urmia who are mentioned in Assyrian and Urartuan texts of the 9th–7th centuries BC. Little is known of their history or culture, though they may have spoken a language related to Hurrian. They were overrun by the SCYTHIANS and MEDES in the 7th century BC. ▷ 1.13

MARI
City in central MESOPOTAMIA beside the Euphrates in modern Syria, strategically situated to control the trade route between SUMERIA and the LEVANT. It was one of the most powerful Mesopotamian city-states in the 3rd millennium BC. Thousands of clay tablets have been found in the palace of the last king, Zimri-lim (c.1790–1757 BC), including diplomatic correspondence, historical and legal archives, and treasury records. The city was destroyed by HAMMURABI of BABYLON in 1757 BC and never regained its former power. ▷ 1.10, 1.11

MASSILIA
The modern Marseilles, founded as a Greek colony by the Phocaeans (from the coast of Asia Minor) in about 600 BC. It exploited the trade routes up the Rhône to the Celtic heartlands of Gaul, and is credited with the introduction of the vine and the olive to France. ▷ 1.23, 1.25

MASTABAS
Egyptian tombs in which the underground chamber is surmounted by a rectangular structure whose walls slope inwards. *Mastabas* were used for royal and noble burials during the early dynasties. The name comes from the similarly shaped benches found outside modern Egyptian homes. ▷ 1.17

MEDES, MEDIAN EMPIRE
INDO-IRANIAN PEOPLE, originally pastoral nomads from central Asia, who settled in northwest Iran in the 9th century BC. The Medes established a unified kingdom in the 8th century BC, with a capital at Hamadan. Little is known about Median culture, as written records have not survived, and most of their works of art appear to be Assyrian-inspired.

Under King Cyaxares (r.c.625–585 BC), the Medes became a major power in the Middle East by destroying the Assyrian empire, sacking ASHUR in 614 BC, and (with the Babylonians) capturing NINEVEH in 612. Cyaxares and his son, Astyages (r.585–550 BC), established a short-lived empire which extended from central Iran to the Persian Gulf and Anatolia. The empire disintegrated in 550 BC when CYRUS the Great of Persia rebelled against Median rule, defeating Astyages at PASARGADAE. The Median aristocracy submitted and were given senior roles in the new administration; Media became a satrapy of the ACHEMENID EMPIRE. ▷ 1.13, 1.15

MEDITERRANEAN TRIAD

The so-called Mediterranean triad consisted of three staple crops: cereals, olives and vines. They could be farmed together on the same land and even in the most disastrous of years, at least one would crop. They formed the backbone of the Greek agricultural economy from the 8th century BC, with olives and vines spreading overseas with Greek settlements.

MEGALITHIC MONUMENT

Ceremonial or mortuary structure built of "large stones" (from the Greek words *megas* and *lithikos*). The term is mainly applied to the NEOLITHIC and BRONZE AGE stone architecture of Europe, including CHAMBERED TOMBS, STONE CIRCLES and avenues, but is also applicable to building traditions such as the IRON AGE MEGALITHIC TOMB CULTURE of India. ▷ 1.04, 1.20, 1.21, 1.26

MEGALITHIC TOMB CULTURE (INDIA)

Small-scale IRON AGE agricultural societies of southern India in the 1st millennium BC that built distinctive MEGALITHIC tombs and other ceremonial monuments. This cultural tradition had indigenous NEOLITHIC origins and developed largely independently of the urban, state-organized societies of northern India. One of the culture's most important sites, Brahmagiri, contains more than 300 tombs and STONE CIRCLES. ▷ 1.26

MEGIDDO

Strategic town in Palestine, founded in the 4th millennium BC. It was often sacked and rebuilt, and owed allegiance to a succession of Egyptian, CANAANITE and Israelite rulers. It was refortified by SOLOMON of ISRAEL in about 1000 BC, and was a major fortress of the kingdom of JUDAH. ▷ 1.14

MEHRGARH

NEOLITHIC village in Baluchistan that was occupied from the 7th to 4th millennia BC. The adoption of Middle Eastern domesticates and similarities with aceramic farming settlements in the FERTILE CRESCENT suggest that agriculture spread rapidly across Iran. The long occupation sequence, with numerous layers of mud-brick houses, also provides important evidence of cultural change from the first village to the proto-urban center of the 4th millennium BC. ▷ 1.26

MEMPHIS

Strategically situated where the narrow Nile valley begins to broaden out into the Delta, Memphis was the natural choice for an Egyptian capital after the first unification of the country in about 3100 BC. The city remained an important administrative center throughout Egyptian history, and only fell into decline when Alexandria was built in the late 4th century BC. ▷ 1.13, 1.15, 1.17, 1.18

MENTUHOTPE II

Egyptian PHARAOH (r.2061–2010 BC) who is remembered for restoring order to the borders of Egypt following the breakdown of authority in the 1st Intermediate period. His impressive burial complex near THEBES, his capital, drew heavily on OLD KINGDOM models, doubtless as a means of asserting his legitimacy. ▷ 1.18

MEROË

Town situated on the Nile in NUBIA. It was the capital city of the Kushite kingdom in the 5th century BC, after the Kushites had retreated southwards from Egypt. An important center for IRON WORKING, the town later gave its name to the Meroitic kingdom, which was at its height from 300 BC to AD 350. Meroitic culture was heavily Egyptianized; its rulers were buried in small PYRAMIDS and worshipped Egyptian gods. ▷ 1.06, 1.15

MESILIM OF KISH

See KISH

MESOAMERICAN CIVILIZATIONS

A series of related Mesoamerican cultures that developed complex societies with STATE systems, ceremonial centers, cities and rich iconography and material culture, as well as the only fully literate culture of the ancient Americas (the Maya civilization of the Classic period). The history of Mesoamerican civilizations is divided into the following periods: ARCHAIC (c.7000–2000 BC), EARLY PRECLASSIC (c.2000–800 BC), MIDDLE PRECLASSIC (c.800–300 BC), Late Preclassic (c.300 BC–AD 300), Classic (c.AD 300–800), and Postclassic (c.AD 800–1520). ▷ 1.04, 1.05, 1.06, 1.07, 1.28

MESOLITHIC

The period of cultural transition in Europe (c.8000–4000 BC), following the end of the last glaciation, when UPPER PALEOLITHIC HUNTER-GATHERERS developed specialized cultural systems adapted to changing climatic conditions and new habitats. Mesolithic communities used sophisticated tool-kits with MICROLITHIC technology and a new emphasis on fishing equipment. In resource-rich coastal areas, such as Brittany and Denmark, the appearance in the late Mesolithic of semi-permanent settlements, ritual sites and formal burials suggests population growth and more complex social systems (e.g. ERTEBOLLE culture). These were the last groups in western Europe to adopt agricultural practices, and the first to build MEGALITHIC tombs. ▷ 1.19, 1.20

MESOPOTAMIAN CIVILIZATION

The distinctive STATE-organized urban cultures of the Tigris and Euphrates river system that formed a core area of civilization from the 4th millennium BC. Its key features include the first cities and large-scale IRRIGATION (by 3500 BC), the earliest writing system (Sumerian pictographs and CUNEIFORM), and

first imperial state (SARGON OF AGADE's Akkadian empire, c.2330 BC). Mesopotamian civilization was highly varied because of its diverse origins in independent city-states and its distinct ethnic communities, but it developed a shared religious and literate tradition with a considerable degree of continuity and integration, as each new dominant state tolerated local customs and adopted cultural and political features of their predecessors.

The complex history of the region can be divided into the following periods (with intermediate periods of political and cultural instability): URUK (c.4300–3100 BC), JEMDET NASR (c.3200–2900 BC), EARLY DYNASTIC (c.2900–2334 BC), Akkadian empire (c.2350–2200 BC), Third Dynasty of UR (c.2100–2000 BC), Old Babylonian and Old Assyrian (c.1900–1600 BC), Middle Assyrian empire (c.1360–1075 BC), Neo-Assyrian empire (c.930–612 BC) and Neo-Babylonian empire (612–539 BC). ▷ 1.04, 1.05, 1.10, 1.11, 1.12, 1.13, 1.14, 1.15

MESSENIA

Plain in the southwest Peloponnese annexed by SPARTA in the 8th century BC. Its native Greek peoples, the HELOTS as they became known, were treated as slaves by the Spartans and forced to work the land for their overlords. The area was liberated from Spartan control by the Thebans in the mid-4th century BC. ▷ 1.24

MEZHIRICH

UPPER PALEOLITHIC settlement in the Ukraine with a hut built partly of mammoth bones, dating from about 20,000 ya. The bones were probably used to weigh down tent awnings, but may also have had some social or religious significance. ▷ 1.19

MICHELSBERG

Late NEOLITHIC post-BANDKERAMIK CULTURE of the Rhineland and northern France, between about 4000 and 2800 BC. It is named after a ceremonial enclosure site in the middle Rhine valley, with distinctive material culture and settlement sites. ▷ 1.20

MICROLITHIC TOOLS

Composite tools made of tiny, stone blade fragments, or "microliths", set in hafts singly (such as arrowheads) or edge-to-edge in groups (such as projectile barbs and sickle blades). Microliths are often geometric in shape and were made by snapping long blades into pieces for more versatile use. Microlithic tools are characteristic of the MESOLITHIC period in Europe but were used by many other cultures. ▷ 1.19

MIDAS

See MITAS

MIDDLE KINGDOM

Period in Egyptian history (c.2055–1650 BC) characterized by stability and prosperity. The

PHARAOH MENTUHOTPE II (12th Dynasty) successfully stabilized the kingdom over a long reign and order was maintained until a succession of weaker pharaohs of the 13th Dynasty lost control of the Delta and allowed the infiltration of the HYKSOS people. At its height the Middle Kingdom saw effective Egyptian control over NUBIA. It was also an age that produced the most famous of the so-called "Wisdom Texts', which extolled the virtues of good administration. ▷ 1.18

MIDDLE PRECLASSIC PERIOD
Period of MESOAMERICAN CIVILIZATION from about 800 to 300 BC, in which OLMEC CIVILIZATION reached the height of its cultural achievement, particularly in stone sculpture, jade carving and temple building, before it collapsed in the 5th to 4th centuries BC. Mayan civilization, which emerged in highland Guatemala and the Yucatán peninsula, has many features in common with the Olmecs, but also developed large-scale IRRIGATION farming systems that facilitated settlement growth and STATE formation (c.600–300 BC). Another complex society emerged in this period in the OAXACA VALLEY, Mexico, where the earliest writing system in the New World (ZAPOTEC hieroglyphic) was invented in the 8th century BC. ▷ 1.06, 1.07, 1.28

MILETOS
Important Greek city-state on the west coast of Asia Minor whose wealth came from its rich territory and trade. In the 6th century BC Miletos was an effective colonizer of the Black Sea coast, and the same period saw the work of its famous philosophers, Thales, Anaximander and Anaximenes. A leader of the unsuccessful IONIAN revolt against the Persians (499 BC), it never fully recovered its prosperity. ▷ 1.22, 1.23, 1.24

MILLET
Several species of grasses that produce small edible seeds, domesticated in different parts of the world at different times, notably in China, sub-Saharan Africa and Ethiopia by the 6th millennium BC, and in the Middle East by the 4th millennium BC. ▷ 1.03, 1.16, 1.27

MINOAN PALACE CIVILIZATION
Important civilization that flourished on CRETE between 2000 and 1450 BC. It was centered on large palaces (KHANIA, KNOSSOS, MALLIA and PHAISTOS), which were also religious and administrative centers. Originally relying on an agricultural economy, the Minoans also traded extensively in the Aegean and were fine craftsmen and fresco painters. Their civilization collapsed, probably as the result of a MYCENAEAN invasion. ▷ 1.07, 1.20, 1.22

MIOCENE EPOCH
Period of the Tertiary era (c.25–5 million ya), marked by cooling climatic conditions in which mammal species increasingly dominat-ed terrestrial fauna, with hominid evolution in eastern Africa. ▷ 1.01

MITAS (MIDAS)
King of PHRYGIA, whose dates are traditionally given as 738–695 BC. A figure of fun for the Greeks, his greed is remembered in the story that he wished for everything he touched to be turned to gold, and then found he could not eat or drink anything. ▷ 1.13

MITTANI
A kingdom of north MESOPOTAMIA and Syria founded by HURRIAN invaders by about 1550 BC, after the decline of the Assyrian and Babylonian states which had ruled the region in the 19–17th centuries BC. Mittani controlled the strategic routes linking Hittite Anatolia, Mesopotamia, the Levantine ports, the Aegean states and Egypt, and was a major regional power from about 1500 to 1350 BC. It collapsed in the early 13th century BC after the HITTITES sacked the capital, WASHUKANNI, and conquered the western part of the kingdom (c.1340 BC), leaving the remainder to be conquered by the Assyrians (by c.1270 BC). Little is known about the political organization or culture of the Mittani state, which left few written records. ▷ 1.12, 1.18

MOAB
Highland region of Palestine to the east of the Dead Sea occupied in biblical times by the Moabites, a Semitic people closely related to the Israelites, who may have settled in Palestine in the 14th century BC. The Moabite kingdom was often at war with ISRAEL and JUDAH, and was destroyed by the Babylonians in about 582 BC. ▷ 1.13, 1.14

MOHENJO-DARO
The largest of the two great cities of the INDUS CIVILIZATION (the other being HARAPPA), situated beside the Indus river in Sind (south Pakistan). The city was probably founded in the early 3rd millennium BC, laid out in a series of residential blocks with a grid street plan and drainage system. On one side of the city was a monumental brick-built citadel which may have served as the royal and religious center of the Indus state, with a huge granary, residential buildings, aisled ceremonial halls and a ritual bath. Massive flooding and local environmental deterioration probably led to its decline and eventual abandonment by about 1700 BC. ▷ 1.26

MOUSTERIAN CULTURE
MIDDLE PALEOLITHIC tool industry of west Eurasia and north Africa, about 150,000 to 40,000 ya, that is often associated with HOMO SAPIENS NEANDERTHALENSIS. The Mousterian culture is characterized by its distinctive flaking techniques and range of tools, including small hand axes, flake tools, and the first hafted projectiles (spears for close-impact hunting of large game). Differences in tool assemblages from site to site may indicate cultural variation or seasonal specializations. ▷ 1.01, 1.19

MUMMIFICATION
The process, used by the ancient Egyptians, of preserving a corpse in preparation for burial, in the belief that only a preserved body ("mummy") could enjoy an afterlife. Carried out in accordance with strict rules over a period of some 70 days, it involved preserving some organs separately, while soaking the rest of the body in natron, a natural drying agent. The body was then bound in cloth and placed in a coffin.

MURSILIS I
King of the HITTITES (r.c.1620–1590 BC). The most successful king of the Old Kingdom period, he extended Hittite rule in Anatolia and northern Syria, and undertook a campaign down the Euphrates, sacking BABYLON in 1595 BC. He was killed in a palace coup. ▷ 1.11

MUSHKI (MYSIANS)
People who were related to the PHRYGIANS and who settled in northeast Anatolia in the 12th century BC, after the collapse of the HITTITE empire. Allied with native HURRIANS and KASKAS, they invaded MESOPOTAMIA but were defeated by TIGLATH-PILESER I of ASSYRIA in 1115 BC. ▷ 1.12

MUWATALLIS II
King of the HITTITES (r.1295–1271 BC). He opposed the Egyptian attempt under PHAROAH RAMESSES II to regain control of Syria and inflicted a strategic defeat on the Egyptian PHARAOH at the Battle of QADESH (c.1285 BC), successfully extending Hittite control as far south as Damascus. ▷ 1.12

MYCENAE
An impressively fortified hilltop city with a palace and lavishly furnished royal tombs in the Peloponnese, occupied from the 16th to 12th centuries BC. Its most famous features are the famous Lion Gate and the so-called "Treasury of Atreus", actually a magnificent THOLOS tomb. Mycenae was excavated in the 19th century by the pioneering German archeologist, Heinrich Schliemann, and many spectacular artifacts, including gold death masks, were discovered. ▷ 1.21, 1.22, 1.23

MYCENAEAN CIVILIZATION
First GREEK-speaking civilization (c.1600–1200 BC), named after MYCENAE, its most important site. The Mycenaean civilization centered on a number of independent rulers, each with their own stronghold. Mycenaeans traded extensively overseas and conquered CRETE in about 1450 BC, where they adapted the LINEAR A script to write their own language (LINEAR B). Excavations at many Mycenaean sites, including Mycenae, indicate that the civilization came to a violent end, though its attackers are unknown. ▷ 1.21, 1.22, 1.23

NABATEAN ALPHABET
Variant of the CANAANITE phonetic alphabet developed by the Nabataeans in Arabia for writing their ARAMAIC LANGUAGE (c.1000 BC). It was most widely used in the Nabataean kingdom of Petra from about 150 BC to AD 150, and gave rise to the Arabic scripts of the Middle Ages. ▷ 1.07

NABONIDUS
The last king of BABYLON (r.555–539 BC). An imperial official crowned by the ruling aristocracy, Nabonidus was defeated by CYRUS the Great of Persia in 539 BC, after which BABYLONIA submitted peacefully to ACHEMENID rule. ▷ 1.13, 1.15

NABOPOLASSAR
King of BABYLON (r.626–605 BC) and the king of the CHALDEAN 11th dynasty, who reasserted Babylonian independence. Nabopolassar drove the Assyrians out of BABYLONIA before attacking ASSYRIA. He destroyed the Assyrian capital at NINEVEH in 612 BC and took over Assyrian domains. ▷ 1.13

NAPATA
District of NUBIA that served as the center of the Kushite kingdom between 1000 BC and 300 BC, before the kingdom moved southwards to MEROË.

NARAM-SIN
King of AKKAD (r.2254–2218 BC), who was the grandson of SARGON OF AGADE and ruled the Akkadian empire at the height of its power. He consolidated Akkadian domains, protected key trade routes, founded numerous temples and may have assumed theocratic powers. ▷ 1.11

NARMER
Early Egyptian ruler who was possibly responsible for the first unification of Egypt (c.3000 BC) and the foundation of the capital at MEMPHIS. The famous Narmer palette found at HIERAKONPOLIS shows for the first time a king wearing the Crowns of both Lower and Upper Egypt. ▷ 1.17

NATUFIAN CULTURE
Late glacial and early Holocene EPIPALEOLITHIC culture, dating from about 12,500 to 10,500 ya (8500 BC), of the LEVANT and Syriax, with an intensive cereal-collecting and gazelle-hunting economy. They became increasingly settled, living in small villages of permanent houses at sites such as JERICHO, with shrines and formal burials, and selectively modified plant-growing conditions that led to incipient farming. ▷ 1.08

NEANDERTHALS
See HOMO SAPIENS NEANDERTHALENSIS

NEBUCHADNEZZAR
King of BABYLON (r.604–562 BC), the son of NABOPOLASSAR. While he was still crown-prince he defeated the Egyptians at CARCHEMISH in Syria in 605 BC, and undertook campaigns in Syria, ELAM and the LEVANT, ensuring Babylonian supremacy in the Middle East by about 590 BC. He crushed revolts in JUDAH in 597 and 587 BC, and deported the population to BABYLONIA. He rebuilt his capital at Babylon on a vast and magnificent scale. His dynasty was overthrown soon after his death. ▷ 1.13, 1.15

NECHO II
Egyptian PHARAOH (r.610–595 BC), the third of the Saite dynasty, who founded Egypt's first navy and reconquered the LEVANT as the ASSYRIAN EMPIRE disintegrated. He was finally checked by the Babylonians in 605 BC. ▷ 1.13

NEOLITHIC
The final phase of the STONE AGE, in which farming was the main form of subsistence production, leading to population growth, village settlements and ranking, while stone remained the principal material used in tool manufacture. The term is still used to refer to early agricultural societies in the Old World. ▷ 1.03, 1.04, 1.06, 1.08, 1.09, 1.10, 1.16, 1.19, 1.20, 1.27

NEW KINGDOM
The third and final of the three great kingdoms of ancient Egypt (1550–1070 BC). The period saw the extension of Egyptian power into Syria and Palestine and the intense exploitation of NUBIA. Among its great PHARAOHS was the conqueror TUTHMOSIS III, the heretic king AKHENATEN and the great builder RAMESSES II; among its most spectacular legacies are the contents of the tomb of TUTANKHAMUN. In the late New Kingdom the power of the temple priesthoods was greatly increased through excessive grants of land by the pharaohs, leading to the decline of royal authority and the loss of Egypt's empire in Nubia and the Near East. ▷ 1.18

NEWGRANGE
Enormous early NEOLITHIC PASSAGE GRAVE located in the Boyne valley ceremonial center in Ireland, built in about 3000 BC. The passage is oriented on sunrise at the midwinter solstice, when the sun's rays illuminate the central chamber. The stone kerb around the mound is elaborately decorated with carvings. Two similar monuments (Knowth and Dowth) are located nearby, as well as numerous satellite tombs. ▷ 1.20

NINEVEH
Assyrian city situated beside the Tigris in central MESOPOTAMIA. Although an important commercial and religious center by 3000 BC, it did not play a major role in Assyrian history until the 9th to 7th centuries BC, when successive rulers built large temples and palaces. It became the Assyrian capital in 705 BC, provided with magnificent buildings and replanned on a grandiose scale, with wide streets, a water-supply system, monumental gates, arsenal and palaces (including ASHURBANIPAL's palace and library, from which thousands of clay tablets have been recovered). The city was destroyed in 612 BC when the Babylonians and MEDES overthrew the Assyrian empire. Nineveh was rediscovered by the pioneering Victorian archeologist, Austen Henry Layard, in 1849. ▷ 1.09, 1.10, 1.11, 1.12, 1.13, 1.15

NIPPUR
Major city and the most important religious center in SUMERIA, founded by 4000 BC. Nippur was the site of the temple of ENLIL, the storm god responsible for sanctifying secular power, making control of the city essential for any ambitious MESOPOTAMIAN king. The final temple sanctuary was built by UR-NAMMU, king of UR, in about 2100 BC. ▷ 1.09, 1.10, 1.12, 1.13

NUBIA
Region along the Nile, south of Egypt, that acted as a corridor between Egypt and the rest of Africa. The more powerful Egyptian kingdoms, especially the NEW KINGDOM, exploited its resources mercilessly, but at times of Egyptian weakness it maintained its own cultures (the KERMA culture) and kingdoms (the Kushite). The Kushite dynasty (747–656 BC) from NAPATA was powerful enough to rule Egypt itself. ▷ 1.14, 1.15, 1.16, 1.17, 1.18

OAXACA VALLEY
Highland area of south Mexico where complex societies developed in the 2nd millennium BC, influenced from about 1200 BC by the OLMECS. It was the core area of ZAPOTEC civilization, which developed in the 1st millennium BC, with an early ceremonial center at Monté Albán and hillside agricultural terraces and settlements. ▷ 1.28

OBSIDIAN
Volcanic glass with flaking properties similar (but superior) to flint, widely used and highly valued for toolmaking in many parts of the world, notably in MESOPOTAMIA, where long-distance trade in obsidian was important by 7500 BC, and in Mesoamerica, where control of obsidian resources was essential for the lowland civilizations of the OLMEC and Maya. ▷ 1.08, 1.09, 1.28

ODYSSEY
Greek epic poem attributed to HOMER (c.700 BC), that tells the story of the hero Odysseus' return from the TROJAN WAR. His adventures include encounters with gods, monsters (the Cyclops) and the hazards of the sea. He eventually arrives at his homeland, Ithaca, to be reunited with his wife, Penelope. The Odyssey is the archetypal story of a hero battling against great odds to reach ultimate happiness. ▷ 1.24

OLD KINGDOM

The first of the great kingdoms of ancient Egypt (2686–2181 BC). It was characterized by powerful rulers who diverted enormous resources towards the building of the PYRAMIDS as their burial places. The strain on the economy, possibly intensified by climatic changes, led to the slow disintegration of the kingdom and a period of disorder (the 1st Intermediate period). ▷ 1.17

OLDOWAN CULTURE

The earliest tool industry (c.2.4–1.4 million ya) that is associated with the first humans (HOMO HABILIS) at sites in east Africa, such as OLDUVAI GORGE (after which it is named), KOOBI FORA and OMO. Flaked pebble tools, choppers and flakes were used for crushing, cutting and scraping. The more consistent Developed Oldowan industry (c.1.5–0.7 million ya), contemporary with early ACHEULIAN industries, was probably employed by hand-ax users for specific tasks. ▷ 1.01

OLDUVAI GORGE

A complex of ravines in the African Rift Valley, Tanzania, cutting through volcanic deposits and ancient lake and river sediments. They contain important early hominid remains (HOMO HABILIS, AUSTRALOPITHECUS ROBUSTUS, HOMO ERECTUS and HOMO SAPIENS), and the longest sequence of PALEOLITHIC tool industries (c.2.1 million–15,000 ya), with a succession of OLDOWAN, ACHEULIAN, MIDDLE PALEOLITHIC and UPPER PALEOLITHIC assemblages. ▷ 1.01

OLMEC CIVILIZATION

The earliest MESOAMERICAN CIVILIZATION, which developed in the humid lowland region along the Gulf coast of southern Mexico from 1250 BC. The Olmecs established a set of political, religious and aesthetic traditions which influenced later Mesoamerican cultures, with large ceremonial centers (notably TRES ZAPOTES, LA VENTA and SAN LORENZO), platform mounds and step pyramids, monumental stone carving, expansive and warlike states, and distinctive religious iconography.

Most stone resources used for the building of monuments (basalt and serpentine) and for portable material culture (OBSIDIAN and jade) had to be imported from highland regions, extending the Olmec sphere of influence. Hieroglyphic writing and a complex calendar had been invented for ritual purposes by about 700 BC, though there is no evidence that the Olmecs developed a literary culture. The decline of Olmec civilization and the destruction of its ceremonial centers took place between about 600 and 400 BC, probably as a result of political fragmentation and economic stresses. The Maya, who were deeply influenced by the Olmecs, became the dominant cultural force in Mesoamerica from about 400 BC. ▷ 1.28

OLYMPIA

Site of the OLYMPIC GAMES, Olympia is situated in the fertile Alpheus valley, in the north west Peloponnese. The site was an important PAN-HELLENIC sanctuary to the god Zeus, whose festivals came to be dominated by the famous games. The temple to Zeus, dating from the mid-5th century BC, contains fine classical sculptures. ▷ 1.24

OLYMPIC GAMES

Games held at OLYMPIA every four years between 776 BC and AD 393, at which aristocratic athletes from throughout the Greek world would compete in a range of events, including athletics, wrestling and chariot racing. The prizes were modest, but the honor of winning was great. ▷ 1.24

OMO

Region at the north end of Lake Turkana in Ethiopia, with ancient lake and river sediments dating from about 4 million ya, rich in early hominid fossil remains (australopithecines and HOMO ERECTUS) and tool industries (early pebble tools). Perhaps most significant is the discovery made there of the earliest fossils – about 135,000 years old – of HOMO SAPIENS SAPIENS. ▷ 1.01, 1.02

OPIS, BATTLE OF

Defeat of the last king of BABYLONIA, NABONIDUS, by CYRUS the Great in 539 BC, removing the last serious threat to the early ACHEMENID EMPIRE. ▷ 1.15

ORACLE BONES

Animal bones, especially ox scapulae and turtle shells, with engraved or painted inscriptions (pictographs), that were used for divination in China during the LONGSHAN and SHANG periods (from c.2500 BC). Cracks in the bone caused by applying heat were interpreted according to their patterns and relation to inscriptions (China's first written script). ▷ 1.27

ORACLE, GREEK

Both city-states and individuals used oracles as a means of divining the future or receiving advice on matters as diverse as marriage, overseas settlement or whether to go to war. The most celebrated oracle was at DELPHI, where answers were given by a priestess who entered a trance to consult the god Apollo. ▷ 1.24

ORKNEY, NEOLITHIC

Group of islands off the north coast of Britain with important NEOLITHIC remains dating from about 3500 to 2000 BC. These include the well-preserved SKARA BRAE settlement, the MAES HOWE PASSAGE GRAVE, and many other MEGALITHIC sites (e.g. the Ring of Brodgar and Stenness STONE CIRCLES). This concentration of monuments offers an unusually detailed view of Neolithic settlement, social organization and ritual practices. ▷ 1.20

OSCANS

Proto-historic inhabitants of southern Italy who are difficult to identify with historically documented groups. The language of the same name – Oscan – was spoken by various Italian groups (notably the SAMNITES, Frentani, Lucani, Bruttii and Apuli). Oscan is an INDO-EUROPEAN Italic language that was widely used until the 1st century BC; it then survived in some local dialects into the imperial period. Many Oscan inscriptions survive, most dating from 300 to 90 BC. ▷ 1.25

PAINTED WARE CULTURES

Earliest farming cultures of Anatolia and the Balkans (c.7000–6000 BC), where native populations adopted Near Eastern domesticates, ceramic technologies and similar social institutions, with village communities, mud-brick houses and long-lived TELL settlement sites. These cultures produced distinctive styles of painted pottery. ▷ 1.20

PALEOINDIANS

Earliest human populations in the Americas, the descendents of HUNTER-GATHERER bands who colonized the New World from at least 15,000 ya, crossing the Bering Straits land-bridge from Siberia. The first "Lower Lithic" cultures remain elusive. The best-known Paleoindian cultures are the CLOVIS-FOLSOM big-game hunters of North America. ▷ 1.02

PALEOLITHIC

The first phase of the STONE AGE of the THREE AGE SYSTEM and the earliest period of human toolmaking. The Paleolithic is itself divided into three stages – the LOWER PALEOLITHIC, MIDDLE PALEOLITHIC and UPPER PALEOLITHIC, each with distinctive stone technologies and tool-kits, and each associated with different human species and different forms of human subsistence and social organization. ▷ 1.01, 1.02, 1.19

PALEOLITHIC, LOWER

Tool industries of the early human species HOMO HABILIS and HOMO ERECTUS, dating from about 2.4 million to 230,000 ya. The earliest pebble tool industries, such as the OLDOWAN, were largely replaced by hand-ax industries, such as the ACHEULIAN. These tools were used mainly for scavenging and food processing, rather than hunting. ▷ 1.01

PALEOLITHIC, MIDDLE

Tool industries of the archaic HOMO SAPIENS and regional variants, such as the NEANDERTHALS in west Eurasia (associated with the MOUSTERIAN industry), characterized by an emphasis on the use of flake tools for a more flexible adaptation to local resources and specialized tasks, including the use of spears for hunting. ▷ 1.01, 1.02, 1.19

PALEOLITHIC, UPPER

Tool industries of HOMO SAPIENS SAPIENS that were based on blade technologies and composite tools developed in Africa from about 70,000 ya and used by humans throughout the world by 12,000 ya. These technologies produced lightweight task-specific tools, and allowed for creative innovation, enabling modern humans to be highly adaptable in exploiting new regions in the course of global colonization. ▷ 1.19

PAN-HELLENIC FESTIVALS
Festivals that drew Greeks from their settlements throughout the Mediterranean and helped to maintain a sense of common Greek identity. Most centered on competitive games (OLYMPIA, DELPHI, Nemea) and were independent of any city-state (POLIS). Others, such as the Panathenaea in Athens, were unashamedly propagandist events for a particular city. ▷ 1.24

PARTHIA
Satrapy of the ACHEMENID EMPIRE located to the southeast of the Caspian Sea, that sent camels and vessels as tribute to the Persian emperor. After the fall of the Achemenid empire, Parthia was settled by the nomadic Parni from the east Caspian steppe region. Their ruling Arsacid dynasty became vassals of the Seleucid kingdom until Arsaces I established Parthia as an independent kingdom in 238 BC. Mithridates I (r.170–138 BC) turned Parthia into a major power by conquering Persia and MESOPOTAMIA. In the 1st century BC, Parthia came under attack by the Roman empire. Despite a crushing victory over the Romans at Carrhae (53 BC), a long series of debilitating wars followed, leading ultimately to the fall of the Arsacid dynasty and the takeover of the Parthian empire by the Persian Sasanian dynasty in AD 224–26. Under the Arsacids Parthia developed as a decentralized feudalistic state. ▷ 1.15

PASARGADAE
The first capital of the ACHEMENID EMPIRE, founded by CYRUS the Great in about 540 BC, near the site of his victory over the MEDES. The extensive un-walled city had splendid palaces, a royal park, monumental buildings and a great citadel, and was the site of Cyrus' tomb. PERSEPOLIS, linked to Pasargadae by a rock-cut avenue, replaced it as the capital in 522 BC. ▷ 1.15

PASSAGE GRAVE
Type of MEGALITHIC MONUMENT of the European NEOLITHIC, constructed in about 4500–2500 BC, that consists of a passage leading to a chamber beneath an earthen or stone mound, usually circular. These were tombs for the collective burial of the dead of a descent group or community. Many have stone carvings, and in some cases the passages were oriented on celestial events. Notable examples of passage graves include GAVRINIS, NEWGRANGE and MAES HOWE. ▷ 1.20

PASTORALISM
A specialized form of farming based on the intensive exploitation of domestic animal herds for meat, leather, fur and secondary products, such as milk and WOOL. Fully nomadic pastoralism developed in the steppe regions of Eurasia from about 2000 BC, when HORSE DOMESTICATION allowed for the increased mobility of herding communities. ▷ 1.03, 1.04, 1.05, 1.06, 1.16

PEISISTRATUS
TYRANT who seized power briefly in Athens in the 560s BC, and then permanently from 546 to 527 BC. He was a relatively benign ruler who presided over Athens at a time of increasing prosperity. He appears to have built temples and may have instituted the great Panathenaic festival. ▷ 1.24

PERSEPOLIS
The royal capital of the ACHEMENID EMPIRE, founded by DARIUS I in 522 BC in a remote mountain region of central Persia, with magnificent palaces and the tombs of the Achemenid kings. It had no significant admininstrative role, as the empire was ruled mainly from SUSA and BABYLON. Persepolis was sacked by Alexander the Great in 330 BC. ▷ 1.15

PHAISTOS
MINOAN palace site on the south coast of CRETE, important from 2000 BC until it was destroyed with the other Minoan palaces in about 1450 BC. It is famous for the Phaistos disk, whose circular inscription – though Minoan in form – is unique and as yet undecipherable. ▷ 1.22

PHARAOHS
The word comes from per-aa ("the great house") and was first used in about 1400 BC, but has come to be used generally for the kings of ancient Egypt. ▷ 1.18

PHILISTINES
One of the SEA PEOPLES who settled on the Levantine coast, expelling the CANAANITES. By 1150 BC they had established a confederacy of city-states (Ashkelon, Gaza, Ashdod, Gath and Ekron). The Philistines were conquered by ISRAEL in about 1000 BC but soon regained their independence. From about 650 BC they were vassals of the Assyrians, Egyptians and Babylonians. ▷ 1.12, 1.13, 1.14

PHOENICIA, PHOENICIANS
A general name for the territory and inhabitants of the ancient city-states of the Levantine coast, including ARVAD, Berytus, SIDON and TYRE. The name is probably derived from the purple dye they produced. The Phoenicians were a Semitic-speaking peoples related to the CANAANITES. They were expert sailors and enterprising traders who, from the 10th to the 5th centuries BC, were heavily involved in Mediterranean trade and

colonization. They had a considerable cultural influence on the Greeks, to whom they gave the alphabet, and on the native peoples of southern Spain, including the Tartessians. Conquered by Persia in the 530s BC, the Phoenicians provided the bulk of the Persian fleet in their wars with the Greeks. After the Persian conquest, the Phoenician settlements in the western Mediterranean became independent under the leadership of Carthage. ▷ 1.13, 1.14, 1.15, 1.23, 1.24, 1.25

PHOENICIAN ALPHABET
The earliest alphabet, based on single signs for the 20 or so consonants, was developed by the CANAANITES in the ancient Near East in about 1600 BC. The PHOENICIANS adapted this between 1300 and 1000 BC, and passed it on to the Greeks in the 8th century BC. ▷ 1.07

PHRYGIA, PHRYGIANS
Central area of western Asia Minor whose native rulers included MITAS. Absorbed into LYDIA, it became part of the ACHEMENID EMPIRE in 545 BC, then fell under Greek and finally Roman influence. The area was divided between the provinces of Asia and Galatia. ▷ 1.12, 1.13, 1.22, 1.23

PIG
Animal that was domesticated independently in the Middle East (by c.6500 BC), Europe (from the wild boar) and East Asia (by c.5000 BC). They were exploited mainly for meat and fat. Modern pig breeds derive from a native southeast Asian species. ▷ 1.03, 1.08, 1.09, 1.20, 1.27

PLEISTOCENE EPOCH
Geo-climatic period following the PLIOCENE. Dating from about 1.6 million ya, it is marked by global temperature oscillations, general cooling and a series of cold glacial phases (ICE AGES). It is arguable whether the present post-Glacial era (from 12,000 ya), termed the Holocene, is a new climatic epoch or simply a warm phase of the Pleistocene. ▷ 1.01, 1.02

PLIOCENE EPOCH
Geo-climatic period following the MIOCENE, dating from about 5 to 1.6 million ya. It is marked by global cooling, numerous extinctions, and the evolution of large mammals (e.g. mastodons) and advanced hominids, such as the australopithecines and earliest humans. ▷ 1.01

PLOW
Agricultural tool used for breaking the soil surface to allow for planting, dragged by oxen, horses or men. The earliest plows, with simple chisel-like blades, were known as ards and were invented in the Middle East by 4500 BC, replacing hoes. Ards usually needed cross-plowing to be effective and were most suited to light soils. Heavy plows for clay soils were invented in Europe in the 1st millennium BC. ▷ 1.03, 1.09, 1.20, 1.21

POLIS
Greek city-state typically centered on a city, complete with temples and other public buildings, that was supported by its surrounding territory. There were many hundreds of city-states scattered throughout the Mediterranean. A high degree of political and social involvement was normally demanded of the citizens of a *polis*. ▷ 1.24

POTATO
Plant with edible tubers that was domesticated in the central Andes of South America by about 1000 BC. It was a staple food throughout the Andean region in the 1st millennium AD. ▷ 1.03, 1.28

POVERTY POINT CULTURE
Complex HUNTER-GATHERER culture of the lower Mississippi valley, North America, from about 1500 to 700 BC. It is named after the site of a ceremonial center with an impressive earthwork enclosure and platform mounds at Poverty Point, Louisiana, possibly influenced by Mesoamerican structures. Little is known about Poverty Point society or economy. ▷ 1.05

PRECERAMIC PERIOD
Period of ANDEAN CIVILIZATION, dating from about 3750 to 2000 BC. It is marked by the development of sedentary settlement and an increasing reliance on farming, the domestication of alpacas and LLAMAS, the continued exploitation of marine resources on the coast and gathered foods and hunting in highland areas, and the earliest construction of monumental architecture at ceremonial centers such as ASPERO. ▷ 1.28

PREDYNASTIC PERIOD
A period of 2,500 years of Egyptian history, between the beginning of farming in the Nile valley and the emergence of the first dynasties (c.2920 BC). Marked by increasingly sophisticated settlements, craftsmanship and religious beliefs, and by an increasingly hierarchical society, the Predynastic period saw the establishment of the main features of EGYPTIAN CIVILIZATION. ▷ 1.17

PTERIA
Site of a defeat of the Lydians by CYRUS the Great in 547 BC. It became a major settlement on the royal road from the ACHEMENID capital at SUSA to SARDIS, the capital of the satrapy of LYDIA, but its exact location is uncertain. Pteria may have been on the site of the former HITTITE capital, HATTUSAS. ▷ 1.15

PYLOS
MYCENAEAN palace site in MESSENIA (southwestern Peloponnese) and, according to Homeric legend, the stronghold of Nestor. Discovered LINEAR B tablets have provided important evidence of Mycenaean society and details of the last days of the palace before its destruction in about 1200 BC. ▷1.22

PYRAMID
A royal burial monument whose four triangular sides slope upwards to a sharp point. True pyramids developed from the earlier so-called STEP PYRAMIDS in OLD KINGDOM Egypt; by the 4th Dynasty, at Giza, they had reached a gargantuan size. Designed to house the bodies of the dead PHARAOHS, pyramids were always part of a much larger burial complex, including mortuary temples in which deceased rulers could be worshipped as gods. Pyramid building ceased at the end of the MIDDLE KINGDOM period. ▷ 1.17

QADESH
Battle between the PHARAOH RAMESSES II and the HITTITES (c.1285 BC), that took place at the town of Qadesh, central Syria, when the Hittites reacted to Ramesses' intrusion into Syria. The first documented battle in history, it was claimed as a victory by Ramesses, though Hittite sources suggest that it was a stalemate, or even defeat, from which Ramesses retreated. ▷ 1.12, 1.18

QAFZEH
MIDDLE to UPPER PALEOLITHIC cave site in ISRAEL with occupation layers containing MOUSTERIAN tools and animal bones. Most important are the skeletal remains of HOMO SAPIENS SAPIENS, dating from about 90,000 ya, suggesting the rapid spread of anatomically modern humans from Africa into Eurasia. ▷ 1.02

QI
A major feudal state of the ZHOU kingdom in northeast China from about 1100 to 250 BC, with a capital at Linzi. It grew in power during the SPRINGS AND AUTUMNS PERIOD and briefly became the leading state (hegemon) in the mid-7th century BC, under Duke Huan and his minister Guan Zhong. Its dominance waned due to internal strife and war with Song. ▷ 1.27

QIN
Feudal state in northwest China and the heartland of the ZHOU kingdom from about 1100 to 770 BC. Its capital was at HAO until barbarian attacks led to the transfer of the capital to LUOYANG. Its power waned during the SPRINGS AND AUTUMNS PERIOD and its revival as a leading power during the WARRING STATES PERIOD (c.480–202 BC) was largely due to the reforms of the 4th century prime minister, Shang Yang. These turned Qin into a centralized, militaristic state and ultimately led to Qin supremacy (from 250 BC) and the unification of China in 221 BC by its king, Zheng (Shi Huangdi). The Qin dynasty was soon overthrown by the Han, who took over the empire in 202 BC. ▷ 1.27

QUATERNARY PERIOD
Geological era following the Tertiary period, from about 1.6 million ya to the present day,
that is represented by glacial and inter-glacial sediments and geomorphological features formed under PLEISTOCENE and Holocene environmental conditions. ▷ 1.01

RAMESSES II (THE GREAT)
Egyptian PHARAOH (r.c.1290–1224 BC). A man of immense ambition, he began his reign with a campaign into Syria that was checked by the HITTITES at QADESH. A subsequent peace treaty stabilized relations and allowed Ramesses to concentrate on a massive building program in Egypt, which included the temples at ABU SIMBEL in NUBIA. The last of the great pharaohs, his mummified remains have survived. ▷ 1.12, 1.18

REHOBOAM
King of ISRAEL (r.928–911 BC) and the son of SOLOMON. Rehoboam became increasingly unpopular and dealt harshly with dissent. Unable to suppress rebellion in the north, he was left in control of JUDAH and the capital, JERUSALEM. Jeroboam became king of Israel, inaugurating a period of dynastic instability. ▷ 1.14

RHODES
Island off the southwestern tip of Asia Minor. Its position made it a center for trade and the ambitions of its neighbors from Minoan times. Its greatest prosperity and proudest period of independence came in Hellenistic times, when it financed the Colossus of Rhodes, a vast statue astride its harbor entrance. Eventually outwitted by Roman diplomacy, the island was absorbed into the Roman empire in the 1st century BC. ▷ 1.22

RICE
Cereal plant (*Orzya sativa*) producing edible starchy grains, collected intensively by HUNTER-GATHERERS in China and southeast Asia. It was domesticated from about 7000 BC, with widespread wet-rice farming in the lower Yangtze region by about 5000 BC. Rice was the staple crop throughout east Asia by the 2nd millennium BC, and in eastern India by about 1000 BC. ▷ 1.03, 1.16, 1.26, 1.27

ROME (ANCIENT CITY)
From modest beginnings in the 10th century BC, Rome became the largest city of the ancient world and the center of the Roman empire. Tradition records a series of kings of

KINGS OF ROME	
Romulus (legendary)	
Numa Pompilius	c.715–673 BC
Tullus Hostilius	c.673–642
Ancus Martius	c.642–617
Tarquin I	c.616–579
Servius Tullius	c.578–535
Tarquin the Proud	c.535–509

Rome until 509 BC when the Roman republic was established.

Relatively little is known archeologically about the city in the regal and earlier republican periods; the extensive remains now visible mainly date to the later republic and empire. The city was embellished by the great patrician families and emperors, with major civic building projects such as forums, temples, theaters and circuses. As Rome's population grew, so did its infrastructure of roads, aqueducts and warehouses. Rome's political importance declined in the 3rd century AD as it was abandoned by the emperors for centers closer to the embattled frontiers. Following the fall of the western Roman empire in the 5th century, Rome's population declined dramatically, but the city retained importance as the leading Christian center in western Europe. ▷ 1.25

SABA
Ancient kingdom of southwest Arabia, known in biblical references as Sheba. Saba was founded by Semitic Sabaeans of the north from about 1200 BC. By the 7th to 5th centuries BC, it was a centralized state with IRRIGATION agriculture, monumental temples, and control over the Red Sea–Indian Ocean trade routes. ▷ 1.05, 1.06

SABEAN SCRIPT AND LANGUAGE
A writing system ultimately based on the proto-CANAANITE phonetic alphabet that was adapted by the Semitic-speaking Sabean people of southwest Arabia from about 1000 BC and used for record-keeping and monument inscriptions. ▷ 1.07

SABINES
A people of ancient Italy occupying the area northeast of ROME, along the west side of the Tiber valley. The Sabines figure largely in the legends of early Rome, though archeological data is scanty. Some recent excavations, however, reveal material culture similarities with LATIUM in the IRON AGE. The Sabines were finally defeated by Rome in 290 BC and were granted full citizenship in 268 BC. ▷ 1.25

SAKAS
INDO-IRANIAN pastoral nomad people of the central Asian steppes who raided the northeastern satrapies of the ACHEMENID EMPIRE in the late 6th and 5th centuries BC. CYRUS the Great built a chain of forts to defend the frontier against the Sakas and was killed fighting them in 530 BC. ▷ 1.06, 1.15

SAMARIA
A city in central Palestine that was founded by King Omri in about 880 BC as the new capital of ISRAEL. Some of Samaria's buildings of the 9th century BC have PHOENICIAN features. The city was destroyed by Shalmaneser V of ASSYRIA in 724 BC, after a three-year siege. ▷ 1.14

SAMARRAN CULTURE
Late NEOLITHIC culture of central MESOPOTAMIA, characterized by painted pottery styles with animal and human figures. Dating from about 6000 to 5500 BC, it follows the HASSUNA CULTURE and marks the extension of agricultural societies southwards. Samarran communities lived in large villages and developed large-scale IRRIGATION systems (at CHOGA MAMI), increasing crop yields and allowing for settlement of the Mesopotamian plains. ▷ 1.09

SAMNITES
A warlike OSCAN-speaking people of ancient Italy in the central-south Apennines, divided into a powerful confederation of the Caraceni, Caudini, Hirpini and Pentri tribes. Even after losing the Samnite wars, they supported Pyrrhus and Hannibal against ROME, fought in the Social War and against Sulla in the civil war. Latin colonies were established at Beneventum (268 BC) and Aesernia (263 BC), but Romanization was relatively slow. ▷ 1.25

SAN LORENZO
Earliest OLMEC ceremonial center, situated on a plateau beside the fertile Coatzacoalcos river plain. The main phase of building (c.1200–900 BC) involved construction work to raise the surface of the natural plateau, huge lateral ridges for access, mounds for timber houses (for an elite community of about 1,000 people), temple mounds, altars with stone carvings, and massive sculpted stone heads (portraits of Olmec kings or gods). It was destroyed in about 900 BC, when many sculptures were deliberately broken and buried. ▷ 1.28

SANXINGDUI
City occupied in the 2nd millennium BC, contemporary with the SHANG dynasty, that was recently discovered in central China. Found bronze objects indicate a high degree of technical sophistication and cultural complexity. The relationship between Sanxingdui and Shang China is uncertain. ▷ 1.27

SAQQARA
Important Egyptian site, close to MEMPHIS, and the burial place of many of Egypt's early kings, including NARMER. The most impressive monument is the STEP PYRAMID (c.2630 BC) built for the PHARAOH DJOSER. After THEBES became the focus for royal burials, Saqqara continued to be used for the burials of Memphis officials. ▷ 1.04, 1.17

SARDIS
Capital of the LYDIAN kingdom of western Anatolia from the 7th to 6th centuries BC, with a large citadel and the earliest known coin mint. It was captured, along with King CROESUS, by CYRUS the Great in 546 BC, and became the capital of a satrapy of the ACHEMENID EMPIRE. ▷ 1.15

SARGON OF AGADE (THE GREAT)
Akkadian king of KISH who founded the first imperial state (c.2334–2279 BC), ruling AKKAD and SUMERIA, north MESOPOTAMIA, the north LEVANT and ELAM. He controlled the maritime trade routes to the Persian Gulf, the Indus and the east Mediterranean, and the land routes to central Anatolia and Iran. He founded the city of Agade as a capital for his empire, but its location has not been discovered. His empire lasted for a century and reached its greatest extent under his grandson, NARAM-SIN, before it disintegrated in the early 22nd century BC. Sargon was a model for later Mesopotamian rulers and his life became the subject of many legends. ▷ 1.10, 1.11

SARGON II
King of ASSYRIA (r.721–705 BC), probably the son of TIGLATH-PILESER III, named after SARGON OF AGADE. Sargon II consolidated the conquests of his father, expanded Assyrian rule in URARTU (714 BC) and conquered south MESOPOTAMIA (710–07 BC). The Assyrian empire reached its greatest power and influence under his reign. He was probably killed in battle in Anatolia in 705 BC. ▷ 1.13

SARMATIANS
INDO-IRANIAN pastoral nomad people of the central Eurasian steppes who were closely related to the SCYTHIANS. The Sarmatians migrated into the Ural region in the 5th century BC, before conquering the Scythians and settling in the Ukraine and Balkans in the 4th–2nd centuries BC. ▷ 1.06

SAUL
First king of ISRAEL (r.c.1020–c.1006 BC), proclaimed ruler by the judge Samuel to unify the Israelites against the PHILISTINES and AMALEKITES. He was killed by the Philistines at the Battle of Gilboa. ▷ 1.14

SCYTHIANS
INDO-IRANIAN pastoral nomads of central Asia who migrated westwards and southwards in the 8th–7th centuries BC, displacing the CIMMERIANS and settling in the Ukraine (Royal Scythians) and the Caspian region (Pointed Hat Scythians). They are famous for their warlike character and rich tradition of metalworking, examples of which have been found in ROUND BARROW tombs. They were later absorbed by local populations or dispersed by further nomad invaders, such as the SARMATIANS, in the 4th–2nd centuries BC. ▷ 1.06, 1.15, 1.23

SEA PEOPLES
Groups of migrants of uncertain origin, who may have included elements from Libya, the northern Aegean, Asia Minor and even Sardinia. They raided widely around the eastern Mediterranean, as far south as Egypt, in about 1200 BC. Relatively little is known

about them, though the HITTITE empire and the MYCENAEAN CIVILIZATION may have disintegrated as a result of their attacks. The Egyptians drove them off the Delta in 1180 BC, though one group, the Peleset (PHILISTINES) settled in Palestine, which is named after them. ▷ 1.12, 1.18, 1.22

SEMITES
Speakers of the Semitic languages, which originated in Arabia and western MESOPOTAMIA, and spread as the Semitic peoples migrated and conquered neighboring regions (3rd–1st millennia BC), either replacing existing populations or establishing ruling elites that imposed their own languages. These peoples include the Akkadians, AMORITES, CANAANITES, HEBREWS, ARAMAEANS, CHALDEANS, PHOENICIANS, Sabaeans and Arabs. ▷ 1.04, 1.05, 1.06, 1.07, 1.11, 1.12, 1.13, 1.14, 1.15

SENNACHERIB
King of ASSYRIA (r.704–681 BC) who maintained Assyrian dominance, though threatened by local or CHALDEAN and Elamite-inspired rebellions in BABYLONIA. He suppressed a revolt in Palestine (701 BC), and undertook six campaigns in Babylonia and ELAM, eventually destroying BABYLON in 689 BC. He moved the Assyrian capital to NINEVEH. ▷ 1.13, 1.14

SHALMANESER III
King of ASSYRIA (r.858–824 BC) who attempted, with varying success, to extend Assyrian dominion over the LEVANT and elsewhere. He was resisted at Qarqar in 854 BC by a coalition of Levantine states, including ISRAEL. The Assyrian empire entered a period of instability after his death. ▷ 1.13

SHAMSHI-ADAD
AMORITE king of SHUBAT-ENLIL (r.1813–1781 BC) who siezed control of ASHUR in about 1813 BC and established the first major territorial state in north MESOPOTAMIA. The kingdom declined thereafter and was under BABYLONIAN control by 1750 BC. ▷ 1.11

SHANG CIVILIZATION
The first state-organized urban culture of China, known from both historical and archeological sources, that was ruled by the Shang dynasty from their heartland in the Yellow river region. The semi-mythical founder of the dynasty, King Tang, is said to have deposed the last of the morally corrupt XIA kings in 1766 BC, though archeological evidence suggests a more gradual centralization from the 19th to 17th centuries BC.

A notable feature of Shang culture is their magnificent bronze work, using unique piece-mould casting processes to produce highly decorated ceremonial vessels and weaponry. A pictographic script, initally written on ORACLE BONES for divination purposes, was adapted for secular use, such

as inscriptions on bronze vessels. Shang cities such as ANYANG were built of rammed earth and timber, with massive ramparts, monumental buildings and large populations. Evidence from inscriptions, later histories and royal burials (accompanied by bronze and jade artifacts and human sacrifices) suggest that Shang society had a clan structure, with a strict social hierarchy and a warrior aristocracy engaged in constant warfare. Shang China became increasingly centralized, bureaucratic (with standard systems of measurement) and expansive. The last king of the Shang, DI-XIN, was overthrown by the ZHOU DYNASTY in 1122 BC. ▷ 1.05, 1.07, 1.27

SHANIDAR
MIDDLE and UPPER PALEOLITHIC cave site in the Zagros mountains, modern Iraq, with important MOUSTERIAN occupation levels. The site contains Neanderthal burials (including a disabled individual who must have been cared for by his companions). ▷ 1.01

SHEEP
Several species of sheep were domesticated in prehistory, the most important being *Ovis orientalis* in the Zagros mountains (by c.9000 BC) and *Ovis vignei* in central Asia (by c.4000 BC). It is possible that other species, such as the European *Ovis musimon*, were also domesticated. Sheep were important sources of meat in NEOLITHIC economies, and later became important for textile manufacture (WOOL). ▷ 1.03, 1.08, 1.09, 1.20, 1.21, 1.22

SHORTHUGAI
An INDUS CIVILIZATION settlement to the north of the Hindu Kush, near the Oxus (Amu Darya) river in north Afghanistan, 500 kilometers (310 miles) from the nearest Indus towns. It was probably a trading colony, founded by 2000 BC, for importing lapis lazuli and other raw materials. ▷ 1.26

SHOSHENQ I
Egyptian PHARAOH (r.945–924 BC) of Libyan extraction, who temporarily regained control of Palestine after a period of Egyptian weakness and withdrawal. ▷ 1.14, 1.18

SHUBAT-ENLIL
City in north MESOPOTAMIA that was founded as a new capital by King SHAMSHI-ADAD of ASSYRIA in about 1800 BC, on the site of an earlier city that had been abandoned in about 2200 BC. The city declined after his death and was destroyed by the Babylonians in about 1726 BC. ▷ 1.11

SICULI (SICELS)
The name given by the Greeks to the indigenous peoples of east Sicily in the later 8th century BC. It has not been possible to distinguish them archeologically from the other local groups, such as the Elymi. ▷ 1.25

SIDON
City on the Levantine coast that was founded in the 3rd millennium BC. Sidon was one of the most important PHOENICIAN city-states from about 1000 BC and became the most prosperous of the coastal cities after the annexation of the region by the Persian empire in about 530 BC. ▷ 1.14

SILBURY HILL
The largest prehistoric mound in Europe, situated in the AVEBURY late NEOLITHIC monument complex in the Kennet valley, England. It was built in three phases in the mid-3rd millennium BC for ceremonial purposes, and was sited so that only the top could be seen from contemporary monuments nearby, though its specific function is unknown. ▷ 1.20

SIWA
Remote oasis site in the desert west of Egypt, known for its oracle to Amun. An expedition under the Persian king CAMBYSES failed to reach it, but Alexander the Great succeeded in getting there, believing that the priests had saluted him as the son of Amun and thus the true PHARAOH. ▷ 1.15

SKARA BRAE
NEOLITHIC farming and fishing village on the coast of the largest of the ORKNEY Islands, northern Britain, inhabited in the 3rd millennium BC. The small nucleated group of stone-built houses linked by paved alleys, with central hearths and stone cupboards, were unusually well-preserved under wind-blown sand and occupation debris. ▷ 1.20

SKUDRA
Region of the southern Balkans (Thrace) on the north side of the Aegean, that was established as the only satrapy of the ACHEMENID EMPIRE on the mainland of Europe after the invasion by DARIUS I in 538 BC. It sent horses and weapons as tribute to the Persian emperor. ▷ 1.15

SLAVERY (ANCIENT WORLD)
Slavery, the ownership of one individual by another, was known throughout the ancient world, but Greece and ROME in particular depended heavily on slave labor. In Greece the subjection of the slave served to emphasize the freedom of the citizen. Slaves were used as domestic servants, on farms, in manufacturing and in mines, and their treatment ranged from the benign to the brutal. In Rome slaves were often seized as the fruits of victories, though a flourishing slave trade was also in existence. By contrast with Greece, in Rome slaves could be given their freedom, and many "freedmen" prospered as a result. Slavery was as prevalent in late antiquity as it had been in earlier times, and the coming of Christianity had no impact on the institution. ▷ 1.10, 1.22, 1.24

SMERDIS

Known as Bardiya in Persian sources and as Smerdis in Greek ones, he was the brother of CAMBYSES, king of Persia. Smerdis was involved in the mysterious events surrounding the death of CAMBYSES in 522 BC and the accession of DARIUS, perhaps as the murderer of Cambyses. Many scholars now believe that Darius murdered him in order to seize the throne himself. ▷ 1.15

SNOFRU

The first PHARAOH of the 4th Dynasty (r.2575–2551 BC) who played a crucial role in the development of the PYRAMID by filling in the space between the steps of a STEP PYRAMID, with the intention of creating the first true pyramid. In order to maintain stability, however, the angle of the sides of the pyramid had to be reduced when it was half built. The result was the unique "bent pyramid". Later pyramid builders were more successful. ▷ 1.17

SOGDIANA

Satrapy of the ACHEMENID EMPIRE in central Asia, to the east of the Aral Sea in modern Uzbekistan, conquered by CYRUS the Great in about 546–39 BC. The province sent horses, weapons and jewelry as tribute to the Persian emperor. ▷ 1.15

SOLOMON

King of ISRAEL (r.c.965–928 BC) and the son of DAVID. Solomon extended his empire through marriage alliances and military campaigns. His control of the trade routes between MESOPOTAMIA, the LEVANT, the Red Sea and Egypt allowed him to amass enormous wealth, which was spent on fortress building and public works such as the Great Temple at JERUSALEM. He reorganized the state administration, but his extravagance and exactions made him unpopular. ▷ 1.14

SOLON

Athenian politician who was awarded the task in 594–593 BC of asserting city authority over the powerful aristocratic families of ATTICA. His stated aim was to bring "good order". He curbed privilege based solely on birth and introduced a comprehensive code of law to which all citizens were equally subject. His reforms were threatened by the TYRANT PEISISTRATUS, but survived to be extended by KLEISTHENES. ▷ 1.24

SOLUTREAN CULTURE

European UPPER PALEOLITHIC tool industry dating from about 23,000–17,000 ya, following the GRAVETTIAN CULTURE. Solutrean toolmakers developed pressure-flaking techniques for the production of exceptionally fine bifacially-worked stone implements, notably leaf-shaped projectile points. They lived in a cold glacial phase, hunting large herd animals such as bison. ▷ 1.19

SORGHUM

Cereal plant with edible starchy seeds that was domesticated in southern Sudan by about 4000 BC. It was widely adopted throughout sub-Saharan Africa by about 1000 BC, as a reliable drought-resistant staple food crop, along with MILLET. ▷ 1.16

SPARTA

Important Greek city-state of the southern Peloponnese. Sparta's power rested on its highly trained HOPLITE forces and on the exploitation of the neighboring plain of MESSENIA. By the end of the 6th century BC, it was the dominant power in the Peloponnese and in 431 BC challenged Athens in the so-called Peloponnesian War. Gaining Persian support, Sparta won (404 BC), but its declining manpower and clumsy diplomacy meant the loss of its advantages. Defeated at Leuctra by Thebes in 371 BC, Sparta never recovered its power. Its rigid institutions and brutal training methods, including the state-supervised upbringing of all male children, were unique in the Greek world. ▷ 1.24

SPHINX, GREAT

Huge ancient Egyptian statue of a seated lion figure with a human head, carved from natural limestone, near the PYRAMID of KHEPHREN at Giza. The lion was traditionally seen as a guardian of the gates to the Underworld, which may explain its use here. The head is probably that of Khephren himself. ▷ 1.17

SPRINGS AND AUTUMNS PERIOD

Phase of the later (Eastern) ZHOU period in China from about 770 to 480 BC, named after the annals of the LU state. The decline of Zhou authority after the transfer of their capital to LUOYANG in 770 BC led to political fragmentation as rival states (dukedoms) within the kingdom struggled for power, some rapidly rising to hegemonic dominance but none sustaining that position (hence "Springs" and "Autumns"). The main hegemons were Zheng (late 8th century BC), QI (early 7th century BC), JIN (late 7th century BC and mid-6th century BC) and CHU (late 7th to early 6th centuries BC). The emergence of seven equally aggressive kingdoms from about 500 BC marked the beginning of the WARRING STATES PERIOD. ▷ 1.06, 1.27

SQUASH

Fruit of the gourd plant family, several species of which were domesticated in low-land areas of Central and South America by 3000 BC, becoming an important food crop in coastal Peru by 2500 BC (ASPERO TRADITION). ▷ 1.03, 1.28

STARCEVO

Early NEOLITHIC settlement beside the Danube in Serbia, occupied in about 6000–4000 BC. The site has given its name to the first Neolithic period in the central Balkans, characterized by TELL settlements, a distinctive pottery style and a mixed agricultural economy. ▷ 1.20

STATE

A form of political organization characterized by "legal-rational" institutions. It involved the codification of rights and obligations of all members of a community within a given territory according to defined social status, ideally implemented impartially according to established law (rather than personal or kin relations). State systems required bureaucracies and writing systems to preserve legal codes and to record precedents, and military institutions to guarantee rights and enforce obligations. Many early states were also theocratic, with elites drawing upon religious doctrines to justify their authority and political decisions. ▷ 1.04, 1.05, 1.06

STEP PYRAMID

A type of Egyptian PYRAMID constructed by raising a number of rectangular layers of stone of decreasing size, one above the other. The step pyramid was first seen at SAQQARA, where the architect Imhotep constructed one over the tomb of the PHARAOH DJOSER (c.2630). The inspiration behind it is believed to be the MASTABAS, an earlier type of Egyptian platform tomb. ▷ 1.17

STONE AGE

A subdivision of the THREE AGE SYSTEM. It was recognized in the 19th century that the idea of a discrete Stone Age is dubious as it subsumes several distinct stages of human biological and cultural evolution. The period was therefore subdivided into three separate periods: the PALEOLITHIC, MESOLITHIC and NEOLITHIC (Old, Middle and New Stone Ages). These terms are still widely used for general descriptive purposes.

STONE CIRCLE

Type of MEGALITHIC MONUMENT, consisting of stones arranged in a circle or ellipse, that is found in many parts of the world but is particularly associated with NEOLITHIC Europe. Stone circles vary greatly in scale, form, location and associations, but all were ceremonial in purpose, some taking account of astronomical alignments in the positioning and arrangement of stones. ▷ 1.20

STONEHENGE

Ceremonial enclosure and MEGALITHIC structure at the center of a concentration of NEOLITHIC and BRONZE AGE monuments on Salisbury Plain in WESSEX, Britain. The site has a long history of construction and use from about 3000 to 1000 BC, with three main building phases representing very different designs. Built in about 2400–2000 BC, the unique sarsen and blue-STONE CIRCLES, with carpentry-influenced design features, are oriented on summer solstice sunrise and winter solstice sunset. ▷ 1.04, 1.20

SUBARTU

Region to the northwest of ASSYRIA that is referred to in southern Mesopotamian texts of the 3rd and early 2nd millennia BC. SHAMSHI-ADAD of Assyria established his short-lived capital, SHUBAT-ENLIL, in Subartu in about 1800 BC, but the region was otherwise of little political or cultural significance in this period. ▷ 1.11, 1.12

SUMER, SUMERIA

The southernmost part of MESOPOTAMIA, and the region in which the first civilization developed in the 5th to 3rd millennia BC. Ubaidian settlers from central Mesopotamia established IRRIGATION systems for intensive farming from about 6000 BC, and introduced brick masonry, pottery and weaving. STATE formation and URBANIZATION in the 4th millennium BC led to the emergence of at least 12 city-states by about 2900 BC, with their own political and religious institutions and distinct cultural traditions. These states competed for regional dominance, the most powerful being KISH, LAGASH, URUK and UR.

Cultural developments in Sumeria during the URUK PERIOD (4300–3100 BC) and EARLY DYNASTIC (c.2900–2334 BC) include writing (Sumerian pictographs), urbanism, state institutions and sophisticated architecture and sculpture. Sumer was united with its northern neighbor, AKKAD, in the 24th century BC, first by LUGALZAGESI of Lagash and then by SARGON OF AGADE, before regaining political pre-eminence under the Third Dynasty of Ur (2112–2004 BC). Sumer merged with Akkad in the 2nd millennium BC (the whole region being known as BABYLONIA), and continued to influence later Middle Eastern civilizations until the Persian conquest in the 6th century BC. ▷ 1.04, 1.05, 1.07, 1.09, 1.10, 1.11

SUPPILULIUMAS

King of the HITTITES (r.1344–1322 BC). He established the Hittite empire as the leading state in the Middle East, conquering the western part of MITTANI and sacking the Mittanian capital, WASHUKANNI (c.1340 BC), fatally weakening the main rival to Hittite expansion. His conquests brought the Hittites into direct conflict with the Egyptians. ▷ 1.12

SUSA

City on the Karkeh river in southwest Iran, with origins in the 6th millennium BC. By 3000 BC it had grown into an urban center similar to those in SUMERIA. It was the capital of ELAM in the 3rd and 2nd millennia BC, with a citadel, palaces and temples, and from 522 BC it became the administrative capital of the ACHEMENID EMPIRE. ▷ 1.09, 1.10, 1.12, 1.13, 1.15

SWANSCOMBE

LOWER PALEOLITHIC site in southeast Britain, with stratified "Clactonian" chopper-tool and ACHEULIAN hand-ax industries, and the fossil remains (c.400,000 ya) of archaic HOMO SAPIENS with cranial features intermediate between HOMO ERECTUS and HOMO SAPIENS NEANDERTHALENSIS. ▷ 1.01

SWARTKRANS

LOWER PALEOLITHIC cave site in South Africa with a sequence of deposits containing numerous fossil remains of AUSTRALOPITHECUS ROBUSTUS and a smaller number of HOMO HABILIS in higher levels, together with OLDOWAN-style tools. Later evidence of the use of FIRE, dating from about 1.6 million ya, may be related to activity by HOMO ERECTUS. ▷ 1.01

SYRACUSE

With its fine harbor and fertile territory in eastern Sicily, Syracuse was first colonized in 734 BC by the Corinthians and gradually became one of the most prosperous city-states in the ancient Mediterranean. Syracuse was able to hold its own militarily against the ETRUSCANS and – under Dionysius I – the Carthaginians (though with much greater difficulty). Despite immense prosperity in the 3rd century BC, Syracuse was conquered by ROME (212 BC) and became the capital of the Roman province of Sicily. ▷ 1.23, 1.25

TADMOR

City in Syria on a trade route across the Syrian desert from the Euphrates to the LEVANT that was probably a settlement from the 3rd millennium BC. Tadmor was ruled by ARAMAEAN kings from about 1200 BC, though it briefly came under Israelite control in the 10th century BC. It later became known as Palmyra. ▷ 1.11, 1.12, 1.13, 1.14

TARTARIA

NEOLITHIC settlement in Transylvania, Romania, where clay tablets dating to about 5000 BC have been found with incised signs, probably a system of notation. It did not develop into a writing system. ▷ 1.20

TARTESSOS

City on the Atlantic coast of Spain (probably modern Huelva), founded by native Tartessians by about 800 BC, and the capital of a powerful state by about 600 BC. It traded with the PHOENICIANS, who had a port nearby at GADES, exporting silver and other metals in return for pottery and luxury goods from the Mediterranean. The Tartessians were influenced by Phoenician styles of art and adapted their alphabetic script. Tartessos was conquered by the Carthaginians in the 4th century BC. ▷ 1.23, 1.25

TARXIEN

One of the late NEOLITHIC stone temple complexes on the Mediterranean island of Malta. It was built by an indigenous farming culture (c.3500–2400 BC), which originally came from Sicily (by 5000 BC), but developed a distinctive religious tradition. The Maltese temples share symmetrical designs with lobed inner chambers, altars and monumental statuary. ▷ 1.20

TASSILI

A plateau region of the central Sahara (southern Algeria) where a rich tradition of ROCK ART (paintings and modified rock forms) flourished (c.6000–1000 BC). Representations of humans and animals indicate that the paintings were mainly the work of agriculturalists (primarily pastoralists), when the region was far less dessicated. There is archeological evidence of MILLET cultivation by 6000 BC and CATTLE-herding by 4000 BC. ▷ 1.16

TEHUACÁN

Desert valley of central Mexico, occupied from about 9000 BC, where especially dry conditions have preserved organic materials and artifacts, including evidence of very early agriculture (the cultivation of peppers and SQUASHES by c.6000 BC). The evidence from Tehuacán provides an exceptionally detailed picture of cultural change in the region. ▷ 1.28

TELL

Mound resulting from the long-term accumulation of debris from buildings and domestic refuse from a settlement. They are commonly found in areas where mud brick is used as the main building material, especially the Middle East and parts of southeast Europe. In the Middle East, where settlements have been occupied continuously for thousands of years, tells can be up to 30 meters (100 feet) high. The word comes from Arabic; alternative forms include *chatal* (Turkish) and *tepe* (Persian).

TELL AWAYLI

Settlement in southern SUMERIA that was founded in the early 6th millennium BC (UBAID PERIOD), with a large granary for the communal storage of agricultural produce. Centralized control of the collection, storage, and redistribution of key resources is a common feature of early complex societies and the development of social hierarchies and political institutions. ▷ 1.09

TELL MUREYBAT

NATUFIAN proto-farming settlement in the upper Euphrates valley in modern Syria, occupied from the 9th to the 7th millennia BC, with evidence of the cultivation of introduced wild cereal plants (einkorn WHEAT) in the 9th millennium BC, and the emergence of a fully agricultural pottery-using community by 6000 BC. ▷ 1.08

TEPE GAWRA

A settlement in central MESOPOTAMIA dating from the HALAFIAN period (c.5500 BC). The early temple, built in the UBAID PERIOD, contains the earliest examples of walls decorated with pilasters and recesses (c.5000

BC), a design feature of later Mesopotamian temples. ▷ 1.09

TEPE YAHYA

Settlement in southern Iran occupied from the 5th millennium BC, with evidence of the earliest bronze metallurgy to use arsenic to improve the casting properties of smelted ores (c.3800 BC). In the 3rd millennium BC it was a major center for the manufacture of soapstone vessels and seals. ▷ 1.10

TERRA AMATA

LOWER PALEOLITHIC occupation site found in fossil beach deposits in southern France, dating from about 230,000 ya. Evidence of oval brushwood shelters (potentially the earliest known human structures) is disputed by most archeologists. ▷ 1.01

THEBES (EGYPT)

The Greek name for the southern Egyptian town of Waset. Thebes rose to prominence after its ruling family initiated the MIDDLE KINGDOM and its local god, Amun, became the dominant Egyptian deity. During the NEW KINGDOM period Thebes, the religious capital of Egypt, reached the height of prosperity, with enormous temples to Amun and other gods erected at LUXOR and KARNAK. ▷ 1.18

THERA

Island in the southern Aegean that was the scene of an immense volcanic eruption in about 1626 BC, which some historians believe may have given rise to the Atlantis legend. Its most flourishing town, Akrotiri, has been rediscovered beneath the lava, providing magnificent examples of MINOAN-style frescoes. ▷ 1.22, 1.24

THESSALY

Large region of northeastern Greece, made up of two plains enclosed by mountains, with little access to the sea. For much of its history Thessaly was a federation of states with only the occasional ruler (e.g. Jason, the TYRANT of the 4th century BC) exercising strong central control. The plains were easily subdued by Philip II of Macedon in the 4th century BC. ▷ 1.24, 1.25

THOLOS

A circular building. The term often refers to the vaulted "beehive" tombs of the Mycenaeans that originated in MESSENIA and reached their most sophisticated form at MYCENAE in the 14th century BC (as in the "Treasury of Atreus"). ▷ 1.22

THRACIANS

People of uncertain origin who occupied the southern Balkans between the Aegean and the Danube (Thrace) from the 7th century BC, known from early historical texts (Herodotus) and archeological sources. They were ethnically heterogenous, with a horse-riding elite, possibly drawn from warrior

pastoralists, who migrated into eastern Europe in the early 1st millennium BC. The Thracians developed close trading and cultural links with the Greeks, and had established a STATE system by the 5th century BC. ▷ 1.05, 1.06, 1.12, 1.15, 1.23, 1.24, 1.25

THREE AGE SYSTEM

An evolutionary classification of human culture, based on tool technologies and materials (STONE AGE, BRONZE AGE and IRON AGE), first proposed by the Danish archeologist Christian Thomsen in 1816–19. It is now accepted that the scheme has no analytical value, being applicable in strict terms only to Eurasia and north Africa (with different temporal parameters in different regions). It is considered too crude a means of characterizing the complexity and variety of ancient cultures, and too simplistic as a way of representing cultural change. The terms Bronze Age and Iron Age are sometimes still used for broad descriptive purposes.

TIBETO-BURMESE

HUNTER-GATHERER peoples with closely-related languages who lived in the Himalayan region and who adopted transhumant PASTORALISM from about 1500 BC. They were influenced by contacts with herding communities in India and by the steppe pastoralists of central Asia. ▷ 1.04

TIGLATH-PILESER I

King of ASSYRIA (r.1115–1076 BC). He resisted invasions by HURRIANS and KASKAS of Anatolia, but failed in his attempt to revive Assyrian dominance by controlling ARAMAEAN settlers. The empire declined after his death, and was reduced to control of the region around ASHUR. ▷ 1.12

TIGLATH-PILESER III

King of ASSYRIA (r.744–727 BC) who re-established Assyrian dominance in the Middle East. Once governor of Calah, he deposed Ashur-nirari V and reorganized the empire as a centralized state with a professional army and a provincial administration under direct royal control. He curbed the power of URARTU and imposed Assyrian rule on BABYLONIA and the LEVANT, resettling conquered populations in border areas. ▷ 1.13, 1.14

TIN

Metal used in COPPER-alloy metallurgy, forming about 10 percent of bronze, added to strengthen and harden cast objects. Tin ore sources were of considerable significance in the ancient Old World, and major deposits were exploited in Europe and Asia from the 3rd millennium BC, with large-scale regional trading networks dating from about 2000 BC. ▷ 1.10, 1.21, 1.23, 1.25, 1.26, 1.27

TINGIS

PHOENICIAN trading colony (modern Tangiers) on the Atlantic coast of Africa, to the west of

the Straits of Gibraltar. It was founded in the 7th century BC as a port for west African trade. By about 500 BC, Tingis was the capital of a province of the Carthaginian empire. ▷ 1.23, 1.25

TORRALBA-AMBRONA

Group of LOWER PALEOLITHIC sites in central Spain where ACHEULIAN hand-ax industries dating from about 600,000–200,000 ya have been discovered, along with evidence of elephant butchery, wooden spears and the use of FIRE. ▷ 1.01

TRES ZAPOTES

An important early OLMEC ceremonial center (c.1200 BC) to the west of the Tuxtla mountains (where basalt for monument construction was obtained), near the Gulf coast in central Mexico. It was the last major Olmec center to be occupied after the destruction of LA VENTA in about 400 BC. ▷ 1.28

TRIPOLYE-CUCUTENI CULTURE

Late NEOLITHIC and early Copper Age culture of the west Ukrainian steppes and Carpathian mountains, dating from about 4200–3800 BC. It is characterized by large fortified villages, painted pottery, and COPPER and gold artifacts such as those deposited in the VARNA cemetery. Tripolye-Cucuteni communities were among the first to domesticate HORSES. ▷ 1.20

TROJAN WAR

Legendary war in which a massed force of Greeks attacked TROY after the abduction of Helen of SPARTA by Paris of Troy. The Greeks eventually sacked the city after a ten-year siege. The war was a major theme in epic poetry and forms the background to HOMER'S ILIAD. The legend may rest on actual events of the MYCENAEAN period. ▷ 1.22

TROY

Ancient city on the eastern side of the entrance to the Dardenelles. Its prosperity resulted from the control of sea routes to the Black Sea and east–west land routes. The complex site was occupied, with short interruptions, from 3000 BC until the 9th century AD, and its detailed history has proved difficult to interpret. No clear evidence of a Greek or MYCENAEAN siege has yet been discovered, though the site was destroyed by fire twice in the 13th century, and again in about 1100 BC. ▷ 1.22

TRUNDHOLM

Ancient bog in Zealand, Denmark, where an outstanding example of middle BRONZE AGE metal craftmanship, the "Chariot of the Sun", was deposited in the mid-2nd millennium BC. The composite cast-bronze model, which consists of a horse pulling a vertical disk (gold-plated on one side), mounted on a wheeled carriage, probably had religious significance. ▷ 1.21

TURDETANIANS

People of southern Spain, related to the Tartessians, who traded with PHOENICIAN and Greek colonies, and later with Carthaginian cities on the Mediterranean coast, in about 900–200 BC. They developed an indigenous sculptural tradition influenced by Greek and Phoenician art, and by about 500 BC had established several kingdoms with urban centers, such as Porcuna. ▷ 1.25

TUTANKHAMUN

Egyptian boy-PHARAOH (r.1333–1323 BC). Tutankhamun was of little importance historically, but achieved worldwide prominence when his unplundered tomb was discovered in the VALLEY OF THE KINGS in 1922. ▷ 1.18

TUTHMOSIS I

Probably the greatest PHARAOH of NEW KINGDOM Egypt, Tuthmosis I (r.1504–1492 BC) founded the Egyptian empire in the LEVANT, as well as extending Egyptian power into NUBIA. He was the first pharaoh to be buried in the VALLEY OF THE KINGS. ▷ 1.12. 1.18

TUTHMOSIS III

Egyptian PHARAOH (r.1479–1425 BC) of the NEW KINGDOM period who became sole ruler in 1458 BC after the death of his domineering stepmother, HATSHEPSUT. A fine military commander, Tuthmosis III systematically reduced the cities and kingdoms of Syria and Palestine, thus consolidating the Egyptian empire in the Near East. ▷ 1.18

TUTHMOSIS IV

Egyptian PHARAOH (r.1401–1391 BC) of the NEW KINGDOM period. By marrying his son to the daughter of the king of the rival Near Eastern state of MITTANI, Tuthmosis IV gained a 50-year period of stability for Egypt and an ally against the growing power of the HITTITE empire of Anatolia. ▷ 1.12

TYRANT

In the turbulent period (650–500 BC) when the Greek city-states were evolving their political systems, it was common for single rulers to seize power – often with popular support – from the aristocratic elite. The term tyrant, possibly PHOENICIAN in origin, was used to describe a ruler who had gained power by his own efforts rather than by inheritance. Tyrants were not initially associated with oppressive government. Many, such as PEISISTRATOS of Athens, were able rulers who enjoyed widespread popular support because they challenged aristocratic privileges. As citizen bodies became more confident, however, one-man rule became an anathema, and most tyrants were overthrown or expelled from their cities. ▷ 1.24

TYRE

A port on the Levantine coast that had become the leading PHOENICIAN city by the 10th century BC, establishing trading colonies throughout the Mediterranean, including Carthage. It was sacked by the Babylonian king, NEBUCHADNEZZAR, in 574 BC but remained an important port into Roman times. ▷ 1.13, 1.14, 1.15, 1.23, 1.25

UBAID PERIOD

Late NEOLITHIC period in which farming communities similar to those of the SAMARRAN and HALAFIAN cultures settled in south MESOPOTAMIA in about 5900–4300 BC. They built large-scale IRRIGATION systems and their distinctive CERAMICS are found throughout Mesopotamia from about 5200 BC. Farming villages in this period grew into small towns, such as ERIDU (by c.5000 BC), some with temple buildings, establishing a pattern of urban development and religious architecture that was central to Mesopotamian civilization. ▷ 1.09

UGARIT

Levantine port that became a major state in the 2nd millennium BC, when it handled Cypriot, MYCENAEAN, HITTITE and Egyptian trade. The cosmopolitan character of Ugaritic culture is evident from trade goods, artifacts and records written in four languages and seven scripts. The city was destroyed, probably by SEA PEOPLES, in about 1200 BC. ▷ 1.08, 1.09, 1.10, 1.11, 1.12, 1.13, 1.14

UJJAIN

One of seven sacred Hindu cities, located in the upland area of central India, founded in the 6th century BC as the capital of the powerful Avanti kingdom. Ujjain was defended by massive earth ramparts enclosing an area about 1.5 kilometers (0.9 miles) in diameter. ▷ 1.26

ULU BURUN SHIPWRECK

Shipwreck on the south Anatolian coast dating from the 14th century BC. Its varied cargo, which included COPPER ingots; bronze weapons; pottery from Greece, Canaan and Cyprus; Anatolian TIN; gold jewelry; Egyptian scarabs, and a range of faience, ivory and glass objects, provides a unique insight into the late BRONZE AGE Aegean system of trade. ▷ 1.22

UMBRIANS

Term applied to various geographical, linguistic and cultural entities. Umbria formed part of the 6th region of Italy under Augustus. Umbrian was an INDO-EUROPEAN Italic dialect of central Italy, attested in a number of inscriptions, notably the Iguvine bronze tables. ▷ 1.25

UMMA

Sumerian city that competed with LAGASH, URUK, UR and AKKAD in the 3rd millennium BC. It briefly achieved regional hegemony under King LUGALZAGESI (c.2350 BC), who defeated Lagash and united SUMER and Akkad under one ruler for the first time. Conquered by SARGON OF AGADE in about 2330 BC, it never regained its former power. ▷ 1.10

UNETICE CULTURE

Culture of north-central Europe dating from about 2500 to 1500 BC, whose features widely typify the Early BRONZE AGE cultures of temperate Europe, including rich single burials under ROUND BARROWS, the widespread use of bronze (from c.2000 BC), the development of CHIEFDOMS, and long-distance trade in bronze, amber, faience and gold prestige goods. ▷ 1.04, 1.21

UR

City in SUMERIA that became a major city-state in the EARLY DYNASTIC period (c.2900–2334 BC), and at times the most powerful city in MESOPOTAMIA. The famous "Royal Cemetery" of the 26th century BC, with spectacular grave goods and human sacrifices (slaves, attendants and guards), suggests a powerful and brutal ruling elite. It competed with rival cities such as KISH, LAGASH and UMMA, and was briefly pre-eminent in the 25th century BC under the First Dynasty of Ur (the first dynasty known from written records).

After a period of domination by Akkadian and Gutian rulers in the 24th–22nd centuries BC, the city revived under the Third Dynasty of Ur (2112–2004 BC), which established an extensive empire in southern Mesopotamia. The great ZIGGURAT built by UR-NAMMU was one of the most impressive structures in ancient Mesopotamia. After the sack of Ur by the Elamites in 2004 BC, the city gradually declined in religious and commercial importance until the massive rebuilding works of the Neo-Babylonian kings, NEBUCHADNEZZAR and NABONIDUS, in the 6th century BC. It was abandoned in the 3rd century BC, when the local IRRIGATION system failed. ▷ 1.09, 1.10, 1.11, 1.12, 1.13

UR-NAMMU

First king of the Third Dynasty of UR (r.2112–2095 BC), who established a new imperial state in MESOPOTAMIA, 80 years after the collapse of the Akkadian empire. His success stemmed largely from control of the trade routes into the Persian Gulf. ▷ 1.11

URARTU

Mountain region between Anatolia and the Caspian Sea, inhabited in the 2nd and 1st millennia BC by Hurrian-speaking peoples. By 850 BC Urartu had become a major state, conquering and developing neighboring areas as far as the Caucasus and upper Euphrates. Its power waned in the 8th century BC, as the Neo-Assyrian empire expanded, culminating in 714 BC in SARGON II's defeat of Rusas (the last Urartian king with imperial aspirations) at Lake Urmia. Urartu was conquered by Armenian invaders in the 7th century BC. ▷ 1.05, 1.07, 1.12, 1.13

URBANIZATION
Process leading to the formation of urban settlements, in which most inhabitants are engaged in non-agricultural activities, living in dense agglomerations of houses, elite residences, public buildings and commercial quarters. Urban life is distinctive in terms of its social complexity, structured by multiple corporate, political and legal institutions (also associated with STATE systems), social stratification, economic specialization and cultural heterogeneity. The earliest cities developed in MESOPOTAMIA from the 5th to 3rd millennia BC, and in the Indus valley and China from the 3rd to 2nd millennia BC. ▷ 1.03, 1.04, 1.09, 1.10, 1.26, 1.27

URNFIELD CULTURES
Although culturally diverse, late BRONZE AGE societies in Europe widely adopted a shared funerary tradition of individual cremation burial in funerary urns that were placed in large cemeteries, sometimes numbering thousands of graves (e.g. Leubingen). This tradition originated in eastern Europe in the mid-2nd millennium BC, spreading to the Rhine and Italy by about 1200 BC and the Atlantic coast by about 1000 BC. ▷ 1.05, 1.06, 1.21, 1.25

URUK
City in SUMERIA that developed from an UBAID farming village, becoming an urban center in the 4th millennium BC (its name is given to the URUK PERIOD of Mesopotamian history). It was a major city-state in the EARLY DYNASTIC period (c.2900–2334 BC), and remained an important religious and commercial center until the 1st millennium BC. ▷ 1.09, 1.10, 1.11, 1.12

URUK PERIOD
Period of Mesopotamian culture following the UBAID PERIOD. During the Uruk period the first civilization in the world developed in SUMERIA (c.4300–3100 BC), marked by processes of STATE formation and URBANIZATION that included the invention of the earliest script for record-keeping, increasingly intensive IRRIGATION agriculture, and the widespread adoption of new technologies (COPPER metallurgy, the potter's wheel, the PLOW and wheeled transport). ▷ 1.09, 1.10, 1.11, 1.12

URUKAGINA
The last king of the 1st dynasty of the city of LAGASH in southern SUMERIA (c.2350 BC). His law code is the earliest surviving record of state legislation and governmental powers, particularly in relation to temple authorities. ▷ 1.10

VALDIVIA TRADITION
Long-lived culture (c.3800–1700 BC) of the PRECERAMIC PERIOD, around the Gulf of Guayaquil, Ecuador. Valdivia communities were sedentary, largely dependent on fishing, shellfish collecting and MAIZE cultivation.

Their CERAMICS were the earliest in South America (from c.3000 BC). ▷ 1.04, 1.28

VALLEY OF THE KINGS
Valley to the west of the Nile at THEBES, used as a burial place by the PHARAOHS of the NEW KINGDOM. Sixty-two tombs were constructed, but most were later discovered and robbed of their rich contents. The exception was the tomb of TUTANKHAMUN, whose opulence revealed the magnificence of what has been lost. ▷ 1.18

VAN LANG
Earliest complex CHIEFDOM society in southeast Asia, based on intensive RICE farming, which emerged in the Red River (Song koi) delta, in the region of modern Hanoi in Vietnam, by about 500 BC. The early history of the area in Vietnamese legends refers to the kingdom of Van Lang (Land of the Tatooed Men), ruled by the legendary Hung dynasty. ▷ 1.06

VARNA
Early Copper Age cemetery (c.4600–4100 BC) in the Danube basin, close to the Black Sea coast. More than 280 burials of men, women and children have been found, with an extraordinary range of artifacts including pottery, gold jewelry and decorative fittings, COPPER tools and weapons, and shell beads. The range and richness of the grave goods may indicate the early development of a complex social hierarchy. ▷ 1.20

VINCA
Large, late NEOLITHIC TELL site in modern Serbia that gave its name to the Vinca culture of the central Balkans (c.5500–4500 BC). It is characterized by large, long-lived agricultural villages and distinctive painted pottery, including figurines and models. ▷ 1.20

VIX
Early IRON AGE (HALLSTATT D) female burial in a timber mortuary house beneath a ROUND BARROW in central France, dating from about 520 BC. It contained a four-wheeled cart, fine metal objects, including a gold diadem, and a huge bronze *krater* (wine mixing vessel) and painted pottery cup from Greece, indicating long-distance trade with the Mediterranean. ▷ 1.23

WARRING STATES PERIOD
Last phase of the later (Eastern) ZHOU period in China (c.480–220 BC), when widespread rejection of Zhou overlordship led to the emergence of seven powerful and aggressive kingdoms competing for dominance, the strongest being QI, CHU and QIN. By about 250 BC, Qin had gained supremacy and finally unified China in about 220 BC. ▷ 1.27

WASHUKANNI
Capital of the HURRIAN kingdom of MITTANI, possibly at the unexcavated site of Tell al-

Fakhariyeh to the east of the Euphrates in northern Syria. It was sacked by the HITTITES in 1340 BC and by the Assyrians in about 1300 BC. Nothing is known of its history, layout or buildings. ▷ 1.12

WATER BUFFALO
See CATTLE

WAVY LINE CERAMICS
One of the earliest CERAMIC traditions in the world, made by HUNTER-GATHERERS in sub-Saharan Africa from the Hoggar massif (Algeria) to the Upper Nile (Sudan), before the adoption of agricultural practices, in about 8000 to 6000 BC. Its name derives from the distinctive incised decoration made by combing catfish spines across the vessel surfaces. ▷ 1.16

WAYWAKA
Burial site in the southern Peruvian Andes where thin sheets of gold foil and a metal-working tool-kit were found with a male inhumation of about 1440 BC. This forms the earliest evidence of metallurgy in the Americas. ▷ 1.28

WEI
Feudal state of the ZHOU kingdom (c.1100–250 BC), with a capital city at Chaoge. It played a minor role in the SPRINGS AND AUTUMNS PERIOD but became a leading state in the WARRING STATES period, particularly during the reign of Duke Wen (c.424–387 BC). ▷ 1.27

WESSEX CULTURE
Early BRONZE AGE culture of southern Britain (c.2000–1500 BC), characterized by groups of large ROUND BARROWS and a rich burial tradition, with grave goods such as bronze daggers, gold work, amber, jet and faience jewelry. These objects demonstrate links with Brittany and central Europe, and the widespead use of bronze. ▷ 1.05, 1.21

WHEAT
Cereal plant species, including emmer, einkorn and spelt wheat, that was domesticated in the FERTILE CRESCENT and Anatolia from about 9000 BC, becoming staple food crops throughout the Middle East, Europe and north Africa by 5000 BC. They were especially important for milling flours suitable for making breads and biscuits. ▷ 1.03, 1.08, 1.09, 1.16, 1.20, 1.22

WHEEL
Circular frame or disk mounted on a central pivot for mechanical purposes, especially for wheeled transport and pottery manufacture. The earliest evidence of the existence of the wheel is wheel-thrown pottery from MESOPOTAMIA, dating from about 4500 BC. Wheeled vehicles were probably first used in the 4th millennium BC, invented either in Mesopotamia or on the west Eurasian steppes

(carts and wagons), and had spread to Europe and India by about 3000 BC. The potter's wheel was also invented independently in China (before 3000 BC). ▷ 1.03, 1.10, 1.20, 1.21, 1.27

WINDMILL HILL
The largest early NEOLITHIC enclosure in northwest Europe, near AVEBURY in southern Britain, built in about 3600 BC. It consists of three concentric circuits of causewayed ditches with internal banks, about 350 meters (1,150 feet) in diameter. It probably had a ceremonial purpose. ▷ 1.20

WOOL
Animal fiber obtained from live animals (mainly SHEEP, GOATS and camelids) that was used to make strong, relatively coarse textiles, including clothes, blankets and carpets. Woollen fabrics were made from about 4000 BC (in MESOPOTAMIA), though the earliest surviving examples date to the 2nd millennium BC (from Egypt, Denmark and China). ▷ 1.03, 1.09, 1.22

WU
Large feudal state of the ZHOU kingdom, with a non-Chinese population, named after its capital city. It gradually grew in power during the SPRINGS AND AUTUMNS period to become the dominant state in southern China by the late 6th century BC (replacing CHU). It was conquered by the neighboring kingdom of Yue in 473 BC. ▷ 1.27

XIA DYNASTY
Legendary 1st dynasty of China (c.2205–1766 BC), founded by YU THE GREAT. There is no archeological or contemporary literary evidence of the Xia dynasty or states in this period, though later literary references may have been based on earlier texts written on materials that have not survived. ▷ 1.27

XIANYUN
Tribal people of northern China who lived beyond the northwest frontier of the ZHOU kingdom in the early 1st millennium BC. Their attacks on the Zhou heartland from the late 9th to early 8th centuries BC led to the abandonment of the ancient capital at Han. ▷ 1.27

YAM
Plant species of the genus *Dioscorea*, with edible tubers, that is found in tropical and subtropical regions and is widely cultivated as a staple food source. The domestication of yams may have occurred as early as about 5000 BC in New Guinea (sweet potatoes) and about 3000 BC in west Africa. ▷ 1.03, 1.16

YAN
Northern feudal state of the ZHOU kingdom (c.1100–250 BC), with a capital city at Ji. It played only a minor role in the power struggles of the SPRINGS AND AUTUMNS PERIOD, as the authority of the Zhou dynasty declined (from c.770 BC). ▷ 1.27

YANGSHAO CULTURE
The earliest farming culture in China with a full agricultural economy (MILLET, PIGS, GOATS and SHEEP), dating from about 5000 to 3200 BC. It developed from indigenous proto-farming societies on the light fertile loess plains of the Yellow river and its tributaries. Yangshao communities lived in large settlements of substantial timber houses and had a rich material culture, with painted pottery, textiles and jade carvings. ▷ 1.27

YAYA-MAMA RELIGIOUS TRADITIONS
Tradition of religious architecture and iconography of the Lake Titcaca region in the high Andes from about 600 to 400 BC, in the area later ruled by the Tiahuanaco state (established by c.AD 500). ▷ 1.06, 1.28

YONG
People who lived to the southeast of SHANG territory, mentioned in late Shang records (from c.1150 BC) when military campaigns conducted by King DI-XIN were directed at hostile barbarians in eastern China. ▷ 1.27

YU THE GREAT
Legendary king and founder of the first ruling dynasty of China, the XIA. In later literary sources he was said to be the chief minister and then successor of the emperors Yao and Shun, and to have ruled China from about 2205 BC. ▷ 1.27

YUE QI
Steppe nomad people of the Altai-Gobi region, also known as the Kushans, who raided the northern states of ZHOU China in the 8th to 2nd centuries BC, until they were forced to move westwards by the expansion of the fierce Xiongnu nomads of Mongolia. ▷ 1.06

ZAPOTECS
People of the OAXACA VALLEY region of south-central Mexico, who developed state societies in the 1st millennium BC, with several ceremonial centers (notably Monté Albán) and the first writing script in the Americas (Zapotec hieroglyphic, used for royal names and calendrical records), from about 800 BC. The cultural and political relationships between Zapotec, OLMEC and Maya states in the 1st millennium BC remain uncertain, though extensive trade networks existed for the exchange of OBSIDIAN, jade and other important materials. The height of Zapotec power and architectural achievement was reached during the 1st to 7th centuries AD. ▷ 1.06, 1.07, 1.28

ZAWI CHEMI SHANIDAR
Proto-farming settlement located in the Zagros mountains, in modern Iraq. It was occupied between the late 10th and early 9th millennia BC, with a subsistence economy based on the intensive management of wild SHEEP herds and wild cereal cultivation. The site provides some of the earliest evidence of animal and plant domestication. ▷ 1.08

ZEBU
See CATTLE

ZEDEKIAH
Last king of JUDAH (r.c.597–586 BC). His attempt to rebel against Babylonian rule in 587 BC led to the destruction of JERUSALEM by NEBUCHADNEZZAR, Zedekiah's imprisonment, and the deportation of his subjects. ▷ 1.14

ZHOU DYNASTY
Ruling dynasty of China (1122–256 BC) that was established by King Wu, who overthrew the last of the SHANG kings, DI-XIN. Wu justified his usurpation by claiming the "Mandate of Heaven", which served as a model for all later imperial ideologies in China, and a feudal system of rule that relied on the obedience of vassal dukedoms.

The Zhou period is divided into two phases, the Western Zhou (1122–770 BC), when the capital was located in their heartland at HAO, and the Eastern Zhou (770–256 BC), initiated when barbarian attacks forced the removal of the capital to the less vulnerable city of LUOYANG. Detached from their heartland, the authority of the Zhou dynasty declined. In the early Eastern Zhou period, also known as the SPRINGS AND AUTUMNS PERIOD (770–480 BC), rival dukedoms vied for dominance, some achieving temporary hegemony, while paying nominal allegience to the Zhou king. The fragmentation of the Zhou state in the late Eastern Zhou period (largely coterminous with the WARRING STATES period, 480–221 BC) finally ended when the last Zhou king was deposed by the triumphant QIN dynasty in 256 BC.

The Zhou period is notable for the spread of urbanism throughout China, its rich artistic tradition, and for the establishment of a fully literate culture and the political and philosophical traditions that pervade much of later Chinese history (especially Confucianism). ▷ 1.05, 1.06, 1.27

ZHOUKOUDIEN
LOWER PALEOLITHIC cave site in northern China, with occupation levels dating from about 500,000 ya. The site contains chopper- and flake-tool industries associated with important fossil remains of HOMO ERECTUS. ▷ 1.01

ZIGGURAT
Rectangular stepped mound on which Mesopotamian temples were built in the 3rd to 1st millennia BC (possibly symbolizing sacred mountains). Most ziggurats were built of mud brick, with an exterior fired-brick casing, ornamental facades, and stairways and ramps for access to the shrines. ▷ 1.09, 1.11

Part 2

THE CLASSICAL

I n the thirty generations between 500 BC and AD 600, the world was rapidly transformed. Across the globe, human populations increased, sometimes startlingly so; many powerful states with complex systems of social and economic control emerged; and food production intensified, allowing specialist workers such as artists, architects, poets and philosophers to develop their skills of adorning, exploring and explaining their world. By AD 600 various empires had come and gone and all the major religions, with the exception of Islam, had begun to take root.

Amidst the mass of vivid detail, certain themes recur. In certain areas, favored by their access to natural resources and their position astride important communication routes, the pace of change accelerated and centers of social or economic innovation sprang up. Powerful individuals commanded their own territories, now known as chiefdoms. They survived by competing with and copying from one another: prestige goods were acquired and displayed during their lives and upon their deaths, for lesser beings and rivals to wonder at. The Scythian chieftain buried at Pazyryk in central Asia about 600 BC was provided in his grave with everything a paramount leader would wish for – a funerary vehicle, feasting and hunting gear and gold; but this collection of finery was as much an opportunity for his family to display the extent of their wealth and power to their rivals as to offer the deceased a comfortable afterlife. Conspicuous consumption and ritual destruction of luxuries by burying them with chieftains meant that a continuous supply of prestige goods was needed. This gave momentum to trade and exchange and, from time to time, encouraged latent hostility between personal or national rivals to flare into outright physical aggression.

In some areas chiefdoms were transformed into states, often through a complex phase of warfare and rapid social reordering. Thus the Mycenaean chiefdoms of the late second millennium BC became the young city-states of Greece two

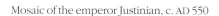

Mosaic of the emperor Justinian, c. AD 550

centuries later. On the other side of the world in about 500 BC, in the Oaxaca valley of Mesoamerica, three competing chiefdoms came together to found a new political capital on the mountain-top of Monte Albán; it remained preeminent in the region for more than a thousand years. The unification of rival polities under a single authority was a recurring pattern, and it was seen on different scales and at different times throughout the world. In 408 BC, a century after the foundation of Monte Albán, three rival Greek cities on the island of Rhodes agreed to found the city of Rhodes. This kind of coalescence the Greeks well understood – they had a special word for it: synoicism.

There was a dynamic, interdependent relationship between these innovating centers and the peripheral areas and entities around them. A complex state system needed raw materials and human power to maintain it. A regular supply of rare metals, exotic stones and woods, furs and fabrics was essential to support the structure of the social hierarchy.

Human power, too, whether in the form of slaves or a supply of food for a free workforce, was a prerequisite for supporting the labor-intensive adjuncts of a state, whether the bureaucracy and professional army of China's Qin empire in the 3rd century BC, or the scholarly elite of Gupta India in the 4th century AD, who created some of the greatest works of law, medicine, astronomy, mathematics and philosophy in the Sanskrit language.

The demands of centralizing powers encouraged trade with the surrounding peripheries. African and Indian communities were drawn into the economic sphere of the Roman empire in the first four centuries AD, despite knowing little or nothing of the Roman state that gave them pottery, coins and trinkets in return for raw materials and slaves. Communities closer to the innovating centers were in a better position to learn from their neighbors and emulate their ways, thus becoming increasingly powerful.

There was a continual drift of creative power and energy from the center to the periphery, as the seeds of innovation took root in the fertile periphery while the core decayed.

WORLD

The early core of Europe developed in the Greek cities around the Aegean in the eighth to sixth centuries BC; later, in the fifth century, the focus for innovation was on the Greek mainland. Power then shifted to the central Mediterranean where, after the third century BC, Rome emerged preeminent. It maintained its leadership for some six centuries, until power moved back to the peripheral Black Sea region with the rise of Constantinople and the Byzantine empire.

Roman merchant ship, c.AD 100

In Mesoamerica a similar pattern can be seen, with the spread of innovating power from the Oaxaca valley in the second half of the first millennium BC to the Valley of Mexico in the central highlands, and then the Maya area of the Yucatán in the early first millennium AD. The pattern is still with us at the beginning of the 21st century, as economic vitality and productivity shift from the north Atlantic toward the Pacific rim.

The cycle of growth and decay and the inexorable shift of centers of power were frequently accelerated by warfare and invasion. The Celtic tribes from eastern France and southern Germany who attacked the Greek and Roman world in the fourth and third centuries BC confronted energetic Mediterranean states that were perfectly capable of defending themselves (and of conquering others); but the succession of attacks by Germanic peoples around AD 400 found the Roman empire in a state of advanced decay. The "barbarian" Germans were able rapidly to overrun the old empire and set up a number of new kingdoms of their own within its carcass.

The collapse of empires – a common theme in this period – is a subject of great fascination. Each case is different, and the reasons are always many and interacting: natural catastrophe, population decline, economic over-extension, invasion, disease. In the purely prehistoric context of Mesoamerica, archeologists can only speculate about "ecological overshoot" and the destructive role of parasitic elites; whereas in China, detailed written records reveal the processes leading to the collapse of the Han empire in AD 220: foreign wars, internal power struggles and recurrent widespread peasant rebellions. In the end, the empire which had held China together for four centuries disintegrated into many rival factions of local warlords.

Yet it is possible to turn the notions of center and periphery inside out and to see the states and empires of Europe, India and China not as centers but as developments on the periphery of the huge, central landmass of Asia – an unending steppe land, home of horse-riding nomads who for century after century moved out rapidly to strike terror into the hearts of their sedentary, civilized neighbors. In Europe the first recorded invaders from the steppes were the Cimmerians in about 700 BC. Then followed the Scythians, the Sarmatians, the Alans and the Huns, the last and most famous contributing to the widespread chaos at the end of the Roman era in the fifth century. Other groups moved through the Indus valley into the heart of the subcontinent, while the northern borders of China were constantly at risk after the eighth century BC – a threat which the Great Wall, with its garrison of half a million troops, was eventually built to avert (and could not do so). Thus the history of Old World civilization was intimately bound up with the pressures of rising populations across the deepest steppes of Eurasia.

During the millennium 500 BC–AD 600, many foundations of the modern world were created. Pyrotechnical skills developed; bronze and iron became widely available throughout the Old World and steel was developed in Han China. Wind and water were harnessed; horse-riding was transformed by the development of the stirrup about 200 BC; and science, astronomy and mathematics made enormous strides in the Hellenistic world, India, China and to some extent in Mesoamerica. By AD 600 a plateau had been reached. There was to be little further advance until the fifteenth century when the arts of navigation and seamanship opened up the world and, in doing so, unleashed new dynamic forces ■

Sasanian silver bowl with hunt scene, c.AD 480

In 500 BC the world's most impressive state was the Achemenid empire of Persia, extending from Libya to the Indus. The empire's first setback occurred when Xerxes I invaded Greece (▷2.07). The quarrelsome Greek city-states united in the face of the common enemy and defeated the Persians at sea at Salamis and on land at Plataea. The Greeks went back to their quarrels and did little to follow up their victory: Persia lost its foothold in Europe but continued to dominate the Middle East for eighty years (▷2.11). Then, in 404, Egypt rebelled and Persian control was not restored until 343. In 380 Persia's Indian provinces were lost.

Late 5th-century Greece was dominated by rivalry between Sparta and Athens, culminating in the Peloponnesian war which engulfed most of the Greek world but settled nothing. Further indecisive wars between shifting alliances ensued. Meanwhile, the Balkan kingdom of Macedon rose unopposed under Philip II and in 338 all the Greek city-states were forcibly enrolled in the Macedonian-dominated Hellenic league. Philip planned to invade Persia but his assassination in 336 left it to his son Alexander to carry out his plans. In only six years he conquered almost all the Persian empire, opening the whole Middle East to Greek influence (▷ 2.09).

By the 4th century the old south Arabian kingdom of Saba had been joined by the new states of Qataban and Hadramaut, driven by a demand from the Mediterranean for the precious gums, frankincense and myrrh, which were produced in the region. By the same period Sabean influence was seen in Damot on the African Red Sea coast.

Through most of the 5th and 4th centuries the main power in the western Mediterranean was Carthage. Carthage was more interested in commerce than conquest and its empire grew little between 500 and 323. Most of central and western Europe was now dominated by Celtic peoples. Around 400, Celts crossed the Alps and invaded Italy, breaking the power of the Etruscans and settling the Po valley. Though still insignificant on the map, by 323 Rome was a major power in Italy, having conquered its Latin and Etruscan neighbors earlier in the century (▷ 2.12).

The strongest state in India in 500 was Magadha in the lower Ganges plain. From 364 it brought most of northern India under its control (▷2.22). Southern India was a mosaic of minor states and chiefdoms with little urban development. The Zhou kingdom of China, which had broken up into a dozen competing states in the 8th century, was still disunited, although many of the smaller states had been absorbed by the bigger players (▷2.24). The continual warfare

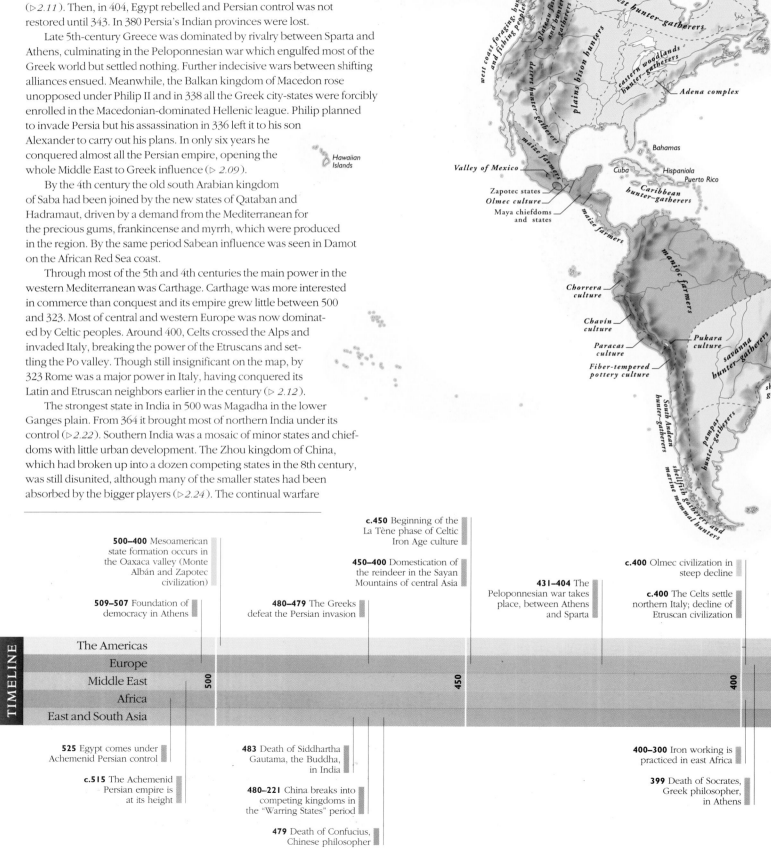

TIMELINE

The Americas

500–400 Mesoamerican state formation occurs in the Oaxaca valley (Monte Albán and Zapotec civilization)

509–507 Foundation of democracy in Athens

c.450 Beginning of the La Tène phase of Celtic Iron Age culture

450–400 Domestication of the reindeer in the Sayan Mountains of central Asia

480–479 The Greeks defeat the Persian invasion

431–404 The Peloponnesian war takes place, between Athens and Sparta

c.400 Olmec civilization in steep decline

c.400 The Celts settle northern Italy; decline of Etruscan civilization

Europe

Middle East

Africa

East and South Asia

500

450

400

525 Egypt comes under Achemenid Persian control

c.515 The Achemenid Persian empire is at its height

483 Death of Siddhartha Gautama, the Buddha, in India

480–221 China breaks into competing kingdoms in the "Warring States" period

479 Death of Confucius, Chinese philosopher

400–300 Iron working is practiced in east Africa

399 Death of Socrates, Greek philosopher, in Athens

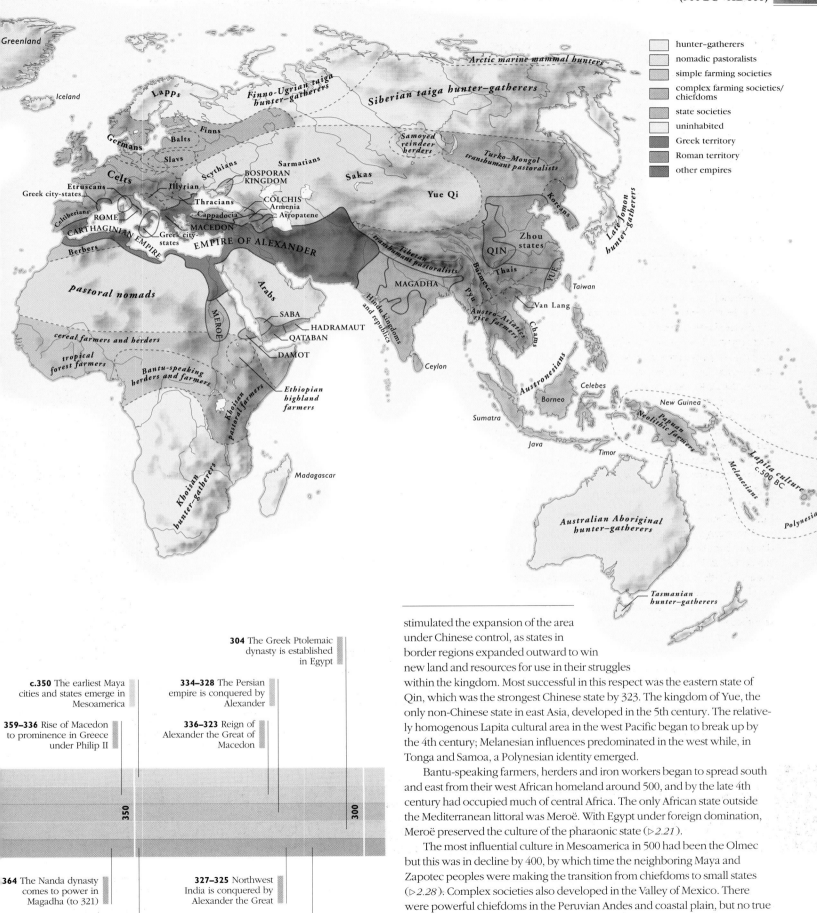

hunter–gatherers
nomadic pastoralists
simple farming societies
complex farming societies/ chiefdoms
state societies
uninhabited
Greek territory
Roman territory
other empires

Greenland
Iceland
Lapps
Finno-Ugrian taiga hunter-gatherers
Arctic marine mammal hunters
Siberian taiga hunter-gatherers
Finns
Germans
Balts
Slavs
Samoyed reindeer herders
Turko-Mongol transhumant pastoralists
Celts
Scythians
Sarmatians
Sakas
Yue Qi
Koreans
Etruscans
Illyrian
BOSPORAN KINGDOM
Greek city-states
Thracians
COLCHIS
Armenia
Cappadocia
Atropatene
Late Jomon hunter-gatherers
ROME
Celtiberians
MACEDON
Greek city-states
Zhou states
QIN
CARTHAGINIAN EMPIRE
EMPIRE OF ALEXANDER
Tibetan transhumant pastoralists
Berbers
MAGADHA
Burmese
Pyu
Thais
YUE
Taiwan
Pastoral nomads
Arabs
MEROE
SABA
HADRAMAUT
QATABAN
DAMOT
Hindu kingdoms and republics
Austro-Asiatic rice farmers
Van Lang
Chams
cereal farmers and herders
Ceylon
tropical forest farmers
Bantu-speaking herders and farmers
Ethiopian highland farmers
Austronesians
Celebes
Borneo
New Guinea
Papuan Neolithic farmers
Khoisan pastoral farmers
Sumatra
Java
Timor
Melanesians
Lapita culture c.500 BC
Madagascar
Khoisan hunter-gatherers
Australian Aboriginal hunter-gatherers
Polynesians
Tasmanian hunter-gatherers

304 The Greek Ptolemaic dynasty is established in Egypt

c.350 The earliest Maya cities and states emerge in Mesoamerica

334–328 The Persian empire is conquered by Alexander

359–336 Rise of Macedon to prominence in Greece under Philip II

336–323 Reign of Alexander the Great of Macedon

350

300

364 The Nanda dynasty comes to power in Magadha (to 321)

327–325 Northwest India is conquered by Alexander the Great

350–320 The Qin state rises to dominance in China

321 Chandragupta Maurya becomes king of Magadha and founds the Mauryan empire

stimulated the expansion of the area under Chinese control, as states in border regions expanded outward to win new land and resources for use in their struggles within the kingdom. Most successful in this respect was the eastern state of Qin, which was the strongest Chinese state by 323. The kingdom of Yue, the only non-Chinese state in east Asia, developed in the 5th century. The relatively homogenous Lapita cultural area in the west Pacific began to break up by the 4th century; Melanesian influences predominated in the west while, in Tonga and Samoa, a Polynesian identity emerged.

Bantu-speaking farmers, herders and iron workers began to spread south and east from their west African homeland around 500, and by the late 4th century had occupied much of central Africa. The only African state outside the Mediterranean littoral was Meroë. With Egypt under foreign domination, Meroë preserved the culture of the pharaonic state (▷2.21).

The most influential culture in Mesoamerica in 500 had been the Olmec but this was in decline by 400, by which time the neighboring Maya and Zapotec peoples were making the transition from chiefdoms to small states (▷2.28). Complex societies also developed in the Valley of Mexico. There were powerful chiefdoms in the Peruvian Andes and coastal plain, but no true states in South America. In North America hunting, gathering or fishing continued as the dominant way of life. Many groups augmented their food supply by cultivating wild plants but this activity was more gardening than farming ■

Alexander's empire did not survive his death in 323 – the immediate cause of its breakup being his failure to provide an heir – and within a few years his generals had become the rulers of independent kingdoms (▷2.10). Seleucos built a state which incorporated most of Anatolia, Mesopotamia, and Iran and extended into central Asia; despite successful rebellions by the Bactrian Greeks in 239 and the Parthians in 238, the Seleucid kingdom was still the largest of the successor states in 200. Ptolemy seized Egypt and founded a dynasty which was to last until 31 BC, ending only with Cleopatra's suicide after the battle of Actium. Macedon itself fell to Antipater, who reasserted Macedonian supremacy in Greece in the face of an Athenian-led rebellion. Macedon was still the leading power in Greece in 200.

The leading power in the western Mediterranean by 200 was Rome. The Romans had completed the conquest of peninsular Italy in 272, and in 264 were drawn into a war with Carthage over Sicily. This, the First Punic War, dragged on for over twenty years until the Romans had wrested control of Sicily, Sardinia and Corsica. Carthaginian expansion in Spain, arousing Roman hostility once again, led in 218 to the outbreak of the Second Punic War. The Carthaginian general Hannibal surprised the Romans by attacking Italy from the north, but counterattacks in Spain and north Africa brought Rome crushing victory, and Carthage was shorn of its empire (▷2.12).

Several centuries of stability on the Eurasian steppes came to an end in the 3rd century as the Sarmatians began to push westward against the Scythians. On the far eastern steppes the Turko-Mongol pastoralists made the transition to a horse-mounted fully nomadic way of life around 300, and by 200 they were united in the powerful Xiong-nu confederation. Their use of the composite bow gave the Xiongnu a decided military advantage over their nomadic Iranian neighbors to the west and made them a formidable adversary for the newly united Chinese (▷2.20).

In 321 Chandragupta Maurya (321–c. 293) seized the throne of the kingdom of Magadha, overthrowing the Nanda dynasty. Chandragupta spent most of his reign building a strong central administration, but he defeated a Seleucid invasion, adding all of northwest India to his domains (▷2.22). His son Bindusara also conquered much of southern India. Under Ashoka the Mauryan empire reached its greatest extent. Appalled by his bloody conquest of the east coast kingdom of Kalinga in 261, Ashoka abjured further warfare and, becoming a Buddhist, tried to impose Buddhist standards of behavior on his people. Little is known

323–280 Wars of the Diadochi: Alexander's generals split up his empire

323 Alexander the Great dies without naming a successor

264 Roman–Carthaginian rivalry in Sicily sets off the First Punic War

272 Rome completes its conquest of peninsular Italy

239 The Bactrian Greeks break away from the Seleucid kingdom

241 A Roman naval victory off Lilybaeum ends the First Punic war

TIMELINE		325	300	275	250
The Americas					
Europe					
Middle East					
Africa					
East and South Asia					

321 Chandragupta Maurya, founder of the Mauryan empire, becomes king of Magadha

c.300 The Turko-Mongol tribes of the eastern steppes adopt a fully nomadic way of life

c.300 Beginning of rice farming in Japan

268–233 Reign of Ashoka: Buddhism spreads through the Mauryan empire

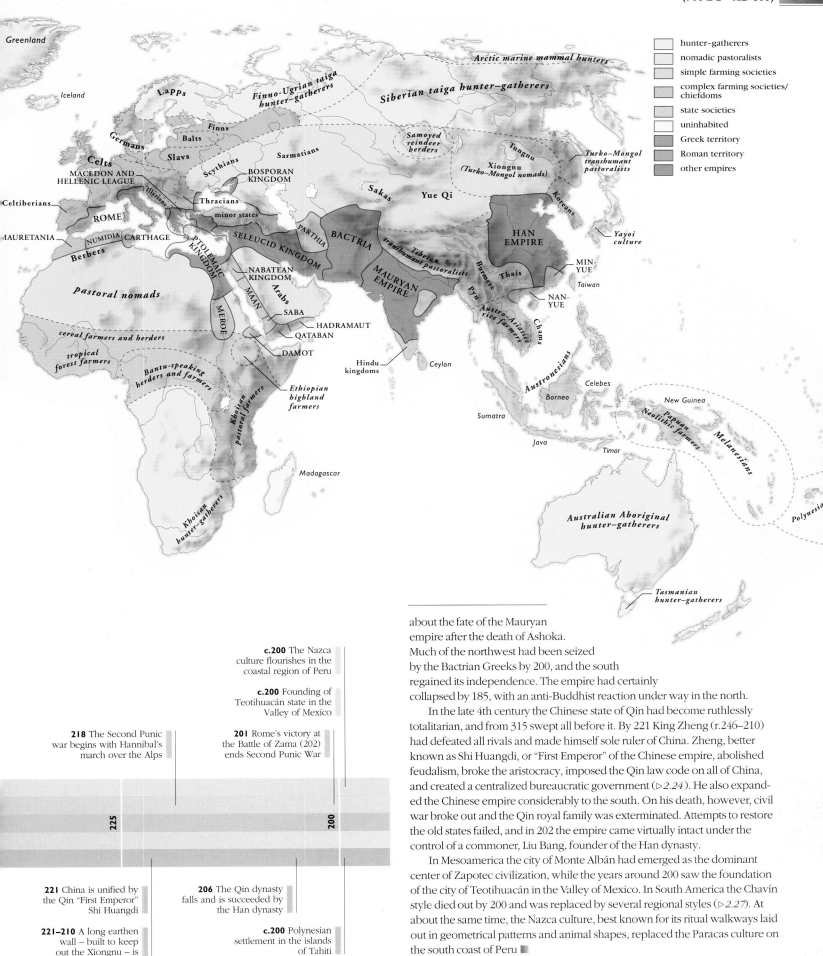

hunter–gatherers
nomadic pastoralists
simple farming societies
complex farming societies/
chiefdoms
state societies
uninhabited
Greek territory
Roman territory
other empires

Greenland

Iceland

Arctic marine mammal hunters

Lapps

Finno-Ugrian taiga
hunter-gatherers

Siberian taiga hunter-gatherers

Finns

Balts

Germans

Celts

Slavs

Samoyed
reindeer
herders

Tungnu

Xiongnu
(Turko-Mongol nomads)

Turko–Mongol
transhumant
pastoralists

MACEDON AND
HELLENIC LEAGUE

Scythians

Sarmatians

BOSPORAN
KINGDOM

Sakas

Yue Qi

Koreans

Celtiberians

Illyrians

Thracians

minor states

HAN
EMPIRE

Yayoi
culture

ROME

MAURETANIA

NUMIDIA

CARTHAGE

PTOLEMAIC
KINGDOM

SELEUCID KINGDOM

PARTHIA

BACTRIA

Tibetan
transhumant pastoralists

MIN-
YUE

Berbers

NABATEAN
KINGDOM

MAURYAN
EMPIRE

Burmese

Thais

Taiwan

NAN-
YUE

MAAN

Arabs

Pyu

Austro-
Asiatic
rice farmers

Chams

Pastoral nomads

MEROE

SABA

HADRAMAUT

QATABAN

DAMOT

Hindu
kingdoms

Ceylon

cereal farmers and herders

tropical
forest farmers

Ethiopian
highland
farmers

Austronesians

Celebes

New Guinea

Papuan
Neolithic farmers

Melanesians

Bantu-speaking
herders and farmers

Sumatra

Borneo

Khoisan
pastoral farmers

Java

Timor

Madagascar

Khoisan
hunter-gatherers

Australian Aboriginal
hunter-gatherers

Polynesians

Tasmanian
hunter-gatherers

about the fate of the Mauryan
empire after the death of Ashoka.
Much of the northwest had been seized
by the Bactrian Greeks by 200, and the south
regained its independence. The empire had certainly
collapsed by 185, with an anti-Buddhist reaction under way in the north.

In the late 4th century the Chinese state of Qin had become ruthlessly
totalitarian, and from 315 swept all before it. By 221 King Zheng (r.246–210)
had defeated all rivals and made himself sole ruler of China. Zheng, better
known as Shi Huangdi, or "First Emperor" of the Chinese empire, abolished
feudalism, broke the aristocracy, imposed the Qin law code on all of China,
and created a centralized bureaucratic government (▷2.24). He also expanded the Chinese empire considerably to the south. On his death, however, civil
war broke out and the Qin royal family was exterminated. Attempts to restore
the old states failed, and in 202 the empire came virtually intact under the
control of a commoner, Liu Bang, founder of the Han dynasty.

In Mesoamerica the city of Monte Albán had emerged as the dominant
center of Zapotec civilization, while the years around 200 saw the foundation
of the city of Teotihuacán in the Valley of Mexico. In South America the Chavín
style died out by 200 and was replaced by several regional styles (▷2.27). At
about the same time, the Nazca culture, best known for its ritual walkways laid
out in geometrical patterns and animal shapes, replaced the Paracas culture on
the south coast of Peru ▮

c.200 The Nazca
culture flourishes in the
coastal region of Peru

c.200 Founding of
Teotihuacán state in the
Valley of Mexico

218 The Second Punic
war begins with Hannibal's
march over the Alps

201 Rome's victory at
the Battle of Zama (202)
ends Second Punic War

225

200

221 China is unified by
the Qin "First Emperor"
Shi Huangdi

206 The Qin dynasty
falls and is succeeded by
the Han dynasty

221–210 A long earthen
wall – built to keep
out the Xiongnu – is
completed in China

c.200 Polynesian
settlement in the islands
of Tahiti

A decisive Roman victory at the battle of Cynoscephalae in 197 BC had broken the power of Macedon, who had supported Carthage in the Second Punic War. This victory opened the way for Roman domination of Greece. In 146 Rome brought the whole of Greece under direct control; and in the same year ruthlessly destroyed Carthage, though it had long ceased to be a threat (▷2.12). The Hellenistic kingdoms of the east were also powerless to prevent Roman expansion. By 64 BC most of Anatolia and the Levant were under Roman rule and Egypt had been made a protectorate. Direct rule was imposed on Egypt in 30 BC (▷2.13).

Rome's successes put its republican system of government – designed for a city-state, not a world empire – under increasing strain: and a succession of civil wars between 50 and 31 BC brought about the collapse of the Roman republic. The eventual victor, Octavian, created a new form of government – in effect, an absolute monarchy. King in all but name, he took the titles *princeps* (first citizen) and Augustus. His successors used the title *imperator* (commander or emperor).

In northern Europe, the Celts found themselves caught between the Romans, who were expanding northward, and the Germans, who were pushing south: by 1 BC the only remaining independent Celts were in the British Isles (▷2.18).

In Africa, the Sabean colonies had developed into the kingdom of Axum around 100 BC. At about the same time the dromedary camel was introduced to the northern Sahara, transforming the lives of the desert nomads much as horse riding had earlier changed the steppe pastoralist way of life, enabling them to range widely and raid settled peoples almost at will. By 1 BC pastoralism had spread among the Khoisan-speaking peoples as far south as the Transvaal region and Bantu-speaking peoples had begun to settle on the east African plateau (▷2.21).

Following his victory in the civil war in China (202), Liu Bang restored prosperity by introducing a series of agricultural and administrative reforms but, despite heroic efforts, failed to stop damaging raids by the nomadic Xiongnu who continued to be a serious threat to China until 38 BC. The Han period saw Chinese expansion in the south (▷2.24), where the non-Chinese kingdoms of Min-yue and Nan-yue were conquered, and in Korea. Small kingdoms had begun to develop in parts of Korea not under Chinese occupation by 50 BC.

The rise of the Xiongnu had a destabilizing effect on the Iranian nomads to the west (▷2.20). In 170 the Xiongnu inflicted a crushing defeat on the Yue Qi, who fled westward, unsettling the Sakas, before overrunning the Bactrian kingdom around 135. The Sakas headed south, first invading the Parthian

c.135 The westward-driven Yue Qi overrun the Bactrian kingdom

170–141 The Parthians conquer the Seleucid kingdom

146 Roman control is extended throughout Greece

c.100 Foundation of the Moche state in the region of Peru

TIMELINE		200		150		100
The Americas						
Europe						
Middle East						
Africa						
East and South Asia						

c.185 Fall of the Mauryan dynasty after Bactrians invade the Punjab

149–146 The Third Punic War: Rome levels the city of Carthage to the ground

101 China under the Han dynasty conquers Van Lang

170 The Hsiung-nu defeat the Yue Qi and dominate the eastern steppes

c.141 The Sakas invade the Parthian empire and northern India

c.100 The beginning of camel nomadism in the Sahara desert

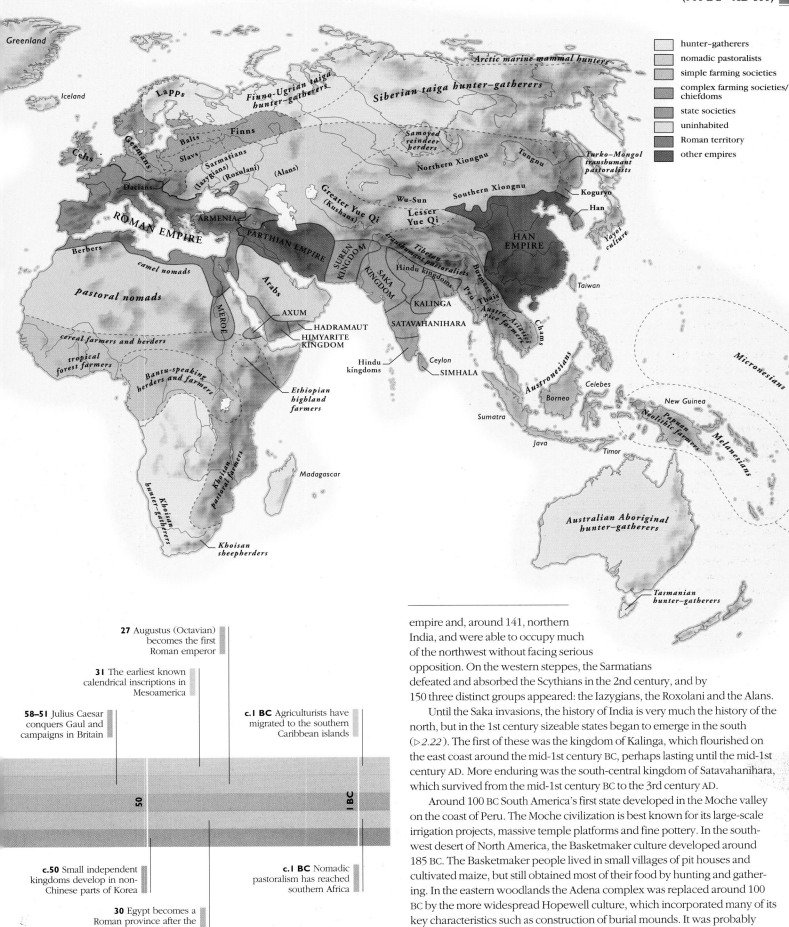

hunter–gatherers
nomadic pastoralists
simple farming societies
complex farming societies/chiefdoms
state societies
uninhabited
Roman territory
other empires

Greenland

Iceland

Lapps

Finno-Ugrian taiga hunter-gatherers

Siberian taiga hunter-gatherers

Arctic marine mammal hunters

Celts

Germans

Balts

Finns

Slavs

Sarmatians
(Iazygians) *(Roxolani)*

(Alans)

Dacians

ROMAN EMPIRE

ARMENIA

PARTHIAN EMPIRE

Samoyed reindeer herders

Northern Xiongnu

Tungnu

Turko–Mongol transhumant pastoralists

Koguryo

Wu-Sun

Greater Yue Qi (Kushans)

Lesser Yue Qi

Southern Xiongnu

Han

HAN EMPIRE

Yayoi culture

SUREN KINGDOM

Tibetan transhumant pastoralists

SAKA KINGDOM

Hindu kingdoms

Burmese

Pyu

Thais

Taiwan

Berbers

camel nomads

Pastoral nomads

Arabs

MEROE

AXUM

HADRAMAUT
HIMYARITE
KINGDOM

KALINGA

SATAVAHANIHARA

Austro-Asiatic rice farmers

Chams

cereal farmers and herders

tropical forest farmers

Hindu kingdoms

Ceylon

SIMHALA

Austronesians

Micronesians

Bantu-speaking herders and farmers

Ethiopian highland farmers

Borneo

Celebes

Sumatra

New Guinea

Papuan Neolithic farmers

Melanesians

Java

Timor

Khoisan pastoral farmers

Madagascar

Khoisan hunter-gatherers

Khoisan sheepherders

Australian Aboriginal hunter-gatherers

Polynesians

Tasmanian hunter-gatherers

---

empire and, around 141, northern India, and were able to occupy much of the northwest without facing serious opposition. On the western steppes, the Sarmatians defeated and absorbed the Scythians in the 2nd century, and by 150 three distinct groups appeared: the Iazygians, the Roxolani and the Alans.

Until the Saka invasions, the history of India is very much the history of the north, but in the 1st century sizeable states began to emerge in the south (▷2.22). The first of these was the kingdom of Kalinga, which flourished on the east coast around the mid-1st century BC, perhaps lasting until the mid-1st century AD. More enduring was the south-central kingdom of Satavahanihara, which survived from the mid-1st century BC to the 3rd century AD.

Around 100 BC South America's first state developed in the Moche valley on the coast of Peru. The Moche civilization is best known for its large-scale irrigation projects, massive temple platforms and fine pottery. In the south-west desert of North America, the Basketmaker culture developed around 185 BC. The Basketmaker people lived in small villages of pit houses and cultivated maize, but still obtained most of their food by hunting and gathering. In the eastern woodlands the Adena complex was replaced around 100 BC by the more widespread Hopewell culture, which incorporated many of its key characteristics such as construction of burial mounds. It was probably around 1 BC that farming peoples began to migrate from the South American mainland to the Caribbean islands ■

---

27 Augustus (Octavian) becomes the first Roman emperor

31 The earliest known calendrical inscriptions in Mesoamerica

58–51 Julius Caesar conquers Gaul and campaigns in Britain

c.1 BC Agriculturists have migrated to the southern Caribbean islands

50

1 BC

c.50 Small independent kingdoms develop in non-Chinese parts of Korea

c.1 BC Nomadic pastoralism has reached southern Africa

30 Egypt becomes a Roman province after the death of Cleopatra

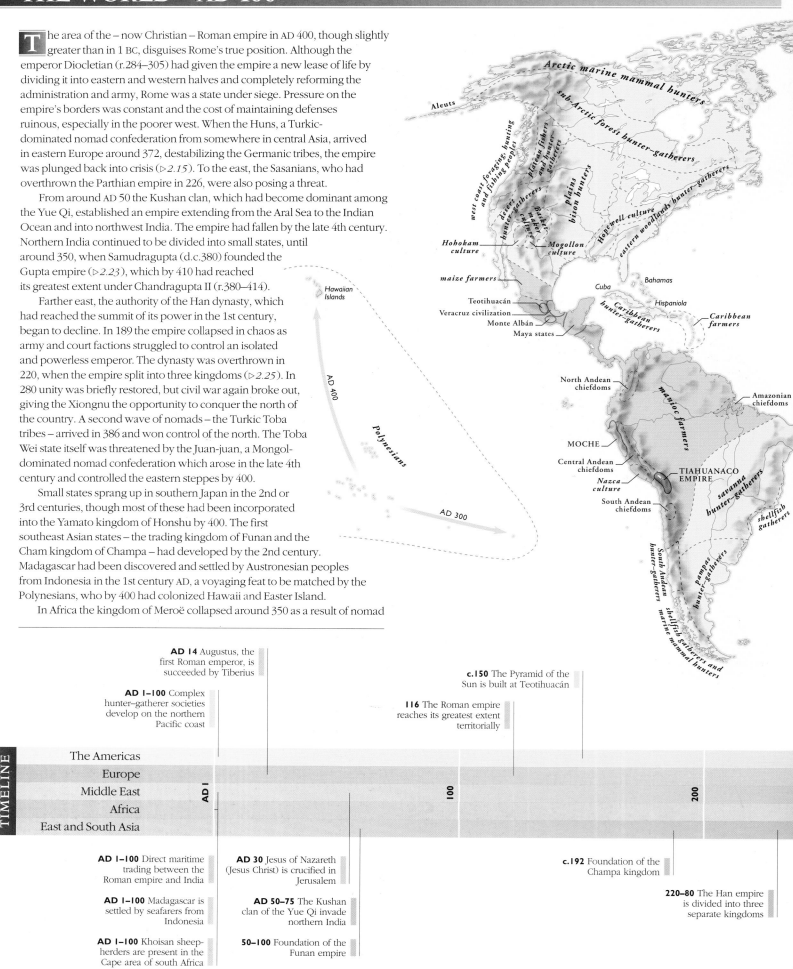

The area of the – now Christian – Roman empire in AD 400, though slightly greater than in 1 BC, disguises Rome's true position. Although the emperor Diocletian (r.284–305) had given the empire a new lease of life by dividing it into eastern and western halves and completely reforming the administration and army, Rome was a state under siege. Pressure on the empire's borders was constant and the cost of maintaining defenses ruinous, especially in the poorer west. When the Huns, a Turkic-dominated nomad confederation from somewhere in central Asia, arrived in eastern Europe around 372, destabilizing the Germanic tribes, the empire was plunged back into crisis (▷2.15). To the east, the Sasanians, who had overthrown the Parthian empire in 226, were also posing a threat.

From around AD 50 the Kushan clan, which had become dominant among the Yue Qi, established an empire extending from the Aral Sea to the Indian Ocean and into northwest India. The empire had fallen by the late 4th century. Northern India continued to be divided into small states, until around 350, when Samudragupta (d.c.380) founded the Gupta empire (▷2.23), which by 410 had reached its greatest extent under Chandragupta II (r.380–414).

Farther east, the authority of the Han dynasty, which had reached the summit of its power in the 1st century, began to decline. In 189 the empire collapsed in chaos as army and court factions struggled to control an isolated and powerless emperor. The dynasty was overthrown in 220, when the empire split into three kingdoms (▷2.25). In 280 unity was briefly restored, but civil war again broke out, giving the Xiongnu the opportunity to conquer the north of the country. A second wave of nomads – the Turkic Toba tribes – arrived in 386 and won control of the north. The Toba Wei state itself was threatened by the Juan-juan, a Mongol-dominated nomad confederation which arose in the late 4th century and controlled the eastern steppes by 400.

Small states sprang up in southern Japan in the 2nd or 3rd centuries, though most of these had been incorporated into the Yamato kingdom of Honshu by 400. The first southeast Asian states – the trading kingdom of Funan and the Cham kingdom of Champa – had developed by the 2nd century. Madagascar had been discovered and settled by Austronesian peoples from Indonesia in the 1st century AD, a voyaging feat to be matched by the Polynesians, who by 400 had colonized Hawaii and Easter Island.

In Africa the kingdom of Meroë collapsed around 350 as a result of nomad

TIMELINE

AD 14 Augustus, the first Roman emperor, is succeeded by Tiberius

AD 1–100 Complex hunter–gatherer societies develop on the northern Pacific coast

c.150 The Pyramid of the Sun is built at Teotihuacán

116 The Roman empire reaches its greatest extent territorially

The Americas

Europe

Middle East

Africa

East and South Asia

AD 1

100

200

AD 1–100 Direct maritime trading between the Roman empire and India

AD 30 Jesus of Nazareth (Jesus Christ) is crucified in Jerusalem

c.192 Foundation of the Champa kingdom

AD 1–100 Madagascar is settled by seafarers from Indonesia

AD 50–75 The Kushan clan of the Yue Qi invade northern India

220–80 The Han empire is divided into three separate kingdoms

AD 1–100 Khoisan sheep-herders are present in the Cape area of south Africa

50–100 Foundation of the Funan empire

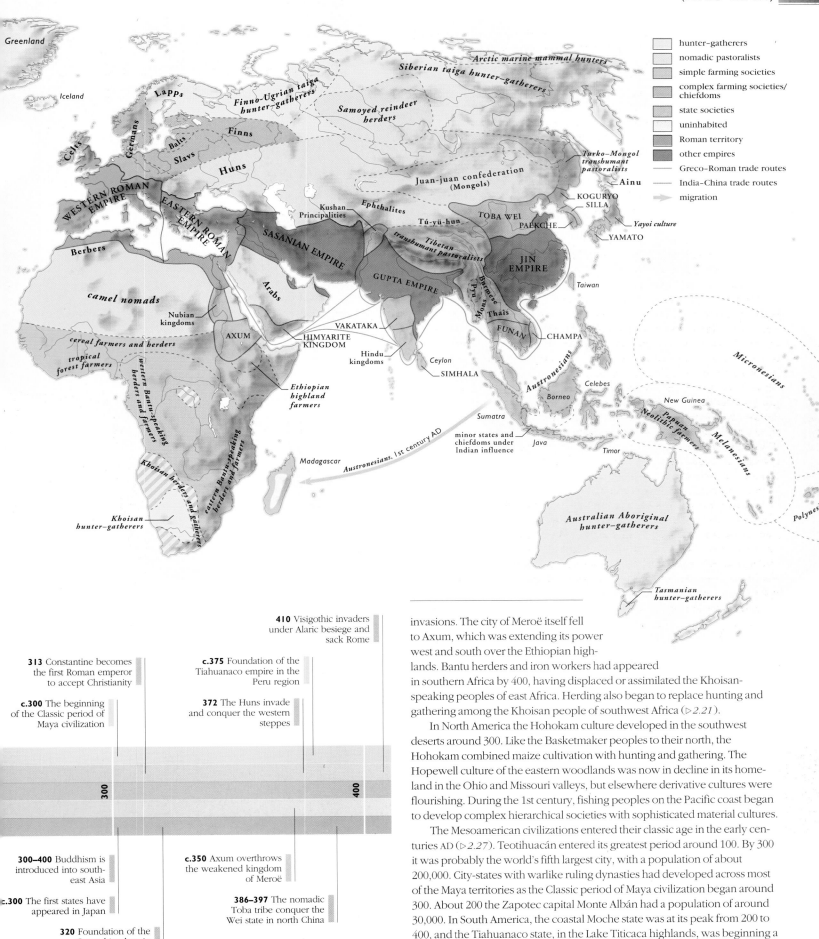

hunter-gatherers
nomadic pastoralists
simple farming societies
complex farming societies/chiefdoms
state societies
uninhabited
Roman territory
other empires
Greco-Roman trade routes
India-China trade routes
migration

410 Visigothic invaders under Alaric besiege and sack Rome

313 Constantine becomes the first Roman emperor to accept Christianity

c.375 Foundation of the Tiahuanaco empire in the Peru region

c.300 The beginning of the Classic period of Maya civilization

372 The Huns invade and conquer the western steppes

300

400

300–400 Buddhism is introduced into south-east Asia

c.350 Axum overthrows the weakened kingdom of Meroë

c.300 The first states have appeared in Japan

386–397 The nomadic Toba tribe conquer the Wei state in north China

320 Foundation of the Gupta kingdom in northern India

invasions. The city of Meroë itself fell to Axum, which was extending its power west and south over the Ethiopian highlands. Bantu herders and iron workers had appeared in southern Africa by 400, having displaced or assimilated the Khoisan-speaking peoples of east Africa. Herding also began to replace hunting and gathering among the Khoisan people of southwest Africa (▷2.21).

In North America the Hohokam culture developed in the southwest deserts around 300. Like the Basketmaker peoples to their north, the Hohokam combined maize cultivation with hunting and gathering. The Hopewell culture of the eastern woodlands was now in decline in its homeland in the Ohio and Missouri valleys, but elsewhere derivative cultures were flourishing. During the 1st century, fishing peoples on the Pacific coast began to develop complex hierarchical societies with sophisticated material cultures.

The Mesoamerican civilizations entered their classic age in the early centuries AD (▷2.27). Teotihuacán entered its greatest period around 100. By 300 it was probably the world's fifth largest city, with a population of about 200,000. City-states with warlike ruling dynasties had developed across most of the Maya territories as the Classic period of Maya civilization began around 300. About 200 the Zapotec capital Monte Albán had a population of around 30,000. In South America, the coastal Moche state was at its peak from 200 to 400, and the Tiahuanaco state, in the Lake Titicaca highlands, was beginning a period of imperial expansion (▷2.28) ∎

The western half of the Roman empire, altogether poorer and less populated than the east, was also more exposed to Germanic barbarian attack. In 406 German tribes – Goths, Franks, Vandals and others – overran the Rhine frontier and by 476 the western Roman empire was almost entirely under their control. The wealthy eastern half of the Roman empire survived more or less unscathed and its emperor Justinian counter-attacked against the barbarians in the 530s, restoring Roman rule in Italy, north Africa and southern Spain (▷2.17). However, the empire was put back on the defensive after Justinian's death; much of Italy fell to the Lombards and most of southern Spain to the Visigoths by 600. The most successful of the Germanic invaders were the Franks, who had settled northern Gaul in the early 5th century. From 486 they were united by Clovis, who extended his kingdom into southern Gaul and east into Germany. By 600 the Frankish kingdom stretched from the Pyrenees almost to the Elbe. The end of Roman rule in Britain saw a revival of Celtic culture but in about 450 Angles and Saxons from north Germany began to settle the fertile east of Britain, driving the Celts to the hillier west.

Fear of the Huns drove the Germanic peoples to invade the Roman empire. The Huns extended their control as far west as the Rhine – further west than any steppe nomads in history – and raided both halves of the Roman empire under Attila (r. 433–453). However, after his death the Hun confederation broke up and returned to the steppes. Between 460 and 515 the Ephthalite (or "White") Huns destroyed the last Kushan principalities of central Asia, raided the Sasanian empire and conquered northwest India, only to be driven out in 528 (▷2.20). On the eastern steppes, the Mongol-dominated Juan-juan confederacy was broken by a rebellion of the Turks in 552. By 600 the Turks had destroyed the Ephthalites and dominated the steppes as far west as the Aral Sea. The Khazars, another Turkic people, were established on the Caspian steppes. A part of the Juan-juan, the Avars, fled from the Turks and arrived on the European steppes in about 562 where they mopped up the remnants of the Huns and raided the Balkans. North of the Caucasus the Alans – the sole remnant of the Iranian peoples who had once dominated the steppes – re-emerged from Hunnic dominance in the 450s.

In Africa, Christianity had spread to Nubia and Axum by the 6th century, strengthening cultural and political links with the eastern Roman empire (▷2.21). With Roman encouragement, the Axumites conquered southwest Arabia in 528 but were expelled by the Sasanians in 574, ending Christian influence in Arabia just four years before the birth of Muhammad at Mecca. In west Africa intensive dry-rice farming led to a rising population on the upper Niger and the foundation of large villages in the 3rd and 4th centuries. One of these, Jenne-jeno, became the center of a wideranging network of west

c.500 Foundation of the Huari empire in the highlands of Peru

481–511 Reign of Clovis, undisputed Frankish king of Gaul from 486

476 Fall of the western Roman empire when the the emperor Romulus is deposed

533–54 Roman emperor Justinian reconquers most of north Africa and Italy

410 The Visigoths, led by Alaric, sack Rome

c.450 The Angles and Saxons begin to settle eastern Britain

TIMELINE		400		450		500		550
The Americas								
Europe								
Middle East								
Africa								
East and South Asia								

c.400 Iron working reaches southern Africa

460–528 The Ephthalite Huns ("Hunas") invade northwest India

531–79 Sasanian Persia achieves its maximum extent under Chosroes I

c.400 Jenne-jeno flourishes as the first town in west Africa

c.470 Decline of the Gupta empire in northern India

c.540 Christianity is introduced into Nubia

429 A wealthy Vandal kingdom is set up in north Africa

c.550 The Turkish khanates are dominant throughout central Asia

Arctic marine mammal hunters

Aleuts

sub-Arctic forest hunter-gatherers

west coast foraging, hunting and fishing peoples

plateau fishers and hunter gatherers

desert hunter-gatherers

Basket-maker culture

plains bison hunters

Hopewell culture

eastern woodlands hunter-gatherers

Hohokam culture

Mogollon culture

maize farmers

Teotihuacán

Veracruz civilization

Monte Albán

Maya states

Cuba

Bahamas

Hispaniola

Puerto Rico

Caribbean hunter-gatherers

Caribbean farmers

Hawaiian Islands

Polynesians

North Andean chiefdoms

Amazonian chiefdoms

manioc farmers

MOCHE

HUARI EMPIRE

TIAHUANACO EMPIRE

farming (replacing hunter-gatherers)

savanna hunter gatherers

pampas hunter-gatherers

South Andean hunter-gatherers

shellfish gatherers and marine mammal hunters

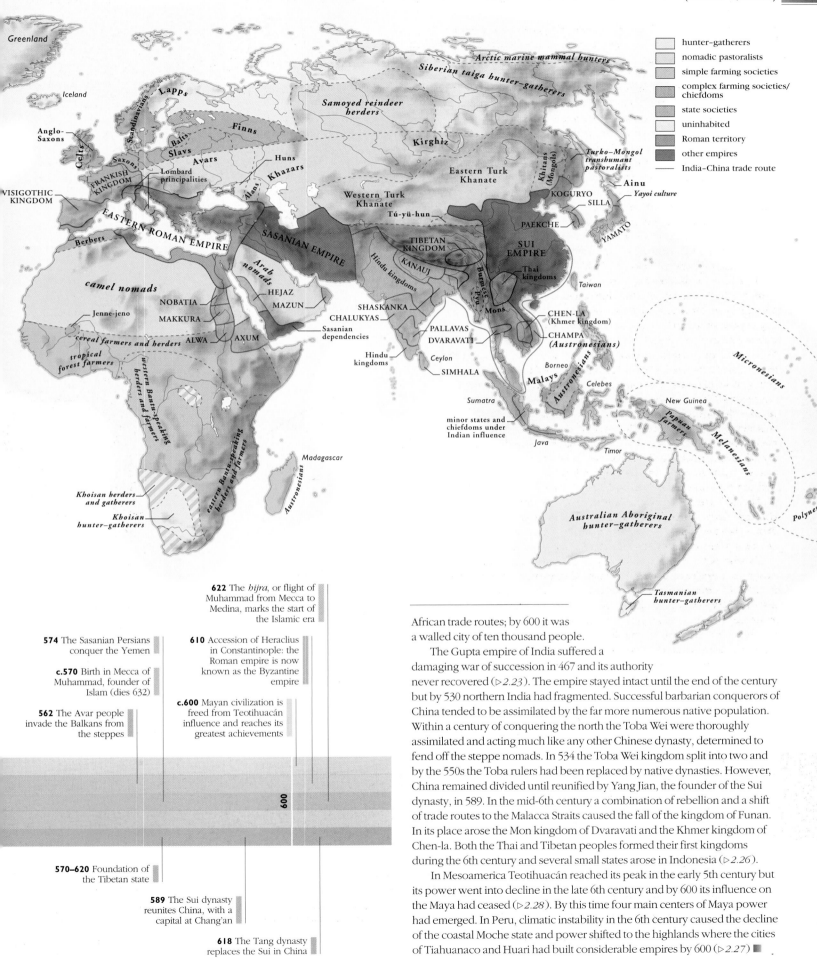

Greenland

Iceland

Arctic marine mammal hunters

Siberian taiga hunter-gatherers

Lapps

Samoyed reindeer herders

Anglo-Saxons

Scandinavians

Finns

Balts

Kirghiz

Celts

Slavs

Avars

Huns

Saxons

Khazars

FRANKISH KINGDOM

Lombard principalities

Eastern Turk Khanate

Turko-Mongol transhumant pastoralists

VISIGOTHIC KINGDOM

Alans

Western Turk Khanate

Khitans (Mongols)

KOGURYO

Ainu

SILLA

Yayoi culture

EASTERN ROMAN EMPIRE

SASANIAN EMPIRE

Tú-yü-hun

PAEKCHE

Berbers

Arab nomads

TIBETAN KINGDOM

KANAUJ

SUI EMPIRE

YAMATO

camel nomads

HEJAZ

Hindu kingdoms

Thai kingdoms

Taiwan

NOBATIA

MAZUN

SHASKANKA

Burmese Pyu

Mons

MAKKURA

Jenne-jeno

CHALUKYAS

CHEN-LA (Khmer kingdom)

cereal farmers and herders

ALWA

AXUM

Sasanian dependencies

PALLAVAS

DVARAVATI

CHAMPA (Austronesians)

tropical forest farmers

Hindu kingdoms

Ceylon

Borneo

Micronesians

SIMHALA

Malays

Austronesians

Celebes

western Bantu-speaking herders and farmers

Sumatra

New Guinea

minor states and chiefdoms under Indian influence

Java

Papuan farmers

Madagascar

eastern Bantu-speaking herders and farmers

Austronesians

Timor

Melanesians

Khoisan herders and gatherers

Polynesians

Khoisan hunter-gatherers

Australian Aboriginal hunter-gatherers

Tasmanian hunter-gatherers

	hunter-gatherers
	nomadic pastoralists
	simple farming societies
	complex farming societies/chiefdoms
	state societies
	uninhabited
	Roman territory
	other empires
—	India-China trade route

622 The *hijra*, or flight of Muhammad from Mecca to Medina, marks the start of the Islamic era

574 The Sasanian Persians conquer the Yemen

c.570 Birth in Mecca of Muhammad, founder of Islam (dies 632)

562 The Avar people invade the Balkans from the steppes

610 Accession of Heraclius in Constantinople: the Roman empire is now known as the Byzantine empire

c.600 Mayan civilization is freed from Teotihuacán influence and reaches its greatest achievements

600

570–620 Foundation of the Tibetan state

589 The Sui dynasty reunites China, with a capital at Chang'an

618 The Tang dynasty replaces the Sui in China

African trade routes; by 600 it was a walled city of ten thousand people.

The Gupta empire of India suffered a damaging war of succession in 467 and its authority never recovered (▷2.23). The empire stayed intact until the end of the century but by 530 northern India had fragmented. Successful barbarian conquerors of China tended to be assimilated by the far more numerous native population. Within a century of conquering the north the Toba Wei were thoroughly assimilated and acting much like any other Chinese dynasty, determined to fend off the steppe nomads. In 534 the Toba Wei kingdom split into two and by the 550s the Toba rulers had been replaced by native dynasties. However, China remained divided until reunified by Yang Jian, the founder of the Sui dynasty, in 589. In the mid-6th century a combination of rebellion and a shift of trade routes to the Malacca Straits caused the fall of the kingdom of Funan. In its place arose the Mon kingdom of Dvaravati and the Khmer kingdom of Chen-la. Both the Thai and Tibetan peoples formed their first kingdoms during the 6th century and several small states arose in Indonesia (▷2.26).

In Mesoamerica Teotihuacán reached its peak in the early 5th century but its power went into decline in the late 6th century and by 600 its influence on the Maya had ceased (▷2.28). By this time four main centers of Maya power had emerged. In Peru, climatic instability in the 6th century caused the decline of the coastal Moche state and power shifted to the highlands where the cities of Tiahuanaco and Huari had built considerable empires by 600 (▷2.27) ■

The years 1000 BC–AD 600 saw the emergence of every major world religion except Islam (a world religion is one that has endured and influenced diverse civilizations). Hinduism and Judaism had earlier roots but assumed their present form at this time; Christianity, Buddhism, Zoroastrianism, Daoism and Confucianism all arose 600 BC–AD 600.

Early Hinduism was based on the Vedas, hymns of the Aryans who invaded India around 1500 BC, but was also influenced by indigenous Dravidian traditions. Vedic Hinduism looked forward to a future existence in heaven; it was not until the 6th century BC that the belief in *karma* and rebirth, central to modern Hinduism, developed. The complex rituals of early Hinduism gave rise to a distinctive feature of Indian civilization, the caste system – the priestly Brahmins forming the highest caste. By 500 BC Hinduism dominated the Indian subcontinent, but discontent with Brahminical traditions grew on the Gangetic plain, where urbanization created a more materialistic society. New sects developed there, the most successful of them being Buddhism.

The founder of Buddhism was Siddhartha Gautama, known as the Buddha, or "Enlightened One." Many legends have become associated with the Buddha and little is known for certain of his life: even his original teachings are a matter of debate as the canon of Buddhist scripture was not written down until four centuries after his death. Buddhism remained a minor sect until the Mauryan emperor Ashoka converted in 260 BC. Under his patronage Buddhist missionaries spread the religion throughout India and to Ceylon and the Iranian nomads in central Asia. In northern India Buddhism supplanted Hinduism as the majority religion. It then spread from central Asia along the Silk Route, reaching China in the 1st century AD; Indian seafarers took it to southeast Asia in the 4th century. By the 3rd century AD Buddhism had divided into two schools: Theravada (Doctrine of the Elders), which adhered strictly to the established Buddhist canon, and Mahayana (Great Vehicle), a more liberal, eclectic

THE MENORAH symbolizes the survival of the Jewish people through the vicissitudes of history, including the Diaspora of the 1st century AD.

tradition. Hinduism responded to the rise of Buddhism by becoming more flexible and tolerant, and by AD 400 it was beginning to recover in India. In the 5th century Hinduism spread to southeast Asia.

The central influence on Chinese thought was the ethical teaching of Confucius. Its emphasis on respect for legitimate authority and moral education made this the official orthodoxy under the Han dynasty (206 BC–AD 220). In the disorder following the fall of the Han, Confucianism declined and Buddhism became a stronger influence in China. Buddhism was itself influenced by Chinese philosophies, particularly Daoism, a system inspired by the teachings of Lao Zi, a philosopher of the 6th century BC. The traditional Chinese practice of ancestor worship remained strong throughout these changes.

Although it was the religion of a minor and relatively unimportant people, the Hebrews, Judaism was the most influential religion of the Middle East. It was the first major monotheistic religion and its

TIMELINE

Middle East and Europe

600 BC	AD 1	AD 600
c.630–553 The life of Zoroaster, founder of Zoroastrianism	**c.6 BC–AD 30** The life of Jesus of Nazareth	**313** The Roman empire under Constantine officially tolerates Christianity
587 The Jews are deported to Babylonia by Nebuchadnezzar. This marks the beginning of the Diaspora	**AD 1–100** Mithraism spreads to the Roman empire	**c. 405** St Jerome completes the Vulgate Latin translation of the Bible
	AD 42–62 St Paul undertakes his missionary journeys throughout Asia Minor, Greece and to Rome	**c. 570** The birth of the prophet Muhammad
	AD 70–100 The Christian Gospels are written	**596** The English conversion to Christianity begins
	220–40 Zoroastrianism is the Persian state religion	

South and east Asia

600 BC	AD 1	AD 600
800–400 The *Upanishads* of Hinduism are composed	**260** The Mauryan emperor Ashoka becomes a Buddhist and sends Buddhist missions to Ceylon and central Asia	**253–333** The life of Ko Hung, founder of religious Daoism
6th century The life of Lao Zi, the inspirer of Daoism		**259** Chinese Buddhists begin pilgrimages to India
c.563–483 Life of Siddhartha Gautama, the Buddha	**c.240 BC** The *Dao De Jing*, the basic text of Daoism, is composed	
551–479 The life of the Chinese sage Confucius	**AD 1–100** Mahayana Buddhism develops	**300–500** The Hindu epics the *Ramayana* and the *Mahabharata* are written down in their final form
600 BC	AD 1	AD 600

1 Although Hinduism is an ancient religion, few physical traces survive before the medieval period.

2 Ellora is the site of rock-cut temples of Buddhist, Hindu and Jain origin, dating from the 6th–8th centuries AD.

3 Southern Britain became Christian by the 4th century but reverted to paganism following the settlements of the Anglo-Saxons in the 5th century.

4 Christian monasticism originated on the edges of the Sahara desert, which developed from communities of hermits in the early 4th century.

5 Mithraism was popular in the Roman army: several Mithraic sites have been discovered on the strongly garrisoned Rhine frontier.

6 Armenia became the first state to adopt Christianity as its official religion, in about 300.

7 A major early Buddhist center developed around *stupas* (mounds) built by Ashoka to house relics of the Buddha and his followers.

8 Sacred Fire, believed to be a manifestation of Ahura Mazda, was the focus of ritual in Zoroastrian temples.

9 The influence of Daoism led Chinese Buddhists to found monasteries on mountains such as at Lingjiu (Vulture Peak).

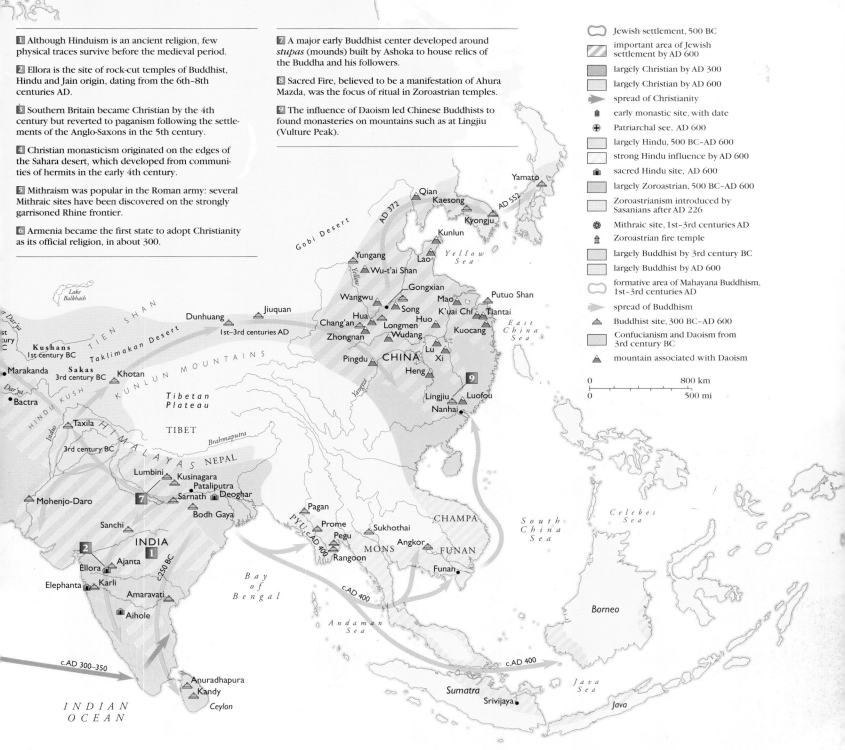

Legend:
- Jewish settlement, 500 BC
- important area of Jewish settlement by AD 600
- largely Christian by AD 300
- largely Christian by AD 600
- spread of Christianity
- early monastic site, with date
- Patriarchal see, AD 600
- largely Hindu, 500 BC–AD 600
- strong Hindu influence by AD 600
- sacred Hindu site, AD 600
- largely Zoroastrian, 500 BC–AD 600
- Zoroastrianism introduced by Sasanians after AD 226
- Mithraic site, 1st–3rd centuries AD
- Zoroastrian fire temple
- largely Buddhist by 3rd century BC
- largely Buddhist by AD 600
- formative area of Mahayana Buddhism, 1st–3rd centuries AD
- spread of Buddhism
- Buddhist site, 300 BC–AD 600
- Confucianism and Daoism from 3rd century BC
- mountain associated with Daoism

0   800 km
0   500 mi

teachings provided the basis of Christianity and Islam. Judaism was a national religion and did not actively seek converts among non-Jews; yet the Hebrews' turbulent history meant that it became very widespread in the Mediterranean and Middle East by AD 600. The Diaspora, or dispersal of the Jews, began in the 6th century BC when communities of exiles from Palestine were established in Egypt and Mesopotamia. The greatest dispersal of Jews occurred in the 1st and 2nd centuries AD, following rebellions in Palestine against Roman rule.

Christianity originated in the teachings of a Jew, Jesus of Nazareth, who rejected the current practice of Judaism. Christianity developed initially as a Jewish sect, but the influence of St Paul and others made

the religion more attractive to non-Jews, and by AD 70 its separation from Judaism was complete. Because of their refusal to pay formal homage to the state gods, Christians often faced persecution by the Roman emperors. Despite this Christianity was well established, especially in the eastern empire, by 312 when the emperor Constantine converted, introducing formal toleration the following year. Christianity made rapid progress after this, and in 391 it became the Roman empire's official religion. Christians came to believe that God had created the Roman empire specifically for the purpose of spreading Christianity.

An early rival to Christianity in the Roman empire was Mithraism, a derivative of the Persian Zoroastrian religion. Zoroaster, the religion's founder,

reformed the ancient Iranian religion, dividing the pantheon into good and evil deities. It developed into a dualist religion which taught that the chief god Ahura Mazda, aided by Mithra, was locked in combat to protect the world from his evil rival Ahriman. Zoroastrianism became the religion of the Achemenid rulers of Persia and flourished under the Parthians and Sasanians. Although in its pure form it won few converts outside Persia, its teaching on the nature of good and evil had an important influence on Hellenistic, Jewish, Christian and Islamic thought.

See also 2.15 (the Christian empire)

After Cyrus, founder of the Persian empire, conquered Lydia in 546 BC, his generals mopped up the relatively insignificant Greek cities of Ionia, but in 499 they rebelled again under the leadership of Aristagoras of Miletos and introduced democratic rule. The rebels received aid from Athens and this provoked the Persian king Darius (r.521–486) to plan a punitive invasion of Greece after the revolt had been crushed in 494.

Darius' first invasion, in 492, was defeated by the weather when the fleet supporting his army was destroyed in a storm rounding Mount Athos. After a second expedition was humiliatingly defeated by the Athenians at Marathon in 490, Darius decided that the conquest of the whole of Greece was needed to secure the Persian position in Ionia. He died before his preparations were complete and it was left to his son Xerxes to carry out his plans. Meanwhile the Greeks prepared for an invasion, with Themistocles persuading Athens – by far the largest and wealthiest *polis* or city-state – to invest in an urgent naval building program.

The history of this invasion was memorably recorded by the Ionian-born Herodotos, the first major Greek prose writer and historian, later in the 5th century. Xerxes' army, said to have been 200,000 strong, was one of the largest forces ever assembled in antiquity and was supported by a fleet of perhaps a thousand ships. Faced with this vast force, most of the northern Greek states opted for neutrality or (in a few cases) alliance with Persia. The southern Greek states, however, united under the leadership of Athens and Sparta and prepared to resist the Persians. The resulting struggle was less uneven than expected. The very size of the Persian army proved a serious handicap; it was difficult to supply and impossible to control effectively on a battlefield; the quality of its troops varied enormously and only around 10,000 were elite troops. In contrast the Greeks, though greatly outnumbered, were heavily armed, experienced, disciplined and highly motivated: they were citizens defending their states, homes and families.

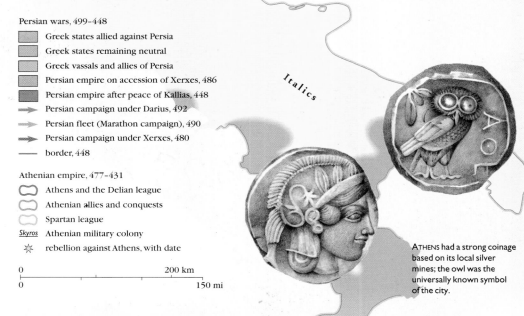

Persian wars, 499–448

- Greek states allied against Persia
- Greek states remaining neutral
- Greek vassals and allies of Persia
- Persian empire on accession of Xerxes, 486
- Persian empire after peace of Kallias, 448
- → Persian campaign under Darius, 492
- → Persian fleet (Marathon campaign), 490
- → Persian campaign under Xerxes, 480
- — border, 448

Athenian empire, 477–431

- Athens and the Delian league
- Athenian allies and conquests
- Spartan league
- *Skyros* Athenian military colony
- ※ rebellion against Athens, with date

```
0                    200 km
0               150 mi
```

Italics

ATHENS had a strong coinage based on its local silver mines; the owl was the universally known symbol of the city.

The Greeks, led by Sparta, attempted to halt the Persian invasion at Thermopylae but were defeated after heroic resistance. The Persians went on to occupy Athens, although its population had been evacuated to Salamis. The Persian fleet, which was needed to outflank Spartan defenses on the Isthmus of Corinth, was now ambushed and destroyed by the Athenian navy at Salamis. Since it was clear that Greece could not now be conquered in a single campaign, Xerxes returned to Asia with half of the army: the remainder wintered in Greece only to be defeated decisively by a Spartan-led army at Plataea in the following year. The threat to Greece ended, the old rivalries of the Greek world resurfaced and Sparta and most of the other states withdrew from the war against Persia. Athens and its allies continued hostilities, destroying the last Persian garrisons in Europe, re-opening the Bosporus to Greek shipping by 475, and freeing the Ionian Greeks from

Persian rule in 468. The Athenians also intervened unsuccessfully against the Persians in Egypt in 454 and captured Cyprus in 450. Hostilities came to a formal end in 448 when the Persians recognized Ionian independence.

To pursue its war aims, Athens created the anti-Persian Delian league of Aegean cities, with a common treasury on the island of Delos to which all members contributed. As its richest member and greatest naval power, Athens dominated the league and came increasingly to regard it as its empire. Some states, such as Aegina, were forcibly enrolled, and if a dissatisfied member tried to withhold contributions, the Athenian fleet was sent to enforce obedience. When the Athenians moved the treasury to Athens in 454 its domination became even more apparent. Despite this, many members remained loyal, being grateful to Athens for its role in the Persian wars and for introducing democracy. After the end of the war with Persia the league became as much a commercial as a military organization, although still serving Athenian interests. Athenian coinage, weights and measures were introduced throughout the league.

Under the leadership of the highly nationalistic Pericles, Athens also extended its power on the mainland and by 460 had achieved a dominant position in central Greece. Sparta – unusual in still having a monarchical constitution – had the strongest army in Greece and was unwilling to surrender its primacy to the increasingly arrogant Athenians. Throughout the 460s the Spartans were preoccupied with a *helot* (serf) revolt, but moves to increase the influence of Athens within the Peloponnese led to the outbreak of war between the two rivals in 457.

Athens was unable to sustain a war against Persia and Sparta at the same time, but the peace treaty with Persia in 448 in some ways weakened the Athenian position. Without the fear of a return to Persian rule, many members of the Delian league felt less closely bound to Athens. Sparta, which had no navy, concentrated its attack on the Athenian position on the mainland of central Greece while attempting to foment rebellion in the league. The Athenians successfully put down rebellions in

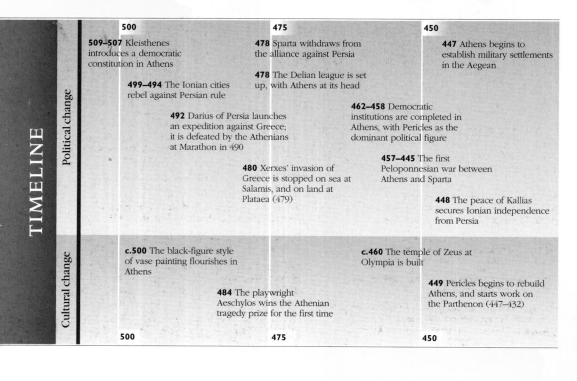

TIMELINE

	500	475	450
Political change	**509–507** Kleisthenes introduces a democratic constitution in Athens	**478** Sparta withdraws from the alliance against Persia	**447** Athens begins to establish military settlements in the Aegean
	499–494 The Ionian cities rebel against Persian rule	**478** The Delian league is set up, with Athens at its head	
	492 Darius of Persia launches an expedition against Greece; it is defeated by the Athenians at Marathon in 490	**462–458** Democratic institutions are completed in Athens, with Pericles as the dominant political figure	
	480 Xerxes' invasion of Greece is stopped on sea at Salamis, and on land at Plataea (479)	**457–445** The first Peloponnesian war between Athens and Sparta	
			448 The peace of Kallias secures Ionian independence from Persia
Cultural change	**c.500** The black-figure style of vase painting flourishes in Athens	**c.460** The temple of Zeus at Olympia is built	
	484 The playwright Aeschylos wins the Athenian tragedy prize for the first time	**449** Pericles begins to rebuild Athens, and starts work on the Parthenon (447–432)	
	500	**475**	**450**

Illyrians

Thracians

Black Sea

Apollonia

Marisa

Epidamnos

*Lake
Ohrid*

*Lake
Prespa*

Strymon

Axios

Pella

MACEDON
Persian vassal, 492

Amphipolis   Eion

7

Akanthos

Abdera

465 ☼ *Thasos*

9

Bosporus
Byzantium
440 ☼

Apollonia

Vjose

Aliakmon

Methone
Poteidaia
432 ☼

2

Mt Athos

Chersonesos **3**
Abydos

Hellespont

Cyzicus

EPIRUS

P I N D O S   M O U N T A I N S

Corcyra

Pinios

Larissa   Kosthanaia

THESSALY

Imbros

Lemnos

Troy

*Northern
Sporades*

LYDIA

Ambracia

ACARNANIA

Anaktorion

Achelous

Artemisium
480

Thermopylae
480

4

Oreos

Euboea

Skyros

*Aegean
Sea*

Mytilene

Lesbos

Phokaia

Gediz

Sardis

I O N I A

PHOCIS

Delphi

LOKRIS

BOEOTIA

EUBOEA
Chalcis 447
Eretria

Erythraia

Kephallenia

Plataea
479

Thebes

Marathon
490

ATTICA

Chios

Buyuk Menderes

Ephesos **6**

ACHAEA

Megara **5**

Athens

Laurion

Andros

Samos *Samos*
440 ☼

Mycale
479

1

Miletos

Elis

ELIS

ARCADIA

Corinth

Salamis
480

Argos

Troizen

Aegina

Ikaria

Delos

8

Halikarnassos

Kos

Zakynthos

Tegea

PELOPONNESE

Sparta

SPARTA

469 ☼ *Naxos*

Rhodes

Mediterranean Sea

Carpathos

Crete

Euboea and Thasos, but by 445 they had lost control in central Greece and agreed to peace terms which recognized Spartan dominance in the Peloponnese.

Despite being almost constantly at war, Athens flourished economically in the 5th century as a result of its dominance of eastern Mediterranean and Black Sea trade and its own rich silver mines – worked by more than 20,000 slaves – at Laurion in Attica. Athenian democratic institutions continued to be developed and by 458 all citizens (excluding slaves, women and foreigners) were eligible to vote for and (except for the poorest) to serve in the highest offices of the government and the judiciary. The triumph in the war with Persia led to an exceptional outburst of cultural confidence in Greece as a whole, and especially in Athens, where vase-painting, sculpture and drama all reached new heights. The

city, and notably its Acropolis, were rebuilt and the "classical" style of art and architecture matured. No other Greek city-state saw such a program of public building at this time.

1 The Greek cities of Ionia, led by Miletos, rebelled against Persian rule in 499 and sacked Sardis.

2 A Persian fleet was destroyed rounding Mt Athos in 492. To avoid the same thing happening in 480, the Persians dug a canal across the peninsula neck.

3 A bridge of boats was built across the Hellespont for Xerxes' expedition in 480.

4 At Thermopylae, the Greeks under Leonidas of Sparta were outflanked; most withdrew, but the Spartans' heroic stand inspired later Greek defense.

5 At the comprehensive Greek victory of Plataea, the Persian general Mardonios was killed and the leading Theban allies of the Persians were executed.

6 The last of the Persian fleet was destroyed at Mycale in 479.

7 Eion, the last important Persian stronghold in Europe, was captured by the Athenians in 475.

8 The common treasury of the Delian league was kept on Delos, but was removed to Athens in 454.

9 Delian league member Thasos rebelled in 465, but the Athenians invaded and tore down the city walls.

See also 2.08 (Peloponnesian war)

The first Peloponnesian War had been indecisive and a second, much larger, war broke out in 431. Although the war eventually broke the power of Athens, it did not leave Sparta, the victor, strong enough to achieve the undisputed dominance in Greece. The war confirmed that no Greek city-state could achieve permanent dominance.

In the 430s, Athens was entering its most exceptional age, with the Parthenon completed in 432, and with values embodied in Periclean rhetoric and the plays of Sophocles and Euripides. In 430 Socrates began his career as teacher and philosopher. The 4th century brought philosophers such as Plato and Aristotle (who was to be the tutor of Alexander of Macedon). And the Peloponnesian War found in Thucydides a great Athenian historian able to record the complex chain of events.

In 435 a minor war broke out between the Corcyreans and Corinth, an ally of Sparta. Anxious that Corinth would seek revenge, the victorious Corcyreans allied with Athens in 433 but this only led the Spartans to fear that the Athenians once again had expansionist ambitions. When Athens attacked the northern city of Poteidaia for defecting from the Delian league, the Spartans demanded that Athens free all members of the league.

Sparta's strength was its army, Athens' its navy: when war broke out between the two in 431, they pursued very different strategies. Sparta's hope was that Athens could be starved into surrender by ravaging its agricultural hinterland in Attica. However, the Athenians had planned for this contingency. Attica was abandoned – its population taken within the city walls – while the city's wealth and command of the sea was harnessed to supply Athens from overseas and to raid the Peloponnese. However this overcrowding led to a plague (430–426) in which a third of the city's population died. By 421 neither side had achieved a decisive advantage and a peace was negotiated but on terms which alienated Sparta's allies Corinth, Elis, Mantineia and Argos, which then allied with Athens in 419. War broke out again unofficially but after a Spartan victory at Mantineia in 418 this new alliance broke up. The war

entered a decisive phase in 416 when the Athenians, to deprive their enemies of Sicilian food exports, agreed to send an expedition to besiege Syracuse. The expedition of the following year was a disaster from which Athens failed to recover. Sparta re-entered the war officially in 414 and sent help to Syracuse. The Athenians were catastrophically defeated in Sicily the following year, losing most of their 45,000-strong force. In the same year, Sparta garrisoned Dekeleia in Attica, forcing the closure of Athens' silver mines.

In 412 Persia, in return for a free hand in Ionia, paid for the construction of a Spartan fleet, tipping the balance of power decisively away from Athens.

Peloponnesian war, 431–404

- Athens and the Delian league, 431
- Athenian allies, 431
- Athenian allies on Sicily or Italian mainland
- Sparta and allied states, 431
- Spartan allies on Sicily or Italian mainland
- other Greeks
- Carthaginian territory in Sicily, 431
- border, 431
- Carthaginian territory in Sicily, c.400
- empire of Dionysios I of Syracuse, 406–367
- dependencies of the empire of Dionysios I
- Persia, 404
- Athenian offensives
- Spartan offensives
- Athenian victory
- Spartan victory
- 4th-century temple
- 4th-century theater

Rise of Macedon

- conquests of Philip II, 359–336
- allies of Philip II
- Corinthian league
- Macedonian victory over Athenian–Theban alliance
- Thebes Macedonian garrison

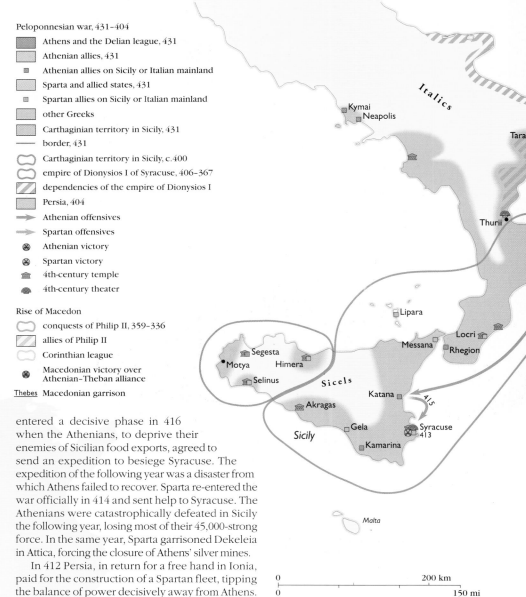

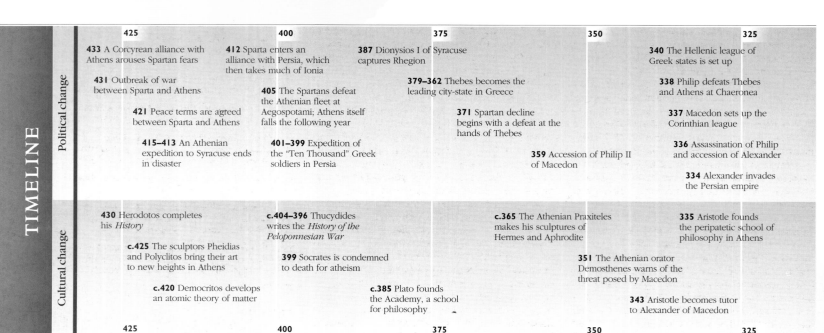

Political change

425	400	375	350	325
433 A Corcyrean alliance with Athens arouses Spartan fears	**412** Sparta enters an alliance with Persia, which then takes much of Ionia	**387** Dionysios I of Syracuse captures Rhegion		**340** The Hellenic league of Greek states is set up
431 Outbreak of war between Sparta and Athens		**379–362** Thebes becomes the leading city-state in Greece		**338** Philip defeats Thebes and Athens at Chaeronea
421 Peace terms are agreed between Sparta and Athens	**405** The Spartans defeat the Athenian fleet at Aegospotami; Athens itself falls the following year		**371** Spartan decline begins with a defeat at the hands of Thebes	**337** Macedon sets up the Corinthian league
415–413 An Athenian expedition to Syracuse ends in disaster	**401–399** Expedition of the "Ten Thousand" Greek soldiers in Persia		**359** Accession of Philip II of Macedon	**336** Assassination of Philip and accession of Alexander
				334 Alexander invades the Persian empire

Cultural change

425	400	375	350	325
430 Herodotos completes his *History*	**c.404–396** Thucydides writes the *History of the Peloponnesian War*		**c.365** The Athenian Praxiteles makes his sculptures of Hermes and Aphrodite	**335** Aristotle founds the peripatetic school of philosophy in Athens
c.425 The sculptors Pheidias and Polyclitos bring their art to new heights in Athens	**399** Socrates is condemned to death for atheism		**351** The Athenian orator Demosthenes warns of the threat posed by Macedon	
c.420 Democritos develops an atomic theory of matter		**c.385** Plato founds the Academy, a school for philosophy		**343** Aristotle becomes tutor to Alexander of Macedon

425	400	375	350	325

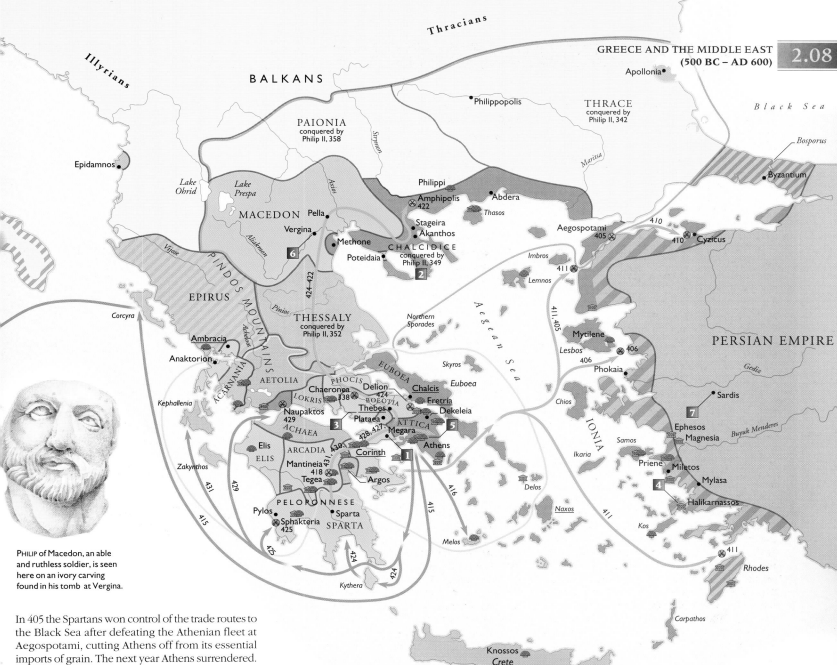

Map labels:

Thracians

Illyrians

BALKANS

Apollonia

Black Sea

Epidamnos

PAIONIA
conquered by
Philip II, 358

Philippopolis

THRACE
conquered by
Philip II, 342

Bosporus

Byzantium

Lake Ohrid

Lake Prespa

MACEDON

Pella

Vergina

6

Methone

Poteidaia

Philippi

⊗ Amphipolis
422

Stageira
Akanthos

Abdera

Thasos

CHALCIDICE
conquered by
Philip II, 349

2

Aegospotami
405

410

410 ⊗ Cyzicus

411 ⊗

Imbros

Lemnos

PERSIAN EMPIRE

EPIRUS

PINDOS MOUNTAINS

Corcyra

Ambracia

Anaktorion

ACARNANIA

Kephallenia

AETOLIA

Naupaktos
429

ACHAEA

Elis

ELIS

Zakynthos

THESSALY
conquered by
Philip II, 352

LOKRIS

PHOCIS

Chaeronea
338

Delion
424

BOEOTIA

Thebes

Plataea

3

Northern
Sporades

Skyros

Euboea

EUBOEA

Chalcis

Eretria

Dekeleia

ATTICA

Megara

Athens

5

1

Corinth

Argos

ARCADIA

Mantineia
418

Tegea

PELOPONNESE

Pylos

⊗ Sphakteria
425

SPARTA

Sparta

Aegean Sea

Chios

Ikaria

Delos

Naxos

Melos

Samos

Kos

Mytilene

Lesbos

406

⊗ 406

Phokaia

IONIA

Priene

411 ⊗

Rhodes

Sardis

Ephesos

Magnesia

7

Gediz

Buyuk Menderes

Miletos

Mylasa

Halikarnassos

4

Carpathos

Kythera

Knossos

Crete

Gortyn

Maritsa

Strymon

Axios

Aliakmon

Vijose

Pinios

Achalon

Aliakmon

431 429 415 425 424 430 431 428 427 415 416 411 405 411

In 405 the Spartans won control of the trade routes to the Black Sea after defeating the Athenian fleet at Aegospotami, cutting Athens off from its essential imports of grain. The next year Athens surrendered. Its democratic constitution was briefly overthrown by a Spartan-supported aristocratic coup and the Delian league was disbanded.

Sparta was now the strongest Greek state but its victory had been paid for by Persian gold. When Sparta went to war against Persia in 400, the Persians simply switched their subsidies to Athens and the increasingly powerful Thebes, and Spartan ambitions faded. The Greek states continued to struggle fruitlessly for another fifty years until unity was imposed on them by Philip II (r.359–336) of Macedon.

Macedon had a mixed population of Greeks, Illyrians and Thracians but, even though the Athenians liked to regard it as a barbarian kingdom, it was a thoroughly hellenized state by Philip's accession. Macedon was now transformed from a backwater into a superpower. Philip ignored the convention of Greek warfare that restricted campaigning to specific times of the year and introduced siege engines to take cities quickly by storm rather than by long blockade. Philip's first conquest, Paionia in the Balkans, paid with its rich mineral resources for the expansion of the Macedonian army and thereafter his progress was inexorable. In 340 Athens made a last-ditch effort to halt Philip's expansion, forming the anti-Macedonian Hellenic league. Philip crushed this alliance at Chaeronea in 338, after which all

the major Greek states, except Sparta, were forced to join the Macedonian-controlled Corinthian league.

Philip now announced a war of all Greece against Persia. The military weakness of Persia had been exposed in 401 when the rebel Persian governor of Sardis recruited an army of 10,000 Greek mercenaries to support his bid for the throne. The "Ten Thousand" marched into the heart of the Persian empire and, when their employer was killed in Babylonia, fought their way home again, demonstrating the military superiority of the Greeks. Philip's confidence was well placed but he was assassinated before his expedition was ready.

In the late 5th century the Greeks came close to being expelled from Sicily after Segesta called on the support of its ally Carthage during a boundary dispute with the aggressive Greek city of Selinus in 410. The Carthaginians went on to occupy the western half of Sicily by 405. The Greeks were united by Dionysios (r.406–367), tyrant of Syracuse, who recovered much of the territory lost to Carthage. Dionysios later extended his power to the Italian mainland where the Greek cities accepted him as their protector against the Italic peoples.

1 Megara was a neighbor and rival of Athens; when Athens blockaded it in the 430s, Sparta found an excuse for war.

2 Athens lost control of Chalcidice as a result of a campaign by the Spartan general Brasidas in 424-422.

3 The war-weariness of Sparta and Athens allowed Thebes to become dominant in Greece 379-362.

4 Halikarnassos was the site of the monument (Mausoleum) to Mausolos, a Lydian king who ruled from Mylasa and tried to build an empire in the 350s.

5 In Athens, Demosthenes spoke passionately about the Macedonian threat but failed to stem it.

6 The opulently furnished tomb of Philip II at Vergina was discovered in 1977. It contained his cremated body, his bronze armor and elegant grave goods.

7 Cyrus, governor of Sardis, recruited 10,000 Greek mercenaries to support his bid for the Persian throne in 401. Their progress was described by Xenophon.

See also 2.07 (5th-century Greece);
2.09 (Alexander); 2.12 (Sicily, Carthage and Rome)

In only eight years of tireless campaigning, Alexander of Macedon (r. 336–323) conquered the Persian empire and the Indus valley. Although his empire broke up on his death, Alexander's conquests determined that Hellenism would be the dominant cultural influence in the Middle East well into the Christian era.

Alexander was eighteen years old when his father, Philip II, was assassinated. He was bold, imaginative, well educated – Aristotle had been his tutor – and a promising soldier. In the first two years of his reign Alexander proved his abilities by securing Macedon's northern borders and subduing the rebellious Greeks. In 334, his home base now stable, Alexander launched his father's planned invasion of Persia, routing the army sent to stop him at the river Granicus. He then marched down the Anatolian coast, liberating and restoring the Greek cities of Ionia. Only Miletos and Halikarnassos, where the garrisons had been supplied by the Persian fleet, offered serious resistance. To prevent further naval interference, Alexander proceeded to conquer Phoenicia and Egypt, after first crushing a large Persian army, commanded personally by Darius III, at the river Issus in 333. With Persian naval power eliminated, Alexander marched into the heart of the Persian empire in 331, and at Gaugamela inflicted another humiliating defeat on Darius. Persian resistance crumbled, and Babylon and the Persian treasury at Susa were captured.

The following year, at the Persian Gates pass, Alexander destroyed the last sizeable Persian army and swept on to loot and burn the Persian capital, Persepolis. It took Alexander three more years of tough campaigning in Bactria and Sogdiana to complete his conquest of the Persian empire, before invading the Indus valley in 327. There, in 326, Alexander won his last major battle, over King Porus at the river Hydaspes. Alexander wanted to press on and invade the Ganges plain, but his soldiers, after marching 25,000 kilometers (15,000 miles), had had enough and they refused. Instead Alexander marched down the Indus to the sea and turned west, reaching Babylon in 324, where, the following year, aged only 32, he died, an overweight alcoholic.

Shortly before his death his adoption of the styles of oriental kingship had lost him the loyalty of some of his original Macedonian followers.

The most important factor in Alexander's success was his military genius, but he was also aided by the centuries-long tradition of imperial rule in the Middle East, which had weakened local identities and loyalties. The provincial populations of the Persian empire were used to foreign rule and, as Alexander respected local customs and did not make unreasonable demands for tribute, a change from Persian to Macedonian rule was a matter of indifference to them. Alexander's empire broke

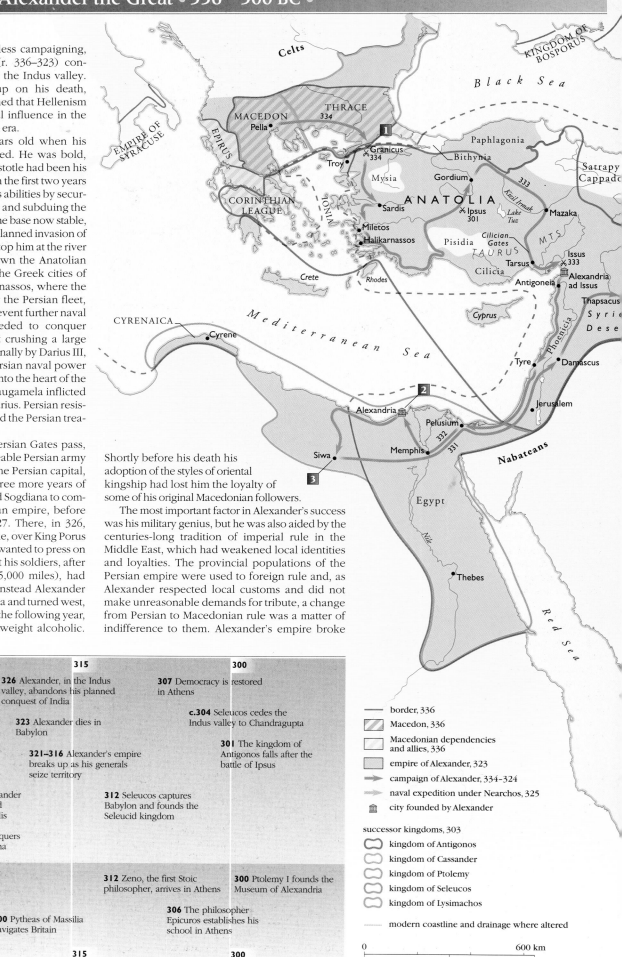

border, 336

Macedon, 336

Macedonian dependencies and allies, 336

empire of Alexander, 323

campaign of Alexander, 334–324

naval expedition under Nearchos, 325

city founded by Alexander

successor kingdoms, 303

kingdom of Antigonos

kingdom of Cassander

kingdom of Ptolemy

kingdom of Seleucos

kingdom of Lysimachos

modern coastline and drainage where altered

0   600 km
0   400 mi

TIMELINE

Political change

334 Alexander invades Anatolia, repulsing a Persian army at the Granicus river

333 Darius III is defeated at the Battle of Issus

332 Alexander conquers Egypt and founds the city of Alexandria

331 At Gaugamela, Alexander defeats Darius again, and goes on to sack Persepolis

329 Alexander conquers Bactria and Sogdiana

326 Alexander, in the Indus valley, abandons his planned conquest of India

323 Alexander dies in Babylon

321–316 Alexander's empire breaks up as his generals seize territory

312 Seleucos captures Babylon and founds the Seleucid kingdom

307 Democracy is restored in Athens

c.304 Seleucos cedes the Indus valley to Chandragupta

301 The kingdom of Antigonos falls after the battle of Ipsus

Cultural change

335 Aristotle founds his school of philosophy in Athens

c.325–300 Pytheas of Massilia circumnavigates Britain

312 Zeno, the first Stoic philosopher, arrives in Athens

306 The philosopher Epicuros establishes his school in Athens

300 Ptolemy I founds the Museum of Alexandria

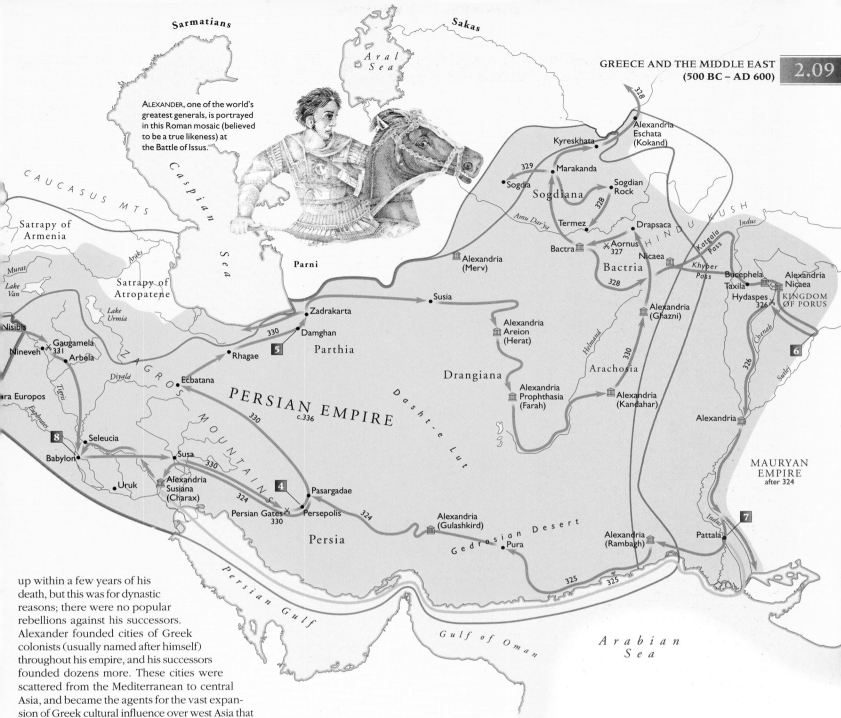

ALEXANDER, one of the world's greatest generals, is portrayed in this Roman mosaic (believed to be a true likeness) at the Battle of Issus.

up within a few years of his death, but this was for dynastic reasons; there were no popular rebellions against his successors. Alexander founded cities of Greek colonists (usually named after himself) throughout his empire, and his successors founded dozens more. These cities were scattered from the Mediterranean to central Asia, and became the agents for the vast expansion of Greek cultural influence over west Asia that was perhaps the most important consequence of Alexander's conquests.

Alexander left as his heirs a posthumous son and a mentally ill brother, neither of whom was capable of ruling in his own right. The regent Perdiccas maintained the central administration until his murder in 321, but under his successor, Antipater (d.319), the governor of Macedon, power in the provinces was seized by the generals and the empire fragmented in a series of conflicts known as the Wars of the Diadochi ("successors"). By 304 five successor kingdoms had arisen. Cassander, Antipater's son, ruled in Macedon; Lysimachos in Thrace; Antigonos had seized power in Anatolia; Seleucos in Mesopotamia and the east; and Ptolemy in Egypt. Of the five, only Antigonos aspired to recreate Alexander's empire, but this simply united the other Diadochi against him. When Antigonos was killed in battle against the combined armies of Seleucos, Lysimachos and Cassander at Ipsus in 301, his kingdom was divided up among the victors: Lysimachos taking Anatolia, Seleucus Syria and Cilicia, and Ptolemy, who had been campaigning separately, Palestine and Cyprus. Although the battle

of Ipsus did not bring an end to the struggles of the Diadochi, it did set the seal on the break-up of Alexander's empire.

During the chaos that followed his death, Alexander's empire had also begun to fray at the edges. His conquests had been rapid and the rulers of the northern satrapies of Bithynia, Paphlagonia, Cappadocia, Armenia and Atropatene had been allowed to retain their provinces after making only token submission. Alexander's early death prevented these provinces being brought into full submission, and during the Diadochan wars they became fully independent kingdoms. The Indus valley was also lost by the Greeks after Alexander's death. Preoccupied with the war against Antigonos, Seleucos ceded the Indian provinces to the Mauryan empire in 304 in return for a herd of war elephants (which he used to good effect at Ipsus). In Greece, now only a small part of the Hellenistic world, the cities of the Corinthian league rebelled unsuccessfully against Macedonian control in 323 and then defected to Antigonos in 307. However, after the defeat of Antigonos at Ipsus, Macedonian control was restored.

1 Alexander won control of Anatolia after defeating an army sent to intercept him at the river Granicus.

2 Founded in 332, Alexandria was to become the largest and richest Greek city in the 3rd century.

3 The oracle of Amun at Siwa claimed Alexander to be son of the god and heir to the Egyptian throne.

4 The burning of the palace of Xerxes at Persepolis in 330 marked the end of the Panhellenic war of revenge but not of Alexander's personal desire for conquest.

5 Darius III was murdered at Damghan by his courtiers as he fled, seeking refuge in Bactria.

6 Only when Alexander's exhausted and homesick army refused to follow him into the Ganges valley did he at last relent and turn back.

7 Nearchos built a fleet of more than 100 ships at Pattala to explore and control the Gulf coast.

8 Alexander died in Babylon in 323, having caught a fever after several days of heavy drinking.

See also 2.08 (rise of Macedon);
2.10 (Hellenistic world)

The struggles of the Diadochi continued for twenty years after the battle of Ipsus (301), during which time Lysimachos's Thracian kingdom was eliminated. Lysimachos himself was killed at the battle of Corupedion in 281, after which Seleucos took control of western Anatolia. Two years later Thrace was overrun by a Gaulish (Celtic) invasion. Some of these Gauls crossed into Anatolia, eventually establishing themselves in the region known subsequently as Galatia, from where they plundered the surrounding countryside for the next fifty years. The spate of Greek colonization of the east begun by Alexander continued until about 250. Dozens of new cities were founded and many established ones were hellenized: Greek became the common tongue from the Mediterranean to central Asia and the Indus valley.

Macedon gradually strengthened its hold on the Greek city-states during the 3rd century, but made an enemy of Rome by supporting Carthage during the Second Punic War (221–201). When Pergamon and Rhodes appealed to the Romans for protection against Macedon, Rome was happy to oblige, and at the battle of Cynoscephalae in 197 broke the kingdom's power and freed the Greek city-states. When Macedon attempted to reassert its position in Greece it was again defeated and annexation followed in 148. By this time the Romans had tired of the constant disputes of the Greek city-states and these were brought under direct Roman rule in 146.

The largest of the Hellenistic kingdoms at the end of the Diadochian wars was the Seleucid, but by the mid-3rd century it had begun a long slow decline. The first loss was the city of Pergamon in 262 BC. In 239 the Bactrian Greeks rebelled and founded an independent kingdom. The history of the Bactrian Greeks is little known, but they won back control of the Indus valley from the ailing Mauryan empire by the early 2nd century. In the 180s Greco-Bactrian rulers campaigned as far east as the Mauryan capital at Pataliputra on the lower Ganges and won temporary control of much of central India. The Greco-Bactrians prospered from their control of the major trans-Asian trade routes and despite their isolation remained in contact with the mainstream of Greek culture. However, Bactria was exposed to attacks by the steppe nomads and around 135 BC most of the kingdom was overrun. Some independent Greek principalities survived in the upper Indus valley but were extinguished by the end of the 1st century BC.

The Seleucid kingdom suffered a further territorial loss in 238 when Parthia became independent

TIMELINE

Political change

c.300 The Parni, Iranian nomads, settle in Parthia

279–278 Gaulish Celts overrun Thrace and invade Anatolia

239 Foundation of the Greco-Bactrian kingdom

238 Foundation of the Parthian kingdom

214-205 The First Macedonian War marks the beginning of Roman intervention in Greece

198 The Seleucids win control of Palestine at the battle of Panion

190 The Romans defeat Antiochus III at Magnesia

c.180 The peak of Greco-Bactrian power

171 and 168 Seleucid invasions of Egypt

166–160 The revolt of Judas Maccabeus in Judea

148–146 Macedon and Greece are annexed by Rome

141 The Parthians conquer Mesopotamia

c.135 The Kushans destroy the Bactrian kingdom

c.94 Taxila becomes the capital of the Saka kingdom

88-63 Mithridates of Pontus fights three wars to free the Greeks from Rome

83 The Seleucid kingdom finally collapses

30 Egypt becomes a Roman province

Cultural change

275 The Pharos lighthouse at Alexandria is completed

c.270 Aristarchos of Samos (c.320–c.250), first proposes a heliocentric universe

c.235 Eratosthenes (c.276–c.194) measures the Earth's circumference

c.140 The Venus de Milo sculpture is completed

c.120 The Greek ambassador Heliodoros erects a monument at Vidisha in central India

c.105 A college of technology is founded at Alexandria

Map legend

— border, c.270
▢ Macedon, c.270
▢ Ptolemaic kingdom, c.270
▢ Roman empire, c.270
▢ Seleucid kingdom, c.270
▢ Greco-Bactrians, c.185
▢ Parthian empire, c.185
▢ Seleucid kingdom, c.185
◯ Parthian empire, c.90
◯ Roman empire, c.90
◯ Seleucid kingdom, c.90

— trans-Asia trade route
▶ migration, with date
▫ cities with Hellenistic foundations
--- modern coastline and drainage where altered

0 — 600 km
0 — 400 mi

Sarmatians

*Aral
Sea*

Tashkent • • Kashgar

Kokand •

Kushans c.140–135

C A U C A S U S   M T S

Marakanda •

C a s p i a n   S e a

A m u   D a r'ya

Bukhara •

HINDU KUSH

Indus

Parni

*Turan
Lowland*

Sakas c.170–100

8

ARMENIA • Artaxata

Araks

Nisa •

Abivard •

Bactra •

□ Ay Khanoum

Murat

*Lake
Van*

ATROPATENE

Merv •

□ Kapisa

*Khyber
Pass*

• Taxila

Tigranocerta •

*Lake
Urmia*

early 3rd century

Bactria

Kabul •

1

Nisibis •

GANDHARA

Chenab

ra Europos •

Z A G R O S

• Herat

Helmand

Tigris

✕ Hamadan
129

M O U N T A I N S

Parthia

D a s h t - e   L u t

Sutlej

Euphrates

M E S O P O T A M I A

□ □

• Gabai

2

• Kandahar

Seleucia •

□

• Farah

Sakastan

Babylon •

• Susa

• Zaranj

• Uruk

□ • Charax

Indus

**SAKA
KINGDOM**
c.94

Persia

Gedrosian Desert

P e r s i a n   G u l f

Gedrosia

COMPLEX poses, as
in this 1st-century
boxer by Apollonios
of Athens, typified
Hellenistic sculpture.

Gulf of Oman

*A r a b i a n
S e a*

under the Arsacid dynasty. The Arsacids were descendants of the ruling house of the Parni, Iranian
nomads who had settled in Parthia earlier in the
century. Under Antiochus III (223–187) the Seleucid
kingdom conquered Armenia, Atropatene and Palestine and contained the expansion of Parthia and
Bactria. Unfortunately, Antiochus's success alarmed
the Romans, who declared war on him in 192 and
two years later inflicted a crushing defeat on him at
Magnesia. Armenia and Atropatene quickly regained
their independence, while the Romans awarded
western Anatolia to their ally Pergamon. Then in 166
Antiochus IV (r.174–163) faced a serious Jewish
revolt. Around the middle of the century the Parthians conquered Persia and overran Mesopotamia,
reducing the Seleucid kingdom to little more than
Syria. However, the Parthians were prevented from
completing the conquest of the Seleucid kingdom
by the invasion of their eastern provinces by the
Sakas in the 130s. The Sakas were contained by
90 BC and their main settlements, later known as
Sakastan, came under the control of the Parthian
Suren family, who founded a semi-independent
kingdom that lasted over a century.

The most enduring of the Hellenistic kingdoms
was the Ptolemaic kingdom of Egypt. Egypt had the
strongest and most recent traditions of independence – it had successfully thrown off Persian rule
from 404 to 341– and its population was resentful of
the Greeks and Macedonians who now dominated
the government and army. To placate the native
Egyptians the Ptolemies adopted many of the trappings of the pharaohs and became patrons of the
traditional religious cults. By the 2nd century some
Egyptians had become hellenized; and some Egyptian cults, such as that of the goddess Isis, had found
favor with the Greeks. Egyptians began to play an
important role in the army. However, there was no
real assimilation of the populations. Alexandria
became the largest and richest Greek city in the
world and even overshadowed Athens as a cultural
center. The Ptolemaic kingdom was the major naval
power of the eastern Mediterranean for most of the
3rd century but began to decline during a period of
dynastic instability after the death of Ptolemy IV in
203. When, in 168, Antiochus IV conquered Egypt,
only the intervention of the Romans secured the
restoration of the Ptolemaic dynasty.

1 The Bactrian kingdom, independent from 239 and
at its peak c.180, was destroyed by the Kushans c.135.

2 The Parthian kingdom, founded by Arsaces in 238,
had conquered Persia and Mesopotamia by 141.

3 The Jewish Maccabean revolt against the Seleucids
in 166-160 led to Judean independence in 142-141.

4 Ptolemaic Egypt, though ruled from the Greek city
of Alexandria, saw its cultural traditions preserved.

5 The Romans broke the power of Macedon at Pydna
in 168, and formally annexed the kingdom in 148.

6 The final remnant of the Seleucid kingdom was
conquered in 83 BC by the Armenian king Tigranes I.

7 Under the Attalids, Pergamon was an important
cultural center with a vast library, and spectacular
architecture.

8 Hellenistic settlers spread Greek institutions across
Asia. Gymnasia – centers of athletics and debating –
have been discovered as far east as Ay Khanoum.

See also 2.09 (Alexander); 2.11 (Parthians and
Sasanians); 2.13 (growth of the Roman empire)

In the chaos that followed the death of Alexander the Great, the Parni, an Iranian nomadic people, migrated from the Caspian steppes into Parthia. There they adopted Parthian language and customs, and their dominant family, the Arsacids, became the local rulers as vassals of the Seleucid kingdom. Arsaces I (r.c.247–c.211) declared his independence in 238, founding the independent Parthian state. The Seleucids contained Parthian expansion until the reign of Mithradates I (170–138), who turned Parthia into a major power by conquering Iran and Mesopotamia. Further expansion was prevented by invasions from the east by the Sakas and the Kushans and by dynastic problems. By 90–80 BC the eastern border was stabilized and the Sakas were settled in a vassal kingdom under the Parthian Suren family. Around the beginning of the Christian era this kingdom extended its control into the Indus valley. After 66 BC the Parthians had an opportunity to expand into Atropatene and seize northern Mesopotamia, where they established a common frontier with the Romans on the Euphrates.

The Romans initially regarded the Parthians as barbarians but learned to respect them when a major Roman army was destroyed at Carrhae by their horse archers almost as soon as it crossed the frontier in 53 BC. Internal troubles in Parthia saved the Romans from paying an even heavier price for their unprovoked attack. The Romans itched to avenge the humiliation, and wars between the two powers were frequent. The Roman infantry never got the measure of the Parthian horse archers and they made little headway until the 2nd century AD when the emperor Trajan took Armenia and Mesopotamia in 115–17. However, Trajan's successor Hadrian gave them up on his accession in 117. The Parthians had previously lost the Suren sub-kingdom to the Kushans, around AD 50–75.

The early Parthian kings adopted the Hellenistic traditions and governmental institutions of the Seleucid kingdom and continued to use Greek as an official language and on coinage. By the 1st century BC, however, the Parthian kingdom had developed into a decentralized feudal state made up of directly ruled provinces, vassal sub-kingdoms under local dynasties, and the fiefs of semi-independent nobles. Hellenistic cultural influence, strong at first, had also begun to decline by this time in the face of a resurgence of Persian traditions.

The frequent wars with Rome sapped the strength of the Parthian dynasty and in AD 224–26 it was overthrown following the rebellion of Ardashir I (r.c.220–40), the sub-king of Persia, who founded the Sasanian dynasty (named for Ardashir's grandfather, Sasan). The Sasanians saw themselves as the successors of the Achemenids and pursued far more aggressive and expansionist policies than the Parthians. Shapur I (r. 240–72) attempted to take Syria from the Romans but despite some spectacular victories, including the capture of the emperor Valerian at Edessa in 260, the Romans held on grimly. Shapur gained some territory from the Armenians and enjoyed spectacular success in the

Legend

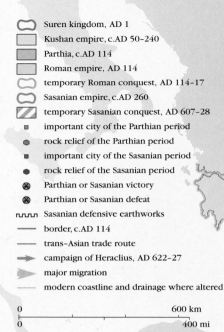

- Suren kingdom, AD 1
- Kushan empire, c.AD 50–240
- Parthia, c.AD 114
- Roman empire, AD 114
- temporary Roman conquest, AD 114–17
- Sasanian empire, c.AD 260
- temporary Sasanian conquest, AD 607–28
- ■ important city of the Parthian period
- ⬡ rock relief of the Parthian period
- ■ important city of the Sasanian period
- ● rock relief of the Sasanian period
- ⊗ Parthian or Sasanian victory
- ⊗ Parthian or Sasanian defeat
- ᴎᴎᴎ Sasanian defensive earthworks
- ── border, c.AD 114
- ── trans–Asian trade route
- ➤ campaign of Heraclius, AD 622–27
- ▶ major migration
- ---- modern coastline and drainage where altered

0 ――――――― 600 km
0 ――――――― 400 mi

TIMELINE

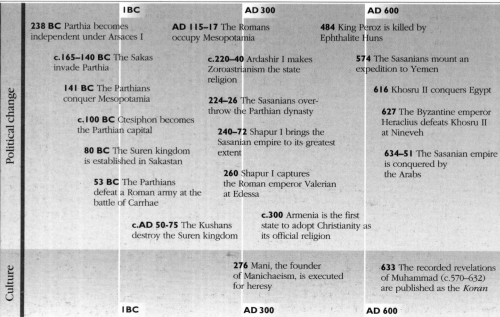

	1 BC	AD 300	AD 600
Political change	**238 BC** Parthia becomes independent under Arsaces I	**AD 115–17** The Romans occupy Mesopotamia	**484** King Peroz is killed by Ephthalite Huns
	c.165–140 BC The Sakas invade Parthia	**c.220–40** Ardashir I makes Zoroastrianism the state religion	**574** The Sasanians mount an expedition to Yemen
	141 BC The Parthians conquer Mesopotamia	**224–26** The Sasanians overthrow the Parthian dynasty	**616** Khosru II conquers Egypt
	c.100 BC Ctesiphon becomes the Parthian capital	**240–72** Shapur I brings the Sasanian empire to its greatest extent	**627** The Byzantine emperor Heraclius defeats Khosru II at Nineveh
	80 BC The Suren kingdom is established in Sakastan	**260** Shapur I captures the Roman emperor Valerian at Edessa	**634–51** The Sasanian empire is conquered by the Arabs
	53 BC The Parthians defeat a Roman army at the battle of Carrhae	**c.300** Armenia is the first state to adopt Christianity as its official religion	
	c.AD 50–75 The Kushans destroy the Suren kingdom		
Culture		**276** Mani, the founder of Manichaeism, is executed for heresy	**633** The recorded revelations of Muhammad (c.570–632) are published as the *Koran*

1 The capital of Arsaces I, founder of the Parthian state, was Abivard. The royal necropolis was at Nisa.

2 A former Parthian winter capital, Ctesiphon was the Sasanian capital from AD 226 until 637.

3 The Kushans were conquered by Shapur I (r.240–72) but briefly regained most of their territory during the minority of Shapur II (r.309–79).

4 At Naqsh-i Rustam a monumental relief carved on a cliff face commemorates the capture of the Roman emperor Valerian by Shapur I in AD 260.

5 "Alexander's Barrier" was actually a Sasanian earthwork built as a defense against steppe nomads.

6 The fire-temples complex at Gushnasp was the holiest site of the Sasanians' Zoroastrian state church.

7 The Sasanian state collapsed after defeats by the Arabs at Al Qadisiya (637) and Nehavend (642).

8 Dura Europos was a major Parthian border fortress city, captured by the Romans in AD 165 and abandoned after it was taken by the Sasanians in 256.

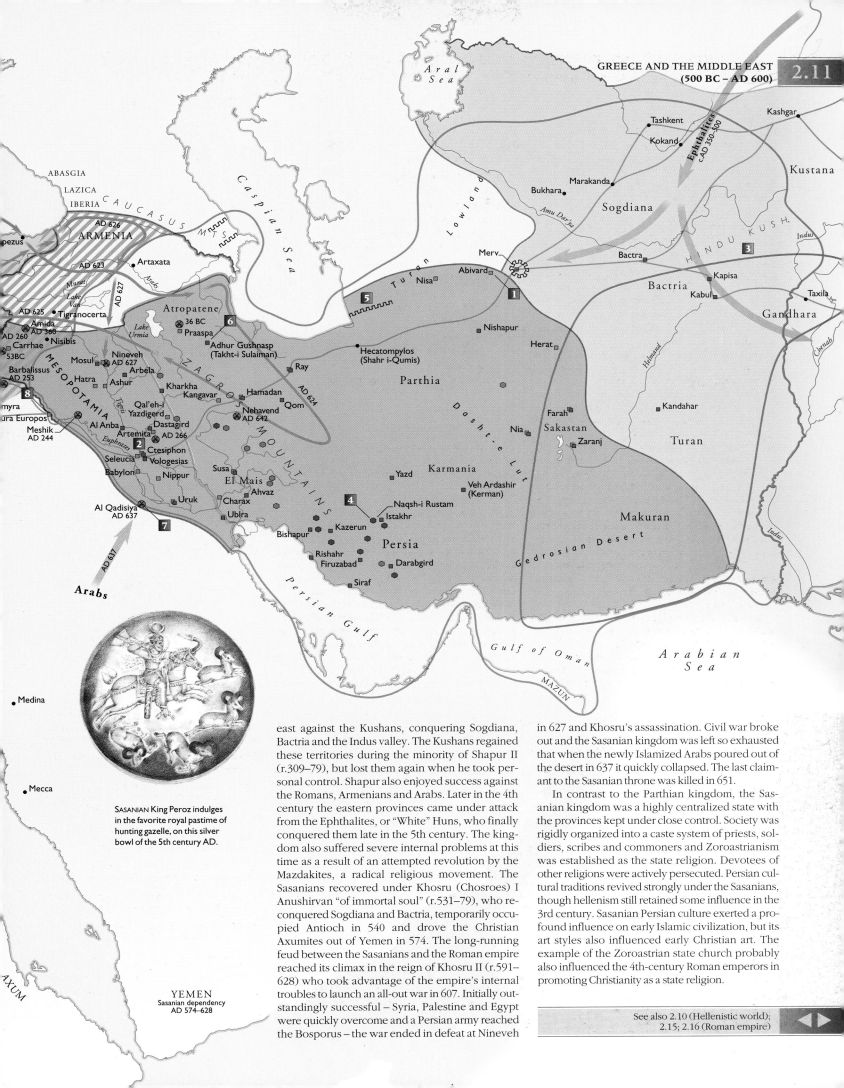

Kashgar

Tashkent

Kokand

Ephthalites
c.AD 350–500

Kustana

Marakanda

Bukhara

Sogdiana

Aral Sea

Amu Dar'ia

Bactra

HINDU KUSH.

Indus

Merv

Abivard

1

Kapisa

Bactria

Kabul

Taxila

Caspian Sea

Nisa

Nishapur

Herat

Gandhara

Chenab

ABASGIA

LAZICA

IBERIA

CAUCASUS MTS

ARMENIA

AD 626

pezus

AD 623

Artaxata

Murat

Araks

Lake Van

AD 627

Atropatene

36 BC

6

Praaspa

Adhur Gushnasp
(Takht-i Sulaiman)

Lake Urmia

Ray

Hecatompylos
(Shahr i-Qumis)

Parthia

Dasht-e Lut

Farah

Nia

Sakastan

Zaranj

Turan

Kandahar

AD 625

Amida

AD 360

AD 260

Carrhae

Nisibis

53BC

Mosul

Nineveh
AD 627

Arbela

Ashur

Hatra

Kharkha

Kangavar

Hamadan

Qom

Nehavend
AD 642

AD 624

Helmand

Barbalissus
AD 253

myra

ura Europos

Meshik
AD 244

MESOPOTAMIA

Tigris

Qal'eh-i
Yazdigerd

Dastagird

Artemita

AD 266

8

Euphrates

2

Ctesiphon

Vologesias

Seleucia

Babylon

Nippur

Al Anba

Susa

El Mais

Ahvaz

Yazd

Karmania

Veh Ardashir
(Kerman)

Makuran

Gedrosian Desert

Indus

Uruk

Charax

Ubira

4

Kazerun

Naqsh-i Rustam

Istakhr

Al Qadisiya
AD 637

7

Bishapur

Persia

Rishahr

Firuzabad

Darabgird

Siraf

AD 637

Arabs

Persian Gulf

Gulf of Oman

Arabian Sea

MAZUN

ZAGROS MOUNTAINS

Turan Lowland

Medina

SASANIAN King Peroz indulges
in the favorite royal pastime of
hunting gazelle, on this silver
bowl of the 5th century AD.

Mecca

AXUM

YEMEN
Sasanian dependency
AD 574–628

east against the Kushans, conquering Sogdiana, Bactria and the Indus valley. The Kushans regained these territories during the minority of Shapur II (r.309–79), but lost them again when he took personal control. Shapur also enjoyed success against the Romans, Armenians and Arabs. Later in the 4th century the eastern provinces came under attack from the Ephthalites, or "White" Huns, who finally conquered them late in the 5th century. The kingdom also suffered severe internal problems at this time as a result of an attempted revolution by the Mazdakites, a radical religious movement. The Sasanians recovered under Khosru (Chosroes) I Anushirvan "of immortal soul" (r.531–79), who reconquered Sogdiana and Bactria, temporarily occupied Antioch in 540 and drove the Christian Axumites out of Yemen in 574. The long-running feud between the Sasanians and the Roman empire reached its climax in the reign of Khosru II (r.591–628) who took advantage of the empire's internal troubles to launch an all-out war in 607. Initially outstandingly successful – Syria, Palestine and Egypt were quickly overcome and a Persian army reached the Bosporus – the war ended in defeat at Nineveh

in 627 and Khosru's assassination. Civil war broke out and the Sasanian kingdom was left so exhausted that when the newly Islamized Arabs poured out of the desert in 637 it quickly collapsed. The last claimant to the Sasanian throne was killed in 651.

In contrast to the Parthian kingdom, the Sasanian kingdom was a highly centralized state with the provinces kept under close control. Society was rigidly organized into a caste system of priests, soldiers, scribes and commoners and Zoroastrianism was established as the state religion. Devotees of other religions were actively persecuted. Persian cultural traditions revived strongly under the Sasanians, though hellenism still retained some influence in the 3rd century. Sasanian Persian culture exerted a profound influence on early Islamic civilization, but its art styles also influenced early Christian art. The example of the Zoroastrian state church probably also influenced the 4th-century Roman emperors in promoting Christianity as a state religion.

See also 2.10 (Hellenistic world);
2.15; 2.16 (Roman empire)

Founded probably around 800 BC, Rome had by about 600 BC fallen under the control of an Etruscan dynasty. Rome benefited from its strategic position on the lowest crossing point of the Tiber but remained a minor city. In 509 the monarchy was overthrown by an aristocratic coup and a republic was founded. The first century of its history was dominated by a struggle between the lower classes (the plebeians) and the leading families (the patricians). By the end of the 5th century the senate had codified the law and granted the plebeians their own representatives: the tribunes. In the 4th century the plebeians also won the right to run for the major offices of state – though voting in the popular assembly was structured to favor the richer classes. The extension of rights to the plebeians helped build a community of interest between the classes that sustained the republic through many crises.

Roman expansion began as a series of minor wars against its immediate neighbors. There was no imperial masterplan at this stage: these wars were intended primarily to make Rome more secure from attack. Around 400 BC, Gauls crossed the Alps and made extensive settlements in the Po valley, which became known as Cisalpine Gaul (Gaul "this side of the Alps") to distinguish it from the Gaulish homeland to the north. The Gauls raided widely, even sacking Rome in 390, but mainly they weakened the Etruscans. In 354 the Romans allied against the Gauls with the Samnites, a powerful tribal confederation, but the alliance did not last. The Romans and Samnites had competing interests in central Italy, which led to the inconclusive First Samnite War (343–341). Rome conquered the Latins (340–338), before renewing its conflict with the Samnites in the Second (327–304) and Third (298–290) Samnite wars. A Roman victory at Sentinum in 295 was followed by the collapse of Samnite power and by 290 Rome dominated central Italy. The Romans planted colonies of Roman citizens in subdued territories

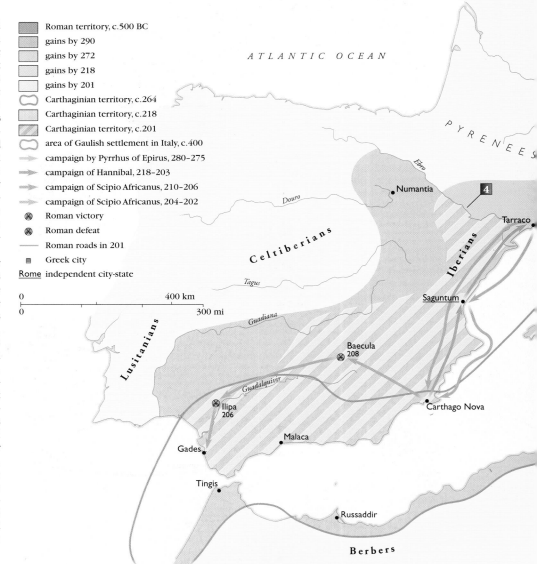

Roman territory, c. 500 BC
gains by 290
gains by 272
gains by 218
gains by 201
Carthaginian territory, c. 264
Carthaginian territory, c. 218
Carthaginian territory, c. 201
area of Gaulish settlement in Italy, c. 400
campaign by Pyrrhus of Epirus, 280–275
campaign of Hannibal, 218–203
campaign of Scipio Africanus, 210–206
campaign of Scipio Africanus, 204–202
⊗ Roman victory
⊗ Roman defeat
Roman roads in 201
■ Greek city
<u>Rome</u> independent city-state

ATLANTIC OCEAN

PYRENEES

Numantia

Tarraco

4

Ebro

Douro

Celtiberians

Iberians

Tagus

Saguntum

Lusitanians

Guadiana

Baecula
208 ⊗

Carthago Nova

Ilipa ⊗
206

Guadalquivir

Malaca

Gades

Tingis

Russaddir

B e r b e r s

and awarded their allies half-citizenship rights which could, if loyalty was proved, eventually be increased to full Roman citizenship.

The Romans began to bring the Greek cities of southern Italy under their sway. The Greeks appealed for protection to King Pyrrhus of Epirus. In 280 Pyrrhus invaded Italy after a hard-fought battle at Heraclea. The king's losses were so great that he remarked after the battle that a few more victories like this and he would lose the war. This is what in fact happened: the Romans resisted doggedly and in 275 Pyrrhus withdrew. Three years later the Romans took Tarentum, completing their conquest of peninsular Italy. Rome was now a Mediterranean power.

In 264 Rome went to war with Carthage, the major naval power of the western Mediterranean, over a dispute about spheres of influence in Sicily. The Romans called the Carthaginians "Poeni" (Phoenicians) – and the wars with Carthage came to be known as the Punic wars. Rome had no tradition of naval warfare but learned quickly, and in 260 its newly built fleet won its first victory over the Carthaginians at Mylae. In 255 the Romans tried to bring the war to a quick conclusion by invading north Africa but were repulsed. The war dragged on until 241, when the Carthaginians were vanquished at sea off Lilybaeum. Sicily became a Roman province; and in 238 the Romans also occupied Corsica

TIMELINE

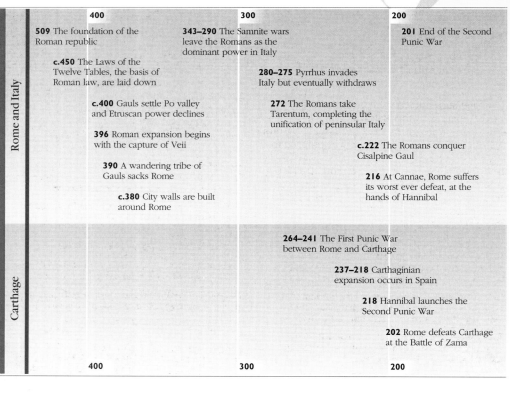

Rome and Italy

509 The foundation of the Roman republic

c. 450 The Laws of the Twelve Tables, the basis of Roman law, are laid down

c. 400 Gauls settle Po valley and Etruscan power declines

396 Roman expansion begins with the capture of Veii

390 A wandering tribe of Gauls sacks Rome

c. 380 City walls are built around Rome

343–290 The Samnite wars leave the Romans as the dominant power in Italy

280–275 Pyrrhus invades Italy but eventually withdraws

272 The Romans take Tarentum, completing the unification of peninsular Italy

c. 222 The Romans conquer Cisalpine Gaul

216 At Cannae, Rome suffers its worst ever defeat, at the hands of Hannibal

201 End of the Second Punic War

Carthage

264–241 The First Punic War between Rome and Carthage

237–218 Carthaginian expansion occurs in Spain

218 Hannibal launches the Second Punic War

202 Rome defeats Carthage at the Battle of Zama

400   300   200

ELEPHANTS carried soldiers to battle, but were used to scare the enemy rather than as cavalry. This Roman plate shows one carrying a fort.

and Sardinia. In the 230s Carthage began to recoup its losses by expansion in Spain; and in the 220s Rome conquered Cisalpine Gaul. In 226 Rome and Carthage agreed on respective spheres of influence, but when Hannibal, Carthage's foremost general, attacked Saguntum, a city within Carthage's sphere but friendly to Rome, the Second Punic War broke out. Roman naval power compelled Hannibal to invade Italy by marching overland and crossing the Alps. In Italy Hannibal found ready allies in the newly conquered Gauls in the north and the Greek cities in the south – and also in the kingdom of Macedon, which viewed with concern the expansion of Roman power into Greece in the 220s. Hannibal was a brilliant general but lacked the strength to take Rome itself and so win the war. The Romans, after a catastrophic defeat at Cannae, did their best to avoid facing Hannibal in open battle, trying simply to contain him in southern Italy. The main Roman counterattack was aimed at Carthage's Spanish possessions. The decisive campaign began in 210 under Scipio Africanus, and by 206 the Carthaginians had been driven out of Spain. Then in 204 Scipio launched an invasion of north Africa and persuaded the Numidian king Massinissa to side with Rome. Hannibal was recalled from Italy to face Scipio, and in 202 the two generals met in battle at Zama. The result was a crushing defeat for Hannibal and

Carthage surrendered on harsh terms. Rome annexed Spain and the Balearic Islands, and the Numidians were given most of Carthage's north African territory. Carthage itself was reduced to a heartland in modern Tunisia: it had to disband its fleet and agree not to go to war without Rome's permission. Although in Spain the Romans faced rebellions – which for seventy years frustrated their attempts to gain control of their new possessions – Rome now dominated the western Mediterranean.

1 The capture of nearby Veii, an Etruscan city, in 396, was the first step in the Roman conquest of Italy.

2 Rome disputed control of Italy with the Samnites, a confederation of the Caraceni, Caudini, Hirpini and Pentri tribes, in a series of wars, from 343 to 290.

3 In the growing rivalry between Rome and Carthage, Sicily was the flashpoint that led in 264 to the outbreak of the First Punic War.

4 In 226 the Ebro was the agreed border between Roman and Carthaginian spheres of influence.

5 A Roman campaign against Illyria was mounted in 229–228 to suppress pirates infesting the Adriatic Sea.

6 Hannibal's crossing of the Alps took 15 days: only a handful of his original 38 elephants survived.

7 Hannibal's base for operations in southern Italy was at Tarentum until the Romans retook the city in 209.

8 Numidia's Berber kingdoms, longtime suppliers of cavalry to Carthage, sided with Rome at Zama in 202.

See also 2.13 (growth of the Roman empire)

Soon after the Second Punic War, Rome was drawn into further wars to protect its position in Italy, Spain and Greece. Cisalpine Gaul was reconquered by 191. The need to protect the new Spanish provinces from native attack drew Rome into a piecemeal conquest of the whole peninsula. Rome also launched a punitive campaign in 200 against Macedon, which had allied itself with Carthage in the Second Punic War. In 197, after the battle of Cynoscephalae, Macedon was forced to liberate the Greek city-states. At this time Rome took no territory for itself. However, the weight of constant disputes among the Greek cities and the Hellenistic kingdoms had become so onerous by 146 that the Romans imposed direct rule on Greece: opposition was ruthlessly suppressed. Also in 146 a Roman army, which had been besieging Carthage for three years, finally razed the city to the ground, its territory becoming the Roman province of Africa. Expansion into the Middle East began in 133, when the last king of Pergamon bequeathed his kingdom to Rome, and Pergamon became the province of Asia. Southern Gaul was conquered and became the province of Gallia Narbonensis in 121.

As the empire grew, the booty of successful campaigns – treasure and slaves – flooded back to Rome. The largest class of the early republic had been peasant freeholders, but they could not compete with the new slave-run estates of the rich and were forced off the land to swell the ranks of the urban poor. Demands for constitutional reform led to bitter class conflict in Rome, as defenders of aristocratic privilege resorted to acts of violence, such as the murder of the reformist tribune Tiberius Gracchus in 133. Gaius Marius then reformed the Roman army, opening recruitment for the first time to landless citizens. These soldiers looked to their commanders to reward their service with grants of land to settle on when discharged. This had a dramatic effect on Roman politics as successful generals could usually count on their armies to support their political ambitions. Success in war was now the surest route to political power: it was the main motive for Pompey's

campaigns in Anatolia and Syria (67–64 BC), Julius Caesar's conquest of Gaul (58–51 BC) and Crassus's ill-fated attack on Parthia, which ended in his death at Carrhae, in 53 BC. The generals' need to reward their veterans led to the foundation of colonies throughout the empire in the late republic: these became important agents of Romanization.

The competition for power between generals led to civil war in 49 BC and ultimately to the fall of the republic. The victor was Caesar, who defeated his opponent Pompey at Ilerda in Spain (49 BC) and Pharsalus in Greece (48 BC). By 44 BC Caesar had crushed all military opposition, but a month after he declared himself dictator for life he was murdered by republican conspirators. Instability and civil war continued until Caesar's nephew Octavian, later known as Augustus, defeated Mark Antony and Cleopatra at Actium in 31 BC. In 27 BC Augustus introduced a new constitutional settlement, which he claimed "restored the republic" but in reality

▨	Roman empire, c.201 BC
▨	gains by 100 BC
▨	gains by 44 BC
▨	gains by AD 14
☐	gains by AD 117
▨	temporary gain, with dates held
⬭	kingdom of Pontus under Mithradates VI, 112–66 BC
■	pre-Augustan Roman colony
■	Augustan Roman colony
■	post-Augustan Roman colony
—	Roman provincial boundary, early 2nd century AD
🏛	Roman provincial capital
🦅	Roman legion stationed, early 2nd century AD
✸	rebellion against Roman rule, with dates
AC	Alpes Cottiae (Roman province)
AM	Alpes Maritimae (Roman province)
AP	Alpes Poeninae (Roman province)

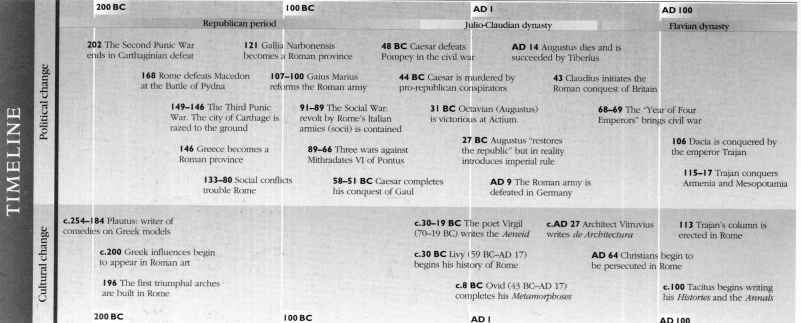

TIMELINE

	200 BC	100 BC	AD 1	AD 100
		Republican period	Julio-Claudian dynasty	Flavian dynasty
Political change	**202** The Second Punic War ends in Carthaginian defeat	**121** Gallia Narbonensis becomes a Roman province	**48 BC** Caesar defeats Pompey in the civil war	**AD 14** Augustus dies and is succeeded by Tiberius
	168 Rome defeats Macedon at the Battle of Pydna	**107–100** Gaius Marius reforms the Roman army	**44 BC** Caesar is murdered by pro-republican conspirators	**43** Claudius initiates the Roman conquest of Britain
	149–146 The Third Punic War. The city of Carthage is razed to the ground	**91–89** The Social War: revolt by Rome's Italian armies (socii) is contained	**31 BC** Octavian (Augustus) is victorious at Actium.	**68–69** The "Year of Four Emperors" brings civil war
	146 Greece becomes a Roman province	**89–66** Three wars against Mithradates VI of Pontus	**27 BC** Augustus "restores the republic" but in reality introduces imperial rule	**106** Dacia is conquered by the emperor Trajan
	133–80 Social conflicts trouble Rome	**58–51 BC** Caesar completes his conquest of Gaul	**AD 9** The Roman army is defeated in Germany	**115–17** Trajan conquers Armenia and Mesopotamia
Cultural change	**c.254–184** Plautus: writer of comedies on Greek models	**c.30–19 BC** The poet Virgil (70–19 BC) writes the *Aeneid*	**c.AD 27** Architect Vitruvius writes *de Architectura*	**113** Trajan's column is erected in Rome
	c.200 Greek influences begin to appear in Roman art	**c.30 BC** Livy (59 BC–AD 17) begins his history of Rome		**AD 64** Christians begin to be persecuted in Rome
	196 The first triumphal arches are built in Rome	**c.8 BC** Ovid (43 BC–AD 17) completes his *Metamorphoses*		**c.100** Tacitus begins writing his *Histories* and the *Annals*
	200 BC	100 BC	AD 1	AD 100

Vänern

Vättern

Lake
Peipus

Baltic Sea

Western Dvina

Volga

Dnieper

Volga

GAULS were respected opponents
of the Romans in the west and in
Anatolia; this statue of a dying
Gaul was made in Pergamon,
2nd century BC.

Germania
12 BC–AD 9
omagus   Teutoburgerwald
✕ AD 9
Colonia Agrippina

Moguntiacum
Augusta Treverorum
21   Agentorate
Agri
Decumates   Castra Regina
Augusta
Vindelicorum   Vindobona   Carnuntum
Raetia   Noricum   Aquincum
mania   Virunum   Pannonia   AD 6–8
perior   Superior
ALPS   Mediolanum   Aquileia   Dalmatia
na   Florentia   AD 6–8 ✕
Segusio   Po   Pannonia
Inferior
menelum   90 BC
Italia   Sava
Corsica   Rome   73–71 BC   91–89 BC
Aleria   Pompeii   2
Sardinia   126–122 BC,   Brundisium
115–111 BC
Carales
Sicily   Epirus
5   Actium
Carthage   31 BC
136–132 BC,   Sicilia
104–101 BC   Syracusae

CARPATHIAN   MTS
Dacia
Sarmizegethusa
Singidunum
Viminacium
Moesia   Novae
Superior   Danube
Salonae   Moesia Inferior
(capital not known)
Thracia
Macedonia   Byzantium
Pydna   Thessalonica   Perinthus
168 BC
Cynoscephalae
197 BC
Pharsalus
48 BC
Achaea   Athens
Corinth
Crete
Creta   Gortyn

Troesmis
Durostorum

Black Sea

KINGDOM OF BOSPORUS
(Roman vassal state)
Panticapaeum

Sinope   Trapezus   3
Satala

Bithynia
and Pontus   Nicopolis
68 BC
Nicomedia   Ancyra   Cappadocia
ANATOLIA   Melitene
Caesarea
Pergamon   Galatia   Tarsus
Magnesia   Asia   1
190 BC   Cilicia
Ephesus   Cyrrhus
Aphrodisias   Antiochia
Myra   Lycia and
Pamphylia   Cyprus
Paphus   Cyprus   Emesa

Armenia
AD 115–117
Tigranocerta

Samosata   Edessa
Carrhae
53 BC
Mesopotamia
AD 115–117

Syria   Palmyra

Ctesiphon

*Mediterranean
Sea*

Malta

Africa

Judaea
Caesarea   Bostra
AD 66–74
Jerusalem

Leptis Magna

Cyrene
Cyrenaica

Alexandria   AD 172
AD 66

Arabia

Aegyptus

0 ——————— 600 km
0 ——————— 400 mi

introduced a monarchical type of government. He took the title *princeps* (first citizen), leaving it to his successors to call themselves *imperator* (emperor).

Expansion continued under the emperors. In Augustus' reign Egypt and Galatia were annexed, the last native resistance was extinguished in Spain, the Alpine tribes were conquered, and the empire's northern frontier was pushed to the Danube. Augustus also tried to conquer Germany but gave up the attempt after a humiliating defeat at the battle of the Teutoburgerwald in AD 9. This defeat convinced Augustus that the empire had reached its natural limits and he advised his successors not to seek any more territories. Despite this advice, the empire continued to expand for another century after the death of Augustus. Much of the expansion was simply a tidying-up operation. The annexation of Lycia (AD 43) and the client kingdom of Mauretania (AD 44)

gave Rome control of the entire Mediterranean coastline. In AD 43, Claudius, a weak emperor who needed a triumph to strengthen his position, began the conquest of Britain but only the southern two-thirds of the island were actually brought under Roman rule. The last emperor to pursue an all-out expansionist policy was Trajan. Between 101 and 106 Trajan conquered the Dacian kingdom, which posed a threat to the security of the Danube frontier. His ambition was to conquer the Parthian empire, and he brought Armenia and Mesopotamia under Roman rule. However, his successor Hadrian (r.117–38), judging these eastern conquests to be undefendable, withdrew from all of them except Edessa. Later in the 2nd century the border was pushed northward in Britain, and northern Mesopotamia was wrested from the Parthians, but from this time on the empire was mainly on the defensive.

1 Willed to the empire by the king of Pergamon, Asia became Rome's first Anatolian province in 133 BC.

2 Rebellions – the "Social War" – forced Rome to concede equal political rights to non-Roman Italians.

3 Mithradates VI of Pontus fought Rome in three wars from 89 until his final defeat in 66 BC.

4 Augustus' victory at Actium in 31 BC ended the civil war and brought Egypt under Roman rule.

5 Carthage, refounded as a Roman colony, became the center of Roman administration in Africa in 29 BC.

6 The Roman conquest of Britain began in AD 43, nearly a century after Caesar's raids in 55 and 54 BC.

See also 2.06 (religion); 2.10 (Hellenistic kingdoms); 2.11 (Persia); 2.14 (later Roman empire)

The Roman empire created a vast free-trade area with a single currency where commerce could flourish without the threat of piracy or war. Good roads, bridges and harbors further aided trade. The empire's prosperity began to falter only in the 3rd century when the high cost of defending the empire caused emperors progressively to debase coinage, setting off runaway inflation.

The vast majority of the population of the Roman empire were peasant farmers or slaves whose needs were adequately met by local producers, but there was also considerable long-distance trade in both luxury goods and basic commodities such as metals, pottery and foodstuffs. The lifestyles of the small wealthy class were geared to conspicuous consumption, and luxury products such as silk, spices, aromatic resins, pigments and ivory were imported from as far afield as China, the East Indies and equatorial Africa to satisfy their tastes. Moralistic Romans worried that these expensive imports were a drain on the wealth of the empire; but finds of Roman metal and glassware, as well as coinage, from India and southeast and central Asia suggest that there was also a healthy demand for Roman exports. Luxury goods apart, the empire was essentially self-sufficient in everyday necessities and what was lacking in one region could easily be supplied by another. Most trade was generated by the needs of the empire's growing urban populations. Rome itself had to import 400,000 tons of grain annually, most of which came from Egypt, Africa and Sicily. The army also generated trade. Over 100,000 tons of grain were needed for rations each year; while the tents for one legion alone required the hides of 54,000 calves. The needs of the army stimulated agriculture and metalworking in the border areas, where most troops were stationed, but also called for much to be brought from elsewhere.

The empire's system of roads was built primarily to provide the army with fast all-weather routes, but they also promoted local trade. However, land transport was expensive because the volumes that could be transported were small. Long-distance cargoes therefore went by water, both by sea and along navigable rivers. Sea-going merchant ships capable of carrying up to 350 tons made it cheaper for

1 The main port for Rome was Puteoli until Claudius improved the harbor at Ostia, though this remained unsafe until Trajan rebuilt it in the early 2nd century.

2 Rome, with about a million inhabitants, was the largest city in the empire. Some 200,000 people relied on state handouts of grain for survival.

3 Egypt was the main granary of the Roman empire: the fertile Nile flood plain was the most productive agricultural area in the empire.

4 Carnuntum was the main center for trading Baltic amber with the German tribes.

5 Northwest Spain was one of the most important mining regions in the Roman empire.

6 Palmyra was a desert city which became an important trading destination for trans-Asian caravans.

7 The Rhineland was an important center of glass manufacturing: much was exported across the Rhine.

the city of Rome to import grain from across the Mediterranean than to cart it into the city from the surrounding countryside. For the same reason the Romans preferred to run frontiers along navigable rivers providing access to border garrisons – and fleets were maintained on the Rhine and the Danube for this purpose.

Although trade was essential to its survival, the empire's commercial classes remained small and enjoyed neither the wealth nor the status of the landowning aristocracy. Goods such as pottery were mass-produced in factories, but most production in the empire was small-scale and under-capitalized, the rich preferring to invest in land. It is in any case doubtful, in view of the poverty of most of the empire's population, whether the markets existed to support a greater degree of industrial production. This is probably one of the factors behind the surprising lack of technological innovation in the empire. Although the Romans were excellent engineers, they did not extensively exploit their under-

standing of the principles of water and wind power. The ready availability of cheap slave labor may also have deterred investment in expensive machinery.

The wealth and population of the empire were not evenly spread: the eastern half was wealthier, more densely urbanized and had a higher population than the western half which, outside Italy, was relatively underdeveloped. In most of the west, as in Gaul and Britain, urbanization was still in its early stages at the time of the Roman conquest, and the promotion of town life became part of the program of Romanization. The Romans founded dozens of new towns, each complete with baths, theaters, amphitheaters and other trappings of Roman civilization. But most of the west was too poor and underpopulated to support this level of urbanization and towns remained primarily administrative or military centers. This contrast between east and west was to have an important bearing on the fate of the empire in the 5th century.

The Roman empire united many different ethnic groups into a single state, but over time, helped by the progressive extension of citizenship, local

TIMELINE		AD 1	150	300
Economic change		**40 BC** Glass-blowing techniques replace the hand-molding of glassware	**c.100** Trajan devalues the coinage and institutes a range of economic reforms	**c.250** A period of high inflation points to impending economic crisis
		27 BC Augustus reduces the army to 28 legions and settles more than 100,000 veterans in frontier colonies	**100** Trajan extends the corn dole in Rome to poor children, as well as to their parents	**286** The empire is divided into eastern and western parts
		24–20 BC Augustus organizes regular grain handouts for the Roman poor, using grain from Egypt	**165–67** A plague epidemic sweeps through the empire	**301** Diocletian, in an attempt to end the inflation, issues an edict on prices
		AD 32 There are protests in Rome over grain shortages; riots recur in 51.	**212** Roman citizenship is granted to all inhabitants of the empire, allowing more taxes to be raised	
Transport		**c.AD 1–50** The first non-stop trading voyages from Egypt to India are undertaken	**c.200** The empire's arterial road system is effectively completed	
		AD 42 Claudius improves the harbor at Ostia		
		AD 1	150	300

Legend:

Roman empire, c.AD 117
main concentration of cities
■ city with population over 100,000
▪ city with population over 30,000
— main road
— sea and river route
— caravan route
- - - division between Greek and Latin languages
CELTIC local language surviving within Roman empire
furs source of goods from outside Roman empire

goods traded within Roman empire

copper — slaves
gold — brass and bronze
iron — glass
lead — pottery
silver — timber
tin — marble
grain — textiles
olive oil — purple dye
wine

0 — 600 km
0 — 400 mi

Map labels:

Vänern *furs*
Vättern
amber
amber
Lake Peipus
Baltic Sea
animal hides, slaves
Colonia Agrippina
Augusta Treverorum
Elbe
Oder
Vistula
Dnieper
animal hides, honey, grain
Castra Regina
Danube
Carnuntum
4
CARPATHIAN MTS
Olbia
Panticapaeum
flax, wine, iron
ALPS
Aquileia
Sarmizegethusa
Danube
Tomi
Black Sea
Milanum
Po
Genua
Ravenna
Salonae
Singidunum
Naissus
Sinope
Trapezus
Ancona
ILLYRIAN
THRACIAN
Byzantium
Nicomedia
Ancyra
Megalopolis
Amida
2
Ostia
Rome
Dyrrhachium
Thessalonica
ANATOLIA
wild animals from Asia
Corsica
Puteoli
1
Brundisium
Pergamon
Smyrna
Tarsus
Edessa
Sardinia
Carthage to Ostia – 3–5 days
Ephesus
Antiochia
silk from China
Athens
Aphrodisias
Corinth
Dura Europus
Hippo Regius
Carthage
Syracusae
Sicily
Rhodus
Rhodes
Cyprus
Palmyra
Ctesiphon
Malta
Crete
Paphus
ARAMAIC/ SYRIAC
6
Theveste
Mediterranean Sea
Gaza to Byzantium – 10–12 days
Tyrus
Damascus
Caesarea to Rome – 20 days
Caesarea
Bostra
Alexandria to Puteoli – 15–20 days
Jerusalem
Gaza
Petra
Cyrene
NABATAEAN
slaves and wild animals from tropical Africa
Leptis Magna
Alexandria
Clysma
LIBYAN
Memphis
DEMOTIC/ COPTIC
3
Myos Hormus
Thebes
Berenice
Syene
perfume, spices and muslin from India
slaves, ivory, ebony and wild animals from tropical Africa
aromatic resins from Arabia

Main text:

identities were weakened, and by the 4th century the vast majority of the empire's citizens considered themselves Roman. In the west local languages were gradually replaced by Latin. Distinct local dialects of Latin developed in Italy, Iberia, Dacia and Gaul, eventually developing into the Romance languages – Italian, Spanish, Portuguese, Romanian and French. Celtic languages survived in Britain, Basque in the Pyrenees and Libyan in much of North Africa. Latin made little headway in the east. Here it was Greek which gradually replaced local languages, such as Phrygian, in Anatolia. However, Greek did not take over as completely as Latin did in the west and there remained large communities of Demotic (late ancient Egyptian) and Aramaic speakers.

MERCHANT ships were slow and heavy but were capable of ocean-going voyages: this illustration comes from Trajan's Column in Rome (AD 113).

See also 2.06 (religion and culture); 2.11 (Persia); 2.13 (Diocletian's reforms);

After Hadrian withdrew from Trajan's eastern conquests in 117, the borders of the Roman empire remained stable for almost 150 years. The only significant change was in the east, where successful campaigning by Septimius Severus between 195 and 198 wrested northern Mesopotamia from the Parthians. The 2nd century was a time of unrivaled peace and prosperity for the empire but this was not to last. The wealth of the empire was attractive to the Germanic tribes along the Rhine and Danube frontiers, and these began to unite in powerful confederations and raid Roman territory. In 167 Marcomannic raiders crossed into Italy, and though the emperor, Marcus Aurelius, successfully secured the borders, pressure on the northern frontier was thereafter continuous. Another problem was the imperial succession: there was no accepted way of deposing an incompetent or tyrannical emperor, nor of selecting a new emperor if a dynasty died out or was overthrown. When the incompetent, tyrannical Nero was overthrown in AD 68 the frontier armies promoted their own candidates for the succession, who then fought it out in a civil war. The same happened after the murder of the mad Commodus.

Pressure on the northern frontiers became critical in the 3rd century, and a new threat appeared in 226 when the Parthians were overthrown by the aggressive Persian Sasanian dynasty. In these conditions, the emperor had to be above all a good soldier. While rival candidates for power, promoted by different legions, fought each other for control of the empire, the borders were left undefended and open to invasion. For example, when Valerian (r. 253–60) withdrew troops from the Rhine to fight a usurper, the Franks immediately invaded Gaul. The efforts of emperors to buy the loyalty of their troops led them to debase the coinage to raise money, but this added runaway inflation to the empire's woes. Urban life now declined, especially in the west, where many towns shrank to a fortified administrative core. Civil war and invasion were incessant between 235 and 284: of the twenty-six emperors who ruled in this period all but one died by violence.

Not all the usurpers aimed at control of the whole empire. After Valerian was captured by the Persians at Edessa in 260, defense of the east devolved on Odenathus, ruler of the desert city of Palmyra. He defeated the Persians but then built an independent kingdom for himself. Under his wife and successor Queen Zenobia, it came to include Egypt, Syria and much of Anatolia. In the west the usurper Postumus founded an independent Gallic empire, winning over the people of Gaul, Britain and Spain; he promised to concentrate on defending the frontiers and not to march on Rome.

The Roman empire began to revive in the reign of Aurelian, with the reconquest of Palmyra (272) and the Gallic empire (274), though Dacia was permanently abandoned to the Germans. Political and economic stability were restored by Diocletian (r. 284–305), who reformed the whole structure of the empire. Diocletian greatly expanded the army and reformed the tax system to pay for it. Price regulation was introduced to curb inflation, though it drove goods off the markets. To restore respect to the imperial office, elaborate court ritual was introduced and the idea of the emperor as "first citizen" was abandoned: he was now "lord and god." Civilian and military authority were separated: provinces

Legend:

	Roman empire, c.235
	Roman territory lost permanently, 163–378
	kingdom of Palmyra, 260–72
	Gallic empire, 260–74
	strong Christian communities by 300
Goths	major Germanic peoples, 3rd century
Picts	other barbarians, 3rd century
→	attacks on Roman empire, with dates
	city sacked
	Roman victory
	Roman defeat
	battle between Roman forces
	frontier wall or rampart
Italia	Diocletianic diocese
	borders of Diocletianic dioceses

TIMELINE

Political change

Flavian | 138–92 Antonine dynasty | 192–235 Severan dynasty | 306–63 Constantinian dynasty

117 Hadrian abandons Trajan's eastern conquests

133 Hadrian's defensive wall across northern Britain is completed

167–80 The Marcomannic wars test the Danube frontier

192–97 Civil war follows the murder of Commodus

197 Severus sacks the Parthian capital Ctesiphon

224–26 The Persian Sasanian dynasty overthrows the Parthian dynasty

c.250 The beginning of a period of runaway inflation

251 The emperor Decius is killed by Goths at Abrittus

260 Sasanians capture the emperor Valerian at Edessa

284 Diocletian becomes emperor (abdicates 305)

286 Diocletian divides the empire into east and west

301 Diocletian tries to control prices and wages by edict

324 Constantinople is founded on the site of Byzantium

376 A large contingent of Visigoths fleeing the Huns is admitted into the empire

378 Visigoths defeat and kill the emperor Valens

391 Paganism is proscribed by Theodosius I

363 The emperor Julian is killed attacking the Sasanians

367 Picts, Scots, Saxons and Franks mount a major attack on Roman Britain

Cultural change

c.125–48 Claudius Ptolemy, astronomer, mathematician and geographer

174–80 Marcus Aurelius writes his Stoic *Meditations*

244 Plotinus (205–70), the neo-Platonist philosopher, arrives in Rome

269 St Antony becomes a hermit – marking the foundation of Christian monasticism

303–11 Christians are violently persecuted under Diocletian and Galerius

313 Constantine's Edict of Milan confirms toleration of all religions

341 The Gothic Christian bishop Ulfilas embarks on a mission to convert his people

361–63 The emperor Julian attempts to revive paganism

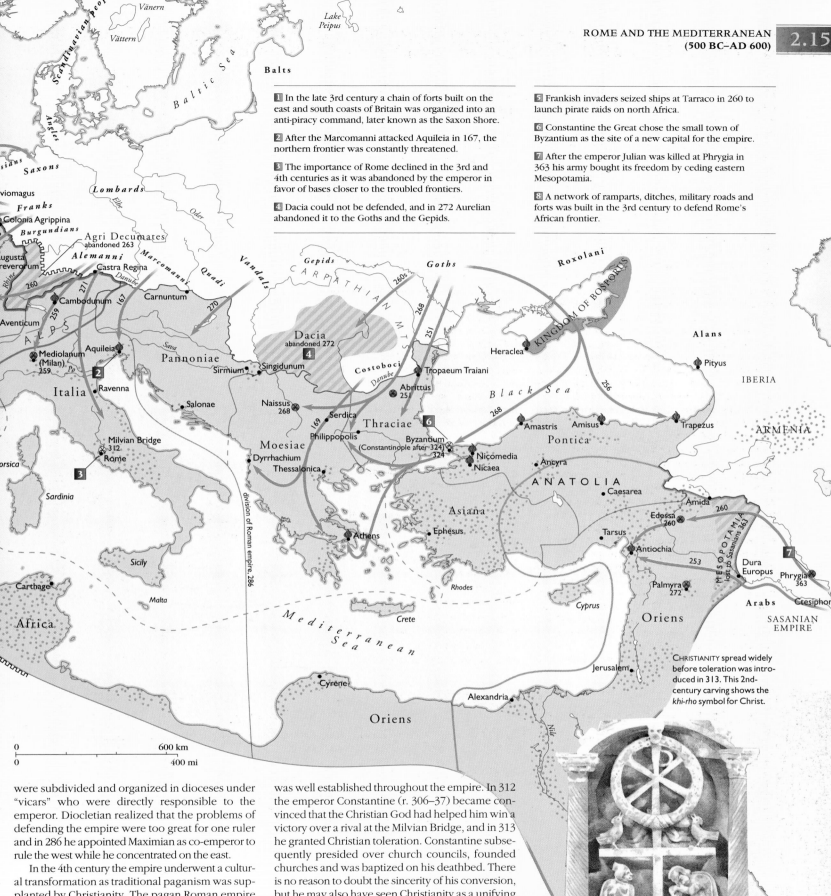

1 In the late 3rd century a chain of forts built on the east and south coasts of Britain was organized into an anti-piracy command, later known as the Saxon Shore.

2 After the Marcomanni attacked Aquileia in 167, the northern frontier was constantly threatened.

3 The importance of Rome declined in the 3rd and 4th centuries as it was abandoned by the emperor in favor of bases closer to the troubled frontiers.

4 Dacia could not be defended, and in 272 Aurelian abandoned it to the Goths and the Gepids.

5 Frankish invaders seized ships at Tarraco in 260 to launch pirate raids on north Africa.

6 Constantine the Great chose the small town of Byzantium as the site of a new capital for the empire.

7 After the emperor Julian was killed at Phrygia in 363 his army bought its freedom by ceding eastern Mesopotamia.

8 A network of ramparts, ditches, military roads and forts was built in the 3rd century to defend Rome's African frontier.

Map labels: Scandinavian Peoples · Vänern · Vättern · Lake Peipus · Baltic Sea · Balts · Angles · Saxons · Lombards · Franks · viomagus · Colonia Agrippina · Burgundians · Augusta Treverorum · Alemanni · Agri Decumates abandoned 263 · Castra Regina · Cambodunum · Carnuntum · Marcomanni · Quadi · Vandals · Gepids · Goths · Roxolani · Aventicum · Rhine · Danube · Mediolanum (Milan) 259 · Aquileia · Sava · Pannoniae · Dacia abandoned 272 · Costoboci · Heraclea · KINGDOM OF BOSPORUS · Alans · Pityus · IBERIA · Italia · Ravenna · Sirmium · Singidunum · Salonae · Naissus 268 · Abrittus 251 · Tropaeum Traiani · Danube · Black Sea · Amastris · Amisus · Trapezus · ARMENIA · Serdica · Philippopolis · Thraciae · Byzantium (Constantinople after 324) 324 · Pontica · Milvian Bridge 312 · Rome · Moesiae · Dyrrhachium · Thessalonica · Nicomedia · Nicaea · Ancyra · ANATOLIA · Corsica · Sardinia · division of Roman empire, 286 · Athens · Asiana · Ephesus · Caesarea · Amida 260 · Edessa 260 · Tarsus · MESOPOTAMIA lost to Sasanians 363 · Sicily · Malta · Rhodes · Antiochia · Dura Europus · Phrygia 363 · Palmyra 272 · Arabs · Ctesiphon · SASANIAN EMPIRE · Carthage · Mediterranean Sea · Crete · Cyprus · Oriens · Africa · Cyrene · Jerusalem · Alexandria · Nile · Oriens

CHRISTIANITY spread widely before toleration was introduced in 313. This 2nd-century carving shows the *khi-rho* symbol for Christ.

0 ____ 600 km
0 ____ 400 mi

were subdivided and organized in dioceses under "vicars" who were directly responsible to the emperor. Diocletian realized that the problems of defending the empire were too great for one ruler and in 286 he appointed Maximian as co-emperor to rule the west while he concentrated on the east.

In the 4th century the empire underwent a cultural transformation as traditional paganism was supplanted by Christianity. The pagan Roman empire was a tolerant state and was prepared to accept any religion that did not involve human sacrifice, so long as its devotees were prepared to pay lip-service to the state gods. Christians were not prepared to do this and had faced frequent persecutions as a result, one of the worst being ordered by Diocletian. Despite this, Christianity had spread steadily through the urban lower and middle classes, and by 300 it was well established throughout the empire. In 312 the emperor Constantine (r. 306–37) became convinced that the Christian God had helped him win a victory over a rival at the Milvian Bridge, and in 313 he granted Christian toleration. Constantine subsequently presided over church councils, founded churches and was baptized on his deathbed. There is no reason to doubt the sincerity of his conversion, but he may also have seen Christianity as a unifying force for the embattled empire. Constantine's successors continued to promote Christianity and, despite a short-lived pagan revival under Julian (r.361–63), the new religion began to exert a strong influence on all aspects of Roman life, from personal morality to art and literature. Christianity finally became the empire's official religion in 391, when Theodosius I abolished pagan worship.

See also 2.11 (Sasanians): 2.14 (earlier Roman empire); 2.16 (fall of the empire); 2.19 (Germans)

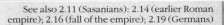

The fragile stability of the 4th-century empire was maintained at great cost to its citizens. Taxation was kept at a high level to pay for the large armies needed to defend the frontiers against increasingly well organized Germanic barbarians; yet the economy, particularly in the west, was in decline. The rich used their political influence to avoid paying taxes, so the tax burden fell heavily upon the poorer classes. Even in Egypt's fertile Nile valley, peasant farmers could not afford to pay their taxes and abandoned their fields. The empire's population contracted and manpower shortages began to affect the armies. The western army relied increasingly on barbarian mercenaries to fill its ranks.

In the 370s pressures on the empire's northern frontier increased dramatically. The Huns, a Turkic nomad people, migrated to the eastern European steppes from central Asia and, around 372, crushed the Ostrogoths. The defeat of this the most powerful Germanic tribe caused panic among the rest. In 376 the Visigoths, seeking sanctuary from the Huns, requested permission to settle in the Roman empire. The eastern emperor, Valens, who saw the Visigoths as a valuable source of recruits for the army, settled them on vacant lands in Thrace. There, however, they were treated badly by the corrupt officials in charge of their settlement; and in 378 they rebelled, defeating and killing Valens in battle at Adrianople. Under a new agreement in 382 the emperor Theodosius gave the Visigoths the status of federates (allies); but they rebelled again in 395 under their ambitious new leader, Alaric. He had previously commanded Gothic troops in the Roman army, but now ravaged Greece and Dalmatia before invading Italy in 401. Stilicho, a Roman general of Germanic origin, drove the Visigoths back into Dalmatia; but the situation deteriorated in 406 when a coalition of Vandals, Suevi and Alans invaded Gaul before crossing the Pyrenees into Spain in 409. They were

followed into Gaul by Franks, Burgundians and Alemanni. In 410 Alaric rebelled yet again, and when his demands were refused the Visigoths sacked Rome. Though no longer the administrative capital of the empire, Rome remained a potent symbol of its history and power, and the attack was deeply shocking. Alaric died soon afterward, and his successors were more inclined to cooperate with the Romans. In 418 the Visigoths, as allies of the Romans, attacked the Suevi, Alans and Vandals in Spain, before being settled on rich lands in Aquitaine as federates under nominal Roman suzerainty.

Although the Huns were indirectly responsible for the empire's woes, they initially maintained good

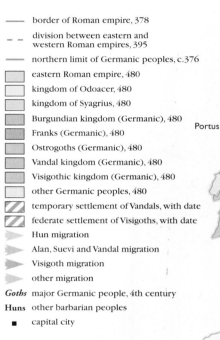

—— border of Roman empire, 378

- - division between eastern and western Roman empires, 395

—— northern limit of Germanic peoples, c.376

eastern Roman empire, 480

kingdom of Odoacer, 480

kingdom of Syagrius, 480

Burgundian kingdom (Germanic), 480

Franks (Germanic), 480

Ostrogoths (Germanic), 480

Vandal kingdom (Germanic), 480

Visigothic kingdom (Germanic), 480

other Germanic peoples, 480

temporary settlement of Vandals, with date

federate settlement of Visigoths, with date

Hun migration

Alan, Suevi and Vandal migration

Visigoth migration

other migration

Goths major Germanic people, 4th century

Huns other barbarian peoples

■ capital city

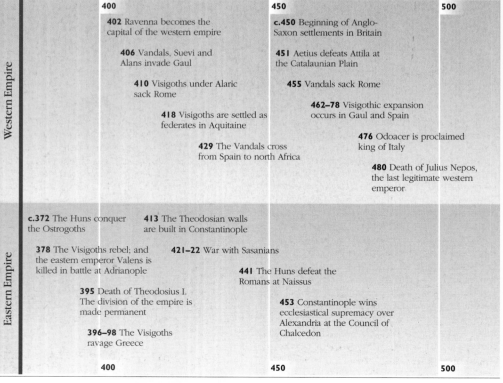

Western Empire

402 Ravenna becomes the capital of the western empire

406 Vandals, Suevi and Alans invade Gaul

410 Visigoths under Alaric sack Rome

418 Visigoths are settled as federates in Aquitaine

429 The Vandals cross from Spain to north Africa

c.450 Beginning of Anglo-Saxon settlements in Britain

451 Aetius defeats Attila at the Catalaunian Plain

455 Vandals sack Rome

462–78 Visigothic expansion occurs in Gaul and Spain

476 Odoacer is proclaimed king of Italy

480 Death of Julius Nepos, the last legitimate western emperor

Eastern Empire

c.372 The Huns conquer the Ostrogoths

378 The Visigoths rebel; and the eastern emperor Valens is killed in battle at Adrianople

395 Death of Theodosius I. The division of the empire is made permanent

396–98 The Visigoths ravage Greece

413 The Theodosian walls are built in Constantinople

421–22 War with Sasanians

441 The Huns defeat the Romans at Naissus

453 Constantinople wins ecclesiastical supremacy over Alexandria at the Council of Chalcedon

1 The arrival of the Huns in eastern Europe around 370 completely destabilized the Germanic tribes, causing many to seek refuge in the Roman empire.

2 In 402 the capital of the western empire was moved from Rome to Ravenna, allowing more rapid communication with the northern frontier and Constantinople.

3 Most of Britain's garrison was withdrawn in 407 by the usurper Constantine to fight in a civil war. In 410 Honorius told the Britons to see to their own defenses.

4 Rome was sacked twice in the 5th century: in 410 by the Visigoths; and in 455 by the Vandals.

5 Saxons, Angles and Jutes from north Germany and Denmark began to settle in eastern Britain c.450.

6 The position and strong fortifications of Constantinople saved Anatolia from barbarian invaders in the 5th century.

7 In the 460s Visigoths, settled by the Romans in Aquitaine in 418, expanded into Gaul and Spain.

8 In 476 Italy came under the rule of Odoacer, a barbarian general, who deposed the "last" western emperor: the puppet usurper Romulus Augustulus, who was still a boy.

STILICHO, part-Roman, part-Vandal, commanded the western empire's armies, but was beheaded by the emperor Honorius in 408.

relations with Rome. The Roman general Aetius used Hun mercenaries widely in the 430s to impose federate status on the Burgundians and other barbarian settlers in Gaul, but in 441 Attila turned on the empire, ravaging the Balkans and pushing his western border to the Rhine. In 451 Attila invaded Gaul but was defeated by a coalition of Romans, Visigoths, Burgundians and Franks under Aetius at the Catalaunian Plain. After Attila's death in 453 the Huns' German subjects rebelled, breaking their power at the battle of Nedao in 454. The collapse of the Huns in fact worked against Rome: fear of them had kept Rome's Germanic allies reasonably loyal, now they had less cause to be cooperative.

In 429 the Vandals had crossed from Spain to Africa and in 439 captured Carthage and set up a completely independent kingdom. This was the most serious blow the barbarians had so far struck against the empire, as north Africa was Italy's main source of grain. The Vandals turned to piracy, and in 455 went on to sack Rome itself. The assassination in

this year of Aetius, the west's most able general, and of Valentinian III, last of the Theodosian dynasty, were further blows. The western empire now began to crumble and by the 470s was reduced to little more than Italy. The last legitimate western emperor, Julius Nepos, was driven out of Italy in 475 by a palace coup which placed a boy usurper, Romulus Augustulus, on the throne. The following year Odoacer, a barbarian general, deposed Augustulus and was proclaimed king by his soldiers. Odoacer recognized the suzerainty of the eastern emperor Zeno and offered to rule Italy as imperial viceroy. The deposing of Augustulus in 476 is widely accepted as marking the end of the western Roman empire, but Julius Nepos continued to rule a rump empire in Dalmatia from 475 until his death in 480. Dalmatia then became part of Odoacer's kingdom.

The main cause of the fall of the western Roman empire was its exposure to barbarian attack – far greater than in the east, which had only a short northern frontier. This problem was exacerbated by

the division of the empire in the 4th century, which deprived the poorer, less populated and more vulnerable west of the resources of the richer east. Eastern emperors did assist their western colleagues, but their main priority was ensuring that the east did not go the same way as the west. The west was also politically less stable than the east. From the time of Honorius onward western emperors were dominated by overbearing generals. After the death of Valentinian III in 455, the western emperors became the puppets of barbarian generals: when they outlived their usefulness or tried to act independently, they were murdered. The high cost of defending the empire undermined positive loyalty to it. There was little popular resistance to the barbarians and, as they were inefficient tax collectors, most people probably felt themselves better off without the empire.

See also 2.11 (Sasanians); 2.17 (rise of Byzantium); 2.19 (Germans and Slavs); 2.20 (steppe peoples)

For twelve years after Odoacer's takeover of Italy, Zeno, the eastern emperor, did nothing. Then in 488 he commissioned Theodoric, king of the Ostrogoths, to overthrow Odoacer and rule Italy until he, the emperor, was able to claim sovereignty in person. By 493 Odoacer was dead and Theodoric was master of Italy. Under Theodoric, who wished to preserve Roman civilization, Italy enjoyed peace and prosperity, but there was no assimilation between Roman and Goth. The main barrier was religion. The Goths had converted to Christianity in the 4th century but were followers of the teachings of Arius, who denied the divinity of Christ – which their Roman subjects regarded as heretical. The Burgundians, Visigoths and Vandals were also Arians and assimilation was equally limited in those kingdoms. Arianism also prevented good relations between the barbarian kingdoms and the eastern emperor, who regarded himself as the guardian of orthodox Christianity. The only barbarians to escape the taint of heresy were the Franks, who converted directly from paganism to orthodox Christianity around 500. This earned them the friendship and support of the eastern emperors and the loyalty and cooperation of their Gallo-Roman subjects. Because of this the Frankish kingdom became the strongest power in western Europe by 600.

Although it was frequently at war with Sasanian Persia, the eastern empire prospered after the fall of the west. The emperor Anastasius (r. 491–518) even managed to cut taxes and still leave his successor, Justin (r. 518–27), with a full treasury. Justin was succeeded by his nephew Justinian (r. 527–65), the last great Roman emperor. Justinian had a very clear idea of the responsibilities of a Roman emperor, chief of which was maintaining the territorial integrity of the empire. To Justinian it was a disgrace that the western provinces of the empire were occupied by barbarians and he launched a concerted effort to recover them. In 533 he sent a force under Belisarius which, against expectations, destroyed the Vandal kingdom in north Africa. The Vandal campaign had been made possible by the cooperation of the pro-Roman Ostrogothic queen Amalasuntha,

who allowed the invasion fleet to use Sicily as a base. Amalasuntha's murder in 534 was used as a pretext for the invasion of Italy in 535. By 540 the Ostrogoth capital at Ravenna had fallen, but resistance was revived by Totila (r. 541–52). War with Persia diverted Roman forces to the east and the resulting stalemate in Italy was only broken in 552 when a new Roman army under Narses arrived from Constantinople. By 554 all of Italy south of the Po was in Roman hands, but north of the river Ostrogothic resistance continued until 562. The last of Justinian's conquests was southern Spain, seized opportunistically during a Visigothic civil war in 554.

Justinian's reconquests restored Roman control of the Mediterranean but put the empire under serious economic strain. The concentration of forces in the west left the Balkans exposed to Slavic raiding and settlement, and the Persians made serious

incursions in the east. Italy was devastated by years of war and much of the province was soon lost again following an invasion by the Lombards in 572. However, north Africa and Sicily proved to be valuable additions to the empire's resources.

In about 560 a new wave of nomads, the Avars, arrived in eastern Europe. The Romans paid them to wipe out the remnants of the Huns, but in 580 a dispute over possession of Singidunum (modern

Legend

- Eastern Roman empire, 527
- Burgundian kingdom, 527
- Frankish kingdom, 527
- Ostrogothic kingdom, 527
- Vandal kingdom, 527
- Visigothic kingdom, 527
- other Germanic kingdoms and peoples
- Frankish kingdom on death of Clothar I, 561
- Roman empire on death of Justinian, 565
- Lombard settlement, with dates
- Sasanian occupation, 607–628
- Roman campaign under Belisarius, 533–34
- Roman campaign under Belisarius, 535–40
- other Roman campaign, 552–54
- Persian-Avar campaigns, with date
- migration, with date
- place fortified by Justinian
- ⊕ patriarchal see

0 ___ 600 km
0 ___ 400 mi

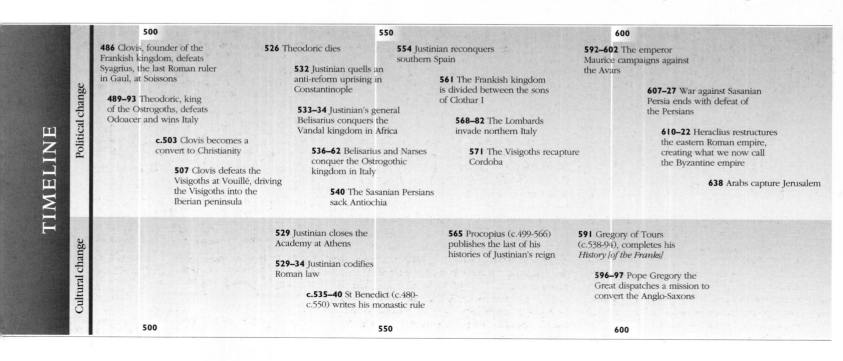

Anglo-Saxons

Bretons

Noviodunum
486

Caesarodunum
Vouillé
507

Augustodunum
48

FRANKISH KINGD

Lugdun

ATLANTIC
OCEAN

Loire

Basques

PYRENEES

Tolosa

SUEVIC
KINGDOM
conquered by
Visigoths 585

Douro

Tagus

Toletum

VISIGOTHIC KINGDOM

Guadiana

Corduba

Gades

Tingis   Septem

Carthago Nova

Iol Caesarea

Balearic
Islands

Liberius

Berbers

TIMELINE

Political change

500

486 Clovis, founder of the Frankish kingdom, defeats Syagrius, the last Roman ruler in Gaul, at Soissons

489–93 Theodoric, king of the Ostrogoths, defeats Odoacer and wins Italy

c.503 Clovis becomes a convert to Christianity

507 Clovis defeats the Visigoths at Vouillé, driving the Visigoths into the Iberian peninsula

526 Theodoric dies

532 Justinian quells an anti-reform uprising in Constantinople

533–34 Justinian's general Belisarius conquers the Vandal kingdom in Africa

536–62 Belisarius and Narses conquer the Ostrogothic kingdom in Italy

540 The Sasanian Persians sack Antiochia

550

554 Justinian reconquers southern Spain

561 The Frankish kingdom is divided between the sons of Clothar I

568–82 The Lombards invade northern Italy

571 The Visigoths recapture Cordoba

600

592–602 The emperor Maurice campaigns against the Avars

607–27 War against Sasanian Persia ends with defeat of the Persians

610–22 Heraclius restructures the eastern Roman empire, creating what we now call the Byzantine empire

638 Arabs capture Jerusalem

Cultural change

529 Justinian closes the Academy at Athens

529–34 Justinian codifies Roman law

c.535–40 St Benedict (c.480-c.550) writes his monastic rule

565 Procopius (c.499-566) publishes the last of his histories of Justinian's reign

591 Gregory of Tours (c.538-94), completes his *History [of the Franks]*

596–97 Pope Gregory the Great dispatches a mission to convert the Anglo-Saxons

500   **550**   **600**

Map labels

Danes
Baltic Sea
Balts
Slavs
Saxons
Thuringians
Vistula
Elbe
Oder
Don
Avars, 533–62 4
Dnieper
Huns
CARPATHIAN MTS
Bulgars
540s–80s
Alans
Rhine
Danube
Lombards 6
568–72
OSTROGOTHIC KINGDOM
ALPS
BURGUNDIAN KINGDOM
Gepids
Singidunum
626
Danube
Cherson
Black Sea
Mediolanum
Po
3
Sava
Naissus 7
Trapezus
572–82
Ravenna
Salonae
Narses
Busta Gallorum 552
Adrianople
8
Nicomedia
1
Rome
Narses
Thessalonica
Constantinople
Nicaea
Corsica
Mons Lactacius 552
ANATOLIA
626
Sardinia
Neapolis
EASTERN ROMAN EMPIRE
Tigris
Nineveh 627
Sicily
Athens
Ephesus
Antiochia
2
Catana
Euphrates
540
Persians
Tricameron 533
Syracusae
Rhodes
Palmyra
Carthage
ad Decimum 533
Cyprus
Ctesiphon
VANDAL KINGDOM
Malta
Liberius
Crete
Damascus
SASANIAN EMPIRE
Mediterranean Sea
Jerusalem
Leptis Magna
Cyrene
Alexandria
Nile
Arabs

JUSTINIAN was portrayed in this mosaic at Ravenna, supported by religious and military forces.

Main text

Belgrade) led to war. For ten years the Avars raided the Balkans until the emperor, Maurice, launched a series of effective counterattacks in 592. Maurice was close to breaking Avar power, when his army mutinied in 602: he was deposed and murdered by his successor, Phocas, an incompetent despot. The administrative structure of the empire now began to fall apart. Slavs and Avars overran the Balkans and the Persians took the fortresses of Roman Mesopotamia one by one. The chaotic state of the empire prompted the governor of Africa to equip his son Heraclius with an army in 610 and send him to Constantinople to overthrow Phocas.

The reign of Heraclius was a turning point. The structure of the empire of Diocletian, Constantine and Justinian could not be revived. Heraclius spent the first years of his reign rebuilding the administrative and military structure of the empire. Greek, which had always been the majority language in the eastern empire, replaced Latin in official documents. Heraclius worked closely with the patriarch of Constantinople, who willingly used the wealth and authority of the church to support the state. While Heraclius was reforming the empire, the war with Persia continued to go badly and by 616 Syria, Palestine and Egypt had been lost. In 622 Heraclius launched a bold campaign directly into the heart of the Sasanian empire and five years later destroyed the Persian army at Nineveh, bringing the war to an end. Heraclius had saved the empire, but his reforms are considered to mark the end of the eastern Roman empire and the beginning of the medieval Greek Byzantine empire (named for the old Greek name for Constantinople).

1 Rome regained importance in the 6th century as the chief center of Christianity in western Europe.

2 The Ostrogothic queen Amalasuntha allowed Justinian's general Belisarius to use Sicily as a base for his attack on the Vandals in 533.

3 Ravenna, the Ostrogothic capital, was taken by Belisarius in 540; resistance continued for many years.

4 The Avars, a Mongol people, migrated to Europe after being defeated by the Turks in central Asia (552).

5 Civil war in the Visigothic kingdom gave Justinian the opportunity to reconquer southern Spain in 554.

6 Originally Roman allies against the Ostrogoths, the Lombards invaded and settled Italy 568–82.

7 Justinian's concentration on the west left the Balkans exposed to frequent Slav raids and settlement.

8 A joint Persian–Avar attack on Constantinople in 626 failed when the Byzantine fleet prevented the two attacking armies from uniting.

See also 2.16 (fall of the western empire);
2.20 (barbarian invaders)

The name Celts was used by Greek writers from the 5th century BC onward to describe a group of peoples of central and western Europe. Roman writers called the same peoples Gauls. The origins of the Celts are uncertain but are probably to be found in the northern Alps in the Bronze Age Urnfield (from mid-2nd millennium BC) and the late Bronze–early Iron Age Hallstatt cultures (1200–450 BC). There were at least two waves of Celtic migration out of central Europe. The first, from around 1000, took the Urnfield culture across western Europe into northern Spain by the 7th century; and a second, beginning in the 8th century, had by 500 BC spread the Hallstatt culture across France, Spain, Portugal, Germany, the Low Countries, and southern Britain.

A new phase of Celtic history began around 450 BC with the development in Germany and France of the La Tène culture. This was distinguished by a vigorous art style based on geometrical patterns and stylized animal images. It developed from Hallstatt art but also showed the influence of Etruscan and Scythian styles. The La Tène culture spread quickly across central and western Europe and reached the British Isles by about 400 BC, passed on partly by trade contacts and partly by smallscale migrations of continental Celts, such as the Parisii, who settled in Yorkshire. The La Tène culture did not spread to Spain, where the earlier Celtic settlers and the native population had become assimilated, forming a distinctive Celtiberian culture.

Around 400 BC there were major migrations of Celtic peoples into Italy and the lower Danube region. In Italy the Celts raided widely, sacked Rome, permanently weakened the Etruscans, and settled densely in the Po valley. The Celts on the lower Danube began to migrate into the Balkans in the 3rd century BC. A major raid on Delphi was repulsed, but the Hellenistic kingdom of Thrace was destroyed by their attacks. Three tribes crossed the Dardanelles and settled in central Anatolia, from where they raided the surrounding kingdoms.

The early 3rd century marked the high tide of Celtic expansion. The Romans began the conquest of the Celts of the Po valley at the battle of Telamon in 225 and captured the last center of resistance in Italy at Bononia (modern Bologna) in 192. The Thracians restored their kingdom around 220; and the Anatolian Celts were pacified by Pergamon in 230. In the 230s the Carthaginians began the conquest of the Celtiberians, and this was continued by the Romans after they had expelled the Carthaginians from Spain in 206. The Roman victory at Numantia in 133 brought them control of most of Spain, but Celtiberian resistance continued in the northwest until 19 BC. By the first century AD the continental Celts were caught firmly in a vise between the northward expansion of the Roman empire and the southward and westward expansion of the Germanic tribes and the Dacians. Between 58

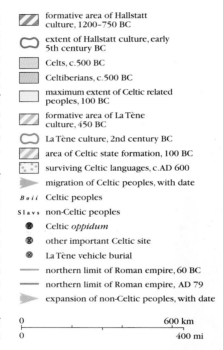

	formative area of Hallstatt culture, 1200–750 BC
	extent of Hallstatt culture, early 5th century BC
	Celts, c.500 BC
	Celtiberians, c.500 BC
	maximum extent of Celtic related peoples, 100 BC
	formative area of La Tène culture, 450 BC
	La Tène culture, 2nd century BC
	area of Celtic state formation, 100 BC
	surviving Celtic languages, c.AD 600
	migration of Celtic peoples, with date
Boii	Celtic peoples
Slavs	non-Celtic peoples
	Celtic *oppidum*
	other important Celtic site
	La Tène vehicle burial
	northern limit of Roman empire, 60 BC
	northern limit of Roman empire, AD 79
	expansion of non-Celtic peoples, with date

0 _____ 600 km
0 _____ 400 mi

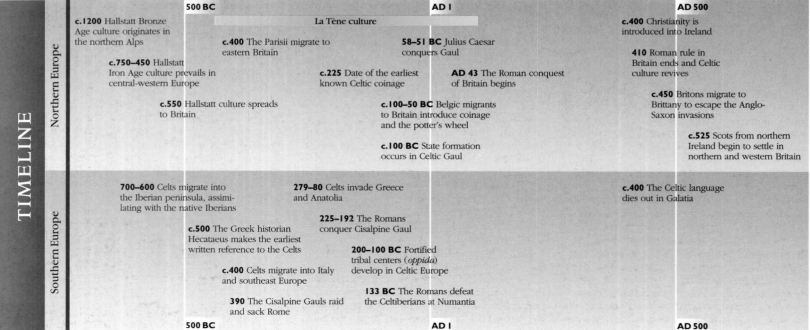

Northern Europe

500 BC

La Tène culture

AD I

AD 500

c.1200 Hallstatt Bronze Age culture originates in the northern Alps

c.750–450 Hallstatt Iron Age culture prevails in central-western Europe

c.400 The Parisii migrate to eastern Britain

c.550 Hallstatt culture spreads to Britain

c.225 Date of the earliest known Celtic coinage

58–51 BC Julius Caesar conquers Gaul

AD 43 The Roman conquest of Britain begins

c.100–50 BC Belgic migrants to Britain introduce coinage and the potter's wheel

c.100 BC State formation occurs in Celtic Gaul

c.400 Christianity is introduced into Ireland

410 Roman rule in Britain ends and Celtic culture revives

c.450 Britons migrate to Brittany to escape the Anglo-Saxon invasions

c.525 Scots from northern Ireland begin to settle in northern and western Britain

Southern Europe

700–600 Celts migrate into the Iberian peninsula, assimilating with the native Iberians

c.500 The Greek historian Hecataeus makes the earliest written reference to the Celts

c.400 Celts migrate into Italy and southeast Europe

390 The Cisalpine Gauls raid and sack Rome

279–80 Celts invade Greece and Anatolia

225–192 The Romans conquer Cisalpine Gaul

200–100 BC Fortified tribal centers (*oppida*) develop in Celtic Europe

133 BC The Romans defeat the Celtiberians at Numantia

c.400 The Celtic language dies out in Galatia

500 BC

AD I

AD 500

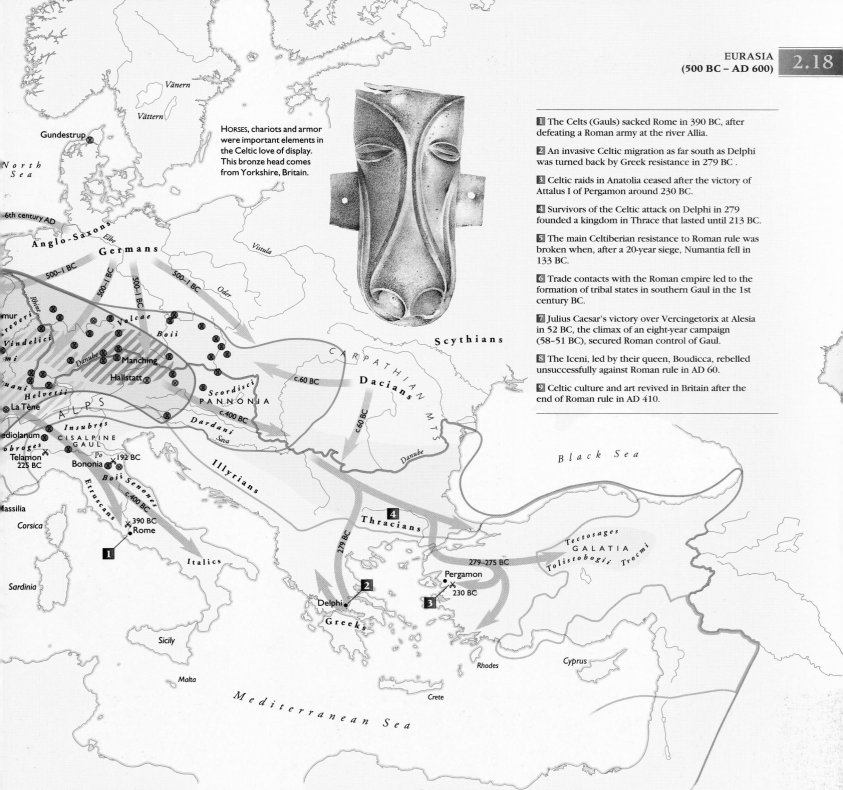

HORSES, chariots and armor were important elements in the Celtic love of display. This bronze head comes from Yorkshire, Britain.

1 The Celts (Gauls) sacked Rome in 390 BC, after defeating a Roman army at the river Allia.

2 An invasive Celtic migration as far south as Delphi was turned back by Greek resistance in 279 BC.

3 Celtic raids in Anatolia ceased after the victory of Attalus I of Pergamon around 230 BC.

4 Survivors of the Celtic attack on Delphi in 279 founded a kingdom in Thrace that lasted until 213 BC.

5 The main Celtiberian resistance to Roman rule was broken when, after a 20-year siege, Numantia fell in 133 BC.

6 Trade contacts with the Roman empire led to the formation of tribal states in southern Gaul in the 1st century BC.

7 Julius Caesar's victory over Vercingetorix at Alesia in 52 BC, the climax of an eight-year campaign (58–51 BC), secured Roman control of Gaul.

8 The Iceni, led by their queen, Boudicca, rebelled unsuccessfully against Roman rule in AD 60.

9 Celtic culture and art revived in Britain after the end of Roman rule in AD 410.

and 51 BC Julius Caesar conquered the Celts of Gaul. Under Augustus the tribes of the Alps and Pannonia were brought under Roman rule. By AD 1 the only independent Celts on mainland Europe were enclaves in German territory north of the Danube.

Celtic society was hierarchical and competitive and by the 2nd century BC was in the early stages of state formation. Fortified centers, or *oppida*, spread across Europe: some, such as Manching on the Danube, were large towns by the 1st century BC. Coinage and, in some areas, writing came into use. In southern Gaul small tribal states in direct contact with the Roman empire had developed by 60 BC. The Roman conquest prevented the Celts from developing a full urban civilization of their own.

The Celtic resistance to Rome failed for two main reasons. The Celts were politically disunited and the Romans easily exploited rivalries between states or

tribes to their own advantage. Also, Celtic warriors saw war as an opportunity to seek personal glory and this put them at a disadvantage to the drilled and disciplined legions. After the Roman conquest the La Tène culture died out on the continent and Celtic language was gradually replaced by Latin; but Celtic religion continued to be practiced. *Oppida* were superseded by planned Romanized towns.

Apart from two punitive raids by Caesar in 55–54 BC, it was AD 43 before the Romans began to subjugate the Celts in Britain. By this time contacts with the Romans across the Channel had already led to considerable Romanization of the southern British tribes and to the development of *oppida* and small tribal states. The Romans could never conquer all of Britain: the closest they came was in AD 83 when they defeated the Caledonians at "Mons Graupius". Harsh weather, mountainous terrain and long lines

of communication meant that the highland tribes of Scotland stayed independent, as did the Celts in Ireland, where pagan Celtic culture survived into the early Middle Ages. La Tène art died out in southern Britain in the 2nd century AD, but Celtic art traditions continued in the far north and Ireland, while Celtic languages survived throughout the British Isles. After the end of Roman rule in Britain in 410, Celtic art revived but was strongly influenced by late Roman and Anglo-Saxon art. The introduction of Christianity to Ireland in the 5th century inspired the development of a Celtic monastic civilization which, through missionary activity, had begun to exert a strong influence in Britain and the continent by 600.

See also 2.13 (growth of the Roman empire); 2.19 (Germans)

The Germans originated in southern Scandinavia and the north German plain in the first half of the 1st millennium BC, probably descended from peoples long settled there. The first contact between the Germans and the Mediterranean civilizations occurred around 350 BC, when the Greek navigator Pytheas of Massilia explored the North Sea coasts. However, his account of his voyage was not widely believed and Mediterranean writers first became aware of the Germans as a group distinct from the Celts only at the end of the 2nd century BC. At this time the Germans' society and way of life resembled that of the Celts, but showed no evidence of power centralization or urban development.

In the second half of the 1st millennium BC the Germans expanded out of north Germany, mainly at the expense of the Celtic peoples to their south and west. These movements were for the most part gradual, but around 120 the Cimbri and the Teutones, two peoples from Jutland, began a twenty-year migration that took them across west-central Europe. When the tribes attacked the Taurisci in 113, their Roman allies sent an army to protect them. The Cimbri and Teutones crushed this army at Noreia but then headed northwest into Gaul. In 109 the tribes invaded southern Gaul and inflicted a succession of defeats on Roman armies, culminating in their victory at Arausio (Orange) in 105. At this point the tribes split up, the Cimbri invading Spain and the Teutones going to northern Gaul. The Roman dictator Marius used the respite to reorganize the legions, and when the Teutones returned to southern Gaul in 102, he defeated them at Aquae Sextiae (Aix-en-Provence). In 101 Marius defeated the Cimbri – who had finally invaded Italy – at Vercellae. Fear of future Germanic invasions was a major motive for Roman expansion northward in the 1st century BC.

Julius Caesar conquered the tribes on the west bank of the Rhine in 56 BC, but these were to be the only Germans permanently under Roman rule. By AD 6 the Germanic tribes as far east as the Elbe were pacified, but a rebellion under Arminius destroyed the Roman army of occupation in AD 9. After AD 12

Key:
- Germanic peoples, c.750 BC
- spread of Germanic peoples, c.50 BC
- spread of Germanic peoples, c.AD 360
- probable formative area of the Slavs (Chernoles complex, c.750 BC)
- Slavs, c.AD 550
- northern frontier of Roman empire, AD 14
- under temporary Roman control, 12 BC–AD 9
- migration of Cimbri and Teutones, 120–101 BC
- Germanic raids and migrations, AD 1–200
- Germanic raids and migrations, AD 200–400
- Slavic migration, AD 540–70
- other migrations
- *Rugii* major Germanic peoples, AD 1–200
- *Rugii* major Germanic peoples, AD 200–400
- **Aesti** other peoples

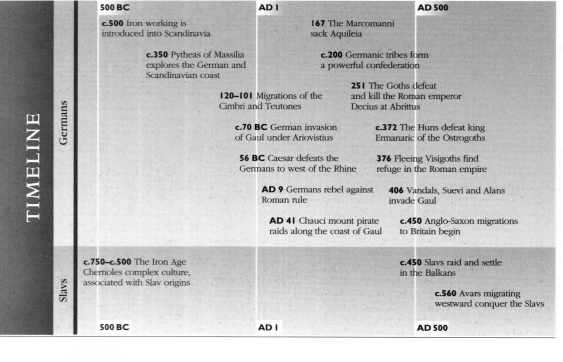

TIMELINE

Germans

500 BC	AD 1	AD 500
c.500 Iron working is introduced into Scandinavia		167 The Marcomanni sack Aquileia
c.350 Pytheas of Massilia explores the German and Scandinavian coast		c.200 Germanic tribes form a powerful confederation
		251 The Goths defeat and kill the Roman emperor Decius at Abrittus
120–101 Migrations of the Cimbri and Teutones		c.372 The Huns defeat king Ermanaric of the Ostrogoths
c.70 BC German invasion of Gaul under Ariovistus		376 Fleeing Visigoths find refuge in the Roman empire
56 BC Caesar defeats the Germans to west of the Rhine		406 Vandals, Suevi and Alans invade Gaul
AD 9 Germans rebel against Roman rule		c.450 Anglo-Saxon migrations to Britain begin
AD 41 Chauci mount pirate raids along the coast of Gaul		

Slavs

500 BC	AD 1	AD 500
c.750–c.500 The Iron Age Chernoles complex culture, associated with Slav origins		c.450 Slavs raid and settle in the Balkans
		c.560 Avars migrating westward conquer the Slavs

1 The Balts were farming peoples whose cultural identity emerged as early as 1800 BC.

2 Two Roman armies were destroyed by the Cimbri and Teutones at Arausio in 105 BC.

3 In AD 9 Rome lost three legions at the battle of the Teutoburgerwald against Germans under Arminius.

4 A Germanic farming village of fifty houses occupied from the 1st century BC to the 5th century AD was found at Feddersen Wierde.

5 Votive offerings were a feature of Germanic religion: one of the richest finds, at Hjortspring, included a ship and many weapons sunk in a bog.

6 A 3rd-century kingdom centered in Stevns controlled the flow of Roman trade in the southern Baltic.

7 The Goths, Burgundians and other Germans believed they had migrated from Scandinavia – called "the womb of peoples" – in the 6th century AD.

8 Some historians think that the "Scythian farmers" were Slavs living under Scythian domination.

9 In the 540s–60s, while the armies of the eastern Roman emperor Justinian (r.527–65) campaigned in Italy, the Slavs raided and settled in the Balkans.

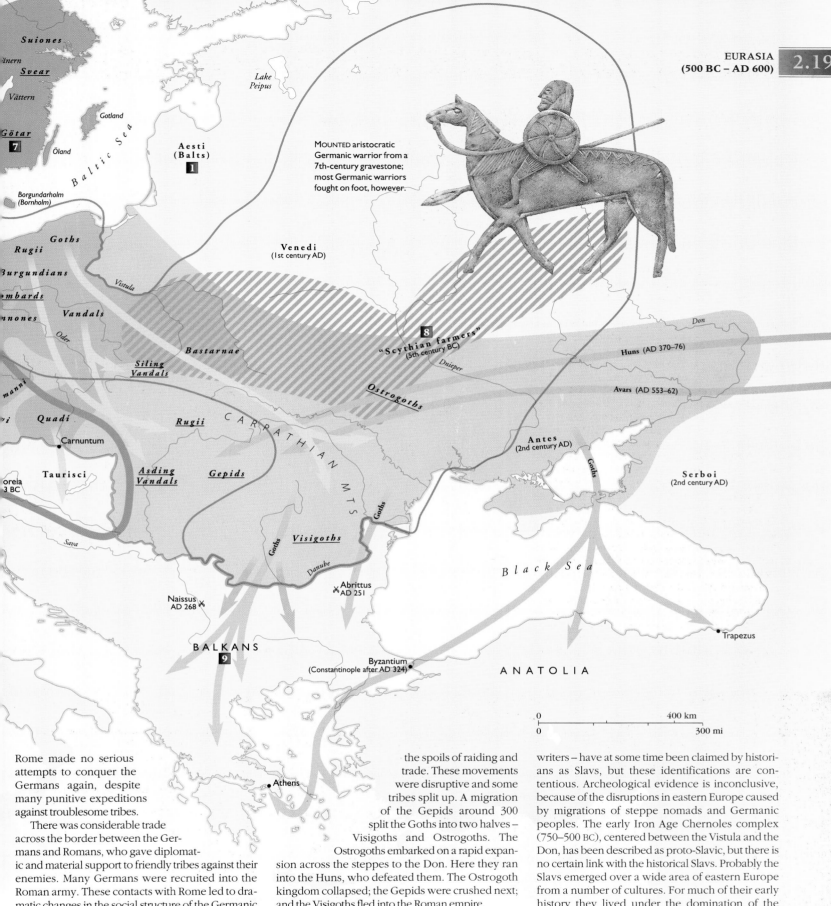

MOUNTED aristocratic
Germanic warrior from a
7th-century gravestone;
most Germanic warriors
fought on foot, however.

Suiones

Svear

Vättern

Götar

7

Gotland

Öland

Lake
Peipus

Baltic Sea

Borgundarholm
(Bornholm)

Aesti
(Balts)

1

Venedi
(1st century AD)

Goths

Rugii

Burgundians

ombards

nnones

Vandals

Vistula

Oder

Siling
Vandals

Bastarnae

"*Scythian farmers*"
(5th century BC)

8

Don

Huns (AD 370–76)

Dnieper

Avars (AD 553–62)

Ostrogoths

manni

Quadi

vi

Taurisci

• Carnuntum

C A R P A T H I A N   M T S

Rugii

Asding
Vandals

Gepids

Antes
(2nd century AD)

Goths

Serboi
(2nd century AD)

oreia
3 BC

Sava

Goths

Visigoths

Goths

Danube

Abrittus
AD 251

B l a c k   S e a

Naissus
AD 268

BALKANS

9

Byzantium
(Constantinople after AD 324) •

A N A T O L I A

• Trapezus

• Athens

0   400 km
0   300 mi

Rome made no serious
attempts to conquer the
Germans again, despite
many punitive expeditions
against troublesome tribes.

There was considerable trade
across the border between the Germans and Romans, who gave diplomat-
ic and material support to friendly tribes against their
enemies. Many Germans were recruited into the
Roman army. These contacts with Rome led to dramatic changes in the social structure of the Germanic
tribes in the late 2nd–early 3rd centuries. Small tribes
merged to form powerful confederations: thus, on
the Rhine, the Chasuarii, Chamavi, Bructeri, Tencteri
and other tribes emerged as the Frankish confederacy in the early 3rd century. These confederations
were dangerous enemies and the empire suffered
from Germanic invasions in the 3rd century. Many
tribes, like the Burgundians, moved closer to the
borders of the Roman empire, hoping to share in

the spoils of raiding and
trade. These movements
were disruptive and some
tribes split up. A migration
of the Gepids around 300
split the Goths into two halves –
Visigoths and Ostrogoths. The
Ostrogoths embarked on a rapid expansion across the steppes to the Don. Here they ran
into the Huns, who defeated them. The Ostrogoth
kingdom collapsed; the Gepids were crushed next;
and the Visigoths fled into the Roman empire.

The earliest records of the Slavs date from the
mid-6th century AD when they began to raid and
settle in the Balkans. They were tribal farming
peoples, ruled by warrior chiefs. By this time Slavs
occupied much of eastern Europe, so peoples
speaking Slavonic languages must have existed long
before this. However, their origins are obscure. The
Venedi, Antes, Serboi and the Scythian farmers – all
eastern European peoples mentioned by classical

writers – have at some time been claimed by historians as Slavs, but these identifications are con-
tentious. Archeological evidence is inconclusive,
because of the disruptions in eastern Europe caused
by migrations of steppe nomads and Germanic
peoples. The early Iron Age Chernoles complex
(750–500 BC), centered between the Vistula and the
Don, has been described as proto-Slavic, but there is
no certain link with the historical Slavs. Probably the
Slavs emerged over a wide area of eastern Europe
from a number of cultures. For much of their early
history they lived under the domination of the
Scythians, Sarmatians, Ostrogoths and Huns, and
they were conquered in the late 6th century by the
Avars. When Avar power declined in the 7th century,
the Slavs emerged to play an important role in the
formation of early medieval Europe.

See also 2.15 (Roman empire); 2.18 (Celts);
2.20 (steppe peoples)

The steppes are a vast area of grassland stretching from eastern Europe across central Asia to Manchuria, which were colonized in the 5th millennium BC by farmers from western Eurasia. The harsh climate was not well suited to arable farming, so the steppe farmers relied primarily on their herds of cattle, horses, sheep and goats. Around 3500 BC wheeled vehicles came into use. This new mobility allowed the farmers to develop a transhumant lifestyle (moving their flocks and herds between summer and winter pastures), significantly increasing the grazing resources available to them. In the second half of the 2nd millennium BC bits and bridles were introduced, which made horseback riding possible. This allowed the steppe peoples to manage large herds over vast ranges, and led to the adoption of a fully nomadic way of life around 900.

The earliest nomads were Iranian-speakers who occupied the steppes as far east as the Ordos desert in China by the 8th century. The Cimmerians on the Russian steppes in the early 1st millennium were the first known nomad power. About 700 they were eclipsed by the Scythians, another Iranian people from central Asia or Siberia. Pursued across the Caucasus by the Scythians, a group of Cimmerians migrated to Anatolia, destroying the Phrygian kingdom on the way. This was the first instance of conflicts on the steppes setting off migrations that had destructive effects on remote urban civilizations – a frequent cycle over the next two millennia.

The Scythians were ruled by powerful chiefs, who were buried in underground chambers with offerings of weapons, jewelry, horses, wagons and human sacrifices, and covered with a *kurgan*, or barrow. An important group of burials at Pazyryk in the Altay mountains, revealed that the Scythians

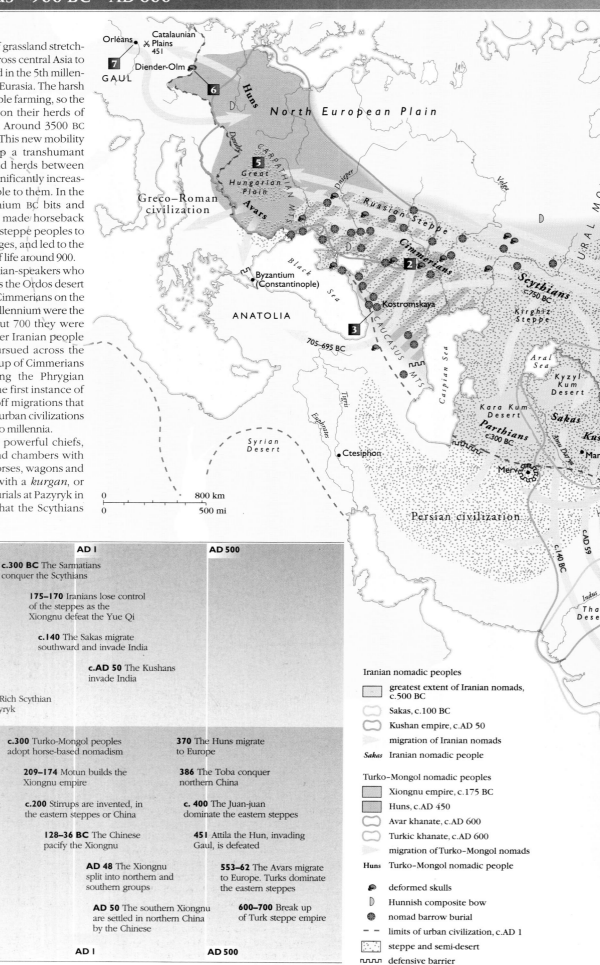

Iranian nomads

c.900 The Iranian steppe peoples adopt horse-mounted nomadism

c.900–700 The Cimmerians dominate the western steppes

705–695 The Cimmerians invade Anatolia

c.700–300 The Scythians now dominate the steppes

500–300 BC Rich Scythian burials at Pazyryk

c.300 BC The Sarmatians conquer the Scythians

175–170 Iranians lose control of the steppes as the Xiongnu defeat the Yue Qi

c.140 The Sakas migrate southward and invade India

c.AD 50 The Kushans invade India

Turko-Mongol nomads

c.300 Turko-Mongol peoples adopt horse-based nomadism

209–174 Motun builds the Xiongnu empire

c.200 Stirrups are invented, in the eastern steppes or China

128–36 BC The Chinese pacify the Xiongnu

AD 48 The Xiongnu split into northern and southern groups

AD 50 The southern Xiongnu are settled in northern China by the Chinese

370 The Huns migrate to Europe

386 The Toba conquer northern China

c. 400 The Juan-juan dominate the eastern steppes

451 Attila the Hun, invading Gaul, is defeated

553–62 The Avars migrate to Europe. Turks dominate the eastern steppes

600–700 Break up of Turk steppe empire

Iranian nomadic peoples

- greatest extent of Iranian nomads, c.500 BC
- Sakas, c.100 BC
- Kushan empire, c.AD 50
- migration of Iranian nomads
- *Sakas* Iranian nomadic people

Turko-Mongol nomadic peoples

- Xiongnu empire, c.175 BC
- Huns, c.AD 450
- Avar khanate, c.AD 600
- Turkic khanate, c.AD 600
- migration of Turko-Mongol nomads
- **Huns** Turko-Mongol nomadic people

- deformed skulls
- Hunnish composite bow
- nomad barrow burial
- limits of urban civilization, c.AD 1
- steppe and semi-desert
- defensive barrier

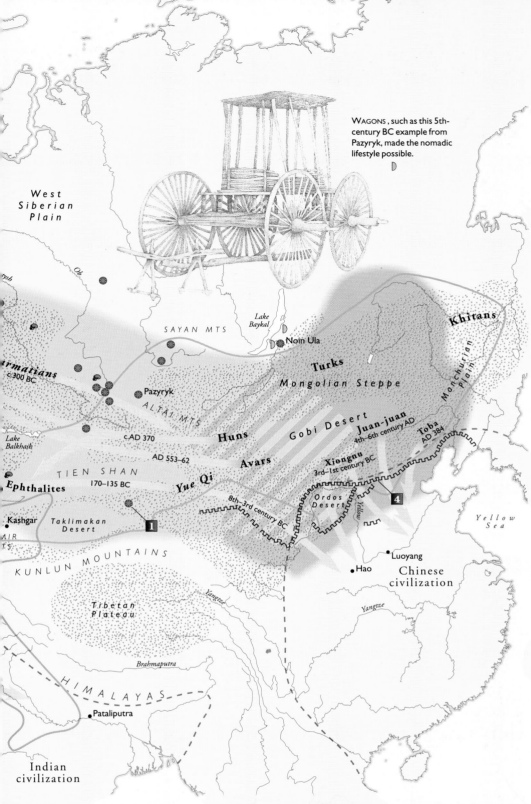

WAGONS, such as this 5th-century BC example from Pazyryk, made the nomadic lifestyle possible.

West Siberian Plain

SAYAN MTS

Lake Baykal

• Noin Ula

Khitans

Sarmatians c.300 BC

Turks

Mongolian Steppe

Manchurian plain

• Pazyryk

ALTAI MTS

c.AD 370

Huns

Gobi Desert

Juan-juan
4th–6th century AD

AD 553–62

Avars

Toba
AD 384

Lake Balkhash

TIEN SHAN

170–135 BC

Ephthalites

Yue Qi

Xiongnu
3rd–1st century BC

• Kashgar

Taklimakan Desert

8th–3rd century BC

Ordos Desert

Yellow Sea

KUNLUN MOUNTAINS

Yellow

• Luoyang

• Hao

Chinese civilization

Tibetan Plateau

Yangtze

Yangtze

Brahmaputra

HIMALAYAS

• Pataliputra

Indian civilization

1 Burials in the Tarim basin indicate that European-type peoples were settled in the eastern steppes around 2000 BC.

2 The Cimmerians, the first steppe peoples to adopt a fully nomadic way of life, dominated the steppes c.900–700 BC.

3 Site of the barrow burial of a Scythian chieftain of the 7th or 6th century BC which included offerings of weapons and sacrificed servants and horses.

4 Chinese rulers began to build great defensive walls to deter nomad raiders, in the 4th century BC.

5 The Hungarian plain, the most westerly area of steppe capable of supporting large herds of horses, became the center of the Hun and Avar empires.

6 Hunnish burials are notable for their distinctively deformed skulls caused by binding children's heads.

7 Orleans, besieged by the Huns in AD 451, was the farthest west that steppe nomads ventured.

Motun (r.209–174 BC) they raided the Han empire of China, exacting huge amounts in tribute. In 170 the Xiongnu defeated the Iranian Yue Qi nomads and drove them to the west, in turn forcing the Sakas to move south around 140 through the Parthian empire into India, where they founded a kingdom which lasted until about AD 400. The dominant Yue Qi clan, the Kushans, built an empire which by AD 50 extended from the Aral Sea to the Indian Ocean and controlled the Asian trade routes.

Between 128 and 36 BC the Chinese fought a series of campaigns that succeeded in reducing the Xiongnu to tributary status. In AD 48 the Xiongnu split into two groups; and they finally disappeared from history around AD 400. In the late 4th century the Huns, a Turkic people, migrated west from central Asia to the steppes of east Europe, destabilizing the Germanic tribes and causing them to invade the Roman empire in search of safer lands to settle. The Huns reached the height of their power under Attila (r.434–53), but their empire collapsed after his death. Another Hunnish people, the Ephthalite ("White") Huns, invaded Persia and India in the late 5th century, preventing the Sasanians from exploiting the problems of the Roman empire and destroying the declining Gupta empire.

For several centuries after the collapse of Xiongnu power, no one people achieved dominance on the eastern steppes. At times of internal weakness China was raided, and in 386 the north was conquered by the Toba nomads, who held power there for over 150 years. Around 400 the Juan-juan, a Mongol-dominated confederation, built an empire which covered much the same area as the earlier Xiongnu empire. The Juan-juan were themselves overthrown in 553 by their Turkish subjects, who went on to create an empire that stretched from Manchuria to the Aral Sea by 600. Part of the Juan-juan confederation, the Avars, fled west and in 562 arrived in eastern Europe where, in alliance with the Sasanians, they almost destroyed the eastern Roman empire. To save the empire reforms had to be introduced – changes so far-reaching that historians consider them the beginning of the Byzantine empire.

decorated their bodies with elaborate tattoos. The Scythians produced a vigorous art style based on stylized animals, and imported Greek metalwork and other goods. Scythian power waned in the 3rd century and their place on the western steppes was taken by the Sarmatians. The defeated Scythians were probably not exterminated, but absorbed by the Sarmatians.

The practice of assimilating defeated rivals explains both the rapid rise of steppe peoples and their rapid extinctions. The numbers of a successful tribe were swelled by assimilated enemies and by other tribes who joined voluntarily to share in the prestige and plunder of the victors. By the same means an apparently numerous and powerful people could suddenly vanish. Although very destructive, nomad armies rarely made lasting conquests outside the

steppe zone. Only on the steppes was there sufficient grazing for the huge numbers of horses that nomad armies needed. Where nomads did make lasting conquests outside the steppe zone, as in India and China, they abandoned their lifestyle and became assimilated into the culture of the more numerous settled population.

The Turko-Mongol peoples of the eastern steppes made the transition from transhumant pastoralism to full horse-mounted nomadism around 300 BC. In the short composite bow (made of glued strips of horn and wood) the Turko-Mongol nomads had a weapon ideally suited to fast moving cavalry warfare, and they soon proved a formidable threat to Iranian nomads and urban civilizations alike. The first nomad power of the eastern steppes was the Xiongnu, a Turkic dominated confederation. Under

See also 2.19 (Germans);
2.23 (Kushans and Guptas); 2.24 (China)

The earliest African state formed in Egypt's Nile valley, where a centralized kingdom had emerged by 3000 BC. By this time desertification had turned the Sahara into a major barrier to travel and the only easy land route between Egypt and tropical Africa lay along the narrow valley of the middle Nile through Nubia. By 2500 several chiefdoms had emerged in Nubia. These were consolidated by 1700 into a large state, known to the Egyptians as Kush, whose capital was at Kerma. Nubia was rich in natural resources, especially gold, and was subjected to Egyptian plundering expeditions. It may, therefore, have been the impetus to organize an effective defense against the Egyptians that provided the impetus for state formation in this area. Kush was conquered by the Egyptians about 1500 at the start of Egypt's imperialistic New Kingdom period. When Egyptian power declined at the end of the New Kingdom (1070 BC), Kush regained its independence. In 770 the kings of Kush conquered southern Egypt and in 712 Shabaka (r.712–698) brought the whole kingdom under Nubian rule. Assyrian attacks on Egypt drove the Nubians from northern Egypt, and by 657 they had lost control of the whole country. The Egyptians expelled the Assyrians in 653 and launched campaigns into Nubia, forcing the Nubians to move their capital south to Meroë around 590. The kingdom of Meroë, as Kush is subsequently known, remained a major power that was taken seriously by the Persians, Greco-Macedonians and Romans who in turn ruled Egypt after 525 BC. In the 4th century Meroë suffered attacks from desert nomads; it collapsed about 350, after the capital was taken by the Axumites. Three small states, Nobatia, Makkura and Alwa, arose as successors to Meroë but Makkura conquered Nobatia in the 8th century.

Nubia was strongly influenced by Egyptian religion, kingship and culture. Until about 200 BC, when an indigenous Meroitic script was developed, Egyptian scripts and language were used for inscriptions, and the use of pyramids for royal burials continued into the Christian era, long after the practice had ceased in Egypt. Christianity was introduced to

Nubia in the 6th century and remained strong until the region was put under pressure by the Arabs in the 13th century.

The second state to develop in tropical Africa, Axum emerged in northern Ethiopia in the 1st century AD. Urban development had begun at sites such as Yeha in the 5th century BC and the cultural development of the area was strongly influenced by the Sabeans of Arabia, whose alphabet, architecture and religion were adopted. In the 1st century AD the port of Adulis was exporting ivory, rhinoceros horn, tortoise-shell, obsidian and aromatic resins to the Roman empire via Red Sea trade routes. The city of Axum itself included complexes of monumental buildings and palaces. Among the most remarkable monuments at Axum are monoliths carved to resemble multistory buildings: the tallest still standing is 69 feet (21 meters) high. The kingdom of Axum reached a peak in the reign of King Ezana around 350. About this time also, Ezana converted to Christianity, the first African ruler to do so. In 522 the Axumites invaded and conquered the Yemen and held it until driven out by the Sasanians in 574. In the 8th century, attacks by the Arabs accelerated the decline of Axum, and by the 10th century power had shifted to the Ethiopian highlands.

Another area of Africa in which state formation occurred was the Maghrib, where the Berber kingdoms of Numantia and Mauretania emerged around 200 BC in the power vacuum left by the defeat of Carthage in the Second Punic War (226–201 BC). However, these states were soon swallowed up by the expanding empire of Rome. The most significant development in north Africa was the introduction of the camel to the Sahara around 100 BC. Camels were ideal for desert warfare, and settled communities on the fringes of the desert soon suffered badly from nomad raids. Camels also had the endurance for long desert crossings – horses, mules and bullocks had previously been the main beasts of burden in the Sahara. Now cross-desert trade began to expand, and by AD 500 camel caravans forged strong trade links between the Mediterranean and west Africa

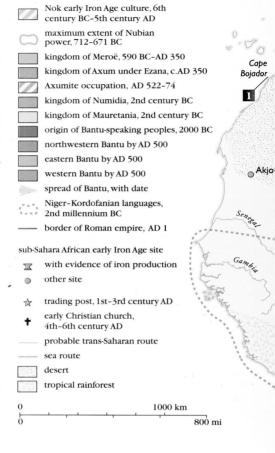

Nok early Iron Age culture, 6th century BC–5th century AD

maximum extent of Nubian power, 712–671 BC

kingdom of Meroë, 590 BC–AD 350

kingdom of Axum under Ezana, c.AD 350

Axumite occupation, AD 522–74

kingdom of Numidia, 2nd century BC

kingdom of Mauretania, 2nd century BC

origin of Bantu-speaking peoples, 2000 BC

northwestern Bantu by AD 500

eastern Bantu by AD 500

western Bantu by AD 500

spread of Bantu, with date

Niger–Kordofanian languages, 2nd millennium BC

border of Roman empire, AD 1

sub-Sahara African early Iron Age site

with evidence of iron production

other site

trading post, 1st–3rd century AD

early Christian church, 4th–6th century AD

probable trans-Saharan route

sea route

desert

tropical rainforest

```
0                    1000 km
0                            800 mi
```

Cape Bojador

Akjo

Senegal

Gambia

(maritime links were never established, because of adverse winds south of Cape Bojador).

The earliest Iron Age culture of west Africa, the Nok culture of Nigeria (c. 500 BC– AD 400), is noted for its sophisticated terracotta sculptures, which are often seen as being ancestral to the art styles of the medieval Ibo and Yoruba peoples. By AD 600 many areas of west Africa had dense farming populations, and one city, Jenne-jeno, had developed as a regional trading center. Many large burial mounds in this region point to the emergence of powerful elites and the beginnings of state formation.

The major development in Africa south of the Equator was the expansion of the Bantu-speaking peoples, mixed farming and, later, iron working. The Bantu languages belong to the Niger-Kordofanian group, confined to tropical west Africa in the second millennium BC. The original homeland of the Bantu was in southern Nigeria and Cameroon, but around 2000 BC Bantu-speakers began to spread into central and east Africa, and by AD 500 they had reached southern Africa. Bantu languages were spread partly by migrations of iron-using farmers, but also by the assimilation to Bantu culture of the Khoisan-speaking Stone Age herders and hunter–gatherers of eastern and southern Africa.

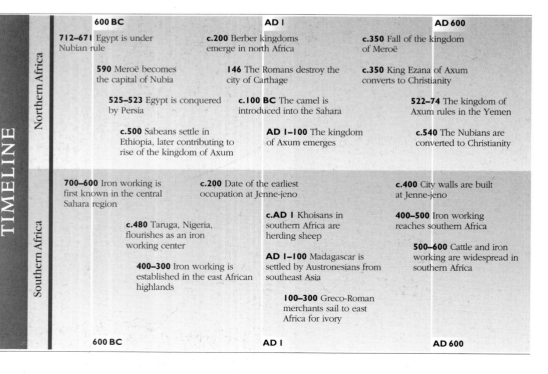

TIMELINE

Northern Africa

600 BC	AD 1	AD 600
712–671 Egypt is under Nubian rule	**c.200** Berber kingdoms emerge in north Africa	**c.350** Fall of the kingdom of Meroë
590 Meroë becomes the capital of Nubia	**146** The Romans destroy the city of Carthage	**c.350** King Ezana of Axum converts to Christianity
525–523 Egypt is conquered by Persia	**c.100 BC** The camel is introduced into the Sahara	**522–74** The kingdom of Axum rules in the Yemen
c.500 Sabeans settle in Ethiopia, later contributing to rise of the kingdom of Axum	**AD 1–100** The kingdom of Axum emerges	**c.540** The Nubians are converted to Christianity

Southern Africa

600 BC	AD 1	AD 600
700–600 Iron working is first known in the central Sahara region	**c.200** Date of the earliest occupation at Jenne-jeno	**c.400** City walls are built at Jenne-jeno
c.480 Taruga, Nigeria, flourishes as an iron working center	**c.AD 1** Khoisans in southern Africa are herding sheep	**400–500** Iron working reaches southern Africa
400–300 Iron working is established in the east African highlands	**AD 1–100** Madagascar is settled by Austronesians from southeast Asia	**500–600** Cattle and iron working are widespread in southern Africa
	100–300 Greco-Roman merchants sail to east Africa for ivory	

| 600 BC | AD 1 | AD 600 |

Tingis •   Caesarea •   • Hippo
     MAGHRIB   Regius
MAURETANIA   NUMIDIA • Timgad   • Carthage
ATLAS MTS   Berbers

Mediterranean Sea

• Leptis Magna   • Cyrene

2

TASSILI MASSIF

S A H A R A   D E S E R T

TIBESTI
MASSIF

Tichit •

⚱ Do Dimmi
c.700–600 BC

TERRACOTTA heads from the Nok
culture of northern Nigeria are
among the earliest surviving
sub–Saharan artworks.

Tondidara •
• Koumbi Saleh

Jenne-jeno •

3

Niani •

Lake Chad

Niger

• Yelwa

Nok •
⚱ Taruga   • Samu
       Dukiya
Benue

W E S T
A F R I C A N
R A I N F O R E S T

6

Libyans

• Alexandria
   • Memphis   • Petra

EGYPT

Nile

• Myos Hormos
• Thebes

• Berenice   • Medina

• Elephantine   Red Sea
Gebel Adda   • Qustul   • Mecca
Ballana ✚ Nobatia
Kerma •   N U B I A
Makkura •   • Napata   **4**
Old Dongola ✚   • Jebel Barkal   Sabeans
   M E R O Ë   ⚱ Meroë   6th century BC
   Wad Ban Naqa •   600 BC   **5**   SABA   HADRAMAUT
Alwa •   • Naqa   AXUM   Kohaito • Adulis   • Miswar
   ✚ Soba   Axum ✚ • Yeha   Muza • • Zafar • Qana
     Blue Nile
       • Avalites ☆   Mosyllon ☆
     E T H I O P I A N   Malao ☆   Opone ☆
     White Nile   H I G H L A N D S

A T L A N T I C
O C E A N

2000 BC onwards
Uele
2000 BC onwards

Congo

Mouila ⚱
200 BC

C E N T R A L
A F R I C A N
R A I N F O R E S T

Lualaba

AD 1–500

Shabelle

• Sarapion ☆
Nikon ☆

*Lake
Turkana*

• Uruwe
Ndora ⚱   *Lake
4th century AD   Victoria*
Katuruka ⚱
5th century BC   • Kwale

Rhapta ☆
7

*Lake
Tanganyika*

AD 1–500

• Sanga   Kalambo
     Falls

*Lake
Malawi*

AD 1–500

Isamu Pati •

Victoria Falls •

Gokomere •
   • Great
   Zimbabwe

9

*Khoisan-speaking
herders and
hunter-gatherers*

*Kalahari
Desert*

Broederstroom ⚱
5th century AD

Castle Cavern
⚱ c.AD 400
8

Austronesians
1st century AD

1. Sailing conditions made it difficult for Mediterranean ships of the period to trade beyond Cape Bojador.

2. Little trans-Saharan trade occurred before camel
caravans became common in the first century AD.

3. Jenne-jeno, the earliest-known town in sub-Saharan
Africa, had become a walled city by about AD 400.

4. A temple complex and royal pyramid burials at
Jebel Barkal mark the site of Nubia's religious center
from the 7th century BC to the 3rd century AD.

5. Axum became an early center of Christianity in
Africa when King Ezana converted, around AD 350.

6. Taruga was the earliest and most important center
of iron production in tropical west Africa c.480 BC.

7. Rhapta, somewhere on the Zanzibar channel, was a
major ivory market used by Greco-Roman merchants.

8. The iron-production center at Castle Cavern
(c.AD 400) was one of the earliest in southern Africa.

9. Khoisan-speaking peoples continued using late
Stone Age technology despite the arrival of iron-
mining peoples in southern Africa.

See also 2.14 (trade and the Roman empire)

◄ ►

I n 500 BC northern India was divided into several Hindu kingdoms, the most powerful being Magadha, ruled by king Bimbisara. Southern India was still dominated by tribal peoples under Hindu influence. In 364 Magadha came under the control of the expansionist Nanda dynasty, which by about 340 dominated northern India. The Nandas' reputation for oppressive taxation, however, led to their overthrow in a coup by Chandragupta Maurya (r. 321–c.293). Chandragupta's origins are obscure but he appears to have been a military commander in the northwest border provinces at the time of Alexander the Great's invasion of the Indus valley: he fought against Greek outposts in the area and may have met Alexander.

By 311 Chandragupta had extended his kingdom to the Indus, bringing him into conflict with Seleucos, who had seized power after Alexander's death. In 305 Chandragupta defeated Seleucos and was ceded control of the whole Indus valley in return for a gift of 500 war elephants. Chandragupta maintained a large standing army and imposed a harsh penal code on his people. He also created an effective central bureaucracy, which controlled economic activity and carried out road building, irrigation and other public works. In about 293 he abdicated in favor of his son Bindusara (r.c. 293–268) and became a Jain monk, dying around 286. Bindusara continued the expansionist program of his father and extended the Mauryan empire far into southern India. In 268 he was succeeded by his son Ashoka, one of India's most remarkable rulers. Reportedly overcome with remorse after a bloody conquest of the east-coast district of Kalinga in 261, Ashoka converted to Buddhism in about 260.

Buddhism had its origins in the teachings of Siddhartha Gautama, the Buddha, (c.563–483), in the heartland of late 6th-century Magadha. It was just one among many sects influenced by, but reacting against, India's traditions of Brahmanic Hinduism,

A CARVING of about AD 100 from Sanchi , exemplifying a common Hindu theme of a dancing woman with a flowering tree.

until the missionary work started by Ashoka in 258 began its transformation from minor sect to major world religion. Ashoka adopted the Buddhist principles of right conduct and non-violence, assured neighboring states of his goodwill, ameliorated his grandfather's penal code and sought to rule as far as possible by moral authority alone. To spread Buddhist values he had edicts on morality and the way of compassion carved on rock-faces and pillars throughout his empire. Over thirty of these survive, forming the most important source of information about Ashoka's reign. Ashoka intervened in doctrinal matters and it was his initiative that led to the defining of the Buddhist canon at the Third Buddhist council at Pataliputra around 240. Ashoka also promoted Buddhism abroad, sending missions to Indonesia, southern India, Ceylon, the Greek states of western Asia and the nomads of central Asia.

Although Ashoka's empire was the largest state to exist in India before the coming of the Mughal empire in the 17th century AD, it did not long survive

Marakanda
Wester Sakas

170–130 BC

HIND U

Herat

Ba

Kandahar

UTTARAPATHA

KIRTHAR RANG

Barbaric

Arabian Sea

TIMELINE

Political change

500 BC	250 BC	AD I
c.540–490 Magadha, under king Bimbisara, becomes the leading Hindu kingdom	**268–233** The reign of the Mauryan king Ashoka	
	c.185 The last Mauryan king is deposed	
c.483 King Vijaya founds the first state in Ceylon		
	141 The Sakas invade northwest India	
364–321 Under the Nanda dynasty Magadha dominates the Ganges plain		
	c.94 BC A Saka kingdom is founded in northwest India	
327–325 Alexander the Great conquers the Indus valley		**c.AD 50** King Kharavela of Kalinga dominates eastern and central India
321 Chandragupta Maurya seizes power in Magadha and founds the Mauryan empire		**AD 50–75** The Kushans invade and conquer northwest India
c.293 Chandragupta abdicates in favor of Bindusara		
c.293–268 Bindusara Maurya conquers southern India		

Cultural change

500 BC	250 BC	AD I
528 Siddhartha Gautama the Buddha (c.563–483) attains "Enlightenment"	**c.260** Ashoka converts to Buddhism	
	c.250 Ashoka introduces Buddhism into Ceylon	
c.500 Sinhalese migrate to northern Ceylon		

Legend

- empire of Alexander the Great, c.325 BC
- kingdom of Magadha under Nanda dynasty, c.324 BC

Mauryan empire
- territory gained by Chandragupta Maurya, 320–305 BC
- territory gained by Bindusara, c.293–268 BC
- territory gained by Ashoka, 268–260 BC
- maximum extent of empire under Ashoka, c.260 BC
- weak or nominal Mauryan control
- provincial capital
- VANGA province under Ashoka
- Ashokan rock edict
- Ashokan pillar edict
- heartland of Satavahanihara kingdom late 1st century BC
- maximum extent of Saka rule, 1st century BC
- Western Sakas, 2nd century AD
- formative area of Buddhism
- Buddhist monument, before 187 BC
- Buddhist monument, 187 BC–AD 50
- migration of peoples
- ancient river course
- modern coastline where altered

his death in 233. Much of the empire was only loosely held and the south was lost almost at once, while by 200 the Bactrian Greeks had conquered the Indus valley and restored Alexander's frontier in India. In the 180s the Bactrians briefly extended their control as far south as Barygaza and as far east as Mathura. The last Mauryan king was overthrown in 185 by Pushyamitra Shunga, one of his generals. Under the Shunga dynasty Magadha continued to be a major power, but after the dynasty fell in 73 BC the kingdom's power collapsed completely and it became just one minor state among many on the Gangetic plain. By this time power had shifted to the northwest where the Sakas, nomadic invaders from central Asia, had established a powerful kingdom around 94 BC. By AD 1 the Saka kingdom was in decline, but around AD 50 a second wave of nomads, the Kushans, invaded and founded another major kingdom in the northwest.

The advent of the Mauryan empire accelerated state formation in southern India – trade contacts, colonies of northerners and Buddhist missions ending the area's relative isolation. The first considerable state in the region, Kalinga, dominated eastern India and extended its power into the Gangetic plain in the middle of the 1st century BC under King Kharavela. Soon after Kharavela's death, however, it sank back into obscurity. More stable was the state of Satavahanihara, centered around Pratisthana, which also rose to prominence in the 1st century BC and remained the dominant power in the south until the 3rd century AD. Ceylon was colonized by Sinhalese from southern India around 500 BC and the native Veddas were pushed into the interior. Traditionally the first state in Ceylon was founded around 483, by King Vijaya in the north of the island. Ashoka's missionaries took Buddhism to Ceylon, where the religion set down particularly deep roots.

1 The trading city of Taxila, occupied successively by Persians, Greeks, Mauryans, Sakas and Kushans, became a melting pot of different cultures.

2 Bodh Gaya, where Buddha gained "Enlightenment" c.528 BC, was and remains a sacred site of Buddhism.

3 Anuradhapura was founded in 437 BC as the capital of a Sinhalese kingdom of northern Ceylon.

4 Pataliputra was capital of Magadha and the Mauryan empire and one of the largest cities in the ancient world, defended by a timber wall with 500 towers.

5 A dam, reservoir and irrigation project of the Mauryan period at Junagadh was one of the first such large projects to be built under government direction.

6 Southern India was (most probably) conquered by Chandragupta's son Bindusara (r. c.293–268 BC).

7 Amaravati was the main Buddhist center in southern India from the 3rd century BC to the 14th AD.

8 A complex of rock-cut Buddhist temples and monasteries with fine wall paintings was built at Ajanta from the 2nd century BC to the 5th AD.

9 Trade in pearls, diamonds and gold led to state formation in southern India by the 1st century BC.

See also 2.09 (Alexander's empires);
2.20 steppe peoples; 2.23 (Guptas)

Around AD 50 the Kushans made northwest India part of an empire stretching from the Ganges to the Aral Sea. They were a clan of the Yue Qi nomads who had overrun the Greek kingdom of Bactria around 135 BC. The Kushan state was set up in Bactria around AD 25 by Kujala Kadphises, who invaded India and conquered Gandhara and the Northern Sakas around AD 50. Kujala's successor, Vima Kadphises (r.c.75–100), conquered the Indus valley and much of the Gangetic plain. The empire reached its peak under Kanishka (r.c.100–130). He was a devout Buddhist and a patron of the arts, supporting both the Indo-Hellenistic school of Gandhara and the Hindu school of Mathura. Under Kanishka's successors, the Kushan empire maintained its borders until the 3rd century, when most of the empire's western provinces were conquered by the Sasanian King Shapur I. Although the Kushans briefly regained their independence in the 4th century, the united Kushan empire was not restored.

The Kushan empire was never highly centralized and the king ruled through a host of dependent sub-kings or *yaghbus*. Kushan rulers used an eclectic range of titles, including *maharaja* (great king), *rajatiraja* (king of kings), the Greek title *basileus* (king) and *kaisara* (from the Latin *caesar*). They also instituted a cult of ruler worship and used the title *devaputra* (son of God). Kushan culture was equally eclectic, mixing Hellenistic, Indian and central Asian styles. Kushan rulers were tolerant in matters of religion. Most of the early rulers were Buddhists and the later ones Hindus, but all showed respect for a wide range of Persian, Greek and even Roman deities. The empire was always wealthy, prospering by its control of all the major trans-Asian overland trade routes. High-quality gold coinage was made by melting down gold Roman coins flooding into the empire to pay for luxury goods such as Chinese silk.

The Kushans did not have a monopoly on east–west trade. By the 1st century AD, Mediterranean seafarers had discovered how to exploit the monsoon winds to sail across the Indian Ocean, bringing increased trade between the Roman empire and southern India. The region's most valuable exports were spices, which the Romans paid for in gold. South Indian rulers did not issue their own coinage and Roman coins circulated freely. The most powerful south Indian state at this period was Satavahanihara; but the influx of wealth led to the formation of several small tribal kingdoms and cities in the region.

The decline of Kushan power made possible the rise of the Gupta kingdom in the 4th century. Minor princes in the Varanasi area in the later 3rd century, the Guptas may have been feudatories of Magadha. The dynasty began with the reign of Chandragupta I (r.320–35), who made an advantageous marriage alliance with the Licchavis. This brought him control of Magadha, the fertile and densely populated heartland of the former Mauryan empire. Chandragupta was succeeded by his son Samudragupta (r.335–80), whose long reign saw the kingdom expand across northern India, reducing the Kushans to tributary status. Samudragupta also fought a major campaign in the southeast, reducing many rulers to tributaries. He formed strong alliances with the Sakas and the Vakatakas (in power in Satavahanihara), but his son and successor, Chandragupta II (r.380–414), turned on the Western Sakas, conquered their kingdom and imposed direct rule. The empire ruled by Chandragupta II was almost as large as the Mauryan empire, but was very loose-knit. Gupta inscriptions approximately cover the area in which the dynasty exercised direct rule – the rest of the empire was ruled by tributary kings and barely-subdued tribes.

The Guptas were patrons of the arts and sciences and the period was one of great creativity. They were devout Hindus and some of the main features of Hinduism, such as image-worship, appeared under their rule. The Hindu epics of the *Ramayana* and the *Mahabharata* reached their final form at this time. Sanskrit poetry and drama flourished, causing the Gupta period to be regarded as the classical age of Indian literature. Advances were made in astronomy and mathematics, including the invention of the decimal system of numerals, later adopted by the Arabs and, through them, by the Europeans.

After the death of Chandragupta II, the empire ceased expanding but remained powerful, and

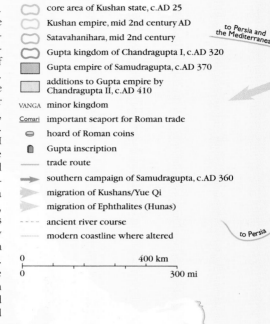

⟅⟆	core area of Kushan state, c.AD 25
⟅⟆	Kushan empire, mid 2nd century AD
⟅⟆	Satavahanihara, mid 2nd century
⟅⟆	Gupta kingdom of Chandragupta I, c.AD 320
▮	Gupta empire of Samudragupta, c.AD 370
▯	additions to Gupta empire by Chandragupta II, c.AD 410
VANGA	minor kingdom
Comari	important seaport for Roman trade
⬮	hoard of Roman coins
▯	Gupta inscription
——	trade route
⟶	southern campaign of Samudragupta, c.AD 360
▷	migration of Kushans/Yue Qi
▷	migration of Ephthalites (Hunas)
- - -	ancient river course
——	modern coastline where altered

0   400 km
0   300 mi

under Skandagupta (r.c.455–67) defeated a major Hunnish invasion. However, a war of succession followed Skandagupta's death and the empire went into decline as tributary kings and nominally conquered tribes reasserted their independence. The final blow came from an invasion of the Hunas (Ephthalite Huns) in 505–11, who founded a kingdom in northwest India, destroying the last remnants of the Kushans. In 528 a coalition of Indian princes defeated the Hunas, but the Guptas played only a minor role in this campaign. Gupta rulers continued in Magadha until around 720, but only as mere princes. Except for a brief period under Harsha (r.606–47) of Kanauj, who united the states on the Gangetic plain, no supraregional state reappeared in India until the 13th century.

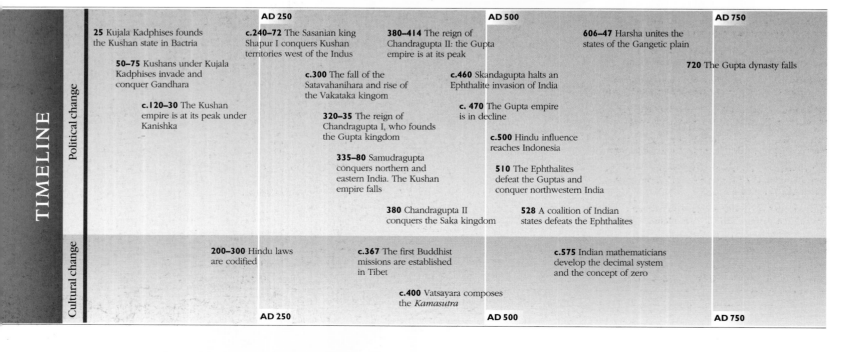

TIMELINE

Political change

25 Kujala Kadphises founds the Kushan state in Bactria

50–75 Kushans under Kujala Kadphises invade and conquer Gandhara

c.120–30 The Kushan empire is at its peak under Kanishka

AD 250

c.240–72 The Sasanian king Shapur I conquers Kushan territories west of the Indus

c.300 The fall of the Satavahanihara and rise of the Vakataka kingom

320–35 The reign of Chandragupta I, who founds the Gupta kingdom

335–80 Samudragupta conquers northern and eastern India. The Kushan empire falls

380 Chandragupta II conquers the Saka kingdom

380–414 The reign of Chandragupta II: the Gupta empire is at its peak

AD 500

c.460 Skandagupta halts an Ephthalite invasion of India

c.470 The Gupta empire is in decline

c.500 Hindu influence reaches Indonesia

510 The Ephthalites defeat the Guptas and conquer northwestern India

528 A coalition of Indian states defeats the Ephthalites

606–47 Harsha unites the states of the Gangetic plain

AD 750

720 The Gupta dynasty falls

Cultural change

200–300 Hindu laws are codified

c.367 The first Buddhist missions are established in Tibet

c.400 Vatsayara composes the *Kamasutra*

c.575 Indian mathematicians develop the decimal system and the concept of zero

AD 250   **AD 500**   **AD 750**

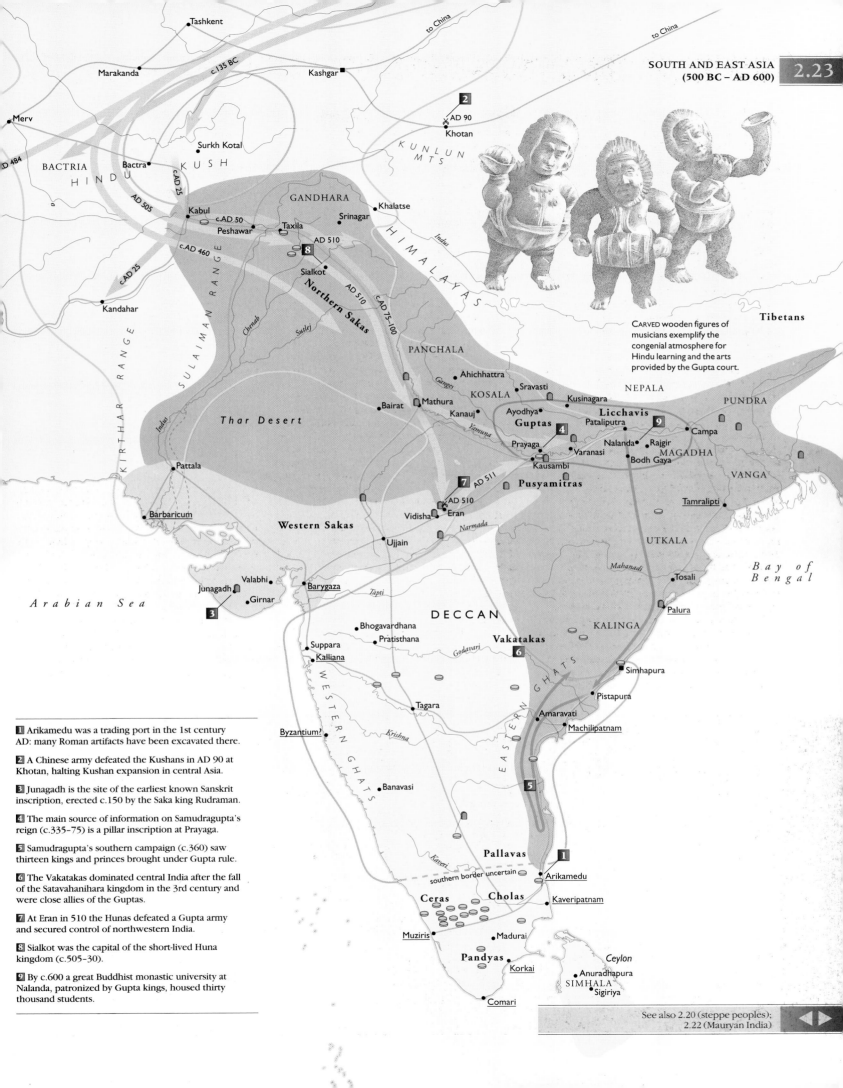

to China

to China

Tashkent

Marakanda

c.135 BC

Kashgar

2
✕ AD 90
Khotan

KUNLUN
MTS

Merv

D 484

BACTRIA

Bactra

Surkh Kotal

HINDU

KUSH

c.AD 25

AD 505

Kabul

c.AD 50

Peshawar

c.AD 460

c.AD 25

Kandahar

GANDHARA

Srinagar

Khalatse

Taxila

AD 510

8

Sialkot

Northern Sakas

AD 510

c.AD 75–100

HIMALAYAS

Indus

CARVED wooden figures of
musicians exemplify the
congenial atmosphere for
Hindu learning and the arts
provided by the Gupta court.

Tibetans

KIRTHAR RANGE

SULAIMAN RANGE

Chenab

Sutlej

Indus

PANCHALA

Ahichhattra

Sravasti

KOSALA

Kusinagara

NEPALA

Ayodhya

Licchavis

PUNDRA

Mathura

Kanauj

Guptas

Pataliputra

9

Bairat

Thar Desert

Yamuna

Prayaga

4

Varanasi

Nalanda

Rajgir

Campa

Bodh Gaya

MAGADHA

VANGA

Pattala

Kausambi

7

AD 511

Pusyamitras

Tamralipti

Western Sakas

AD 510

Vidisha

Eran

Barbaricum

Narmada

UTKALA

Ujjain

Mahanadi

Bay of
Bengal

Arabian Sea

Valabhi

Junagadh

Girnar

Barygaza

Tapti

Tosali

3

DECCAN

Palura

KALINGA

Bhogavardhana

Vakatakas

Pratisthana

Godavari

6

Simhapura

Suppara

Kalliana

Pistapura

Tagara

Amaravati

Byzantium?

Machilipatnam

Krishna

Banavasi

WESTERN GHATS

EASTERN GHATS

5

Pallavas

1

Kaveri

Arikamedu

southern border uncertain

Ceras

Cholas

Kaveripatnam

Muziris

Madurai

Ceylon

Pandyas

Korkai

Anuradhapura

SIMHALA

Sigiriya

Comari

1 Arikamedu was a trading port in the 1st century
AD: many Roman artifacts have been excavated there.

2 A Chinese army defeated the Kushans in AD 90 at
Khotan, halting Kushan expansion in central Asia.

3 Junagadh is the site of the earliest known Sanskrit
inscription, erected c.150 by the Saka king Rudraman.

4 The main source of information on Samudragupta's
reign (c.335–75) is a pillar inscription at Prayaga.

5 Samudragupta's southern campaign (c.360) saw
thirteen kings and princes brought under Gupta rule.

6 The Vakatakas dominated central India after the fall
of the Satavahanihara kingdom in the 3rd century and
were close allies of the Guptas.

7 At Eran in 510 the Hunas defeated a Gupta army
and secured control of northwestern India.

8 Sialkot was the capital of the short-lived Huna
kingdom (c.505–30).

9 By c.600 a great Buddhist monastic university at
Nalanda, patronized by Gupta kings, housed thirty
thousand students.

See also 2.20 (steppe peoples);
2.22 (Mauryan India)

Zhou China (1122–256 BC) was a decentralized feudal state: the king exercised direct authority only over his own domain, while the provinces were held as fiefs by dukes who ruled in his name. Gradually the dukes became, in effect, the rulers of independent states; the Zhou king reigned from his capital at Luoyang but did not rule. The Warring States period (480–221 BC) saw the stronger states eliminate the weaker and absorb their territory: by 300 eleven states were left, and by 256, when the last Zhou king was deposed, there were seven. By 221 one state – Qin – was supreme.

Qin's rise to dominance began under Xiao (r.361–338). Shang Yang, Xiao's prime minister, ended the power of the feudal aristocracy and enacted a series of reforms that turned Qin into a centralized state based on a settled and productive peasantry and a strong army. Qin's frontier position gave it opportunities for expansion at the expense of the tribal peoples to the west, while its mountainous borders protected it from the aggression of other states. By 315 it was the strongest of the surviving states. The Qin dukes had already abandoned the pretence of subservience to the Zhou by adopting the title of king. In the 3rd century Qin waged almost constant warfare against the other Chinese states, which failed to combine against it and were picked off one at a time. The unification of China was completed in a series of lightning campaigns by Zheng (r.246–210) between 230 and 221, after which he adopted the title Shi Huangdi, the "First Emperor".

Shi Huangdi is regarded as the founder of the Chinese empire and the pattern of centralized totalitarian government he established has endured to the present day. Qin laws and institutions were extended to the whole of China. The aristocracies of the defeated states were deported, the remnants of feudalism were abolished and a non-hereditary central and local bureaucracy was created. The empire was divided into 36 districts or commanderies, governed by civilian and military officials responsible directly to the autocratic emperor. Coinage, weights and measures, scripts and even the axle sizes of wagons were standardized. In an attempt to ensure that Chinese history began with him, Shi Huangdi ordered the destruction of all works of history, along with all "subversive" works of literature: scholars who protested were executed. Military campaigns extended the empire in the south while armies of conscripted laborers linked the frontier walls, which had been built by the Warring States against nomad invasions, into a continuous defensive system.

The cost of Shi Huangdi's reforms ruined the economy and his despotic rule caused such discontent that, after his death in 210, a civil war broke out. In 206 rebels massacred the entire Qin royal family. However, there was no restoration of the old states and the empire passed intact under the rule of Liu Bang, a commoner who had become a Qin official, and who became the first ruler of the Han dynasty. Gaozu (to use his more common posthumous title) ameliorated the severe Qin laws, reduced taxes and introduced reforms to restore prosperity. He rewarded some generals and bureaucrats with small fiefs but these were strictly controlled and the centralized state of Shi Huangdi was preserved.

The Former Han period (206 BC–AD 9) saw major territorial gains in central Asia and the south but northern China suffered severely from raids by the Xiongnu nomads until they were pacified in a long series of Han campaigns between 128 and 36 BC.

A TERRACOTTA army, six thousand men and horses strong, was buried with Shi Huangdi at Xianyang.

Jin, c.500 BC
Warring States border, c.300 BC
Qin state, c.350 BC
Qin gains by 300 BC
Qin gains, 300–250 BC
Qin gains, 230–221 BC
Qin gains by 206 BC
empire of the former Han dynasty, c.AD 6
Han protectorates, c.59 BC–AD 23, AD 73–127
territorial gains of Later Han dynasty
independent kingdom of Nan-yue, 206–113 BC
Warring States capital
capital of Zhou empire
capital of Qin dynasty
capital of former Han dynasty and Later Han dynasty
Qin fort
frontier wall
Chinese campaign
Xiongnu campaign
modern coastline and drainage where altered

Turfan
105 BC
108 BC
Dunhuang
Cherchen
Gansu Corridor
Changye
Wu-su
QILIAN MTS
Lake Qinghai
Tibetans
Yu
Q

TIMELINE

	400 BC	200 BC	AD 1	AD 200
	Warring States period	Former Han	Later Han	Three kingdoms period

Political change

c.500 Jin becomes the leading Chinese state

c.400 Breakup of the Jin state

361–338 Shang Yang turns Qin into a militaristic state

c. 350–315 Qin becomes the leading state in China

256 Qin deposes the last Zhou king

230–221 King Zheng of Qin unifies China

221–210 Zheng unites China under the Qin dynasty and takes the title Shi Huangdi

209–202 Civil war: the Qin dynasty is overthrown and Han dynasty established

117–115 BC Han conquer Gansu corridor

128–36 BC The Han launch a series of campaigns to pacify the Xiongnu

57 BC Traditional date for foundation of the first Korean state, Silla

AD 9 Courtier Wang Mang overthrows Han dynasty

AD 23 Restoration of Han dynasty

126 Peasant revolts against landowners

189 Provincial warlords seize the Han capital, Luoyang

190 General Tung Cho installs a puppet emperor on Han throne

220 Deposition of last Han emperor: China splits into three kingdoms

Cultural change

c. 500 Sun Tzu writes *The Art of War*

371–289 Mencius (Mengzi), Confucian philosopher

c.350 Crossbow invented

175–150 Iron weapons and tools come into widespread use in China

c. 100 Sima Qian writes the history of China from the beginning to his own times

c.100 Introduction of Buddhism to China

400 BC   200 BC   AD 1   AD 200

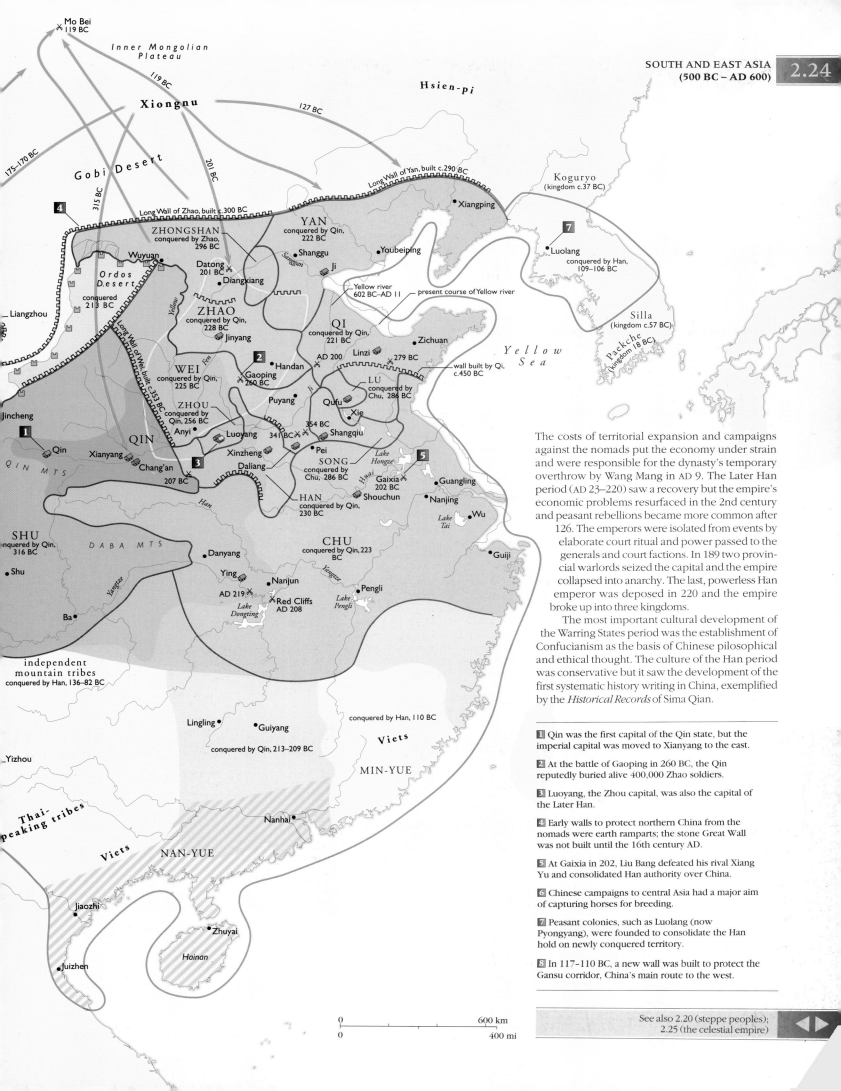

Mo Bei
119 BC

Inner Mongolian
Plateau

Hsien-pi

119 BC

127 BC

Xiongnu

Gobi Desert

201 BC

175–170 BC

315 BC

Koguryo
(kingdom c.37 BC)

Long Wall of Yan, built c.290 BC

Xiangping

Long Wall of Zhao, built c.300 BC

4

ZHONGSHAN
conquered by Zhao,
296 BC

YAN
conquered by Qin,
222 BC

Shanggu

Youbeiping

7

Luolang
conquered by Han,
109–106 BC

Wuyuan

Datong
201 BC

Ji

Ordos
Desert
conquered
213 BC

Diangxiang

Sangan

Silla
(kingdom c.57 BC)

Liangzhou

Yellow river
602 BC–AD 11

present course of Yellow river

ZHAO
conquered by Qin,
228 BC

QI
conquered by Qin,
221 BC

Zichuan

Yellow
Sea

Jinyang

Long Wall of Wei, built c.353 BC

AD 200

Linzi

279 BC

Paekche
kingdom 18 BC

2

Handan

wall built by Qi,
c.450 BC

Jincheng

WEI
conquered by Qin,
225 BC

Gaoping
260 BC

LU
conquered by
Chu, 286 BC

ZHOU
conquered by
Qin, 256 BC

Puyang

Qufu

Xie

1

Qin

Anyi

Luoyang

341 BC

354 BC

Shangqiu

Xianyang

QIN

Chang'an

3

Xinzheng

Pei

SONG
conquered by
Chu, 286 BC

Lake
Hongze

5

Guangling

Daliang

207 BC

Gaixia
202 BC

Nanjing

QIN MTS

Han

HAN
conquered by Qin,
230 BC

Shouchun

Hwai

Lake
Tai

Wu

SHU
conquered by Qin,
316 BC

DABA MTS

Shu

Danyang

CHU
conquered by Qin, 223
BC

Guiji

Yangtze

Ying

Nanjun

Pengli

Ba

AD 219

Lake
Dongting

Red Cliffs
AD 208

Lake
Pengli

independent
mountain tribes
conquered by Han, 136–82 BC

Yizhou

Lingling

Guiyang

conquered by Han, 110 BC

Viets

conquered by Qin, 213–209 BC

MIN-YUE

Thai-speaking tribes

Nanhai

Viets

NAN-YUE

Jiaozhi

Zhuyai

Hainan

Juizhen

The costs of territorial expansion and campaigns against the nomads put the economy under strain and were responsible for the dynasty's temporary overthrow by Wang Mang in AD 9. The Later Han period (AD 23–220) saw a recovery but the empire's economic problems resurfaced in the 2nd century and peasant rebellions became more common after 126. The emperors were isolated from events by elaborate court ritual and power passed to the generals and court factions. In 189 two provincial warlords seized the capital and the empire collapsed into anarchy. The last, powerless Han emperor was deposed in 220 and the empire broke up into three kingdoms.

The most important cultural development of the Warring States period was the establishment of Confucianism as the basis of Chinese pilosophical and ethical thought. The culture of the Han period was conservative but it saw the development of the first systematic history writing in China, exemplified by the *Historical Records* of Sima Qian.

1 Qin was the first capital of the Qin state, but the imperial capital was moved to Xianyang to the east.

2 At the battle of Gaoping in 260 BC, the Qin reputedly buried alive 400,000 Zhao soldiers.

3 Luoyang, the Zhou capital, was also the capital of the Later Han.

4 Early walls to protect northern China from the nomads were earth ramparts; the stone Great Wall was not built until the 16th century AD.

5 At Gaixia in 202, Liu Bang defeated his rival Xiang Yu and consolidated Han authority over China.

6 Chinese campaigns to central Asia had a major aim of capturing horses for breeding.

7 Peasant colonies, such as Luolang (now Pyongyang), were founded to consolidate the Han hold on newly conquered territory.

8 In 117–110 BC, a new wall was built to protect the Gansu corridor, China's main route to the west.

0   600 km

0   400 mi

See also 2.20 (steppe peoples);
2.25 (the celestial empire)

2.25 China disunited and the rise of Japan • AD 220 – 600 •

China's "period of disunion" between the fall of the Han dynasty in 220 and the reunification of the empire under the Sui in 589 saw constant warfare and nomad invasion. It was also critically important in Chinese cultural and economic history.

None of the warlords whose rivalries had brought down the Han could command universal allegiance, and the empire split into three kingdoms. The strongest – and the most populous – was the northern state of Wei, which included the wealthy Yellow river valley. The weakest and least populated kingdom was Shu, which relied on its mountainous frontiers for protection. Wu was the largest by area but its population was only slightly more than that of Shu. Each kingdom considered itself the legitimate successor to the Han, and wars between them were frequent and devastating: many towns were ruined and the total population of China fell sharply.

The first kingdom to fall was Shu. In 263 the Wei general, Sima Yen, sent an army through hundreds of kilometers of trackless mountain country to descend unexpectedly on Chengdu, the Shu capital. Shu capitulated but many of its nobles and troops fled west, eventually finding a refuge in Persia. Two years later Sima Yen seized power in Wei and, as Wudi (r.265–89), became the first emperor of the Jin dynasty. Wudi's main interest was his harem but he found time to conquer Wu in 280, briefly reuniting China. Shortly after Wudi's death, civil wars broke out between his sons, reaching their peak in the "rebellion of the eight princes" (291–306). To support their struggles the princes recruited troops from among the steppe peoples, but this made the weakness of the empire only too obvious to the nomads, who turned on their employers: northern China fragmented into a mosaic of Chinese and nomad states. Southern China stayed under the stable but oppressive rule of the Jin dynasty until 420, after which several short-lived dynasties ruled until 589.

The destruction afflicting northern China caused large numbers of landowners and peasants to flee

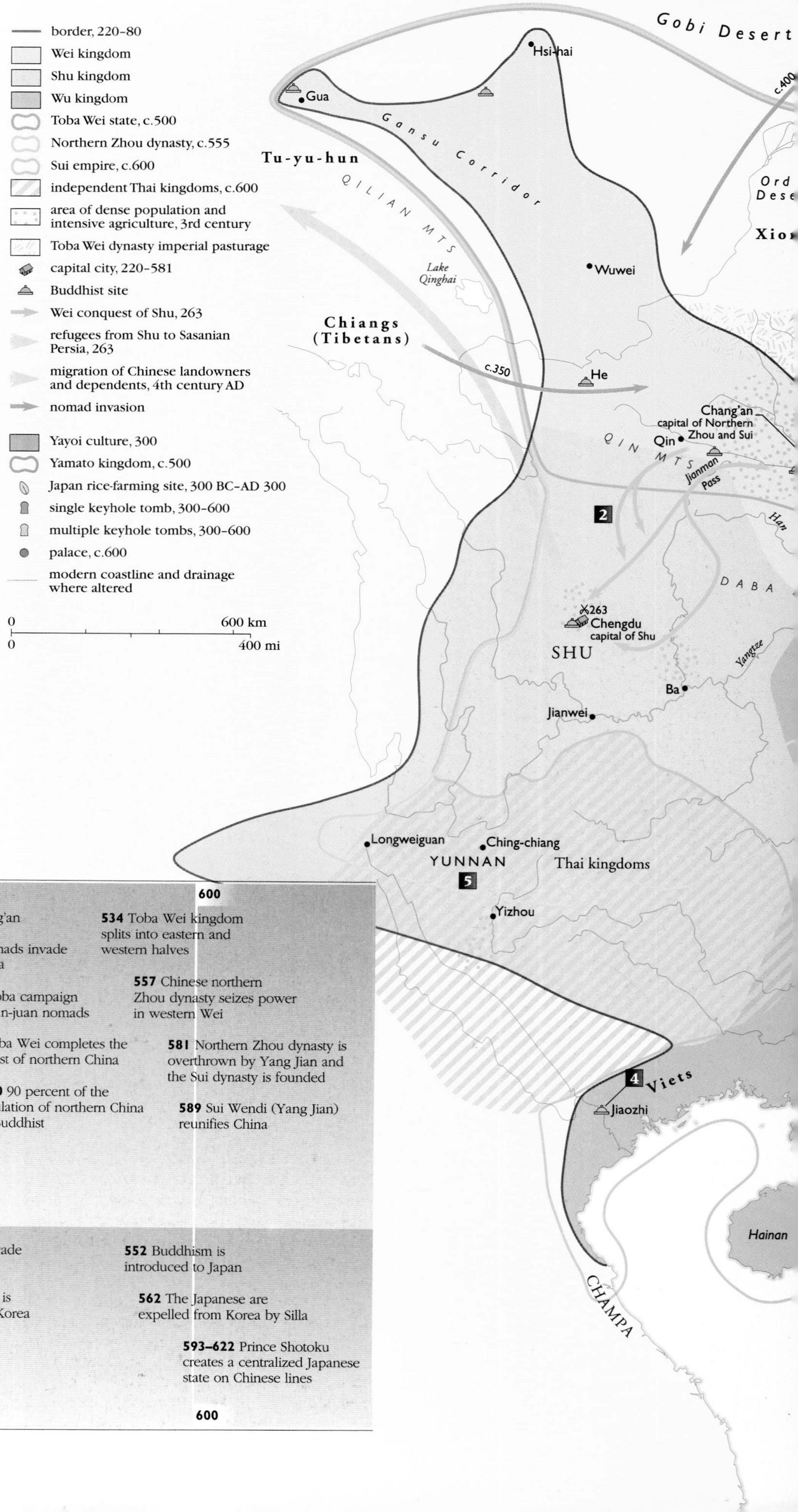

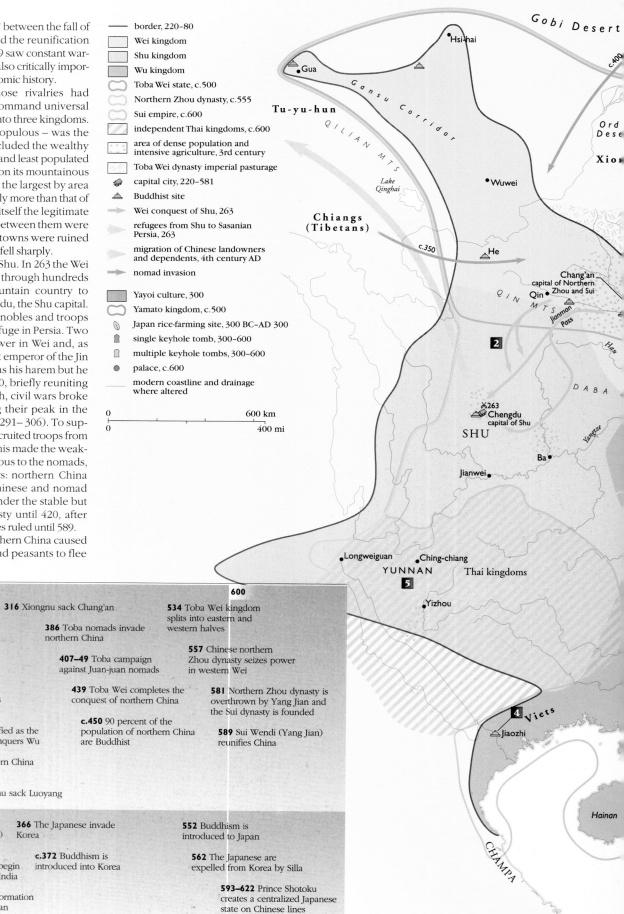

border, 220–80
Wei kingdom
Shu kingdom
Wu kingdom
Toba Wei state, c.500
Northern Zhou dynasty, c.555
Sui empire, c.600
independent Thai kingdoms, c.600
area of dense population and intensive agriculture, 3rd century
Toba Wei dynasty imperial pasturage
capital city, 220–581
Buddhist site
Wei conquest of Shu, 263
refugees from Shu to Sasanian Persia, 263
migration of Chinese landowners and dependents, 4th century AD
nomad invasion
Yayoi culture, 300
Yamato kingdom, c.500
Japan rice-farming site, 300 BC–AD 300
single keyhole tomb, 300–600
multiple keyhole tombs, 300–600
palace, c.600
modern coastline and drainage where altered
0 600 km
0 400 mi
Gobi Desert
Hsi-hai
Gua
Gansu Corridor
Tu-yu-hun
QILIAN MTS
Lake Qinghai
Wuwei
Chiangs (Tibetans)
c.350
He
Chang'an capital of Northern Zhou and Sui
Qin
QIN MTS
Jianmen Pass
Han
DABA
263
Chengdu capital of Shu
SHU
Yangtze
Ba
Jianwei
Longweiguan
Ching-chiang
YUNNAN
Thai kingdoms
Yizhou
Viets
Jiaozhi
Hainan
CHAMPA
c.400
Ord Dese
Xio
2
4
5

TIMELINE

China

- **200–300** Growth of Buddhist influence in China
- **220** Deposition of last Han emperor
- **263** Kingdom of Wei conquers Shu
- **265** Jin dynasty comes to power in Wei
- **280** China is reunified as the kingdom of Jin conquers Wu
- **291–306** Northern China fragments
- **311** Xiongnu sack Luoyang
- **316** Xiongnu sack Chang'an
- **386** Toba nomads invade northern China
- **407–49** Toba campaign against Juan-juan nomads
- **439** Toba Wei completes the conquest of northern China
- **c.450** 90 percent of the population of northern China are Buddhist
- **534** Toba Wei kingdom splits into eastern and western halves
- **557** Chinese northern Zhou dynasty seizes power in western Wei
- **581** Northern Zhou dynasty is overthrown by Yang Jian and the Sui dynasty is founded
- **589** Sui Wendi (Yang Jian) reunifies China

Neighboring states

- **239** Embassy from Queen Himiko of Wa (Japan) to China
- **259** Chinese Buddhists begin to make pilgrimages to India
- **c. 300** State formation begins in Japan
- **366** The Japanese invade Korea
- **c.372** Buddhism is introduced into Korea
- **552** Buddhism is introduced to Japan
- **562** The Japanese are expelled from Korea by Silla
- **593–622** Prince Shotoku creates a centralized Japanese state on Chinese lines

300 600

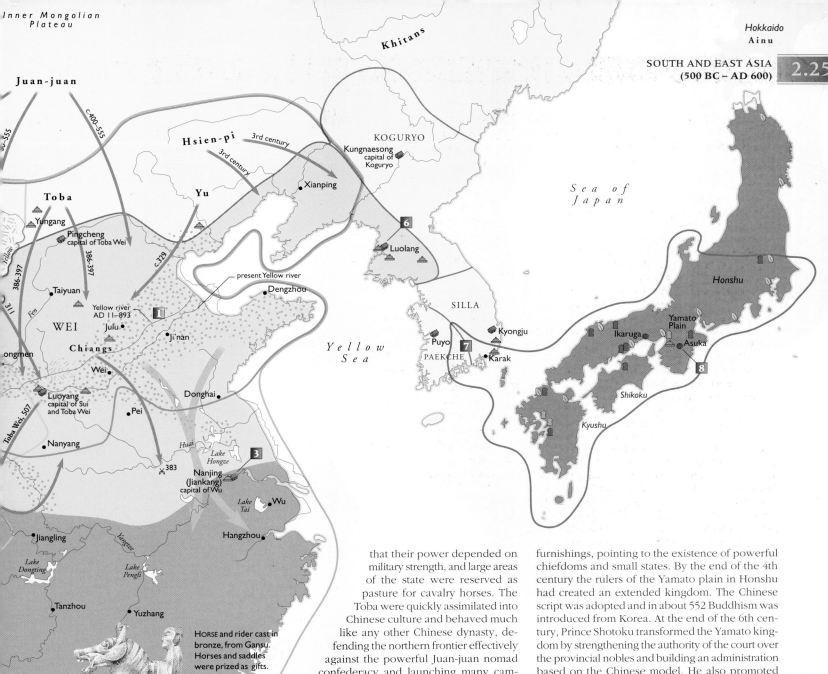

Juan-juan

Khitans

Hsien-pi   3rd century
Toba
Yu   3rd century

KOGURYO

Kungnaesong
capital of
Koguryo

Xianping

Hokkaido
Ainu

Sea of Japan

6

Luolang

Honshu

Yungang
Pingcheng
capital of Toba Wei

Taiyuan

present Yellow river

Dengzhou

SILLA

Kyongju

Yamato
Plain

Ikaruga

Yellow river
AD 11–893

WEI   Julu

Ji'nan

Yellow
Sea

Puyo
PAEKCHE

Karak

7

Asuka

8

Chiangs   Wei

Donghai

Shikoku

Luoyang
capital of Sui
and Toba Wei

Pei

Kyushu

Nanyang

Huai   Lake
Hongze

383

Nanjing
(Jiankang)
capital of Wu

Lake
Tai   Wu

Jiangling

Yangtze   Lake
Pengli

Hangzhou

Lake
Dongting

Tanzhou   Yuzhang

HORSE and rider cast in
bronze, from Gansu.
Horses and saddles
were prized as gifts.

WU

Guangzhou
Nanhai

south and settle on the fertile but sparsely populated Yangtze plain. This sparked a period of economic and population growth in southern China which, within a few centuries, saw it overtake the north as the most populous and prosperous part of China.

The position in the north began to stabilize after the Toba, a Turkic nomad confederation, invaded the north in 386–97 and re-established the Wei state. The Toba were a small minority among the Chinese population and they had little administrative expertise. However, they gained the cooperation of the northern landowners who saw the restoration of strong government as a way to protect their interests against a discontented peasantry. The Toba knew

that their power depended on military strength, and large areas of the state were reserved as pasture for cavalry horses. The Toba were quickly assimilated into Chinese culture and behaved much like any other Chinese dynasty, defending the northern frontier effectively against the powerful Juan-juan nomad confederacy and launching many campaigns to extend their authority over all of China. The Toba Wei state split into eastern and western halves after a civil war in 534. The Chinese Northern Zhou dynasty seized power in western Wei in 557. The Northern Zhou expanded into southwest China and in 577 conquered eastern Wei, reuniting the north. Four years later the Northern Zhou were overthrown by one of their generals, Yang Jian, who founded the Sui dynasty. In 589 he launched a campaign against the southern Chen dynasty and reunified China under his rule.

The major cultural development of this period of disunion was the rise of Buddhism. Buddhism was introduced into China in the 1st century AD but it only became popular after the fall of the Han: its emphasis on personal salvation and otherworldliness being attractive to a deeply troubled society. Buddhism introduced Indian art, architecture, philosophy and science and was the strongest outside influence on China before the 19th century AD.

While China was undergoing disunion, the first states appeared in Japan. Complex societies began to develop in Japan in the Yayoi culture (300 BC–AD300) which saw rice farming become established in Kyushu, Honshu and Shikoku. Early in the Yamato period (AD 300–710) large tombs appeared (called "keyhole tombs" for their shape) with rich

furnishings, pointing to the existence of powerful chiefdoms and small states. By the end of the 4th century the rulers of the Yamato plain in Honshu had created an extended kingdom. The Chinese script was adopted and in about 552 Buddhism was introduced from Korea. At the end of the 6th century, Prince Shotoku transformed the Yamato kingdom by strengthening the authority of the court over the provincial nobles and building an administration based on the Chinese model. He also promoted Chinese esthetic values, and introduced Chinese craftworkers and the Chinese calendar.

1 The fertile, densely populated river region made Wei the most powerful kingdom in the 3rd century.

2 The Wei conquest of Shu involved forced marches through difficult terrain.

3 Nanjing (Jiankang) was capital of southern Chinese dynasties 220–280 and 317–589 and was a major cultural center.

4 The Viets, an Austroasiatic people, carried out an unsuccessful rebellion against Chinese rule in 541–47.

5 Thai-speaking peoples of Yunnan founded several independent kingdoms by 600, benefitting from Chinese weakness.

6 Luolang became the capital of Koguryo after its capture in 313.

7 The southern Korean peninsula was conquered by the Japanese 366–562.

8 Asuka, capital of the late Yamato kingdom, was a complex of palaces, tombs and temples, c.550–650.

See also 2.06 (spread of Buddhism);
2.24 (the first emperor)

In AD 600 the Austronesian language group spanned the Indian and Pacific oceans. Austronesian-speaking peoples had originated in Taiwan around 3000 BC. The introduction of rice farming from China a millennium earlier led to population growth, followed by expansion into the Philippines, Indonesia and Malaysia, where Austronesians had become the dominant peoples by about 2000 BC. In the early first millennium BC Austronesians settled the coast of modern Vietnam and in the 1st century AD Austronesians from the Indonesian archipelago sailed west to colonize the uninhabited island of Madagascar.

Australia, New Guinea and the Solomon Islands had been settled many millennia earlier by Australoid peoples. Around 2000 BC Austronesians began moving into the coastal regions of New Guinea (they did not penetrate the highlands) and the islands. The Lapita culture (named for a site in New Caledonia), characterized by tools of shell and by distinctive pottery, developed here around 1600. By 1000 the Lapita culture had spread eastward to New Caledonia, Fiji, Samoa and Tonga. This migration probably followed the inventions of the sail-powered canoe with outrigger and the twin-hulled voyaging canoe.

The Australian Aborigines remained (except in the far north) isolated from the rest of the world, and the hunter–gatherer way of life established at least 40,000 years ago survived, adapting to environmental changes, until European contact in the 18th century AD. Differing styles of art have been found widely dispersed across the continent.

In the middle of the first millennium BC the Lapita culture-area began to divide. In the west the culture was absorbed into the diverse cultural traditions of the long-established Australoid peoples, ancestors of the modern Melanesians. In the Fiji–Samoa–Tonga triangle the Lapita developed into the ancestral Polynesian culture. The early Polynesians lived

0 | 2000 km
0 | 1500 mi

1 Austronesian languages originated in Taiwan before 3000 BC and began to spread through the southeast Asian islands before 2000 BC.

2 The Lapita culture originated in the Bismarck archipelago (New Britain and New Ireland) c.1600 BC and by 1000 had spread to New Caledonia, Fiji and Tonga.

3 Polynesian culture developed in the Fiji–Samoa–Tonga triangle c.500–300 BC, but was later displaced in Fiji by waves of Melanesian settlers.

4 Important trade routes crossed the Kra isthmus in the early centuries AD, stimulating the growth of several small short-lived kingdoms.

5 Oc Eo was a major trading port in the 2nd and 3rd centuries AD, declining in the 4th century when trade routes shifted to the Malacca straits.

6 By AD 400 the kingdom of Funan dominated most of the territory of modern Cambodia and Thailand.

7 Powerful chiefdoms, megalithic monuments and a system of pictographic writing developed on Easter island in the 17th century AD.

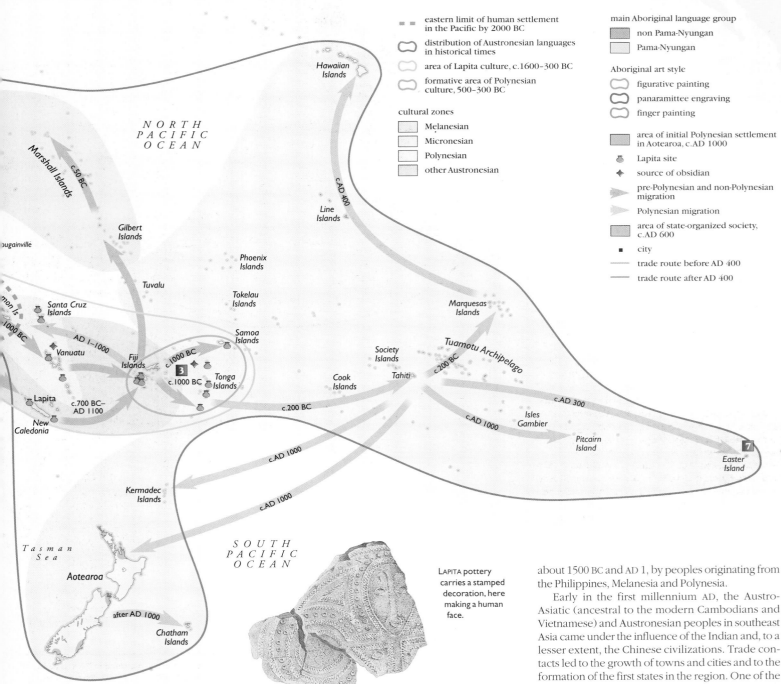

Map legend:

- - - eastern limit of human settlement in the Pacific by 2000 BC

distribution of Austronesian languages in historical times

area of Lapita culture, c.1600–300 BC

formative area of Polynesian culture, 500–300 BC

cultural zones

Melanesian

Micronesian

Polynesian

other Austronesian

main Aboriginal language group

non Pama-Nyungan

Pama-Nyungan

Aboriginal art style

figurative painting

panaramittee engraving

finger painting

area of initial Polynesian settlement in Aotearoa, c.AD 1000

Lapita site

source of obsidian

pre-Polynesian and non-Polynesian migration

Polynesian migration

area of state-organized society, c.AD 600

city

trade route before AD 400

trade route after AD 400

Map labels:

NORTH PACIFIC OCEAN

SOUTH PACIFIC OCEAN

Tasman Sea

Hawaiian Islands

Marshall Islands — c.50 BC

Gilbert Islands

Line Islands — c.AD 400

Phoenix Islands

Tuvalu

Tokelau Islands

Santa Cruz Islands

Vanuatu — AD 1~1000

Fiji Islands

Samoa Islands — c.1000 BC

Tonga Islands — c.1000 BC

Marquesas Islands

Society Islands

Tahiti — c.200 BC

Cook Islands

Tuamotu Archipelago

Isles Gambier

Pitcairn Island — c.AD 300

Easter Island

Lapita — c.700 BC–AD 1100

New Caledonia

Bougainville

Kermadec Islands — c.AD 1000

Aotearoa — after AD 1000

Chatham Islands

c.200 BC

c.AD 1000

LAPITA pottery carries a stamped decoration, here making a human face.

by a mixture of farming, fishing and gathering tree-products such as coconuts; their crops and domestic animals – taro, yams, breadfruit, pigs, dogs and chickens – had been brought by their ancestors from southeast Asia.

The Polynesians migrated farther east to Tahiti, the Tuamotu archipelago and the Marquesas Islands by about 200 BC. Polynesian settlement of the Pacific was the result of planned voyages of discovery. Polynesian seafarers accumulated extensive practical knowledge of the stars, weather, ocean wildlife, sea conditions and currents, and this enabled them to navigate accurately across vast distances of open ocean. Easter Island was settled around AD 300 and the Hawaiian islands a hundred years later. The final pulse of Polynesian expansion took place around AD 1000 with the settlement of Aotearoa (New

Zealand). Few of the Polynesians' traditional crops would grow in Aotearoa's temperate climate, so the Maoris cultivated native plants and hunted sea mammals and flightless birds. There was also migration westward in the first millennium AD to the Solomon Islands, but the Polynesians here were cut off from the main Polynesian regions by a Melanesian migration from Vanuatu to Fiji around 1100. Some Polynesians probably made contact with the Americas, as the Maoris and eastern Polynesians cultivated the sweet potato, a native of South America. The Polynesians formed simple tribal societies in the colonization period, but by 1200 chiefdoms appeared throughout the region.

The third Pacific culture-area, Micronesia, has a much more confused history but scattered islands of this region seem to have been settled between

about 1500 BC and AD 1, by peoples originating from the Philippines, Melanesia and Polynesia.

Early in the first millennium AD, the Austro-Asiatic (ancestral to the modern Cambodians and Vietnamese) and Austronesian peoples in southeast Asia came under the influence of the Indian and, to a lesser extent, the Chinese civilizations. Trade contacts led to the growth of towns and cities and to the formation of the first states in the region. One of the earliest states to emerge was Funan, centered on the lower Mekong, which by AD 100 became an intermediary in trade between China and India. In the 4th century Funan became an imperial power and for a time dominated mainland southeast Asia. Another important kingdom was Champa in southern Vietnam. In the 4th and 5th centuries Champa took advantage of Chinese divisions to launch cross-border raids, but its kings were forced to pay tribute to China after 586. State formation began later in island southeast Asia, but by 600 many small Buddhist- and Hindu-influenced states had arisen in Sumatra, Java and Borneo. An important factor here was a shifting of trade routes away from Funan, south to the Malacca straits in the 4th century.

See also 2.05 (the world 600)

The foundations of Mesoamerican civilization were laid in the Middle Preclassic period (900–300 BC) by the Olmec peoples of the Gulf coast and the Zapotecs of the Oaxaca valley. The influence of the Olmec civilization had declined by the start of the Late Preclassic (300–1 BC), but the Zapotec remained influential, particularly with regard to its hieroglyphic script. However, by the end of the period the Zapotec civilization was overshadowed by Teotihuacán and the Maya.

Teotihuacán first appeared around 200 BC as one of many large, prosperous farming communities in the fertile and well watered Valley of Mexico. The growth of Teotihuacán began at the beginning of the Classic period (AD 1–650), when a monumental ceremonial center, palaces and a large urban settlement were built on a carefully planned grid pattern. At its peak around AD 500, Teotihuacán covered twenty square kilometers (eight square miles) – a greater area than ancient Rome, although with a rather smaller population (between one and two hundred thousand). Considerable areas of the city were devoted to craft workshops, including those of obsidian workers, potters, stonemasons, plasterers and bricklayers. The city also contained quarters for foreign residents, such as Zapotec merchants. Trade was important to Teotihuacán, and it is likely that the caste of armed merchants, known in Aztec times as *pochteca*, had their origins there.

In its heyday Teotihuacán was the most important cultural, religious and economic center in Mesoamerica. The art, architecture, religions and costume of the Olmec, Maya and Zapotecs all show the influence of Classic Teotihuacán. Although the Teotihuacán civilization was probably literate, no inscriptions or other written records have survived. For unknown reasons – possibly soil erosion caused by overcultivation and deforestation – Teotihuacán began to decline around AD 600. Soon after 700 the city was sacked and burned, probably by forces from the nearby city of Cholula. The site continued to be occupied on a small scale, but by the time of the Aztecs – the cultural heirs of Teotihuacán – its origins had been forgotten.

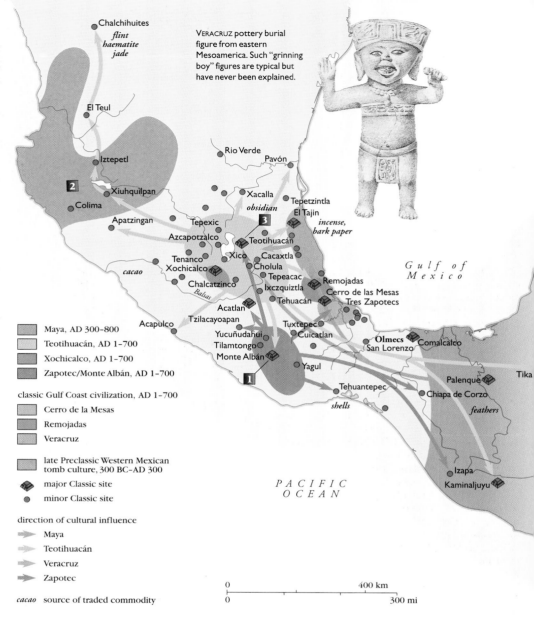

VERACRUZ pottery burial figure from eastern Mesoamerica. Such "grinning boy" figures are typical but have never been explained.

Maya, AD 300–800
Teotihuacán, AD 1–700
Xochicalco, AD 1–700
Zapotec/Monte Albán, AD 1–700

classic Gulf Coast civilization, AD 1–700
Cerro de la Mesa
Remojadas
Veracruz

late Preclassic Western Mexican tomb culture, 300 BC–AD 300
major Classic site
minor Classic site

direction of cultural influence
Maya
Teotihuacán
Veracruz
Zapotec

cacao source of traded commodity

0 — 400 km
0 — 300 mi

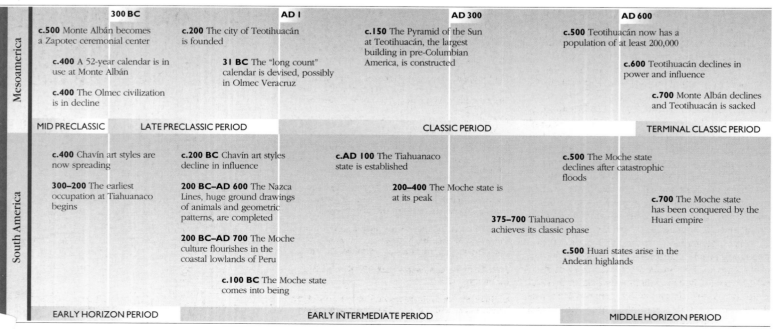

TIMELINE

		300 BC	AD I	AD 300	AD 600
Mesoamerica	**c.500** Monte Albán becomes a Zapotec ceremonial center		**c.200** The city of Teotihuacán is founded	**c.150** The Pyramid of the Sun at Teotihuacán, the largest building in pre-Columbian America, is constructed	**c.500** Teotihuacán now has a population of at least 200,000
	c.400 A 52-year calendar is in use at Monte Albán		**31 BC** The "long count" calendar is devised, possibly in Olmec Veracruz		**c.600** Teotihuacán declines in power and influence
	c.400 The Olmec civilization is in decline				**c.700** Monte Albán declines and Teotihuacán is sacked
	MID PRECLASSIC	LATE PRECLASSIC PERIOD		CLASSIC PERIOD	TERMINAL CLASSIC PERIOD
South America	**c.400** Chavín art styles are now spreading	**c.200 BC** Chavín art styles decline in influence		**c.AD 100** The Tiahuanaco state is established	**c.500** The Moche state declines after catastrophic floods
	300–200 The earliest occupation at Tiahuanaco begins	**200 BC–AD 600** The Nazca Lines, huge ground drawings of animals and geometric patterns, are completed		**200–400** The Moche state is at its peak	**c.700** The Moche state has been conquered by the Huari empire
		200 BC–AD 700 The Moche culture flourishes in the coastal lowlands of Peru		**375–700** Tiahuanaco achieves its classic phase	**c.500** Huari states arise in the Andean highlands
		c.100 BC The Moche state comes into being			
	EARLY HORIZON PERIOD		EARLY INTERMEDIATE PERIOD		MIDDLE HORIZON PERIOD

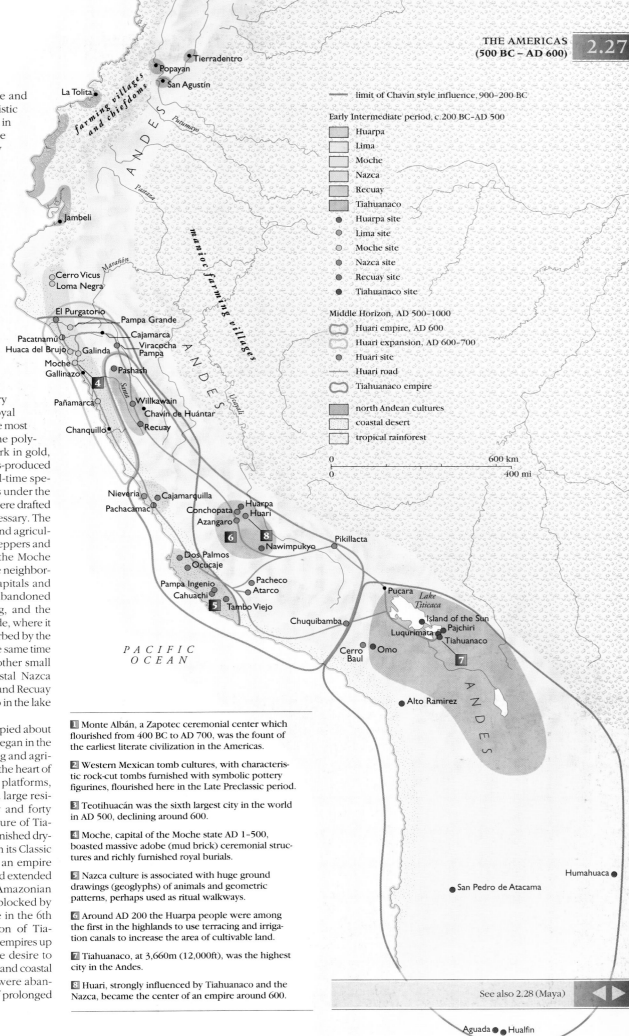

Intensive irrigation-based agriculture and powerful chiefdoms, sophisticated artistic and architectural traditions all developed in many areas of the central Andes during the Initial period (1800–800 BC) and Early Horizon period (800–200 BC). The dominant cultural influence over a wide area of highland and coastal Peru by about 400 BC was the Chavín art style; its declined about 200 BC and it was succeeded by a variety of local styles.

The decline of Chavín influence marks the start of the Early Intermediate period (200 BC–AD 500), which saw the first states and empires in South America. Warfare was more prevalent and large fortifications were built through the region. The earliest state formed around the coastal site of Moche in about 100 BC. Moche was a vast ceremonial center, including two huge adobe (mud brick) platforms: the pyramids of the Sun and the Moon. Between the two is a cemetery which has yielded richly furnished royal burials. Moche craftsmen were among the most skilled in the New World, producing fine polychrome ceramics, textiles and metalwork in gold, silver and copper. Some pottery was mass-produced using molds. Moche craftsmen were full-time specialists, some of whom worked in teams under the direction of supervisors, while laborers were drafted for work on major public projects as necessary. The Moche economy was based on fishing and agriculture, growing maize, potatoes, cotton, peppers and peanuts in irrigated fields. By AD 200 the Moche culture was spread by conquest to all the neighboring coastal valleys, where provincial capitals and fortresses were built. Moche itself was abandoned around AD 500, after massive flooding, and the capital was moved north to Pampa Grande, where it remained until the Moche state was absorbed by the Huari empire between 600 and 700. At the same time that Moche became an imperial state, other small states were emerging among the coastal Nazca people and among the highland Huarpa and Recuay peoples and, farther south, at Tiahuanaco in the lake Titicaca basin.

The site of Tiahuanaco was first occupied about 300 BC, but its growth as a major power began in the period AD 100–375, when major building and agricultural improvement projects began. At the heart of Tiahuanaco was a precinct of temples, platforms, tombs and palaces around which was a large residential area, housing between twenty and forty thousand people. The outstanding feature of Tiahuanaco architecture is its meticulously finished drystone walls and monolithic sculptures. In its Classic period (AD 375–700) Tiahuanaco built an empire which dominated the southern Andes and extended to the Pacific coast and the edge of the Amazonian rainforest. Expansion to the north was blocked by the rise of the aggressive Huari empire in the 6th century. The motive for the expansion of Tiahuanaco, and all the successive highland empires up to the Inca in the 15th century, was the desire to achieve control over supplies of lowland and coastal products. Both Tiahuanaco and Huari were abandoned around 1000, possibly because of prolonged drought conditions.

1 Monte Albán, a Zapotec ceremonial center which flourished from 400 BC to AD 700, was the fount of the earliest literate civilization in the Americas.

2 Western Mexican tomb cultures, with characteristic rock-cut tombs furnished with symbolic pottery figurines, flourished here in the Late Preclassic period.

3 Teotihuacán was the sixth largest city in the world in AD 500, declining around 600.

4 Moche, capital of the Moche state AD 1–500, boasted massive adobe (mud brick) ceremonial structures and richly furnished royal burials.

5 Nazca culture is associated with huge ground drawings (geoglyphs) of animals and geometric patterns, perhaps used as ritual walkways.

6 Around AD 200 the Huarpa people were among the first in the highlands to use terracing and irrigation canals to increase the area of cultivable land.

7 Tiahuanaco, at 3,660m (12,000ft), was the highest city in the Andes.

8 Huari, strongly influenced by Tiahuanaco and the Nazca, became the center of an empire around 600.

Map legend:

limit of Chavín style influence, 900–200 BC

Early Intermediate period, c.200 BC–AD 500
Huarpa
Lima
Moche
Nazca
Recuay
Tiahuanaco
Huarpa site
Lima site
Moche site
Nazca site
Recuay site
Tiahuanaco site

Middle Horizon, AD 500–1000
Huari empire, AD 600
Huari expansion, AD 600–700
Huari site
Huari road
Tiahuanaco empire

north Andean cultures
coastal desert
tropical rainforest

0   600 km
0   400 mi

See also 2.28 (Maya)

The most sophisticated of the pre-Columbian civilizations of the Americas was the Maya of Guatemala, Petén and Yucatán. By draining and canalizing the swamplands, agricultural production rose in the Middle Preclassic period (700–300 BC), making it possible to support large populations. Chiefdoms and small states appeared and the first towns and monumental structures were built. During the Late Preclassic (300 BC–AD 300) powerful city-states emerged, writing came into use, advanced mathematical and astronomical studies were pursued, and a calendrical system was adopted. The new states were competitive and warlike and many cities were fortified. Underlying these developments may have been such factors as population pressure, agricultural intensification, long-distance trade and increased warfare. The main influences on the development of Mayan civilization were the Olmecs and the Zapotecs, from whom the Maya received, among other things, the 52-year "long count" calendar, writing and the sacred ball game.

The most important Maya center of the Late Preclassic period was the city of El Mirador, occupied 150 BC–AD 150. It had large temple pyramids, a fortified palace area, marketplaces and a population approaching 80,000. Causeways known as *sacbes* linked El Mirador with its subordinate villages. Although there is some evidence of writing at El Mirador, the best evidence for its use by the Preclassic Maya comes from the southern highland area, where many *stelae* (stone monuments) were erected at sites like Kaminaljuyú, in the 1st and 2nd centuries AD, to commemorate royal ancestors. The earliest known inscription, found at El Baul, carries a "long-count" date equivalent to AD 36. The Maya did not invent writing themselves, but their hieroglyphic script was the only pre-Columbian script that could fully express the spoken language. The Mayan script included both ideographic and phonetic elements. About 800 glyphs are known. The southern Maya declined in the 3rd century AD and the tradition of erecting commemorative *stelae* died out. The cause was probably a volcanic eruption that blew apart

Mount Ilopango, covering thousands of square kilometers with ash and ruining agriculture for years.

Commemorative *stelae* with hieroglyphic inscriptions began to be erected by the Maya in the central lowland rainforest area around AD 300, a development that marks the beginning of the Classic period (AD 300–800). The earliest show clear stylistic links with the highland Maya. Until about AD 400 *stelae* were only erected at Tikal, Uaxactún and a few nearby centers, but thereafter the practice spread throughout the central area. Palenque, Yaxchilán, Copán and Calakmul all developed into major regional powers, but the dominant city-state for much of the Classic period was Tikal, with a population of 75,000–100,000. At its peak under King Stormy Sky (r.411–57), Tikal dominated most of the central area and maintained cultural and trade links

with Teotihuacán, the greatest power in Mesoamerica. Tikal went into decline after its defeat by Caracol in 562; and although it recovered under Ah Cacau (r.682–723) it did not regain its preeminence.

Warfare was common among the Classic Maya city-states, although the aim was more often to exact tribute and take prisoners than to annex territory permanently. The normal fate of prisoners was ritual torture and mutilation, after which they were sacrificed to the gods. Human sacrifices were needed to dedicate new temples, to accompany the dead and to mark important events such as the completion of calendrical cycles. Mayan rulers were expected to take part in painful bloodletting rites as a means of communicating with ancestral spirits. Marriage alliances were the usual means of forging friendly relations between states.

Key

◈	late Preclassic site with monumental sculpture, 300 BC–AD 300
○	other late Preclassic site, 300 BC–AD 300
▨	area of Classic Maya civilization, AD 300–800
▨	Puuc style
▨	Chenes style
▨	Rio Bec style
▨	Cotzumalhuapan style
◈	major Classic site
●	minor Classic site
◈	pre-eminent regional center
	influence of Tikal, 5th century AD
<u>Tikal</u>	dynastic histories deciphered
——	city-state border, AD 790
——	trade route
cacao	source of traded commodity

area with intensive agriculture
▢	raised fields
▢	stone-faced terraces

0 ———————————— 200 km
0 ———————————— 150 mi

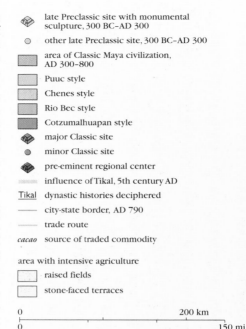

MOSAIC jade mask found at Palenque, possibly a representation of Pacal, ruler of Palenque in the 7th century.

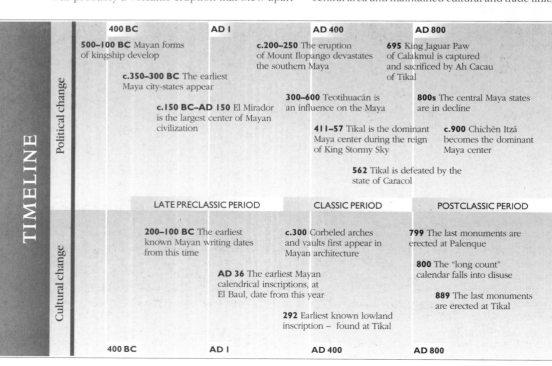

TIMELINE

Political change

400 BC	AD 1	AD 400	AD 800
500–100 BC Mayan forms of kingship develop		**c.200–250** The eruption of Mount Ilopango devastates the southern Maya	**695** King Jaguar Paw of Calakmul is captured and sacrificed by Ah Cacau of Tikal
c.350–300 BC The earliest Maya city-states appear			
c.150 BC–AD 150 El Mirador is the largest center of Mayan civilization		**300–600** Teotihuacán is an influence on the Maya	**800s** The central Maya states are in decline
		411–57 Tikal is the dominant Maya center during the reign of King Stormy Sky	**c.900** Chichén Itzá becomes the dominant Maya center
		562 Tikal is defeated by the state of Caracol	

	LATE PRECLASSIC PERIOD	CLASSIC PERIOD	POSTCLASSIC PERIOD

Cultural change

	200–100 BC The earliest known Mayan writing dates from this time	**c.300** Corbeled arches and vaults first appear in Mayan architecture	**799** The last monuments are erected at Palenque
	AD 36 The earliest Mayan calendrical inscriptions, at El Baul, date from this year		**800** The "long count" calendar falls into disuse
			889 The last monuments are erected at Tikal
		292 Earliest known lowland inscription – found at Tikal	

400 BC	AD 1	AD 400	AD 800

1 El Mirador was the largest Maya center in the Late Preclassic period, before being abandoned c.AD 150.

2 Lake Ilopango now fills the crater left by the catastrophic eruption of Mount Ilopango c.AD 200-250, which caused the decline of the southern Maya .

3 Tikal was the largest Maya city. It reached its peak under King Stormy Sky (r.AD 411-57) and dominated the central Maya until conquered by Caracol in 562.

4 Classic Maya ceremonial centers were often aligned on astronomical events. The earliest such center, at Uaxactún, was aligned on the midwinter, equinoctial and midsummer sunrises.

5 Copán, a major Maya center during the Classic period, was supplanted by Quirigua in 738.

6 The raised causeway, or *sacbe*, linking Cobá with Yaxuná runs for some 100 kilometers (62 miles).

7 Murals at Bonampak celebrating a victory of King Chan Muan c.790 provide vivid evidence of the warlike character of Maya civilization.

8 Power and population moved to the north in the Early Postclassic period (AD 900-1200), when Chichén Itzá became the dominant Maya center.

Gulf of
Mexico

*Isla de
Cozumel*

*Yucatán
Peninsula*

NORTHERN AREA

Candelaria

CENTRAL AREA

PETÉN

*Lago Peten
Itzán*

*marine products
and shells*

SOUTHERN AREA

G u a t e m a l a n   H i g h l a n d s

*Lago de
Izabal*

*Lago de
Atitlán*

PACIFIC
OCEAN

*Lake
Ilopango*

The civilization of the Classic Maya was not uniform: several regional decorative styles are known, and there was considerable variation in architectural styles. The Maya were highly skilled craftsmen, producing monumental stone sculpture, jade carving, pottery, paintings and obsidian tools of the highest quality. A few gold and copper objects have been found at Mayan sites, but metals were little used before Postclassic times.

The Classic period came to an end around the beginning of the 9th century, when the city-states of the central lowlands began to collapse. The population declined dramatically, new building ceased, and the tradition of erecting commemorative *stelae* was abandoned. The last monuments were erected at Palenque in 799, at Yaxchilan in 808, at Quirigua 810, at Copán in 822 and Tikal in 889. By 950 all the major central Mayan cities lay in ruins. The "long count" calendar fell out of use.

The collapse is thought to be an indirect consequence of the fall of Teotihuacán around 750. Mayan rulers competed, through warfare and by commissioning more and more ambitious building projects, to fill the power vacuum created by the fall of Teotihuacán. Pressures on the peasantry to supply food and labor increased to such a point that the agricultural economy collapsed; malnutrition, population decline and political collapse followed. Classic Mayan civilization did not die out, but continued to flourish in the semiarid north of the Yucatán peninsula until around 1000, when the area was invaded by the Toltecs, from central Mexico.

See also 2.27 (Teotihuacán)

Cross-referencing
References to other dictionary entries are identified in small capitals (e.g. CHRISTIANITY); references to map spreads are denoted by the use of an arrow (e.g. ▷ 2.21).

Dating
For the purposes of this dictionary, the end of the Paleolithic period of early human prehistory, about 10,000 BC/12,000 years ago (i.e. the end of the Pleistocene Ice Age), is taken as the boundary between geological and historical time. Earlier dates are therefore given in years ago (ya), while dates after the end of the Paleolithic are given using the conventional BC/AD system.

Chinese spellings
Since 1979 the standard international system for the transliteration of Chinese names into Roman characters has been Pinyin and this is the system used throughout this dictionary.

ACADEMY
Originally a gymnasium (training ground for athletes) on the outskirts of ATHENS, named after the hero Academeus. The philosopher PLATO (429–347 BC) turned it into a school for the training of philosophers. It remained in use until it was closed down by the Christians in the 6th century AD. ▷ 2.08, 2.17

ACTIUM, BATTLE OF
Battle of 31 BC in which Octavian (AUGUSTUS) blockaded the fleet of MARK ANTONY and CLEOPATRA at Actium on the Ambracian Gulf in northwest GREECE. Although Mark Antony and Cleopatra managed to evade the blockade and escape south, this defeat meant the loss of their campaign. ▷ 2.02, 2.13

ADRIANOPLE
City of northern Thrace, funded by HADRIAN in about AD 125. It was the site of a battle in AD 378, at which the Roman emperor VALENS was defeated and killed by the VISIGOTHS, supported by the OSTROGOTHS. As a result of the defeat, the new emperor THEODOSIUS supplied food to the GOTHS in return for help in defending the border against other intruders. The city was taken by the Turks in 1361 and renamed Edirne. ▷ 2.16

ADULIS
An ancient port on the Red Sea coast of AXUM (now in Eritrea) and important staging post in the trade between the Mediterranean and southern Arabia, east Africa and the Indian Ocean. It was probably founded by the Egyptians and rose to prominence in the mid-3rd century BC, boosted by PTOLEMAIC trade. ▷ 2.21

AEGOSPOTAMI, BATTLE OF
Aegospotami, at the entrance to the Black Sea, was the site of a devastating defeat of the Athenian navy by the Spartan commander Lysander, in 405 BC. The battle marked the end of the PELOPONNESIAN WAR. ▷ 2.08

AESCHYLOS
Athenian playwright (c.525–456 BC) seen as the founder of Greek tragedy, though very few of his plays survive. For the first time, individual characters rather than a chorus were used to tell a story. His famous trilogy, the *Oresteia*, dealt with the problems of justice and revenge in the city-state. ▷ 2.07

AETIUS
(c.AD 390–454) One of the last effective generals of the ROMAN EMPIRE, who was responsible for the defeat of ATTILA and the HUNS at the Battle of the Catalaunian Plains in AD 451. Despite his success, the empire continued to crumble under BARBARIAN pressure, and Aetius was assassinated by the emperor VALENTINIAN III in 454. ▷ 2.16

AETOLIA
Mountainous region of west-central GREECE that remained outside the mainstream of Greek history until the 4th century BC, when the settlements of the area united in the Aetolian league. The league absorbed neighboring cities and shrines, including DELPHI, in the 3rd century BC, but its forces were defeated by ROME in 168 BC. ▷ 2.08

AGRI DECUMATES
Roman name for a region of southwestern Germany, north of the Danube and east of the Rhine. It was annexed to the ROMAN EMPIRE from about AD 75 but abandoned in 263 to the ALEMANNI. ▷ 2.13, 2.15

AH CACAU
Ancient MAYAN king of TIKAL (r.AD 682–723). Under his reign Tikal began its second major period of expansion and key monuments were built. His magnificently furnished tomb was discovered in 1961. ▷ 2.28

AHURA MAZDA
The chief god of ZOROASTRIANISM – the religion of Achemenid and Sasanian PERSIA first preached by Zoroaster in the 7th century BC. Ahura Mazda – also known as Ormazd or "supreme knowledge" – was said to have created the world and created the twin spirits of good and evil, though he was associated with the spirit of good in its struggle against evil. ▷ 2.06

AJANTA
Sacred Buddhist site in Maharashtra state, western India, some 106 kilometers (66 miles) northwest of Aurangabad. It comprises temples and monasteries carved by hand from the rock face between the 1st century BC and the 7th century AD, and adorned with fine carvings and frescoes of Buddhist legends. The caves were rediscovered in 1819. ▷ 2.22

ALANS
Sarmatian pastoral nomad tribe from the Black Sea steppes, first recorded in the 1st century AD raiding the Persian empire. In the late 4th century they were driven westward by the HUNS. They entered the ROMAN EMPIRE in 406; some settled in GAUL, others became closely associated with the VANDALS and migrated to southwest Spain and north Africa. ▷ 2.16, 2.17, 2.19

ALARIC
Powerful leader of the GOTHS who created a fighting force from refugee VISIGOTHS in the ROMAN EMPIRE. His main aim was to find land in which they could settle, but when the Romans refused to negotiate with him he sacked Rome in AD 410. He died shortly afterwards. ▷ 2.16

ALBION
Ancient name for Britain – first used by GREEK writers in the 4th century BC – that is presumed to refer to the white chalk cliffs of Dover. It was also used by medieval CELTIC writers and later became applied specifically to England.

ALEMANNI
Literally meaning "all men", a grouping of Germanic peoples who began raiding across the borders of the ROMAN EMPIRE in the mid-3rd century AD, sometimes reaching as far south as Italy. They were never truly defeated. The French word for Germany, "Allemagne", is a reminder of their impact. ▷ 2.15, 2.16, 2.19

ALESIA
Celtic stronghold in Central GAUL (modern France) and the site of the last stand of VERCINGETORIX – the most formidable of the Celtic leaders – against JULIUS CAESAR in 52 BC. The defeat of Vercingetorix after a long and difficult siege allowed Gaul to become incorporated into the ROMAN EMPIRE. ▷ 2.13, 2.18

ALEXANDER THE GREAT
One of the great conquerors in world history, Alexander inherited the throne of MACEDONIA in 336 BC from his father, PHILIP II. A charismatic leader who always fought at the front of his troops, Alexander subdued mainland GREECE before invading the Persian Achemenid empire in search of the treasure and prestige he needed to maintain his position. After spectacular victories at the rivers Granicus (334) and Issus (333), and at Gaugamela in Assyria (331), Persian resistance collapsed. In 330 Alexander captured Persepolis, the Persian capital: DARIUS III, the last Achemenid king, was murdered shortly afterwards. Alexander spent another four years subduing the Persian empire's eastern provinces and invading India (326) before his army mutinied, forcing him to end his campaigns.

Alexander's conquest of the Persian empire made Greco-Macedonian civilization the dominant cultural influence as far east as India. The strain of constant fighting, effects of wounds and heavy drinking took their toll, and Alexander died in 323 BC aged only 32, probably in the belief that his victories had earned him the status of a god. Alexander had not given his empire any centralized institutions, and it fell apart during the Wars of the Diadochi. ▷ 2.08, 2.09, 2.11, 2.22

ALEXANDRIA
City on the Egyptian coast founded by Alexander the Great in 332 BC and seat of the Ptolemaic dynasty. The Ptolemies successfully preserved its independence from Egypt proper, but used Egyptian wealth to make it one of the most flourishing cities of the ancient Mediterranean. Its museum and library made it a center for mathematicians, scientists and poets. Alexandria was incorporated into the Roman empire, along with the rest of Egypt, in 30 BC, after the death of the last Ptolemaic queen, Cleopatra. ▷ 2.09, 2.10, 2.16, 2.21

ALKIBIADES
(451–404 BC) Ambitious, aristocratic Athenian general who persuaded the Athenians to launch an ill-fated campaign in Sicily in 415 BC. He then defected to Sparta and, though he later commanded an Athenian fleet, never regained the trust of the city. ▷ 2.08

ALTAIC LANGUAGES
A subfamily of the Ural-Altaic languages found in eastern Europe and across Russia, that comprises the Turkic, Mongolian and Tungusic languages.

AMALASUNTHA, QUEEN
Daughter of Theodoric, the Ostrogothic king of Italy. On his death in AD 526 she became regent for her son. She respected Roman culture and built links with Justinian, the emperor in the east, that led to her murder by Ostrogoth nobles in AD 534. ▷ 2.17

AMARAVATI
Buddhist site in Andhra Pradesh state, eastern India, the most important Indian Buddhist site from the 3rd century BC to the period of Islamic rule, and the capital of the Buddhist kingdom of Andhra. Its stupa (from 200 BC) was of exceptional size and contained sculptures of fine detail and narrative power. The Amaravati style spread throughout southern India, as far as southeast Asia. ▷ 2.22

AMBROSE
Formidable Christian bishop of Milan from AD 374 to 397. Appointed because of his administrative skills, he turned out to be a powerful upholder of Christian orthodoxy (against the Arians) and a scourge of paganism. He even excommunicated the emperor Theodosius I for the massacre of some opponents.

ANASTASIUS
Ruler of the eastern Roman empire (r.AD 491–518). Although elderly when he came to the throne, Anastasius was an excellent administrator and left a full state treasury. He was disliked in his capital, Constantinople, for favoring the eastern provinces of his empire above the city. ▷ 2.17

ANGLES
Germanic tribe of northern Germany and southern Denmark from the early centuries AD, and one of the three main groups to invade Britain in the mid-5th century. They settled mainly in Northumbria, Mercia and East Anglia, and gave their name to England. ▷ 2.16, 2.19

ANGLO-SAXONS
The Germanic invaders and settlers of southern and eastern Britain in the 5th century AD, made up of the Angles, Saxons and Jutes. About 200 years later the three groups had merged into a single Anglo-Saxon identity. The term was used by Gallic writers to distinguish the invaders from the Romano-British population. Anglo-Saxon England flourished until the Norman invasion of 1066. ▷ 2.16, 2.17, 2.19

ANTIGONOS
(c.382–301 BC) Macedonian commander whose ambitions were to win control of the empire of Alexander the Great after the latter's death. The task was too great for any one man, and Antigonos was continually outmaneuvered by rivals until he was killed at the Battle of Ipsus. His grandson (also Antigonos) managed to regain control of Macedonia and establish a stable kingdom there. ▷ 2.09

ANTIOCH, ANTIOCHIA
The royal capital of the Seleucid kingdom founded in 300 BC on the banks of the Orontes in Syria. It flourished as both an administrative and trading center, and later became the capital of the Roman province of Syria. It was home to an important and influential early Christian community. ▷ 2.11, 2.17

ANTIOCHUS III
The most successful of the Seleucid kings, (r.223–187 BC). Known as "the Great", he re-established his dynasty's control over much of the old Persian empire, including Babylon. An attempt to regain influence in Greece led to a successful counteroffensive by Rome. Antiochus was humbled and his kingdom lost the west coast of Asia. ▷ 2.10

ANTIOCHUS IV
The ambitious son of Antiochus III and a Seleucid king from 174 to 163 BC. His attempt to take over Egypt was thwarted by the Romans, and his plans to Hellenize Judaea led only to a successful Jewish revolt. He died while campaigning in Persia. ▷ 2.10

ANTONINE DYNASTY
Roman dynasty composed of the emperors Antoninus Pius (AD 138–61), Marcus Aurelius (AD 161–80) – who initially shared the reign with his adoptive brother Lucius Verus (AD 161–69) – and Commodus (AD 177–92), the son of Marcus Aurelius. ▷ 2.15

ANTONINE WALL
Built for Antoninus Pius in AD 139–42 by Q. Lollius Urbicus, this was a massive undertaking – a frontier wall running 59 kilometers (37 miles) across modern Scotland, from the Forth to the river Clyde. Made of turf on a cobbled foundation with a ditch in front, it had 17 forts as well as signaling platforms and fortlets. Excavation has revealed two main phases of occupation, between about 139 and 164. The circumstances of its abandonment are not known. ▷ 2.15

ANTONINUS PIUS
Roman emperor (r.AD 138–161) who served as proconsul in Asia during the 120s. He was adopted by the emperor Hadrian and on succeeding him in 138 ruled the empire efficiently and frugally. He was succeeded by Marcus Aurelius.

ANTONY, MARK
(c.83–30 BC) Roman statesman and general. After the assassination of Julius Caesar in 44 BC, Antony formed the Second Triumvirate with Lepidus and Octavian (Augustus) against the republican conspirators. Following Antony's defeat of Cassius and Brutus at Philippi in 42 BC, the triumvirs divided the empire between them, Antony taking the rich eastern Mediterranean. In Egypt Antony met Cleopatra (41 BC) and they became lovers. They also allied politically to challenge Octavian's dominance in the west. However, Antony's relationship with Cleopatra allowed Octavian to cast him in the role of a traitor. In 31 BC Antony and Cleopatra were defeated by Octavian at Actium; Antony committed suicide in 30 BC as Octavian entered Alexandria. ▷ 2.13

ANTONY, ST
(c.AD 251–356) Ascetic Christian who lived much of his long life in the Egyptian desert. Often seen as the founding figure of Egyptian monasticism, he was idealized in a famous Life (357), the first of many to glorify early saints. ▷ 2.15

ANURADHAPURA
Ceylonese city, the capital of a kingdom of the same name from the 5th century BC. The city was abandoned following raids from southern India in the 10th century AD, and the capital moved to Polonnaruva. During its period of supremacy Anuradhapura became a cultural center for the arts. Later forgotten, the city was not rediscovered until the late 19th century. Its remains include vast stupas and imposing statues. ▷ 2.22

APOLLONIUS OF PERGE
Greek mathematician (fl.c.200 BC) whose work on cones remained the standard text on the subject for centuries.

AQUILEIA
In 181 BC the Romans founded a Latin colony here at the head of the Adriatic – a strategic position controlling routes across the Julian Alps, the trade in Baltic amber and local gold deposits. Aquileia became a great military, commercial and industrial center, and one of the largest cities in the world, with about 100,000 inhabitants. It was sacked by ATTILA in AD 452 but revived in the medieval period. ▷ 2.15, 2.19

AQUITANIA, AQUITAINE
The area enclosed by the Garonne, Pyrenees and Bay of Biscay. It was inhabited by the Gaulish tribes of the Aquitani, who were conquered by the Romans between 56 and 27 BC. Under AUGUSTUS, Aquitania became an imperial province extending as far north as the Loire, and prospered from agriculture and trade. It was settled by the VISIGOTHS in the early 5th century. ▷ 2.13, 2.16, 2.18

ARACHOSIA
Ancient province of the Persian and Alexandrian empires, now in southern Afghanistan. Its capital was probably at the modern city of Kandahar. ▷ 2.09

ARAUSIO, BATTLE OF
Defeat in southern France (near modern Orange) of the Romans (105 BC) at the hands of the CIMBRI and TEUTONES. Following this defeat, GAIUS MARIUS became Roman consul and reorganized the army. ▷ 2.19

ARCHIMEDES
Outstanding Greek mathematician (c.287–212 BC) of the ancient world. His fertile mind transcended conventional mathematical thinking in fields as varied as astronomy, the measurement of volumes, hydrostatics and notation. He is also remembered for his inventions, such as a screw used to raise water, and ingenious devices to protect his native city SYRACUSE from a Roman siege in which he was killed. ▷ 2.10

ARDASHIR
Two kings of Sasanian PERSIA. Ardashir I (r.c.AD 220–40) was the grandson of SASAN, after whom the dynasty was named. He was king of Persia and founded the SASANIAN DYNASTY by overthrowing the Parthian dynasty in 224–26. Ardashir II (r.379–383) succeeded SHAPUR II. A weak king, he was soon deposed. ▷ 2.11

ARIANISM
The early Christian belief, developed by Arius (a priest in ALEXANDRIA) and others, that JESUS was a distinct creation of God the Father. ARIANISM was condemned as a heresy at the COUNCIL OF NICAEA in 325 (which proclaimed the orthodox view that Jesus had always been part of God), but remained strong in the eastern empire.

ARIKAMEDU
Trading port near Pondicherry on the coast of southeast India in the early centuries AD. Roman artifacts, including coins and pottery, have been excavated there since 1945. It may have been known as Poduce in ancient times. It has been suggested that contact with the Mediterranean began well before the Roman period. ▷ 2.23

ARIOVISTUS
Germanic leader who invaded eastern GAUL in about 70 BC and fought with the Sequani CELTS before dominating the region in the 60s BC. Despite an earlier alliance with Rome, JULIUS CAESAR defeated him in eastern Gaul in 58 BC. ▷ 2.19

ARISTAGORAS OF MILETUS
(c.505–496 BC) Powerful figure in the Ionian city of MILETUS who played a leading part in organizing a revolt of the Ionian cities against their Persian overlords. He failed to coordinate the cities and their resources effectively, and died while fighting in Thrace. ▷ 2.07

ARISTARCHOS OF SAMOS
Greek astronomer of the early 3rd century BC, and the first to propose that the sun revolved around the stars. He also assumed that the Earth moved on an axis and attempted, unsuccessfully, to measure the size of the solar system. ▷ 2.10

ARISTOTLE
Greek philosopher born in the northern Aegean (384–322 BC). Aristotle studied with PLATO in ATHENS before embarking on an extraordinary intellectual career which penetrated almost every area of philosophy, the sciences, ethics and politics. He is chiefly remembered for his system of logic, as a founder of the discipline of zoology and for his thoughts on the nature of man. His work dominated medieval scientific thinking and some aspects of it were of value as late as the 19th century. ▷ 2.08, 2.09

ARMAGH
Ancient city in Ireland (now in Northern Ireland) and the ecclesiastical capital established by ST PATRICK in about AD 445.

ARMINIUS
GERMAN war leader born in about 19 BC who inflicted a humiliating defeat on the Romans in the TEUTOBURGERWALD (near modern Osnabruck) in AD 9, effectively ending the Roman attempt to conquer Germany. ▷ 2.19

ARSACIDS
Dynasty ruling the Parthian empire in PERSIA, founded by Arsaces I (r.c.247–c.211 BC). He was a king of the IRANIAN-speaking PARNI peoples, who asserted the independence of the kingdom of Parthia from the SELEUCIDS in 238 BC. His successors extended their rule over Persia and Mesopotamia, notably under Mithradates I in the 2nd century BC. Under their rule the Parthians emphasized continuity with the Achemenids, but adopted a great deal of HELLENISTIC culture. The dynasty was overthrown by the SASANIANS in the 3rd century AD. ▷ 2.10, 2.11

ARVERNI
Celtic tribe of southern GAUL (in modern Auvergne), whose leader, VERCINGETORIX, led a revolt against the Romans. It was eventually crushed by JULIUS CAESAR at ALESIA (52 BC). ▷ 2.18

ASHOKA
MAURYAN king of India (r.268–233 BC) who brought the Mauryan empire to its zenith by conquering KALINGA in 261. Horrified by the violence of the conquest, Ashoka converted to BUDDHISM, which he made the state religion, promulgating its teachings throughout his empire in laws carved on rock faces and pillars. He convened a Buddhist council at PATALIPUTRA that confirmed the Buddhist canon. His empire broke up through internal factionalism and external pressures in the 50 years after his death. ▷ 2.22

ASIA (ROMAN PROVINCE)
Originally the kingdom of PERGAMON. Made the Provincia Asia in 133 BC, and enlarged under the empire, it occupied much of modern west-central Turkey. A fertile region with abundant natural resources, it was known for its manufactured goods, such as woollen fabrics. It flourished in the early empire but suffered Gothic invasions in the AD 250s and 260s. Many fine archeological remains have survived. ▷ 2.13

ASUKA
Capital of YAMATO Japan from the mid-6th century AD to 710, when Nara became the first permanent capital. The city was a center of Buddhist culture. ▷ 2.25

ATHENS
The dominant Greek city-state of the 5th century BC. Its large territory, ATTICA, and fine trading connections led to Athens' increasing wealth in the 6th century BC. In the 5th century it pioneered a democratic system of government, led the Greeks successfully against two Persian invasions and established a large Aegean empire. Athens brimmed with self-confidence. Culturally it fostered the birth of drama and was an important center for vase painting and sculpture. The PARTHENON, the temple to Athena on the Acropolis, was an architectural and sculptural masterpiece. In the late 5th and 4th centuries BC Athens was home to the philosophers SOCRATES, PLATO and ARISTOTLE. After its defeat by Sparta in

404 BC Athens sank into decline, but the city remained a major cultural center for centuries. ▷ 2.07, 2.08, 2.09, 2.10

ATREBATES

A Gaulish people (probably of continental origin) encountered by the Romans in the area between west Sussex and the rivers Thames and Test. They made treaties with Rome and three *civitates* ("communities") were created: of the Atrebates (capital at Silchester), of the BELGAE (capital at Winchester) and of the Regni (capital at Chichester). ▷ 2.18

ATROPATENE

One of the successor kingdoms of ALEXANDER THE GREAT's empire in northern PERSIA and the Caucasus (now Azerbaijan) set up by the Persian general, Atropates, in 328 BC. Its capital was at Gazaca. It came under Roman control (in the 1st century BC), Parthian and later Sasanian control. ▷ 2.09, 2.10, 2.11

ATTALIDS

Dynasty of kings who ruled over PERGAMON, a kingdom in western Asia Minor carved from the SELEUCID empire, from 241 to 133 BC. Their capital, Pergamon, was an important center of HELLENISTIC culture. ▷ 2.10

ATTALUS I

Founding king (r.238–197 BC) of the ATTALID dynasty, following a major defeat of the (Celtic) Galatians of Asia Minor. He later fought successfully as an ally of Rome against the resurgent power of MACEDONIA. ▷ 2.18

ATTILA

King of the HUNS (r.AD 435–53), Attila undertook a series of military campaigns against Rome from AD 442 until his death in 453. He attacked the Balkan Roman province (442–43, 447), invaded GAUL, where he was defeated by Roman and allied forces at the Catalaunian Plain (451), and finally sacked various Italian cities (452). ▷ 2.16, 2.20

AUGUSTINE, ST

(AD 354–430) Major theologian and preacher who was appointed bishop of Hippo in his native north Africa. Augustine is remembered above all for his autobiographical *Confessions* and *City of God* (which proclaimed that the heavenly kingdom was more important than any earthly city). Augustine was dedicated to upholding the authority of the Latin church as it moved away from its roots in the Greek world and redefined itself.

AUGUSTULUS, ROMULUS

Last emperor (r.AD 475–76) of the western ROMAN EMPIRE who came to power – and was overthrown – while still a child. ▷ 2.16

AUGUSTUS

Born in 63 BC under the name of Octavian, and adopted by JULIUS CAESAR as his heir, he

was a skilled and ruthless politician and military leader. He had a long struggle to gain the leadership of Rome, finally defeating MARK ANTONY (his leading opponent) and CLEOPATRA at ACTIUM in 31 BC. In 27 BC Augustus introduced a new constitutional settlement, which he claimed "restored the republic" but in reality introduced a monarchical type of government. He took the title of *princeps* (first citizen), leaving it to his successors to call themselves *imperator* (emperor) – a term derived from *imperium*, the supreme power to execute the law and command in war, which had belonged to the kings of Rome and then to consuls and other officials.

He received from the senate the title "Augustus" and ruled until his death in AD 14. He enlarged the empire and did much to improve and modernize the living conditions and city control of Rome through such measures as the introduction of safeguards against flood, fire and famine. He also enhanced both Rome's and his own prestige with a major building program that included a new forum, temples, and the creation of the splendid suburb of the Campus Martius. ▷ 2.03, 2.04, 2.13, 2.14, 2.18

AURELIAN

(r.AD 270–75) Born in about AD 215 in the Danube region, he rose to fame by the common route of military success and became emperor in 270 on the death of Claudius II. In his short reign he protected Rome from BARBARIAN invasions (this included the construction of the great Aurelianic wall around Rome), defeated the VANDALS in PANNONIA and the Carpi on the Danube, crushed revolts in PALMYRA and conquered the GALLIC EMPIRE with his defeat of Tetricus in 274 at Chalons. He was murdered in 275 on a campaign against PERSIA. ▷ 2.15

AURELIUS, MARCUS

(AD 121–80) Born in Baetica (Spain), he was related to HADRIAN, of whom he became a favorite. He succeded ANTONINUS PIUS as emperor in 161 and ruled jointly with his adoptive brother, Lucius Verus, until the latter's death in 169. He successfully defended the empire's frontiers in Britain, Spain, Upper Germany, along the Danube and in the east, but by allowing his patently unworthy son COMMODUS to succeed him, he condemned the empire to a long period of political instability. Marcus Aurelius was widely admired as a STOIC philosopher and his *Meditations*, as well as some of his correspondence have survived. ▷ 2.15

AUSTRALIAN ABORIGINALS

The original inhabitants of Australia who first reached the continent 40,000–60,000 ya, at a time when the land bridge with New Guinea still existed. The first settlements in southern Australia and Tasmania date from about 30,000 ya. They lived as hunter-gatherers,

most being nomadic. Engraved and painted figurative art developed about 29,000 ya, and different cultural areas have been identified, based on techniques. Exchange of stones, shells and pigments along a complex of long-distance trade and cultural routes ensured an overall cultural unity, despite the diversity imposed by linguistic and environmental differences (some 260 language groups have been identified). This was expressed above all in the concept of "dreamtime", an awareness of the spirit in the environment.

At the time of the first European contact, there were perhaps 3 million Australian Aboriginals, of whom the largest concentration was in the Murray-Darling region of southeastern Australia. ▷ 2.26

AUSTRO-ASIATIC PEOPLES

Ancestral peoples of mainland southeast Asia – especially Cambodia and Vietnam. Rice farmers, they settled the region before 2000 BC. The relationship between the Austro-Asiatic and AUSTRONESIAN languages is a subject of continuing dispute. ▷ 2.26

AUSTRONESIAN

Cultural group of southeast Asia based on the Austronesian language group that originated in Taiwan before 2000 BC. They spread through the Indonesian and Malayan archipelagoes and into the Pacific islands, where the POLYNESIAN culture developed. Austronesians from Sumatra settled Madagascar in the 1st century AD. The term is also applied to the modern languages of Malaya and Indonesia. ▷ 2.26

AVANTI

Ancient kingdom (*mahajanapadas*) of west-central India. In about 600 BC its capital was at Mahismati (later moved to UJJAIN). It was a major regional power until it was conquered by MAGADHA in the late 4th century BC. The kingdom revived after the fall of the SAKAS but the region gradually became known as Malwa. ▷ 2.22

AVARS

Nomadic people originating from the eastern Asiatic steppes who were driven westward from the region in the mid-6th century AD. By 600 they had established a khanate based on the Great Hungarian Plain and encompassing much of modern Ukraine and eastern Europe. They unsuccessfully besieged Constantinople in 626 in alliance with the Sasanians. They were defeated by CHARLEMAGNE in 791, finally submitting in 795. ▷ 2.17, 2.20

AXUM, AXUMITES

Important trading kingdom in northern Ethiopia that successfully exploited its position on the Red Sea to survive for nearly 1,000 years (1st to 10th centuries AD). CHRISTIANITY arrived at the time of its most powerful king, EZANA, in the mid-4th century, opening up links with Byzantine Egypt. In the 6th century the Axumites temporarily occupied southern Yemen. ▷ 2.21

BACTRIA
Ancient region of central Asia, with its capital at Bactra (modern Balkh), and a province of the Achemenid empire from the 6th century BC. It broke away from the SELEUCID KING-DOM to become an independent HELLENISTIC kingdom in 239 BC, extending its sway into the Indus valley in the early 2nd century BC and campaigning deep into central India. Bactrian influence helped to introduce Hellenistic culture to India. The kingdom was overrun by KUSHAN nomads in about 135 BC. ▷ 2.09, 2.10, 2.11, 2.22, 2.23

BALLCOURT, MESOAMERICAN
Distinctive feature of Mesoamerican cultures from Preclassic times, a large I-shaped court with retaining walls and (in examples from the Classic period) sloping playing areas. The ball game was played between two teams who had to pass a solid rubber ball through a stone ring attached to the side wall. Players wore body protection. The game had cosmological significance and was sometimes associated with human sacrifice.

BARBARIAN
Originally used by the Greeks as a term of abuse for anyone who did not speak GREEK; in the CLASSICAL PERIOD it became a general term for the peoples of north and east Europe and the Asian steppes who did not enjoy a settled or civilized existence. ▷ 2.15, 2.16, 2.17

BASKETMAKER CULTURE
Aceramic cultural group of hunter-gatherers and early farmers in the southwestern region of North America, and precursors of the Pueblo and Anasazi. The tradition began in the early 1st millennium BC (Basketmaker I); Basketmaker II (185 BC–AD 500) saw initial maize cultivation; Basketmaker III (from 500) saw more complex agriculture and developed into the Anasazi tradition. ▷ 2.03, 2.04, 2.05

BASQUES
Indigenous people of northern Spain, culturally distinct since Paleolithic times. Known as Vascones, they successively resist-ed Roman, VISIGOTH and Moorish rule. In the 3rd century AD they were converted to CHRISTIANITY. In the 9th century AD they nominally recognized the overlordship of Charlemagne, but they maintained their own language and identity, and fought for autonomy from France and Spain into the late 20th century. ▷ 2.14, 2.16, 2.17

BELGAE
JULIUS CAESAR subdued a group of this name to the north of the rivers Seine and Marne (modern northern France). They were said to have settled in southeast Britain, but

archeological evidence suggests that there were close contacts across the Channel, rather than major movements of people. ▷ 2.18

BELGICA
The Roman province of Gallia Belgica was formed some time after the Gallic BELGAE were subdued by JULIUS CAESAR in 57 BC. Both archeological remains and ancient sources indicate that this was not an area of uniform culture. ▷ 2.13

BELISARIUS
(c.AD 500–65) General of the eastern ROMAN EMPIRE who reconquered northern Africa and parts of Italy, including Rome, for the emperor JUSTINIAN in the 530s. When Belisarius took RAVENNA in 540 the OSTROGOTHS offered to make him king of Italy. Although he declined the offer, Justinian never trusted him again. ▷ 2.17

BENEDICT, ST
(c.AD 480–c.550) Italian founder of the Benedictine monastic order and author of the famous rule of St Benedict, which served as a model for monastic life throughout the Middle Ages. It stressed obedience, silence and humility. Benedict's first foundation was at Monte Cassino in central Italy. ▷ 2.17

BENEVENTUM (BENEVENTO)
A center, named Malventum, of the Hirpini Samnites that was taken by the Romans some time after 300 BC. It became a flourishing Latin colony, with the more auspicious name of Beneventum, in 268 BC. Under the empire it became a colony for veteran soldiers, and the famous arch of TRAJAN was erected in AD 114. ▷ 2.12

BERBERS
Indigenous people of the northern Sahara and Mediterranean region of north Africa, mainly sedentary farmers in the CLASSICAL PERIOD. Berbers are shown in Egyptian Old Kingdom tomb paintings (c.2400 BC). The Berber kingdoms of NUMANTIA and MAURETANIA arose in about 200 BC but were colonized by the Romans and con-quered by the Arabs in the 7th century AD. In the medieval period invading Bedouins forced them to become nomadic. ▷ 2.15, 2.16, 2.17, 2.21

BETHLEHEM
City of the ancient Holy Land south of Jerusalem, home of King David and birth-place of JESUS. HADRIAN built a shrine to Adonis on the original site of the nativity in AD 135, but CONSTANTINE built the church of the Nativity there in 333 (it was rebuilt by JUSTINIAN I in the 6th century). ▷ 2.06

BINDUSARA
MAURYAN king of India (r.c.293–268 BC), father of ASHOKA. Bindusara campaigned in the Deccan as far south as Karnataka. ▷ 2.22

BITHYNIA
Ancient region of northwest Anatolia that, despite its strategic position, mostly main-tained its independence from Achemenid, Greek and Macedonian rule until the 2nd century BC, when a HELLENISTIC Bithynian kingdom flourished, its capital at Nicomedia. In 74 BC the last ruler bequeathed the state to the Romans, who created a single province of BITHYNIA and PONTUS. Its prosperity continued until the early 2nd century AD. ▷ 2.09, 2.10, 2.13

BODH GAYA
Village in Bihar state, northern India, and the reputed site of the enlightenment of Siddhartha Gautama, the Buddha. ASHOKA built a shrine there in the 3rd century BC that was restored and rebuilt several times, notably in the 7th century AD (and in the 19th century). Bodh Gaya was an important monastic and pilgrimage center until it was abandoned in the 15th century. ▷ 2.22

BONAMPAK
MAYAN site of the late Classic period (AD 600–800), now in Chiapas province, southern Mexico. Discovered in 1946, the site includes several temples as well as some of the best-preserved Mayan frescoes. Showing scenes of war, they revised the old view of Mayan civilization as essentially peaceful. ▷ 2.28

BONONIA, BATTLE OF
Battle fought at the site of modern Bologna in the Po valley in 192 BC, in which the Romans finally conquered the GALLIC Boii, who, along with other Gallic tribes, had occupied the region for centuries. The Latin colony of Bononia was founded in 189 BC. ▷ 2.18

BOSPORUS, KINGDOM OF
Kingdom on the northern coast of the Black Sea from 438 BC to the 3rd century AD. Greek in origin, it was influenced by the local Scythian cultures. Although the kingdom never forgot its Greek roots, it became a loyal ally of ROME and was eventually absorbed by BARBARIAN tribes. ▷ 2.01, 2.02, 2.09, 2.10, 2.15

BOUDICCA
The wife of Prasutagus, a client king of the ICENI of East Anglia. Ill treatment of his family by imperial officials after his death prompted an uprising in AD 60–61. The Iceni, helped by the Trinovantes and led by Boudicca, sacked Camulodunum (Colchester), Londinium and Verulamium (St Albans), but were defeated by Suetonius Paulinus, the local Roman gover-nor, and Boudicca took poison. ▷ 2.18

BRAHMINISM
Early form of HINDUISM that developed from VEDISM in the 2nd millennium BC. It focused on the sacrificial role of the Brahminic (priest-ly) caste and stressed the importance of the supreme power (absolute Self), known as Brahma. By about 500 BC Brahminism had

ossified and was challenged by other forms, including BUDDHISM. Hinduism, which emerged in response to this challenge, placed relatively greater emphasis on other deities and devotional practices. ▷ 2.06

BRASIDAS

Spartan general who captured a number of important Athenian cities in the northern Aegean in the early part of the PELOPONNESIAN WAR, before being killed in 422 BC. ▷ 2.08

BRIGANTES

The largest Iron Age tribe in Britain, with an OPPIDUM at Isurium (Aldborough, north Yorkshire). Queen Cartimandua maintained amicable relations with Rome, but later conflicts resulted in Roman annexation in AD 71–79, the development of a Roman town at Isurium, villas in the countryside, and the exploitation of the local lead deposits by AD 81. ▷ 2.18

BRITANNIA

Name given to Britain as a Roman imperial province. Initially governed from London, it was divided into Upper (capital London) and Lower (York) in the early 3rd century AD, and was further subdivided under DIOCLETIAN. Britannia was prosperous and stable, with agriculture the main occupation, some metal extraction and craft production, and varying degrees of Romanization across the region. Attempts to conquer the whole island of Great Britain failed and Roman power rarely extended north of the Forth–Clyde isthmus. Britannia, in effect, became independent in 410 when the emperor HONORIUS instructed the BRITONS to arrange their own defenses. Most of the former province was settled by the ANGLO-SAXONS in the late 5th century AD. ▷ 2.03, 2.13, 2.15, 2.18

BRITONS, ANCIENT

The Iron Age cultural groups of Britain exhibited a variety of social organizations, though all were mainly dependent on agriculture and separated into tribal chiefdoms with settlement hierarchies headed by various forms of enclosed settlements. Contacts with the continent were especially strong in the south and southeast, where cross-channel trade brought products such as Gallo-Belgic coinage and wine amphorae. ▷ 2.16

BRUTTIANS

An Italic people attested from the 4th century BC in the largely mountainous region of modern Calabria, southern Italy. They ousted the encroaching LUCANIANS and became independent in about 356 BC. In the 4th and 3rd centuries BC they harassed the Greek cities on the coast, and from the 3rd century had a stormy relationship with Rome, alternately becoming an ally and rebelling. ▷ 2.12

BRUTUS, MARCUS JUNIUS

(c.85–42 BC) Roman senator and politician who supported POMPEY the Great but was made governor of CISALPINE GAUL after JULIUS CAESAR's victory in the civil war. In 44 BC he was leader of the republican party and a principal conspirator, with Gaius Cassius Longinus, in the assassination of Caesar. He was defeated at Philippi by Octavian (AUGUSTUS) in 42 BC.

BUDDHISM

Religious philosophy that emerged in India in the 5th century BC, following the teaching of Siddhartha Gautama, the Buddha ("Enlightened One"), who lived and taught in MAGADHA, northern India. In its pure form Buddhism rejects belief in the gods, emphasizing instead the possibility of salvation through an enlightenment achieved by following Buddhist precepts (the Eightfold Path). Some forms of Buddhism, however, worship the Buddha as a god. In the 3rd century AD the tradition divided into two forms: MAHAYANA (Great Vehicle) and THERAVADA (Doctrine of the Elders). Buddhism was taken to China from the 1st century AD, and Japan in AD 552; it traveled to southeast Asia in about AD 400. It lost its hold in India to a Hindu revival (c.600–700), and to the Muslims after 1200. ▷ 2.06, 2.22, 2.23, 2.24

BURGUNDY, KINGDOM OF

The Burgundians were a Germanic peoples who crossed over the Rhine into the ROMAN EMPIRE in strength in AD 406. They formed a kingdom, first in northern GAUL, then in southwestern France, until they were absorbed into the kingdom of the FRANKS in 534. ▷ 2.15, 2.16, 2.17

BUSTA GALLORUM, BATTLE OF

Battle fought in Italy in AD 552 in which the eastern Roman forces, led by NARSES, defeated the OSTROGOTHS, securing imperial control of Italy south of the Po. ▷ 2.17

CAESAR, GAIUS JULIUS

(100–44 BC) Roman general and statesman. Born to a great patrician family, he rose to eminence through military distinction and astute political maneuvering during a troubled period in Roman history. A skilled orator known for his vanity, he was also prepared to take great risks – both personal and financial – to secure advancement. In 49 BC, after lucrative campaigns in GAUL, he invaded Italy and began a civil war as a means of ridding himself of enemies and competition. He eventually defeated POMPEY, his major opponent, and appointed himself dictator for life in 44 BC, so bringing about the final collapse of the ROMAN REPUBLIC.

His liasion with CLEOPATRA did little to increase his popularity. As dictator he introduced the Julian calendar, reorganized the eastern provinces, founded many colonies and increased the number of patrician families, senators, priests and magistrates. Although he refused the title of *rex* (king), he aimed at deification and became increasingly unpopular with his fellow nobles, who eventually assassinated him in 44 BC. ▷ 2.03, 2.13, 2.18, 2.19

CALEDONIA, CALEDONII

The Roman terms for the Scottish Highlands beyond the river Forth, and its inhabitants. This hostile upland zone was never completely conquered by the Romans, though Agricola waged a campaign in 82–83 BC and won the BATTLE OF MONS GRAUPIUS. In AD 197 the Caledonii broke their treaty with Rome. They were suppressed in 209 by SEPTIMIUS SEVERUS, but rose up again in 210–11. ▷ 2.18

CALIGULA

See GAIUS CAESAR

CAMEL

One of two domesticated species: the two-humped Bactrian camel was native to central Asia and may have been used in central and southern Asia by 2000 BC; the single-humped dromedary or Arabian camel was domesticated earlier in the Middle East, but was not introduced to Egypt or the Sahara until about 100 BC – a development that made possible the emergence of trans-Saharan trade. ▷ 2.21

CANNAE, BATTLE OF

Remarkable victory for the CARTHAGINIAN general HANNIBAL (216 BC) against the Romans in southern Italy. The Romans had superior forces but were surrounded by the Carthaginian cavalry. Military historians describe the battle as a classic example of the use of an encircling tactic to defeat the compact Roman forces. ▷ 2.12

CAPPADOCIA

Large region in northeastern Asia Minor bordering on the Black Sea. Originally part of the Achemenid empire, it was partially Hellenized after ALEXANDER's conquests, then became a client kingdom of Rome. Officially made a province of the ROMAN EMPIRE in AD 17, its border marked the empire's eastern frontier. ▷ 2.09, 2.10, 2.13

CARACALLA

Emperor of Rome (r.AD 211–17) who was renowned for his exceptional cruelty. He succeeded SEPTIMIUS SEVERUS and murdered his brother Geta to become sole ruler of the empire. He also extended citizenship to all free inhabitants of the empire.

CARNUNTUM

Important site on the Danube, originally part of NORICUM, then added to PANNONIA in about AD 14. A Roman military base was established there, with a civil settlement some 5 kilometers (3 miles) to the west. MARCUS

Aurelius wrote the second book of his *Meditations* here. The site was destroyed in the Marcomannic wars, then rebuilt. ▷ 2.14

CARRHAE

Ancient Mesopotamian city (also known as Haran) founded by the Assyrians. It was the site of a battle in 53 BC in which the Parthians, relying mainly on their archers, halted a Roman invasion led by Marcus Licinius Crassus. ▷ 2.11, 2.13

CARTHAGE, CARTHAGINIANS

A Phoenician colony on the coast of north-east Tunisia, traditionally founded in 814–813 BC. Carthage enjoyed a good harbor, fertile hinterland and a strategic position in the Mediterranean, and soon planted colonies of its own along the north African and Spanish coasts. It fought the Greeks over Sicily for 300 years, made treaties with Rome in 508 and 348 BC that were favorable to Carthage's monopoly of maritime trade, and developed a large empire. Carthage and Rome eventually came into conflict over Sicily. The three Punic wars (264–146 BC) ended in defeat by Rome and the city's complete destruction. Carthage was refounded as a Roman colony by Julius Caesar, became the capital of Africa Proconsularis and by the 2nd century AD was second only to Rome and Alexandria. Held by the Vandals in AD 439–533, it was captured by Muslim forces in 697. ▷ 2.12

CASSANDER

Son of Antipater who stabilized Macedonia after his father's death in 319 BC and was proclaimed "King of the Macedonians" in 305 BC. His death in 297 saw Macedonia racked by fresh power struggles. ▷ 2.09

CASTE SYSTEM

Social system most fully elaborated in early Hindu India, whereby all members of society are placed within ranked hereditary social groups. The original system allowed for four castes: the *brahmins* (priests) were the highest caste, followed in order by *kshatriyas* (warriors), *vaishyas* (tradesmen) and *shudras* (servants). Further groupings were later introduced. ▷ 2.06

CATO, MARCUS PORCIUS

"Cato the Censor" (234–149 BC) was best known as a leading Roman orator. He served in the army and government, and worked as a lawyer. A forthright man and champion of traditional Roman values, he was also a gifted writer. His output was encyclopedic in breadth but his only surviving work is *De Agri Cultura* (On agriculture).

CAUDINE FORKS

Battle (321 BC) in which the Romans, seeking control of southern Italy, were defeated by the Samnites. The Roman army was forced to pass "beneath the Samnite yoke", a humiliation unique in Roman history. ▷ 2.12

CELTIBERIANS

Graeco-Roman name for the peoples living around the Ebro valley in the eastern Meseta of Spain. Their culture was influenced by Celtic migrants in the 7th to 6th centuries BC and an important type of settlement was the hillfort (*castro*). After a series of wars with locals and Carthaginians (2nd to 1st centuries BC), Rome was victorious. ▷ 2.12, 2.18

CELTIC LANGUAGE

A branch of Indo-European, Celtic is divided into Insular Celtic (Goidelic – comprising Irish, Scots-Gaelic and Manx, and British – comprising Welsh, Cornish and Breton), and Continental Celtic, of which the best known is Gaulish, with many inscriptions dating from the 2nd to 1st centuries BC. Continental Celtic was effectively extinct by the early Middle Ages. Welsh and Breton are the most important surviving Celtic languages. Smaller communities of Scots and Irish-Gaelic speakers survive in remote areas. ▷ 2.14, 2.18

CELTS

An important group of proto-historic Celtic-speaking peoples of central and western Europe and the British Isles. Their origins are probably in the Bronze Age Urnfield and Hallstatt cultures. From the 5nd century BC they were associated with the distinctive La Tène style, which became widespread in central-western Europe and in Britain.

The Celts were organized into aristocratic chiefdoms. Tradition described them as fierce fighters and fine horsemen. They invaded the Classical world, settled in Cisalpine Gaul, sacked Rome in 390 BC, raided Greece, crossed the Hellespont in 278 BC and settled in Galatia in central Anatolia. The Celts worshipped a multitude of gods, they mostly associated with specific localities, such as springs and groves, and had a priestly class known as the druids. From 225 BC Rome gradually extended control over the Celtic territories in northern Italy, Spain and Provence (by the later 2nd century BC). At the same time the Celts in central Europe were being conquered by the Germans. In 58–52 BC Julius Caesar subdued the Celtic groups in Gaul and from AD 43 those in Britain were also defeated. By the 2nd century AD only the Celts in Ireland and the Scottish highlands remained free. ▷ 2.05, 2.09, 2.10, 2.12, 2.18, 2.19

CERRO DE LAS MESAS

Archeological site that was part of the classic Veracruz Gulf Coast civilization, which reached its height between about AD 300 and 600. Its artifacts resemble those of surrounding civilizations of the period and indicate trading links with Teotihuacán, though links with the Olmecs are not clear. ▷ 2.27

CERROS

Late Preclassic period Mayan city in eastern Yucatán, Mexico. A trading center surrounded by extensive canal systems, it was mainly built in the 1st century BC but collapsed not much more than a century later. ▷ 2.28

CHAERONEA

Ancient city of northern Boeotia in Greece and the site of a battle in 338 BC at which Philip II of Macedon defeated the Athenians and Thebans, so winning control of Greece. A second battle (86 BC) saw the defeat of Mithradates VI of Pontus by the Roman general, Sulla. ▷ 2.08

CHAERONEA, BATTLE OF

Decisive battle of 338 BC in which Philip II of Macedon crushed the combined armies of Athens and Thebes. It can be said to be the moment when the great age of the independent city-state came to an end. ▷ 2.18

CHALCEDON, COUNCIL OF

A major council of the early church held at the city of Chalcedon, near Constantinople, in AD 451. It proclaimed that Jesus was of two distinct natures – human and divine. Although many Christian groups refused to accept this, the Chalcedonian formula is still accepted by Christian churches of the West. ▷ 2.16

CHANDRAGUPTA I

Founder of the Gupta dynasty in Magadha, northeast India (r.AD 320–35). He was a local chief who married into the nearby Licchavi tribe in 320 and by the time of his death he controlled a region that included much of modern Oudh and Bihar. ▷ 2.23

CHANDRAGUPTA I MAURYA

Founder of the Mauryan dynasty of north India (r.321–c.293 BC). He conquered Nanda Magadha and came to control most of northern India. In about 305 he defeated Seleucos I to take over the Indus valley and part of Afghanistan. In c.293 he abdicated in favor of his son Bindusara. According to tradition, he became a Jain monk and starved himself to death in 286. ▷ 2.22, 2.23

CHANDRAGUPTA II

Gupta emperor of India (r.AD 380–414) who brought the Gupta empire to its peak by conquering the Western Saka kingdom in Gujarat and Malwa, western India. He made his capital at Ayodhya, supported learning and the arts, and maintained a prosperous and tolerant empire. ▷ 2.23

CHENGDU

City of southwestern China, now capital of Sichuan province. It rose to prominence under the Qin (3rd century BC) and has long been the key to communications between western and eastern China. In AD 221 it became capital of the kingdom of Shu, but fell to Wei in 263. An important trading center since 600, it became a major industrial center in the later 20th century. ▷ 2.25

CHERNOLES
Early Iron Age site (c.750–500 BC) in Moldova and a culture complex characterized by its distinctive pottery, which is found from Poland to the upper reaches of the river Don. This culture is sometimes identified with the ancestral Slavic peoples. ▷ 2.19

CHOLULA
Mesoamerican city, close to modern Mexico City. First occupied in about 500 BC, it later came under the influence of nearby TEOTIHUACÁN. During this period the largest pyramid in Mexico – 55 meters (170 feet) high – was built there. Its forces probably destroyed Teotihuacán in about AD 700, whereafter it became a TOLTEC, MIXTEC and then AZTEC center. It was destroyed by Cortes in 1519, and its inhabitants were massacred. ▷ 2.27

CHOSROES
See KHOSRU

CHRISTIANITY
Religion that developed in the eastern part of the ROMAN EMPIRE in the 1st century AD, that proclaimed the teacher and healer JESUS of Nazareth as the Son of God and savior of the world. Beginning as a Jewish sect, Christianity was given more of a Greek flavor and its beliefs were systematized. The faith spread to Asia Minor, GREECE and eventually to Rome itself, through ST PAUL, by the year AD 60.
Despite frequent persecution at the hands of the Romans, Christianity spread through the empire and was given a major boost by the conversion of the emperor CONSTANTINE in AD 312. It became the official faith of the empire in AD 391, and the Christian church, focused on the pope in Rome, became a force of enduring civilization in the face of BARBARIAN invasions. Conversion of the barbarian kings ensured that Christianity became the dominant religion of Europe, and despite doctrinal divisions (notably between the Orthodox and Catholic churches in 1054, and the Protestant and Catholic churches in the 16th century), it has survived and spread to become the world's largest religion in the 20th century. ▷ 2.06, 2.15, 2.17

CHRYSOSTOM, JOHN
One of the "fathers of the church" (c.AD 347–407), brought up in ANTIOCH. He was a popular preacher and writer on Christian life. Made patriarch of Constantinople in 398, he sought to reform the clergy and bring the court to adhere to strict standards of morality. He fell out with the emperor in 403 and was exiled.

CICERO
A famous Roman orator (106–43 BC) who held political posts and worked as a leading lawyer. His fortunes suffered various reversals during the upheavals of the 1st century BC.

He eventually fell out with the emperor AUGUSTUS and died in 43 BC, a victim of the proscriptions. ▷ 2.13

CILICIA
The eastern part of southern Asia Minor, the more fertile areas of which were settled by Greeks. Its coastline later proved a haven for pirates and it was absorbed as a province of Rome in 80 BC. Its most famous governor was the Roman statesman CICERO, its most famous citizen ST PAUL and its most famous romantic encounter was that between MARK ANTONY and CLEOPATRA at Tarsus. Cilicia later became part of the Byzantine empire. ▷ 2.09, 2.10, 2.13

CIMBRI
Germanic tribe whose migration in the late 2nd century BC from its homeland in Jutland threatened the borders of Roman Italy. The Cimbri defeated the Romans at ARAUSIO in 105 BC, but following a reorganization of the Roman army were themselves destroyed at Vercellae in 101 BC. ▷ 2.19

CLASSICAL PERIOD
The period in Greek history dating from 480 BC (the defeat of the Persians) until the death of ALEXANDER in 323 BC. The Classical period is normally seen as the height of Greek civilization. It includes the great years of Athenian democracy and empire (480–430 BC), the work of the historians HERODOTUS and THUCYDIDES, the major philosophers, SOCRATES, PLATO and ARISTOTLE, and the flourishing of Greek drama.

CLAUDIUS
(r.AD 41–54) Until he was unexpectedly proclaimed emperor of Rome by the Praetorians following the assassination of Caligula (AD 41), Claudius had held a low position in the imperial family. Hampered from childhood by a limp and speech defect (perhaps cerebral palsy), he led a retiring scholarly life, writing histories (in this he was advised by LIVY). As emperor he preserved the peace, enlarged the empire, and paid attention to the welfare of the populace, but he was thought over-influenced by his wives and freedmen. He was poisoned by his wife Agrippina, so that she could ensure the succession of NERO, her son by a previous marriage. ▷ 2.13, 2.14

CLEOPATRA
Last of the Ptolemies, Cleopatra (r.51–30 BC) used her charisma and astuteness to lure two Roman generals, JULIUS CAESAR and MARK ANTONY, into supporting her disintegrating kingdom. She had children by them both. Her stratagems failed when Mark Antony and Cleopatra's forces were defeated by Octavian (later the emperor AUGUSTUS) at ACTIUM in 31 BC, and she committed suicide. She has remained an object of fascination ever since. ▷ 2.13

CLOTHAR
Two Frankish kings of the 6th to 7th centuries AD. Clothar I (r.511–61) was the son of CLOVIS and ruled a third of the Frankish kingdom from Soissons; by 558 he had outlived his brothers to reunite his father's kingdom, conquer BURGUNDY and campaign in Spain. His grandson, Clothar II, was king of Neustria (r.584–629), but ruled the entire Frankish kingdom from 613. ▷ 2.17

CLOVIS
King of the FRANKS (r.AD 481–511) and founder of the Merovingian dynasty. A tribal chieftain, he fought against the Romans and drove them from GAUL in 486. In 493 he married a Burgundian princess and was baptized in about 503, following a victory against the ALEMANNI. A champion of Catholicism, Clovis united the Franks, made Paris his capital and defeated the VISIGOTHS in 507. ▷ 2.17

COBÁ
Classic period MAYAN regional capital in northeastern Yucatán, Mexico, and one of the largest Mayan cities at its peak in AD 400–800. A network of raised roads linked it to neighboring cities. Cobá was defeated by Chichén Itzá in about 900. In the 1970s it was the site of a major excavation. ▷ 2.28

COMMODUS, LUCIUS AURELIUS
Emperor of Rome (r.AD 180–92). Born in about AD 161, Commodus succeeded his father MARCUS AURELIUS in 180, survived an assassination attempt in 182 and from then on effectively left the running of government to a series of favorites. By 191 Commodus was apparently insane, occupying much of his time performing as a gladiator and otherwise abusing his position (this included renaming Rome as the Colonia Commodiana and executing many senators). Laetus had him strangled in 192 and his memory was condemned. ▷ 2.15

CONSTANTINE THE GREAT
(r.AD 306–37) Proclaimed emperor of Rome by his troops in AD 306, Constantine is known for his support of CHRISTIANITY. He defeated Maxentius, his rival for control of the western empire, in 312 with a smaller force. In response to a vision, he had sent his soldiers into battle with crosses on their shields and apparently believed his victory was aided by the Christian God. Constantine subsequently granted Christians toleration (EDICT OF MILAN, 313) and actively promoted Christianity during the remainder of his reign. In 324 he defeated Licinius, who controlled the eastern empire, to become the sole ruler of the ROMAN EMPIRE. In the same year he founded Constantinople on the site of Byzantium as a new capital. Constantine was baptized shortly before his death in 337, near Nicomedia. ▷ 2.04, 2.06, 2.15, 2.16

CONSTANTINIAN DYNASTY

Roman dynasty founded by CONSTANTINE THE GREAT after he won control of the western ROMAN EMPIRE in AD 306. Constantine legitimized and supported CHRISTIANITY. On his death in 337 the empire was divided between his three sons – Constantine II, Constantius and Constans. By 350, however, Constantius was the only survivor. Constantius was succeeded by his cousin JULIAN (361–63), the last of the dynasty, who attempted to restore PAGANISM but died fighting in PERSIA. ▷ 2.15

CONSTANTINOPLE, COUNCILS OF

Two ecumenical councils of the church, held to resolve Christian doctrine. The first (AD 381) was called by the emperor THEODOSIUS and confirmed the doctrine of the Trinity, reiterating the conclusions of the COUNCIL OF NICAEA (325). The second (553) is considered the fifth ecumenical council, convened by JUSTINIAN. It condemned the doctrine of Monophysitism.

COPÁN

Classic period MAYAN city, now in western Honduras. The site was settled by 1000 BC and the city was built from 200 BC, with an artificial acropolis topped by temple-pyramids and a large number of inscribed hieroglyphs. There is also a BALLCOURT. The city reached its peak in the 7th century AD under King Smoke Jaguar, but in 738 it was defeated by its neighbor, QUIRIGUA. By 900 the city had been abandoned. ▷ 2.28

COPTIC LANGUAGE

The Egyptian language written with GREEK letters. It was used in early Christian texts in Egypt and is still used in the ceremonies of the Coptic church. ▷ 2.14

CORINTHIAN LEAGUE

League of Greek cities established at Corinth in 338 BC by PHILIP II OF MACEDON as a means of perpetuating Macedonian control over GREECE. The league was sustained by ALEXANDER THE GREAT but broke up on his death. ▷ 2.08, 2.09

CRASSUS, MARCUS LICINIUS

Roman military commander and politician of the 1st century BC who defeated the rebel slave leader, Spartacus, and was a patron of JULIUS CAESAR. He was killed in battle in 53 BC against the Parthians near CARRHAE in northern Mesopotamia, in a disastrous attempt to emulate Caesar's military achievements. ▷ 2.13

CTESIPHON

Ancient city near Baghdad in modern Iraq that was the winter residence of the Parthian kings from about 100 BC, and was occupied by the Romans in the 1st century AD. It became the SASANIAN capital in AD 226 and was conquered by the Arabs in 63. It was abandoned after the foundation of Baghdad in the following century; the ruined palace of KHOSRU I survives. ▷ 2.11, 2.15

CYNOSCEPHALAE, BATTLE OF

Major battle fought in 197 BC between Philip V of MACEDON and the Romans, which ended in the defeat of the Macedonians and the beginnings of Roman hegemony in GREECE. ▷ 2.10, 2.13

CYRENE

The leading Greek colony in Africa, founded from Thera in about 630 BC. Located in a fertile region near the coast (modern Shahat), Cyrene was prosperous and was noted for its agricultural products and horses. It came under Roman control in 96 BC and continued to exist until the Arab invasions of the 7th century AD. ▷ 2.21

CYRUS THE YOUNGER

Son of Darius II and Achemenid governor of Lydia and Phrygia (western Anatolia) in the late 5th century BC. In a bid for the Persian throne in 401 he assembled an army including more than 12,000 Greek mercenaries, but died in battle at Cunaxa in Babylonia. The campaign was described by XENOPHON, a leader of the Greek army. ▷ 2.08

DACIA

Located in central Europe north of the Danube, roughly equivalent to modern Romania, Dacia was a fertile area with good metal reserves. It became a powerful kingdom under Decebalus in the late 1st century AD. TRAJAN defeated the Dacians in the First (101–02) and Second Dacian Wars (105–06), which are commemorated on TRAJAN'S COLUMN. Under HADRIAN Dacia was divided into three provinces. Gothic invasions in the 3rd century drove out the Romans by AD 270. ▷ 2.03, 2.13, 2.14, 2.15, 2.18

DAKSHINAPATHA

Kingdom of ancient southern India that was conquered by the MAURYAN king BINDUSARA in the 3rd century BC. ▷ 2.22

DAO DE JING

The central text of Daoism, traditionally ascribed to LAO ZI (6th century BC), but composed in about 240 BC. It consists of about 40 short, allusive pieces comprising advice to a ruler or man of wisdom, emphasizing the mysterious energy (qi) unifying and informing all things, and the principles and virtue (te) by which union with this energy can be maintained – the principle of non-action being the most important. The principles of Daoism came to underlie the religious philosophy of much of east Asia. By the early centuries AD, Daoism had incorporated many indigenous beliefs in China and included worship of many deities (including Lao Zi himself) and sacred places. It also developed a distinctive form of monasticism. ▷ 2.06

DARIUS I

Achemenid king of PERSIA (r.521–486 BC). After securing his authority against a series of local revolts, he strengthened the satrap system of government. He continued the policy of restoring the Jewish state and contributed to the rebuilding of the Temple at Jerusalem. His campaign against the SCYTHIANS (513) led him into Thrace, where he crossed the Danube and, following a revolt of the Greek cities of Lydia in 499, he sent an expedition against the mainland Greeks in 490; it was turned back at MARATHON. He planned a second expedition, but died before it could go ahead. ▷ 2.07

DARIUS III

Achemenid king of PERSIA (r.336–330 BC). During his reign, ALEXANDER THE GREAT of MACEDON invaded, defeating Darius at Issus (333) and Gaugamela (331). Darius fled to BACTRIA but was murdered, bringing the Achemenid empire to an end. ▷ 2.09

DEAD SEA SCROLLS

Manuscripts discovered in 1947 in a cave at QUMRAN in the West Bank, near the Dead Sea. They contain fragments of the Old Testament and other biblical texts, and formed the library of the ESSENES Jewish community, which was destroyed in AD 68. They have revealed much about the diversity of the Jewish faith at the time of JESUS.

DECIUS

Roman emperor (r.AD 249–51) whose short reign was occupied with war against the Carpi and GOTHS, and the attempt to shore up the empire by reinvigorating the Roman state cults. Decius was defeated and killed in 251 in a battle with the Goths at Abrittus. ▷ 2.15, 2.19

DEKELEIA

Village in Attica that came to prominence during the PELOPONNESIAN WAR, when it was occupied by the Spartans (413 BC). The Spartans closed the Athenian silver mines and lured part of the slave population from ATHENS. ▷ 2.08

DELIAN LEAGUE

League of Aegean city-states formed under the leadership of ATHENS in 478 BC to continue hostilities against PERSIA. Its original meeting place was DELOS, but Athens assumed ever greater control of the league and its meetings were moved there in about 454 BC. By the 440s the league had effectively become an Athenian empire. ▷ 2.07, 2.08

DELOS

Aegean island and important cult center of Apollo and Artemis from the 8th century BC onwards. It was the headquarters of the DELIAN LEAGUE between 478 and 454 BC. In Roman times the island became a major slave-trading center. ▷ 2.07

DEMOCRACY, GREEK
Greek democracy had its roots in the people's assemblies of Dark Age Greece. In some city-states, predominantly in ATHENS in the 5th century BC, the assembly – which all male citizens had the right to attend – eventually became the center of political power, with the *demos* (the people) also taking turns to be magistrates and jurors. With its demands for intense commitment from citizens, Greek democracy would not have been possible without slave labor. ▷ 2.01, 2.07, 2.09

DEMOCRITOS
Greek philosopher from Abdera in Thrace famous for the theory (c.420 BC) that all matter was made up of atoms which moved through empty space to make different combinations, and thus the observable substances of the physical world. ▷ 2.08

DEMOSTHENES
The greatest of the Athenian orators (384–322 BC), he is remembered above all for his impassioned denunciations of the ambitions of PHILIP II OF MACEDON. He could do little to save his city, however, and ATHENS was defeated by Philip in 338 BC. Despite the defeat, Demosthenes remained a leading statesman in Athens until his death. ▷ 2.08

DEMOTIC LANGUAGE
The language used by the people of ancient Egypt. The word "demotic" also described the script used to write everyday documents. Demotic Egyptian was resilient enough to survive centuries of rule by GREECE and Rome. ▷ 2.14

DIADOCHI, WARS OF THE
General term for the wars that broke out at the death of ALEXANDER THE GREAT in 323 BC and lasted until the BATTLE OF IPSUS (301 BC), stabilizing the empire as a number of smaller states. Diadochi is Greek for "successors". ▷ 2.02, 2.09, 2.10

DIASPORA, JEWISH
Literally "scattering", the forcible dispersal of the Jews and by extension the communities that formed as a result. The exile into Babylon (587–537 BC) was the first such dispersal, and led to permanent Jewish settlements in Mesopotamia and Egypt. A second Diaspora occurred in the AD 130s: following the crushing of a Jewish revolt by the Romans, Jews were banished from much of JUDEA and from Jerusalem. They settled widely throughout the Middle East, north Africa, GREECE and southern Italy. Further dispersals of Jews took place in and after the Middle Ages. ▷ 2.06

DIOCLETIAN
Roman emperor from AD 284 to 305. After 50 years of debilitating civil war and BARBARIAN raids, Diocletian reorganized the empire so that power was shared between four imperial rulers (the TETRARCHY) and resources were organized more effectively in the service of defense. The emperor's status was elevated to that of a semi-divine figure closely associated with the traditional Roman gods. One result of this was the persecution of Christians. It was largely due to Diocletian that the empire survived into the 5th century. ▷ 2.14, 2.15

DIONYSIOS I, KING OF SYRACUSE
A talented general, Dionysios (430–367 BC) seized power in Syracuse in 405 BC and mobilized the city's power against the CARTHAGINIANS, who occupied western Sicily. Though he effectively organized resources and men from mainland Italy, he never dislodged the Carthaginians. He prided himself on his Greek heritage, even competing as a dramatist in ATHENS. ▷ 2.08

DUMNONII
A local tribe occupying Devon, Cornwall and part of Somerset, probably defeated by VESPASIAN. After 43 BC it became a self-governing *civitas* ("community") under the FLAVIAN DYNASTY, with a capital at Isca (Exeter). Romanization mainly affected Isca, while many continued to live in traditional enclosed farmsteads. ▷ 2.18

DURA EUROPOS
An ancient Mesopotamian city founded in about 300 BC by a SELEUCID general. In the late 2nd century BC the city was taken by the Parthians and became a center for trade between the Mediterranean and central Asia. In AD 165 it was seized by the Romans and built up as a frontier fortress, but in 256 it was taken and destroyed by the Sasanians. Archeological excavations of the site during the 1920s and 1930s provided considerable detail about the everyday life of the period. ▷ 2.11

EARLY INTERMEDIATE PERIOD
The period in South America between the Early Horizon and MIDDLE HORIZON periods, dating from 200 BC to AD 500. This period saw the first states in the Andean region, notably MOCHE and TIAHUANACO. ▷ 2.27

EASTER ISLAND
Remote island in the eastern Pacific Ocean, settled in about AD 300 by the Polynesians. By 1000 a great phase of building and artistic production had begun, including the island's great stone sculptures. A unique writing system, known as Rongorongo, was developed. The first Europeans arrived briefly in 1722, but, before the visit of Captain Cook in 1774, deforestation brought social collapse, civil war and severe population decline. ▷ 2.26

ECNOMUS, BATTLE OF MOUNT
A decisive victory, fought off the southern coast of Sicily, of the Roman fleet, led by Regulus, over the CARTHAGINIANS (256 BC) in the First PUNIC WAR. Regulus went on to invade north Africa but was captured. ▷ 2.12

EDESSA
HELLENISTIC city of northern Mesopotamia, taken by the Romans in the 1st century AD. In AD 260 it was seized by the SASANIANS under SHAPUR I, following a prolonged siege in which the Roman emperor VALERIAN was captured. An important Christian center within the Byzantine empire, it fell to the Arabs in 639. ▷ 2.11, 2.13, 2.15

EL BAUL
Ancient MAYAN site in the southern Guatemalan highlands dating from the late Preclassic and Classic periods (c.AD 100–800). Its monumental sculptures include the earliest example of the "long-count calendar", dated to AD 36. ▷ 2.28

EL MIRADOR
Ancient MAYAN site in central Yucatán, Mexico, and one of the earliest important Mayan centers. It flourished from 150 BC to AD 150, when it lost its pre-eminence to nearby TIKAL. It included the largest known pyramid of the Western Hemisphere, some 70 meters (230 feet) high. The site was rediscovered in 1926, but not excavated until the 1970s. ▷ 2.28

EL TAJÍN
Large Mesoamerican site in eastern Mexico, the chief ceremonial center of the late Classic period VERACRUZ civilization, mostly built between AD 600 and 900. The Pyramid of the Niches (with 365 niches in four storeys) is the oldest of its structures. The site includes at least three separate BALLCOURTS. El Tajín displays close cultural contacts with the Classic MAYA. ▷ 2.27

ELLORA
Religious site in Maharashtra state, western India. Cut into a cliff face are more than 30 temples of Hindu, Buddhist and Jain origin dating from AD 500 to 900. Covered in sculptures, the Hindu Kailasa temple (mid-8th century), dedicated to Shiva, is the finest of the group. ▷ 2.06

EPAMINONDAS
(c.420–362 BC) Outstanding general and leader of THEBES in the 370s BC. His victory at Leuctra in 371 broke the power of Sparta and made Thebes the leading Greek city-state. Theban power collapsed following his death at the BATTLE OF MANTINEA in 362.

EPHESUS
Important Ionian city on the coast of Asia Minor whose earlier remains include a great temple to its patron goddess Artemis (c.600 BC). It flourished in HELLENISTIC times and was adopted as the center of the Roman administration of the province of Asia. It

received a famous visit from St Paul. Ruins of the ancient city, many of them from late antiquity, remain in abundance. ▷ 2.06, 2.07, 2.08, 2.13, 2.14, 2.15

Ephthalite ("White") Huns
Group of central Asian peoples of uncertain origin, but probably from the eastern steppes. Their relationship with the Huns, who invaded Europe under Attila, is uncertain. They conquered the eastern provinces of the Sasanian empire in the AD 480s and in the early 6th century gained control of northwestern India, where they were known as the Hunas. They were driven out of India in 528, and from Persia in 557. By 600 they had been defeated in central Asia by the Turks. ▷ 2.11, 2.20, 2.23

Epicuros
Greek philosopher (341–270 BC) who believed that the search for pleasure is the true end of life. By pleasure Epicuros did not mean luxury or decadence but peace of mind through friendship and intellectual pursuits. He believed that there was no life after death and that the gods had no role in a world that was physically self-sufficient. ▷ 2.09

Eratosthenes
Greek intellectual and scholar (c.285–194 BC) who was chief librarian at the famous library in Alexandria. Remembered as a poet, historian, literary critic, philosopher, geographer and mathematician, among his achievements was the most accurate measurement of the Earth's circumference. ▷ 2.10

Ermanaric
Ostrogothic king (d.c.AD 372) who ruled in the Ukraine region. He was killed – or committed suicide – when the Huns invaded the region. ▷ 2.19

Essenes
The smallest of the three Jewish sects of the last centuries BC, who lived a communal life apart from the rest of society. Their main center was probably at Qumran, where the Dead Sea Scrolls were found. The relationship between the teachings of the Essenes and those of Jesus remains controversial.

Euboea
Large Greek island running north–west to south–east alongside the east coast of central Greece. Its prominence in Greek history dates from the 10th to 8th centuries BC, when it occupied an important position in the reviving Aegean trade. The settlement at Lefkandi (10th century BC) was the most advanced in Greece. The cities of Chalcis and Eretria established many colonies in the northern Aegean and pioneered Greek trade in the west in the 8th century BC, but exhausted themselves in the Lelantine War (late 8th century BC). The island later came under strong Athenian influence. ▷ 2.07

Euclid
Greek mathematician (fl.300 BC) remembered for his *Elements*, a textbook of elementary mathematics, which remained the standard introduction to the subject for 2,000 years.

Euripides
Major Athenian tragedian (c.480–407 BC) whose plays explore the full breadth of human emotions – from religious ecstasy (the *Bacchae*) to the desperation of a thwarted woman driven to infanticide (*Medea*), and the obsessive nature of lust (of Phaedra for her stepson in *Hippolytus*). Euripides was inventive and controversial, prepared to question the justice of war, even when Athens was in the midst of one, and ready to rewrite traditional myths so as to heighten their emotional impact. ▷ 2.08

Ezana
King of Axum (r.c.AD 325–55) who conquered the kingdom of Kush and established Axum to include most of modern Ethiopia. In about 350 he was converted to Christianity by Frumentius, a Syrian. He set up the Ethiopian church and resisted the attempts of the Roman emperor Constantine II to bring Axum under the influence of the Roman Catholic church. ▷ 2.21

Flavian dynasty
Roman dynasty composed of the emperors Vespasian (r.AD 69–79), his elder son Titus (r.79–81) and younger son Domitian (r.81–96). ▷ 2.15

Former Han
See Han dynasty

Franks
Germanic tribal confederation settled in the eastern Rhineland in the 3rd century AD. They were divided into the Salian Franks and the Ripuarian Franks. The Salian Franks, under their leader Clovis, defeated the Romans in Gaul in 486. Thereafter he re-united the two groups and established a kingdom that included most of modern France and the Rhineland. ▷ 2.15, 2.16, 2.17, 2.19

Funan
The first kingdom of Cambodia. Founded in the 1st century AD, it grew to become a regional power by 400. Funan was heavily influenced by Hindu culture from India and flourished as a result of trade with India and China. Its capital was at Vyadhapura, near Banam. Funan was overthrown by Chen-la in the mid-6th century. ▷ 2.26

Gaius Caesar
Emperor of Rome (r.AD 37–41), often known as Caligula ("Little Boot"), who succeeded Tiberius. He had a reputation for extravagence, cruelty and megalomania, and he may have suffered from epilepsy. He was assassinated in 41.

Galatia
A region in central Asia Minor that was settled by migrating Celtic tribes in the 260s BC; it retained a Celtic flavor throughout the imperial period. Galatia was also a Roman province from 25 BC, in much the same area. It was to these Galatians that St Paul addressed his epistle. ▷ 2.10, 2.13, 2.18

Galen
(c.AD 130–c.201) One of the most important physicians of the ancient world. Originally from Pergamon, Galen spent much of his life working in Rome. His work covered every area of medicine, but he is particularly remembered as a pioneer in physiology and anatomy, drawing careful conclusions through the dissection of animals. His intellectual authority, based on the 3 million words of his surviving work, dominated the later Western medical tradition.

Galerius
(AD 250s–311) Roman general who was appointed by the emperor Diocletian as a Caesar in 293, one of two subordinates of the emperor himself, to help coordinate the defense of the Roman empire. Galerius was responsible for a massive defeat of the Persians (AD 298), which brought lasting peace on the empire's eastern frontier. Initially a persecutor of the Christians, he announced a policy of toleration shortly before his death. ▷ 2.15

Galla Placidia
Roman empress (r.AD 388–450) who was the daughter of Theodosius. After being held hostage by the Visigoths, she married the Visigothic king Ataulf. After his death she became co-empress with Constantius, and later ruled as regent for her son, Valentinian III.

Gallia, Galliae
See Gaul

Gallic empire
"Empire" declared in AD 260 by a usurper, Postumus, on the northern frontier of Gaul. A former Roman commander, Postumus, had his own legions and the support of the local aristocracy, and at one point he claimed control over Gaul, Britain and France. He successfully defended the frontier against German tribes, but after his death his territory was reabsorbed into the empire (AD 274). ▷ 2.15

Gandhara
Satrapy in the remote far east of the Achemenid empire that was conquered by Alexander the Great and was the scene of one of his greatest victories (at Hydaspes in 326 BC). Ceded by the Seleucids to the Indian Mauryan empire in 303 BC, it was an important avenue for east–west trade. ▷ 2.10, 2.23

GAOZU (LIU BANG)

Emperor of China (r.206–195 BC) and the founder of the HAN DYNASTY. He was born a commoner, Liu Bang, but rebelled against QIN rule following the death of SHI HUANGDI. He won control of the kingdom of Han (western China) in 206 and unified China by 202 BC, firmly suppressing internal dissent. Gaozu, his posthumous title, meant "high progenitor". ▷ 2.24

GAUGAMELA, BATTLE OF

See ALEXANDER THE GREAT

GAUL

The fertile and prosperous area roughly equivalent to modern France. Occupied by Celtic and related tribes, the south was influenced by Greek colonization. Gaul gradually came under Roman control. The Mediterranean south formed Provincia (modern Provence) in 121 BC, and in 58–50 BC JULIUS CAESAR conquered the rest. AUGUSTUS divided it into four provinces – Narbonensis, Lugdunensis, AQUITANIA and BELGICA. It was seized by GERMAN peoples in the 5th century AD. ▷ 2.10, 2.12, 2.13, 2.14, 2.15, 2.16, 2.17, 2.18, 2.19

GAUL, CISALPINE

The prosperous region of northern Italy, comprising the Po plain and mountain fringes from the Apennines to the Alps, that was influenced and settled by CELTS from the mid-1st millennium BC. By 191 BC the region had fallen to Rome. It was heavily colonized and soon became a Roman province. ▷ 2.12, 2.13, 2.18

GAULS

See CELTS; GAUL

GEDROSIA

Desert area along the coast of the Arabian Sea, originally part of the Achemenid empire, then conquered by ALEXANDER and ceded by the SELEUCIDS to the Indian MAURYAN empire in 303 BC. ▷ 2.10

GEPIDS

A Germanic tribe that lived in the southern Baltic region during the early centuries AD and had moved to central Europe (modern Hungary) by AD 300. The Gepids attacked the ROMAN EMPIRE but were defeated at the Battle of Naissus in 296. They were instrumental in the defeat of the HUNS at the BATTLE OF NEDAO in 454. ▷ 2.15, 2.16, 2.17, 2.19

GERMANIA

The Roman name for the lands east of the Rhine occupied by "free" GERMANS, and for the imperial provinces (Germania Inferior, Germania Superior) on the west bank of the lower and middle Rhine. These were lost in the 5th century AD to Frankish and Alamannic peoples. ▷ 2.13

GERMANS

Tribes of the ancient world that originated in southern Scandinavia and moved into central Europe and Germany in the last centuries BC. The German language was distinct by about 500 BC; a thousand years later it had split into its distinctive northern, eastern and western forms. The German peoples included the GOTHS, LOMBARDS, FRANKS, ANGLO-SAXONS, Burgundians and Scandinavians. ▷ 2.19

GOSPELS

The accounts of the life of JESUS that form the first four books of the NEW TESTAMENT of the Bible, probably written by the evangelists Mark (the earliest), Matthew, Luke and John from AD 70 to 100, using oral reminiscences and perhaps a common lost written source, sometimes known as Q.

GOTHS

One of the ancient GERMAN peoples. According to legend they derived from southern Scandinavia and crossed to northern Germany, where they defeated the VANDALS. In the 2nd century AD they moved to the Black Sea region and began to raid the ROMAN empire. They divided into the OSTROGOTHS (eastern Goths, living in the Ukraine) and VISIGOTHS (western Goths, in modern Bulgaria). ▷ 2.19

GRACCHUS, TIBERIUS

(163–133 BC) Roman reformer. As tribune of the plebs in 133, he attempted to enact a land reform policy. He was opposed by the senatorial elite – many of whom had acquired large areas of public land illegally – who murdered him. Tiberius' brother GAIUS attempted to continue his work, but he too was murdered in 121 BC. ▷ 2.13

GREECE, ANCIENT

Greece is a mountainous country and the ancient Greeks were a hardy, independent people. Their first civilization, the Mycenaean, rested on agriculture but also extended trade networks. A Dark Age followed the collapse of the Mycenaeans (1100 BC), but by the 8th century BC a growing population saw the emergence of small city-states – urban centers dependent on their local territory. The city-state fostered sophisticated politics, marble temples, drama and philosophy. There were also shrines – Olympia and Delphi among them – that offered a cultural focus for all Greeks, including those who migrated through the Mediterranean.

After success in the PERSIAN WARS (490 and 480 BC) there were no limits to Greek self-confidence, and the 5th century BC saw the achievements of the CLASSICAL PERIOD. In the late 5th century BC, however, the PELOPONNESIAN WAR between ATHENS and Sparta (which Athens lost) heralded the decline of the city-state and Greece was crushed by Macedonian expansion in the late 4th century BC. Following ALEXANDER's conquests, Greek culture spread throughout Asia and into Egypt in the HELLENISTIC PERIOD, and remained intact after absorption into the ROMAN EMPIRE. The Byzantine empire that emerged in the 6th century AD was still culturally a Greek state. ▷ 2.07, 2.08, 2.09, 2.10, 2.13, 2.14, 2.15, 2.16, 2.17

GREEK LANGUAGE

Greek is known to have been spoken by the Mycenaeans. By the 8th century BC there were numerous dialects, though these were mutually intelligible and the Greeks themselves spoke of being united by language. The first written Greek texts date from the 8th century BC. By the 3rd century BC a standardized Greek, *koine*, was used across the expanded Greek world.

GREGORY OF TOURS

(AD 538–93) Born into an aristocratic Romano-Gallic family, Gregory became – like many of his family before him – bishop of Tours. He is chiefly remembered for his history of the 6th century FRANKS. ▷ 2.17

GREGORY THE GREAT, POPE

Roman aristocrat and pope from AD 590 to 604, who founded the modern papacy. Breaking with the older eastern Christian centers, Gregory the Great invoked the supremacy of Rome and worked tirelessly to impose his authority on the church in the west. The conversion of the English was his most lasting achievement. ▷ 2.17

GULF COAST CIVILIZATIONS

The Mesoamerican cultural traditions that flourished in eastern Mexico in the first seven centuries AD (Classic period). Based on the styles found in urban centers, three such traditions have been identified, those of Cerro de las Mesas, Remojadas and VERACRUZ. All showed considerable exchange with the more dominant TEOTIHUACÁN, as well as Olmec and MAYAN influences. ▷ 2.27

GUPTA EMPIRE

Indian dynasty, rulers of the northeastern state of MAGADHA, who extended their sway across the north and east of the subcontinent from AD 320 until the mid-6th century. The influence of the dynasty was felt even more widely. It was founded by CHANDRAGUPTA I; other notable figures were his son SAMUDRAGUPTA and CHANDRAGUPTA II. Despite their shrinking empire, the dynasty continued to rule Magadha until 720. The Gupta period is considered a time of classic Hindu culture in India. ▷ 2.23

HADRIAN

Emperor of Rome from AD 117 to 138. Born in Spain, he became the ward of TRAJAN, his father's cousin, who adopted him as his successor. He spent much of his reign touring the provinces, notably building Rome's first artificial frontiers – the limes – a continuous palisade linking the frontiers of the Rhine and Danube, and HADRIAN'S WALL in northern England. He made an impact on the empire by these provincial tours, his frontier policy and his intellectual and reforming interests. Worn out and ill, he spent his last years in Rome and died in AD 138. He was buried at his great mausoleum, the present Castel Sant'Angelo, in the center of Rome. ▷ 2.11, 2.13, 2.15

HADRIAN'S WALL
The frontier wall between the Roman province of BRITANNIA and the unconquered tribes to the north, it runs 129 kilometers (80 miles) from Wallsend-on-Tyne to Bowness-on-Solway. Built for the emperor HADRIAN in about AD 122–26 (the eastern part in stone, and the western in turf), it had fortified gateways every Roman mile, observation towers in between and 12 forts, including Housesteads and Chesters. It was replaced in about 142 by the ANTONINE WALL further north, then came back into use during the 160s, until the garrison was finally removed in the 4th or early 5th century AD. ▷ 2.15

HAN DYNASTY
Dynasty of ancient China that came to power in 206 BC and ruled until AD 220 (with a brief interruption in AD 9–23, when the usurpur WANG MANG seized power). Before AD 9 the dynasty was based at Chang'an and is sometimes known as the Western or Former Han; in the period after the capital was moved to Luoyang in 23, it is known as the Eastern or Later Han. Established by GAOZU, the dynasty introduced many of the traditional forms of Chinese imperial rule, including the centralized education system and bureaucracy. ▷ 2.24

HANNIBAL
Among the greatest of generals, Hannibal led CARTHAGE's forces in the Second PUNIC WAR (218–202 BC), attempting to weaken Rome so that it no longer presented a threat to the CARTHAGINIAN empire. In spite of his military brilliance he underestimated Rome's strength. He surprised the Romans by invading Italy from the north, across the Alps, but despite the astounding victories at the rivers of Ticinus and Trebia, at Lake Trasimenus and at CANNAE, Hannibal was eventually bottled up in southern Italy. With the Carthaginians under pressure in Spain and north Africa, he returned to Carthage in 205 BC and was defeated by the Romans under SCIPIO AFRICANUS at the Battle of Zama (202 BC). Enemies at home forced him into exile in the east. In 183–182 BC Rome persuaded Prusias I of BITHYNIA to surrender him, but Hannibal avoided this by taking poison. ▷ 2.02, 2.12

HASMONEANS
See MACCABEES

HECATAEUS
Geographer from Miletus who wrote an account of the Mediterranean and its peoples in about 500 BC. His critical approach to the stories he was told foreshadows the more sophisticated work of the historian HERODOTUS, who acknowledged his debt to Hecataeus. ▷ 2.18

HELLENIC LEAGUE
An alliance of THEBES and ATHENS that was established after clever Athenian diplomacy in 340 BC, in the vain hope of defending GREECE against PHILIP II OF MACEDON. The combined Greek armies were defeated at the BATTLE OF CHAERONEA in 338 BC. ▷ 2.01, 2.02, 2.08

HELLENISTIC PERIOD
Period in Greek history dating from the death of ALEXANDER THE GREAT (323 BC) to the conquest of Egypt by Rome (30 BC), and a time when Greek culture spread across Asia and into Egypt as a result of Alexander's conquests. Kingdoms rather than city-states formed the centers of power, but it was a time of vigorous intellectual activity in the sciences, mathematics and astronomy (above all in ALEXANDRIA) and in philosophy (EPICURUS and the STOICS in ATHENS). In the event, the Hellenistic kingdoms were unable to offer a coordinated response to the expansion of Roman power, and the Greek world became part of the ROMAN EMPIRE. ▷ 2.10

HELLESPONT
The first part of the straits at the entrance to the Black Sea, control of which was essential for exporting the resources of the sea to the Mediterranean world. It is the site of a famous bridge that was constructed by XERXES of PERSIA to convey his troops from Asia to Europe in 480 BC. ▷ 2.07

HERACLEA, BATTLE OF
A battle fought in 280 BC in southern Italy between the Romans and King PYRRHUS of Epirus (319–272 BC), who was supporting the Hellenic Tarentines against Rome. Pyrrhus won, but suffered crippling losses, giving rise to the term "Pyrrhic victory". ▷ 2.12

HEROD THE GREAT
The son of a local Judaean ruler, Herod was used by the Romans as a client king of JUDAEA (r.40–4 BC) and the surrounding area. For much of his reign he was a trusted king who utilized his wealth flamboyantly in a number of building projects (most notably in the rebuilding of the Temple at Jerusalem), as well as in lavish benefactions in the Greek world. The last years of his reign were marked by increasing unrest, which resulted in full Roman control of Judaea on his death. As he was the Herod of the Nativity stories, the date of his death has helped to date the birth of JESUS to about 4 BC. ▷ 2.13

HERODOTOS
Greek historian (c.484–c.425 BC) best known for his history of the PERSIAN WARS, as much a survey of the known world as a narrative account of the wars themselves. He was the first chronicler of the past to test his sources critically and is seen as the father of history. Throughout his historical work, Herodotos stresses the moral supremacy of the Greeks over their opponents on the grounds that Greeks lived in free states, while the Persians lived under a tyranny. ▷ 2.07, 2.08

HIMYARITE KINGDOM
Kingdom of southern Arabia from the 2nd to 6th centuries AD. The Himyars were a tribe within the kingdom of Saba, and they maintained Sabean culture in their kingdom. The capital was at San'a. The kingdom was destroyed by an invasion from the Ethiopian kingdom of AXUM in the 520s. ▷ 2.21

HIPPARCHOS OF BITHYNIA
Important Greek astronomer of the second half of the 2nd century BC, who used Babylonian records and his own careful observations to predict the movements of the stars and eclipses. In the course of his work he invented trigonometry. He was an important influence on the astronomer CLAUDIUS PTOLEMY. ▷ 2.11

HIPPO REGIUS
Ancient city on the north coast of Africa, near modern Annaba, Algeria, founded by the CARTHAGINIANS in the 4th century BC. It was later the capital of the kingdom of NUMIDIA. From the 2nd century BC it was a Roman colony. During the Christian era it became a bishopric and St AUGUSTINE was bishop there from AD 395 to 430. The city was taken by the VANDALS in the 430s and later flourished under the Arabs.

HIPPOCRATES
Greek physician of the 5th century BC, from the island of Cos. A highly influential figure in medical history, he is associated with the idea that the patient must be treated as a whole, and that the physician must put the needs of the patient first. He also stressed the importance of diet.

HISPANIA, HISPANIAE
Roman provinces of the Iberian peninsula. Two provinces were formed in 197 BC from territory conquered during the Second PUNIC WAR – Hispania Citerior and Ulterior. Both were gradually extended inland in campaigns against native peoples, and were renamed TARRACONENSIS and Baetica respectively after AUGUSTUS completed the conquest of Iberia in 19 BC. ▷ 2.15

HOHOKAM CULTURE
An early culture of southern Arizona in southwestern North America, that flourished from c.AD 300 or earlier. Beginning as hunter-

gatherers who also grew maize, they had developed a full farming way of life by AD 800 and built a complex system of canals to irrigate the land. Cotton was also developed as a major crop. BALLCOURTS have been discovered at some of their ritual centers, including Snaketown, suggesting the influence of Mesoamerica. The Hohokam culture collapsed during the early 15th century. ▷ 2.04

HONORIUS

Roman emperor who ruled the western empire from AD 395 to 423. While he secluded himself at RAVENNA, Rome was sacked by the VISIGOTHS under ALARIC (AD 410) and a massive BARBARIAN invasion of GAUL (406–07) led to the beginning of the disintegration of the empire. ▷ 2.16

HSIEN-PI (XIANBI)

TUNGUSIC nomadic people from Manchuria who threatened the northeastern border of China in the 3rd century AD, and overran the northern plains in the following century. The TOBA were a branch of the Hsien-pi. ▷ 2.24, 2.25

HSIUNG-NU

See XIONGNU

HUARI (WARI)

Site in the highlands of PERU around which an empire emerged in about AD 500 to dominate the region from Cuzco to the coast throughout the MIDDLE HORIZON PERIOD. The site was abandoned by about 1000. The Huari built roads and well-planned cities (notably Pikillacta), features that were later adopted by the INCAS. ▷ 2.27

HUARPA CULTURE

Site in the Peruvian highlands around which a small state was created during the EARLY INTERMEDIATE PERIOD (200 BC–AD 500). The Huarpa developed terracing and irrigation canals. ▷ 2.27

HUNS

TURKIC nomadic pastoralist peoples from central Asia, who moved westward into Hungary in about AD 372, causing many Germanic tribes in eastern Europe to flee to the ROMAN EMPIRE. They forced the Roman emperor THEODOSIUS to pay them tribute in 432. In the 440s the HUNS, under ATTILA, invaded the Balkans, followed in 451 by GAUL and Italy. After Attila's death in 453 they were destroyed by a confederation of Germanic tribes at the BATTLE OF NEDAO in PANNONIA. ▷ 2.16, 2.17, 2.19, 2.20, 2.23

IAZYGIANS

Sarmatian tribe that threatened the Danube region and the northern borders of the ROMAN EMPIRE from the 1st century AD. DIOCLETIAN successfully campaigned against them at the end of the 3rd century.

IBERIANS

Ancient inhabitants of southeast Spain who are of unknown origin and spoke a non-Indo-European language. By the mid-1st millennium BC they were in the early stages of state formation, but further development was halted after conquest by the CARTHAGINIANS. They lost their distinctive identity under Roman rule. ▷ 2.11, 2.15, 2.18

ICENI

British tribe in Norfolk and Suffolk that made a treaty with CLAUDIUS but subsequently rebelled in AD 60–61 under BOUDICCA. After its defeat a *civitatis* ("community") was established at the capital of Venta (Caistor-by-Norwich). The wealth of this area is expressed in gold and silver hoards, such as those from Mildenhall and Thetford. ▷ 2.18

ILLYRIANS

Large group of related Indo-European peoples found in Classical times, east of the Adriatic. They harassed MACEDONIA and Epirus, sided with POMPEY during the civil war, and were only slowly brought under effective Roman control. By 11 BC they were incorporated in the Roman province of Illyricum, which was later divided into the provinces of Dalmatia and PANNONIA. ▷ 2.01, 2.02, 2.07, 2.08, 2.12, 2.18

INDO-SCYTHIANS

See YUE QI

IPSUS, BATTLE OF

Decisive battle fought in central Phrygia in 301 BC, at which ANTIGONOS, contender for ALEXANDER THE GREAT's empire, was defeated and killed by SELEUCOS. It marked the end of any attempt to maintain Alexander's empire intact. ▷ 2.09, 2.10

IRANIAN LANGUAGES

Group of languages within the Indo-European family. It includes Avestan and Old Persian (the languages of ancient Iran), as well as the languages of many of the historic nomadic peoples of central Asia, including Parthian, Soghdian and Saka (also known as Khotanese). Modern Persian has an Iranian basis, as have the languages of Afghanistan, Kurdistan and Tajikistan. ▷ 2.20

ISSUS RIVER, BATTLE OF

See ALEXANDER THE GREAT

JAINISM

A religion of India founded in the 6th century BC by Mahavira as an offshoot of Vedic Hinduism. Its central tenet is the release from the material world through austerity, and a strict code of *ahimsa* (non-violence) to all living creatures. Jainism rivaled BUDDHISM in the early centuries BC, but declined after 100 BC. Its influence has remained strong in India; it affected Mahatma Gandhi, among others. ▷ 2.06

JEBEL BARKAL

Archeological site in Sudan, the burial site of the kings of Mero from 590 BC to AD 330. The tombs were built in the form of steep pyramids; many other signs of Egyptian influence were discovered there. ▷ 2.21

JENNE-JENO

Ancient town on the upper Niger, now in Mali, west Africa. The site was occupied from AD 400 or earlier. Its walls, the first to be built in sub-Saharan Africa, were erected in 400–800, and a distinctive style of terracotta pottery developed there. It flourished as a center for trade and agriculture until the 14th century, when the site was abandoned in favor of the nearby city of Jenne. ▷ 2.21

JEROME, ST

(c.AD 347–420) Outstanding biblical scholar responsible for the translation of the GREEK and Hebrew texts of the Old and NEW TESTAMENTS into an authoritative LATIN version (the VULGATE BIBLE). A troubled and abrasive figure, Jerome found it difficult to reconcile his love of the classics with his Christian faith, but his own learning survives in his works on monasticism and celibacy. ▷ 2.06

JESUS OF NAZARETH

Teacher and healer (c.6 BC–AD 30) of JUDEA, believed by Christians to be the Christ or Son of God. He preached a form of messianic Judaism, but was crucified on the charge of blasphemy against the Jewish faith. His followers believed in his resurrection and a sect grew up in which he was the Savior. Initially limited to Jews, this sect – known as the Christians – was broadened to accept Greeks and other non-Jews by ST PAUL, who proclaimed the message throughout the Roman world. The life and teachings of Jesus were set down in the four GOSPELS between AD 70 and 100. ▷ 2.06

JIN

Wealthy and powerful kingdom of northern China that emerged in the Springs and Autumns period (8th–6th centuries BC) and flourished in the early part of the Warring States period (from 480 BC). It gradually weakened and split up in about 400 BC to form the nucleus of Wei, ZHAO and HAN. ▷ 2.24

JIN DYNASTY

Chinese dynasty ruling from AD 265 to 420. Its founder, WUDI, ruler of the northern kingdom of Wei, conquered the southern kingdom of Wu, briefly uniting China under his rule. His successors lost control of Wei after 280, but the dynasty retained its control in the south. ▷ 2.24, 2.25

JUAN-JUAN

A confederation of nomadic peoples of east Asia, dominated by the Mongols, who succeeded the XIONGNU to control Manchuria in AD 400–553, frequently threatening northern China. Following the collapse of the confederation at the hands of the Blue Turks, part of the Juan-juan known as the Avars moved into eastern Europe. ▷ 2.20

JUDAS MACCABEUS
See MACCABEES

JUDEA
A kingdom of southern Palestine that gained its independence briefly from the SELEUCIDS in the 160s BC, and again from 140 BC. Judea became a Roman province in the 40s BC under a client king, later King HEROD (r.37–4 BC). Judea came under Roman rule in AD 6 and was ruled alternately by Herod's descendants and by Roman officials. The province was renamed Syria Palestina after the Jewish revolt of the AD 120s.

JUGURTHA
King of NUMIDIA who reigned from 118 to 104 BC and the grandson of MASSINISSA. From 112 Jugurtha tried to maintain the independence of Numidia from Roman rule, but he was captured in 105 and executed the following year.

JULIAN
(AD 331–63) After some highly successful campaigns on the northern borders of the ROMAN EMPIRE, Julian succeeded his cousin Constantius as emperor in 361. The last of the pagan Roman emperors, he attempted, without success, to stem the advance of CHRISTIANITY. He was killed campaigning in PERSIA. ▷ 2.15

JUNAGADH
Town in Gujarat state, west India, with Buddhist and Hindu remains which date from the 3rd century BC. It was the capital of Gujarat in the early centuries AD. A large-scale irrigation project was carried out there by ASHOKA in the mid-3rd century BC and a rock outside the town bears an inscription by him. ▷ 2.22, 2.23

JUSTINIAN
(AD 482–565) Ruler of the eastern ROMAN EMPIRE from 527. One of the dominating figures of late antiquity, Justinian attempted the reconquest of the western empire, with some success, in north Africa, southern Spain and Italy. Counted among Justinian's major achievements was the codification of Roman law and the construction in Constantinople of Hagia Sophia – one of the great buildings of antiquity. He hoped to create a united Christian church but his attempts to enforce doctrinal unity simply led to greater fragmentation among Christian groups in the east. Justinian's wife Theodora, a former circus artiste, often played an influential role, particularly in his religious policies. ▷ 2.17

JUTES
Germanic tribe from Jutland, one of the three main groups to invade Britain in the 5th century AD. Little is known of their history prior to the invasion. The Jutes mainly settled in Kent and the Isle of Wight. ▷ 2.16

KALINGA
Ancient kingdom of eastern India, now in northern Andhra Pradesh state. It was conquered by MAGADHA in about 340 BC, but seceded before being reconquered by ASHOKA in 261 BC. Following the collapse of the MAURYAN EMPIRE Kalinga regained independence and its prosperity was based on flourishing trade with southeast Asia. It was conquered again by the GUPTAS, and finally disappeared in 1324 at the hands of the Delhi sultanate. ▷ 2.22

KAMINALIJUYÚ
Ancient Mesoamerican site, close to Guatemala City. It was first inhabited in about 1500 BC and flourished from 300 BC. Under the influence of TEOTIHUACÁN, it was one of the largest MAYAN cities of the Classic period, with more than 200 mounds and pyramids. The site was abandoned by AD 1000. ▷ 2.28

KANISHKA
King of the KUSHAN state of central Asia (r.c.AD 100–30). Ruled from Peshawar, his kingdom encompassed northern India, Afghanistan and part of central Asia. Remembered as a patron of BUDDHISM, his empire provided early contacts that led to the introduction of Buddhism to China. He was also in contact with the ROMAN EMPIRE, and the Gandhara style of art, which fused Hellenistic and Indian traditions, flourished under his rule. During his reign a Buddhist council was held in Kashmir that led to the formation of MAHAYANA BUDDHISM. ▷ 2.23

KARMA
In Hinduism, the law that governs the effects of actions on the subsequent condition of the soul, especially with regard to the process of reincarnation. The doctrine of *karma* developed in the 5th century BC.

KEYHOLE TOMBS (KOFUN)
Monumental tombs of the YAMATO period monarchs of Japan (3rd to 7th centuries AD). Named after their distinctive shape (also known as "square-front, round-back tombs"), the largest examples were built on the Yamato plain. The tomb of the emperor Nintoku, at Mozu in central Honshu, is up to 500 meters (1600 feet) in length, and consists of a mound surrounded by a triple moat. ▷ 2.25

KHARAVELA
King of KALINGA in east India (r.c.AD 50). He was a follower of JAINISM but campaigned successfully both in the Deccan and in southern India. ▷ 2.22

KHOSRU (CHOSROES) I ANUSHIRVAN
SASANIAN emperor of PERSIA (r.AD 531–79), known as "of immortal soul" and as "the just". He extended Sasanian power in BACTRIA, Sogdiana, the Middle East and the Yemen, and reformed the empire, reorganizing taxation and the bureaucracy and maintaining a mainly professional army. He encouraged the arts and welcomed many Greek scholars to Persia. The palace at CTESIPHON is said to date from the period of his reign. ▷ 2.11

KHOSRU II
SASANIAN emperor of PERSIA (r.AD 591–628) who campaigned successfully against the eastern ROMAN EMPIRE in Mesopotamia from 602, taking Damascus in 613, ALEXANDRIA in 616 and CHALCEDON in 617. His conquests were reversed in 622–27 by the eastern Roman emperor, Heraclius, despite an expedition to besiege Constantinople in 626. Following final defeat at Nineveh, Khosru was assassinated. His reign is remembered as a time of courtly splendor and administrative centralization, but his war with the eastern ROMAN EMPIRE fatally weakened Persia on the eve of the Arab invasions. ▷ 2.11

KHOTAN
City now in Xinjiang province, western China, one of the oasis cities on the SILK Route, and the site of the first introduction of BUDDHISM to China in the 3rd century BC. It was the scene of a battle in AD 90 when the Chinese defeated the Kushans. The city's main period of prosperity came during the Islamic era, from the mid-8th century. ▷ 2.23

KO HUNG
Chinese philosopher, alchemist and theorist of Daoism (AD 253–333) who developed the Daoist search for the elixir of life in his work, *He Who Holds to Simplicity*. His work incorporated Confucian ethics and criticized the individualism of earlier Daoists.

KOFUN PERIOD
Name given to the early YAMATO period of Japanese history (AD 300–550), named after its distinctive "old tombs" (*kofun*) and especially the huge KEYHOLE TOMBS. During this period the first states and confederations emerged in Japan, and Shinto shrines, such as those at Ise, were built.

KUJALA KADPHISES
Founder of the KUSHAN state (r.c.AD 25–75) in BACTRIA. He invaded north India and conquered the Western Sakas in about 50. ▷ 2.23

KURGAN
Distinctive barrow of the STEPPE peoples of southern Russia and eastern Europe, usually the burial site of a chieftain or group of notables. The earliest *kurgans* date from the 4th millennium BC, and distinctive culture areas can be traced as far west as the Danube

and Adriatic regions. The practice continued through the Catacomb grave cultures of the Bronze Age into historical times, among the Scythians and Sarmatians. ▷ 2.20

KUSHAN EMPIRE
Central Asian empire, established by a sub-group of the YUE QI nomads, that was based in BACTRIA and founded by KUJALA KADPHISES in the 1st century AD. The empire grew by 100 to incorporate most of modern Afghanistan, Pakistan and much of northern India as far east as Varanasi, as well as Turkmenistan and Uzbekistan. BUDDHIST in faith and eclectic in culture, the Kushans contributed to a mixing of Greek, Roman, Persian, Indian and Chinese influences throughout the region. The empire declined in the 4th century. ▷ 2.10, 2.11, 2.20, 2.21, 2.22, 2.23

LA TÈNE CULTURE
A Swiss lakeside deposit of votive metalwork at La Tène that has given its name to an archeological culture, and to the later Iron Age period in Europe, dating from about 450 until the Roman conquest. The La Tène style first developed in the area from the Marne to the upper Danube, and was used on fine bronze vessels, armor, horse gear and jewelry for the aristocracy. It is characterized by elegant, stylized curvilinear animal and vegetable forms, with elements from Scythian animal designs and the Hallstatt geometric tradition. La Tène cultural material soon appeared over a larger area, including parts of Britain. ▷ 2.18

LAO ZI
Chinese philosopher (fl.6th century BC), traditionally the author of the DAO DE JING (now known to have been compiled in the 3rd century BC) and founder of Daoism. Little is known about his life for certain, but many legends survive, including stories of his meeting in old age with his younger contemporary, Confucius. ▷ 2.06

LAPITA CULTURE
A cultural tradition of the western Pacific, named after an archeological site in New Caledonia, where a distinctive style of pottery decoration was discovered in the 1950s. It arose in the Bismarck archipelago in about 1600 BC and spread through the island chains of MELANESIA, reaching Fiji, Samoa and Tonga by 1000 BC. The Lapita culture is considered ancestral to the Polynesian identity and can be used to trace the migration routes of the Polynesians. ▷ 2.26

LATER HAN
See HAN DYNASTY

LATIN LANGUAGE AND ALPHABET
Belonging to the Italic group of Indo-European languages (including Faliscan, Umbrian and Oscan), Latin is first attested by inscriptions from Latium dating to the early 1st millenium BC. The alphabet is based on a southern Etruscan type, which is itself adapted from a Greek model. As Rome extended its territory, Latin spread as the main language of Italy and many other parts of the ROMAN EMPIRE. Classical Latin is best defined by the Latin literature of about 90 BC to about AD 120. Vulgar Latin was the spoken language of the mainly illiterate population, and its regional dialects developed into the ROMANCE LANGUAGES. ▷ 2.14, 2.17, 2.18

LAURION
The Laurion silver mines in southern Attica were among the most productive in the Greek world, and made a vital contribution to ATHENS' prosperity. The Athenian navy, which defeated the Persians, was built largely out of their proceeds. The mines were owned by the state, leased out to citizens and mined by slaves, whose working conditions were appalling and life expectancy short. ▷ 2.07

LEONIDAS OF SPARTA
King of Sparta (r.490–480 BC) who was responsible for the defense of the pass at THERMOPYLAE against the invading Persian army of XERXES. He and his 300 companions died heroically after they were outflanked by the Persians. ▷ 2.07

LEPTIS MAGNA
Phoenician trading station founded in about 600 BC on the coast of Tripolitania, north Africa. The continued prosperity of the city derived largely from the fertile hinterland, which by the late republic was producing considerable quantities of olive oil. The city was embellished with fine municipal buildings, built by the emperor SEPTIMIUS SEVERUS (who was born there), and many Roman remains are visible. It fell into decline from the 4th century AD. ▷ 2.21

LICCHAVIS
Tribe of northern India in modern Bihar state that maintained a distinct identity from the 6th century BC to the 4th century AD, when they established a dynasty in NEPALA. Unlike other states of the region, they maintained a republican form of government. ▷ 2.23

LIU BANG
See GAOZU

LIVY
Roman historian (59 BC–AD 17) who formed part of the circle of AUGUSTUS and encouraged the young CLAUDIUS to become a historian. He spent 40 years writing his own monumental history of Rome, from its origins to 9 BC, in 142 books (of which 35 have survived) – the Ab Urbe Condita. ▷ 2.13

LOMBARDS
Ancient Germanic peoples, one of the SUEVI tribes, who lived in northwest Germany in the 1st century AD. In 400 they lived in modern Austria and in the mid-6th century they settled PANNONIA. In 568, led by Alboin, they invaded northern Italy, setting up a Lombard kingdom that flourished in the 7th and 8th centuries.

LONG WALLS OF WEI, ZHAO AND YAN
Walls built in the north and west of China by three of the leading kingdoms in the Warring States period, in the 4th and 3rd centuries BC, to protect China from nomadic incursion (and, in the case of Wei, from invasion by QIN). Mainly built of earth, the northern walls were about 100 kilometers (60 miles) further north than the line of the later Great Wall of China. ▷ 2.24

LUCANIA, LUCANIANS
Roughly equal to modern Basilicata, southern Italy, this mountainous zone was said to be occupied by a group of tribes, including the Oenotrians, Chones, and Ausonians. Greek colonization began along the coast in about 700 BC, and between about 420 and 390 BC the Oscan Lucani took control of the region (except for the Greek cities). Urban sites developed in about the 4th century BC, which may have been organized in a league. The area was generally hostile to Rome, but came under its control by the late republic and prospered under the empire. ▷ 2.12

LUOLANG
Ancient name for Pyongyang, capital of a HAN Chinese colony (also known as Nangnang) founded in about 108 BC on the site of an earlier Korean town. It was capital of the Korean Koguryo kingdom from AD 313, and later of Koryo. ▷ 2.24, 2.25

LUSITANIA, LUSITANIANS
A Celticized region of western Iberia that was inhabited by various groups, including the Lusitani, Vettones and Celtici. The Lusitani were attacked by Rome and finally fell to JULIUS CAESAR in 61 BC. The region formed part of Hispania Ulterior and in 27 BC became part of the Augustan province of Hispania Lusitania. It was an important source of metals and its fish sauce was widely exported. By AD 411 Lusitania had come under BARBARIAN control. ▷ 2.12, 2.13, 2.18

LYSIMACHOS
General of ALEXANDER THE GREAT who built up a large kingdom after his death in 323 BC. It eventually included Thrace (the province allocated to Lysimachos by Alexander), MACEDONIA and parts of Asia Minor. Lysimachos was defeated and killed by SELEUCOS in 281 BC and his kingdom disintegrated. ▷ 2.09, 2.10

MACCABEES
Priestly Jewish family who led a revolt against the SELEUCID dynasty in the mid-2nd century BC. From 166 it was led by Judas Maccabeus,

who occupied Jerusalem in 164 and rededicated the Temple, but was killed in 161. The conflict continued until the late 140s BC, after which JUDEA became an independent kingdom ruled by the Maccabees (or Hasmonean) family until civil war in 63 BC led to Roman intervention by POMPEY. The family continued to resist the Romans until 30 BC, when Hyrcanus II was put to death. ▷ 2.10

MACEDON, MACEDONIA

Macedonia occupies the strategically important area between the Greek peninsula and the Balkans. Ruled by the Teminid dynasty from about 650 BC, Macedonia was converted into a powerful and prosperous state by PHILIP II (r.360–336 BC), who laid the economic and military foundations for the success of his son, ALEXANDER THE GREAT. Macedonia survived as a kingdom into HELLENISTIC times, but was eventually defeated by Rome at the BATTLE OF CYNOSCEPHALAE (197 BC) and later broken up (148 BC). It is not clear whether the Macedonians spoke a GREEK dialect or a language independent of Greek, but they had absorbed many Greek influences by the 4th century BC and Alexander's conquests spread Greco-Macedonian culture far into Asia. ▷ 2.07, 2.08, 2.09, 2.10, 2.12, 2.13

MACEDONIAN WAR, FIRST

Conflict between Philip V of MACEDON and ROME in 214–205 BC, and the first time Rome directly intervened in the Greek peninsula. Rome had been roused by Philip's alliance with HANNIBAL. The war ended in stalemate but warfare was to be renewed in 201 BC and Philip was comprehensively defeated at CYNOSCEPHALAE in 197 BC. ▷ 2.10

MAGADHA

Kingdom of the lower Ganges valley and by about 700 BC one of the 16 *mahajanapadas*, ("great realms"), with a capital at PATALIPUTRA. Under King Bimbisara (c.543–491 BC) Magadha became the dominant power in India, annexing neighboring kingdoms such as Anga and Kosala. From the 4th to 2nd centuries BC it was the center of the NANDA and MAURYAN empires. ▷ 2.22, 2.23

MAGNESIA, BATTLE OF

Important battle fought in 190 BC, the climax of the war between the SELEUCID king ANTIOCHUS III and ROME. Antiochus was defeated and forced to cede the west coast of Asia Minor to Rome's ally, PERGAMON. ▷ 2.10, 2.13

MAHABHARATA

Indian religious and literary epic poem comprising more than 90,000 couplets. Compiled from earlier sources by about AD 400, it tells the story of a princely feud said to have occurred before 1000 BC and offers insights into the proper conduct of kings and warriors, and the correct behavior for those seeking rebirth. Part of the text, known as the *Bhagavad Gita*, comprises the most important Hindu text and describes advice given by the god Krishna to a prince, Arjuna, as he prepares for battle.

MAHAYANA BUDDHISM

Literally meaning "greater vehicle", the tradition of BUDDHISM mainly practiced in China, Japan and Tibet. This tradition taught that the Buddha himself was the temporary earthly manifestation of a transcendent quality, and that the goal of Buddhists should be to achieve the status of *bodhisatva* – one who has postponed his enlightenment while working for the salvation of all. ▷ 2.06

MAIDEN CASTLE

One of the largest hillforts in Britain, near Dorchester, southern England. Begun in the early Iron Age, the hillfort was later extended to fortify the entire hill and rebuilt until the hilltop was defended by four massive concentric sets of ramparts and ditches. By 50 BC the site had become the tribal capital of the Durotriges, with coinage and imported Gallo-Roman luxuries. Excavation has revealed evidence of its sack by VESPASIAN's legion, including piles of slingshot and a war cemetery. The population was moved to the site of Durnovaria (Dorchester) and the hill-fort was abandoned.

MAKKURA

Ancient kingdom of Africa centered on the Nile in the modern Sudan. Arising in the 6th century AD, it was converted to CHRISTIANITY in about 550 and conquered its northern neighbor Nobatia in the 8th century. It was overthrown by the Arabs in 1317. ▷ 2.21

MANCHING

Large Celtic oppidum in Bavaria, southern Germany, on low-lying ground on the southern bank of the Danube. By the 2nd century BC it had earth ramparts 7 kilometers (4.5 miles) long, containing a complex of regularly laid out houses with workshops supplying a wide range of crafts. Manching fell to the Romans in 50 BC. The site was excavated from 1955. ▷ 2.18

MANETHO

Egyptian priest (fl.c.305–285 BC) who composed an important history of Egypt in Greek. His division of the Egyptian pharaohs into dynasties has survived; though confusing in parts, it has proved of great value to historians.

MANI

Persian philosopher (c.AD 216–76) and founder of MANICHAEISM. He was of Zoroastrian background but the religion he preached from 242 incorporated aspects of BUDDHISM and CHRISTIANITY. He successfully sought converts throughout the SASANIAN empire until 272, when his followers were persecuted. He was executed for heresy in 276. ▷ 2.11

MANICHAEISM

The religion preached by MANI, combining elements of ZOROASTRIANISM, BUDDHISM and CHRISTIANITY, in the 3rd century AD in PERSIA. Following Mani's death in 276, the religion spread throughout the ROMAN EMPIRE (especially north Africa), where it became a powerful Christian heresy by the 4th century, proscribed by the emperor JUSTINIAN. Manichaeans preached the fundamental conflict between the spiritual, good realm of God, and the material, evil realm of Satan. The term was generally used for any similar dualist heresy in the Middle Ages, but a truly Manichaean sect survived in central Asia until the 13th century. ▷ 2.06

MANTINEIA, BATTLE OF

Battle of 418 BC fought in the central Peloponnese during the PELOPONNESIAN WAR. The SPARTANS crushed a combined force of Athenians, Argives and Mantineians, and in doing so ensured their control of the Peloponnese for another 30 years. One of the largest hoplite battles known, it involved perhaps 20,000 infantry. ▷ 2.08

MARATHON, BATTLE OF

Famous Athenian victory in 490 BC over the Persians on the plain of Marathon in northern Attica, that effectively marked the defeat of DARIUS I's invasion of GREECE. Outnumbered, the Athenians stretched their lines and enveloped the Persian army. Some 192 Greeks and an estimated 6,400 Persians died. The victory helped create the myth of Athenian pre-eminence among the Greeks, though the "run" with the good news from Marathon to ATHENS – the inspiration for the modern marathon – is probably fictional.

MARCOMANNI

GERMAN tribe that forms part of the SUEVI group. In the 1st century BC they migrated from central Germany into Bohemia and were trading partners of the Romans. In AD 167 they invaded the ROMAN EMPIRE but were expelled from Italy by MARCUS AURELIUS. ▷ 2.15, 2.19

MARCOMANNIC WARS

Wars fought by Rome in AD 166–73 and 177–80 against the MARCOMANNI, a west GERMAN (Suevic) tribe which had migrated from Saxony and Thuringia (c.100 BC) and finally settled in Bohemia, establishing a powerful kingdom there. The wars began when they invaded PANNONIA and DACIA in 166. The most dangerous period for Rome was when MARCUS AURELIUS was defeated in 170 and the Marcomanni and Quadi of Slovakia crossed the Danube, swept over the Julian Alps and besieged AQUILEIA. Rome fought back and the Marcomanni were defeated as they tried to recross the Danube with their booty. The wars continued until 180, and were depicted on the column of MARCUS AURELIUS in Rome. ▷ 2.15

MARDONIUS
Persian general and son-in-law of DARIUS I. He played an important part in settling the Ionian revolt and restoring PERSIA's prestige in Thrace in the 490s BC. Chosen by XERXES to be his leading general for the invasion of 480 BC, Mardonius was left in charge of the campaign of 479 BC but was defeated and killed at the BATTLE OF PLATAEA. ▷ 2.07

MARIUS, GAIUS
(c.157–86 BC) Roman politician and soldier responsible for perfecting Rome's legionary army. Beginning in 104 Marius reformed the Roman army and turned it into a professional force. His reforms immediately proved their worth when he defeated the TEUTONES at Aquae Sextiae and the CIMBRI at Vercellae in 102 and 101 BC, both peoples who had previously inflicted serious defeats on Roman armies. He came into conflict with Sulla in 88 BC over command of an expedition to the east and was forced into exile. Returning in 87, he was elected consul but died shortly afterwards. ▷ 2.13, 2.19

MASADA
Small plateau, 457 meters (1,500 feet) high, on the Dead Sea. Accessible only by a steep path, it became the site of King HEROD's most spectacular fortress residences, including two lavishly decorated palaces, a garrison-block, baths and storerooms. In the ZEALOT rebellion against Rome it was the last stronghold to be taken, falling in AD 73 or 74, after a six-month seige by Flavius Silva. Most of the 960 defenders were reported to have commited suicide rather than surrender. ▷ 2.13

MASSINISSA
King of NUMIDIA, north Africa (r.c.202–148 BC), who fought in Spain in 212 for the Carthaginians against Rome. He changed sides in 204; in return the Romans helped him gain the throne. He built a strong Numidian state in the early 2nd century and forcibly developed agriculture there among the previously pastoralist BERBERS. ▷ 2.12

MATHURA
Ancient city of central India, now in Uttar Pradesh state. It is the traditional birthplace of the Hindu god Krishna and one of the seven holy cities of Hinduism. It was the center of a school of Hindu arts and culture from the 2nd century BC, notably in the KUSHAN and GUPTA periods. Most of the Hindu remains were destroyed by Muslims from the 16th century. ▷ 2.22, 2.23

MAURETANIA
Area of north Africa whose name means "land of the moors". Its population mainly

consisted of the Moorish branch of the BERBER group. Much of the region was mountainous or rocky, but the lowland zones were fertile and its chief exports were wine, precious woods and purple dye. Phoenician trading stations were established along the coast in the 8th and 7th centuries BC. Kingdoms were formed by the late 3rd century BC, and were gradually amalgamated. In 33 BC Mauretania passed to Roman control, and in c.AD 44 CLAUDIUS constituted two Mauretanian provinces. ▷ 2.13, 2.21

MAURICE
Eastern Roman emperor (r.AD 582–602) who, despite inheriting a virtually bankrupt empire that was threatened by BARBARIANS, successfully kept its borders intact. Maurice benefited from peace with the Persians, which allowed him to concentrate on other enemies, such as the AVARS. His armies mutinied in 602 and Maurice was murdered by the mutineers' leader, Phocas. ▷ 2.17

MAURYAN DYNASTY
The first dynasty to build an empire extending across most of the Indian subcontinent. It was founded by CHANDRAGUPTA I MAURYA (r.321–c.293 BC), who took over MAGADHA and built an empire that reached beyond the Indus into Afghanistan, claiming part of ALEXANDER's easterly conquests. Its capital was PATALIPUTRA. His successors BINDUSARA and ASHOKA extended the empire to the south. It began to decline in the late 3rd century BC, and the dynasty finally collapsed c.185 BC. ▷ 2.22

MAUSOLEUM
The burial place of MAUSOLOS of Caria at Halikarnassos, one of the Seven Wonders of the Ancient World, completed in about 350 BC. A gargantuan structure complete with a central platform, colonnades and a pyramid, it was typical of the more extravagant approach to rulers' tombs seen in the HELLENISTIC PERIOD. ▷ 2.08

MAUSOLOS
Ruler of Caria (377–353 BC), Mausolus enjoyed a semi-independent role within the Persian empire and had extensive contacts with the Greek world, annexing neighboring islands such as Rhodes and Cos in the 350s BC. He instigated the building of the MAUSOLEUM as his tomb. ▷ 2.08

MAXIMIAN
Roman emperor (r.AD 286–305) who ruled as the western "Augustus" after DIOCLETIAN divided the empire into two. He abdicated with Diocletian in 305, but subsequently became embroiled in a civil war for the succession and committed suicide in 310.

MAYAN CIVILIZATION
Ancient Mesoamerican civilization centered on the Yucatán peninsula of modern Mexico,

Guatemala and Honduras. The Maya people settled the region by about 1000 BC; the so-called Preclassic period continued to AD 250, by which time the first Mayan cities – such as TIKAL – were established. In the Early Classic period (AD 300–600) Tikal and the other cities of the central lowlands were dominant, and in the Late Classic period (600–800) Mayan civilization reached its peak, based on a large number of small, independent city-states. In the Postclassic period the center of gravity shifted to the north, as CHICHÉN ITZÁ, influenced by the Toltecs, became dominant, while environmental crisis caused civilization to decline in the south. The Maya were gradually conquered by the Spanish; the last state fell in 1697. ▷ 2.28

MELANESIA, ANCIENT
Region of the Pacific northeast of Australia, south of the Equator, comprising New Guinea, the Solomon Islands, New Hebrides, New Caledonia, the Bismarck archipelago and Fiji. Melanesia was the home of the LAPITA culture (which was to develop into the Polynesian culture) in about 1600 BC, though other pottery traditions, including that of Mangaasi on Vanuatu, also flourished from 700 BC. ▷ 2.26

MENCIUS (MENGZI)
Chinese philosopher (371–289 BC) who traveled throughout China promoting the teachings of Confucius to the kings of the various Warring States. His teaching is known from his writings, *The Book of Mencius*. His reputation languished until the 11th century AD, when his work was republished as one of the *Four Books* of Confucianism.

METAURUS RIVER, BATTLE OF
Battle fought in 207 BC in Umbria between Roman forces and the younger brother of HANNIBAL, Hasdrubal, who was bringing reinforcements to Hannibal from Spain and GAUL. Hasdrubal was defeated and killed, so ending CARTHAGE's last hope of victory in Italy. ▷ 2.12

MEXICO, VALLEY OF
One of the centers of ancient civilization in Mesoamerica, known to the indigenous population as Anahuac. About 80 x 60 kilometers (50 x 40 miles), the valley was fertile and agriculturally productive by 200 BC, when the city of TEOTIHUACÁN was founded. It later became the center of the Toltec and Aztec civilizations. ▷ 2.27

MICRONESIA
The western Pacific north of the equator, comprising the Caroline, Marshall, Mariana and Gilbert islands, as well as Nauru. The archeology of this region is incomplete, but it appears that it was settled in the 1st millennium BC from the south, west and southeast. Most Micronesians speak Malayo-Polynesian languages. A remarkable ceremonial center

was built at Nan Madol on the island of Pohnpei (Caroline Islands) from the 9th century AD; it was probably no longer in use by the 16th century. ▷ 2.26

MIDDLE HORIZON PERIOD
Period in South America from AD 500 to 1000, distinguished by the spread of the HUARI culture around the region. The period culminated with the collapse of both the Huari and TIAHUANACO empires, marking the start of the Late Intermediate period. ▷ 2.27

MILAN, EDICT OF
Edict issued in AD 313 by CONSTANTINE THE GREAT and his co-emperor Licinius, granting toleration of all religious sects throughout the ROMAN EMPIRE. The main beneficiary was CHRISTIANITY, which, in addition to toleration, gained the financial and moral support of the emperor. ▷ 2.15

MILVIAN BRIDGE, BATTLE OF
Major battle fought north of Rome in AD 312, in which CONSTANTINE THE GREAT defeated Maxentius, his rival for the western empire, and assumed control of the west. Later legends told of the support, through a vision of a cross, of God. ▷ 2.15

MIN-YUE
Ancient state of the AUSTRO-ASIATIC YUE peoples of southeast China, now in Fujian province. It flourished from the 4th century BC and was conquered by the HAN DYNASTY in the late 2nd century BC. ▷ 2.02, 2.03, 2.24

MITHRADATES VI
(r.120–63 BC) The greatest HELLENISTIC king of PONTUS in Asia Minor, and Rome's most dangerous enemy in the 1st century BC. He extended his control to include the Crimea, CAPPADOCCIA and Paphlagonia, and finally annexed BITHYNIA. Rome intervened and three Mithridatic wars were fought between 89 and 66 BC. Sulla won the first for Rome and Mithridates was allowed to retire to Pontus. The second war (c.83–81 BC) was inconclusive. Mithridates invaded Bithynia in 74 or 73 BC, beginning the third war, which was won by POMPEY. Mithridates retired to the Crimea but refused to give up the war against Rome. He was planning an invasion of Italy when his son Pharnaces led a revolt against him, and he took his own life in 63 BC. ▷ 2.10, 2.13

MITHRAISM
Religion of the late ROMAN EMPIRE that originated in PERSIA as an offshoot of ZOROASTRIANISM. By the 5th century BC Mithra had become the main Persian deity, and the cult expanded throughout the Roman world in the 1st century AD. Mithraism emphasized the cosmic conflict between light and darkness, and took the form of a mystery religion centered around the rite of bull sacrifice. It had declined by AD 400. ▷ 2.06

MOCHE
Ancient culture of coastal PERU, named after a site with vast ceremonial structures and royal graves. The Pyramid of the Sun was the largest adobe structure in the ancient Americas (it was partly destroyed by the Spaniards in the 16th century). The site was in occupation from about 100 BC and the state's influence was widely felt in the area from about AD 200. It declined in about 500. Mochica pottery showed a high degree of skill and character, deriving in style from the Chavín culture. ▷ 2.27

MONGOLIAN LANGUAGES
Group of languages, including Kalmyk, Buryat and Khalka (also known as Mongolian), spoken in eastern Russia, Mongolia and northwest China. They became distinct from the TURKIC languages early in the 1st millennium AD.

MONS GRAUPIUS, BATTLE OF
Fought in the difficult terrain of north Scotland in 83 BC between the local CALEDONII and the Romans under Agricola. Although Agricola won the battle, he did not succeed in conquering the Caledonii. ▷ 2.18

MONTÉ ALBÁN
Zapotec ceremonial center and political capital built on several hills in the Oaxaca valley, central Mexico, from about 500 BC. The earliest structures include a temple platform with a series of figurative sculptures of defeated enemies and hieroglyphic inscriptions. The city reached the height of its grandeur in about AD 100–700. ▷ 2.27

MUSEUM
A place of the Muses, or one where the arts sponsored by them were practiced. The most celebrated museum was in ALEXANDRIA. Founded by the Ptolemies, it was not primarily concerned with the collection of objects but supported scholars who carried out original research, particularly on earlier GREEK literary texts.

MYLAE, BATTLE OF
In the First PUNIC WAR (264–241 BC) the Romans saw the need to wrest command of the sea from CARTHAGE and in 260 BC built a fleet of 100 quinqueremes, fitted with a rotatable boarding bridge. The Roman fleet under Duilius defeated Carthage in this naval battle at Mylae (modern Milazzo, Sicily). ▷ 2.12

NABATEA
Ancient kingdom of the Middle East, now in Jordan. With its capital at PETRA, the Nabatean kingdom was established during the late 4th century BC, and by 85 BC controlled the northern Red Sea coast, Damascus and the Lebanon. Following the conquests of POMPEY in the Levant in 63 BC, Nabatea became an ally of the Romans; the kingdom was

annexed by TRAJAN in AD 106, becoming the Roman province of Arabia. The Nabateans used a consonantal script that was ancestral to Arabic. ▷ 2.10

NAN-YUE
Ancient state of southern China and north Vietnam inhabited by the AUSTRO-ASIATIC YUE peoples. Nan-yue flourished between 206 and 113 BC, after which it was incorporated within the HAN empire. ▷ 2.24

NANDA DYNASTY
Dynasty that ruled in MAGADHA, in ancient India, founded by Mahapadma in about 364 BC. Under Nanda rule Magadha began a period of expansion, and the dynasty controlled a vast army. It was overthrown by CHANDRAGUPTA I, founder of the MAURYA dynasty, in 321 BC. ▷ 2.01, 2.02, 2.22

NAQSH-I RUSTAM
Archeological site in southern PERSIA, the site of the tombs of many of the early Achemenid kings, as well as several Sasanian sculptures, including a carving depicting the capture of the Roman emperor VALERIAN in AD 260. ▷ 2.11

NARSES
(AD 480–573) Armenian eunuch, general and adviser to the eastern Roman emperor JUSTINIAN. As commander of the imperial bodyguard, Narses played a major part in suppressing the Nika riots of 532, which nearly overthrew Justinian. He was later responsible for completing the conquest of the OSTROGOTHIC kingdom of Italy between 551 and 562. ▷ 2.17

NAZCA
Ancient culture of coastal PERU that flourished from 200 BC to AD 600, during the EARLY INTERMEDIATE PERIOD. The desert-based Nazca culture produced fine textiles and pottery, but is distinguished for its geometric patterns (geoglyphs) formed by clearing areas of desert of their stones. The significance of these patterns is controversial, but they appear to have been ritual walkways associated with the cult of the rain-god. The Nazca culture declined with the rise of TIAHUANACO. ▷ 2.02, 2.03, 2.04, 2.27

NEARCHOS
Naval commander who performed the remarkable feat of sailing ALEXANDER THE GREAT's fleet from the Indus river to the mouth of the Persian Gulf, without the loss of a single ship, in 325 BC. He later wrote his memoirs of the voyage and of Alexander's earlier Indian campaigns. ▷ 2.09

NEDAO, BATTLE OF
Battle fought in AD 454 in modern Hungary at which the Huns were defeated by a coalition of GERMAN tribes. The Hunnish empire abruptly collapsed. ▷ 2.16

NEO-PLATONISM
Development of PLATO's philosophy, notably by PLOTINUS (AD 205–70). Plotinus argued that there was a single supreme force that was the source of all existence and values. It was possible for human beings to grasp the essence of this force through reasoned reflection on its nature. Christian thinkers, notably AUGUSTINE, equated Plotinus' supreme force with the Christian God. ▷ 2.15

NEPALA
Ancient kingdom of Nepal, first referred to in the Vedic texts. It was the birthplace of Siddhartha Gautama, the Buddha, in the 6th century BC. The kingdom was extended by the LICCHAVI dynasty from the 4th century AD. In the 10th century the Malla dynasty introduced thoroughgoing Hinduism and established contact with China and India.

NEPOS, JULIUS
Roman emperor of the west from AD 474 to 475. He recognized Visigothic sovereignty in Spain and southern GAUL. Deposed by the general Orestes, who placed his son ROMULUS AUGUSTULUS on the throne, Nepos fled to Dalmatia. He continued to be recognized as the western emperor by Zeno, the emperor of the east, until his murder in 480. ▷ 2.16

NERO
Roman emperor (r.AD 54–68) and the stepson and successor of CLAUDIUS. In his early years in power he was dominated by his mother Agrippina, whom he had murdered in 59. He took delight in the arts, particularly music, and the THEATER, and became increasingly extravagant and unpopular. In AD 64 Rome suffered a devastating fire, which Nero used as an excuse to begin persecution of the young Christian church in Rome. Serious plotting against him began in 68, and he killed himself.

NEW TESTAMENT
The Christian part of the Bible, comprising 27 books written in GREEK: the four GOSPELS, the Acts of the Apostles, letters of ST PAUL and other apostles to the early churches, and the Revelation of St John. The canonical version of the complete New Testament was assembled in AD 367 by St Athanasius.

NICAEA, COUNCIL OF
Ecumenical council of the Christian church, called (and presided over) by the emperor CONSTANTINE in AD 325. It resolved the conflict between the Arians and the Orthodox view over whether the Son and the Father were "of one substance", and produced the Nicene creed as a statement of the faith.

NOK CULTURE
Early Iron Age farming culture of the Benue plateau region, modern Nigeria, from about 600 BC to AD 400. Nok craftsmen produced striking terracotta sculptures of human heads, animal figurines, fine pottery and iron artifacts, though little is known of Nok culture or social organization. ▷ 2.21

NOMADISM
Way of life typified by the lack of permanent settlement and usually cyclical movement from place to place. Hunter-gatherers are usually nomadic, but most nomads are pastoralists, moving in search of new grazing for their herds. Those who have permanent homes but leave them periodically are said to be semi-nomadic; those who move seasonally are said to practice transhumant pastoralism. Nomadism has been typical of the Eurasian steppes and of north Africa. The sudden arrival of large groups of nomads frequently caused severe alarm to more settled societies. Nomadism arose in the 8th century BC, and continued as an important force in world history until the 18th century AD. ▷ 2.20

NORICUM
A predominantly Celtic region in the eastern Alps, whose main tribe was the Taurisci. It is a fertile area with iron reserves. In the early 2nd century BC Noricum was the name of a Celtic federal state. It was incorporated into the ROMAN EMPIRE in 16 BC and became the province of Noricum. In the 5th century AD the region was occupied by Germanic peoples. ▷ 2.13

NORTHERN ZHOU
Minor dynasty based at Chang'an that ruled northern China from AD 557 until its overthrow by the SUI DYNASTY in 581. ▷ 2.25

NUMANTIA, SIEGE OF
A CELTIBERIAN walled city by the 4th century BC, Numantia was the last Celtiberian stronghold to resist Rome. After an eight-month seige, the 4,000 inhabitants surrendered in 133 BC to the Romans under SCIPIO AFRICANUS. The city was then destroyed and the survivors were sold into slavery. ▷ 2.18

NUMIDIA
Originally the country of the Numidiae, African nomads to the west and south of CARTHAGE. Numidia sided with Rome during the Third PUNIC WAR, but supported POMPEY in 47–46 BC and the indigenous dynasty was overthrown. Eastern Numidia was established as the Roman province of Africa Nova in 46 BC. The African provinces were rearranged under AUGUSTUS and again under SEPTIMIUS SEVERUS, who created the province of Numidia in AD 197–98. Numidian bears, leopards and lions were supplied for shows in Roman amphitheaters. ▷ 2.12, 2.21

OCTAVIAN
See AUGUSTUS

ODOACER
Germanic king of Italy (r.AD 476–93). As leader of the German mercenaries he deposed the last Roman emperor, ROMULUS AUGUSTULUS, in 476. He maintained the existing Roman institutions. His rule was not recognized by the eastern emperor Zeno, who, in 488 sent THEODORIC to depose him. Odoacer agreed in 493 to share his authority with Theodoric, who then assassinated him. ▷ 2.16, 2.17

OPPIDUM
A large, complex type of settlement, generally fortified, that developed across Celtic Europe in the 2nd and 1st centuries BC. They were central areas involved in long-distance trade, specialized craft production, sometimes minting of coinage, and tribal administration. JULIUS CAESAR found that each Gaulish tribe had several *oppida*, though not all were of equal importance. *Oppida* were superseded by planned Romanized towns. ▷ 2.18

OSTIA
The port of Rome, at the mouth of the Tiber river in central Italy. The earliest remains at the site date to the late 4th century BC. Most of what is visible has been dated to the 2nd and 3rd century AD. About 75 percent of the inner city was uncovered in excavations between 1938 and 1942, and the findings confirm Ostia's important role in Rome's commerce, communications and naval history. Great storehouses and port facilities were built during the empire. There were also lavish civic buildings reflecting the relative wealth of much of the population, and seaside villas along the coast. Ostia was abandoned in the 5th century AD. ▷ 2.14

OSTROGOTHS
Major group of Gothic tribes, settled in the Ukraine region in the late 4th century AD, when they were defeated by the HUNS. In the mid-5th century they were living in PANNONIA and then invaded Italy, where their king THEODORIC set up a kingdom in 493. The kingdom was destroyed by the eastern Roman emperor JUSTINIAN between 535 and 562. ▷ 2.16, 2.17, 2.19

OVID
Roman poet (43 BC–AD 17) who turned from public life to poetry, becoming the leading poet in Rome. In 8 BC Ovid was banished (for his erotic poem, *The Art of Love*, and an undisclosed indiscretion) to a wretched outpost of the empire – Tomis on the Black Sea – where he eventually died. His works include the *Metamorphoses*. ▷ 2.13

PACAL
MAYAN king of PALENQUE (r.AD 615–83), whose magnificent pyramid-tomb was excavated in 1949. It included a jade mask and breastplate.

PAGANISM
Literally, the religion of the countryside, but used by extension to describe any polytheistic

religion, including the official faiths of the Classical world, in contrast to CHRISTIANITY.

PALENQUE
Ancient MAYAN city in Chiapas, southern Mexico, that flourished in the second half of the Classic period (AD 300–800). Its monuments are among the most remarkable of the region, notably the Temple of the Inscriptions (where PACAL's tomb was found) and the Great Palace. Palenque was one of the first Mayan sites to be rediscovered (by a Spanish soldier) in 1786. ▷ 2.28

PALLAVA DYNASTY
Indian dynasty originating in the north, who established a capital at Kanchipuram (Tamil Nadu state) and came to hold sway in the south. They rose to prominence in the 4th century AD. They were defeated by the GUPTAS in about 360, but continued to rule until the late 9th century, when they fell to the Chola dynasty. At the height of their dynasty architecture flourished, notably in the temples of Mahabalipuram and Mamallapuram. ▷ 2.23

PALMYRA
Syrian trading town based on a desert oasis, Palmyra grew rich from trade between east and west during the Roman period. In the AD 260s it declared its independence, first under Odaenathus and then under his wife, ZENOBIA, but was reconquered by VALERIAN in 272. ▷ 2.14, 2.15

PAMA-NYUNGAN LANGUAGES
The main language group of the Aboriginal inhabitants of Australia, spoken throughout the continent, except the northwest. ▷ 2.26

PAMPA GRANDE
Archeological site in the Lambayeque valley of PERU to which the capital of the Mochica state was moved after MOCHE itself was abandoned in about AD 500. ▷ 2.27

PAMPHYLIA
Region of central-southern Asia Minor settled by the Greeks from the 8th century BC, but later (AD 43) linked with Lycia as a province of the ROMAN EMPIRE. It enjoyed great prosperity under Roman rule. ▷ 2.13

PANNONIA, PANNONIAE
The Pannonii were an ILLYRIAN group with Celtic influences, south and west of the Danube. From the late 2nd century BC they were in conflict with Rome, invaded Istria in 14 BC and were ruthlessly suppressed by TIBERIUS. The Roman province of Pannonia was established in AD 9. In 106 AD it was divided into Pannonia Superior and Pannonia Inferior, and further subdivided under DIOCLETIAN. In the 4th century AD Panonnia suffered BARBARIAN invasions and finally fell to Radagaisus and the OSTROGOTHS in AD 405. ▷ 2.13, 2.15, 2.18

PAPACY
See ROME, BISHOP OF

PARACAS CULTURE
A farming and fishing culture of the Early Horizon period on the south Peruvian coast (c.650–150 BC), within the area of Chavín influence. It is mostly known from Paracas tomb sites, which contain distinctive painted ceramics and mummified human remains, fine decorated textiles and other objects preserved in dry conditions.

PARNI
Ancient nomadic IRANIAN-speaking peoples from the eastern Caspian who entered the former Persian empire in the early 3rd century BC. In 238 BC they founded the semi-independent Parthian kingdom under the ARSACID dynasty and assimilated with the native Parthian peoples. ▷ 2.09, 2.10, 2.11

PARTHENON
Major temple to Athene the Maiden (Greek Parthenos) built on the Athenian Acropolis in the 430s BC and renowned for the splendor of its marble, the ingeniousness of its design (achieved through sloping its columns slightly inwards) and its sculptured reliefs. ▷ 2.07

PATALIPUTRA
Ancient city of northern India, on the site of Patna in Bihar state, founded in the 5th century BC as the capital of MAGADHA; it was also the MAURYAN capital. The city was sacked by the Bactrian Greeks in 185 BC, but revived to become the GUPTA capital in the 4th century AD. It was abandoned three centuries later but was rebuilt by the Mughals. ▷ 2.10, 2.22

PATRIARCHS
The five senior bishops of the Christian church, all of whom exercised authority over a wide area. The patriarchal sees were Rome, Constantinople, ANTIOCH, ALEXANDRIA and Jerusalem, and their pre-eminence over other bishoprics was confirmed by JUSTINIAN in the 6th century AD. ▷ 2.17

PATRICK, ST
Romano-British aristocrat and Christian evangelist (c.AD 385–461), probably born in Wales. Few firm facts are known of his life. He is said to have introduced CHRISTIANITY to Ireland after he was taken there as a young man by pirates and escaped to GAUL. He studied at a monastery in Auxerre before being sent as bishop to Ireland in 432. He made his first converts at the ancient royal center of TARA. In the mid-440s he set up the archbishopric at ARMAGH.

PAUL, ST
Major figure of the early Christian church who combined a relentless missionary zeal (which took him to Christian communities throughout the eastern Mediterranean) with

an effective theology based on faith in the risen Christ. His letters offer important insights into the early Christian communities. He probably died a martyr in Rome in about AD 65. ▷ 2.06

PAZYRYK
Archeological site on the Altai Mountains, Russia. Among its 40 burials is that of a nomadic Scythian chieftain, together with a dismantled wagon, rich grave-goods and human sacrifices, dating from about 600 BC. The goods include bronze mirrors and SILK from China. The bodies, preserved in the permafrost, display extensive tattooing. ▷ 2.20

PELOPONNESIAN WAR
Major struggle between Sparta and ATHENS, and their allies, that lasted from 431 until 404 BC, when Athens was defeated. Neither side had any effective means of destroying the other, but Athens was weakened by the massive losses of the Sicilian expedition (415–413 BC) and Sparta was strengthened by Persian support. Sparta's final naval victory at AEGOSPOTAMI (405 BC) broke Athens' link with its Black Sea grain supplies and led to its surrender. ▷ 2.08

PERGAMON
Important stronghold in western Asia Minor that became capital of the ATTALID dynasty (241–133 BC) and a showpiece of HELLENISTIC art and architecture. The city's name was extended to that of the surrounding Attalid kingdom. Attalus III bequeathed his kingdom to Rome and Pergamon remained prosperous in Roman times. ▷ 2.10, 2.13, 2.18

PERICLES
Major statesman of ATHENS in the 5th century BC (r.490–429 BC). Pericles masterminded the coming of DEMOCRACY (461 BC) and retained a leading role as one of the city's generals for 30 years. He was associated in particular with the glorification of the city, not only in his famous funeral speeches, but in buildings such as the PARTHENON. ▷ 2.07, 2.08

PERSIA, ANCIENT
Region east of the Fertile Crescent and south of the Caspian, and home of several major civilizations of the Classical world. It was named by the Greeks after the Parsua tribe of southwestern Iran, who inhabited Persis (the modern region of Fars). The Persians were descendants of Indo-Iranian nomads who had occupied the region in the 8th century BC. They conquered Babylon in 539 BC under Cyrus, founder of the Achemenid dynasty, who built an empire across the Middle East. It was overthrown by ALEXANDER THE GREAT, but a·new Persian empire was built, first by the Parthians and then the SASANIANS (from AD 224). The Sasanians were defeated by the Byzantines in the 620s, and the region was overrun by the Arabs in the following decades. ▷ 2.11

PERSIAN WARS
The Persians invaded GREECE twice. The first invasion, a punitive expedition against ATHENS in 490 BC, was defeated at MARATHON. The second, in 480 BC, was an all-out attempt at conquest by XERXES, who led a massive invasion force into Greece. After initial victories and the burning of Athens, the Persians were defeated at sea at SALAMIS (480) and Mycale (479), and on land at PLATAEA (479). The victory brought a surge of self-confidence to the Greeks and above all to Athens. ▷ 2.07

PERU, ANCIENT
Center of ancient South American civilization. Peru's first cultures alternated between the desert- and river-valley-based cultures of the coastal regions and those of the Andes. The history of the region is divided into the following periods: the Initial period (1800–800 BC); the Early Horizon period (800–200 BC), dominated by the Chavín culture; the EARLY INTERMEDIATE PERIOD (200 BC–AD 500), during which the MOCHE state flourished; the MIDDLE HORIZON PERIOD (AD 500–1000), dominated by the HUARI and by TIAHUANACO; the Late Intermediate period (1000–1470), the time of Sícan and Chimú, and finally, the Late Horizon period (1470–1530), during which the Inca empire controlled Peru and much of western South America. ▷ 2.27

PETÉN
Highland and forested region of northern Guatemala, south of the Yucatán peninsula, and home of the Mayan city-states of the Classic period, such as TIKAL. It was the last part of the Maya region to be conquered by the Spaniards. ▷ 2.28

PETER, ST
Traditionally the first apostle or follower of JESUS and the founder and first bishop of the church of Rome (d.c.AD 64). A former fisherman, he was depicted in the GOSPELS as the leader of the Twelve Disciples. After the crucifixion he emerged as the leading figure in the group of surviving followers, credited with miracles and with defending the Christian faith, though his reluctance to open the faith to non-Jews was criticized by ST PAUL. He traveled to Rome in about AD 55, where he headed the nascent church and was martyred in NERO's reign. The NEW TESTAMENT books, traditionally said to be his epistles, are widely considered not to have been written by him.

PETRA
Ancient desert city, now in Jordan, and the capital of the Nabatean kingdom from the 4th century BC until AD 106, when the Romans occupied it. Petra became a center for overland trade with the east until the Islamic period. Its tombs, with elaborate facades, are carved into the rock of a narrow gorge.

PHARISEES
The largest of the three main Jewish sects, it came to prominence in the 2nd century BC. The Pharisees sought to maintain the oral Jewish tradition, as well as placing great stress on the strict interpretation of the scriptures and the Law. The Pharisees were criticized by JESUS, but they continued to dominate Jewish thought until the destruction of the Temple in AD 70.

PHAROS LIGHTHOUSE
Famous lighthouse constructed by Sosistratos of Cnidus on the island of Pharos, off ALEXANDRIA, in about 300–280 BC. More than 100 meters (328 feet) high, it was one of the Seven Wonders of the Ancient World and survived until the 12th century AD. ▷ 2.10

PHARSALUS, BATTLE OF
The final confrontation between JULIUS CAESAR and POMPEY. Fought in 48 BC at Pharsalus in Thessaly, GREECE, Pompey was defeated and escaped to Egypt, where he was murdered. ▷ 2.13

PHEIDIAS
Greek sculptor of the second half of the 5th century BC, considered one of the greatest sculptors of the ancient world. Pheidias was responsible for the massive statues of Athena in the PARTHENON and of Zeus at Olympia. He was probably responsible for overseeing the sculptured reliefs of the Parthenon. ▷ 2.08

PHILIP II OF MACEDON
Ruler of MACEDON (r.359–336 BC) who united and expanded his kingdom to make it the dominant power in the Greek world, with control of much of northern GREECE. His secret lay in his brilliantly trained and well-led army, one of whose most crushing victories was over the Athenians and Thebans at CHAERONEA in 338 BC. Philip laid the political and military foundations for the conquests of his son, ALEXANDER. ▷ 2.08, 2.09

PHRAATES
Name given to five Parthian kings of PERSIA. Phraates I (r.c.191–176 BC) began a policy of expansion in the north. Phraates II (r.138–128 BC) definitively defeated the SELEUCIDS, but faced nomadic invasions in the east. Phraates III (r.70–57 BC) and Phraates IV (r.c.37–2 BC) intrigued with the Romans for control of Armenia. Phraates V (r.2 BC–AD 4) confirmed Roman control over that area.

PHRYGIAN LANGUAGE
Ancient language related to GREEK that (written in Greek characters) survived as one of the local languages of the ROMAN EMPIRE. ▷ 2.14

PICTS
The name Pictae or "painted people" was first used by the Romans in AD 297 for the Celtic peoples to the north of the ANTONINE WALL in Scotland. They lost their independence when they were defeated in the 9th century AD by Kenneth MacAlpin of Dalriada. ▷ 2.15

PILATE, PONTIUS
Roman governor of JUDAEA (r.AD 26–36). Appointed by TIBERIUS, his actions were frequently provocative to Jewish religious feeling, and he was dismissed for his handling of an anti-Roman demonstration in Samaria. He is best known for his ambiguous role in the crucifixion of JESUS and was venerated as a saint by the Coptic church of Egypt.

PLATAEA, BATTLE OF
The final decisive land battle of the PERSIAN WARS of 480–479 BC. After a series of maneuvers on the borders of Attica, the Persians were tempted to attack a Greek army which seemed in disarray, but which, under Spartan leadership, rallied to defeat them. The Persian commander MARDONIUS was killed. ▷ 2.07

PLATO
(c.429–347 BC) Athenian by birth, Plato was one of the great Greek philosophers. Much of his writings survive in the form of dialogues, in which a group of characters follows a discussion through to its conclusion. Plato believed that ideas such as goodness and justice existed as real – if invisible – entities, to be understood through reasoned thought on their nature. In the *Republic* he argued that effective government could be based on such understandings. Plato founded the ACADEMY, a school for philosophers which survived for centuries after his death. ▷ 2.08

PLAUTUS
Comic playwright, probably from Umbria, whose plays, written between about 250 and 184 BC, are the earliest LATIN works to have survived intact. He was strongly influenced by contemporary Greek drama. ▷ 2.13

PLOTINUS
Neoplatonist philosopher (AD 205–70) who lived and traveled in GREECE and PERSIA before settling in Rome at the age of 40 to teach philosophy. He was at the center of an intellectual circle, and from the age of 50 wrote a series of philosophical essays, the *Enneads*. ▷ 2.15

POLYCLITOS
A Greek sculptor from Argos of the late 5th century BC who believed that the parts of the human body related to each other in mathematical ratios. His sculpture of a spear holder, which survives only in copies, was supposed to provide a model of the correct proportions. ▷ 2.08

POLYNESIA
The largest of the three divisions of Oceania, in the central and southern Pacific. It consists

of the Hawaii islands, Samoa, Tonga, Tahiti and EASTER ISLAND; New Zealand is also considered part of Polynesia. Polynesia was settled from MELANESIA between 1000 BC and AD 1000. Its languages are a branch of AUSTRONESIAN. ▷ 2.26

POMPEII

The early history of settlement at this site in southern Campania is unclear. Originally an Etruscan settlement, it was occupied by the Oscan-speaking Samnites in the 5th century BC. In 80 BC Sulla imposed a colony of Roman citizens and LATIN replaced Oscan as the official language. The city flourished through the late republic and early empire, but suffered a severe earthquake in AD 62 and was destroyed by the eruption of Vesuvius in AD 79. Preserved under layers of pumice, large-scale excavations of the site after the late 1700s revealed in poignant detail evidence of Roman daily life. ▷ 2.13

POMPEY

(106–48 BC) Roman military commander and skilled politician. His greatest military achievements were his eastern campaigns (66–62 BC), in which he defeated MITHRIDATES VI, founded colonies, annexed Syria and turned JUDEA into a client kingdom. By this and other means he accrued great wealth and both official and unofficial power. He engaged in lengthy and complex rivalry against CRASSUS and JULIUS CAESAR for the leadership of Rome. He was finally defeated by Caesar in 48 BC at PHARSALUS in GREECE, and fled to Egypt, where he was murdered. ▷ 2.13

PONTUS

Mountainous region on the south edge of the Black Sea, east of BITHYNIA, with fertile valleys, fine timber and mineral reserves. Greek colonies were established on the coast, but had relatively little effect on the interior. The kingdom of Pontus reached its largest extent under MITHRIDATES VI, who challenged Roman power in Asia Minor. In 63 BC POMPEY organized Pontus as a province, but it drifted out of Roman control under MARK ANTONY and was gradually brought back into the empire under AUGUSTUS. ▷ 2.10, 2.13

POSTUMUS

Roman general responsible for guarding the Rhine from BARBARIAN attacks, who seized power for himself in AD 260 and established a GALLIC empire, which at its height controlled GAUL, Britain and Spain. He was killed in 269 and his territory was regained for the ROMAN empire in 274. ▷ 2.15

POTEIDAIA

One of the most important of the colonies of Corinth established in about 600 BC to exploit trade with MACEDONIA. It became an uneasy subject of the Athenian empire and the help

that was given by Sparta, in support of Corinth when Poteidaia revolted from ATHENS in 432, was one of the factors leading to the PELOPONNESIAN WAR. ▷ 2.08

PRAXITELES

Influential Athenian sculptor of the mid-4th century BC whose masterpiece, a statue of the goddess Aphrodite, broke with convention by its show of nudity. Rejected by the more conservative cities of GREECE, it was displayed in a circular shrine in the city of Cnidus. ▷ 2.08

PROCOPIUS

(c.AD 499–566) Important historian who was responsible for a detailed history of the campaigns of JUSTINIAN in Africa and Italy. He also completed a notorious "secret history" of Justinian's reign, and a study of the emperor's building projects. ▷ 2.17

PTOLEMAIC EGYPT

From 305 BC until its annexation by Rome in 30 BC, Egypt was ruled by the Greek Ptolemaic dynasty. Their capital at ALEXANDRIA was maintained separately from the rest of Egypt, though there were Greek enclaves along the Nile. The country was heavily exploited to sustain the high living and cultural interests of the Ptolemies. At their peak in the 3rd century BC the Ptolemies dominated the eastern Mediterranean, but after 168 BC they relied increasingly on Roman support. The last Ptolemy, CLEOPATRA, was reduced to manipulating her lovers, JULIUS CAESAR and MARK ANTONY, in the vain hope of keeping her country independent. ▷ 2.09, 2.10

PTOLEMY, CLAUDIUS

Alexandrian astronomer, geographer and mathematician of the mid-2nd century AD. His *Almagest* brought together the findings of earlier astronomers, notably HIPPARCHOS, and consolidated and extended them to form a coherent astronomical system that was to remain influential for more than 1,000 years. ▷ 2.15

PTOLEMY I

General of ALEXANDER THE GREAT who on Alexander's death seized the Egyptian part of his empire and declared himself king (r.305–284 BC). He set up his capital at ALEXANDRIA and successfully established a GREEK-speaking administration, though it was heavily exploitative of the native peoples. He also annexed Cyprus and some Aegean islands. ▷ 2.09, 2.10

PTOLEMY IV

Ruler of Egypt from 244 to 205 BC. During his reign PTOLEMAIC control of Egypt began to disintegrate, with THEBES coming to enjoy virtual independence. Ptolemy was eventually murdered by his courtiers and the loss of Ptolemaic possessions in the Aegean followed soon afterwards. ▷ 2.10

PUNIC WARS

Fought between 264 and 146 BC, the Punic wars ended with the defeat of the CARTHAGINIAN empire by Rome. "Punic" derived from "Poeni", the Roman name for the Carthaginians. The First Punic War (264–41) erupted after Rome became ruler of Magna Graecia (a Greek territory in southern Italy and Sicily), where Carthage also had territory; the action was mostly confined to Sicily. In 241 an exhausted Carthage made peace with Rome, losing its territories in Sicily, Corsica and Sardinia.

In 219 HANNIBAL took SAGUNTUM in Spain, provoking the Second Punic War (218–201 BC), famous for the campaigns of Hannibal and SCIPIO AFRICANUS. After Hannibal's victory at CANNAE (216), much of southern Italy rebelled against Rome. He remained invincible but failed to widen the area of revolt sufficiently. With the other armies occupied in Spain and north Africa, Carthage could not supply him with enough reinforcements. Scipio Africanus eventually took the war to north Africa, won over the Numidian princes and defeated Hannibal at Zama in 202 BC. Carthage sued for peace once more, losing its empire in Spain. Rome still saw Carthage as a threat and initiated the Third Punic War (149–146 BC), which ended in a Roman victory, the destruction of the city and the enslavement of its people. Carthage's territory became the Roman province of Africa. ▷ 2.10, 2.12, 2.13, 2.21

PUSHYAMITRA SHUNGA

Indian ruler, a soldier who assasinated the last MAURYAN king of MAGAHDA in 185 BC and founded the SUNGA dynasty. ▷ 2.22

PYDNA, BATTLE OF

Decisive battle (168 BC) between the Romans and Perseus of MACEDONIA (son of Philip V) in northwest GREECE. The Macedonians were heavily defeated and their country was divided into four republics (in 148 BC it was annexed as a province), which represented a turning point in the Roman annexation of Greece. ▷ 2.10, 2.13

PYRRHUS

Ambitious king of Epirus (r.297–272 BC) who restored the strength of his kingdom and is remembered for his campaigns against the Romans (280–275 BC) in support of the Greek colonies in Italy. He won several battles, but his losses were so great that the term "Pyrrhic victory" was coined to describe them. He eventually withdrew to GREECE, but died on campaign in the Peloponnese. ▷ 2.12

PYTHEAS OF MASSILIA

Greek navigator of the late 4th century BC whose most famous voyage took him through the Straits of Gibraltar to explore the coasts of western Europe, circumnavigating Britain, perhaps reaching Norway and sailing into Arctic waters. ▷ 2.09, 2.19

PYU
Ancient Tibeto-Burmese peoples of the Irrawaddy valley of Burma, who dominated the region from the 3rd century BC. By the early centuries AD they had come into contact with Indian and Chinese culture and were followers of THERAVADA BUDDHISM. They controlled some 20 small kingdoms in southern Burma. Their chief city, Sri Ksetra, was abandoned in the 6th century, and they were overrun by the Burmese in the 9th century AD. ▷ 2.26

QATABAN
Ancient kingdom of the southern Arabian peninsula that flourished in the second half of the 1st millennium BC, one of the so-called "incense kingdoms", which relied on trade in aromatic gums for their prosperity. Its capital was at Miswah. Qataban was gradually superseded by the HIMYARITE KINGDOM, and was finally conquered in the 1st century AD. ▷ 2.01, 2.02

QIN DYNASTY
Dynasty that ruled China between 221 and 206 BC, traditionally considered the first to unite the country, and from which China derives its name. The Qin originated in the west of the country, but in the late 4th and 3rd centuries BC conquered the competing kingdoms. Zheng (r.246–210 BC) completed the unification of the country and took the title SHI HUANGDI, the "First Emperor". Under his rule from the capital at XIANYANG (near Xi'an in modern Shaanxi province), an administrative centralization was carried out and he sought to obliterate many traces of the past. He also built a series of border ramparts to resist nomad attack from the north. These are generally seen as the origins of the later Great Wall. Soon after his death civil war destroyed the dynasty. ▷ 2.24

QUIRIGUA
Classic period Mayan city in the southern area, now in Honduras. It has notable carved *stelae* (stone monuments), including the largest monolithic monument of the MAYA, the portrait of an unidentified ruler. Quirigua challenged the power of the nearby COPÁN in the 8th century BC. ▷ 2.28

QUMRAN
Ancient village near the Dead Sea, in the modern West Bank. From the 2nd century BC it was home to an ESSENE community and was destroyed several times by the Romans, prior to its abandonment in AD 68. It was here that the DEAD SEA SCROLLS were discovered in 1947.

RAETIA (RHAETIA)
Roman province in Europe, now southwest Germany, Austria and Switzerland. It was conquered by Rome in 15 BC and was the hub of strategic communications routes to the north and east. ▷ 2.13

RAMAYANA
Classical Indian epic composed in SANSKRIT in the 3rd century BC, from earlier legends and Vedic sacred material. Said to be the work of a single author – the poet Valmiki – it contains up to 40,000 couplets and tells the story of Rama and the princess Sita, who eventually gain the throne of Ayodhya. Like the MAHABHARATA, the Ramayana has been immensely influential in Indian culture. ▷ 2.23

RAVENNA
City on the Adriatic (northern Italy) chosen as a capital of the western ROMAN EMPIRE by HONORIUS in AD 402, because of its good sea communications with Constantinople and easily defendable position in marshland. ODOACER and the Ostrogothic king THEODORIC also made it their capital (late 5th century). Rivalry between Arian OSTROGOTHS and native Latin Christians led to the building of its magnificent churches and their mosaics. Ravenna was retaken by JUSTINIAN's general, BELISARIUS, in 540. ▷ 2.16, 2.17

RECUAY CULTURE
Ancient culture of northern highland PERU that flourished in the EARLY INTERMEDIATE PERIOD (200 BC–AD 500). It is typified by distinctive resist-painted ceramics. Recuay inherited much of the dominance of Chavín, and influenced the contemporary MOCHE culture on the coast. ▷ 2.27

REMOJADAS
Classic period civilization of the VERACRUZ lowlands of the Gulf Coast of Mexico that flourished from AD 1 to 700. Distinctive clay models – including "laughing figures" – and larger sculptures have been found in its burial mounds. They reveal the influence of both the MAYAN and TEOTIHUACÁN cultures. ▷ 2.27

RHAPTA
Ancient trading port in east Africa, possibly in the Rufiji delta or Zanzibar channel, that is mentioned by Greco-Roman writers of the early centuries AD. It exported ivory, tortoise-shell and coconut oil, and imported weapons and iron tools from the Mediterranean. ▷ 2.21

ROMAN EMPIRE
From 27 BC Rome and its territories were ruled by a series of emperors, beginning with AUGUSTUS. By the 2nd century AD the empire covered about 13 million square kilometers (5 million square miles), with an estimated population of 55 million. Rome's main aims were to maintain peace within the empire and to extract money and other resources, mostly through taxation. The empire was administered as a series of provinces. Local elites became increasingly important and were given various administrative posts: by the 3rd century AD they had become highly Romanized. In the 3rd and 4th centuries the empire declined through internal conflict and external threat, the latter coming especially from the Germanic peoples, including the VISIGOTHS, FRANKS, VANDALS and OSTROGOTHS. From the late 3rd century it became usual for the eastern and western halves of the empire to be ruled separately. The western empire was occupied by Germanic peoples in the 5th century. The eastern empire survived and was gradually transformed into the medieval Byzantine empire. ▷ 2.13, 2.14, 2.16, 2.19

BISHOPS OF ROME TO AD 600

Peter	to c.64	Fabian	236–50	Celestine I	422–32
Linus	c.67–76/79	Cornelius	251–53	Sixtus III	432–40
Anacletus	76–88 or 79–91	Lucius I	253–54	Leo I	440–61
		Stephen I	254–57	Hilary	461–68
Clement I	88–97 or 92–101	Sixtus II	257–58	Simplicius	468–83
		Dionysius	259–68	Felix II	483–92
Evaristus	c.97–c.107	Felix I	274	Gelasius I	492–96
Alexander I	105–15 or 109–19	Eutychian	275–83	Anastasius II	496–98
		Gaius	283–96	Symmachus	498–514
Sixtus I	c.115–c.125	Marcellinus	291/296–304	Hormisdas	514–23
Telesphorus	c.125–c.136	Marcellus I	308–09	John I	523–26
Hyginus	c.136–c.140	Eusebius	309/310	Felix III	526–30
Pius I	c.140–55	Miltiades	311–14	Boniface II	530–32
Anicetus	c.155–c.166	Sylvester I	314–35	John II	533–35
Soter	c.166–c.175	Mark	336	Agapetus I	535–36
Eleutherius	c.175–89	Julius I	337–52	Silverius	536–37
Victor I	c.189–99	Liberius	352–66	Vigilius	537–55
Zephyrinus	c.199–217	Damasus I	366–84	Pelagius I	556–61
Calixtus I (Callistus)	217–22	Siricius	384–99	John III	561–74
		Anastasius I	399–401	Benedict I	575–79
Urban I	222–30	Innocent I	401–17	Pelagius II	579–90
Pontian	230–35	Zosimus	417–18	Gregory I	590–604
Anterus	235–36	Boniface I	418–22		

ROMAN REPUBLIC

The period in Rome's history between 509 BC, when the ruling Tarquinian dynasty was expelled, and the beginning of the ROMAN EMPIRE under AUGUSTUS in 27 BC. Republican Rome was governed by officials called magistrates (consuls, censors, etc.), who were elected by the Roman people, and the Senate, an assembly of ex-magistrates. The republic saw the dramatic expansion of Rome's territories both in and beyond Italy, and the successful waging of war against various powerful opponents, notably the Samnites, GAULS and CARTHAGINIANS. The later republic was a time of political corruption and power struggles between the leading generals and families, and growing popular discontent. The republic finally collapsed into civil war and was replaced by the monarchical government of AUGUSTUS in 27 BC. ▷ 2.12

ROMANCE LANGUAGES

A group of related European languages descended from LATIN, including French, Italian, Spanish, Catalan, Portuguese and Romanian. In the regions where these are spoken, the language developed from the vernacular Latin during the ROMAN EMPIRE and was influenced, but not destroyed, by the languages of the invading Germanic peoples.

ROME, BISHOP OF

By tradition (though not accepted beyond the Roman Catholic church) the head of the Christian church, also known as the pope. The first bishop of Rome, from AD 55, was ST PETER. The primacy of the bishopric is based on Christ's appointment of him as the foundation of the church. The position rose to prominence during the period of BARBARIAN invasion, when it preserved the tradition of Roman imperialism and civilization.

ROME, SACKS OF

Rome was first sacked by the GAULS in 390 BC: a Roman garrison held out on the Capitoline Hill and the Gauls were persuaded to leave by a payment of tribute. The most famous sack of Rome took place in AD 410, after the Romans refused to make concessions to the Visigothic leader, ALARIC. Rome was not seriously damaged, and though by this time it was no longer capital of the empire, it was a serious blow to Roman prestige. Rome was sacked a third time by the VANDALS in 455, after a marriage treaty involving the Vandal king Gaiseric's son had been broken by Rome. The seizure of Sicily, Rome's oldest province, by the Vandals soon followed. ▷ 2.12, 2.16, 2.18

ROMULUS

See AUGUSTULUS, ROMULUS

ROSETTA STONE

Granite stone discovered at Rosetta in 1799 that contains a PTOLEMAIC decree (of 196 BC) in three scripts – hieroglyphic, DEMOTIC and GREEK. The Rosetta Stone provided vital clues in the decipherment of hieroglyphics by the French scholar Champollion in 1822.

ROYAL ROAD

Road from the Achemenid winter capital of Susa to Sardis in Lydia. It covered some 2,200 kilometers (1,500 miles) and 111 relay stations along the route provided couriers with overnight accommodation and fresh horses. The journey took three months on foot, but the fastest couriers could cover it in a week.

SACBE

Mesoamerican causeway, named after the Mayan word for "white road". Typically up to 1 meter (3 feet) high and 5 meters (16 feet) wide, they are made of stone plastered with lime; some run up to 100 kilometers (60 miles). Many *sacbes* have been found around COBÁ. ▷ 2.28

SADDUCEES

One of the main strands of Jewish thought of the early 2nd century BC. Unlike the PHARISEES, the Sadducees accepted only the scriptures as a source of authority, and were monastic and conservative in their approach. They died out after the destruction of the Temple at Jerusalem in AD 70.

SAGUNTUM

North of modern Valencia, Spain, this was a citadel of the Edetai, who were allied to Rome. HANNIBAL beseiged Saguntum, thereby precipitating the Second PUNIC WAR. Captured by the Romans by 212 BC, the city became a Roman *municipium* (township) by the Augustan period. It survived until the mid-5th century AD, as attested by finds from its harbor of Grau Vell. ▷ 2.12

SALAMIS, BATTLE OF

Crucial naval battle between the Greek (predominantly Athenian) and Persian navies during the Persian invasion of GREECE in 480. Desperate after the sacking of ATHENS, the Greeks lured the Persian fleet into the channel between the island of Salamis and the mainland, and inflicted heavy casualties. Their victory prevented Persian forces from invading the Peloponnese and completing the conquest of Greece. ▷ 2.07

SAMNITE WARS

Series of wars fought between Rome and the powerful Samnites for control of central Italy. The First Samnite War (343–341 BC) gave Rome control of Campania. The Second Samnite War (327–304 BC) saw the Romans defeated at CAUDINE FORKS (321), but the Samnites could not follow up their victory. The Third Samnite War (298–290 BC) drew in the GAULS, Umbrians and Etruscans against Rome. The Romans defeated this coalition at Sentinum in 295 and had conquered most of peninsular Italy by 290. The Samnites were forced to become Roman "allies". ▷ 2.12

SAMUDRAGUPTA

Indian emperor of the GUPTA dynasty (r.AD 335–80). He consolidated the Gupta empire and then, building from his base near Delhi, extended it in the west by defeating the KUSHANS, as well as extending southward. He is said to have defeated or killed more than 20 other monarchs. His reign is considered a high point in Hindu Indian culture and society, and he is personally remembered as a poet and musician. ▷ 2.23

SANSKRIT

The classical literary language of India, still used for sacred or learned purposes. Vedic Sanskrit, one of the oldest surviving Indo-European languages, was used from about 1500 BC to 200 BC; classical Sanskrit was used from about 500 BC, developed first as a court language, then adapted for literary and religious purposes.

SASAN

Persian ruler of the 2nd century AD who gave his named to the SASANIAN DYNASTY founded by his grandson ARDASHIR I. Little is known about his life, but he was probably a prince in Persis (modern Fars). ▷ 2.11

SASANIAN DYNASTY

Dynasty ruling PERSIA, founded in AD 224 by ARDASHIR I, and destroyed by the Arab invasions of the 630s. The capital was at CTESIPHON. Under the Sasanians, Persia reached the peak of its ancient glory, rivaling that of Rome; they revived Achemenid traditions and made ZOROASTRIANISM their state religion. Notable monarchs include SHAPUR I (r.240–72), SHAPUR II (r.309–79), KHOSRU I (r.531–79) and KHOSRU II (r.591–628). ▷ 2.11

SATAVAHANIHARA

Ancient kingdom of western and central India from the 1st century BC to the 3rd century AD, with its capital at Pratisthana. It was the first state of the Deccan to build an empire in the south. Its greatest ruler was Gautamiputra (r.AD 106–30). ▷ 2.22, 2.23

SATRAPY

Unit of provincial government of Achemenid PERSIA, created by DARIUS I. The satrap was a royal appointee.

SAXON SHORE

Military command consisting of a chain of ten late Roman forts in southeast Britain, built to defend the province against Germanic pirates. The command also covered two other forts on the coast of GAUL. ▷ 2.15

SCIPIO AFRICANUS

(236–185 BC) Roman general who played a key role in the Second PUNIC WAR (218–01 BC) against CARTHAGE. After conquering Carthaginian Spain he took the battle to north Africa, won over the Numidian princes and defeated HANNIBAL at Zama in 202 BC. His

EMPERORS OF ROME

JULIO-CLAUDIAN DYNASTY

Augustus	27 BC–AD 14
Tiberius	14–37
Gaius (Caligula)	37–41
Claudius	41–54
Nero	54–68
Galba	68–69
Otho, Vitellius	69

FLAVIAN, NERVO-TRAJANIC AND ANTONINE DYNASTIES

Vespasian	69–79
Titus	79–81
Domitian	82–96
Nerva	96–98
Trajan (**97–98** with Nerva)	97–117
Hadrian	117–38
Antoninus Pius	138–61
Marcus Aurelius	161–80
(**161–69** with Lucius Verus)	
Commodus	180–92

SEVERAN DYNASTY

Pertinax	193
Didius Julianus	193
Septimius Severus	193–211
Caracalla (**211–12** with Geta)	211–17
Macrinus	217–18
Elagabalus	218–22
Alexander Severus	222–35

PERIOD OF POLITICAL ANARCHY AND DISORDER

The many usurpers are not listed

Maximinus	235–38
Gordian I and II (in Africa)	238
Balbinus and Pupienus (in Italy)	238
Gordian III	238–44
Philip	244–49
Decius	249–51
Trebonianus Gallus	251–53
Aemilianus	253
Valerian	253–60
Gallienus	253–68
(**253–60** with Valerian)	
Claudius II	268–70
Quintillus	270
Aurelian	270–75
Tacitus	275–76
Probus	276–82
Carus	282–83
Carinus and Numerian	283–84

DIVISION OF THE EMPIRE

Diocletian (sole ruler) 284–87

West		East	
Maximian	287–305	Diocletian	284–305
Constantius	305–06	Galerius	305–11
Severus	306–07	Maximinus	309–13
Maxentius	306–12		
Constantine	306–24	Licinius Augustus	308–24
Constantine (sole ruler) 324–37			
Constantine II	337–40	Constantius II	337–61
Constans	340–50		
Magnentius (usurper)	350–53		
Gallus Caesar	355–61		
Julian Caesar	355–61		
Julian (sole ruler) 361–63			
Jovian (sole ruler) 363–64			
Valentinian	364–65	Valens	364–78
Gratian	375–83	Theodosius	379–95
Theodosius (sole ruler) 394–95			
Valentinian II (Italy, Illyricum)	375–92		
Maximus (usurper)	383–88		
Eugenius (usurper)	392–94		
Honorius	395–423	Arcadius	395–408
Constantius III	421	Theodosius II	408–50
Iohannes (usurper)	423–25		
Valentinian III	425–55	Marcian	450–57
Petronius Maximus	455		
Avitus	455–56	Leo	457–74
Majorian	457–61		
Libius Severus	461–65		
Anthemius	476–72		
Olybrius	472		
Glycerius	473		
Julius Nepos	473–75	Zeno	474–91
Romulus Augustulus	475–76		
		Anastasius	491–518
		Justin	518–27
		Justinian	527–65
		Justin II	565–78
		Tiberius II Constantine	578–82
		Maurice	582–602
		Phocas	602–10
		Heraclius	610–41

success bred enmity, however, and in 184 he faced accusations of embezzlement and bribe-taking in Asia. He avoided trial by going into voluntary exile in Campania, where he died in 183 BC. ▷ 2.12

SEGESTA
Native city of the Elymi in western Sicily. It agreed to support the Athenian invasion of Sicily in 415 BC, in the hope of strengthening itself against its rival, the Greek city of Selinus. Soon afterwards, however, the CARTHAGINIANS sacked Selinus, but the Segestans had to pay the price of coming under Carthaginian control themselves (409 BC). ▷ 2.08

SELEUCID KINGDOM
Kingdom carved by SELEUCOS I from the Asian possessions left by ALEXANDER THE GREAT. It originally stretched from the west coast of Asia Minor to the borders of India. A mass of different peoples and cultures, its history, perhaps inevitably, was one of gradual disintegration. Its last territory, Syria, and capital, ANTIOCH, succumbed to Rome in 64 BC. ▷ 2.09, 2.10, 2.11

SELEUCOS I
The founding king (r.312–281 BC) of the SELEUCID KINGDOM. Using Babylonia as a base, Seleucos gradually fought his way to control much of Asia, fighting against or making coalitions with rival successors to ALEXANDER's empire as occasion demanded. He founded Seleucia-on-the-Tigris, his first capital, and ANTIOCH, his western capital (300 BC). ▷ 2.09, 2.10

SENTINUM, BATTLE OF
See SAMNITE WARS

SEVERAN DYNASTY
Dynasty composed of the five Roman emperors, SEPTIMIUS SEVERUS (r.AD 193–211), CARACALLA (r.211–17), Macrinus (218), Elagabalus (r.218–22) and Alexander Severus (r.222–35). ▷ 2.15

SEVERUS, SEPTIMIUS
Proclaimed emperor of Rome in PANNONIA in AD 193, following the murder of Helvius Pertinax, he then marched on Italy to remove Didius Julianus. Severus then defeated Pescennius Niger, who had been proclaimed emperor in Syria. He campaigned successfully in Parthia, Africa and, with his son CARACALLA, in northern Britain. He died of gout at York in AD 211. ▷ 2.15

SHABAKA
King of Kush (r.712–698 BC) who conquered the whole of Egypt and made his capital at THEBES. He adopted the traditional style of the king of Egypt, setting up the 25th Dynasty of Egypt and initiating the Late period of Egyptian civilization. ▷ 2.21

SHANG YANG
The Wei-born prime minister of the QIN state in western China (d.338 BC), responsible for replacing an ancient aristocratic society with a centralized, militaristic state. In doing so, he laid the foundations for the future dominance of Qin, and of the forms of imperial government in China. ▷ 2.24

SHAPUR I
SASANIAN king of PERSIA (r.AD 240–72), the son of ARDASHIR I. He consolidated Sasanian power in Armenia and Mesopotamia, and in 260 defeated and captured the Roman emperor VALERIAN at EDESSA – an event celebrated in rock carvings throughout the empire. He supported the teachings of MANI. ▷ 2.11

SHAPUR II
SASANIAN king of PERSIA (r.AD 309–79). He came to the throne as an infant and, after assuming his full royal power at the age of 16, campaigned successfully in central Asia, taking Sasanian cultural influence as far as China. He campaigned against the Romans, but almost lost CTESIPHON to JULIAN in 363. He recovered Armenia and initially persecuted the Christian community there to force it to convert to ZOROASTRIANISM, though he later tolerated CHRISTIANITY. ▷ 2.11

SHI HUANGDI (FIRST EMPEROR)
The "First Emperor" of China (r.221–210 BC), formerly known as king Zheng of QIN (r.246–221). By defeating the states of Chu and Qi in 221 and 223, he unified the country for the first time. Establishing a centralized, bureaucratic empire, he laid the foundations for the Chinese empire, even though his dynasty did not long survive his death. He created a single Chinese script and system of weights and measures, and improved the communications systems. He also burned the works of many earlier scholars, including Confucius. His tomb at XIANYANG, near Xi'an in modern Shaanxi province, was discovered in 1974, guarded by a unique "terracotta army" of 6,000 life-sized soldiers, as well as hundreds of sacrificed horses and elaborate grave goods. ▷ 2.02, 2.24

SHU
Kingdom in the Sichuan basin of western China following the fall of the HAN in the AD 220s, with its capital at CHENGDU. It was conquered by Wei in 263. ▷ 2.24, 2.25

SHUNGA DYNASTY
Dynasty ruling the northern Indian kingdom of MAGADHA from 185 to 73 BC, founded by PUSHYAMITRA SHUNGA. ▷ 2.22

SILK
Fiber produced in the cocoons of moth caterpillars (silkworms). The manufacture of silk textiles, which began in China by 3000 BC (and remained a Chinese secret until AD 550), involved the care of silkworms and the cultivation of their food source, mulberry trees. The light, lustrous fabric was highly valued in antiquity. The silk trade began in the 1st millennium BC by caravan along the trans-Eurasian "Silk Route" from China, through the Gobi region, across the Pamir mountains into central Asia, and from there to the Middle East.

SIMA QIAN
Chinese scholar (c.145–85 BC) known as the "father of Chinese history", who was also the chief astronomer and expert of the calendar at the court of the HAN emperor, Wu. He developed his father's project of writing a definitive history of the whole of China, despite three years of imprisonment and castration for offending the emperor. His completed work, *Shih Chi*, ran to 130 chapters and included annals and genealogies of China's early kingdoms. ▷ 2.24

SKANDAGUPTA
The last king of the GUPTA dynasty of India (r.c.AD 455–67) to assert the power of the dynasty. His main achievement was the defeat of the EPHTHALITE HUNS in about 460. ▷ 2.23

SLAVIC (SLAVONIC) LANGUAGES
Part of the Indo-European group of languages, which includes Russian, Ukrainian and Belorussian (East Slavic); Polish, Czech and Slovak (West Slavic), and Serbo-Croat, Macedonian, Croatian, Slovenian and Bulgarian (South Slavic). Its common ancestral form, known as Proto-Slavic, was widely used in the 1st century BC, but the individual Slavic languages emerged during the 1st millennium AD. ▷ 2.19

SLAVS
A linguistic group that emerged as settled farmers in eastern Europe and the Balkans by the 5th century AD. The Slavs have little ethnic unity. In the Middle Ages a Slavic empire was built up in Moravia. ▷ 2.19

SOCIAL WAR
The Social or Italic War (91–87 BC) was fought between Rome and the *socii* – Rome's allies in Italy. The system of alliance devised by Rome was clever – the native communities were theoretically independent, but in practice merely subjects who supplied troops for Roman campaigns. The system became increasingly exploitive and the *socii* rose against Rome when denied citizenship. Rome was only able to defeat the rebellion by granting citizenship to those *socii* who returned to their allegiance. ▷ 2.13

SOCRATES
Athenian philosopher (469–399 BC), one of the most influential and perplexing figures of antiquity. Socrates devoted himself to finding the nature of goodness, which he believed

provided the key to happiness. He unsettled many through his continuous questioning of conventional wisdom, and his proclamation that it was the wise man who understood that he knew nothing. Eventually put to death for corrupting the young, he was a hero to PLATO, who reproduced or developed many of the teachings of Socrates in his own work. ▷ 2.08

SOISSONS, BATTLE OF
Important battle (AD 486) in the rise to power of CLOVIS, king of the FRANKS. Clovis defeated Syagrius, one of the last Roman generals to hold power in the disintegrating empire, and was then free to overawe the less powerful chieftains of GAUL, thus achieving a unified Frankish kingdom. ▷ 2.17

SOPHOCLES
Important Athenian tragic dramatist who was active from 468 to 406 BC. Sophocles is remembered for the intensity of his tragedies, in which flawed personalities are confronted by appalling choices. He was the first dramatist to portray women (Antigone, Electra) trapped within their emotions and instincts, though his most celebrated character was a king, Oedipus, who gouged out his eyes after he learned that he had murdered his father and married his mother. ▷ 2.08

SPARTAN LEAGUE
A loose organization of Sparta and its allies formed in the late 6th century BC. Members followed a common foreign policy, though Sparta was the dominant member throughout, and the league's power collapsed as Sparta's did. It was dissolved in 366 BC. ▷ 2.07

SPHAKTERIA, BATTLE OF
Climax of Athenian success in the PELOPONNESIAN WAR of 425 BC, when a Spartan force on the island of Sphacteria was forced into surrender. Sparta was so humiliated that it eventually sought peace (421 BC), though the war resumed in 418 BC. ▷ 2.08

STEPPE NOMADS
Collective term for the peoples who inhabited the steppes of Eurasia from Classical times, made up mainly of loose confederations of tribes which could build and usurp huge empires very quickly, and which periodically threatened settled civilizations from Rome to China. The steppe nomads relied on herds of horses and lost their effectiveness when they were unable to find sufficient grazing for them. There were three main groups of Eurasian nomads: the IRANIAN-speaking (including the Scythians, Sarmatians and Kushans); the TURKIC-speaking (including the HUNS) and MONGOLIAN-speaking (including the JUAN-JUAN). ▷ 2.20

STILICHO
Half-German generalissimo and effectively ruler of the western ROMAN EMPIRE during the infancy of the emperor HONORIUS (from AD 395). Stilicho attempted, without much success, to quell a mass of BARBARIAN invaders. He was eventually charged with treason and executed in 408 by Honorius' advisers. ▷ 2.16

STIRRUP
Foot support for the rider of a horse. Stirrups gave a rider greater balance, and made it possible to fight effectively from the saddle. The use of stirrups was probably pioneered by STEPPE NOMADS in the early centuries BC, though there is a suggestion that stirrups may have existed in Assyria in 850 BC. The first stirrups were seen in India before 100 BC. They were not known in China until the 5th century AD, the same time they were introduced into Europe by the HUNS. The adoption of stirrups allowed the development of the knight fighting from horseback in medieval Europe, a change that was pioneered by Charles Martel in the Frankish kingdom in the 730s.

STOICS
Group of philosophers whose discussions (led by ZENO of Citium) took place in a stoa at ATHENS from 313 BC. The Stoics believed in one united world order moving onwards to an unknown purpose. Human beings had to learn how to understand and accept their own role within this order, having the freedom to live a good life, but always subject to greater powers. The Romans, and later the Christians, found Stoicism appealing. ▷ 2.09

STUPA
A decorated hemispherical stone mound surrounded by a paved walkway, distinctive of BUDDHISM, and built to house relics. The first *stupas* were built in northern India from the 3rd century BC, and represented the first form of religious architecture in the subcontinent. The form spread throughout the Buddhist world (in China and Japan it was modified into the pagoda form). The terraced temple of Borobudur in Java is also based on the *stupa* form. ▷ 2.06

SUEVI
Group of Germanic peoples that included the ALEMANNI, the MARCOMANNI and the LOMBARDS. In the 1st century AD they inhabited the east Elbe region, but invaded the ROMAN EMPIRE in the early 5th century. By 450 the Suevi controlled much of the Iberian peninsula, before being ousted by the VISIGOTHS. ▷ 2.16, 2.17, 2.19

SUI DYNASTY
Chinese dynasty (AD 589–618) founded by SUI WENDI, who unified China and introduced new bureaucratic controls to ensure the country's prosperity. His son Yang (r.604–18) continued to build the prestige of his father's empire, beginning the Grand Canal and the rebuilding of the Great Wall.

He campaigned in Korea in the 610s, but a popular revolt forced him to abdicate and the Tang dynasty was set up. ▷ 2.25

SUI WENDI (YANG JIAN)
Emperor of China (r.AD 589–618) and founder of the SUI DYNASTY. A soldier, he married a princess of the NORTHERN ZHOU and then overthrew the dynasty in 581. He campaigned against the Chen in the south, unifying the country for the first time in 350 years. He also campaigned effectively in Turkestan and Mongolia, and attempted to extend the power of China to the south. From 601 he became increasingly absorbed in public Buddhist observances, following the model of ASHOKA. ▷ 2.25

SUN TZU
Chinese writer (c.500 BC) whose volume, *The Art of War*, was the first major Chinese work on strategy. He emphasized the importance of political considerations to the military strategist and his work profoundly influenced later Chinese military thinking.

SUREN
Ancient kingdom of eastern Iran, Afghanistan and the Indus valley established by the Parthian Suren family in the 1st century BC, but conquered by the KUSHANS in about AD 50. ▷ 2.10, 2.11

SUTTON HOO
Aristocratic, pagan ANGLO-SAXON cemetery in Suffolk, England, dating from the late 6th to late 7th centuries AD. It is best known for its royal burial of a clinker-built ship, complete with opulent grave goods drawn from many parts of the then-known world. Other ships and aristocratic burials have since been discovered on the site, but none of such opulence.

SYPHAX
Numidian leader of the late 3rd century BC who tried to exploit the rivalry of the Romans and Carthaginians to his advantage. He was eventually defeated by the Romans after he allied with the Carthaginians, and died in Italy in 201 BC. ▷ 2.12

TABGATCH
See TOBA

TACITUS
Roman historian, born in about AD 56 in GAUL. He moved to Rome by AD 75 and held some political offices there, but was mainly occupied with writing. His works include *Agricola* (AD 98), a biography of Agricola (his father-in-law and governor of Britain for seven years), and the *Germania* (AD 98), a description of the Germanic tribes. The surviving books of his *Histories* (c.AD 109–10) and *Annals* (c.AD 120) record the events of AD 69–70 and the reigns of TIBERIUS, GAIUS (Caligula), CLAUDIUS and NERO. ▷ 2.13

TARA

Located in County Meath, Ireland, Tara was the original residence of the high kings of Ireland. There are many archeological remains of the early historic period – mainly forts and burial mounds. The site was most important as a political center from the 3rd to the 6th centuries AD. ▷ 2.18

TARRACONENSIS

The largest early imperial province in Spain, originally the province of HISPANIA Citerior (197 BC), renowned for its fine wine, fish sauce and silver mines. It was taken by the VISIGOTHS in about AD 475. ▷ 2.13

TARUGA

Early Iron Age site of the NOK CULTURE in the Benue region, Nigeria, with evidence of iron metallurgy (smelting furnaces) dating to the 5th century BC, and possibly as early as 800 BC. ▷ 2.21

TAXILA

City in the upper Indus valley, north Pakistan, and the capital of GANDHARA. It was conquered by the Persians in about 500 BC, when the region became the easternmost province of the Achemenid empire. The irregular layout of the site suggests that it was not a planned settlement, but expanded as its commercial importance increased on the strategic caravan route between India and Iran, via the Khyber Pass. ▷ 2.10, 2.22

TEN THOUSAND

Greek mercenary force raised by the Spartan commander Lysander, in support of a rebellion by the Persian, Cyrus, against his brother the king (401 BC). The rebellion was a failure but the ensuing Greek retreat of the "Ten Thousand" was immortalized by the historian XENOPHON. ▷ 2.08

TEOTIHUACÁN

Ancient city of Mesoamerica, close to modern Mexico City. First occupied in about 200 BC, by AD 500 it had became one of the world's largest cities, with a cultural and economic influence that was felt deep into the Maya region. Laid out on a strict grid, its monuments include the vast Pyramids of the Sun and Moon, as well as hundreds of other temples. There are no written records of its civilization, but its gods were worshiped by later Mesoamerican cultures, including the Toltecs and Aztecs. The city was sacked in about 700 and was excavated during the 1960s. ▷ 2.27, 2.28

TETRARCHY

Name given to the system of government introduced by DIOCLETIAN in the late 3rd century AD, in which rulership of the ROMAN EMPIRE was shared between four emperors. The empire was divided into eastern and western halves, each under a senior emperor, or "Augustus". Each Augustus ruled with the assistance of a junior colleague, or "Caesar", designated the successor to the Augustus. The system was intended to provide effective defense and bring stability to the imperial succession, but it quickly broke down after Diocletian's abdication in 305. ▷ 2.15

TEUTOBURGERWALD, BATTLE OF

Battle in AD 9, in which a Roman army under Varus was destroyed on the march by GERMANS under ARMINIUS, losing three legions and ending Roman attempts to conquer Germany. Recent finds of Roman military equipment have located the battlefield – about 16 kilometers (10 miles) north of the modern city of Osnabrück. ▷ 2.13, 2.19

TEUTONES

One of the ancient GERMAN tribes from Jutland in the late 2nd century BC. They invaded the ROMAN EMPIRE with the CIMBRI and were finally defeated at Vercellae in 101 BC. Their name was sometimes applied to the entire group of Germanic peoples. ▷ 2.19

THASOS

Island in the north Aegean known for its fertility and mineral wealth. Settled by the Greeks in about 650 BC, Thasos became prosperous and often extended its power onto the mainland of Thrace. A member of the DELIAN LEAGUE, it was occupied by ATHENS when it rebelled (465 BC). Later subdued by PHILIP II OF MACEDON, the island regained its prosperity in Roman times. ▷ 2.07

THEATER

The Greek theatron was originally the sitting place for an audience, though the word came to include the stage and buildings which formed the backdrop to it. Rudimentary at first, by the 4th century BC theaters were grandly built in stone or marble (as at Epidauros), and spread to the Roman world.

THEBES (GREECE)

Ancient settlement in southeastern Boeotia, an important Mycenaean center and the legendary birthplace of Heracles. The city re-emerged in the 6th century BC and for much of its history was preoccupied with maintaining control of the rich plain of Boeotia against the ambitions of ATHENS and Sparta. A stunning victory over Sparta at Leuctra in 371 BC saw Thebes become the most powerful state in GREECE for a short period, but after 360 BC it was of little importance. ▷ 2.08, 2.21

THEMISTOCLES

(c.524–459 BC) Athenian politician who was remembered for his skills in diplomacy and generalship. He was instrumental in building the Piraeus, the harbor in ATHENS, constructing a new navy from the city's silver resources, and masterminding the victory at SALAMIS. His later career was less fortunate. He was exiled from Athens and entered the service of the Persians before he died. ▷ 2.07

THEODORIC

King of Italy (r.AD 493–526), the OSTROGOTH Theodoric occupied the vacuum left by the collapse of the western empire. He tolerated Roman culture and his reign was a stable and effective one, though his Arian beliefs meant that Roman and Ostrogothic cultures remained distinct. He extended his kingdom to include parts of France and Spain. ▷ 2.17

THEODOSIAN DYNASTY

Dynasty founded by THEODOSIUS I. After his death in AD 395 it was divided, with one son, Arcadius, taking the east of the empire and another, HONORIUS, the west. Honorius saw only disintegration and withdrawal, but under Arcadius' successor, his son Theodosius II (emperor from AD 408 to 450), Constantinople was consolidated as the effective capital of the remaining empire. ▷ 2.16

THEODOSIUS I

Roman emperor from AD 379 to 395. Rising to power through his own abilities, Theodosius emerged as emperor in the east (AD 379) and, after campaigns in Italy, in the west (AD 387). He was the last emperor to rule the empire as a single unit. A devout Christian heavily influenced by AMBROSE, bishop of Milan, he ruthlessly imposed orthodox CHRISTIANITY on the empire. During his reign Gothic tribes were allowed to settle within Roman territory in return for providing armed support. ▷ 2.15, 2.16

THERAVADA BUDDHISM

The "Doctrine of the Elders", one of the major divisions of BUDDHISM, and the form most prevalent in Sri Lanka and southeast Asia. Theravada Buddhism was promoted by ASHOKA in the 3rd century BC, under whose influence it spread southward; it was taken to southeast Asia in the 11 to 14th centuries AD. It tends to be conservative and orthodox; the goal of the adherent is to achieve individual enlightenment. There is a strong monastic tradition. ▷ 2.06

THERMOPYLAE, BATTLE OF

Battle fought at the pass of Thermopylae by the Greeks, under the leadership of LEONIDAS and his force of Spartans, against the invading Persian army of 480 BC. Eventually the Persians crossed through the mountains behind the pass, but the Spartans fought heroically to the death, buying time for the rest of the Greek army to escape. ▷ 2.07

THREE KINGDOMS (CHINA)

The period of Chinese history between AD 220 and 265, following the collapse of the HAN DYNASTY. During these years, China was divided into the kingdoms of Wu, Wei and SHU. The Three Kingdoms period was briefly followed by the JIN DYNASTY. The period saw many Indian cultural influences enter China and is remembered in Chinese chivalry and folklore. ▷ 2.25

THREE KINGDOMS (KOREA)
Early period of Korean history (1st century BC to 7th century AD) in which the Korean peninsula was divided between the kingdoms of Koguryo, Silla and Paekche. ▷ 2.25

THUCYDIDES
(c.455–c.396 BC) One of the leading Greek historians, remembered for his detailed history of the PELOPONNESIAN WAR, written while the war was still being fought. Showing no illusions about the brutalities of war and power politics, Thucydides' work stands out for its colorful narratives and the powerful speeches he put in the mouths of its main characters. ▷ 2.08

TIAHUANACO (TIWANAKU)
Former city and religious center in the Andes, near Lake Titicaca, Bolivia. The site was occupied in the early centuries BC, but the Tiahuanaco state was formed in about AD 100. Its cultural influence spread throughout the Andean region. The site was abandoned in about 1000. Tiahuanaco is notable for its monolithic architecture, notably the Gateway of the Sun, carved with hieroglyphs and gods, and an intricate system of raised, irrigated fields capable of feeding its population of up to 50,000, despite an altitude of 4,000 meters (13,000 feet). ▷ 2.27

TIBERIUS
(r.AD 14–37) Born in 42 BC, he became the stepson of Octavian (AUGUSTUS) in 38 BC. After a successful military career, he was proclaimed emperor on Augustus' death in AD 14. A generally competent ruler, Tiberius became unpopular due to his unappealing manner, family jealousy and unscrupulous use of treason laws to destroy his political enemies – real or imagined. He retired to Campania in AD 27 and then to Capri, where he died in AD 37. The rumors of Tiberius indulging in vice on Capri are unsubstantiated. ▷ 2.04, 2.13

TIGRANES I
Armenian ruler (r.c.100–56 BC) who created a short-lived empire, which stretched from Parthia in the east to Syria and the Levant in the west, incorporating much of the decaying SELEUCID KINGDOM in the process (83 BC). Such expansion aroused Roman concern and Tigranes was forced back into Armenia by POMPEY. ▷ 2.10

TIKAL
Classic period MAYAN lowland city, now in northwestern Guatemala. Tikal came to prominence in the 5th century AD, when it had trading contacts throughout Mesoamerica, reaching as far as TEOTIHUACÁN. It contained five temple-pyramids and several palaces. It was excavated in the 1950s and 1960s. ▷ 2.28

TIWANAKU
See TIAHUANACO

TOBA (TABGATCH)
TURKIC-speaking nomadic people from Mongolia who invaded northern China in the 4th century AD. ▷ 2.25

TOBA WEI KINGDOM
Kingdom established in north China by the TOBA people in AD 439. The capital was initially at Pingcheng in the far north, but in 494 it was moved to Luoyang. The state endured until 534, when it split into eastern and western halves. ▷ 2.25

TOTILA
OSTROGOTHIC king (r.AD 541–52) who reconquered much of central and southern Italy, including Rome, from the eastern ROMAN EMPIRE. He died in battle, and the Romans regained the initiative once more. ▷ 2.17

TRAJAN
Roman emperor from AD 98 to 117. Born in AD 53 to a high-ranking family in Spain, he became emperor of Rome after the death of Nerva. Noted for his fair and considerate conduct, Trajan was respected by the senate, was reasonable in his dealings with the provinces, beloved by his troops – in whom he took a personal interest – and concerned with the welfare of the Roman people. He undertook a number of building projects to beautify and improve the facilities of Rome, including the construction of a new harbor at OSTIA, the Via Traiana and the new forum and basilica. He conquered DACIA (AD 101–02, 105–06), removing a potential threat to the empire's Danube frontier, but his conquests in Armenia and Parthia (115–17) were given up by his successor HADRIAN as being undefendable. ▷ 2.11, 2.13, 2.14, 2.15

TRAJAN'S COLUMN
Dedicated in AD 113 as part of TRAJAN's forum at Rome, this 29-meter (95-foot) high marble column on a square sculpted base celebrated the emperor's military achievements. The detailed spiral reliefs on the shaft of the column, depicting Trajan's Dacian wars (AD 101–02, 105–06), were probably added after his death as a form of commemoration. ▷ 2.13

TRIREME
The standard Greek warship that was used most effectively by the Athenians in the 5th century BC (as at the BATTLE OF SALAMIS). Rowed by three banks of coordinated oarsmen, the galley was designed to ram its opponents at speed. Meticulous training and high morale were essential for its successful use. ▷ 2.07

TÚ-YÜ-HUN
TURKIC-speaking nomadic people of central Asia who threatened northwestern China in the 4th to 6th centuries AD. ▷ 2.25

TUNGUSIC
Language group spoken in eastern Siberia and northern Manchuria. Its speakers include the Tung-nu and the Manchus.

TURKIC LANGUAGES
Group of languages forming a subdivision of the ALTAIC languages, today including Turkish, Uzbeg, Azerbaijani, Tatar and Uighur, but historically also including many languages of the nomads of the east Asian steppes. ▷ 2.20

TURKISH KHANATES
The TURKIC-speaking confederation of tribes that established its authority over much of the central and east Asian steppes in the 6th century AD. ▷ 2.20

TWELVE TABLES
Tradition records that the Laws of the Twelve Tables – the basis of Roman law – were compiled in about 450 BC. Although the tradition cannot be confirmed, it is probable that they underlay the colonial charters of the late 4th century BC and were revised from the early 3rd century BC. ▷ 2.12

UAXACTÚN
Former MAYAN city of PETÉN in northern Guatemala, north of TIKAL. Although a minor site historically, it has yielded sufficient pottery remains to enable archeologists to construct a sequence of types of Mayan pottery. Important Preclassic discoveries were made at Uaxacún in the 1980s. The city flourished in the Classic period and declined in about AD 1000. ▷ 2.28

ULFILAS, BISHOP
(c.AD 311–83) Born into a Christian family and captured by the GOTHS, Ulfilas took on the mission of converting the Goths to Arian CHRISTIANITY, and translated the Bible into Gothic. The Arian Goths were shunned by orthodox Christians, which helps to explain the reluctance of the empire to come to terms with them. ▷ 2.15

UPANISHADS
Sacred texts of Hinduism and the final stage of the Vedas. There are more than 100 separate works, the most important of which were written from about 800 to 400 BC; the last date from AD 300 or later. They deal with speculative and philosophical issues in prose and verse, and stress the importance of Brahman, the doctrine of pure being.

VAKATAKA
Indian dynasty in the Deccan, said to have been founded by Vindhyasakti in about AD 260. From about 400 they were allied with the GUPTAS, but they took advantage of the Hunas invasions in the late 5th century to seize an empire in central India. The last known Vakataka king was Prithvishena II (c.470). ▷ 2.23

VALENS

Eastern Roman emperor from AD 364 to 378 and the brother of the western emperor, Valentinian I. He supported ARIANISM and began the persecution of orthodox Christians. He campaigned successfully against the VISIGOTHS but then allowed them into the empire in 376. He was killed at the BATTLE OF ADRIANOPLE. ▷ 2.15, 2.16

VALENTINIAN III

Western Roman emperor (r.AD 425–55) who presided over the final period of a determined defense of the empire by his military chief, AETIUS. Valentinian himself killed AETIUS in 454, fearing his political ambitions. The following year Valentinian was killed in a revenge attack by one of Aetius' retainers. Following Valentinian's death the western ROMAN EMPIRE lost all political stability and began its final disintegration. ▷ 2.16

VALERIAN

Roman emperor of senatorial origin who shared power with his son, Gallienus, between AD 253 and 260, at the height of the 3rd-century crisis. His main concern was to restore Roman control in the east, but he was captured, humiliated and killed by the Persian ruler SHAPUR I in 260. ▷ 2.11, 2.15

VANDALS

Germanic peoples who crossed over the Rhine in AD 406 and spread remorselessly through GAUL, Spain and eventually (under their impressive leader Gaiseric) into the rich Roman provinces of north Africa (429). They sacked Rome in 455, but were eventually conquered by JUSTINIAN's general, BELISARIUS, in 533. ▷ 2.15, 2.16, 2.17, 2.19

VANGA

Ancient kingdom of east Bengal, one of the *mahajanapadas* ("great realms") of the 6th century BC. It formed part of the MAURYAN empire and was later conquered by the GUPTAS. ▷ 2.22, 2.23

VANGIONES

GERMAN tribe that inhabited the west bank of the Rhine in the 5th century AD, and whose chief center was at modern Worms (known as Civitas Vangionum). The city was disputed by the Romans and Burgundians, and sacked by the HUNS (as Roman allies) in 436. It was rebuilt by the Merovingian kings. ▷ 2.16

VEII

The most southerly of the great Etruscan cities, 16 kilometers (10 miles) north of Rome, that was famous in antiquity for its terracotta statuary. In 396 BC the city was destroyed following a long siege by Rome, but a small settlement survived. Excavation has revealed extensive Villanovan cemeteries and the imposing extra-urban sanctuary of Portonaccio. ▷ 2.12

VENETI

The name given to two different groups in antiquity: a Celtic group in Brittany and part of Normandy which had strong links to southwest England (they were finally subdued by Rome in a naval battle of 56 BC), and a group that inhabited the fertile country around the head of the Adriatic; cultivated traders and horse-breeders, they were friendly to Rome and were probably granted full Roman citizenship in 49 BC. ▷ 2.18

VERACRUZ

Ancient civilization of the Gulf Coast of eastern Mexico of the Classic period (AD 1–700); its major center was at EL TAJÍN. It incorporated the remains of Olmec civilization and it was probably in Veracruz that the "long-count" calendar was devised, in the late 1st century BC. Veracruz was also deeply influenced by TEOTIHUACÁN. The BALL-COURT was a distinctive feature of Veracruz culture. ▷ 2.27

VERCINGETORIX

The son of a Gallic nobleman, he raised a coalition of peoples of central GAUL against JULIUS CAESAR in 52 BC. Caesar finally defeated Vercingetorix by successfully beseiging him at ALESIA, thereby effectively completing the Roman conquest of Gaul. Vercingetorix surrendered and was executed after Caesar's triumph of 46 BC. ▷ 2.18

VERGINA

A site in MACEDONIA that is now confirmed as the ancient capital of the Macedonian Teminid dynasty and the burial place of their kings. The most spectacular find has been the tomb, body and associated grave goods of PHILIP II. ▷ 2.08

VESPASIAN

Emperor of Rome from AD 69 to 79 and the founder of the FLAVIAN DYNASTY. Vespasian served as a soldier in Britain, Germany and Judaea, and asserted his claim to the throne by force. He sought to restore the finances of the state and celebrated the start of a new age of peace (despite completing the destruction of Jerusalem during a Jewish rebellion). He was succeeded by Titus.

VIJAYA

According to legend Vijaya was a prince of the 5th century BC, Bengali by origin, who was banished from his father's kingdom in Gujarat. He first colonized the island of Ceylon and established a dynasty on the west coast in 483 BC. The third king of the Vijaya dynasty established the kingdom of ANURADHAPURA and his descendants continued to rule there until AD 65. ▷ 2.22

VIMA KADPHISES

Kushan king from about AD 75 to 100 who conquered much of northern India. ▷ 2.23

VIRGIL

Roman poet (70–19 BC) from Mantua who was in the circle of AUGUSTUS. Most famous for his epic poem the *Aeneid*, which claims a Trojan origin for the Roman people, he also wrote the *Eclogues* and the *Georgics*, both celebrations of country life. ▷ 2.13

VISIGOTHS

Distinct group of GOTHS (probably western Goths) that emerged in the 4th century AD. They were admitted to the ROMAN EMPIRE in 376 as refugees from the HUNS. Badly treated, they rebelled in 378, defeating and killing the emperor VALENS in 378 at ADRIANOPLE. In search of land in the empire for themselves, they ravaged their way through GREECE and Italy (sacking Rome under ALARIC in 410), and were eventually settled in Aquitaine as foederati in 418. By 480 they had taken over southern GAUL and most of Spain. ▷ 2.04, 2.05, 2.15, 2.16, 2.17, 2.19

VITRUVIUS POLLIO, MARCUS

Roman military architect who served JULIUS CAESAR and AUGUSTUS. He is best known for his treatise, *De Architectura*, which was addressed to Augustus and stressed the intellectual and technical demands of the profession. ▷ 2.13

VOTADINI

Celtic tribe inhabiting the Scottish lowlands in the Roman period. Their capital was at Traprain Law, but they moved to Edinburgh in about AD 500, when they established the kingdom of Gododdin.

VOUILLÉ, BATTLE OF

Decisive battle in western France (AD 507) between the FRANKS, led by CLOVIS, and the VISIGOTHS. As a result, the Franks established their domination over present-day France and confined the Visigoths to the Iberian peninsula. The battle also ensured the victory of Catholicism over ARIANISM in the Frankish kingdoms. ▷ 2.17

VULGATE BIBLE

Translation by ST JEROME (AD 347–420) of the Old Testament and NEW TESTAMENT from Hebrew and GREEK into LATIN. The first accessible and reliable text of the Bible for the ordinary (Latin-speaking) reader in western Europe, it represents one of the great achievements of early Christian scholarship.

WANG MANG

Chinese nobleman, also known as "the usurper", who overthrew the western HAN DYNASTY in AD 6 and became regent for the child he had made emperor. Three years later Wang Mang claimed the throne himself, as the first of the Xin dynasty. He attempted to introduce land reform, without success. Rebellions occurred after devastating floods and famine in northern China and the Han were restored in AD 23. ▷ 2.24

WUDI (SIMA YEN)
First emperor of the short-lived JIN DYNASTY of China (r.AD 265–89), who came to power as a soldier in the northern kingdom of Wei and usurped its throne in 265. He attempted to reduce the power of the aristocracy, but was unable to protect China from BARBARIAN invasions. His title, Wudi, meant "martial emperor". ▷ 2.25

XENOPHON
(c.428–354 BC) Aristocratic Greek historian, soldier and politician. Originally from ATHENS, in his varied career he also served with a Spartan army. Xenophon is remembered for his vivid account of the March of the TEN THOUSAND and the *Hellenica*, an outline of Greek history from 411 to 362 BC and one of the few sources for the period, even if not now seen as a reliable one. ▷ 2.08

XERXES I
Son of DARIUS I and king of PERSIA from 486 to 465 BC. Xerxes is remembered in European history for his meticulously planned invasion of GREECE in 480 BC, which ended in failure. The expedition was probably only a minor incident during his reign, which was one of comparative stability. ▷ 2.07, 2.09

XIANYANG
The site in China, some 60 kilometers (40 miles) from Xi'an in modern Shaanxi province, of the tomb of the first QIN emperor, SHI HUANGDI. The tomb contained a terracotta army of 6,000 life-sized models of soldiers and horses. ▷ 2.24

XIAO GONG
King of QIN from 361 to 338 BC and – in partnership with his minister SHANG YANG – initiator of Qin's rise to dominance in China. Their reforms of administration, military service and trade strengthened Qin in both peace and wartime. ▷ 2.24

XIONGNU (HSIUNG-NU)
TURKIC-speaking nomadic peoples of the east Asian steppes. From 300 BC they repeatedly threatened northern China, prompting the Chinese to begin building a system of defensive walls. Raids continued until the late 2nd century BC, after which the Xiongnu split in two. The Xiongnu were permitted to settle inside the wall and their generals claimed to control northern China briefly in the 4th century AD, but from the 5th century the Xiongu disappeared. Xiongnu graves have revealed goods from Iran and GREECE. ▷ 2.20, 2.24, 2.25

YAMATO PERIOD
Period of Japanese history (AD 300–710) in which the authority of the emperor was first established and the distinctive Japanese culture began to emerge. During this period vast KEYHOLE TOMBS were built for the emperors, indicative of a hierarchical society.

From about AD 600 political centralization began, following the model of China; by 700 the state had established its authority over most of Japan. The capital was at ASUKA. BUDDHISM was introduced from Korea in 552, and ambassadors were sent to China in the 7th century.

YAXCHILÁN
Late Classic MAYAN city of the central area (now in Mexico). It is a river-based center, and its first *stelae* (stone monuments) date from about AD 300; the last date from the early 9th century. ▷ 2.28

YAYOI CULTURE
The Bronze and Iron Age culture of Japan (300 BC–AD 300), marked by the spread of wet-rice cultivation and the establishment of the first petty states. The potter's wheel was also known. Yayoi culture, a development of Jomon culture, was first established in Kyushu, Shikoku and southern Honshu, and gradually spread northward. It is named after the district of Tokyo where its artifacts were discovered. ▷ 2.25

YEAR OF FOUR EMPERORS
After NERO's suicide in AD 68 civil war erupted over the succession. Galba (r.68–69), Otho (r.69) and Vitellius (r.69) all reigned briefly, until stability was restored by VESPASIAN (r.69–79). ▷ 2.13

YUE
Vietnamese-speaking tribes in northern Vietnam and southern China who formed the kingdoms of NAN-YUE and MIN-YUE in the late 1st millennium BC. ▷ 2.24

YUE QI (INDO-SCYTHIANS)
IRANIAN-speaking nomads of central Asia and the Gansu region around the time of JESUS. Driven from their homelands by the XIONGNU in the early 2nd century BC, they moved to BACTRIA and eventually formed the KUSHAN empire. The Yue Qi were influential in the spread of BUDDHISM from India to China. ▷ 2.20, 2.23, 2.24

ZEALOT
Jewish faction, deriving from the revolt of the MACCABEES in the 2nd century BC, that fought to establish an independent Jewish kingdom according to the Torah. The Zealots became an organized force during the reign of HEROD (r.37–4 BC) and led a rebellion against a Roman census in AD 6. They were known as *sicarii* ("dagger-men") for their policy of assassination. After their revolt of AD 66–73, which led to the destruction of the Temple of Jerusalem by the Romans, the Zealots were much weakened.

ZENO
(335–263 BC) Greek philosopher who arrived in ATHENS in 313 BC and founded Stoicism (so-called because his discussions were held under a stoa, an open-air colonnade). Followed by the STOICS, it was a highly influential philosophy not only for the Greeks, but for Romans and Christians as well. ▷ 2.09

ZENOBIA
Formidable queen of the Syrian trading city of PALMYRA. Zenobia established an independent empire, which extended as far as Egypt and Asia Minor, during a crisis in the ROMAN EMPIRE in the AD 260s. At first tolerated by the Romans as a bulwark against PERSIA, she was subdued by the emperor AURELIAN in 272, though her life was spared. ▷ 2.15

ZHANG QIAN
Chinese explorer (d.114 BC) who was the first to travel to central Asia (from 138) and bring back a reliable account of his journeys. On his first journey he visited the YUE QI and was held for ten years by the XIONGNU. His second journey took him to BACTRIA and Soghdiana, and brought China in contact with HELLENISTIC civilization.

ZHAO
Northern Chinese kingdom and one of the strongest states of the Warring States period. In 307 BC it introduced new cavalry techniques, imported from the nomads of the north, to China. However, it was conquered by QIN in 228 BC. ▷ 2.24

ZHENG (FIRST EMPEROR)
See SHI HUANGDI

ZHONGSHAN
Small northern Chinese kingdom of the Warring States period, conquered by ZHAO in 296 BC. ▷ 2.24

ZHOU, NORTHERN
See NORTHERN ZHOU

ZOROASTRIANISM
Ancient religion that emerged in PERSIA in the 6th century BC, founded by the prophet Zoroaster (c.630–c.550 BC), about whose life little definite is known. Its holy books are the *Avesta* and the *Zend Avesta*. Zoroastrianism sees the world in terms of a cosmic struggle between the forces of good (and light), led by AHURA MAZDA, and those of evil (and dark). Its ceremonies often show particular veneration for fire. Zoroastrianism was the religion of Achemenid, Parthian and SASANIAN Persia. Through its offshoot, MITHRAISM, it influenced the ROMAN EMPIRE and CHRISTIANITY in particular. It is still practiced in Iran and elsewhere; Indian adherents are known as Parsis. ▷ 2.06, 2.11

Acknowledgments

Text, timelines and maps

The authors and publishers readily acknowledge the work of a large number of scholars and published works, on which they have drawn in the preparation of this atlas. Many of these works remain in print, and can be used as reliable secondary reading on the many topics covered in this atlas. Among them are the following:

al Faruqi, Ismail Ragi (ed) *Historical Atlas of the Religions of the World* (New York and London, 1974)

Allchin, B and R *The Birth of Indian Civilization: India and Pakistan before 500 BC* (London, 2nd ed 1994)

Bahn, Paul G (ed) *Cambridge Illustrated History of Archaeology* (Cambridge and New York, 1996)

Baines, John and Malek, Jaromir *Atlas of Ancient Egypt* (Oxford and New York 1980)

Barraclough, G (ed) *The Times Atlas of World History* (4th ed, London 1993 and New York, 1994)

Beek, MA *Atlas of Mesopotamia* (London 1962)

Blunden, Caroline and Elvin, Mark *Cultural Atlas of China* (London and New York, 1986)

Boardman, J *The Greeks Overseas* (London 1964)

Bolton, Geoffrey (ed) *The Oxford History of Australia* (Oxford and Melbourne 1994)

Bonsall, C *The Mesolithic in Europe* (Edinburgh 1989)

Chadwick, Henry and Evans, Gillian R (eds) *Atlas of the Christian Church* (London and New York, 1987)

Champion, T, Gamble, C, Shennan, S and Whittle, A *Prehistoric Europe* (London 1984)

Chang, KC *The Archaeology of Ancient China* (Yale 1977)

Chard, CS *Northeast Asia in Prehistory* (Madison, USA 1974)

Coe, Michael, Snow, Dean and Benson, Elizabeth *Atlas of Ancient America* (London and New York, 1986)

Coe, Michael *Mexico: from the Olmecs to the Aztecs* (London and New York, 4th ed 1994)

Cohn-Sherbok, D *Atlas of Jewish History* (London and New York, 1994)

Coles, JM and Harding, AF *The Bronze Age in Europe* (London 1979)

Connah, G *African Civilizations: Precolonial cities and states in tropical Africa* (Cambridge and New York, 1987)

Cook, JM *The Persian Empire* (London 1983)

Cornell, Tim and Matthews, John *Atlas of the Roman World* (London and New York, 1982)

Cotterell, A *East Asia* (London 1993, New York 1995)

Crawford, M *The Roman Republic* (London 1978, Cambridge, Mass. 1993)

Cunliffe, Barry (ed) *The Oxford Illustrated Prehistory of Europe* (Oxford and New York, 1994)

Davies, JK *Democracy and Classical Greece* (London, 2nd ed 1993)

Davis, Norman *Europe: a History* (Oxford and New York, 1996)

de Lange, Nicholas *Atlas of the Jewish World* (London and New York, 1984)

Elliott, JH (ed) *The Hispanic World* (London and New York, 1991)

Fagan, Brian M *The Journey from Eden: the Peopling of our World* (London and New York, 1990)

Fagan, Brian M *Ancient North America* (London and New York, 1995)

Fagan, Brian M *People of the Earth* (New York and London, 7th ed 1992)

Fage, JD and Oliver, R (eds) *The Cambridge History of Africa* (Cambridge and New York, 1975)

Fage, JD *An Atlas of African History* (London 1978)

Falkus, M and Gillingham J *Historical Atlas of Britain* (London and New York, revised ed 1987)

Fiedel, SJ *Prehistory of the Americas* (Cambridge and New York, 2nd ed 1992)

Freeman-Grenville, GSP *Historical Atlas of the Middle East* (New York 1993)

Frye, RN *The Heritage of Persia* (London, 2nd ed 1976)

Gamble, C *The Palaeolithic Settlement of Europe* (Cambridge 1986)

Gamble, C *Timewalkers: the Prehistory of Global Colonization* (Stroud 1993, Cambridge, Mass. 1994)

Gaur, A *A History of Writing* (London 1984, New York 1994)

Gilbert, Martin *The Atlas of Jewish History* (London and New York, 5th ed 1996)

Green, MJ *The Celtic World* (London and New York, 1995)

Grosser Historischer Weltatlas (3 vols, Munich 1981)

Hall, DGE *A History of South-east Asia* (London, 4th ed 1981)

Hood, S *The Minoans* (London and New York, 1973)

Johnson, Gordon, Bayly, C and Richards JF *The New Cambridge History of India* (Cambridge 1987)

Johnson, Gordon *Cultural Atlas of India* (London 1995, New York, 1996)

Kemp, BJ *Ancient Egypt* (London 1989, New York 1992)

Kinder, H and Hilgemann, W *Atlas of World History* (2 vols, Munich, London and New York, 1974)

Kuhrt, A *The Ancient Near East* (2 vols, London and New York ,1995)

Kulke, H and Rothermund, D *A History of India* (London 1990)

Langer, William L *An Encyclopedia of World History* (5th ed, London and New York, 1973)

Levi, Peter *Cultural Atlas of the Greek World* (London and New York, 1984)

Ling, T *A History of Religion East and West* (London 1968)

Mallory, JP *In Search of the Indo-Europeans* (London 1989, New York 1991)

Moore, RI (ed) *The Hamlyn Historical Atlas* (London 1981)

Moseley, ME *The Incas and their Ancestors* (London and New York, 1993)

Murray, Oswyn *Early Greece* (London, 2nd ed 1993)

Phillipson, DW *African Archaeology* (Cambridge, 2nd ed 1993)

Roaf, Michael and Postgate, Nicholas *Cultural Atlas of Mesopotamia and the Ancient Near East* (London and New York, 1990)

Roberts, JM *The Hutchinson History of the World* (London 1976)

Rogerson, John *Atlas of the Bible* (London and New York, 1985)

Scarre, Dr Chris *Past Worlds: The Times Atlas of Archaeology* (London and New York, 1988)

Schmidt, KJ *An Atlas and Survey of South Asian History* (New York and London, <None> 1995)

Schwartzberg, Joseph E (ed) *A Historical Atlas of South Asia* (Chicago and London, 2nd ed 1992)

Sharer, RJ *The Ancient Maya* (Stanford, Ca. 5th ed 1994)

Shepherd, William R. *Shepherd's Historical Atlas* (New York and London, 9th ed 1974)

Sinor, D (ed) *The Cambridge History of Early Inner Asia* (Cambridge 1990)

Smith, BD *The Emergence of Agriculture* (New York 1995)

Taylour, W *The Mycenaeans* (London and New York, 2nd ed 1990)

The Times Atlas of the World (London and New York, 8th ed 1990)

Todd, M *The Early Germans* (Oxford and Cambridge, Mass. 1992)

Twitchett, D and Fairbank, J (eds) *The Cambridge History of China* (15 vols, Cambridge and New York 1978–91)

Vincent, Mary and Stradling, RA *Cultural Atlas of Spain and Portugal* (London 1994, New York 1995)

Walbank, FW *The Hellenistic World* (London 3rd ed 1992, Cambridge, Mass. 1993)

Watson, F *India, a Concise History* (London and New York 1993)

Whittle, A *Neolithic Europe: a Survey* (Cambridge and New York 1985)

Artwork

Artwork references have been assembled from a wide variety of sources. Any individual or institution who can demonstrate that copyright may have been infringed is invited to contact Andromeda Oxford Ltd.

Figures refer to map numbers; **bold** type indicates major references.

A

Abasgia 2.11
Abrittus, Battle of 2.15, 2.19
Abu Hureyra 1.08
Abu Simbel 1.29
Academy 2.08, 2.17, 2.29
Acarnania 1.24, 2.07–08
Achaea, Achaeans 1.23–24, 1.29, 2.07–08, 2.13
  see also Mycenae, Mycenaean civilization
Achemenes 1.15, 1.29
Achemenid empire 1.06, **1.15**, 1.26, 1.29, 2.01, 2.06, **2.07**
  Egypt 2.01, 2.21
  India 2.01
  Persian wars 2.01
Acheulian culture 1.01, 1.29
Acropolis 1.29
Actium, Battle of 2.02, 2.13, 2.29
Adab 1.10
Adad-nirari I 1.12
Adad-nirari II 1.13, 1.29
Adena 1.06, 1.29, 2.01–03
Adrianople, Battle of 2.16, 2.29
Adulis 2.21, 2.29
Aegina 2.07
Aegospotami, Battle of 2.08, 2.29
Aegyptus 2.03, 2.10, 2.13–14, 2.17.
  See also Egypt
Aeolia, Aeolian Greeks 1.23–24, 1.29
Aeschylos 2.07, 2.29
Aesti 2.19
Aetius 2.16, 2.29
Aetolia 2.08, 2.29
Afanasevo culture 1.04, 1.29
Africa 2.01, 2.03
  Arab conquests 2.01
  hominid remains 1.01
  Iron Age **1.16**, 2.04–05, **2.21**
  Neolithic **1.16**
  nomad invasions 2.04
  Roman province 2.13, 2.17
  single-origins theory 1.01–02
  see also individual states and peoples
African Rift Valley 1.01
Agade 1.11
Agamemnon 1.22, 1.29
Agri Decumates 2.13, 2.15, 2.29
agriculture 1.02, **1.03**, 1.04, 1.06, 1.08
  Africa **1.16**, 2.05, 2.21
  Agricultural Revolution (Neolithic) see Neolithic
  Americas 1.03, 1.28, 2.28
  animal domestication 1.03, 1.05–06, 1.08–09, 1.11, 1.16, 1.19–20, 1.26, 1.28, 2.01, 2.03, 2.21, 2.26

Bronze Age Europe 1.21
  Caribbean 2.03
  cereals 1.03, 1.05, 1.08–09, 1.16, 1.20, 1.28
  China 2.25
  chinampas 1.28
  and desertification 1.04
  east Asia 1.27
  Egypt 1.03, 1.17
  Fertile Crescent **1.08–09**
  food plant cultivation 1.03, 1.08–09, 1.16, 1.20–21, 1.27–28, 2.02, 2.05
  irrigation 1.03, 1.08–09, 1.17, 1.28, 2.03, 2.22, 2.27
  Japan 2.25
  legumes 1.20
  Mediterranean 1.22
  Neolithic and proto-Neolithic **1.08**, 1.19–20
  pastoralism 1.05–06, 1.16
  plow 1.09
  Polynesia 2.26
  slash-and-burn 1.28
  south Asia 1.26
Agrigentum, Battle of 2.12
Ah Cacau 2.28, 2.29
Ahab 1.14, 1.29
Ahar 1.26
Ahhiyawa 1.12
Ahmose 1.18, 1.29
Ahura Mazda 2.06, 2.29
Ajanta 2.22, 2.29
Akhenaten 1.12, 1.18, 1.29
Akkad 1.04, 1.07, 1.10–11, 1.29
  Sargon the Great 1.04, 1.10–11
  Third Dynasty 1.11
  see also Babylon, Babylonia
Akrotiri 1.22
Akshak 1.10
Al Mina 1.23
Alans 2.03, 2.05, 2.16–17, 2.19, 2.29
Alaric 2.04–05, 2.16, 2.29
Albion, 2.29.
  See also Britain
alcohol 1.10, 1.20
Alemanni 2.15–16, 2.19, 2.29
Aleppo 1.12
Alesia, Battle of 2.13, 2.18, 2.29
Aleuts 1.04–06, 1.29, 2.01–05
Alexander the Great 1.18, 2.01–02, 2.08, **2.09**, 2.11, 2.22, 2.29
  "Alexander's Barrier" 2.11
Alexandria 2.09–10, 2.16, 2.21, 2.29
  Museum 2.09
  Pharos lighthouse 2.10
Ali Kosh 1.08
Alkibiades, 2.29
Allia river, Battle of 2.18
Allobroges 2.18
alpaca 1.28
alphabets see writing
Altai mountains 2.20
Altaic languages, 2.29
Altamira 1.19, 1.29
Alwa 2.05–06, 2.21

Al-Qadisiya, Battle of 2.11
Amalasuntha, Queen 2.17, 2.29
Amalekites 1.14, 1.29
Amaravati 2.22, 2.29
Amazonia 1.05–06
amber 2.14
Ambrose, 2.29
Amekni 1.16
Amenemhet I 1.18, 1.29
Amenophis IV 1.18
Americas 1.06
  agriculture 1.03
  Amerindians 1.04
  Andean civilizations see Andean civilizations
  Archaic period 1.05
  Mesoamerica see Mesoamerica
  first civilizations **1.28**
  North America 2.01–05
  Paleoindians 1.02
Ammon 1.14
Amorites 1.04, 1.11, 1.13, 1.29
amphictonies 1.24, 1.29
Amun, Oracle of 2.09
Anastasius 2.17, 2.29
Anatolia 1.04–09, 1.11–13, 2.03, 2.10, 2.13–16, 2.18, 2.20
  Alexander the Great 2.09
  Celts 2.18
  Palmyra 2.15
  Seleucids 2.02
Andean civilizations 1.03, 1.06, **1.28**, 1.29, 2.01–05, **2.27**
  Archaic period 1.05
  Early Horizon period 1.28, 2.27
  Early Intermediate period 2.27
  Initial period 1.28, 2.27
  Preceramic period 1.28
  Middle Horizon Period 2.27
Anga 1.26
Angles 2.05, 2.16, 2.19, 2.29
Anglo-Saxons 2.05–06, 2.17–19, 2.29.
  See also Saxons
Aniba 1.18
animal domestication
  see agriculture
Antes 2.19
Antigonos 2.09, 2.29
Antioch, Antiochia 2.11, 2.17, 2.29
  sack 2.17
Antiochus III 2.10, 2.29
Antiochus IV 2.10, 2.29
Antipater 2.02, 2.09
Antonine dynasty 2.15, 2.29
Antonine Wall, 2.29
Antoninus Pius, 2.29
Antony, Mark 2.13, 2.29
Antony, St 2.15, 2.29
Anuradhapura 2.22, 2.29
Anyang 1.27, 1.29
Aotearoa 2.26
Apollonios of Athens 2.10
Appollonius of Perge, 2.30
Aquae Sextiae, Battle of 2.19
Aquileia 2.15, 2.19, 2.30

Aquitania, Aquitaine 2.13, 2.16, 2.18, 2.30
Arabia, Arabs 1.06, 1.09, 1.15, 2.01–05, 2.11, 2.13, 2.16–17, 2.23
  Arab expansion and conquests 2.01, 2.17
  Roman province of Arabia 2.13
  Saba see Saba
Arabic language and script 1.07
Arachosia 1.15, 2.09, 2.30
Aram, Aramaeans 1.05, 1.12–14, 1.29
Aram-Damascus 1.14, 1.29
Aram-Zobah 1.14
Aramaic language and alphabet 1.05, 1.07, 1.15, 1.29, 2.14
Arausio, Battle of 2.19, 2.30
Arcadia 1.24, 1.29, 2.07–08
  Archaic period, 1.29
Archimedes, 2.30
Ardashir I 2.11, 2.30
Ardipithecus ramidus 1.01, 1.29
Arganthonios 1.25
Argos 1.24, 1.29, 2.08
Aria 1.15
Arianism, 2.30
Arikamedu 2.23, 2.30
Ariovistus 2.19, 2.30
Aristagoras of Miletos 2.07, 2.30
Aristarchos of Samos 2.10, 2.30
Aristotle 2.08–09, 2.30
Arius 2.17
Armagh, 2.30
Armenia, Armenians 1.11, 1.15, 2.06, 2.10–11, 2.13, 2.15
  Satrapy of Armenia 2.09
Arminius 2.19, 2.30
Arpachiyeh 1.09
Arrapna 1.13
Arretium 1.25
Arsaces I 2.11
Arsacids 2.10–11, 2.30
Artemisium 2.07
Arvad 1.12, 1.14, 1.30
Arverni 2.18, 2.30
Aryans 1.05–06, 1.26, 1.30, 2.06
Arzawa 1.12, 1.30
Asding Vandals 2.16, 2.19
Ashkelon 1.14
Ashoka 2.02, 2.06, 2.22, 2.30
Ashur 1.05, 1.11–13, 1.30
Ashur-Dan II 1.13
Ashurbanipal 1.13, 1.15, 1.30
Ashurnasirpal II 1.13, 1.30
Ashuruballit I 1.12
Asia (Roman province) 2.13, 2.30
Asiana 2.15
Aspero tradition 1.04, 1.28, 1.30
Assaka 1.26
Assyrian empire 1.05–07, **1.13**, 1.14–15, 1.18, 1.23, 1.30, 2.21
  Middle Empire **1.12**

Old Assyrian period **1.11**
Astyages 1.15
Asuka, 2.30
Aten (Egyptian deity) 1.18
Athens 1.06, 1.15, 1.22, 1.24, 2.01, **2.07**, 2.08–10, 2.30
  Academy 2.17
  Acropolis 1.24
  Delian league 2.07–08
  democracy 2.01, 2.07, 2.09
  Parthenon 2.07–08
  Peloponnesian War 2.01, 2.07, **2.08**
  Periclean 2.07–08
  Persian Wars **2.07**
Athos, Mount 2.07
Atiebates 2.18
Atlas mountains 2.21
Atrebates 2.30
Atropatene 2.09–11, 2.30
Attalids 2.10, 2.30
Attalus I 2.18, 2.30
Attica 1.24, 1.30, 2.07–08
Attila 2.05, 2.16, 2.20, 2.30
Augustine, St 2.30
Augustodunum, Battle of 2.17
Augustulus, Romulus 2.16, 2.30
Augustus, Gaius Julius Caesar Octavianus 2.03–04, 2.13–14, 2.18, 2.30
Aurelian 2.15, 2.30
Aurelius, Marcus 2.15, 2.30
Aurignacian culture 1.19, 1.30
Australia 2.26
Australian Aboriginals 1.02, 1.04–06, 2.01–05, 2.26, 2.30
Australoid peoples 2.26
Australopithecus afarensis 1.01, 1.30
Australopithecus africanus 1.01, 1.30
Australopithecus robustus 1.01, 1.30
Austro-Asiatic peoples 2.01–03, 2.26, 2.30
Austronesian languages 2.26
Austronesians 1.04–06, 2.01–05, 2.21, 2.26, 2.30
Avanti 1.26, 2.22, 2.30
Avar khanate 2.05, 2.17, 2.19–20
Avaris 1.18, 1.22, 2.30
Avebury henge, 1.30
Axum, Axumites 2.03–06, 2.11, 2.21, 2.30.
  See also Sabeans
Ay Khanoum 2.10
Aztec civilization 2.27

B

Ba 1.27, 1.30
Babylon, Babylonia 1.05–07, 1.11–13, **1.13**, 1.14–15, 1.23, 1.30, 2.09
  Akkad see Akkad
  Alexander the Great 2.09
  dark ages 1.11–12
  Neo-Babylonian empire **1.13**

Old Babylonian period 1.11
  Persian conquest 1.15
  sack of Babylon 1.11–12
Bactria 1.15, 2.02–03, 2.09–11, 2.22–23, 2.31
Baerica 2.13
Bahrain 1.11
Baipu 1.27
Balearic Islands 1.21, 1.23, 1.25, 2.12
Balkans 1.07, 2.05, 2.16–17, 2.19
  Celts 2.18
  Slavs 2.19
Ballcourt, Mesoamerica, 2.31
Balts 1.06, 2.01–02, 2.04–05, 2.16–17, 2.19
Baluchistan 1.26
Banas culture **1.26**, 1.30
Bandkeramik culture 1.03, 1.20, 1.30
Bantu languages 1.06, 1.30, 2.01–05, **2.21**
Barbalissus, Battle of 2.11
barbarians 2.05, 2.15–17, 2.31
Barger-Oosterveld 1.21
barley 1.03, 1.08–09, 1.16, 1.30
barrow, long, 1.30
barrow, round, 1.30
Barygaza 2.22
basileus, 1.30
basileus 2.23
Basketmaker culture 2.03–05, 2.31
basketry 1.09
Basque language 2.14
Basques 2.14, 2.16–17, 2.31
Bastarnae 2.19
Baykal, Lake 2.20
Belgae 2.18, 2.31
Belgica 2.13, 2.31
Belisarius 2.17, 2.31
Bell Beaker cultures 1.04, 1.20–21, 1.30
Benedict, St 2.17, 2.31
Benedictine order 2.17
Beneventum 2.12, 2.31
Berbers 1.04–06, 1.23, 1.25, 2.01–05, 2.12, 2.15–17, 2.21, 2.31
Bering Straits 1.02
Beringia, 1.30
Beth-horon 1.14
Beth-shean 1.14
Bethlehem 1.14, 2.06, 2.31
Bhojas 2.22
Bible
  Book of Judges 1.14
  Gospels 2.06
  Old Testament 1.10, 1.14
  Vulgate Latin translation 2.06
Bible lands **1.14**, 1.30
Bimbisara 1.26, 1.30, 2.22
Bindusara 2.02, 2.22, 2.31
Bismarck Archipelago 1.05
bison see buffalo
bit and bridle 2.20
Bithynia 2.09–10, 2.13, 2.31
Bituriges 2.18

Bluefish Cave (Alaska) 1.02
boat-building 1.02, 1.17
  dug-out canoe 1.19
  Greek civilization 1.23
  outrigger canoe 1.05
  sail 1.09, 1.16
boats and ships
  outrigger canoe 2.26
  Roman empire 2.14
  voyaging canoe 2.26
Bodh Gaya 2.22, 2.31
Boeotia 1.24, 1.31, 2.07–08
Boii 2.18
Bonampak 2.28, 2.31
Bononia, Battle of 2.18, 2.31
Book of the Dead, 1.31
Borneo 2.26
Bosporus 1.15, 2.07, 2.11
  Kingdom of 2.01–02, 2.09–10, 2.15, 2.31
Boudicca 2.18, 2.31
bow and arrow 1.18, 1.31, 2.02, 2.20, 2.24
Bowl cultures 1.20, 1.31
Boxgrove, 1.31
Brahmagiri 1.26
Brahmins 2.06, 2.22, 2.31
Brasidas 2.08, 2.31
bread 1.08
Bretons 2.16–17
Brigantes 2.18, 2.31
Britain 1.05, 1.23, 1.25, 2.14
  Anglo-Saxons 2.05, 2.16–19
  Belgic migrants 2.18
  Celts 2.03, 2.05, 2.14, 2.18
  Christianity, introduction 2.06
  England 2.06
  Hadrian's Wall 2.15
  Romans 2.03, 2.13, 2.15, 2.18
  Saxon Shore 2.15
  Scotland 2.15, 2.18
  Scots 2.15, 2.18
Britannia, 2.31
Britanniae see Britain
Britons 2.16, 2.31
Brittany 1.25, 2.18
Bronze Age 1.04–06, 1.09–10, 1.20, 1.31
  Africa 1.16
  Europe 1.21, 1.25
  Middle East 1.11–12
  south Asia 1.26
Bronze Age Europe 2.18
bronze working 1.03–06, 1.10, 1.16, 1.18, 1.20–23, 1.27
Bructeri 2.19
Bruttians 2.12, 2.31
Brutus, Marcus Junius, 2.31
Buddha (Siddhartha Gautama) 1.06, 1.26, 1.31
Buddha (Siddhartha Gautama) 2.01, 2.06, 2.22
Buddhism 1.06, 1.26, 2.02, 2.04, 2.06, 2.22–24, 2.31
  Ashokan rock edicts 2.22
  Ceylon 2.06, 2.22
  China 2.06, 2.24–25
  Gandhara 2.23
  India 2.02, 2.06, 2.22–23
  Iranian nomads 2.06
  Japan 2.25

Korea 2.25
Mahayana 2.06
Mathura 2.23
  monasteries 2.06, 2.23
  Pacific and southeast Asia 2.06, 2.26
  spread 2.06
Theravada 2.06
Third Buddhist council 2.22
Tibet 2.23
buffalo 1.06
Buhen 1.17
buildings
  glazed bricks 1.12
  mud brick 1.08–09
  pyramids 1.16
  ziggurats 1.09, 1.11
Bulgaria, Bulgars 2.17
Burgundy 2.15–17, 2.19
  Kingdom of 2.16–17, 2.31
burial sites, prehistoric 1.04–06, 1.08–09, 1.19–21, 1.26
Burmese 1.05–06, 2.02–05
Busta Gallorum, Battle of 2.17, 2.31
Byblos, 1.31
Byzantium, Byzantine empire 2.05, 2.10, 2.15, 2.17
  origins 2.17
  see also Constantinople

C
Cabeço da Arrunda 1.19
Caesar, Gaius Julius 2.03, 2.13, 2.18–19, 2.31
Cai 1.27
Calakmul 2.28
Caledonii 2.18, 2.31
calendar, 1.31
  Chinese 2.25
  "long count" 1.28, 2.27–28
  Mayan 2.28
  Mesoamerica 2.03
  Monté Albán 2.27
Cambodia 2.26
Cambyses 1.15, 1.31
camel 1.03, 2.03, 2.05, 2.21, 2.31
Cameroon, Cameroons 2.21
Campa 1.26
Campana 2.27, 2.32
Canaan, Canaanites 1.05, 1.07, 1.12, 1.14, 1.23, 1.31
canal systems
  Egypt 1.17
  Mesoamerica 1.28
  Mesopotamia 1.09
  Nile to Red Sea 1.15
Cannae, Battle of 2.12, 2.31
Cao 1.27
Cape Bojador 2.21
Cape of Good Hope 2.04
Cappadocia 1.15, 2.01, 2.09–10, 2.13, 2.31
Caracalla, 2.31
Caraceni 2.12
Caracol 2.28
Carchemish 1.12–13, 1.31
  Battle of 1.13–14
Caria 1.15
Caribbean 2.03–04
Carnac 1.20, 1.31
Carnuntum 2.14, 2.31
Carnutes 2.18
Carpathian mountains 2.19
Carrhae, Battle of 2.11, 2.13, 2.32

Carthage 1.06, 1.16, 1.23, 1.25, 2.01–03, 2.08, 2.10, 2.12–13, 2.16, 2.18, 2.21, 2.32
  destruction 2.13
  Punic wars 2.02–03, 2.12, 2.13, 2.21
Carthage ad Decimum, Battle of 2.17
Cassander 2.09, 2.32
caste system, 2.32
Castle Cavern 2.21
Catacomb Grave cultures 1.04, 1.21, 1.31
Catalaunian Plain, Battle of 2.16, 2.20
Cato, Marcus Porcius, 2.32
cattle 1.03, 1.05, 1.08–09, 1.16, 1.20, 1.31
Caucasus 1.06, 2.20
Caudine Forks 2.12, 2.32
Caudini 2.12
causewayed camp, 1.31
cave- and rock-art 1.02, 1.16, 1.19, 1.31
Celtiberians 1.05–06, 1.23, 1.25, 2.01–02, 2.12, 2.18, 2.32
Celtic language 2.14, 2.18, 2.32
Celts 1.06, 1.23, 1.25, 2.01–03, 2.05, 2.09–10, 2.12, 2.18, 2.19, 2.32
ceramics 1.04, 1.06, 1.08–10, 1.31
  Americas 1.28
  Chinese 1.27
  earliest 1.03
  Egyptian 1.17
  glazed 1.12
  Greek 2.07
  Japanese 1.03
  kiln 1.03, 1.09
  Lapita 2.26
  Mayan 2.28
  Moche 2.03, 2.27
  Neolithic 1.03–04, 1.20
  painted 1.20
  potter's wheel 1.03, 1.09, 1.26–27, 2.18
  Roman 2.14
  south Asia 1.26
  Teotihuacán 2.27
  wavy-line 1.16
Ceras 2.23
Cerro de la Mesas 2.27, 2.32
Cerros, 2.32
Ceylon 2.06, 2.22.
  See also Simhala
Chad, Lake 1.16
Chaeronea, 2.32
Chaeronea, Battle of 2.08, 2.32
Chalcedon, Council of 2.16, 2.32
Chalcidice 2.08
Chaldeans 1.12–13, 1.31
Chalukyas 2.05
Chamavi 2.19
chambered tomb, 1.31
Champa 2.04–06, 2.25–26
  see also Viets
Chams 2.01–04
Chan Muan 2.28
Chandragupta I Maurya 2.01–02, 2.22–23, 2.32
Chandragupta I, 2.32
Chandragupta II 2.04, 2.23, 2.32
Chang'an 2.05, 2.25
Chaoxian see Korea
chariot 1.11, 1.18, 1.22, 1.27
Chasuarii 2.19

Chatal Huyuk 1.03, 1.09, 1.31
Châtelperronian culture 1.19, 1.31
Chatti 2.19
Chauci 2.19
Chavín de Huántar 1.06, 1.28, 1.31, 2.02, 2.27
Chayonu 1.08, 1.31
Chedi 1.26
Chen 1.27
Chen dynasty 2.25
Chen-La 2.05, 2.26
Chengdu, Battle of 2.25, 2.32
Chernoles complex culture 2.19, 2.32
Cherusci 2.19
Chesowanja 1.01, 1.31
chicken 1.03
chiefdom, 1.31
China 1.03–05, 1.27, 1.27, 2.20, 2.24
  Eastern Zhou 1.27
  First Emperor 2.02, 2.24
  Former Han 2.24
  Great Wall 2.24
  Han dynasty see Han Dynasty
  Iron Age 2.24
  Jin dynasty see Jin dynasty
  Later Han 2.24
  Longshan culture 1.04–05, 1.27
  Northern Zhou 2.25
  Period of Disunion 2.25
  Qin dynasty 2.01–02, 2.24
  Shang dynasty 1.07, 1.27
  Song dynasty 2.24
  Springs and Autumns Period 1.06, 1.27
  Sui dynasty 2.05, 2.25
  Tang dynasty 2.05
  Three kingdoms 2.24
  Toba Wei nomads 2.20
  unification 2.24, 2.25
  Warring States period 1.27, 2.01, 2.24
  Western Zhou 1.27
  Xia dynasty 1.27
  Yue kingdom 2.01
  Zhou dynasty see Zhou dynasty
Chinchoros tradition 1.04–06, 1.15, 1.31
Chinese language and script 2.25, 1.04, 1.07, 1.31
Chiripa culture 1.05, 1.28, 1.31
Choga Mami 1.09, 1.31
Cholas 2.22
Cholula 2.27, 2.32
Chorasmia 1.15
Chorrera culture 1.05–06, 1.28, 1.31, 2.01
Chosroes I 2.05
Choxian see Korea
Christianity 2.06, 2.15, 2.17, 2.32
  Africa 2.05, 2.21
  Arians 2.17
  Armenia 2.06, 2.11
  Axum 2.05
  Bible 2.06
  Britain 2.06
  Franks 2.17
  Ireland 2.18

monasteries 2.06, 2.15, 2.17–18
  Nubia 2.05, 2.21
  patriarchates 2.17
  Roman empire 2.04, 2.06, 2.13, 2.15
  spread 2.06
Chrysostom, John, 2.32
Chu 1.27, 1.31, 2.24
Cicero, 2.32
Cilicia 1.13, 1.15, 2.09–10, 2.13, 2.32
Cimbri 2.19, 2.32
Cimmerians 1.05, 1.13, 1.31, 2.20
Cisalpine Gaul 2.12–13, 2.18
Classical period, 2.32
Claudius 2.13–14, 2.32
Cleopatra 2.02–03, 2.13, 2.32
climatic change 1.01–03, 1.08, 1.16, 1.19
Clothar I 2.17, 2.32
Clovis 2.05, 2.17, 2.32
Clovis culture 1.02, 1.32
Cobá 2.28, 2.32
coinage 1.24, 1.32
Colchis 1.15, 1.23, 1.32, 2.01
Commodus 2.15, 2.32
Confucianism 1.27, 2.06, 2.24
Confucius 1.06, 1.27, 1.32, 2.01, 2.06
Constantine the Great 2.04, 2.06, 2.15–16, 2.32
Constantinian dynasty 2.15, 2.33
Constantinople 2.05, 2.15–17
  Theodosian walls 2.16
  see also Byzantium, Byzantine empire
Constantinople, Councils of, 2.33
Copán 2.28, 2.33
copper working 1.03, 1.06, 1.08–10, 1.16–17, 1.20, 1.26, 1.32
Coptic language 2.14, 2.33
Corcyreans 2.08
Cord Impressed Ware culture, 1.32
Córdoba 2.17
Corinth 1.22–24, 1.32, 2.07–08
Corinthian league 2.08–09, 2.33
Corsica 1.21, 1.25, 2.02, 2.12–13
Cortaillod, 1.32
Corupedion, Battle of 2.10
Costoboci 2.15
cotton 1.03, 1.26, 1.28, 1.32
cowpea 1.16
Crassus 2.13, 2.33
Crete 1.05, 1.20, 1.24
  Minoan civilization 1.04–05, 1.20, 1.22
  Mycenaean civilization 1.05, 1.22–23
Crimea 1.23
Croesus 1.15, 1.32
crossbow 2.24
Ctesiphon 2.11, 2.15, 2.33
Cumae see Kymai
cuneiform writing 1.07, 1.10, 1.15, 1.32
Cynoscephalae, Battle of 2.03, 2.10, 2.13, 2.33
Cynossema see Kymai
Cyprus 1.05, 1.15, 1.22–23, 2.07, 2.09, 2.13

Cyrenaica 1.23, 2.13
Cyrene 2.21, 2.33
Cyrillic alphabet 1.07
Cyrus II (the Great) 1.06, 1.13–15, 1.32
Cyrus, governor of Sardis 2.08, 2.33

D
Dacia 2.03, 2.13–15, 2.18, 2.33
Dakshinapatha 2.22, 2.33
Dalmatia 2.13, 2.16
Damascus 1.12–14
Damghan 2.09
Dan 1.14
Danes 2.16–17, 2.19
Danube river 2.13–15, 2.19
Dao De Jing 2.06, 2.33
Daoism 2.06
Dardani 2.18
Darius 1.15, 1.32
Darius I, King of Persia 2.07, 2.33
Darius III, King of Persia 2.09, 2.33
Datong, Battle of 2.24
David 1.14, 1.32
Dead Sea Scrolls, 2.33
Deccan 2.22–23
decimal system 2.23
Decius 2.15, 2.19, 2.33
Dekeleia 2.08, 2.33
Delian league 2.07–08, 2.33
Delos 1.24, 2.07, 2.33
Delphi 1.24, 1.32, 2.07, 2.18
Democracy, Greek, 2.33
Democritos 2.08, 2.33
Demosthenes 2.08, 2.33
Demotic language 2.14, 2.33
Denmark 1.19
Der 1.13
desertification 1.02–04, 1.16
devaputra 2.23
Di-xin 1.27, 1.32
Diadochi 2.09–10
  Wars of the 2.02, 2.09–10, 2.33
diamonds 2.22
Diaspora 1.14, 1.32, 2.06, 2.33
diet
  and animal domestication 1.08–09, 1.16
  bread 1.08
  fishing 1.16
  food plant cultivation 1.08–09, 1.16
  salt 1.08
Dilmun 1.11, 1.32
Diocletian 2.04, 2.14–15, 2.33
  Edict of 2.14–15
Dionysios I, King of Syracuse 2.08, 2.33
Dionysus (Greek deity) 1.23
divination 1.24, 1.27
Djoser 1.17, 1.32
Do-Dimmi 1.16
dog 1.03, 1.08, 1.32
dolmen, 1.32
Don river 2.19
Dongyi 1.27
Dorians 1.12, 1.22–24, 1.32
Dravidians 1.04–06, 1.26, 1.32
Drangiana 1.15, 2.09
Drepanum, Battle of 2.12

Dumnonii 2.18, 2.33
Dur-Kurigalzu 1.13, 1.32
Dur-Sharrukin 1.13
Dura Europos 2.11, 2.33
Dvaravati 2.05, 2.26.
    See also Mons
Dyukhtai tradition 1.02,
    1.32

E

Eannatum of Kish 1.10
Early Dynastic period 1.32
Early Horizon period 1.32
Early Intermediate period
    2.33
Early Preclassic period
    1.32
Easter Island 1.07, 2.04,
    2.26, 2.33
Eastern Turk Khanate 2.05
eastern woodlands (North
    America) 1.05–06,
    2.01–05
Eastern Zhou 1.27
Ecbatana see Hamadan
Ecnomus, Battle of 2.12,
    2.33
Edessa 2.13, 2.33
    Battle of (260) 2.11,
    2.15
Edom, Edomites 1.13–14,
    1.32
Egypt 2.01, 2.09–10
    Achemenid empire
    2.01, 2.21
    Alexander the Great
    2.09
    Greeks in 2.01
    Nubian rule 2.21
    Ptolemaic 2.01–03,
    2.09–10
    Roman empire 2.03,
    2.10, 2.13–14, 2.17
    Sasanian empire 2.11
    Seleucid invasions 2.10
    see also Aegyptus;
    Egyptian civilization
Egyptian civilization 1.05,
    1.07, 1.10, 1.13–16,
    1.23, 1.32
    1st Dynasty 1.17
    2nd Intermediate
    period 2.21
    4th Dynasty 1.17
    11th Dynasty 1.18
    17th Dynasty 1.18
    18th Dynasty 1.18
    21st Dynasty 1.18
    25th Dynasty 1.18
    1st Intermediate period
    1.17
    2nd Intermediate
    period 1.18
    3rd Intermediate period
    1.18
    agriculture 1.03,
    1.16–17
    Assyrian conquest 1.13,
    1.18
    Babylonian campaign
    against 1.13
    Bronze Ages 1.11
    Early Dynastic period
    1.17
    foundation 1.04, 1.16,
    1.17
    Greek colonies 1.23
    invasion of Judah and
    Israel 1.14
    kings of, 1.33
    Kushite rulers 1.06
    Late period 1.18
    Middle Kingdom
    1.04–05, **1.18**, 1.38
    Naqada period 1.17

New Kingdom 1.05,
    1.12, **1.18**, 1.39, 2.21
    Old Kingdom 1.04,
    1.17, 1.39
    Persian conquest 1.06,
    1.15, 1.18
    pyramids 1.04, 1.16–18
    Sea Peoples 1.05, 1.12,
    1.18
    urbanization 1.16
Eion 2.07
El Baul 2.28, 2.33
El Mais 2.11
El Mirador 2.28, 2.33
El Paraiso tradition 1.05,
    1.28, 1.32
El Tajín, 2.33
el-Amarna 1.18, 1.33
Elam, Elamites 1.04–05,
    1.07, 1.10–13, 1.15, 1.32
Elba 1.25
eleusine 1.16
Eleusis, 1.33
Elijah 1.14, 1.33
Elis 1.24, 2.07–08
Elisha 1.14, 1.33
Ellora 2.06, 2.33
Elteken, Battle of 1.14
Emutbal 1.11
England 2.06.
    See also Britain
Enlil (Sumerian god) 1.11,
    1.33
ensete 1.16
Epaminondas, 2.33
Ephesus 2.06, 2.33
Ephthalite (White) Huns
    2.04–05, 2.11, 2.20,
    2.23, 2.34
Epicuros 2.09, 2.34
epidemics
    plague 2.14
Epipaleolithic period
    1.16, 1.33
Epirotes 1.23
Epirus 1.24–25, 1.33,
    2.07–10, 2.12–13
Eran 2.23
Eratosthenes 2.10, 2.34
Eridu 1.09–11, 1.33
Erlitou culture 1.27, 1.33
Ermanaric 2.19, 2.34
Ertebolle culture, 1.33
Esarhaddon 1.13, 1.33
Eshnunna 1.11, 1.33
Essenes, 2.34
Ethiopia 1.06, 1.16,
    2.03–04, 2.21
Ethiopic script 1.07
Etruscan league 1.25
Etruscans 1.06–07, 1.23,
    1.25, 1.33, 2.01, 2.12,
    2.18
Euboea 2.07, 2.34
Euclid, 2.34
Eudoxes 2.19
Euphrates river 1.09–12
Eurasian steppes 2.02
Euripides 2.08, 2.34
Europe
    Bronze Age **1.21**, 2.18
    first Mediterranean
    civilizations **1.22**
    Iron Age 2.18–19
    Neolithic **1.20**
    Paleolithic **1.19**
Germans, proto- 1.06,
    1.34
Euzena 2.21, 2.34
Ezion-geber 1.14

F

Faiyum 1.17
farming see agriculture
Feddersen Wierde 2.19
Fertile Crescent 1.03,
    1.08–09, 1.12, 1.33

Fiji 2.26
Finno-Ugrians 1.04–06,
    2.01–04
Finns 1.06, 2.01–05
fire, earliest use 1.01, 1.33
First Emperor of China see
    Shi Huangdi
fishing 1.04, 1.16, 1.19,
    1.28
Flavian dynasty 2.15, 2.34
Flood, the 1.10, 1.33
Folsom culture 1.02, 1.34
food plant cultivation 1.16
Former Han 2.24
Franks 2.05, 2.15–17, 2.19,
    2.34
French language 2.14
Frisians 2.15–17, 2.19
Funnel-necked Beaker
    culture, 1.34

G

Gades 1.23, 1.25, 1.34
Gaius Caesar, 2.34
Gaixia, Battle of 2.24
Galatia 2.10, 2.13, 2.18,
    2.34
Galen, 2.34
Galerius 2.15, 2.34
Galicia 1.25
Galla Placidia, 2.34
Gallaeci 2.18
Gallia, Galliae 2.15, 2.34
    Lugdunensis 2.13
    Narbonensis 2.13
    see also Gaul
Gallic empire 2.15, 2.34
Gandhara 1.15, 1.26, 1.34,
    2.10, 2.23, 2.34
Ganges plain 1.03,
    1.05–06
Ganges river 2.09
Gangetic plain 2.01,
    2.22–23
Gansu Corridor 2.24
Gaoping, Battle of 2.24
Gaozu (Liu Bang)
    2.02–03, 2.24, 2.34
Gaugamela, Battle of 2.09
Gaul 1.23, 2.05, 2.10,
    2.12–18, 2.34
    Aquitani 2.18
    Belgae 2.18
    Celts 2.12, 2.18
    Cisalpine 2.12–13, 2.18,
    2.34
    Franks 2.05
    German invasion 2.05,
    2.19
    Roman empire 2.03,
    2.12–13, 2.17–18
    Teutones 2.19
    see also Gallia, Galliae
Gauls see Celts; Gaul
Gavrinis, 1.34
Gaza 1.14, 1.18
Gedrosia 2.10, 2.34
Gepids 2.15–17, 2.19, 2.34
Germania 2.13, 2.34
Germanic tribes 2.01–05,
    2.13–15, 2.18, **2.19**,
    2.20, 2.34
    attacks on Roman
    empire 2.05, 2.16–17
Germans, proto- 1.06,
    1.34
Gezer 1.14, 1.34
Gilboa, Battle of 1.14
Gindarus, Battle of 2.11
Girsu 1.10
Giza 1.16–17
glass 1.12, 2.14
goat 1.03, 1.08–09, 1.16,
    1.20, 1.34

Godavari river 1.26
gold 1.03, 1.18, 1.20–22,
    2.21–23, 2.28
Gordion 1.13, 1.34
Gospels, 2.34
Götar 2.16, 2.19
Goths 2.05, 2.15–17, 2.19,
    2.34
    see also Ostrogoths;
    Visigoths
Gracchus, Tiberius 2.13,
    2.34
Granicus river 2.09
Gravettian culture 1.19,
    1.34
Great Wall of China 2.24
Greek alphabet 1.07, 1.34
Greek civilization
    1.04–06, 1.15, 1.20,
    1.23, 2.09, 2.12, 2.18,
    2.22, 2.34
    5th century BC **2.07**
    aristocracy 1.24
    Celts 2.18
    city-states 1.06, 1.15,
    1.24, 2.01, 2.08, 2.10
    colonies 1.23–25
    Delian league 2.07–08
    dark ages 1.05, 1.22–24
    democracy 1.15, 1.24,
    2.01, 2.07, 2.09
    Hellenic league
    2.01–02, 2.08
    Hellenistic 2.03, **2.10**
    Macedonian
    supremacy 2.02
    monarchy 1.24
    Mycenae see Mycenae,
    Mycenaean civilization
    oligarchy 1.24
    pan-Hellenic festivals
    1.24
    Peloponnesian War
    2.01, 2.07, **2.08**
    Persian invasion
    defeated 1.23
    Persian Wars 2.01, 2.07,
    2.07
    Roman rule 2.03,
    2.12–13
    Spartan league 2.07
    trade 1.23–24
    Trojan War 1.22
    tyrants 1.24
    Visigoth invasion 2.16
    see also Athens; Bactria;
    Sparta
Greek language 2.10–11,
    2.14, 2.17, 2.34
Gregory of Tours 2.17,
    2.34
Gregory the Great, Pope
    2.17, 2.34
Guadalquivir valley 1.25
Guatemala 2.28
Gulf Coast civilization
    2.27, 2.34
Gupta empire 2.04, 2.20,
    2.23, 2.34
    fall 2.05, 2.23
Gushnasp 2.11
Gutians 1.10–12, 1.34
Guyana 1.04
gymnasia 2.10

H

Habuba Kabira 1.10
Hadar 1.01, 1.34
Hadramaut 2.01–03, 2.21
Hadrian's Wall 2.15, 2.34
Hadrian, Emperor 2.11,
    2.13, 2.15, 2.34
Halafian culture 1.09, 1.34
halberd 1.21
Halikarnassos 2.08–09

Hallstatt culture 1.06,
    1.25, 1.34, 2.18
Hamadan 1.13, 1.15
Hamadan, Battle of 2.10
Hamath 1.14
Hamazi 1.10
Hammurabi 1.11, 1.34
Han 2.03, 2.24
Han dynasty 2.02–04,
    2.06, 2.20, **2.24**, 2.25,
    2.35
Hannibal 2.02, 2.12, 2.35
Hao 1.27, 1.34
Harappa 1.26, 1.34.
    See also Indus Valley
    civilization
Harran 1.13
Harsha 2.23
Hassuna culture 1.09, 1.34
Hastinapura 1.26
Hatshepsut 1.18, 1.34
Hatti 1.12, 1.34
Hattusas 1.12, 1.34
Hawaii 2.04, 2.26
Hazor 1.14
Hebrew language and
    alphabet 1.07, 1.34
Hebrews 1.05, 1.12–14,
    1.18, 1.23, 1.34, , 2.06.
    See also Jews
    exile 1.14
    see also Jews
Hebron 1.14
Hecataeus 2.18, 2.35
Hejaz 2.05
Heliodorus 2.10
Hellenes 1.24, 1.34
Hellenic league 2.01–02,
    2.08, 2.35
Hellenistic Greece 2.03,
    2.10, 2.35
Hellespont 1.15, 2.07,
    2.35
helot, 1.34
Helvetii 2.18
henges 1.04, 1.20, 1.34
Heraclea, Battle of 2.12,
    2.35
Heraclius 2.05, 2.11, 2.17
hermits 2.06
Hermunduri 2.19
Herod the Great, 2.35
Herodotus 2.07–08, 2.35
Heuneburg 1.25, 1.34
Hezekiah 1.14
Hierakonpolis 1.17
hieroglyths, 1.34
hijra 2.05
hillforts 1.05, 1.34
Himalayas 2.20, 2.22
Himiko 2.25
Himyarite kingdom
    2.03–04, 2.35
Hindu Kush 1.26, 2.22–23
Hinduism 1.06, 1.26, 1.34,
    2.02–06, 2.22–23
    Brahmanic 2.06, 2.22
    and Buddhism 2.06
    caste system 2.06
    Dravidian 2.06
    Indonesia 2.23
    karma 2.06
    Mahabharata 2.06,
    2.23
    Mathura 2.23
    Pacific and southeast
    Asia 2.26
    Ramayana 2.06, 2.23
    spread **2.06**
    Upanishads 2.06
    Vedas 2.06
Hipparchos of Bithynia
    2.11, 2.35
Hippias 1.24, 1.34
Hippo Regius, 2.35

Hippocrates, 2.35
Hiram 1.23, 1.34
Hirpini 2.12
Hispaniae 2.15, 2.35
Hit 1.10, 1.34
Hittites 1.04–05, 1.07,
    1.11, **1.12**, 1.13–14,
    1.18, 1.21–22, 1.35
    Neo-Hittites 1.13–14
Hjortspring 2.19
Hohokam culture
    2.04–05, 2.35
Homer 1.22, 1.24, 1.35
hominoid apes 1.01, 1.35
Homo erectus 1.01–02,
    1.35
Homo habilis 1.01, 1.35
Homo Neanderthalensis
    1.02, 1.35
Homo sapiens 1.01–02,
    1.35
Homo sapiens
    neanderthalensis 1.01,
    1.35
Homo sapiens sapiens
    1.01–02
Honorius 2.16, 2.35
Honshu 2.04, 2.25
Hopewell culture 2.03–05
horse 1.03, 1.06, 1.11,
    1.16, 1.19–22, 1.35,
    2.02, 2.20, 2.24–25
Hoshea 1.14
Hsien-pi 2.24–25, 2.35
Hsiung-nu see Xiongnu
Huang Di 1.27, 1.35
Huari empire 2.05, 2.27,
    2.35
Huarpa culture 2.27, 2.35
Huelva 1.25
Hunas 2.23
    see also Ephthalite
    Huns
Hungarian Plain 2.20
Huns 2.04–05, 2.16–17,
    2.19–20, 2.23, 2.35
    Ephthalite (White)
    see Ephthalite Huns
    Hun confederation 2.05
hunter–gatherers 1.01–06,
    1.08, 1.16, 1.19–20,
    1.35, 2.01–05, 2.26
Hurrians 1.04, 1.07,
    1.11–12, 1.35
Hydaspes river, Battle of
    2.09
Hyksos 1.18, 1.35

I

Iazygians 2.03, 2.35
Iberia, Iberians 1.23, 1.25,
    2.11, 2.15, 2.18, 2.35
Iberian Celts 1.25
Ibo 2.21
Ice Age 1.01–03, 1.08,
    1.16, 1.18–19, 1.35
"ice man" 1.20, 1.35
Iceni 2.18, 2.35
Ikaruga 2.25
Ilerda, Battle of 2.13
Iliad, 1.35
Illyrians 1.05–06, 1.23–25,
    2.01–02, 2.07–08, 2.12,
    2.18, 2.35
Ilopango, Lake 2.28
Impressed Pottery
    cultures 1.04, 1.20–21,
    1.35
Inca civilization 1.07
India 1.03, 1.06, **1.25**,
    2.02, 2.04, 2.06
    Achemenid empire 2.01
    Aryan invasion 2.06
    caste system 2.06
    Ephthalites 2.05, 2.23

Gupta empire *see*
Gupta empire
Hunas 2.23
Kushan empire 2.04,
2.22, **2.23**
Magadha *see* Magadha
Mauryan empire *see*
Mauryan empire
religions 2.06, 2.22.
See also Buddhism;
Hinduism; Islam;
Jainism
Saka invasions 2.03,
2.22
Satavahanihara 2.03,
2.22–23
Suren 2.11
see also Indus Valley
civilization
Indian script 1.07
Indo-European
languages, 1.35
Indo-Iranian peoples
1.13, 1.35
Indonesia 2.04–05, 2.26
Austronesians 2.04
Buddhism 2.22
Hinduism 2.23
Indus valley 2.10
Alexander the Great
2.09, 2.22
Bactrian Greeks 2.10,
2.22
Mauryan empire 2.10,
2.22
Parthian empire 2.11
Sasanian empire 2.11
Suren 2.11
Indus Valley civilization
1.04–05, 1.07, **1.26**,
1.35
Insubres 2.18
Intial period, 1.35
Ionia, Ionian Greeks 1.15,
1.23–24, 1.35, 2.07–09
Ipsus, Battle of 2.09–10,
2.35
Iran 1.05–06, 1.10–11,
1.13, 1.15, 2.11
see also Persia, Persians
Iranian language 2.20,
2.35
Iranian nomads 2.02–03,
2.10, 2.20, 2.20.
See also Parni
Ireland 1.21
Celts 2.18
Christianity 2.18
Scots 2.18
Iron Age 1.06, 1.21, 1.24,
1.35
Africa **1.16**, 2.04–05,
2.21
China 2.24
Europe 1.06, 1.25,
2.18–19
Middle East **1.12**
south Asia **1.26**
iron working 1.03,
1.05–06, 1.12, 1.16,
1.18, 1.21, 1.27, 2.01,
2.04–05, 2.19, 2.21, 2.24
irrigation 1.03, 1.08–09,
1.17, 1.26, 1.28, 1.35
Isaiah 1.14, 1.35
Isin 1.11, 1.35
Isis (Egyptian deity) 2.10
Islam 2.05–06, 2.11
hijra 2.05
Koran 2.11
Israel 1.02, 1.05–06, 1.08,
1.13–14, 1.35
Assyrian conquest 1.13
Egyptian invasion 1.14,
1.18

Jewish settlement 1.14
split with Judah 1.14
Issus river, Battle of 2.09
Isthmus of Corinth 2.07
Italian language 2.14
Italics 1.23, 1.25, 1.36,
2.08, 2.18
Italy 1.07, 1.23, 2.13, 2.15
Celts 2.01, 2.18
Cimbri 2.19
Etruscans *see* Etruscans
Greeks 2.08, 2.12
Lombards 2.05,
2.15–17, 2.19
Odoacer 2.16–17
Romans *see* Roman
empire; Roman
republic; Rome
Visigoths 2.16
ivory 2.21

J

Jaguar Paw, King 2.28
Jainism 1.26, 2.22, 2.35
janapadas 1.26, 1.36
Japan 1.03, 1.07
first states 2.04, **2.25**
Yamato period 2.25
Yayoi culture 2.02–05,
2.25
Java 1.07, 2.26
Jebel Barkal 2.21, 2.35
Jebusites 1.14, 1.36
Jehu 1.14
Jemdet Nasr 1.10, 1.36
Jenne–jeno 2.05, 2.21,
2.35
Jericho 1.08, 1.36
Jerome, St 2.06, 2.35
Jerusalem 1.12, 1.14, 1.23,
1.36, 2.06
Arab conquest 2.17
Hebrew capture 1.14
patriarchal see 2.17
religious importance
1.14
sack 1.14
temple 1.14
Jesus of Nazareth 2.04,
2.06, 2.35
Jews 1.14, 2.06
Bible lands 1.14
Diaspora 1.14, 2.06
exile 1.14
Jewish resettlement by
Nebuchadnezzar 1.13
Maccabean revolt 2.10
Old Testament 1.10,
1.14
see also Hebrews
Jin 1.27, 1.36, 2.04, 2.24,
2.35
Jin dynasty 2.04, 2.24–25,
2.35
Koguryo *see* Koguryo
Silla *see* Silla
Jomon 1.03, 1.05, 1.36
Jomon 2.01
Joppa 1.14
Jordan river 1.05
Joshua 1.14, 1.36
Josiah 1.14, 1.36
Juan-juan 2.04–05, 2.20,
2.25, 2.35
Judah 1.13–14, 1.18, 1.36
Judaism *see* Jews
Judas Maccabeas 2.10
Judea 2.10, 2.13, 2.36
independence 2.10
Maccabean revolt 2.10
Jugurtha, 2.36
Julian, Roman emperor
2.15, 2.36
Junagadh 2.22–23, 2.36
Justin 1.17
Justinian 2.05, 2.17, 2.19,
2.36

Jutes 2.16, 2.19, 2.36
Jutland 2.19

K

kaisara 2.23
Kalhu 1.13, 1.36
Kalibangan 1.26
Kalinga 2.02–03, 2.22,
2.36
Kallias, peace of 2.07
Kamasutra 2.23
Kaminaljuyú 2.28, 2.36
Kanauj (Harsha) empire
2.05, 2.23
Kanesh 1.12, 1.36
Kanishka 2.23, 2.36
Kar-Tukulti-Ninurta 1.12
Karasuk culture 1.05, 1.36
Karkheh 1.13
karma 2.06, 2.36
Karmania 2.11
Karnak 1.18, 1.36
Kaskas 1.12, 1.36
Kassites 1.04, 1.10–12,
1.36
Kastri 1.22
Kausambi 1.26, 1.36
Kelheim 1.21
Keralaputras 2.22
Kerma 1.18, 1.36, 2.21
keyhole tombs 2.25, 2.36
Khania 1.22
Kharavela 2.22, 2.36
Kharga Oasis 1.15
Khazars 2.05
Khendjer 1.18
Khephren 1.17, 1.36
Khilakku 1.13
Khitans 2.20, 2.25
Khoisan 1.04–06, 1.36,
2.02–05, 2.21
Khosru I Anushirvan 2.11,
2.36
Khosru II 2.11, 2.36
Khotan 2.22, 2.36
Battle of 2.23
Khufu 1.17, 1.36
Kirghiz 2.05
Kish 1.10–11, 1.36
Kition 1.23
Kizzuwatna 1.12, 1.36
Kleisthenes 1.15, 1.24,
1.36, 2.07
Kleomenes, 1.36
Knossos 1.22, 1.36
Ko Hung 2.06, 2.36
Kofun period, 2.36
Koguryo 2.03–05, 2.24–25
Komchen 1.28
Koobi Fora, 1.36
Koran 2.11
Korea 1.03–07, 2.02–03,
2.24–25
Koguryo *see* Koguryo
Silla *see* Silla
Kosala 1.26, 1.36, 2.23
Kostromskaya 2.20
Kotosh tradition 1.28, 1.36
Kow Swamp, 1.36
Kra isthmus 2.26
Kufic Arabic 1.07
Kujala Kadphises 2.23,
2.36
Kulli 1.26, 1.36
Kultepe 1.11
Kummukhu
(Commagene) 1.13
Kungnaesong 2.25
Kunlun mountains 2.20,
2.22
kurgan 2.20, 2.36
Kuru 1.26
Kush 1.05–06, 1.16, 1.18,
1.36

Kushans 2.04–05,
2.10–11, 2.20–22, **2.23**,
2.36
Kusinagara 1.26
Kustana 2.11
Kymai (Cumae) 1.23,
1.25, 1.36
Kynouria 1.24
Kyreskhata 1.15
Kythera 1.22, 1.24
Kyushu 2.25

L

La Tène culture 2.01, 2.18,
2.36
La Venta, 1.36
Lachish 1.14, 1.37
Laconia 1.24, 1.37
Lagash 1.10, 1.37
Laitoli (Laetoli) 1.01, 1.37
Lao Zi 2.06, 2.36
Lapita culture 1.05–06,
2.01, 2.26, 2.36
Lapps 1.05–06, 2.01–05
Lascaux 1.19, 1.37
Latin language and
alphabet 1.07, 2.14,
2.17–18, 2.36
Latins, Latium 1.25, 1.37,
2.12
Laurion 2.07, 2.36
Lazica 2.11
lead working 1.09
Lebanon 1.08
Leonidas of Sparta 2.07,
2.36
Lepenski Vir 1.19, 1.37
Leptis Magna 2.21, 2.36
Leubingen 1.21
Levant 1.05, 1.07–09,
1.11–14, 1.18, 1.23,
1.37, 2.03
Aurignacian culture
1.18–19
Libya, Libyans 1.12, 2.21
Libyan language 2.14
Licchavis 2.23, 2.36
Ligurians 1.23, 1.25, 1.37,
2.12
Lilybaeum, Battle of 1.25,
2.02, 2.12
Lima 2.27
Linear A script 1.22, 1.37
Linear B script 1.22, 1.37
Linear Pottery culture *see*
Bandkeramik culture
linen (flax) 1.03, 1.08–09,
1.16, 1.37
Lingjiu (Vulture Peak)
2.06
Lipari Islands 1.25
Lirong 1.27
literacy 1.07
Liu Bang *see* Gaozu
Livy 2.13, 2.36
llama 1.28, 1.37
logographic scripts, 1.37
Lokris 2.07–08
Lombards 2.05, 2.15–17,
2.19, 2.36
Long Wall of Wei 2.24,
2.36
Long Wall of Yan 2.24,
2.36
Long Wall of Zhao 2.24,
2.36
longhouses 1.20, 1.37
Longshan culture 1.04–05,
1.27, 1.37
Los Millares, 1.37
lost-wax process 1.10
Lothal 1.26, 1.37
Lu 1.27, 1.37
"Lucy" (*Australopithecus
afarensis*) 1.01, 1.37

Lucanians 2.12, 2.36
Lugalzagesi 1.10–11, 1.37
Lukka 1.12
Lullubians 1.11, 1.37
Lumbini 1.26, 1.37
Luolang 2.24–25, 2.36
Luoyang 1.27, 1.37,
2.24–25
Lusitania, Lusitanians
1.25, 2.12–13, 2.18, 2.36
Luvians 1.05, 1.12, 1.37
Luxor, 1.37
Lycia, Lycians 1.23–24,
2.13
Lydia, Lydians 1.15,
1.23–24, 1.37, 2.07
Lysimachos 2.09–10, 2.36

M

Maan kingdom 2.02
Maccabean revolt 2.10
Maccabees, 2.36
Macedon, Macedonia
1.15, 1.23–25, 2.01–02,
2.07–10, 2.12–13, 2.37
Alexander the Great
1.18
Corinthian league 2.08
Hellenic league
2.01–02, 2.08
rise of 2.01, **2.08**
see also Alexander the
Great
Macedonian War, First
2.10, 2.37
Madagascar 2.04, 2.21,
2.26
Maes Howe, 1.37
Magadha 1.06, 1.26,
2.01–02, 2.22–23, 2.37
Seleucid invasion 2.02
see also Mauryan
empire
Magdalenian 1.19, 1.37
Maghrib 2.21
Magna Graecia, 1.37
Magnesia, Battle of 2.10,
2.13, 2.37
Magnia Graecia 2.12
Mahabharata 2.06, 2.23,
2.37
mahajanapadas 1.26
maharaja 2.23
Mahavira 1.26
Mahayana Buddhism
2.06, 2.37
Mahismat 1.26
Maiden Castle, 2.37
maize 1.03–04, 1.28, 1.37,
2.03–05
Makkura 2.05–06, 2.21,
2.37
Makuran 2.11
Malacca straits 2.26
Malatya 1.12
Malaya 2.05, 2.26
Malayo-Indonesians 2.05
Malla 1.26
Mallia 1.22
Manching 2.18, 2.37
Manchuria 2.20
Manetho, 2.37
Mani 2.11, 2.37
Manichaeism 2.11, 2.37
Mannea 1.13, 1.37
Mantineia 2.08
Battle of 2.08, 2.37
Maoris 2.26
Marathon, Battle of 1.15,
2.07, 2.37
Marcomanni 2.15, 2.19,
2.37
Marcomannic wars 2.15,
2.37

Mardonios, Mardonius
2.07, 2.37
Marduk (Babylonian god)
1.15
Marhashi 1.11
Mari 1.10–11, 1.37
Mariana Islands 2.26
Marius, Gaius 2.13, 2.19,
2.37
Marquesas Islands 2.26
Marsi 2.19
Masada, 2.37
Massilia 1.23, 1.25, 1.37
Massinissa 2.12, 2.37
mastabas 1.17, 1.37
Mathura 2.22–23, 2.37
Matsva 1.26
Mattiaci 2.19
Mauretania 2.02, 2.13,
2.21, 2.37
Caesariensis 2.13
Tingitana 2.13
Maurice 2.17, 2.37
Mauryan empire 1.26,
2.01–03, 2.09–10, **2.22**,
2.37
Mausoleum 2.08, 2.37
Mausolos 2.08, 2.37
Maximian, 2.37
Mayan civilization
1.06–07, 1.28
Mayan civilization
2.01–05, 2.27, **2.28**,
2.37
Classic period 2.04
Mazdakites 2.11
Mecca 2.05
Medes 1.06, 1.13, 1.15,
1.37
Median empire 1.15
Medina 2.21
Mediolanum (Milan),
Battle of 2.19
Mediteranean triad, 1.38
Mediterranean, first
civilizations **1.22**
megalithic monuments
1.04, 1.20–21, 1.26, 1.38
Megalithic Tomb culture,
1.38
Megara 2.08
Megiddo, Battle of 1.14,
1.18, 1.38
Mehrgarh 1.26, 1.38
Mekong 2.26
Melanesia 1.04–05, 2.01,
2.37
Melanesians 2.02–05, 2.26
Meluhha 1.26
Memphis 1.13, 1.15, 1.17,
1.38, 2.09, 2.21
Mencius (Mengzi) 2.24,
2.37
menorah 2.06
Mentuhotpe II 1.18, 1.38
Meroë 1.06, 1.15, 1.38,
2.01–04, 2.21
Meroitic script 2.21
Mesilim of Kish 1.10
Mesoamerica 1.07, 1.38,
2.01, 2.04–05, **2.27–28**
Archaic and Preclassic
periods 1.03, 1.05–06,
1.28, 2.27
Classic period 2.04,
2.27–28
Early Postclassic period
2.28
Late Preclassic period
2.27–28
Middle Preclassic
period 2.28
Mid Preclassic period
2.27
Postclassic period 2.28

Terminal Classic period 2.27
Western Mexican tomb cultures 2.27
see also individual cultures
Mesolithic 1.03, 1.19–20, 1.38
Mesopotamia 1.03, 1.06, 1.08–09, 1.12, 1.26, 1.38, 2.09, 2.11, 2.15, 2.21
Amorites 1.11
Aramaeans 1.05
Bronze Age **1.11–12**
earliest cities 1.09, **1.10**
Early Dynastic period 1.10
Iron Age **1.12**
Parthians 2.10–11
Roman empire 2.11, 2.13, 2.17
Seleucids 2.02, 2.10
Uruk period 1.04, 1.09–10
see also Akkad; Assyrian empire; Babylon, Babylonia; Chaldeans; Hittites; Kassites; Sumeria
Messapians 1.25, 2.12
Messenia 1.24, 1.38
metal working
casting 1.27
lost-wax process 1.10
smelting 1.03
see also bronze working; copper working; gold; iron working; silver; tin
Metaurus river, Battle of 2.12, 2.37
Mexico **2.27**, 2.28
tomb cultures 2.27
see also Mesoamerica
Mexico, valley of 2.01–02, 2.27, 2.37
Mezhirich 1.19, 1.38
Michelsberg, 1.38
microlith tools 1.19, 1.38
Micronesians 2.03–04, 2.26, 2.37
Midas 1.13
Middle Horizon period, 2.38
Middle Kingdom, 1.38
Middle Preclassic period, 1.38
migration, single–origins theory 1.01, **1.02**
Milan
Edict of 2.15, 2.38
see also Mediolanum
Miletos 1.22, 1.38, 2.07, 2.09
millet 1.03, 1.16, 1.27, 1.38
Milvian Bridge, Battle of 2.15, 2.38
Min-yue 2.02–03, 2.24, 2.38
Minoan palace civilization 1.04–05, 1.07, 1.20, **1.22**, 1.38
Miocene epoch 1.01, 1.38
Missouri valley 2.04
Mitas (Midas) 1.13, 1.38
Mithradates I 2.11
Mithradates VI 2.10, 2.13, 2.38
Mithraism 2.06, 2.38
Mittani 1.12, 1.18, 1.38
Mixtec civilization 1.07
Mixu 1.27
Mo Bei, Battle of 2.24

Moab, Moabites 1.13–14, 1.38
Moche state 2.03–05, 2.27, 2.38
Moesia, Moesiae 2.15
Inferior 2.13
Superior 2.13
Mogador 1.23
Mogollon culture 2.04–05
Mohenjo-Daro 1.26, 1.38
Mongolia, Mongols 1.05, 1.07, 2.04, 2.38
see also Juan-juan; Turko-Mongols; Xiongnu
Mons 2.04–06
Mons Graupius, Battle of 2.18, 2.38
Mons Lactacius, Battle of 2.17
Mont Bibracte, Battle of 2.18
Monté Albán 1.28, 2.01–05, 2.27, 2.38
Moon, Pyramid of the 2.27
Motun 2.20
Motya 1.25
Mousterian culture 1.01, 1.19, 1.38
Mu-ti defensive wall 1.11
Muhammad 2.05–06, 2.11
mummification, 1.38
Mursilis 1.11, 1.38
museum, 2.38
Mushki (Mysians) 1.12, 1.38
Muwatallis II 1.12, 1.38
Mycale, Battle of 2.07
Mycenae, Mycenaean civilization 1.05, 1.07, 1.12, **1.21–23**, 1.38
Mylae, Battle of 2.12, 2.38
Mylasa 2.08
Mysia 2.09
Mysians see Mushki

N
Nabatean alphabet 1.07, 1.39
Nabateans, Nabataean kingdom 2.02, 2.09–10, 2.38
Nabonidus 1.13, 1.15, 1.39
Nabopolassar 1.13, 1.39
Nahal Hemar 1.08
Naissus, Battle of 2.16, 2.19
Nakbe 1.28
Nakum 2.28
Nalanda 2.23
Nan-yue 2.03, 2.24, 2.38
Nanda dynasty 2.01–02, 2.22, 2.38
Nanjing 2.25
Napata 1.39, 2.21
Naqada 1.17
Naqsh-i Rustam 2.11, 2.38
Naram-Sin 1.11, 1.39
Naranjo 2.28
Narmer 1.17, 1.39
Narses 2.17, 2.38
Natufian culture 1.03, 1.08, 1.39
navigation 1.23, 2.04, 2.26
Nazca 2.02–04, 2.27, 2.38
Lines 2.27
Neanderthals 1.01–02, 1.19
Nearchos 2.09, 2.38
Nebuchadnezzar 1.13–15, 1.39, 2.06
Necho II 1.13, 1.39
Nedao, Battle of 2.16, 2.38

Nehavend, Battle of 2.11
Neo-Babylonian empire 1.13
Neo-Hittites 1.13–14
neo-Platonism 2.15, 2.38
Neolithic 1.03–04, 1.06, 1.09–10, 1.19, 1.39
Africa **1.16**
east Asia 1.27
Europe **1.20**
Middle East **1.08**
Nepala 2.23, 2.38
Nepos, Julius 2.16, 2.38
Nero, 2.38
Nervii 2.19
New Caledonia 2.26
New Guinea see Papua New Guinea
New Kingdom, 1.39
New Testament, 2.38
New Zealand
see Aotearoa
Newgrange, 1.39
Nicaea, Council of, 2.38
Nicopolis, Battle of (68 BC) 2.13
Niger river 2.05
Niger-Kordofanian languages 2.21
Nigeria 1.16
Nile river 1.16–17, 2.21
canal to Red Sea 1.15
Cataracts 1.17
Delta 1.17
Nina 1.10
Nindowari 1.26
Nineveh 1.09, 1.12–13, 1.39
sack 1.13, 1.15
Nineveh, Battle of 2.11, 2.17
Nippur 1.11–12, 1.39
Nisa 2.11
Nobatia 2.05–06, 2.21
Nok culture 1.16, 2.21, 2.38
nomadism 1.03–06, 2.02–05, 2.17, 2.19, **2.20**, 2.22–25, 2.38
Noreia, Battle of 2.19
Noricum 2.13, 2.38
North America 2.01–05
Northern Zhou, 2.38
Noviodunum, Battle of 2.17
Nubia 1.04–06, 1.14–18, 1.39, 2.04–05, 2.21
Numantia 2.21
Numidia 2.02, 2.12, 2.21, 2.38
Battle of 2.18, 2.38
Numidia 2.02, 2.12, 2.21, 2.38
nuraghe 1.21

O
oats 1.03, 1.21
Oaxaca valley 1.28, 1.39, 2.27
obsidian 1.08–09, 1.39, 2.26–28
Oc Eo 2.26
oca 1.28
Octavian see Augustus, Gaius Julius Caesar Octavianus
Odenathus 2.15
Odoacer 2.16–17, 2.38
Odyssey, 1.39
Ohio 2.04
oil palm 1.16
Old Kingdom, 1.39
Oldowan culture 1.01, 1.39
Olduvai Gorge 1.01, 1.39
Oleneostravski 1.19

olive 1.22
Olmec civilization 1.05–06, **1.28**, 1.39, 2.01–03, 2.27–28
Olympia 1.24, 1.39
Olympia, Temple of Zeus 2.07
Olympic Games 1.24, 1.39
Omo 1.01, 1.39
Omri 1.14
Opis, Battle of 1.15, 1.39
oracle bones, 1.39
oracle, Greek, 1.39
Ordos desert 2.20
Oriens 2.15
Orkney 1.20, 1.39
Orleans 2.20
Oronsay 1.19
Orontes river 1.12
Orthodox church 2.17
Oscans 1.25, 1.39
Ostia 2.14, 2.38
Ostrogoths 2.16–17, 2.19, 2.38. See also Goths
Otztaler Alps 1.20
Ovid 2.13, 2.38

P
Pacal 2.28, 2.38
Pacific islands 2.26
Paekche 2.04–05, 2.24–25
paganism 2.15, 2.38
Painted Ware cultures 1.20, 1.39
Paionia 2.08
Palenque 2.28, 2.39
Paleoindians 1.02, 1.39
Paleolithic
Europe **1.19**, 1.39
Lower 1.01, 1.39
Mid 1.01–02, 1.19, 1.39
Upper 1.19, 1.39
Palestine 1.15, 1.22, 2.09–10
Roman empire 2.17
Sasanian empire 2.11
Pallava dynasty 2.05, 2.39
Palmyra 2.14–15, 2.39
Pama-Nyungan languages 2.26
Pampa Grande 2.27
Pamphylia 2.13
pan-Hellenic festivals, 1.40
Panchala 1.26, 2.23
Pandya state 2.22
Panion, Battle of 2.10
Pannonae 2.15, 2.18, 2.39
Inferior 2.13
Superior 2.13
Paphlagonia 2.09–10
Papua New Guinea 1.05, 2.01–05, 2.26
Paracas culture 1.06, 1.28, 2.01–02, 2.39
Parisii 2.18
Parni 2.09–10, 2.11, 2.39
see also Iranian nomads
Parsees 1.15
Parthenon, 2.39
Parthia, Parthians 1.15, 1.40, 2.02–04, 2.06, 2.09–10, **2.11**, 2.13, 2.15, 2.20
Parthian language 2.11
Pasargadae 1.15, 1.40
Battle of 1.15
passage grave, 1.40
pastoralism 1.03–06, 1.16, 1.40, 2.01–03
Patagonia 1.02
Pataliputra 2.10, 2.22, 2.39
patriarchs 2.17, 2.39
Patrick, St, 2.39

Pattala 2.09
Paul, St 2.06, 2.39
Pazyryk 2.20, 2.39
pearls 2.22
Peisistratus 1.24, 1.40
Peloponnese 1.04, 1.22, 1.24
Peloponnesian War 2.01, 2.07, **2.08**, 2.39
Pelusium 2.09
Pelusium, Battle of 1.15
Pentri 2.12
Perdiccas 2.09
Pergamon 2.10, 2.18, 2.39
Battle of 2.18
Roman empire 2.13
Pericles 2.07–08, 2.39
Period of Disunion (China) 2.25
Peroz 2.11
Persepolis 1.15, 1.40
palace of Xerxes 2.09
sack 2.09
Persia, Persians 1.06, 1.13, 1.15, 1.18, 1.24–25, 2.01, 2.08–11, 2.17, 2.22, 2.39
Achaemenid empire see Achaemenid empire
alliance with Sparta 2.08
conquest of Egypt 2.21
Parni see Parni
Parthians 1.15 see also Parthia, Parthians
Persian-Avar campaigns 2.17
Phoenicians conquered by 1.23
Sasanian empire see Sasanian empire
war with Roman empire 2.17
Persian Gates pass 2.09
Persian Wars 2.01, **2.07**, 2.39
Peru 1.03–05, 1.07, 2.01–05, 2.27, 2.39
Petén 2.28, 2.39
Peter, St 2.39
Petra, 2.39
Phaistos 1.22, 1.40
pharaohs 1.18, 1.40
Pharisees, 2.39
Pharos lighthouse 2.10, 2.39
Pharsalus, Battle of 2.13, 2.39
Pheidias 2.08, 2.39
Philip II, King of Macedon 2.01, 2.08–09, 2.39
Philippines 2.26
Philistia 1.13–14
Philistines 1.12, 1.14, 1.40
Phocas 2.17
Phocis 2.07–08
Phocs 1.24
Phoenicia, Phoenicians 1.05–07, 1.13–14, 1.16, 1.23, 1.24, 1.40, 2.09
alphabet, 1.40
Babylonian conquest 1.23
Greek conquest 1.23
trade and colonies 1.05, 1.13, **1.23**, 1.23, 1.25
Phrygia, Phrygians 1.05, 1.12–13, 1.22–23, 1.40, 2.15, 2.20
Phrygian language 2.14, 2.39
Phyraates, 2.39
Pictones 2.18
Picts 2.15, 2.39
pig 1.03, 1.08–09, 1.40

Pilate, Pontius, 2.39
Pisidia 2.09
Pithekoussai 1.23
plague 2.14
Plataea, Battle of 1.15, 2.01, 2.07, 2.39
Plato 2.08, 2.39
Plautus 2.13, 2.39
Pleistocene epoch 1.01–02, 1.40
Pliocene epoch 1.01, 1.40
Plotinus 2.15, 2.39
plow 1.03, 1.09, 1.20–21, 1.40
Po valley 2.01
Po-lo 2.26
pochteca 2.27
Poeni 2.12
Polar ice caps 1.01
polis 1.24, 1.40
Polyclitos 2.08, 2.39
Polynesia, Polynesians 1.05–07, 2.01–05, 2.26, 2.39
Pompeii 2.13, 2.40
Pompey 2.13, 2.40
Pontica 2.15
Pontus 2.10, 2.13, 2.40
population growth 1.03, 1.09–10, 1.20
Populonia 1.25
Portuguese language 2.14
Porus 2.09
Postumus 2.15, 2.40
potato 1.28, 1.40
Poteidaia 2.08, 2.40
pottery see ceramics
Poverty Point culture 1.05, 1.40
Praaspa, Battle of 2.11
Pratisthana 2.22
Praxiteles 2.08, 2.40
Prayaga 2.23
Preceramic period, 1.40
Prednosti 1.19
Predynastic period, 1.40
priesthood 1.10, 1.17
printing 1.09
Procopius 2.17, 2.40
Psammeticus III 1.15
Pteria 1.15, 1.40
Ptolemaic Egypt 2.01–03, 2.09–10, 2.40
Ptolemy I 2.01, 2.09, 2.40
Ptolemy IV 2.10, 2.40
Ptolemy, Claudius 2.15
Pukara culture 2.01–02
Pulindas 2.22
Pundra 2.23
Punic Wars 2.10, **2.12**, 2.40
First 2.02, 2.12
Second 2.02–03, 2.12–13, 2.21
Third 2.03, 2.13
Punjab 2.03
Pushyamitra Shunga 2.22, 2.40
Pusiamitras 2.23
Pydna, Battle of 2.10, 2.13, 2.40
Pylos 1.22, 1.40
pyramids 1.16, 1.40
Egyptian 1.04, **1.17–18**
Mayan 1.28
Mesoamerican 1.28
Nubian 2.21
Teotihuacán 2.04, 2.27
Pyrrhus 2.12
Pytheas of Massilia 2.09, 2.19, 2.40
Pyu 2.03–04, 2.26, 2.40

Q

Qadesh 1.18, 1.40
  Battle of 1.12, 1.18
Qafzeh 1.02, 1.40
Qarqar, Battle of 1.13–14
Qataban 2.01–02, 2.40
Qi 1.27, 1.40
Qin 1.27, 1.40
Qin dynasty 2.01–02,
  2.24, 2.40
Quadi 2.15–16, 2.19
Quaternary period 1.01,
  1.40
quinua 1.28
Quirigua 2.28, 2.40
Qumran, 2.40

R

Raetia 2.13, 2.40
rainforests 1.01
rajatiraja 2.23
Ramayana 2.06, 2.23,
  2.40
Ramesses II (the Great)
  1.12, 1.18, 1.40
Ramesses III 1.18
Rathikas 2.22
Ravenna 2.16–17, 2.40
Recuay culture 2.27, 2.40
Red Cliffs, Battle of 2.24
Rehoboam 1.14, 1.40
reindeer 1.19
religion
  ancestor worship 2.06
  paganism 2.15
  Paleolithic 1.19
  religion 1.10
  shrines 1.09
  spread of world
  religions **2.06**
  see also individual
  religions
  temples 1.09, 1.1
Remi 2.18
Remojadas 2.27, 2.40
Reudingi 2.19
Rhaetians 1.25
Rhapta 2.21, 2.40
Rhegion 2.08
Rhine river 1.19, 2.14–16
Rhodes 1.22, 1.40, 2.10
Riben *see* Japan
Riblah 1.13
rice 1.03, 1.16, 1.26–27,
  1.40, 2.02, 2.05, 2.25–26
road systems 2.12, 2.14,
  2.27
Roman empire 2.03–05,
  2.13, 2.15, **2.16**, 2.19,
  2.23, 2.40
  Africa 2.13, 2.17
  Antonine dynasty 2.15
  Arabia 2.13
  Armenia 2.13
  Asia 2.13
  barbarians 2.05,
  2.15–17
  Britain 2.03, 2.13, 2.15,
  2.18
  Celts 2.18
  Christianity 2.04, 2.06,
  2.13, 2.15
  citizenship 2.12, 2.14
  colonies 2.12–13
  Constantinian dynasty
  2.15
  Dacia 2.13
  dioceses 2.15
  division 2.04, 2.16
  eastern 2.04–05,
  2.14–17.
  See also Byzantium,
  Byzantine empire
  economy **2.14**, 2.15
  Egypt 2.03, 2.13–14

Flavian dynasty 2.15
frontiers 2.19
Galatia 2.13
Gaul 2.03, 2.12–13,
  2.17–18
German and Slav tribes
  2.05, 2.13, 2.15–16,
  2.19
  greatest extent of 2.04
  languages 2.14, 2.17
  Macedon 2.10, 2.13
  Mesopotamia 2.11,
  2.13, 2.17
  Mithraism 2.06
  paganism 2.15
  provinces **2.13**
  Sasanian wars 2.11
  Severan dynasty 2.15
  social organization
  2.12, **2.14**, 2.17
  Spain 2.12–14, 2.17
  taxation 2.14
  trade 2.04, 2.13, **2.14**,
  2.18–19, 2.21, 2.23
  urbanization 2.14–15
  western 2.04–05,
  2.14–16, **2.16**
Roman republic 1.06,
  1.25, 2.01, **2.12**, 2.41
  Civil War 2.13, 2.15
  collapse 2.03, 2.13
  colonies 2.12–13
  conquest of peninsular
  Italy 2.02
  domination of Greece
  2.03, 2.10, 2.12–13
  Punic Wars 2.02–03,
  2.12, 2.13, 2.21
  Samnite wars 2.12
  Social war 2.13
  tribunes 2.12
  Twelve Tables 2.12
Romance languages 2.14
Romanian language 2.14,
  2.41
Rome 1.25, 2.01–02, **2.12**,
  2.14
  as center of Christianity
  2.17
  bishops of, 2.41
  city walls 2.12
  emperors of, 2.41
  Etruscans 2.12, 1.25
  foundation 1.25, 1.40,
  2.12
  kings of, 1.40
  patriarchal see 2.17
  sack (390 BC) 2.12,
  2.18, 2.41
  sack (410 AD) 2.04–05,
  2.16, 2.41
  sack (455 AD) 2.16,
  2.41
  Trajan's column 2.13
Romulus 2.05, 2.41
Rongorongo 1.07
Rosetta Stone, 2.41
Roxolani 2.03, 2.15
Royal Road, 2.41
Rudna Glava 1.20
Rudraman 2.23
Rugians, Rugii 2.16, 2.19
runic 1.07
Ruzhen dynasty
  see Jin dynasty

S

Saba 1.05–06, 1.41,
  2.01–02, 2.21
Sabean script and
  language 1.07, 1.41,
  2.21
Sabeans 2.03, 2.21, 2.21.
  See also Axum,
  Axumites

Sabines 1.25, 1.41, 2.12
Sacbe, 2.41
saches 2.28
Sacred Fire 2.06
Sadducees, 2.41
Sagartia 1.15
Saguntum 2.12, 2.41
Sahara 1.02–04, 1.16, 2.03,
  2.06, 2.21
Sahel 1.16
Sakas 1.06, 1.15, 1.41,
  2.01–03, 2.09–11, 2.20,
  2.22–23
  Northern 2.22–23, 2.25
  Western 2.22–23
Sakastan 2.10–11
Salamis 2.07
  Battle of 2.01, 2.07, 2.41
Salamis, Battle of 1.15,
  1.23, 1.24
salt 1.08
Samaria 1.14, 1.41
Samarran culture 1.09,
  1.41
Samnite Wars, 2.41
Samnites 1.25, 1.41, 2.12
Samoa 1.05, 2.01, 2.26
Samoyeds 2.01, 2.03–05
Samudragupta 2.04, 2.23,
  2.41
San Lorenzo 1.28, 1.41
Sanchi 2.22
Sanskrit 2.23, 2.41
Sanxingdui 1.27, 1.41
Saqqara 1.04, 1.17, 1.41
Sardinia 1.21, 1.23, 2.02,
  2.12–13
Sardis 1.15, 1.41, 2.07–08
Sargon II 1.13, 1.41
Sargon of Agade
  (the Great) 1.04,
  1.10–11, 1.41
Sarmatians 1.06, 1.41,
  2.02–03, 2.10, 2.19–20
Sasan 2.11, 2.41
Sasanian empire 2.04–06,
  2.11, 2.15–17, 2.20–21,
  2.23, 2.25, 2.41
  dependencies 2.05
Satavahanihara 2.03,
  2.22–23, 2.41
Satiyaputras 2.22
Satrapy, 2.41
Saul 1.14, 1.41
savanna 1.03
Saxon Shore 2.15, 2.41
Saxons 2.05, 2.15–16, 2.19
  see also Anglo-Saxons
Sayan mountains 2.20
Scandinavia,
  Scandinavians 2.05,
  2.19
Scipio Africanus 2.12, 2.41
Scordisci 2.18
Scotland 2.15, 2.18
  Celtic tribes 2.18
  see also Britain
sculpture 1.09
Scythians 1.06, 1.15, 1.23,
  1.41, 2.02–03, 2.18–20
  Black Sea 1.15
  Caspian 1.15
  pointed-hat 1.15
  "Scythian farmers" 2.19
Sea Peoples 1.05, 1.12,
  1.18, 1.22, 1.41, 2.41
Segesta 2.08, 2.42
Seleucid kingdom
  2.02–03, 2.09, 2.11, 2.42
  fall 2.10
  invasion of Egypt 2.10
Seleucos 2.02, 2.09, 2.22,
  2.42
Selinus 1.25, 2.08
Semites 1.04, 1.41

Semnones 2.19
Sennacherib 1.13–14, 1.41
Senones 2.18
Sentinum, Battle of 2.12
Senwosret III 1.18
Seqenenre II 1.18
Sequani 2.18
Serboi 2.19
Sethos I 1.18
Severan dynasty, 2.42
Severus, Septimus 2.15,
  2.42
Shabaka 2.21, 2.42
Shalmaneser I 1.12, 1.41
Shalmaneser III 1.13
Shalmaneser V 1.13–14
Shamshi-Adad 1.11, 1.41
Shang dynasty 1.05, 1.07,
  1.27, 1.41
Shang Yang 2.24, 2.42
Shanidar, 1.41
Shapur I 2.11, 2.23, 2.42
Shapur II 2.11, 2.42
Shaskanka 2.05
Shechem 1.14
sheep 1.03, 1.08–09, 1.16,
  1.20, 1.22, 1.41, 2.20–21
Shi Huangdi
  (First Emperor) 2.02,
  2.24, 2.42
Shikoku 2.25
Shorthugai 1.26, 1.41
Shoshenq I 1.14, 1.18,
  1.41
Shotoku 2.25
Shu 2.24–25, 2.42
Shu-Sin 1.11
Shubat-Enlil 1.11, 1.41
Shunga dynasty 2.22, 2.42
Sialkot 2.23
Siberia 2.01–05
Sibury Hill 1.41
Sicani 1.25
Sicels 2.08
Sicily 1.06, 1.23–25, 2.02,
  2.08, 2.12–13, 2.17
Siculi 1.25, 1.41
Siddhartha Gautama
  see Buddha
Sidon 1.14, 1.41
Siling Vandals 2.16, 2.19
Silk Route 1.06, 2.06
silk, 2.42
Silla 2.04–05, 2.24–25
silver 2.07–08
Sima Qian 2.24, 2.42
Sima Yen *see* Wudi
Simhala 2.03–05
Sinai 1.17
Sind 1.15
Singidunum 2.17
single-origins theory 1.02
Sinhalese 1.26, 2.22
Siwa 1.15, 1.41, 2.09
Skandagupta 2.23, 2.42
Skara Brae, 1.41
Skudra 1.15, 1.41
slavery 1.10, 1.41
  Africa 2.21
  early Mediterranean
  civilizations 1.22
  Greek civilization 1.24,
  2.07
  Romans 2.13–14
Slavic languages 2.19,
  2.42
Slavs 1.06, 2.01–02, 2.04,
  2.16–17, **2.19**, 2.42
smelting 1.09, 1.12
Smerdis 1.15, 1.42
Snofru 1.17, 1.42
Social War 2.13, 2.42
Socrates 2.01, 2.08, 2.42
Sogdiana, Soghd 1.15,
  1.42, 2.09, 2.11

Soissons, Battle of 2.17,
  2.42
Solomon **1.14**, 1.23, 1.42
Solomon Islands 1.02,
  2.26
Solon 1.24, 1.42
Solutrean culture 1.19,
  1.42
Song dynasty 1.27, 2.24
Sophocles 2.08
sorghum 1.16, 1.42
Spain 1.23, 1.25, 2.16
  Celtiberians 2.18
  Cimbri 2.19
  Roman empire 2.12–14,
  2.17
  Visigoths 2.05
Spanish language 2.14
Sparta 1.24, 1.42, 2.01,
  2.07–08, 2.10
  constitution 2.07
  helot revolt 2.07
  Peloponnesian war
  2.01, 2.07, **2.08**
Spartan league 2.07, 2.42
Sphakteria, Battle of 2.08,
  2.42
Sphinx, Great, 1.42
Springs and Autumns
  period 1.06, 1.27, 1.42
squash 1.28, 1.42
Starcevo 1.20, 1.42
state, 1.42
stelae 2.28
Step Pyramid 1.17, 1.42
steppe nomads 2.02, 2.05,
  2.10, 2.19, **2.20**, 2.25,
  2.42
steppe pastoralist cultures
  1.04
steppes 1.02–06, 1.19,
  2.05, **2.20**
  Caspian 2.05, 2.11
  European 2.05
  Iranian domination
  2.20
  Russian 2.20
Stevns 2.19
Stilicho 2.16, 2.42
stirrup 2.20, 2.42
Stoics 2.09, 2.15, 2.42
Stone Age, 1.42.
  See also Mesolithic;
  Neolithic; Paleolithic
stone circle, 1.42
Stonehenge 1.04, 1.20,
  1.42
Stormy Sky, King 2.28
stupas 2.06, 2.42
Subartu 1.12, 1.42
Sudan 1.16
Suevi 2.16–17, 2.19, 2.42
Sui dynasty 2.05, 2.25,
  2.42
Sui Wendi (Yang Jian)
  2.05, 2.25, 2.42
Suiones 2.19
Sumatra 2.26
Sumeria 1.04–05, 1.07,
  1.09–11, 1.42
  Early Dynastic period
  1.10
  King List 1.10
  trade 1.10
Sun Tzu 2.24, 2.42
Suppuliumas 1.12, 1.42
Surasena 1.26
Suren 2.03, 2.10–11, 2.42
Susa 1.10, 1.13, 1.15, 1.42,
  2.09·
Sutton Hoo, 2.42
Svear 2.19
Swanscombe, 1.42
Swartkrans 1.01, 1.42
sweet potato 2.26

Syagrius 2.16–17
Syphax 2.12, 2.42
Syracuse 1.23, 1.25, 1.42,
  2.08–09
Syria 1.03, 1.08, 1.11, 1.13,
  1.15, 2.09–11, 2.13
  Palmyra 2.15
  Roman empire 2.17
  Sasanian empire 2.11
Syriac language 2.14

T

Tacitus 2.13, 2.42
Tadmor 1.12, 1.14, 1.42
Tahiti 2.02, 2.26
taiga 1.04
Taiwan 2.26
Takkola 2.26
Tamar 1.14
Tang dynasty 2.05
Tara, Battle of 2.18, 2.43
Tarentum 2.12
Tarim basin 2.20
Tarraco 2.13
Tarraconensis 2.13, 2.43
Tartaria 1.20, 1.42
Tartessos, Tartessians
  1.23, 1.25, 1.42, 2.18
Taruga 1.16, 2.21, 2.43
Taruma 2.26
Tarxien 1.20, 1.42
Tasmania 1.04–06,
  2.01–04, 2.26
Tassili 1.16, 1.42
Taurisci 2.19
Taxila 1.26, 2.10, 2.22,
  2.43
Tectosages 2.18
teff 1.16
Tehuacán, 1.42
Telamon, Battle of 2.18
Tell al-Fakhariyeh 1.12
Tell Awayli 1.09, 1.42
Tell Mureybat 1.08, 1.42
Tell Umm Dabaghiyeh
  1.09
Tell, 1.42
Tencteri 2.19
Teng 1.27
"Ten Thousand" 2.08,
  2.43
Teotihuacán 2.02–05,
  2.27–28, 2.43
  Classic period 2.04
  sack 2.27
Tepe Gawra 1.09, 1.43
Tepe Yahya 1.10, 1.43
Tepecik 1.09
Terra Amata 1.01, 1.43
Tertiary period 1.01
Tetrarchy, 2.43
Teteuburgerwald, Battle
  of 2.13, 2.19, 2.43
Teutones 2.19, 2.43
textiles 1.03, 1.08–10
  cotton 1.03, 1.26, 1.28
  linen 1.03, 1.08–09,
  1.16
  printed 1.09
  silk 1.03, 1.06
  spinning 1.03
  weaving 1.03, 1.09–10
  wool 1.03, 1.09, 1.22
Thai language 2.24–25
Thailand, Thais 1.04–06,
  2.02–05, 2.25–26
Thames river 1.19
Thasos 2.07, 2.43
Theater, 2.43
Thebes 1.13, 1.15,
  1.17–18, 1.43, 2.08,
  2.21, 2.43
Themistocles 2.07, 2.43
Theodoric 2.17, 2.43

Theodosian dynasty 2.16, 2.43
Theodosius I 2.15–16, 2.43
Thera 1.22, 1.24, 1.43
Theravada Buddhism 2.06, 2.43
Thermopylae, Battle of 2.07, 2.43
Thessaly 1.24–25, 1.43, 2.07
tholos 1.22, 1.43
Thrace, Thracians 1.05–06, 1.12, 1.15, 1.23–25, 1.43, 2.01–02, 2.07–10, 2.13, 2.15–16, 2.18
Three Age system, 1.43
Three Kingdoms (China) **2.24**, 2.43
Three Kingdoms (Korea) , 2.43
Thucydides 2.08, 2.43
Thuringia, Thuringians 2.17, 2.19
Tiahuanaco empire 1.28
Tiahuanaco empire 2.03–05, 2.27, 2.43
Tiber river 1.25
Tiberius 2.04, 2.13, 2.43
Tibet, Tibetans 1.05–07, 2.02, 2.04–05, 2.23–25
Tibeto-Burmese 1.04, 1.43
Ticinus river, Battle of 2.12
Tien Shan mountains 2.20
Tiglath-pileser I 1.12, 1.43
Tiglath-pileser III 1.13–14, 1.43
Tigranes I 2.10, 2.43
Tigris river 1.09–12
Tikal 2.28, 2.43
Timor 2.26
tin 1.10, 1.21, 1.23, 1.25, 1.27, 1.43
Tingis 1.23, 1.43
Titicaca, Lake 1.28, 2.04, 2.27
Toba 2.25, 2.43
Toba Wei 2.04–05, 2.20, 2.25, 2.43
Tolistbogii Trocmi 2.18
Toltec civilization 2.28
Tonga 1.05, 2.01, 2.26
Toniniá 2.28
toolmaking cultures 1.01, 1.03, 1.19–20
Torralba-Ambrona, 1.43
Totila 2.17
trade 2.07
    Africa 2.05, 2.21
    Americas 2.27
    Assyria 1.11
    Black Sea 2.08
    Britain 1.23, 1.25
    Bronze Age 1.09, 1.21
    early Mediterranean civilizations 1.22

Egyptian civilization 1.17–18
Greek civilization **1.23–24**, 2.07
India 2.22–23
Indus valley civilization 1.26
Iron Age Africa 2.21
Malacca straits 2.26
Mayan 2.28
Mycenaean 1.21
Neolithic 1.08–09
Olmecs 1.28
Pacific and southeast Asia 2.26
Phoenicians 1.05, 1.13, 1.23
pochteca 2.27
Roman empire 2.04, 2.13, **2.14**, 2.18–19, 2.21, 2.23
Silk Route 1.06, 2.06
Sumerians 1.10
trading colonies 1.05–06, 1.23
Teotihuacán 2.27
Trajan 2.11, 2.13–15, 2.43
Trajan's column, 2.43
transhumance 1.05–06, 2.01–03, 2.20
transport
    wheeled vehicles 1.03, 1.20–21
    see also boat-building; boats and ships; canal systems; road systems
Trasimenus, Lake, Battle of 2.12
Trebia river, Battle of 2.12
Tres Zapotes 1.28, 1.43
Treveri 2.18
Tricameron, Battle of 2.17
Tripolye-Cucuteni culture 1.20, 1.43
Trireme, 2.43
Troy 1.22, 1.43
    Trojan War 1.22, 1.43
Trundholm 1.21, 1.43
Tú-yü-hun 2.04–05, 2.25, 2.43
Tuamotu archipelago 2.26
Tukulti-Ninurta I 1.12
tundra 1.02–03
Tung Cho 2.24
Tung-nu 2.02–03
Tungri 2.19
Tungusic, 2.43
Tunis, Tunisia 1.16, 1.23
Turan 2.11
Turdetanians 1.25, 1.43
Turkey 1.03.
    See also Anatolia
Turkic languages, 2.43
Turkish khanates 2.05, 2.20, 2.43
Turko-Mongols 1.05, 2.01–03, 2.20, 2.20.
    See also Xiongnu

Turks 2.05, 2.20
    Kirghiz 2.05
Tutankhamun 1.18, 1.43
Tuthmosis I 1.12, 1.18, 1.43
Tuthmosis III 1.18, 1.43
Tuthmosis IV 1.12, 1.43
Twelve Tables 2.12, 2.43
tyrant, 1.43
Tyre 1.13–14, 1.23, 1.25, 1.43

U
Uaxactún 2.28, 2.43
Ubaid culture 1.09, 1.43
Ubii 2.19
Ugarit, 1.43
Ujjain 1.26, 1.43
Ukraine 1.23
Ulfilas, Bishop 2.15, 2.43
ullucu 1.28
Ulu Burun shipwreck 1.22, 1.43
Umbrians 1.25, 1.43, 2.12
Umma 1.10, 1.43
Unetice culture 1.04, 1.21, 1.43
Upanishads 2.06, 2.43
Ur 1.04, 1.09–13, 1.43
    Chaldean occupation 1.12
    sack 1.11
    Third Dynasty 1.11
Ur-Nammu 1.11, 1.44
Urartu, Urartians 1.05, 1.07, 1.12–13, 1.43
urbanization 1.04, 1.09, **1.10**, 1.44, 2.14–15
    and agriculture 1.03–04, 1.08–10
    China 1.27
    early Mediterranean civilizations 1.22
    Egypt 1.16
    Indus valley civilization 1.26
Urmia, Lake, Battle of 1.13
Urnfield cultures 1.05–06, 1.21, 1.25, 1.44, 2.18
Uruk 1.04, 1.07, 1.09–12, 1.44
Urukagina 1.10, 1.44
Uttarapatha 2.22

V
Vakataka 2.04, 2.23, 2.43
Valdivia tradition 1.04, 1.28, 1.44
Valens 2.15–16, 2.44
Valentinian III 2.16, 2.44
Valerian 2.11, 2.15, 2.44
Valley of Mexico 2.27
Valley of the Kings 1.18, 1.44
Vallon Pont d'Arc 1.19
Van Lang 1.06, 1.44, 2.02
Vandals 2.05, 2.15–17, 2.19, 2.44

Vanga 2.22–23, 2.44
Vangiones, Battle of 2.16
Vanuatu 1.05, 2.26
Varanasi 2.23
Varna, 1.44
Vatsa 1.26
Vatsayara 2.23
Vedas, *Vedic Hymns* 1.26, 2.06, 2.22
Veddas 1.26
Vedic Aryans 1.05–06, 1.26
Veii 2.12, 2.44
Venedi 2.19
Veneti 2.18, 2.44
Venice 2.12
Veracruz 2.04–05, 2.27, 2.44
Vercellae, Battle of 2.19
Vercingetorix 2.18, 2.44
Vergina 2.08, 2.44
Vidisha 2.10
Viennensis 2.15
Viets 2.24–26.
    See also Champa
Vijaya 2.22, 2.44
Villanova culture 1.25
Vima Kadphises 2.23, 2.44
Vinca, 1.44
Vindelici 2.18
Virgil 2.13, 2.44
Visigoths 2.04–05, 2.15–17, 2.19, 2.44.
    See also Goths
Vistula river 2.19
visual arts 1.09
Vitruvius Pollio, Marcus 2.13, 2.44
Vix 1.23, 1.44
Volcae 2.18
Votadini 2.18, 2.44
Vouillé, Battle of 2.17, 2.44
Vrijji 1.26
Vulgate Bible, 2.44

W
Wadi Kubbaniya 1.16
Wang Mang 2.24, 2.44
Warring States period 1.27, 1.44, 2.01, **2.24**
warrior class 1.04
Washukanni 1.12, 1.44
water buffalo 1.03
wavy line ceramics, 1.44
weaving 1.03, 1.09–10
Wei 1.27, 1.44
Wei 2.24–25
Wessex culture 1.05, 1.44
Western Turk Khanate 2.05
Western Zhou 1.27
wheat 1.03, 1.08–09, 1.16, 1.20, 1.22, 1.44
wheel 1.03, 1.10, 1.20–21, 1.27, 1.44, 2.20

White Huns *see* Ephthalite Huns
Willendorf, Venus of 1.19
Windmill Hill, 1.44
"womb of peoples" 2.19
wool 1.03, 1.09, 1.22, 1.44
writing 1.04, **1.07**, 1.09–10, 1.20
    Arabic 1.07
    Aramaic alphabet 1.05, 1.07, 1.15
    Canaanite alphabet 1.07, 1.12
    Chinese script 1.07, 2.25
    cuneiform 1.07, 1.10, 1.15
    Cyrillic alphabet 1.07
    Greek alphabet 1.07, 1.24
    Hebrew alphabet 1.07
    hieroglyphs 1.06–07, 1.17, 1.22, 1.28, 2.27–28
    Kufic Arabic 1.07
    Latin alphabet 1.07, 2.14, 2.17–18
    Linear A script 1.22
    Linear B script 1.22
    logographic 1.07
    Meroitic script 2.21
    Nabatean alphabet 1.07
    parchment 1.15
    Phoenician alphabet 1.05, 1.07, 1.23–25
    phonetic alphabet 1.05, 1.07
    pictographs 1.07, 1.10, 1.26–27, 2.26
    Rongorongo 1.07
    runic 1.07
    Sabean script 1.07, 2.21
    Sanskrit 2.23
Wu 1.27, 1.44. 2.25
Wu-su 2.24
Wu-Sun 2.03
Wudi (Sima Yen) 2.25, 2.44
Wuzhong 1.27

X
Xenophon 2.08, 2.44
Xerxes I 1.13, 1.15, 2.01, 2.07, 2.09, 2.44
Xia dynasty 1.27, 1.44
Xiang Yu 2.24
Xianyang 2.24, 2.44
    Terracotta army 2.24
Xianyun 1.27, 1.44
Xiao Gong 2.24, 2.44
Xiongnu 2.02–04, 2.20, 2.24–25, 2.44
Xochicalco 2.27
Xu 1.27

Y
yaghbus 2.23
yak 1.03
yam 1.16, 1.44

Yamato period 2.04–05, 2.25, 2.44
Yan 1.27, 1.44
Yang Jian *see* Sui Wendi
Yangshao culture 1.27, 1.44
Yangtze valley 1.03, 1.27, 2.25
Yavadyipa 2.26
Yaxchilán 2.28, 2.44
Yaxuná 2.28
Yaya-Mama religious traditions 1.06, 1.28, 1.44
Yayoi culture 2.02–05, 2.25, 2.44
Year of Four Emperors 2.13, 2.44
Yeha 2.21
Yellow river 1.27, 2.25
Yemen 2.05, 2.11, 2.21
Yong 1.27, 1.44
Yoruba states 2.21
Yu the Great 1.27, 1.44
Yucatán 1.28, 2.28
Yue 1.27, 2.01, 2.44
Yue Qi 1.06, 1.44, 2.01–04, 2.23–24, 2.44
Yunnan 2.25–26
Yuxian 1.27

Z
Zagros mountains 1.03, 1.08–09, 1.11
Zama, Battle of 2.02, 2.12
Zapotec civilization 1.06–07, 1.28, 1.44, 2.01–02, 2.04, 2.27–28
Zawi Chemi Shanidar 1.08, 1.44
Zealot, 2.44
Zedekiah 1.14, 1.44
Zeno 2.09, 2.16–17, 2.44
Zenobia 2.15, 2.44
zero, concept of 2.23
Zhang Qian, 2.44
Zhao 2.24, 2.44
Zheng (First Emperor) *see* Shi Huangdi
Zheng 1.27
Zhongshan 2.24, 2.44
Zhou dynasty 1.05–06, 1.27, 1.44, 2.01, 2.24–25
Zhoukoudien, 1.44
ziggurats 1.09, 1.11, 1.44
Zobah 1.14
Zoroaster 1.15, 2.06
Zoroastrianism 2.06, 2.11, 2.44